EurographicSeminars

Tutorials and Perspectives in Computer Graphics

Edited by W. T. Hewitt, R. Gnatz, and D. A. Duce

G. Garcia I. Herman (Eds.)

Advances in Computer Graphics VI

Images: Synthesis, Analysis, and Interaction

With 186 Figures, 2 in Color

Springer-Verlag
Berlin Heidelberg New York
London Paris Tokyo
Hong Kong Barcelona
Budapest

EurographicSeminars

Edited by W. T. Hewitt, R. Gnatz, and D. A. Duce
for EUROGRAPHICS –
The European Association for Computer Graphics
P. O. Box 16, CH-1288 Aire-la-Ville, Switzerland

Volume Editors

Gérald Garcia
Ecole cantonale d'art de Lausanne
Unité de Synthèse de l'Image Numérique
46, rue de l'Industrie
CH-1030 Bussigny, Switzerland

Ivan Herman
Centre for Mathematics and Computer Sciences (CWI)
Department of Interactive Systems
Kruislaan 413
NL-1098 SJ Amsterdam, The Netherlands

ISBN 3-540-53455-5 Springer-Verlag Berlin Heidelberg New York
ISBN 0-387-53455-5 Springer-Verlag New York Berlin Heidelberg

Library of Congress Cataloging-in-Publication Data
Advances in computer graphics VI / G. Garcia, I. Herman, editors. p. cm. –
(EurographicSeminars)
"Collection of several tutorials from the EUROGRAPHICS '90 conference in Montreux."
Includes bibliographical references.
ISBN 0-387-53455-5
1. Computer graphics – Congresses. I. Garcia, G. (Gérald), 1942–. II. Herman, I. (Ivan)
III. EUROGRAPHICS (1990: Montreux, Switzerland) IV. Title: Advances in computer graphics
6. V. Title: Advances in computer graphics six. VI. Series: Eurographics seminars.
T385.A3645 1991 006.6 – dc20 90-23983 CIP

45/3140-543210 – Printed on acid-free paper

Preface

This book is a collection of several tutorials from the EUROGRAPHICS'90 conference in Montreux. The conference was held under the motto "IMAGES: Synthesis, Analysis and Interaction", and the tutorials, partly presented in this volume, reflect the conference theme. As such, this volume provides a unique collection of advanced texts on 'traditional' computer graphics as well as of tutorials on image processing and image reconstruction. As with all the volumes of the series "Advances in Computer Graphics", the contributors are leading experts in their respective fields.

The chapter *Design and Display of Solid Models* provides an extended introduction to interactive graphics techniques for design, fast display, and high-quality rendering of solid models. The text focuses on techniques for Constructive Solid Geometry (CSG). The following topics are treated in depth: interactive design techniques (specification of curves, surfaces and solids; graphical user interfaces; procedural languages and direct manipulation) and display techniques (depth-buffer, scan-line and ray-tracing techniques; CSG classification techniques; efficiency-improving methods; software and hardware implementations).

The chapter *State of the Art in Image Synthesis* covers all aspects of creating realistic images of complex modelled environments. The major focus of the chapter is, however, on global reflection models and the algorithms which are used to implement them. A short introduction to colour science, CRT technology and its relation to the human visual system is given as background material. Local reflection models which are currently built into hardware are also covered briefly. The section on global algorithms covers ray tracing and the radiosity method for image synthesis. Recent advances which have been developed to make these algorithms more efficient are discussed in detail.

Many architectures and algorithms have been proposed for applying massively parallel methods to computer graphics. This fact is the starting point of the chapter *Distributed Graphics And Parallelism.* A few massively parallel graphics systems have now actually been implemented. One can expect to see many more very soon. Can it really be expected to attain, through parallel systems, the six orders of magnitude speedup necessary to produce today's most expensive imagery in real time? Answers may lie in looking at some current approaches to massive parallelism in graphics and the bottlenecks they leave. It will also help to look carefully at what is required to make images and how information must flow from shape descriptions to pixels. The chapter gives also a survey of existing parallel graphics systems.

The main problem in computer vision is to understand 3D (and possibly time varying) scenes by analyzing 2D images. Thus, as in computer graphics, a major issue is the relationship between 3D scenes and their 2D perspective views. It is not surprising then that the two fields can learn much from each other. The goal of the chapter *Computer Vision* is to give an introduction to researchers in computer graphics into some of the important concepts, techniques, and approaches in computer vision. Three interrelated topics are discussed: the representation, acquisition, and utilisation of 3D (especially geometrical) information.

Volume, surface, and relational representations are described briefly, followed by a discussion of various depth acquisition schemes including laser ranging, structured-light illumination, passive stereo and shape from shading. Two important examples of utilisation are discussed in some detail: 3D object recognition and motion estimation.

The chapter *3D Volume Visualisation* deals with a rapidly growing field of computer graphics. Just as raster graphics superseded line drawing graphics for visualising surfaces, volumetric graphics is now superseding raster graphics for visualising volumes. A volumetric object, typically represented as a large 3D grid of voxels (volume elements), is derived from discrete samples of a natural phenomenon or may be synthesised by a computer model. Topics covered by this chapter include: volume representation, viewing and rendering algorithms, 3D discrete topology, commercial and special purpose architectures, and applications such as medical imaging, biology, geology, oceanography, 3D image processing, CAD, simulation and scientific visualisation.

The chapter *Introduction to Digital Image Processing* presents in its first part the fundamentals of digital image processing and their applications. The problem of transforming an analogue scene into digital data, involving sampling and quantisation, are discussed both on theoretical and practical levels. Basic two or three-dimensional signals and linear processing systems are described, including tools like the multidimensional Fourier transform, the z transform and the correlation functions. The design and use of higher-dimensional linear filters are also introduced. Finally, the basic restoration and enhancement methods are presented. In the second part of the chapter the state of the art is criticised, showing weaknesses and strong points of conventional techniques. New perspectives are emphasised with examples taken from multidimensional visual information representation and coding.

The chapter *X/PEX Programming* examines the principles underlying the development of the X Windows System and its fundamentals of operation. A look at the internals of X helps in gaining a better understanding of how it works, and how to best use it. PEX, the PHIGS Extension to X, adds 3-dimensional graphics to X. The goals of PEX are considered, and also its definition as an extension to the X protocol.

The image processing capacities of the human visual system are truly remarkable. Neurophysiological and psychological data indicate that humans are capable of correctly identifying upwards of 100000 different objects and scenes on the basis of only 100 to 150 msec of visual processing. By comparison, the abilities of even the most sophisticated artificial vision systems seem feeble. Researchers in visual neuroscience, experimental psychology and neural modelling are beginning to unravel the mysteries of biological vision. The chapter *Image Processing by the Human Visual System* makes an attempt to review the progress made in recent years. It can be expected that a better understanding of the human visual system may give ideas for the development of more advanced methods in the fields of image understanding, computer vision and realistic image synthesis.

The chapter *Intelligent CAD Systems* addresses an important trend in CAD technology, resulting from recent advances in artificial intelligence, including expert systems and knowledge-based systems. It draws on the results of the series of four workshops organised by Eurographics. The application of such techniques offers a structured approach to handle the complexity inherent in many large CAD systems. Specific areas addressed include: theoretical basis for the approach (design processes, design objects, design activities); innovative AI theories (quantitative physics and truth maintenance); advanced implementation techniques (object-oriented and logic programming). The text gives a comprehensive overview of these topics and clarifies the state of the art and future trends.

Since the introduction of the first brain scanner almost twenty years ago, computer reconstructed images have become commonplace in medicine. However, while tomographic images are now as familiar as conventional X-rays, many of the underlying reconstruction techniques are less well known. The aim of the chapter *Image Reconstruction for Medical Applications* is to review these techniques, both for the well-established domain of two-dimensional tomography and for three-dimensional tomography which is becoming increasingly important in medical imaging. The chapter is subdivided into four parts: (1) review of the basic mathematical tools and concepts required, such as Fourier transforms, convolution, sampling and shift invariance, (2) presentation of the reconstruction problem as the inversion of the Radon transform, (3) two-dimensional reconstruction techniques, including both interactive and direct methods, and (4) three-dimensional reconstruction by inversion of the X-ray transform.

The chapter *Direct Manipulation Techniques for Human-Computer Interfaces* presents methods and tools for the design of object-oriented, direct manipulation interfaces. It introduces the major principles and techniques used in direct manipulations, like visual metaphors, object-oriented interaction and their psychological implications. Guidelines for designing efficient and consistent user interfaces are presented.

This volume will be a source of state-of-the-art knowledge in the areas covered and we hope that it will be helpful for system designers, application programmers as well as for researchers. We would like to express our gratitude to all the contributors of this volume for the enthusiasm with which they have approached the project; we would also like to thank the other organisers of EUROGRAPHICS'90 who have all made their contribution in defining the topics of the conference and the tutorial programme which served as a basis for the present volume. In particular, we would like to mention the names of David Duce, Michel Grave, Bertrand Ibrahim, Thierry Pun, Michel Roch and Carlo Vandoni.

Lausanne, June 1990 Gérald Garcia, Ivan Herman

Table of Contents

Design and Display of Solid Models

Willem F. Bronsvoort, Frederik W. Jansen, and Frits H. Post

ABSTRACT

Solid modelling plays an important role in CAD/CAM and other advanced applications of 3D graphics. This survey presents an overview of graphics techniques for the design, fast display, and high-quality rendering of solid models (*ie. Graphics for Solid Modelling).* Emphasis will be on techniques for Constructive Solid Geometry (CSG).

After an introduction on representation techniques, the following topics on interactive design of solid models will be covered: input and editing of curves, surfaces and solids, assembly modelling, parametrization, constraints, modelling languages and direct manipulation. The second part of the survey will discuss display techniques: ray tracing, scanline and depth-buffer algorithms, CSG classification techniques and efficiency-improving methods.

1. Introduction

In this section the use of solid modelling in different application areas, the types of solid modelling representations, and the role of graphics in solid modelling will be discussed. Graphics enhances the design of solid models by providing interactive tools for *direct manipulation* on graphical representations of these models, and by providing techniques for *direct display* of solid models.

1.1 Modelling from an Application Point of View

An increasing number of application areas are using geometric representations of three-dimensional (3D) objects. Most important are CAD/CAM, animation and visual simulation, and scientific visualization. In CAD/CAM, the geometric model represents the object to be designed, in visual simulation and animation it models the learning, training or entertaining environment, and in scientific visualization it is used to model objects and surfaces to visualize multi-dimensional data in the form of scalar and vector fields such as temperature, flow and pressure.

Although these applications all use 3D geometric representations, each will pose different requirements on the modelling with respect to consistency, completeness and complexity. For instance, for animation and artistic purposes, the visual appearance may be most important, whereas for visual simulation the emphasis is on real-time display. In CAD/CAM, the consistency and validity of a model is most important, to ensure that the model can exist and can be produced automatically. Other criteria could be mentioned as well such as the modelling domain (how much of the required geometry can actually be described) and ease of definition and manipulation.

In general we can distinguish three modelling approaches.

In *animation* and *visual simulation* one often wants to achieve visual realism in the display of natural phenomena such as clouds, trees and mountains. It is not required here that objects are modelled accurately, as long as they give a good visual impression. Much can be achieved with procedural models, such as fractals and particle systems, and the use of texture mapping to model surface details. Another important aspect is modelling the behaviour of objects, so-called *physically-based modelling*. The emphasis in this approach is on the procedural definition of shape and movements, and the interactive design of the objects is not so important, except for the specification of general characteristics and motion patterns.

Scientific visualization is concerned with the visualization of the characteristic properties and spatial distribution of entities in large data collections that are obtained from scanning devices, or from computer simulations of physical processes. Modelling and visualization here is the result of several processing steps, which may include filtering, data segmentation, surface reconstruction and calculation of iso-surfaces. The modelling is done in a semi-automatic way, and user intervention is only needed for the fine-tuning of the different steps. A widely used modelling method here is volume modelling, the representation of solids as a regular array of identical volume elements *(voxels)*. Another important function of geometric modelling in scientific visualization is the representation of the environment, and of auxiliary objects such as particles.

In *CAD/CAM*, on the other hand, the emphasis is on the design of correct and accurate models. Interactive input and manipulation of the model is very important. The user wants to specify a shape accurately and as easily as possible. The resulting model should be correct and complete, and the modelling scheme should cover a large modelling domain, including free-form surfaces and blend surfaces. The techniques to model 3D objects in this sense are generally referred to as *solid modelling*.

Therefore, although 3D modelling is used in many applications, and will increasingly be used for these purposes, one should be aware that there are large differences between these applications in the use of modelling. This survey will focus on solid modelling, and in particular on methods for interactive design and display of solid models.

1.2 Solid Modelling Representations

In solid modelling, two types of internal representations are widely used: the Boundary representation (B-rep) and the Constructive Solid Geometry representation (CSG-rep). The boundary representation describes a solid by a complete specification of the boundary of the object, and with CSG a solid is defined as a set combination of primitive solids, such as the block, cylinder and sphere.

Both approaches have their advantages and disadvantages. With the B-rep, an explicit description of the boundary is available, and it is therefore rather straightforward to make a picture of the object, to calculate its volume or to calculate any other property related to the boundary information. The CSG representation, on the other hand, does not give an explicit description of the boundary of the solid; it is called a procedural definition because it tells how the object can be constructed from elementary volumes, but it does not give the explicit volume or boundary of the resulting model. The boundary of the CSG model is only a subset of the boundaries of its primitive solids. The composite solid can therefore not be displayed without classification of the surfaces, ie. determination of whether a surface is on the boundary of the

CSG model. This classification, however, is not that expensive, and commercial workstations will soon be available that will display CSG models in real-time (see also section 7).

An important advantage of CSG is that objects can easily be modified and manipulated. A boundary representation, on the other hand, is hard to modify. Each incremental operation requires a (local) boundary evaluation, and it may happen that small changes will result in a completely new topology of the object. CSG is therefore often preferred for interactive design: it provides a method for high-level specification and is intuitively clear. After the design phase, the end result can always be converted into a B-rep, when needed. In this survey we will therefore concentrate on the design and visualization of CSG models.

1.3 Graphics for Solid Modelling

The design of CSG models involves two aspects. The first one relates to the mathematical representation of the surfaces and their specification. The second aspect relates to the organization of the model; it includes the set composition, but also the relations between solids as specified by dimensions, tolerances, and other constraints. Also the structure of the design process - top-down refinement or a step-by-step procedure - may be part of the interaction. For this wide range of modelling activities, we will describe the interactive graphical methods developed so far. A preferred mode of interaction is *direct manipulation,* which enables the user to interact with entities by means of their visual representation on the screen; instead of specifying alphanumeric commands or editing a file of numbers or a computer program, the user can directly manipulate the entity by selecting and manipulating its graphical representation.

Direct display of CSG models can be done as described above by classifying the surfaces of the primitive solids as part of the display process. We will discuss CSG versions of the ray tracing, scanline and depth-buffer algorithm. The ray tracing algorithm is used for high-quality rendering for presentation purposes. The scanline and depth-buffer algorithms are projective algorithms which lack the rendering quality of ray tracing, but are an order faster, and can be used for interactive viewing.

The outline of the survey is as follows. Section 2 will introduce the curve and surface representation techniques for defining primitive solids and the techniques to combine them to solid models. It also discusses boundary evaluation from CSG to B-rep. Section 3 presents the techniques for interactive design of geometric models, in particular the geometric specification of the primitive solids. Section 4 discusses the techniques for structuring and parametrization of models. This concludes the part on design. The following three sections describe CSG display methods, the ray tracing algorithm (section 5), the scanline algorithm (section 6) and the depth-buffer algorithm (section 7), and their associated CSG classification techniques. Section 8 concludes the survey.

2. Shape Representations

In this section the two most common representation schemes for solid modelling, constructive solid geometry (CSG) and boundary representation, are discussed. A representation scheme determines the method to represent a solid object, and the related data structures. The schemes will be introduced in a stepwise manner: first it will be explained how surfaces can be represented, then how primitive objects can be constructed from surfaces, and finally how more complex objects can be constructed from primitive objects.

2.1 Surface Representations

There are two types of surfaces that are used for the representation of solid objects: implicit surfaces and parametric surfaces.

An *implicit surface* is defined by an equation of the form $F(x,y,z) = 0$, in which F is a "well-behaved" function, which can, in general, contain logarithms, exponentials and trigonometric functions (Mortenson 1985). For some functions it is possible to solve the implicit equation for one of the variables as a function of the other two, eg. $z = f(x,y)$. This form is the explicit equation of the surface.

A class of simple implicit surfaces consists of the *algebraic surfaces*. These can be written as a finite number of terms with x, y and z raised to a positive integral power only. Their equation is thus

$$\sum_{i=0}^{p} \sum_{j=0}^{q} \sum_{k=0}^{r} a_{ijk}\, x^i y^j z^k = 0$$

The simplest algebraic surface is linear in all variables:

$$ax + by + cz + d = 0$$

This equation defines an unbounded *planar surface*. If the equation is of degree two, a *quadric surface* is defined. Examples of this are:

$$x^2 + y^2 - r^2 = 0$$

which defines an unbounded cylindrical surface, and

$$x^2 + y^2 + z^2 - r^2 = 0$$

which defines a spherical surface. Such simple algebraic surfaces are most often used in solid modelling, because most objects occurring in engineering applications can be modelled with them.

An implicit surface divides 3D space into two parts, the part where $F(x,y,z) \geq 0$ and the part where $F(x,y,z) < 0$. These parts are called *halfspaces*. For example, a spherical surface divides 3D space into the halfspace inside the surface, and the halfspace outside the surface.

A parametric surface is defined in a completely different way (Mortenson 1985; Farin 1988). 3D *parametric curves* are introduced first. These are defined by a 3D vector function of one parameter:

$$\mathbf{p}(u) = \begin{bmatrix} x(u) \\ y(u) \\ z(u) \end{bmatrix} \qquad u_0 \leq u \leq u_1$$

As the parameter u varies from u_0 to u_1, the point $\mathbf{p}(u)$ traces out the curve. The coordinate functions $x(u)$, $y(u)$ and $z(u)$ are again "well-behaved" functions. Very often they are *polynomial functions*, ie. functions of the type

$$f(u) = \sum_{i=0}^{n} a_i u^i$$

In practice, it is very difficult to specify the right coefficients a_i of the polynomial functions to get the shape one has in mind for a curve. Therefore, the most important curve-defining techniques work with a set of control points that are either interpolated or approximated by the curve defined by those points. The modelling system can then compute the coefficients of the polynomial coordinate functions from these control points.

For example, *Bézier curves* are defined by:

$$p(u) = \sum_{i=0}^{n} p_i B_{i,n}(u) \qquad 0 \leq u \leq 1$$

where p_i $(i = 0,1,\ldots,n)$ are the control points, and $B_{i,n}(u)$ $(i = 0,1,\ldots,n)$ the *blending functions*, which are in this case defined by

$$B_{i,n}(u) = \binom{n}{i} u^i (1-u)^{n-i} \qquad 0 \leq u \leq 1$$

Only two of the properties that can be proved for a Bézier curve are mentioned here. The degree of a Bézier curve is always one less than the number of control points, and the curve interpolates the first and last control points. In figure 2.1 a cubic Bézier curve with its 4 control points is shown.

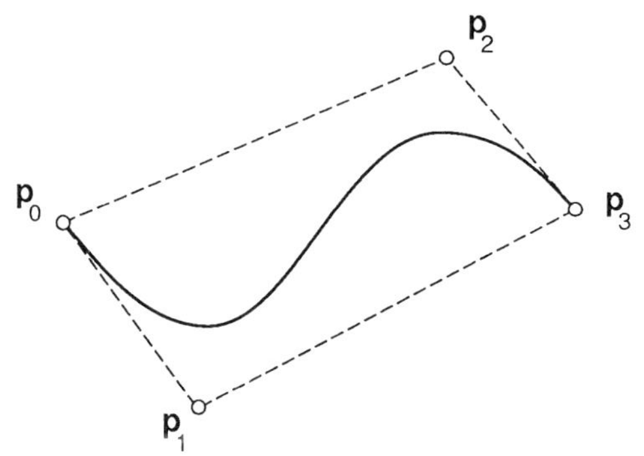

Figure 2.1. A cubic Bézier curve with its control points p_0, p_1, p_2 and p_3.

Two other types of parametric curves that are very important in geometric modelling are *B-splines* and *rational B-splines*. These differ in the types of blending functions used, and therefore have other properties than Bézier curves. The degree of a B-spline is not determined by the number of control points, but by the *order* of the curve: the degree is one less than the order. B-splines are defined on a larger parameter interval than [0,1]. This interval is divided into *spans* in a uniform or non-uniform way by a sequence of knot values, together forming the *knot vector*. The choice of the knot vector determines the interval where a certain blending function (and hence the control point associated with it) can influence the curve; thus it allows additional control over the shape of the curve. B-splines are piecewise polynomials on the spans. *Rational* B-splines have as extra parameters a *weight factor* for each control point that affects the contribution of the control point to the curve (Tiller 1983). They are defined as the ratio of two polynomial functions. Of particular importance are *non-uniform rational B-splines (NURBS)*, because quadric algebraic curves (such as circles, ellipses, and hyperbolas) can also be modelled with them.

A parametric surface can be composed of several surface patches. A *patch* is defined by a 3D vector function of two parameters:

$$p(u,v) = \begin{bmatrix} x(u,v) \\ y(u,v) \\ z(u,v) \end{bmatrix} \qquad u_0 \le u \le u_1,\ v_0 \le v \le v_1$$

As the parameter u varies from u_0 to u_1 and v from v_0 to v_1, the point $p(u,v)$ traces out the patch. The coordinate functions $x(u,v)$, $y(u,v)$ and $z(u,v)$ are again often (rational) polynomial functions.

Bézier patches are defined by:

$$p(u,v) = \sum_{i=0}^{n} \sum_{j=0}^{m} p_{i,j} B_{i,n}(u) B_{j,m}(v) \qquad 0 \le u \le 1,\ 0 \le v \le 1$$

Bézier patches have similar properties as Bézier curves. In figure 2.2 a bicubic Bézier patch with its 16 control points is shown; on the surface, several Bézier curves are drawn. *B-spline* and *rational B-spline patches* are defined in the same way, but again with their own specific blending functions.

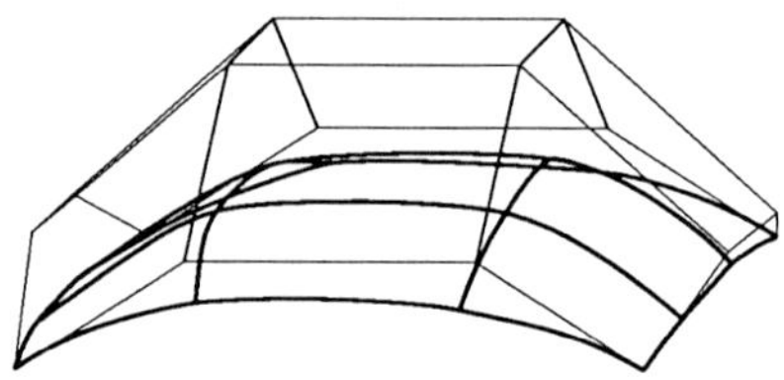

Figure 2.2. A bicubic Bézier patch with its 16 control points.

As defined, the parameter ranges of a surface patch $p(u,v)$ are restricted to $[u_0,u_1]$ and $[v_0,v_1]$. Stated differently, the domain of $p(u,v)$ is the rectangle that can be defined as the intersection of four halfplanes, which are 2D equivalents of 3D halfspaces, in parameter space:

$$\{(u,v) \mid u \ge u_0\}$$

$$\{(u,v) \mid u \le u_1\}$$

$$\{(u,v) \mid v \ge v_0\}$$

$$\{(u,v) \mid v \le v_1\}$$

See figure 2.3a. Parts of a patch can be removed by defining another halfplane in u and v, and further restricting the domain to the intersection of this halfplane and the rectangular area just defined. For example, the corner $p(u_0,v_0)$ can be removed from the patch $p(u,v)$ by taking the intersection of the rectangle with the halfplane

$$\{(u,v) \mid (u - u_0)^2 + (v - v_0)^2 \ge \tfrac{1}{4}(u_1 - u_0)^2\}$$

and restricting the domain of **p**(u,v) to the intersection (see figure 2.3b). Such patches with parts removed from it are called *trimmed patches* (Casale 1987). Trimming of a patch can be used to remove sections of the patch that are not on the boundary of a solid object.

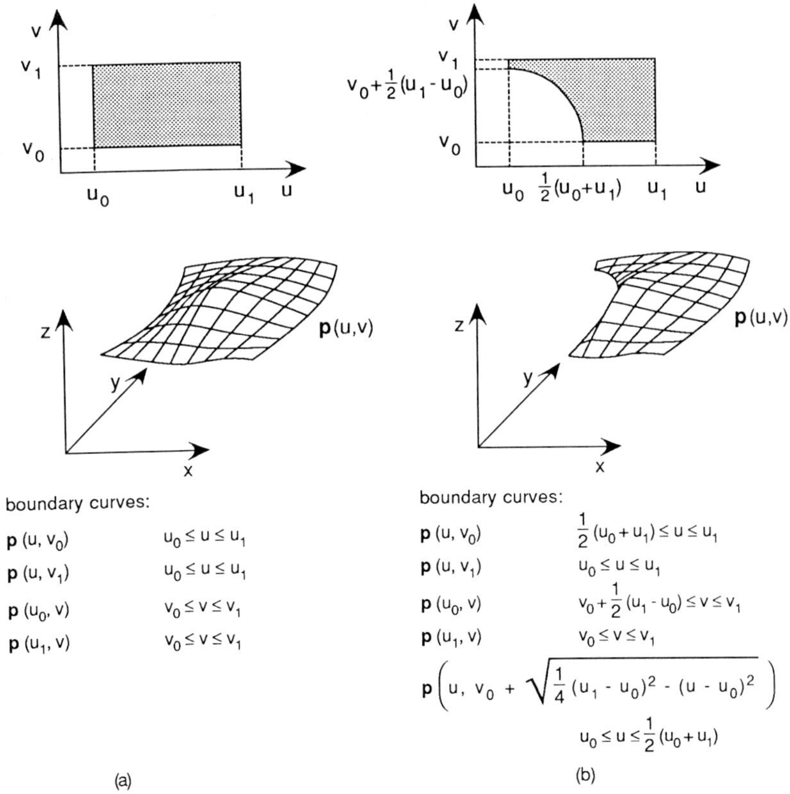

Figure 2.3. The domain (at the top), the shape (in the middle), and the boundary curves (at the bottom), for a non-trimmed patch (a) and a trimmed patch (b).

Parametric surfaces can be used for the modelling of freeform surfaces. Also, the quadric algebraic surfaces often used in solid modelling can be rewritten as NURBS. Compared to implicit surfaces, parametric surfaces have as advantages that they are generally easy to bound by trimming them, and that it is simple to compute points on them, which is convenient for drawing, tesselation and subdivision operations. Implicit surfaces have as advantage that they define two halfspaces, which makes it possible to classify points with respect to a surface, ie. to determine whether a point is on the surface, on one side of the surface, or on the other side of the surface; this is, eg, useful in boundary evaluation algorithms (see 2.4).

2.2 Object Representations for Primitive Objects

Using the types of surfaces discussed in the previous subsection, primitive objects can be defined. A primitive object can either be defined by a halfspace representation, or by a boundary representation (Requicha 1980; Mortenson 1985; Mäntylä 1988).

Halfspace representations define primitive objects as the intersection of a number of halfspaces. In the representation, the coefficients of the surface equations defining the halfspaces are stored. As an example, consider the tetrahedron of figure 2.4. This object can be defined as the intersection of four halfspaces, each determined by a planar surface through three vertices of the tetrahedron.

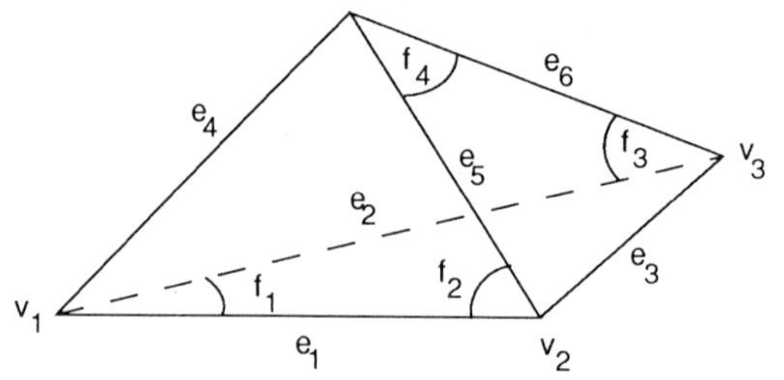

Figure 2.4 . A tetrahedron.

Another example is a cylinder with radius r and height h, which can be defined as the intersection of the halfspaces

$$x^2 + y^2 \leq r^2$$

$$z \geq 0$$

$$z \leq h$$

Boundary representations are based on the observation that a solid object can be considered as being bounded by a number of faces, which are bounded by a number of edges, which in turn are bounded by two vertices. Information is stored about these boundary elements and their adjacency relations.

A face, which may be planar or curved, can be represented by the equation of the surface of which it is a part, and references to its bounding edges. An edge can be represented by the equation of the line or curve of which it is a part, and references to its bounding vertices. A vertex can be represented by its (X, Y, Z)-coordinates. A surface can be represented by either an implicit equation or a (rational) parametric equation, or, in case of a *dual representation*, by both. A dual representation has the advantage that for certain purposes the implicit equation can be used, whereas for other purposes the parametric equation can be used. A line or curve is often represented by a parametric equation.

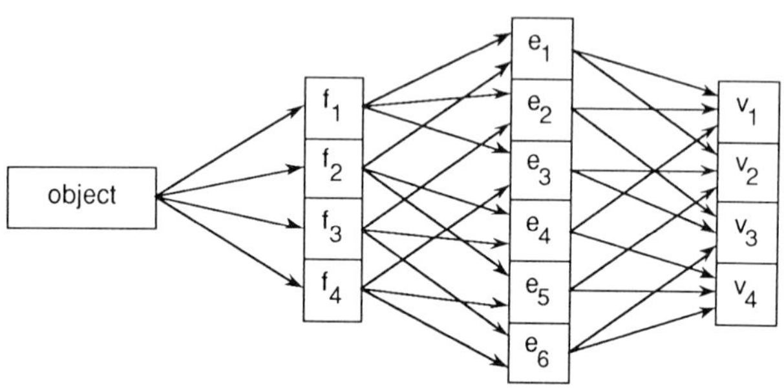

Figure 2.5. Boundary representation of the tetrahedron of figure 2.4.

The data structure is a graph, with nodes (data records) for the boundary elements, and links (pointers) for the references between these elements. The links between the nodes represent the *adjacency relations* between the boundary elements. In fact there are many variants, both in the types of references stored (the *topological information*), and in the types of equations and coordinates stored (the *geometrical information*). See figure 2.5 for a possible boundary representation of the tetrahedron of figure 2.4. An often used variant is the winged-edge data structure, which contains much topological information, and is well suited to the kind of queries often performed on boundary representations (Baumgart 1975).

2.3 Constructive Solid Geometry (CSG)

CSG is based on a collection of primitive solids, such as cubes, cylinders and spheres. Instances of these are scaled, rotated and translated in 3D space, and then combined with the set operations union (∪), difference (-) and intersection (∩) to form more complex, composite objects (Requicha 1980; Mortenson 1985; Mäntylä 1988). The primitives can either be represented by halfspaces, or by a boundary representation, as described in 2.2.

The data structure of a CSG representation is a binary tree called the *CSG tree*. All nodes in the tree are records. At a leaf node, also referred to as a primitive node here, information about a primitive is stored. This may consist either of its type and the applied transformations if halfspaces are used, or of a boundary representation. At an internal node, also referred to as a composite node here, the set operation to be applied to the objects defined by the left and right branches of that node, and pointers to these branches, are stored. See figure 2.6 for a CSG model and a schematic representation of its CSG tree.

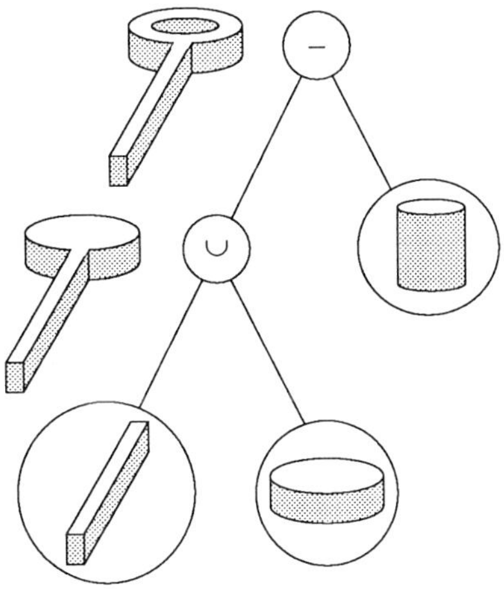

Figure 2.6. A CSG model and its CSG tree.

The main advantage of a CSG representation is the simplicity of the data structure. The main disadvantage is that there is no explicit information in the representation about the faces, edges and vertices of the composite object, which makes it less suitable for certain purposes.

Many solid modellers based on CSG model specification maintain the CSG representation as their main model representation, or as one of their auxiliary model representations.

2.4 Boundary Representation and Boundary Evaluation

For many applications, a boundary representation of an object is required, also of objects modelled with CSG. Such a boundary representation is similar to one for a primitive, but usually contains far more faces, edges and vertices. A boundary representation can be computed from a CSG model by a *boundary evaluation* algorithm.

Many boundary representations provide only planar faces, because such a representation is simpler, and many operations, eg. display, are simpler and faster. The disadvantage is that curved faces have to be approximated by planar faces, which gives inaccurate results and requires more memory. Objects with planar faces only are called *polyhedral objects*. If an object also has quadric algebraic faces, it is called a *quadric object*.

The main advantage of boundary representations is that information about faces, edges and vertices is explicitly stored in the representation, which is useful for many purposes, eg. fast display. The main disadvantages are the complexity of the data structure and the large amount of memory needed. Another problem with boundary representations is that boundary evaluation algorithms are difficult to implement, time-consuming and sensitive to numerical inaccuracy.

A general framework for boundary evaluation algorithms has been suggested by Requicha and Voelcker (1985). Their algorithms are based on the generate-and-test paradigm for faces and edges. Candidate faces and edges are first generated, which are then classified as belonging, or not belonging, to the CSG model. Candidate faces and edges are the faces and edges of the primitives to be combined, and newly generated *cross edges*, ie. intersections between faces of different primitives. The first have to be computed only when the primitives are represented by halfspaces, because they are already known when the primitives are represented by a boundary representation. The generation of the cross edges is one of the most difficult steps in the algorithm: it requires that each face of each primitive be checked for intersection with every face of the other primitives, and this checking can lead to numerical difficulties when, eg, faces are nearly coplanar.

The second step is to test which of the candidate faces and edges belong to the composite object. This is done by a method called *set membership classification*. The classification of a candidate set with respect to a primitive divides the candidate set into subsets of elements that are inside, on the boundary of, or outside the primitive. To find the classification with respect to a composite object that consists of two primitives, the classification subsets of the primitives are combined according to rules for the appropriate set operator. The same is done to find the classifications at higher level nodes in the CSG tree. If there are no special cases, such as coplanar faces, this is a simple operation; if there are, however, ambiguities can occur. These can be resolved by adding neighbourhood information to the classifications, ie. information on where the material of the object is. For example, neighbourhood information for a face could indicate on which side the object lies. The classification-combination algorithm uses the neighbourhood information to resolve ambiguities.

Polyhedral primitives are assumed, although the authors claim that the basic algorithms can also handle primitives with curved faces if the appropriate procedures for determining intersection curves between faces are available. However, they give no details on this.

Boundary evaluation for polyhedral objects

Mäntylä (1983) has given a simple boundary evaluation algorithm for polyhedral objects, which, however, cannot handle special cases such as coplanar faces. The boundaries of two primitives to be combined, A and B, are both divided along their intersection lines into two parts. The boundary of A is divided into $AinB$, which consists of the part inside B, and $AoutB$, which consists of the part outside B. Likewise, the boundary of B is divided into $BinA$ and $BoutA$ (see figure 2.7a).

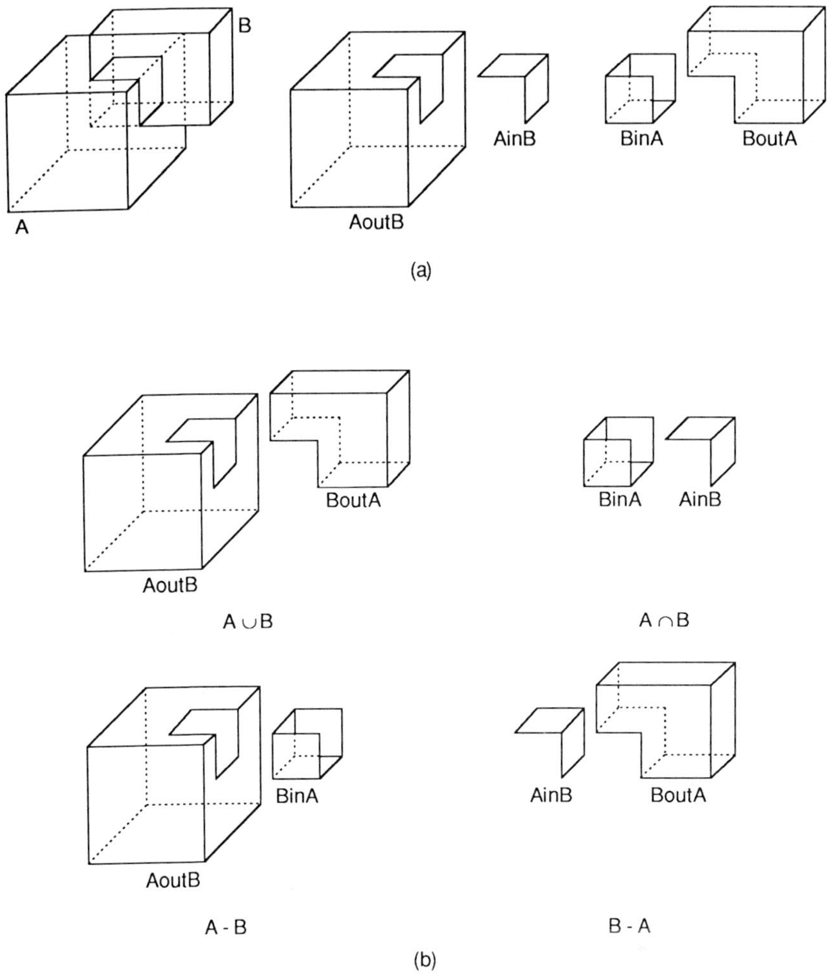

Figure 2.7. *(a) Division of the boundaries of two primitives A and B.*
(b) Parts of the boundaries selected depending on the applied set operator.

To determine the boundary of the composite object, the relevant parts of the boundaries of A and B have to be selected (see figure 2.7b). This is dependent on the set operator:

- $A \cup B$: *AoutB* and *BoutA*
- $A \cap B$: *AinB* and *BinA*
- $A - B$: *AoutB* and *BinA*
- $B - A$: *BoutA* and *AinB*

The two selected parts are combined to make up the boundary of the resulting object. From figure 2.7b it can be seen that in all cases the correct object results.

Laidlaw et al (1986) and Mäntylä (1986) have extended the work on boundary evaluation for polyhedral objects. The basic ideas are the same: candidate faces and edges are first generated, which are then classified as being on, or not on, the boundary of the composite object. The most important extension is that methods are provided for handling special cases (coplanar faces, collinear edges, coincident vertices, etc). Both papers give detailed descriptions of the algorithms, and can therefore serve very well as a starting point for implementation.

Laidlaw et al (1986) give an analysis of the different types of intersections that may occur in the generate phase, and also give methods for handling coplanar faces correctly and efficiently. Mäntylä (1986) gives a new method for the classification phase, based on *vertex neighbourhood classification*. All special cases are reduced to a collection of classification problems that involve pairs of coincident vertices. The vertex neighbourhoods used for the classification are implicitly represented as ordered cycles of edges and faces around a vertex. Mäntylä claims that his method efficiently exploits adjacency information usually already available in boundary representations.

Both papers report that numerical difficulties still remain. These arise from the restricted accuracy of floating-point computation, and there is not yet a set of algorithms that consistently answers geometric queries, such as do two faces intersect, does an edge intersect a face, and does a vertex lie inside a face. Segal and Séquin (1988) suggest a scheme in which the boundary evaluation algorithm can detect, and if possible overcome, the effects of numerical inaccuracies by using tolerances; when this does not work, the user is consulted. Hoffmann et al (1989) claim to have implemented a robust algorithm by using reliable basic routines, by avoiding numerical redundancy and numerical computation based on derived quantities as much as possible, and by using symbolic reasoning to resolve possible ambiguity. Although their approach looks promising, much remains to be done in this area.

Boundary evaluation for quadric objects

The basic idea underlying boundary evaluation algorithms for objects with quadric surfaces, in particular the most commonly occurring *natural quadrics*, plane, sphere, cylinder and cone, is the same as for polyhedral objects (Requicha and Voelcker 1985). Miller (1988) distinguishes a generate and a test phase for quadric objects also. The test phase is again based on set membership classification. The main differences are in the generate phase, where the intersection curves of quadric surfaces are even more difficult to compute than the intersection lines of planar surfaces.

A distinction is made between algebraic and geometric approaches for determining the intersection curves (Miller 1987, 1988). Algebraic methods are based on unified representations and algorithms for all types of planar and quadric surfaces; this minimizes the amount of code, but requires numerically sensitive tests on quantities that have no direct geometric significance. Geometric methods require separate algorithms for each pair of surface types, but use only tests on quantities with direct geometric significance, such as points and radii, and their numerical stability is therefore easier to achieve. In particular, special cases such as touching faces, can be handled more accurately. Miller (1987) gives an exhaustive description of methods for determining the intersection curves between the natural quadrics. Piegl (1989a) describes a purely geometrical approach, in which conic sections as intersection curves are computed exactly on the basis of the orientation of the primitives, and the more general intersections are handled by computing a number of points on and tangents to the intersection curve, and determining a spline curve on the basis of these.

Efficiency of boundary evaluation
Another aspect worth mentioning is the efficiency of boundary evaluation. If, eg, each face of one primitive were actually compared with every face of all other primitives, then the generate phase would become unacceptably slow. Requicha and Voelcker (1985) already suggest a number of methods to improve the efficiency, such as the avoidance of unnecessary face intersections by using bounding boxes or space subdivision (see also Mäntylä and Tamminen 1983), but work in this direction has continued in the meantime. For example, Navazo et al (1987) use a special type of octtree for primitives to localize the intersection computations in the generate phase.

The previous methods can be characterized as *spatial* or *geometric localization* methods. Another approach is *structural localization*, which is based on the observation that not every cross edge of a primitive with another primitive will be on the boundary of the resulting composite object. Rossignac and Voelcker (1986) have shown how the *active zone* of a primitive can be expressed as an intersection of the primitive with a subset of the CSG tree. Using the active zone will restrict the search for cross edges to those needed for the boundary evaluation.

2.5 Direct Display Algorithms

Because of the problems involved in boundary evaluation, the following approach has emerged for display of CSG models. A complete boundary evaluation is avoided by applying a *direct display algorithm* to the CSG model. In such an algorithm the classification of faces is performed as part of the display process. Besides the usual task of determining which face is nearest to the observer on the relevant area of the screen, a direct display algorithm also has to determine whether that face is on the boundary of the composite object. In fact what is done here, is a partial boundary evaluation over a limited area on the screen, for the visible parts of the model only. Also, in display algorithms based on point sampling, the classification has to be done only locally at the sampling points, and not for the whole model. Details of the classification depend on the display algorithm that is taken as the basis for the direct display algorithm.

The advantages of this approach are:

- it is relatively easy to extend display algorithms for classification, and thus the burden of writing complex software for a complete boundary evaluation can be avoided
- it is much more efficient than first applying a boundary evaluation, and then a standard display algorithm
- numerical inaccuracies can be resolved much easier
- because of its simplicity, the classification can be implemented in special-purpose display hardware; this would be very difficult for a complete boundary evaluation.

The main disadvantage is that no boundary representation of the composite model is produced, and this may be needed for other applications. However, similar techniques working directly on CSG models have also been successfully used in other applications, such as computing the volume and other integral properties (Lee and Requicha 1982). An interesting research topic would be to identify the types of applications in which the evaluation of the CSG models could be incorporated into the corresponding algorithms for boundary representations. Another disadvantage is that the classification is viewpoint dependent, but this is of minor importance, since the classification overhead in the display algorithm is relatively small.

3. Model Input and Modification

In this section we will discuss input and modification techniques for solid models. We will concentrate here on creating a model of a single complex part; methods for assembly involving multiple parts will be discussed in section 4. First, we will distinguish between different modes and levels of input, such as elementary geometric data, predefined components, and input from engineering drawings or 3D wire frame models. Then we will review some tools for procedural input of new models and for modifying existing models, and finally we will discuss two types of user interfaces for solid modelling: modelling languages, and interactive graphical modelling.

3.1 Input of Geometric Models

Input of a geometric model is the construction of an internal representation from commands and geometric data. It has the nature of a representation conversion: the input data and commands can be viewed as an input representation, which is converted to the main representation by applying an algorithm, which builds eg. a boundary model or a CSG tree from the input representation. The input representation should thus contain a complete and valid description of the model, and these qualities should be preserved by the conversion algorithm.

Model input is concerned with the following problems:

- Correspondence to the user's frame of reference: a designer is usually neither a programmer, nor a mathematician; internal details of mathematics and data structures should therefore be hidden, and the modelling system should be responsible for checking the validity of the models.
- Level of modelling operations: low-level input consists of elementary geometric data (eg. points), and simple commands for creation and modification. In this case, usually a good understanding of the underlying mathematical concepts and the implementation is required, but it gives the skilled user access to all facilities of the internal model.
  High-level input uses more powerful commands and requires less input of geometric data. An example of this is the creation of a solid from predefined parameterized primitives, instead of specifying all the basic geometric entities, such as edges, faces and vertices. Research on model input is a quest for higher level input techniques, eventually allowing specification on a functional rather than a geometric level.
- Feedback during interactive input: spatial and shape information can be provided by graphical display of models, using line drawings or shaded images. For a good judgment of the quality of a shape, special types of visual output are necessary, eg. showing contour lines, reflection lines or curvature lines (Farin 1988; Farouki 1987).

Model input can be divided into the following categories: geometric data, predefined components, or input from existing representations. These types will be discussed in some detail below.

Geometric data

From elementary geometric data, such as 3D points, surfaces or solids can be constructed, using geometric algorithms for interpolation or approximation of the data. The simplest form of this is generation of polygon meshes, by using triangulation algorithms (eg. Watson 1981). The data points are connected to form a coherent mesh of non-overlapping triangles.

Another form is the definition of smooth curves, surfaces, or solids, using parametric polynomial methods, such as Bézier methods or B-splines (see 2.1; Farin 1988). The input points must then be ordered in a grid with regular topology; often a rectangular topology is required, sometimes a triangular topology is allowed. The points can then be used as control points.

These methods are often used in modelling complex smooth surfaces, especially for input of existing physical shapes. They are of limited use for solid modelling, because it is difficult to guarantee that the surfaces defined will form complete and valid solids. One exception is the *hyperpatch*, an extension of surface modelling methods to solids, using a 3D grid of control points and parametric blending functions of three variables (Casale and Stanton 1985).

Another important application of geometric data input for solid modelling is the definition of 2D curves for sweeping, lofting, and other methods of cross-sectional design. These will be discussed in section 3.2.

Predefined components
In solid modelling, predefined components are widely used. A standard set of primitive objects is available, such as blocks, cylinders, cones, and spheres. Of each of these primitives, a predefined template representation is available, which can be instantiated using a limited set of parameters (the radius of a sphere, the radius and height of a cylinder), and appropriate transformations (translation, rotation) to specify a position and orientation in space. The template representation can be a boundary representation, containing the full topology of the primitive; for each instance, geometry is computed from the parameters. In this simple form, we have a *primitive-instancing* specification (Requicha 1980). To facilitate the building of complex models, additional facilities can be provided to define hierarchical structures, in which spatial relationships between parts can be defined (see 4.1).

In almost every solid modelling system, the primitives can be combined using the set operations (union, difference, and intersection) described in section 2.3. By specifying the primitives, their parameters and transformations, and their combinations, a complete CSG tree can be built interactively. This method allows specification of highly complex models in a step by step fashion. However, input of the parameters and transformations separately for each primitive is a rigid bottom-up design process, that does not allow easy modification of global dimensions of the model, and does not preserve the spatial relationships between the various parts of a model. Also, specifying positions by independent translations and rotations is a tedious process. Therefore, in section 4, more flexible and powerful methods will be described to interactively specify CSG models.

Input from existing representations
With the previously described techniques, the designer does not use any existing representations of the model to be defined. Below we will describe some techniques that start from existing drawings or models.

The first group of methods, known as 3D reconstruction, is the creation of 3D models from 2D engineering drawings. Mostly multi-view orthographic drawings are used, but sometimes also quasi-isometric sketches; drawings are pasted onto a 2D digitizer for input. We can distinguish two methods: the entity method, and the bottom-up method.

With the *entity method*, a CSG representation is constructed interactively from two or three view engineering drawings. The user must visually identify the primitives and the relevant set operations, and from input of certain critical data points for each primitive, dimensions and positions are derived (Aldefeld 1983; Ho Bin 1986; figure 3.1).

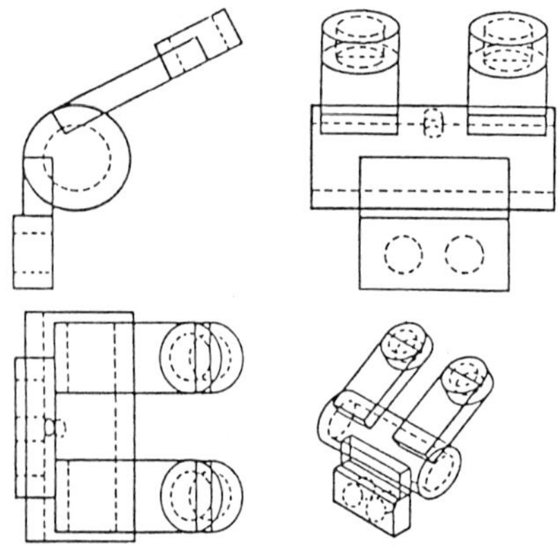

Figure 3.1. CSG model constructed from drawing input (Ho Bin 1986).

The *bottom-up method* generates boundary representations of all possible objects that can be constructed from digitized input points in two or more projected views. If more than one solution exists, the user selects the correct one. 3D (candidate) vertex coordinates are found by identifying the same 2D point in two or more views. The vertices are assembled in (candidate) edges and faces, and adjacency relations are found by searching the sets of candidate elements using combinatorial algorithms, until one ore more consistent candidate objects result, from which the user can choose (Wesley and Markowski 1981; Sakurai and Gossard 1983; Lequette 1988).

Instead of engineering drawings, sometimes 3D wire frame representations of the model already exist. In this case slightly different methods must be applied to generate solid boundary representations. This is done using similar combinatorial algorithms, with occasional user input to resolve ambiguities (Courter and Brewer 1986; Wesley and Markowski 1980).

These methods depend upon the existence of consistent and accurately dimensioned drawings, and also on the accuracy of the input device and the human operator. They are mainly important as a one-time conversion operation from drawings (or wire frame based CAD systems) to solid modelling systems.

3.2 Procedural Specification of Models

Procedural specification is a form of input in which not the shape itself is defined, but a procedure to generate it. Only a small amount of geometric data is then needed to produce the shape. Examples of this principle are sweeping, lofting, and skinning, or more generally, methods of cross-sectional design. These methods can be considered as a separate class of shape representations, but they are described here because of their suitability for input. A few examples will be given here.

Sweeping is a method of defining a shape from two curves: a 2D closed curve (the contour) and a 3D open or closed curve (the trajectory or spine curve). The contour is the cross section of the shape, the trajectory is the axis. A surface is generated as the contour moves orthogonally along the trajectory curve. The contour and trajectory may be defined in any way: as polygons, parametric curves, or algebraic curves. If the trajectory is closed, the sweep surface fully defines the boundary of a solid; if it is open, end planes can be added to form a closed boundary. In this way a *sweep object* is defined.

There are four basic types of sweep objects (figure 3.2):

- *translation sweep*: the trajectory is a straight line segment; the resulting objects are beams or prisms;
- *rotation sweep*: the trajectory is a circular arc; solids of revolution are defined with a full circular trajectory;
- *circle sweep*: the contour is a circle, the trajectory is an arbitrary space curve (van Wijk 1984b);
- generalized cylinders: both contour and trajectory are arbitrary curves (Bronsvoort et al 1989)

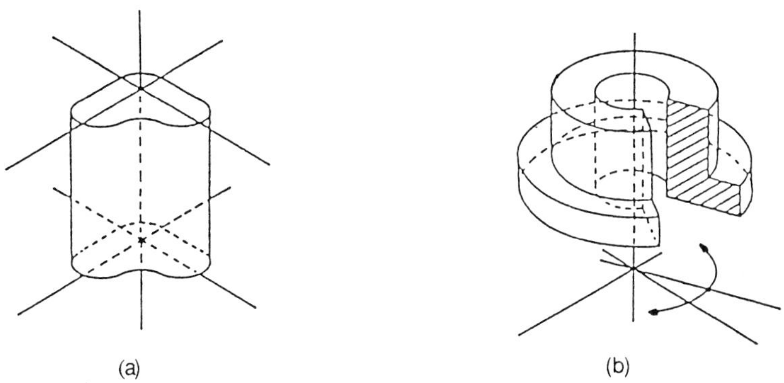

Figure 3.2. Two basic forms of sweeping: (a) translation sweeping; (b) rotation sweeping (van Wijk 1986b).

The concept can be extended in several ways. One way is to take a 3D shape as a contour, such as a sphere (van Wijk 1984b). Another way is to allow the size of the contour to vary gradually as it moves along the trajectory. The contour can be scaled in its plane in two perpendicular directions, according to smoothly varying *profile curves*, which specify scale factors at each point of the trajectory. Thus we will get *profiled prisms* when the trajectory is linear, and *profiled generalized cylinders* when the trajectory is an arbitrary space curve (figure 3.3; Bronsvoort et al 1989; see also Coquillart 1987).

Most types of sweep objects can be easily converted into explicit polygonal boundary models; and so they can serve as primitives in polygonal CSG modelling systems (Post and Klok 1986; Bronsvoort et al 1989). For display, polygon conversion is not always necessary, because display algorithms have been developed for sweep objects that directly use the procedural representation (van Wijk 1984a,b; Bronsvoort and Klok 1985; Bronsvoort et al 1989).

The validity of a solid object defined by sweeping is not guaranteed; for example, several types of self-intersections may occur, especially with the extended forms of sweeping using general 3D trajectories. Also, the range of shapes generated is restricted.

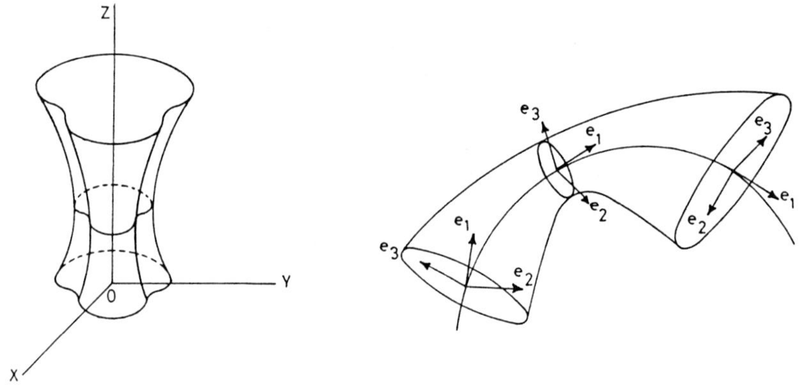

Figure 3.3. Profiled sweep objects: (a) profiled prism; (b) profiled generalized cylinder.

Lofting is a related technique: a series of open or closed curves is specified by the user, and a free-form surface is generated that smoothly interpolates these curves. The curves are often defined as cross sections in a number of parallel planes (Filip and Ball 1989). This method is often used to define ship hulls or aircraft fuselages.

With *skinning*, a number of different planar closed curves are defined as cross sections, and positioned orthogonally at points along a 3D spine curve. A skin surface is then defined that smoothly interpolates all cross sections (Tiller 1983; Woodward 1986). In this way, *ducts* can be defined; solids can be obtained by adding end planes as with sweeping.

Sweeping, lofting and skinning are all members of a family of shape specification techniques called *cross-sectional design* methods (Faux and Pratt 1979; Woodward 1986). The general idea is to specify a solid or surface by a number of 2D longitudinal or transverse cross sections, and an algorithm for generating a surface that smoothly interpolates these cross sections.

Cross-sectional design is very suitable for input of shapes and solids. Cross sections and planar trajectories or spine curves can be specified using common 2D input procedures, eg. for control points of parametric curves, and the amount of geometric data input is small. Specifying 3D trajectory curves is more difficult, but in practice it seldom happens that both contour and trajectory of a sweep object are complex shapes. In lofting and skinning, each cross section has to be explicitly positioned in relation to the spine curve; in sweeping, this relation is governed by a rule which specifies the orientation of the contour in each plane normal to the trajectory (sweeping frame; see Bronsvoort et al 1989).

The amount of geometric data input needed for cross-sectional design is generally very small, even for quite complex shapes. The spatial relation between cross sections and the resulting surface is clear. However, surfaces may result that cannot be easily used in defining valid solids. For example, local or global self-intersections may occur.

3.3 Shape Operations

After input of an initial model, it can be extended and modified. In top-down design, rough shapes are refined, and more detail is added; in a bottom-up strategy, a complex shape is composed by combining separate elementary shapes. Methods for editing existing models are known as shape operations. We will briefly review some operations here; some of them are purely facilities offered by a particular representation (local operations, Euler operations, shape handles), whereas others can be considered as analogies of design and manufacturing operations (deformations, blending, and offsetting).

Local operations

Boundary models allow access to low-level entities, such as vertices, edges, and faces, and thus operations can be defined to make local changes to them (Jared and Stroud 1983). Some operations can only change geometry (tweaking), whereas others affect both geometry and topology (gluing).

Some examples are given below.

- *Gluing*: joining two objects with (partially) coincident faces. The data structures for the two objects are merged, and topology is adjusted to make a single object. The result is that the two objects are 'glued' together.
- *Tweaking*: changing the geometry of an existing face, by translating or rotating it, or by changing its definition, such as replacing a planar face by a free-from surface patch (see also Beeker 1986).
- *Chamfering*: an edge or vertex is replaced by a face. This is a simple form of *blending* (see below).

Local operations are simple and fast to perform, but the validity of a model can be easily ruined. An implementation should therefore provide careful checking of data and handling of special cases to avoid this, but robustness is not an inherent characteristic as with set operations.

Euler operations

For the topology of a valid boundary model, the following relation must hold:

$$v - e + f = 2,$$

where v, e, and f are the number of vertices, edges, and faces. This relation, known as Euler's rule, applies to simple objects without internal holes. It can be generalized by adding three other parameters: r for the number of rings (loops) in faces, h for the number of holes through an object, and s for the number of disjoint parts (shells). The generalized form is:

$$v - e + f = 2\ (s - h) + r$$

Euler operations are sets of unit changes to the variables, that preserve the validity of the relation (Mäntylä 1988). They consist of creating and destroying elements in the data structure, increasing and decreasing two or more variables by one. An example is: "make edge and face" (mcf): e and f are both incremented by one. In figure 3.4, the complete set of ten Euler operations is shown.

Individual Euler operations are not primarily intended as shape operations directly available to the user, but as internal access functions to modify the data structure. However, high-level operations, such as set operations, can be implemented using (compound) Euler operations. They can also be used for a permanent procedural representation, which requires less storage than a full boundary model. The description does not depend on the internal representation, and can thus also be used as an external interface.

Conservation of Euler's rule is a necessary, but not a sufficient condition to guarantee validity of a boundary model. Not only topology, but also geometry must be valid, and for geometry there are no similar simple rules. Checking geometric validity is quite complex, and must be performed separately.

Operator	Transition Vector						Description
	v	e	f	h	s	r	
mvfs	1	0	1	0	1	0	Make Vertex, Face, Shell
mev	1	1	0	0	0	0	Make Edge, Vertex
mef	0	1	1	0	0	0	Make Edge, Face
kemr	0	-1	0	0	0	1	Kill Edge, Make Ring
kfmrh	0	0	-1	1	0	1	Kill Face, Make Ring, Hole
kvfs	-1	0	-1	0	-1	0	Kill Vertex, Face, Shell
kev	-1	-1	0	0	0	0	Kill Edge, Vertex
kef	0	-1	-1	0	0	0	Kill Edge, Face
mekr	0	1	0	0	0	-1	Make Edge, Kill Ring
mfkrh	0	0	1	-1	0	-1	Make Face, Kill Ring, Hole

Figure 3.4. Euler operators (after Mäntylä 1988).

Shape handles for parametric curves and surfaces

Similar to local operations on boundary models, the shape of parametric curves and surfaces can be modified by moving, inserting, or multiplying control points, which has a more or less localized and predictable effect on the shape. Also, operations on *knot vectors* of B-spline curves and surfaces (see 2.1) are possible; insertion of new knots (Böhm 1980; Cohen et al 1980) will lead to generation of extra control points in a certain region, which can then be locally modified. Generally, the effects of knot vector manipulations are more difficult to predict, and require more knowledge about the mathematics on the part of the user than control point manipulations.

When rational B-splines are used, each 3D control point $[x\ y\ z]$ will be assigned a *weight* w, and is thus transformed to a 4D homogeneous point $[wx\ wy\ wz\ w]$. These weights can also play a role in controlling the resulting shape. If $w = 0$, the control point does not affect the shape at all; if $w \rightarrow \infty$, the shape will interpolate the control point.

In Piegl (1989b,c), a series of new shape operations for rational B-spline curves and surfaces are described, based on manipulation of control points, for computing weights and inserting knots. These operations, called shape handles, can be used for both curves and surfaces. They are intended to have a predictable geometric effect on the shapes, without requiring knowledge of the mathematics. Three examples will illustrate this.

- *Inverse knot insertion*: the user does not specify knots, but simply new control points in a region to be modified; the appropriate knots are computed by the system, and inserted in the knot vector.
- *Weight recomputation:* the user specifies a direction in which the curve or surface is to be displaced, determined by a control point and a point on the surface. The amount of push toward or pull away from the control point is specified, and the weight of the relevant control points is recomputed to achieve this. These push-pull operations can also be performed simultaneously on a larger region of a curve or surface.
- *Segmented modifications*: local control is a desirable property of (rational) B-splines. This operation enables the user to precisely restrict changes to a region on the curve or surface indicated by the user. Knot vectors are refined and new control points generated that are guaranteed to affect only the part indicated by the user.

These operations are attractive because they are oriented towards graphical interaction (mainly specifying and moving points) and do not require thorough knowledge of the underlying geometry. They are applicable to rational B-spline curves and surfaces, an important class of shapes that is also suitable for use in solid modelling, because they can exactly represent conic sections and natural quadric surfaces.

Deformations
Deformations are geometrical analogies of physical deformations, such as bending, twisting, and tapering. The geometry of an existing model is modified without changing topology; the effect is as though the object were made of clay or rubber.

One method of deforming objects was described by Barr (1984). Each type of deformation is characterized by a deformation function, by which position vectors for a deformed object are calculated from those of the undeformed object. Using the Jacobian matrix of a deformation function, surface tangents and normals can also be derived.

In free-form deformation (FFD) (Sederberg and Parry 1986), an object is deformed by enclosing it in a rectangular box. In this box, a 3D rectangular grid of control points is generated, and a Bézier function of three variables (hyperpatch) is used as a deformation function. When control points (individual points, rows, or planes of points) are moved, the shape of the box is deformed, and so is the object inside it.

FFD is conceptually simple and powerful; it can be applied globally or locally, preserving continuity between deformed and undeformed parts, or in a hierarchical scheme. Deformations can be combined in any order; simple constraints can be imposed, so that the volume of a deformed object does not change. FFD can be applied to any kind of model, provided that any number of surface points can be calculated.

Other approaches to deformation are specific for a certain type of models. Fournier and Wesley (1983) described an algorithm for localised bending of a polygonal model, by inserting a bending zone with a cylindrical geometry. Another example is the deformation of generalized sweep objects described by Post and Klok (1986); a sweep object is bent by bending the trajectory, twisted by rotating the contour, and tapered by scaling the contour during sweeping.

The deformations mentioned above are purely geometrical operations, and do not attempt to model physical reality; the mechanics of deformation can be modelled using finite element analysis or similar techniques.

Blending
Angular forms and discontinuous transitions between surfaces can be smoothed using blending operations. Blending is a general term, covering many types of smoothing techniques, such as filleting, fairing, chamfering, and rounding (Woodwark 1987). We will briefly describe two types of blending here: by insertion of curved surfaces, and by recursively cutting off corners. Both types start from rough polyhedral solids.

Sharp edges or vertices can be smoothed by replacing them with curved faces, that must have at least tangent continuity with all surrounding faces (Chiyokura 1988). For geometry, both free-form parametric surfaces, and algebraic surfaces can be used. Besides the smooth interpolation of the adjacent faces, additional geometric constraints can be imposed on the geometry of blend surfaces; for example, they can be restricted to a given range or volume, or to having a constant radius (Rossignac and Requicha 1984). Blending can be incorporated in CSG modelling systems, smoothing intersections between pairs of primitive solids (Middleditch and Sears 1985).

Depending on the topology of the original solid, the new faces can have three, four, or five edges. With four edges, simple cylindrical or conical algebraic surfaces, or parametric patches can be used. Special types of parametric surfaces have been developed with three or five edges (Chiyokura 1988).

Complex geometric and topological problems may easily occur in blending, for instance where different blend surfaces interact. No single universal blending operation is known which can be used in all cases, but the technique described by Holmström (1987) based on piecewise quadric surfaces can be applied in many situations.

A second type of blending is obtained by recursively cutting off corners of the initial polyhedron (Nasri 1987). Edges and vertices are replaced by small faces, and the newly created edges and vertices are again replaced by smaller faces, and so on, until a certain smoothness criterion is satisfied. In this way, a polyhedral approximation of a rounded solid is created (figure 3.5). Problems can again occur where non-four-sided faces are generated. Singular areas can appear, consisting of non-planar faces; these are reduced in size, but will not vanish by further subdivisions.

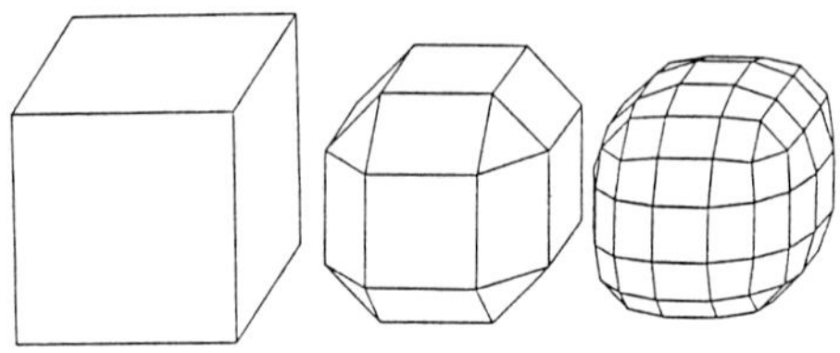

Figure 3.5. Blending by recursive subdivision.

Offsetting

With offsetting, a new object is defined as the set of points that lie within or at a certain distance *r* from an existing base object (Rossignac and Requicha 1986a). The base object can be a point, a curve segment, a surface, or a solid. If the offset is positive, a larger object results; with a negative offset, the base object is reduced in size. The (positive) offset of a point is a sphere; the offset of a line segment is a (rounded) cylinder. Generally, an offset surface does not have the same geometric representation as its base surface. As computation of explicit offset surfaces is difficult (Farouki 1985), offsetting is often considered as a procedural representation.

Offsetting has a variety of applications, such as modelling of tolerances, NC tool path generation, clearance testing in robot motion planning, modelling of surface finish, and blending of solids. Simple (constant-radius) blending of solids can be achieved by a series of positive and negative offsetting operations (Rossignac and Requicha 1986a). A 2D example of this is shown in figure 3.6.

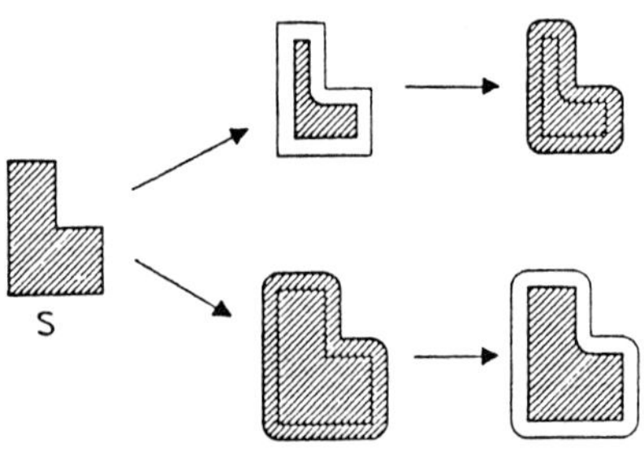

Figure 3.6. Blending using offsetting operations (Rossignac and Requicha 1986a).

3.4 User Interfaces for Solid Modelling

User interfaces for solid modelling can be divided into two classes: command language and graphical interfaces. In a command language interface, a model is described in a model description language, which is an explicit input representation. It can be stored in a text file, which is read and translated by the modelling system to its main representation. The modelling commands can also be entered interactively, to be interpreted and executed immediately by the modelling system.

Model description languages can be simple (low-level) or more advanced (high-level). For a CSG modelling system, the language must at least have commands for creation of primitives, for specifying their parameters, and their position and orientation in space, and for set operations. More advanced languages are more like modern procedural programming languages. They can have facilities such as predefined geometric data types and data structures, naming of objects for repeated use, variables and arithmetic expressions, and conditional and repetition constructs.

Of particular importance are facilities for the definition of object families by means of parameterized functions and procedures. Instances are created by calling such a procedure, specifying values for the parameters. For instance, a cog-wheel could be characterized by its diameter and number of teeth. This is an implementation of parametric design (see 4.2). An example of this, taken from the language SML (van Wijk 1986a), is shown in figure 3.7.

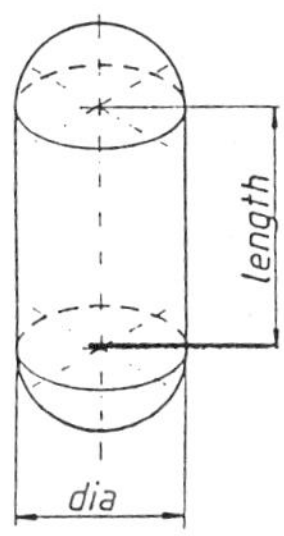


```
function Rcyl(dia, length);
begin
   Rcyl := cyl(dia, length);
   S1 := sph(dia);
   S2 := sph(dia);
      mov(z, length);
   Rcyl := Rcyl + S1 + S2
end;

Capsule := Rcyl(10, 30) - Rcyl(8, 30);
```

Figure 3.7. Model description language SML (van Wijk 1986a).

High level model description languages provide a compact, structured method to specify geometric models. Existing model descriptions are easily stored and changed, and libraries with parametric objects can be built. Language input is also easily portable, requiring only text input and an input translator. A disadvantage is that writing model descriptions is more akin to programming than to engineering design. The user is often not a programmer, but a design engineer, who may not be familiar with the algorithmic style imposed by the language.

Graphical user interfaces are based on the idea of building a model in a dialogue with the modelling system, with visual feedback reflecting the state of the model. The designer uses a graphical workstation with input devices, and appropriate graphical software. The dominant graphical user interface on CAD workstations is the window manager interface, with multiple overlapping windows, menu control, and a mouse as a pointing and positioning device (Myers 1988). Command input is typically done by menu selection using the mouse. Menus can be permanently on the screen, but can also be *pop-up* or *pull-down* menus, which appear only when called, and disappear again after a selection has been made.

Menu selection is often used in combination with command language input. The main advantage of menu selection is that it is easy to learn; only the limited set of commands available at any given moment is presented to the user. A disadvantage is that many steps are often needed to perform even a simple operation, with menus flashing on and off the screen, which can be distracting to the user. Also, with menus it is difficult to specify operands; for this, additional text or graphical input is required.

Interactive graphical user interfaces are often based on the text editor analogy: a model is read from a file, modified, and saved again in a file. Basic editing operations are creating, moving, copying, and deleting objects. Besides this, there must be a set of shape operations (as described in 3.3) for refining shapes or composing shapes from separate parts. Interactive procedures for these can be inspired by metaphors from engineering design, manufacturing, or the visual arts. Some of the shape operations mentioned are analogies of sculpturing or sheet metal work.

A style of interaction in which the user acts directly upon a visual representation of a model (realistic or symbolic) is called *direct manipulation* (Shneiderman 1983). Parts of a model to be used in some operation can be selected by *pointing* at them on the screen, and thus no names need be given. Some actions, such as moving and rotating objects, or performing shape operations, can be carried out by *dragging* objects, or control points, on the screen. In each case, a clear relationship must exist between the action and the effect of the action on the visual representation. In this style of interaction, a 3D cursor can be a very useful aid (van Overveld 1989). In section 4, an example will be described of a system that uses direct manipulation techniques for definition of CSG models.

Viewing commands must be available to control visual feedback: to specify viewing parameters such as viewpoint and view direction, projection, or lighting conditions, and to determine the mode of display, such as line drawings, or different types of shaded images.

Visual feedback of models must satisfy two conflicting criteria: it must be fast, and give a clear impression of spatial form and structure. Display algorithms that give more spatial information are computationally more expensive; wire frame pictures can be generated within seconds, whereas line drawings with hidden lines removed, or medium-quality shaded images may take a few minutes. Ray tracing takes even more time, and is therefore seldom used in an interactive environment; it produces high-quality pictures for presentation of the final design.

The value of the various modes of display in giving spatial information cannot be objectively determined. Clarifying one part of a picture may well imply loss of information in another part, as happens in removing hidden parts. Line drawings only give good information at silhouettes and edges; shaded images give a good impression of curved surfaces. To let the user decide on the most suitable form of visual feedback, a range of display styles must be available, possibly including the types of display mentioned in 3.1 that are especially suitable for judging the geometrical quality of a shape.

4. Assembly Modelling

Solid modelling representations and input techniques discussed so far allow the definition of consistent and valid models. The design of these models, however, is an iterative process (ie. a process of trial and error). Even simple changes to the geometry often require much computation. To be able to design complex objects and assemblies, a flexible modelling scheme is needed that provides techniques to easily modify and manipulate shapes, and to structure and manipulate assemblies. Further, we need techniques to structure and capture the design process for undo, replay and other manipulations, and to provide an interactive graphics environment for direct manipulation.

In this chapter, some of these techniques will be discussed, covering parametrization, definition and use of form features, constraints specification and evaluation, and use of knowledge-based techniques. Further we will discuss how these higher-level capabilities can be embedded in an interactive graphical user interface.

4.1 Structuring

A geometric model can be defined by specifying the coordinates of vertices or control points, or by specifying the coefficients for the equations of boundary surfaces. However, this explicit geometry does not give much flexibility in manipulating the model, nor does it capture the relations between different parts of the model. Hierarchical structuring of the object is useful to model assemblies and to manipulates these. In most cases, binary tree structures are used, such as the CSG tree and the PHIGS data structure. In the geometric hierarchy, each child node is positioned with respect to its parent node by a transformation matrix. Modifying the matrix allows one to move or rotate the subsolid defined by the subtree of that node. Although every point can be used for reference, it is convenient to use the local coordinate systems of the primitives as leaf nodes in this tree.

An extension to the geometric hierarchy is proposed in (van Emmerik 1988), where the tree (called the *geometric tree*) is extended to sub-primitive level. The leaf nodes of the tree are linked to control points that govern the main dimensions of the primitive (see figure 4.1). A sphere, block and cylinder all have one base coordinate system and one extra control point to specify the diameter or length, width and height. Although the hierarchical geometric ordering of an object has some topological aspects, topological ordering is related to the representation of regular patterns and to set compositions. Note that the geometric tree does not have to coincide with the set expression, although often it does.

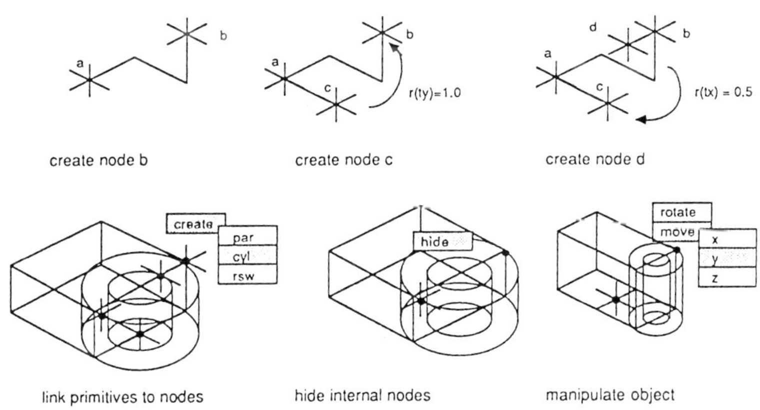

Figure 4.1. Geometric tree and method for linking primitives and composite objects (van Emmerik 1988).

4.2 Parametrization

Geometry is seldom specified in an absolute sense. Engineers, for instance, specify their designs by adding tolerances to the dimensions to avoid a too accurate and hence too expensive machining of parts. Also, during the design process, modifications are often made to adjust size and configuration. Variational geometry can be specified in two ways: *geometric parametrization* specifies dimensions as variables and structures the geometric relations by specifying dependencies between dimensions, and *topological parametrization* is used to create and manipulate regular patterns and structural dependencies. In topological parametrization the number of elements and the dimensions of the elements are a function of one or more (discrete) parameters.

Parametric design makes explicitly use of pre-defined parametrized components, by which a family of simple objects (primitive instancing), and also more complex objects is represented with variable dimensions (figure 4.2). An instance of such a part can be obtained by specifying a set of parameters, which may be related by mathematical functions, and subject to validity tests (Newell and Parden 1983; Gossard and Lin 1983).

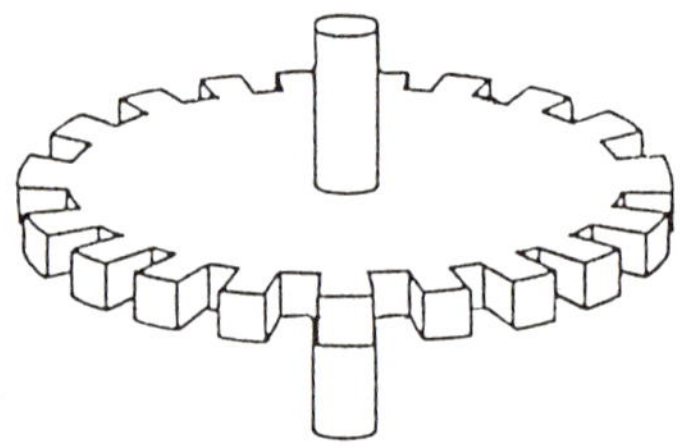

Figure 4.2. Parametrized object. The parameters here are the diameter and the number of teeth.

Although there are several methods to implement parametrization, a convenient way is the use of a procedural language (see section 3.4).

4.3 Feature Modelling

By using geometric modelling techniques in CAD/CAM, several disadvantages of the current modelling schemes have become apparent. First of all, the specification of elementary volumes and surfaces is not in accordance with the way an engineer looks at a design: he sees the product in terms of functional characteristics and functional elements, such as holes, rims, roundings and fixtures, and not as cylinders, spheres and vertices. So there is a level above the individual primitives that is of interest to the designer. It is thus worthwhile to make this level explicit and manageable. Second, the functional information (how the object is to be made, how the surface finish should be) is not easily incorporated in a geometric model. Attaching this information to faces or solids is not adequate, and can lead to loss of information (for instance, the notion that several different surfaces can be processed with the same machining operation). Also, for application programs it is often hard to interpret the multitude of small surface elements in a meaningful way. Third, the exchange of geometric data between different CAD/CAM-systems is hampered by the different solid and surface representations schemes that are used by the different systems. It is far from trivial, or even impossible, to convert a bicubic B-spline surface into an algebraic representation, or to convert a winged-edge B-rep into a CSG model. Therefore, a standardized shape description method, ie. *feature modelling*, which describes the object characteristics on a higher level, has been proposed.

A feature is a characteristic part of the object with a certain functional meaning or denotation. Features can be *design features* or *manufacturing features*. Design features refer to entities with relation to the product's function or use. Manufacturing features refer to certain manufacturing operations. The definition and specification of features is part of the product exchange standardization effort undertaken under the name STEP/PDES (Wilson 1987). See figure 4.3.

Form feature	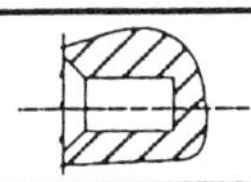	Connected set of primitive surfaces or volumes related to manufacturing	- holes - slots - roundings
Pattern feature	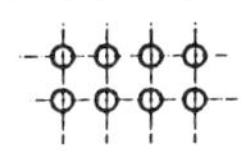	Regular pattern of simular entities	- circular pattern - rectangular pattern - linear pattern
Connection feature	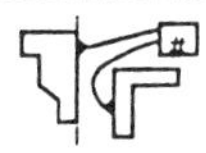	Local geometric property applied between features, parts or assemblies	- parallelity - concentricity
Property feature		Property not related to explicitgeometric or topologic organization	- heat treatment - surface finish
Application feature	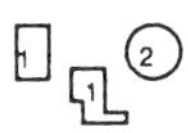	Related only by process planning requirements	- assembly sequence - simultaneous painting

Figure 4.3. Examples of features (van Emmerik and Jansen 1989).

Features can be internally represented in a CAD/CAM or geometric modelling system by a parametrized and/or procedural description. Whether a B-rep or a CSG representation is the most suitable solid modelling representation underlying the feature definition, is still an issue for discussion. However, being able to read and write a neutral STEP-file and to communicate the product description, every system can use the internal representation that suits its applications best.

4.4 Geometric Constraints

One of the elements of a feature description is a specification of tolerances imposed on the geometric relations between elements and parts. Tolerances can be expressed as constraints to maintain tangency, parallellity, adjacency or a certain distance between two elements. Constraints (Freeman-Benson et al 1990) describe geometric relations that have to be satisfied. In contrast to a procedural definition of geometric models, constraints offer a declarative specification: the user tells how the end result should be and which relations will have to be maintained, rather than how the system can reach this result. A configuration of elements may be *under-constrained,* which leaves some degrees of freedom, *determined*, which means that there is one solution while all constraints can be satisfied, and *over-constrained*, which means that not all constraints can be satisfied and that an optimum solution has to be found that meets most constraints. Also in the under-constrained case, one often wants to find an optimum solution, given the fact that there are many *admissible* solutions. Constraints may be given strength or weight factors to establish a priority or quantitative measure of influence. Constraints can form a hierarchy of required constraints that must be met, and desired constraints with different weight factors that only partly have to be met. See also Freeman-Benson et al (1990).

There are several methods to solve a set of constraints. Constraints can be expressed as a set of (in)-equalities, which can then be solved by numerical methods. For interactive use, incremental forms of constraint solving are attracting interest (Freeman-Benson et al 1990). Because of the declarative character of the constraints, logic programming (rule-based) techniques are also used to solve the constraints specification.

Logical representation techniques are also used to describe other relations such as "part-of" and "dependent-on". In theory it is possible to convert all the geometric data into a logical format, such as first-order predicates. However, it is still an open issue whether a complete logic representation of all geometric data should be used or not. Expressing all geometric data in, for instance, first-order logic may be desirable from a conceptual point of view (it unifies the processing), but is not very attractive from an efficiency point of view.

Knowledge processing may also be used to enhance the interactive design of models and assemblies. With conventional, procedural specification methods, the user has to specify the model by entering a sequence of elementary modelling instructions that will eventually lead to the desired result. Higher-level operations are seldom available. For example, complex objects can often be described as a set combination of primitive solids with smooth transitions (blends, roundings and fillets) between these elementary volumes. It is easy to specify the object without the blends, but it takes quite an amount of work to define and position the blends. It would be much easier for the designer to issue a command: 'blend this object', and that the system would have the expertise to detect where and how the blends and fillets should be added to the model (figure 4.4).

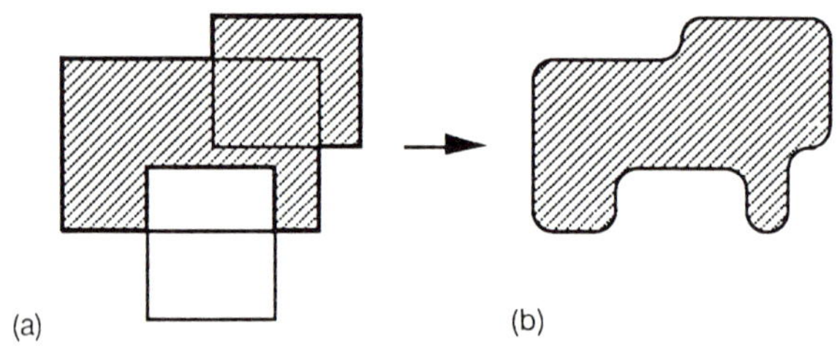

Figure 4.4. Shape as result of set operations upon primitives (a) and rounded version (b).

Use of knowledge processing in geometric modelling is often referred to as *geometric reasoning* (Arbab and Wing 1985; Kapur and Mundy 1989; Woodwark 1989), although this term is used for other application areas as well, eg. theorem proving. In Ando et al (1989) an interesting application of geometric reasoning is described for the design of products. At an early stage of the design process it is assumed that the designer has only a vague idea of the model. The constraints specified by the designer do not completely specify the product. The system first generates a tentative solution and then applies refinement rules to generate a model that is simpler and can be easier manufactured. The system formulates the constraints as logical expressions and uses forward reasoning. An ATMS (Assumption-Based Truth Maintenance System) is used as a logical database to maintain the dependencies between elements. In Shimada et al (1989) an application of geometric reasoning is described for the representation of features with constraints. In Gero (1990) a method is described that allows the specification of a "prototype", which is an ordered set of geometric elements with a specific behaviour and properties that captures the design intention and history. After modifying the configuration, the system will automatically generate a new instance of the prototype.

4.5 User Interface

Parametrization and constraints specification are described most compactly by a procedural language. However, from the user point of view, the programmer's interface is not very attractive, and a graphical user interface will always be preferred. Unfortunately, manipulating the geometry directly does not capture any notion of parametrization. Takala (1984) suggests to use log files that record the command sequences during the interactive edit session. Editing sub-sequences and combining these sub-sequences allows the re-use and combined use of these sequences. Rossignac (1986) also proposes the use of command sequences, but in his system the sequences are kept as active 'objects' and are only written to a file for storage. The commands are formulated as geometric constraints that impose relationships between new and existing elements, such as aligning the axes of two primitive solids. If an earlier sequence is modified, the later sequences are replayed and because the commands are defined as constraints, a new and correct configuration is obtained. In all the sequence methods some kind of history mechanism is applied. This has the drawback that the commands cannot be directly related to the visible entities on the screen.

A user interface based on direct manipulation is proposed in van Emmerik (1988, 1989, 1990), and van Emmerik and Jansen (1989). Both the geometric and topological parametrization and constraints (figure 4.5) are visualized on the screen as objects that can be manipulated by the user.

constraint	sub-type	description	example	fixes	order	icon
equal	z_equal	z-position of entities in evaluated model equal	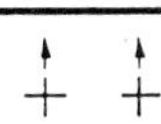	tz	1	
linear distance	y_distance	orthogonal y-distance between two entities	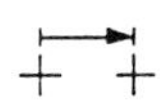	ty	1	
ratio	x_ratio	positioning as a ratio between two entities	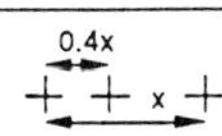	tx	1	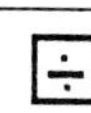
parallel	yz_parallel	plane through x-axis and y-axis of both entities parallel		ry,rz	1	
pointto	x_pointto	x_axis of entity points to other entity	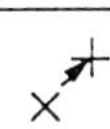	ry, rz	1	
radial distance	xy_distance	fixed distance between two entities in xy_plane	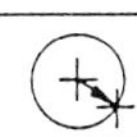	tx or ty	2	

Figure 4.5. Examples of constraints (van Emmerik 1989).

Internally, the system converts all operations into a procedural format which is interpreted to generate the visible representation. Constraints can be specified incrementally and will overrule earlier specifications as far as needed to find a solution. The system signals when a constraint is added that will over-constrain the model. See figure 4.6.

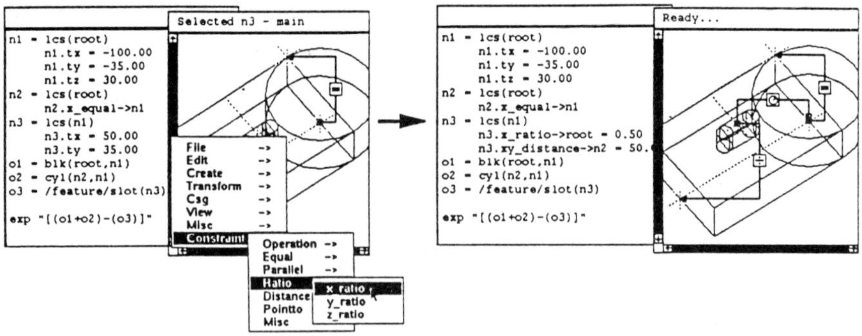

Figure 4.6. User interface for direct manipulation. The geometric and topological parametrization can be manipulated with the geometric tree. Constraints are visualized by symbols and arrows (van Emmerik 1990).

5. CSG Ray Tracing

Until here, modelling techniques have been discussed, with different types of geometries and representations. In the next three sections, we will be concerned with display generation techniques for one specific type of solid models: CSG models (see 2.5).

A CSG model, as specified by a CSG tree, can be displayed in two different ways. First, the model can be converted into a boundary representation, which can then be displayed using any of the standard types of display algorithms, such as scanline or depth buffer algorithms. To avoid the problems of boundary evaluation during the interactive design process, the model can also be displayed directly from the CSG tree, performing CSG classification as a part of the display process, restricted to the visible parts of the model. The latter class is referred to as *direct display algorithms* for CSG models.

The first type of direct display algorithm for CSG models developed was ray tracing (Roth 1982), which is a *non-projective* display technique. In this section, we will first discuss some of the general principles of ray tracing, especially intersection algorithms and efficiency techniques, and then explain CSG ray classification as an extension. In the following sections, two types of *projective* display algorithms will be discussed: the scanline algorithm (section 6) and the depth buffer algorithm (section 7). It will be shown how each type can be extended for direct display of CSG models, by applying appropriate classification techniques.

5.1 General Principles of Ray Tracing

Ray tracing has become popular as a technique for generating high-quality images (Whitted 1980; Glassner 1989). It is conceptually simple and elegant (figure 5.1). The model or scene to be displayed resides in *object space*, and is observed through an imaginary rectangular window, located between the eye of the observer and the object space. To display a picture on a raster screen similar to what is visible in the window, the object space is sampled by sending rays from the eye point through the window into object space, and determining the points where rays hit the surface of the model. In terms of geometry, these points are the intersections of the rays with the surfaces. If for each pixel of the raster screen one ray is sent, a colour is assigned to a pixel by calculating the light reflected at the ray/surface intersection point that is nearest to the eye, which is on the visible surface.

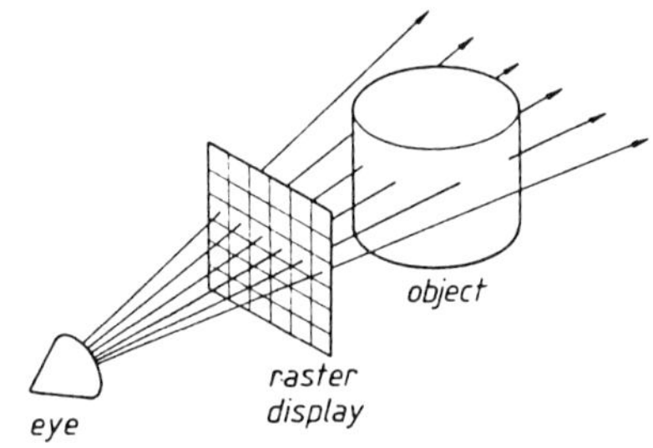

Figure 5.1. Basic principle of ray tracing (van Wijk 1986b).

To add more realism to a picture, several optical effects can be modelled with ray tracing, such as specular reflection, transparency (with refraction), and shadows. This is done by sending rays from the first intersection point into the scene; these *secondary rays* can also contribute to the colour of the pixel (figure 5.2). Sending rays in the reflected direction has the effect of generating mirror images of other objects reflected in the first (specular reflection). Rays may also be sent in the refracted direction into transparent material, thus simulating transparency with refraction. In both cases, the secondary rays may hit other objects, where more reflections and refractions may occur. This results in a tree structure of rays, to be traced in a recursive process. A ray may also be sent in the direction of each light source, to test whether the point receives direct light, or direct illumination is blocked by another opaque object. In this way, shadows can be simulated.

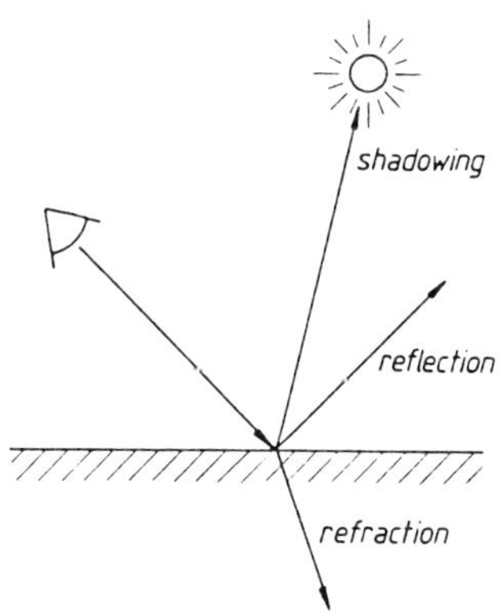

Figure 5.2. Secondary rays for specular reflection, transparency, and shadows (van Wijk 1986b).

When a ray hits a visible surface, a lighting calculation is performed at the intersection point, to determine a colour contributed to the pixel by the surface hit. This calculation uses the surface normal at the intersection point, the direction and intensity of the light sources, the direction from the intersection point to the eye point, and optical properties of the surface, such as reflection coefficients, glossiness, transparency, and refraction index. A typical lighting calculation would take at least into account the contributions of ambient light, diffuse reflections, specular reflections, and transparency (Hall 1989).

Ray tracing in effect models the behaviour of light rays passing from light sources through the scene to the eye. To capture the small fraction that will ever reach the eye, the rays are traced backwards from the eye to the light source (Glassner 1989). Essentially, ray tracing models only the effects of directed light; it does not account for diffuse reflections. Secondary rays are usually only traced in the geometrically ideal direction of reflection or refraction, and thus only specular effects and smooth, glossy surfaces and clear transparent materials are represented. This is a limitation of ray tracing.

Another limitation is that ray tracing is a point sampling technique, and thus liable to aliasing problems, due to the limited sampling frequency. To compensate for this, the sampling frequency can be increased by tracing more than one ray for each pixel. This can be done adaptively, taking more samples in areas of high contrast (Glassner 1989). In *distributed ray tracing*, samples are taken in a controlled random pattern for each pixel, using stochastic sampling techniques. In this way, aliasing is reduced at the cost of introducing noise (Cook 1989). With distributed ray tracing, also some non-specular optical effects (or fuzzy effects) can be obtained, such as soft shadows, translucency (blurred transparency), blurred reflections, and even depth of field and motion blur. It does not, however, model diffuse interreflections.

The effects of distributed ray tracing are obtained only at the high cost of tracing a stochastically distributed bundle of rays for each pixel, regardless of its information content. More general forms of ray tracing based on stochastic sampling adaptively sample the scene, guided by estimates of its local information content (Painter and Sloan 1989).

An approach which can model diffuse lighting effects is the *radiosity method* (Hall 1989). This method is based on balancing the distribution of light energy that is passed around in a scene by diffuse reflection from each surface to all other surfaces. Radiosity and ray tracing have been combined in the two pass method (Wallace et al 1987; Sillion and Puech 1989), which models both diffuse and specular components to achieve a high degree of realism. Ray tracing is also used here as a probing technique for estimating the *form factors* for modelling the diffuse inter-reflections.

5.2 Intersection Calculations and Efficiency

To determine whether a ray hits an object, intersections have to be calculated between the ray and all faces of the object. This intersection calculation is a critical part of ray tracing: we can only display objects when intersection calculations can be performed for all surfaces of an object; also, the intersection calculations are for a large part responsible for the high computational cost of ray tracing.

The calculation amounts to intersecting a straight line with a surface. Mathematically, the parametric equation of the ray is substituted into the surface equation, and the equation is solved for the ray parameter. For most types of surfaces, the roots of a polynomial equation must be found. If the equation cannot be solved analytically, approximate methods must be used. Intersection algorithms exist for many types of surfaces, such as simple algebraic surfaces (Roth 1982), complex algebraic surfaces (Hanrahan 1983), parametric surfaces (Kajiya 1982; Joy and Bhetanabhotla 1986); fractal surfaces (Kajiya 1983), deformed surfaces (Barr 1986), and several types of objects defined by sweeping, such as translation and rotation sweeping (Kajiya 1983; van Wijk 1984a), sweeping a circle and a sphere (van Wijk 1984b), generalized cylinders (Bronsvoort and Klok 1985), and profiled sweep objects (Bronsvoort et al 1989).

As an example of a simple intersection calculation, the intersection of a ray and a sphere is given here.

The parametric equation of the ray is:

$$\boldsymbol{r} = \boldsymbol{e} + t \,.\, \boldsymbol{d} \qquad\qquad t > 0$$

in which $\boldsymbol{e}$ $[x_e\ y_e\ z_e]$ is the eye point, $\boldsymbol{d}$ $[x_d\ y_d\ z_d]$ is the unit direction vector of the ray determined by the eye position and the sample point on the screen, and t is the ray parameter. The equation of the spherical surface with radius r and center $[x_c\ y_c\ z_c]$ is:

$$(x - x_c)^2 + (y - y_c)^2 + (z - z_c)^2 = r^2$$

Substituting the ray equation into this equation yields:

$$(x_e + t.x_d - x_c)^2 + (y_e + t.y_d - y_c)^2 + (z_e + t.z_d - z_c)^2 = r^2,$$

which can be simplified to a quadratic in t:

$$At^2 + Bt + C = 0,$$

with:

$$A = x_d^{\ 2} + y_d^{\ 2} + z_d^{\ 2} = 1$$

$$B = 2\,(x_d\,(x_e - x_c) + y_d\,(y_e - y_c) + z_d\,(z_e - z_c))$$

$$C = (x_e - x_c)^2 + (y_e - y_c)^2 + (z_e - z_c)^2 - r^2$$

Solving for t, we find zero or two (possibly identical) real roots. No roots means that the ray does not hit the sphere; with two roots, there are two intersection points, and with two identical roots, the ray touches the sphere. The intersection points are calculated by inserting the values for t in the ray equation. Note that only intersection points with positive values of t lie before the eye point.

The intersection points with the surfaces of an object must be checked to see whether they are within the boundary of the faces of the object. If so, the ray intersects the object. In practice, it is often easiest to perform the calculation in the local coordinate space of the object. The ray must then first be transformed to this local coordinate system, and the intersection points found must be transformed back to object space. As a last step, all intersection points found for a ray are sorted on increasing distance from the eye point, or increasing value of the ray parameter t.

For each visible intersection point, a surface normal must be determined for the lighting calculations. A normal can be determined directly from the surface equation, or be obtained as the vector product of two tangent vectors at the intersection point.

One major problem of ray tracing, its high computational cost, is mainly caused by the high number of rays and hence the high number of intersection calculations. In principle, each ray must be intersected with each surface of the model. To reduce the number of intersection calculations, a variety of techniques have been developed. We will briefly describe three types of techniques here.

Bounding volumes and hierarchies (Roth 1982; Rubin and Whitted 1980; Kay and Kajiya 1986). Every primitive object in a model is tightly enclosed by a simple bounding volume, such as a rectangular box or a sphere. The bounding volume is tested first for intersection with the ray, and if the ray does not hit the bounding volume, it does not hit the object inside it. Of course the intersection test for the bounding volume must be more efficient than for the enclosed object.

The method can be improved by organizing the bounding volumes in a hierarchical structure. A group of bounding volumes is enclosed by a larger bounding volume, and so on, until a bounding volume is defined for the whole model. Thus a tree structure of bounding volumes is formed. If a ray does not hit a bounding volume, the contents (which may be several levels of smaller bounding volumes) need not be examined further.

Space subdivision (Glassner 1984, Fujimoto et al 1986). The whole model is enclosed in a rectangular bounding volume, which is subdivided into rectangular cells, which may contain (parts of) one or more objects. In a data structure, it is recorded which object is (partly) contained in which cell. During ray tracing, the ray path is traced through the cells, computing intersections only with the surfaces of objects contained in a cell encountered on the ray path. Thus only a small part of the objects is intersected with each ray.

The cell structure can be a regular grid of identical cells, regardless of the number of objects in the cell. The structure can also be hierarchical; only the cells that contain more than a given number of objects are subdivided further, until all cells contain less than the specified number of objects. Thus the object space is subdivided adaptively, with large cells in empty parts of the model, and small cells in dense parts. The data structure often used here is the octtree, in which cells are recursively subdivided into eight sub-cells.

Ray traversal in a regular grid structure is generally faster, but a ray may encounter more objects in a single cell; a hierarchical cell structure takes more time to traverse, but the number of cells visited may be much less, especially in sparse regions of the model. The choice between the two types of cell structures depends on the model: for homogeneous models (objects of about equal size, evenly distributed in space), the regular grid is preferred; for inhomogeneous models, the octtree structure may be preferable.

Reducing the number of rays (Bronsvoort et al 1984). The total number of rays to be traced can be considerably reduced by adaptive sub-sampling in screen space. Ray tracing starts at a low sampling density (eg. one ray for each area of 8×8 pixels), and sampling density is increased only in areas of high contrast, which most likely occur near silhouettes or details. Contrast is determined by performing shading calculations, and comparing the colours calculated for neighbouring areas. A disadvantage is that fine details or small objects may be missed.

The efficiency of ray tracing can be improved in many other ways, such as using more efficient intersection algorithms, or by exploiting ray coherence (using the intersection points found for one ray in the calculations for the next ray). For an overview, see Arvo and Kirk (1989).

5.3 CSG Ray Classification

Once we have a ray tracing system that can display all types of primitive objects available in a solid modelling system, it can be adapted for direct display by performing *CSG ray classification* for each ray. The purpose of this is to determine which parts of the primitive objects found along the ray path belong to the composite model.

The intersection algorithms must be able to find all intersections along the ray path with the whole model, and the intersection points are sorted as usual on increasing distance from the eye point. For each primitive object, one or more ray intervals (or ray segments) can be indicated between the points where the ray enters and leaves the primitive. Thus, the ray can be divided into a number of intervals indicating which parts are inside each primitive. These intervals can be combined using rules according to the set operations specified in the CSG tree. In this way, the intervals belonging to the evaluated CSG model can be found by traversal of the CSG tree. An example of this is illustrated in figure 5.3. An algorithm to perform ray classification by recursive, top-down tree traversal is shown in figure 5.4.

As a final step, overlapping and adjacent intervals belonging to the evaluated object can be merged. The problem of classification is thus reduced to a one-dimensional operation: combining intervals on a straight line. This is a great simplification compared with a full 3D boundary evaluation, and even compared with the 2D classification used in the scanline algorithm discussed in section 6.

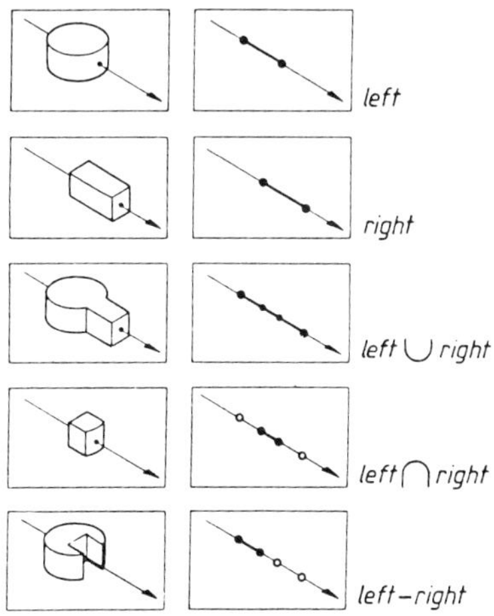

Figure 5.3. Ray classification (van Wijk 1986b).

```
function rayclass (object): raysegments;
var leftsegments, rightsegments: raysegments;
begin
   if object.type = primitive then
      { compute segments of ray inside primitive object }
   else { object.type = composite }
      begin
         leftsegments := rayclass (object.left);
         rightsegments := rayclass (object.right);
         rayclass := combine (leftsegments, rightsegments, object.operator)
      end
end
```

Figure 5.4. Top-down ray classification algorithm.

If the intersection points are found in depth order along the ray path (which can for instance be achieved using spatial subdivision methods), a more efficient depth order classification method using *bottom-up* tree traversal can be used. This method is described in detail in section 6.

To improve the efficiency of CSG ray classification, the size of the CSG tree can be reduced. If the ray tracing process proceeds in scanline order, a list of 'active' primitives can be kept that intersect the horizontal plane through a given scanline. The tree can be dynamically pruned at every scanline transition where new primitives become active, or a primitive in the list becomes inactive, and thus can be removed from the list, leaving only the nodes that may be visited during a traversal for classification on the current scanline (Bronsvoort et al 1984). The pruning is done as follows.

First, all leaf nodes of inactive primitives, and internal nodes with inactive left and right subnodes, can be removed. If an internal node contains the union operator, and one of its two children is inactive, then that node can be skipped. Similar rules apply to internal nodes with difference and intersection operators. The complete set of rules for the reduction of an internal node combining an active child A and an inactive child I is:

$$
\begin{aligned}
A \cup I &= A \\
I \cup A &= A \\
A - I &= A \\
I - A &= I \\
A \cap I &= I \\
I \cap A &= I
\end{aligned}
$$

If an inactive node results, then it can be removed from the tree. To implement this tree pruning, every internal node has pointers to its currently active subtrees.

6. CSG Scanline Algorithms

The CSG scanline algorithm for polyhedral objects introduced by Atherton (1983) will be discussed in this section. The algorithm can be used in the context of a solid modelling system based on CSG to draw shaded images of models on a raster display fast enough for interactive work. It requires the primitives to be approximated by planar faces, and to be described by a boundary representation. No boundary evaluation to create a boundary representation containing explicit information about the faces, edges and vertices of the composite object is needed. Instead, the boundary representations of the primitives, and the CSG tree indicating how these are combined, are kept, and the classification of faces is performed during image generation. Several techniques for efficient classification, and for efficiency improvements of CSG scanline algorithms in general, will be discussed.

CSG scanline algorithms for objects with quadric faces are also known (Chung 1984; Pueyo and Mendoza 1987). These work basically in the same way as the algorithms for polyhedral objects.

6.1 Standard Scanline Algorithms

The basic idea of the scanline visible-surface algorithm (Hearn and Baker 1986) is that an image is generated in scanline order, from top to bottom of the screen. The plane of the screen is taken as the XY-plane of the viewing coordinate system (see figure 6.1a). Before the actual drawing, in a preprocessing step all objects in the model are transformed to viewing coordinates, and all edges are sorted on their highest Y-value. This is done by a bucket sort: each edge is inserted into a list, called a bucket, belonging to the first scanline at which it occurs (see figure 6.1b). The array of buckets, with one bucket for each scanline, is used to maintain an *active-edge list.*

During the processing of a scanline, the active-edge list always contains the edges that intersect that scanline (for brevity, 'edges that intersect a scanline' is used here, instead of 'edges whose projections on the screen intersect a scanline'). Since the scanlines are processed sequentially, the active-edge list can be updated at the transition from one scanline to the next. If there are edges in the list that do not intersect the next scanline, then these are removed from the list. If there are edges in the bucket belonging to the next scanline, then these are removed from the bucket, and inserted into the list. Furthermore, the list is kept sorted on the X-coordinates of the intersection points of the edges with the scanline. The X-coordinate of the intersection point of an edge with the next scanline is incrementally computed. Figure 6.1c shows the active-edge list at a particular scanline. The active-edge list is, in its turn, used to maintain an *active-face list*.

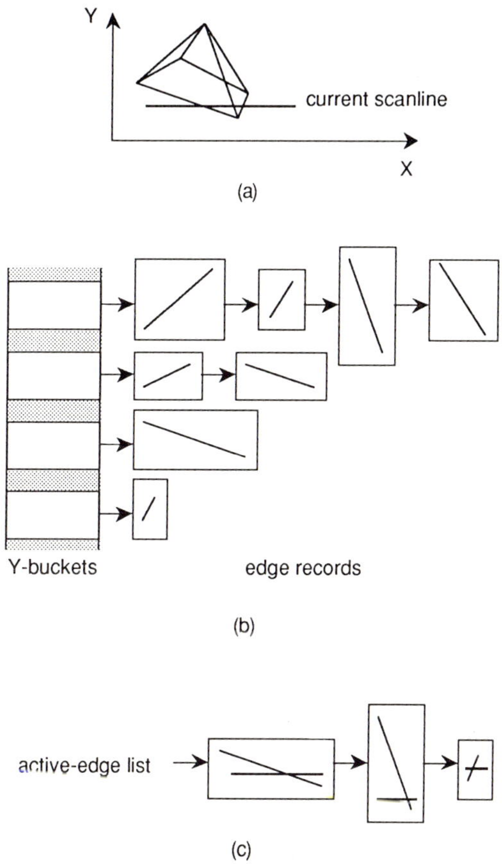

Figure 6.1. Schematic representation of data structures for the scanline algorithm.
(a) An image on the screen with the current scanline indicated.
(b) The associated Y-buckets lists with edge information.
(c) The active-edge list while processing the current scanline.

At a given point on a scanline, the active-face list always contains the faces that are active, ie. potentially visible, at that point. The list is updated at every edge in the active-edge list as a scanline is traversed from left to right: the face(s) left of the edge are removed from the list, and the face(s) right of the edge are inserted into the list; since most edges have a face at both sides, usually the left face can be replaced by the right face. In this way, the active-face list always contains the faces behind the part of the scanline between the current edge and the next edge in the active-edge list; such a part is called a *span*. This is illustrated in figure 6.2, in which the cross-sections of two objects with the *scanplane*, ie. the plane determined by the scanline and the Z-direction, are shown in 3D screen space and in this plane.

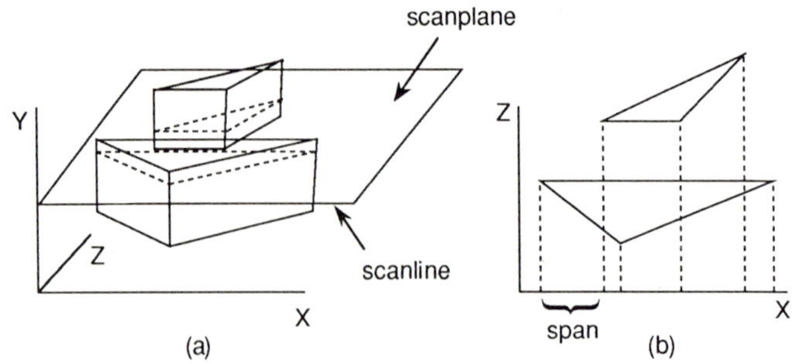

Figure 6.2. (a) A scene in 3D screen space; the screen is in the XY-plane, and the XZ-plane through the current scanline (the scanplane) is drawn.
(b) The scanplane with the scanline divided into spans.

Figure 6.3 gives the basic scanline algorithm in pseudo code. The procedure 'handlespan' sorts for the current span the faces in the active-face list on depth in the scanplane (see figure 6.2), ie. on distance from the screen, takes the nearest, and draws the span with the colour of that face. If intersecting faces are allowed, then the depth comparison has to be done on both ends of the span, or, in practice, on positions on the scanline displaced from the ends by a small distance, to make it possible to sort faces that have the same depth values at the ends. If the nearest faces found on both ends are different, then the intersection point of the scanline and the intersection line of these faces is determined, the span is subdivided at that point, and the two new spans are handled recursively in the same way.

```
perform viewing transformation;
sort edges on highest Y-value;
for each scanline do
begin
   update active-edge list;
   while active-edge list not processed do
   begin
      get edge from list;
      remove face(s) left of edge from active-face list;
      insert face(s) right of edge into active-face list;
      handlespan(X-value of edge, X-value of next edge)
   end
end;
```

Figure 6.3. Basic scanline algorithm.

Scanline algorithms for objects with quadric faces work basically in the same way as those for polyhedral objects. There are, however, a number of differences that make these algorithms more complicated. First, besides the edges in the boundary representation of a primitive, also the silhouette edges of the primitive have to be processed by the algorithm. Second, several computations, eg.those to determine the depths of the faces at a span boundary, are more complicated because of the quadratic equations for the faces. Third, the handling of intersecting faces requires more attention, eg.because, instead of one single intersection line, there can now be several intersection curves between two faces.

Still more complicated are scanline algorithms for general algebraic surfaces (Sederberg and Zundel 1989) and for freeform surfaces (Lane et al 1980; Pueyo and Brunet 1987).

Scanline algorithms are efficient visible-surface algorithms. The reason for this is that several types of coherence in the model and the image are exploited:

- coherence between scanlines: the edges that intersect one scanline, will probably also intersect the next scanline, and the order of the X-coordinates of their intersection points with a scanline will change only gradually between scanlines; this is exploited by maintaining an active-edge list, and by computing the X-coordinate of the intersection point of an edge with the next scanline incrementally, and sorting the list with a bubble sort
- coherence between spans: the active faces and their depth order will change only gradually as a scanline is traversed from left to right; this is exploited by maintaining an active-face list, and by sorting the list at the span boundaries with a bubble sort
- coherence on a span: on a span, the visible face usually remains the same; this is exploited by comparing depths only at the ends of the span, and, if the same nearest face is found at both ends, by drawing the whole span in one operation.

In the next subsection, the extension of standard scanline algorithms to CSG scanline algorithms is described.

6.2 Extensions for CSG

CSG scanline algorithms (Atherton 1983) must be able to handle intersecting faces, because primitives in CSG models often intersect. Further, more than depth-sorting the faces is needed at a span boundary, because not all faces are on the boundary of the composite object as specified by the CSG tree. The extra task is to find the first face on the boundary of the composite object in the sorted active-face list, because that face is the visible one. Determination of whether a face is on the boundary of the composite object is done by classification of that face (see the end of this subsection).

If, on both ends of a span, the same faces are found from the nearest face up to and including the first face on the boundary of the composite object, and thus visible face, then the span can be drawn with the colour of the face visible on both ends, because that face is visible over the entire span. If, on the other hand, different sequences of faces are found, then the span is subdivided at the intersection point of the intersection line of the first two different faces and the scanline, and the new spans are handled recursively in the same way (see figure 6.4, in which a scanplane is shown). Figure 6.5 gives the procedure 'handlespan', used in figure 6.3, for a CSG scanline algorithm in pseudo code.

During the depth-order classifications, a list of all faces up to and including the first face on the boundary of the composite object is built for use in the comparison of the faces encountered at both ends of a span. In the recursive calls, repeated sorting and classifications at positions where these operations have already been executed can be avoided by checking whether a list of faces for that position already exists.

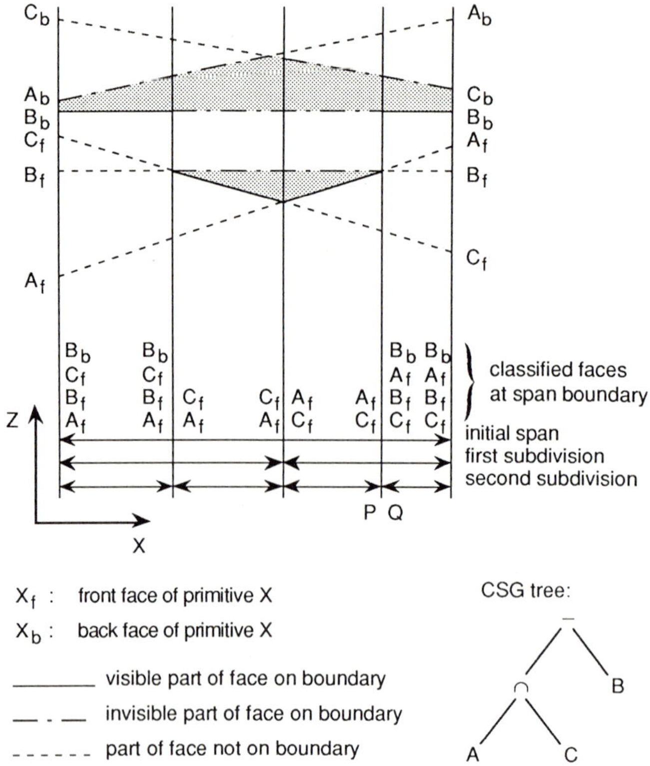

Figure 6.4. Example of the determination of the first face on the boundary of the composite object at span boundaries, and subdivisions of spans.

```
procedure handlespan (left, right : real);
(*epsilon is a small constant*)
begin
   sort faces in active-face list at position left + epsilon;
   repeat
      classify next face in active-face list
   until (face on boundary of composite object) or (all faces handled);
   sort faces in active-face list at position right - epsilon;
   repeat
      classify next face in active-face list
   until (face on boundary of composite object) or (all faces handled);
   if faces up to and including first face on boundary of composite object equal
   for left and right end of span then
      drawspan(left,right)
   else
   begin
      determine intersection point ip of first pair of different faces;
      handlespan(left,ip);
      handlespan(ip,right)
   end
end; (*handlespan*)
```

Figure 6.5. Procedure 'handlespan' for a CSG scanline algorithm.

The determination, at each span boundary, of the first face on the boundary of the composite object from the sorted active-face list can be done in the following way. To each primitive node in the CSG tree, a Boolean variable is added to indicate the *status* (inside/outside) of a point with respect to that primitive. The status variable of a primitive is 'inside' if the intersection point of the line through the span boundary in the Z-direction (see figure 6.4) and the face currently being classified is on a front face of or inside the primitive, and 'outside' if it is on a back face of or outside the primitive. These status variables can be set while classifying faces in order along this line: when a face of some primitive is encountered, the status variable of that primitive is set to 'inside' if it was 'outside', and to 'outside' if it was 'inside'. All status variables are initialized to 'outside'.

The determination now proceeds as follows. The first face is taken from the sorted active-face list, the status variable of the primitive to which the face belongs is set to 'inside', and it is checked whether the face is on the boundary of the composite object by classification of that face. If so, the determination is completed. If not, the next face is taken from the active-face list, the status variable of the primitive to which that face belongs is set to 'inside' (or 'outside' if it was already 'inside'), and this face is classified, and so on. This is continued until a face on the boundary of the composite object has been found, or all faces in the active-face list have been processed.

Classification of a face is done by traversing the CSG tree, and looking at the Boolean status variables to determine whether the face is on the boundary of the composite object. Strictly speaking, it is not the whole face that is classified, but only the intersection point of the line through the span boundary in the Z-direction with the face. This, however, results in the classification of the face at that point, and, for convenience, it will be called classification of the face.

6.3 Bottom-up Classification

The standard classification technique for a face uses a top-down function, which recursively determines the status at all composite nodes by looking at the statuses at the left and right branches and the set operator. For example, the status at a composite node with the union operator is 'inside' if the status at its left branch or its right branch (or at both branches) is 'inside', because a point is on the front face of or inside the union of two objects if it is on the front face of or inside at least one of these objects. Similar rules hold for composite nodes with the difference and intersection operators. The function is initially called with the root node of the CSG tree as parameter. If the function delivers the value 'inside', ie. if at the root node, representing the complete composite object, the status is 'inside', then the face is on the boundary of the composite object.

However, this recursive procedure incorporated in a CSG scanline algorithm consumes a disproportionate amount (about 65-75%) of the total computing time for some representative models (Bronsvoort 1986). A much more efficient classification technique is *bottom-up classification*, in which the classification process proceeds from the leaf nodes (the bottom) of the CSG tree to the root node (the top), in contrast to the top-down direction of the standard procedure (Sato et al 1985; Bronsvoort 1986).

The bottom-up classification works as follows. To each node in the CSG tree, a pointer to its parent node is added, and a Boolean variable to indicate the status (inside/outside) of a point with respect to the object represented at that node. All these status variables are initialized to 'outside'.

For the first face in the depth-sorted active-face list, the leaf node in the CSG tree of the primitive to which the face belongs is directly located by a table look-up, and the status variable there is set to 'inside'. Next the parent of the leaf node is visited, and it is checked whether the status variable there has to be changed, by examining the operator, and if necessary, the status variable of its other child. Progression up the CSG tree is continued until either the status variable of a node is not changed (see figure 6.6 - step 1), or the root node is reached. If the root node is reached, and the status variable there is changed to 'inside', then the face is on the boundary of the composite object.

Otherwise, the face is not on the boundary of the composite object, in which case the next face from the active-face list is taken. The leaf node of the primitive to which this face belongs is located, the status variable of that primitive is changed, and the CSG tree again is traversed in the way described above. This is continued until a face on the boundary of the composite object has been found (see figure 6.6 - step 2), or all faces in the active-face list have been processed.

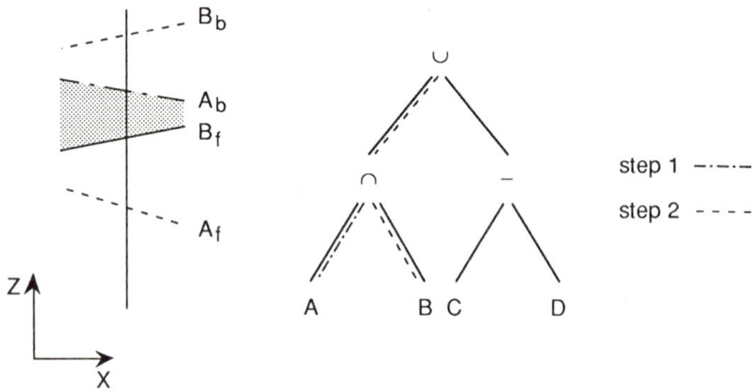

Figure 6.6. Two bottom-up classifications: the first face in the sorted active-face list is from primitive A, the second from primitive B.

The bottom-up technique has two major advantages over the top-down technique. First, the number of nodes visited in the CSG tree is minimized by taking the path directly from the leaf node where the status variable is modified, to the root node. Second, traversal of the tree is terminated as soon as the status variable of a composite subobject is not modified, and it is thus certain that the status variables of all nodes higher in the CSG tree, and thus of the root node, will not be modified.

After completing the classifications at one span boundary, in general several Boolean status variables in the CSG tree will have the value 'inside'. To start the classifications at the next span boundary, all these variables would have to be reset to 'outside'. If this were to be done by re-initializing the whole CSG tree, eg.by a recursive procedure, which is easiest, then the required CPU time would largely cancel the gain of using the bottom-up classification technique. The CSG tree is therefore not re-initialized at each new classification position, but instead, starting from the tree as it stands, the status variables are adjusted to the new situation only as far as necessary. This will be explained using figure 6.4. When the new classification position Q is reached, the sorted active-face list (C_f,B_f,A_f,B_b) is compared, item by item, with the face list of the previous classification position P (C_f,A_f), starting from the beginning. As long as the faces are the same (C_f), no tree traversal is needed. However, if a difference is found at a particular index, then this index is noted, and tree traversals, as previously described, are carried out for the remaining faces in the face list of the previous classification position P (A_f). This is done to reset all status variables in the CSG tree to their values before the classifications of these faces. Finally, tree traversals for the active-face list, starting at the same index, are carried out until the first face on the boundary of the composite object is found (B_f,A_f,B_b). It turns out that this scheme is much more efficient than re-initialization at each new classification position.

If the bottom-up classification technique is used instead of the top-down technique, a reduction of about 55-70% in computing time is achieved (Bronsvoort 1986).

6.4 Other Efficiency-improving Techniques

In this subsection three ways to further improve the efficiency of CSG scanline algorithms are briefly described.

Partial back-face elimination
In CSG visible-surface algorithms, it is impossible to apply full back-face elimination as in standard (non-CSG) visible-surface algorithms, because a back face of a primitive may become a visible face if, eg, the primitive is subtracted from another primitive, and the back face is the first face on the boundary of the composite object encountered. Also, both the back faces and the front faces are needed in the classification process to maintain the statuses at all primitive and composite nodes. However, if only union operators are encountered on the path in the CSG tree from the root node to a primitive, then the back faces of that primitive need not be processed (Bronsvoort 1986). For if, during a sequence of classifications, a front face of that primitive is encountered, and no intersection or difference operation is applied to that primitive, then that face is on the boundary of the composite object and thus visible, and the sequence of classifications can terminate.

The number of faces that can be eliminated depends on the structure of the model, ie. how primitives are combined by set operators, and can range from zero, if eg.one primitive is subtracted from the rest of the model, to about half the number of faces, if only union operators occur in the model.

Using strips instead of scanlines
Bronsvoort (1987) describes a variant of CSG scanline algorithms working with strips that can contain more than one scanline. Inside these strips, areas are determined where only one face is visible, which may involve subdivision of an area into smaller areas. Both visible-line and visible-surface versions of the algorithm are given.

The visible-surface version is more efficient than the CSG scanline algorithm for simple models. For more complex models, this is no longer true because of increasing overheads. This has strengthened the view that sampling on a scanline basis is a very effective way to exploit coherence in an image, and that algorithms based on this principle are probably the most efficient available on general-purpose machines.

The idea of using strips turned out to be a good starting point for a visible line algorithm for CSG models. For complex models, however, a scanline-based sampling technique is again resorted to.

Local updating
Crocker (1987) and Bronsvoort and Garnaat (1989) describe techniques for local updating of a CSG model and its image with a CSG scanline algorithm. Local updating is a strategy for making incremental changes to a geometric model and its displayed image for a fixed viewing

position. Only those parts of a model that are affected by modifications are recomputed and redisplayed, which can considerably increase efficiency compared to updating the complete model and its image.

The CSG scanline algorithm is able to support local updating very effectively. The coherence-exploiting techniques of the original algorithm also work very well with local updating. The computing time for a locally-updated image is mostly considerably less than the time needed for a complete redraw of the image. Interactive editing of CSG models with immediate reasonable-quality image feedback therefore becomes feasible with a modeller using a CSG scanline algorithm with local updating.

7. CSG Depth-buffer Algorithms

In the CSG ray tracing and scanline algorithms, images are generated in image order on a pixel-by-pixel or scanline-by-scanline basis. However, it is often convenient to process surfaces in object order, ie. on a surface-by-surface basis. Most rendering hardware systems obtain their speed by pipe-lining the transformation, shading and rendering operations, or by performing the rendering operations for a surface for multiple pixels in parallel. Hidden-surface removal is done with depth-buffering techniques. The depth-buffer algorithm fits well in an object-order processing scheme and can be suitably implemented in hardware.

CSG objects can be displayed with a depth-buffer algorithm by classifying the surfaces with respect to the CSG object, in addition to the depth test. This classification may be done in software by evaluating analytic expressions that characterize the primitives and combining the signs of these analytic functions according to the set expression of the CSG tree (Rossignac and Requicha 1986b). This type of classification, however, is not very well suited for hardware. An alternative method is to classify surfaces by depth comparisons using multiple depth buffers. In this chapter we will discuss several versions of the CSG depth-buffer algorithm. In the first section the terminology is introduced that will be used in the other sections.

7.1 Tree Representations

The CSG expression can be internally represented as a binary tree. The leaf nodes of the tree represent the primitive solids, and the internal nodes represent the subsolids defined by applying the operations of the associated subtrees to its primitive solids. The root represents the composite solid. The *depth* of a tree is the maximum number of nodes along a path in the tree from the root to a primitive. Nodes whose path to the root contains an odd number of "-" nodes, are said to be *negative*. Nodes that are not negative are *positive*.

The *positive form* of the Boolean function associated with a CSG tree is an expression that uses only the union and intersection operator. Any CSG tree may be converted into its positive form by replacing the difference operators by an intersection operator under inversion of the right subtree:

$$A - B = A \cap \overline{B}$$

and applying De Morgan's laws:

$$\overline{A \cap B} = \overline{A} \cup \overline{B}$$

$$\overline{A \cup B} = \overline{A} \cap \overline{B}$$

$$\overline{\overline{A}} = A$$

recursively to the complemented subtree. The resulting CSG tree of intersection and union set operators has primitives (*positive* primitives) and complemented primitives (*negative* primitives, ie. voids) at the leaves. See figure 7.1.

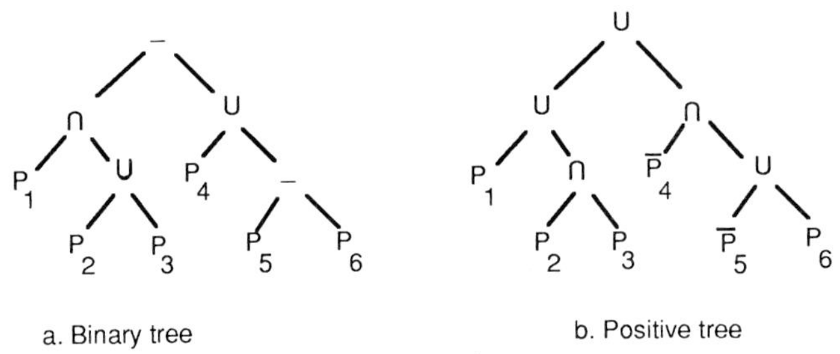

Figure 7.1. CSG-tree (a) and its positive form (b).

If each level of a tree has only one node with a depth larger than one (not a primitive), then the tree can be restructured as a *linear tree* of the form

$$S = P_1 \text{ op}_1 \ P_2 \text{ op}_2 \ P_3 \text{ op}_3 \ \ldots \text{op}_{n-1} \ P_n$$

where the absence of parentheses indicates that the association is from left to right. Fig. 7.2a shows a linear tree. The tree of figure 7.1b cannot be converted into a linear tree because of the subtree $\overline{P_5} \cup P_6$.

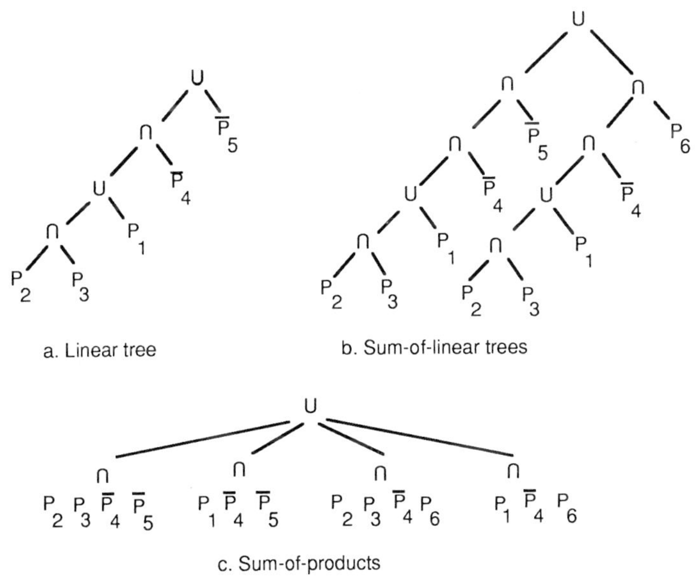

Figure 7.2. Linear tree (a), sum-of-linear trees (b) and sum-of-products form (c).

Any CSG tree that is not a linear tree can be converted into a union of linear trees:

$$S = \bigcup_i P_{i1}\ \mathrm{op}_{i1}\ P_{i2}\ \mathrm{op}_{i2} \cdots \mathrm{op}_{in-1}\ P_{in}$$

by performing the following substitution to the subtrees of the internal nodes with a depth higher than one:

$$A \cap (B \cup C) = (A \cap B) \cup (A \cap C)$$

Fig. 7.2b shows the resulting CSG tree. Note that the same primitive can now appear at several places in the tree.

Applying the same substitution to all the union combinations in a subtree results in a union of subtrees (figure 7.2c) with only set intersection operations (*sum-of-products* form):

$$S = \bigcup_i \bigcap_j P_{ij}$$

A product may also be called a *simple tree* (Goldfeather et al 1986). See also Thomas (1983) and Okino et al (1984) for similar definitions.

The tree-restructuring reduces the depth of the CSG tree at the cost of a larger number of leaf nodes: a primitive may now appear in several subtrees. In pathological cases, the sum-of-products form may grow exponentially with the number of primitives. However, because complex objects are generally defined as assemblies of simpler objects, the union operations will dominate at the top of the tree, keeping the number of products low. Furthermore, *pruning*

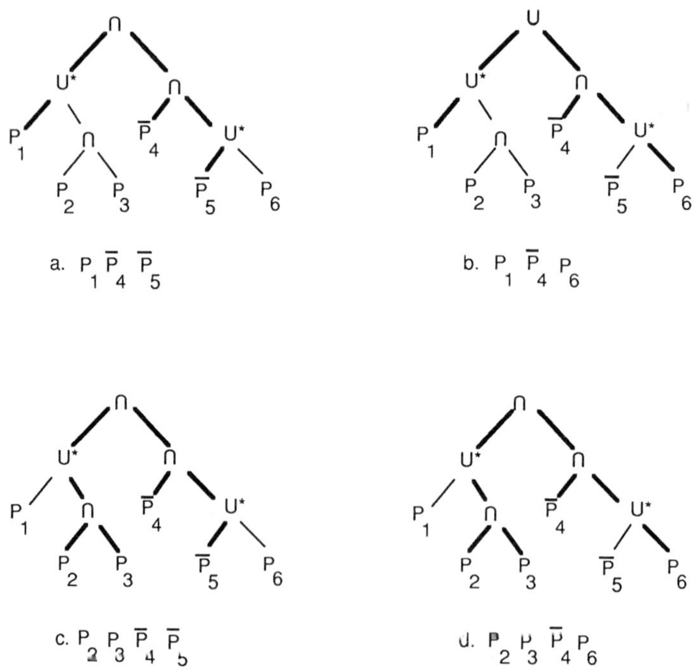

Figure 7.3. Tree traversal for product extraction.

techniques may be applied in both object and image space to eliminate empty and non-active products (Thomas 1983; Goldfeather et al 1989).

The CSG tree can be converted into a sum-of-linear trees or a sum-of products form by an explicit re-ordering or re-structuring of the tree. However, these forms can also be extracted from the tree by a specific traversal of the tree that selectively visits or re-visits nodes. These dynamic versions of the corresponding tree conversions are often preferred, because their representation is compact and the conversion can be done adaptively. The sum-of-products form can be obtained by a repeated traversal of the tree, where each traversal extracts a product from the tree representing a unique sub-set of the tree. The tree traversals to find the subsets are guided by the following rules:

- at each internal node with a set union operation, only one of the subtrees at a time is visited,
- at each internal node with a set intersection operation, both subtrees are visited.

Figure 7.3 shows the different traversals to extract the products. At the union set operators, alternatively the left and right subtree is selected. A variation on this basic algorithm can generate a sum-of-linear trees.

7.2 Depth-Buffering Classification Techniques

The standard depth-buffer algorithm (Catmull 1974; Fournier and Fussell 1988) for displaying (non-CSG) objects operates on a depth buffer (z-buffer) and an intensity buffer (frame buffer). At each pixel, the depth buffer stores a depth value (distance to the viewpoint), and the intensity buffer stores a shading intensity value (the intensity of the light that is reflected by the surface of the object towards the view point). The depth buffer is initialized to the maximum depth and the intensity buffer to the background colour. Surfaces can be scan-converted in any order. At each pixel covered by a surface, the value of the surface covering the pixel is compared to the corresponding value in the depth buffer: if the depth of the point is smaller than the corresponding value in the buffer, the depth and intensity values of the surface are written into the buffers, replacing the old values.

To display CSG objects, the points on the surfaces that project onto the pixels have to be classified in addition to the standard depth buffer test. To be on the boundary of the CSG model, the point has to 'in' the set definition of the CSG model. This can be tested by performing a point-in-primitive test for each primitive, and combining these tests according to the set definition of the CSG object. How the point-in-primitive test is done depends on the definition of the surfaces. For a block, for instance, the point should be inside all the halfspaces defining the block. Only if the point classifies as 'in', the surface is rendered into the frame buffer for that pixel, on condition that it passes the depth test. In most cases it is advantageous to do the depth test before the CSG classification. If the point fails the depth test, then there is no need to do the classification (Rossignac and Requicha 1986b).

Alternatively, a point-in-solid test can be done by comparing the depth value of the point with the depth values of corresponding points on the boundaries of the other primitives, and combining these individual point classifications according to the set operations specified in the CSG tree. In the depth-buffer algorithm the depth comparisons may be done on the depth values of the surfaces that project on the same pixel.

To classify a point $\mathbf{p}$ on the boundary of primitive A with respect to primitive B, $\mathbf{p}_z$, the depth (z-coordinate) of $\mathbf{p}$ is compared to the depth value of corresponding points on the boundary of B. If B, or its complement, is convex, there are at most two points on the boundary of B (one on a front face and one on a back face) that correspond to any given point **p** (project onto the same pixel).

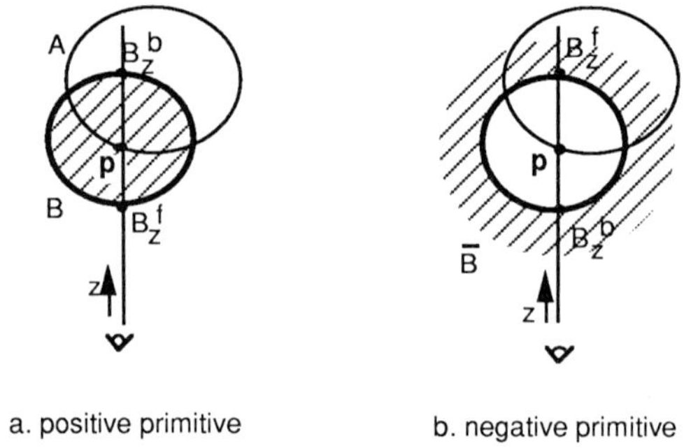

Figure 7.4. Point-in-solid classification by performing depth comparisons.

Let $B_z^f(p)$ *and* $B_z^b(p)$ denote the z-coordinates of the front and the back faces of a convex primitive B at points that correspond to a point **p** and thus project onto the same pixel p as **p.** If p_z, the depth value of **p**, lies between $B_z^f(p)$ and $B_z^b(p)$, then **p** is 'in' B if B is positive, and 'out' of B if B is negative (see figure 7.4).

Consequently, a point p on the boundary of a primitive A will be 'in' a primitive B, if

$$p_Z \geq B_z^f(p) \;\; \textbf{and} \;\; p_Z \leq B_z^b(p), \quad \text{if } B \text{ is positive,}$$

or

$$p_Z \leq B_z^b(p) \;\; \textbf{or} \;\; p_Z \geq B_z^f(p), \quad \text{if } B \text{ is negative.}$$

This test can be conveniently implemented using an extra depth buffer to store the front faces of A. The front and back faces of all other primitives are then scan-converted and their depths compared with the depth values in the buffer at each pixel. (Primitives are assumed to be convex; non-convex primitives require additional processing). Additional to the point-in-primitive tests, the 'in' or 'out' classification with respect to the primitives are combined using the set operators, as specified in the CSG tree. Only points that classify as 'in' or 'on' with respect to the composite solid are rendered in a final frame buffer with an additional depth test to select the visible faces (Jansen 1986).

In this way each primitive will be compared with all the other primitives in the CSG tree. This will lead to quadratic performances with respect to the number of primitives. However, for a given primitive, not all other primitives will be of interest and for these primitives the classification can be simplified. For instance, if only union operations have to be taken into account, the CSG algorithm reduces to the standard depth-buffer algorithm (the depth buffer test automatically takes care of the union operation). A generalization of this idea, the 'active zone' theory of Rossignac and Voelcker (1986), describes the subset of the CSG tree for a primitive that is relevant for the classification of candidate points on the boundary of that primitive.

According to active zone theory, the CSG tree can be re-ordered with respect to a primitive into a subtree (I-tree) that forms an intersection with the primitive, and a subtree (U-tree) that is unioned to the primitive (see figure 7.5). To classify the boundary of a primitive, only the part of the boundary that is outside the I-tree has to be clipped off. The part inside the U-tree will be removed by the depth test.

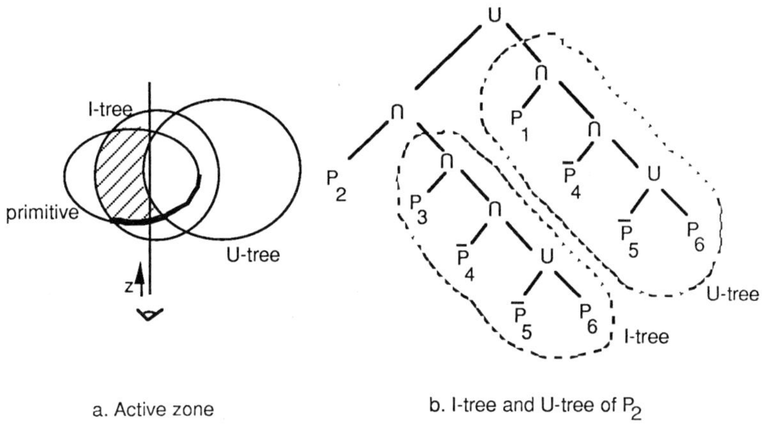

Figure 7.5. Active zone of primitive.

Further, if primitives are spatially disjoint, their contribution to each other's classification can be determined *a priori* (Tilove et al 1984). It is therefore often worthwhile to 'localize' the CSG expression for a given primitive in a pre-processing stage. Also, an image subdivision may reduce the complexity of the CSG classification (Woodwark and Quinlan 1982; Thomas 1983; Bronsvoort et al 1984; Jansen and Sutherland 1987). For instance, if in the example of figure 7.5, P_2 does not intersect P_4, then $\overline{P_4}$ can be removed from the I-tree of P_2.

However, these improvements do not suffice to reduce the amount of processing, and parallelism at the pixel level has to be used to achieve real-time performance. This is offered by logic-enhanced frame buffer systems that incorporate a large number of pixel processors for performing elementary operations for pixels in parallel (Fuchs et al 1985), and by specialized rendering engines that can perform operations on multiple pixels simultaneously. If the classification for each surface is done independently at each pixel, then the intermediate results of the logical combine operations (the 'in' or 'out' classification with respect to the individual primitives) have to be stored (at least temporarily) locally at the pixel level (ie. in the pixel memory).

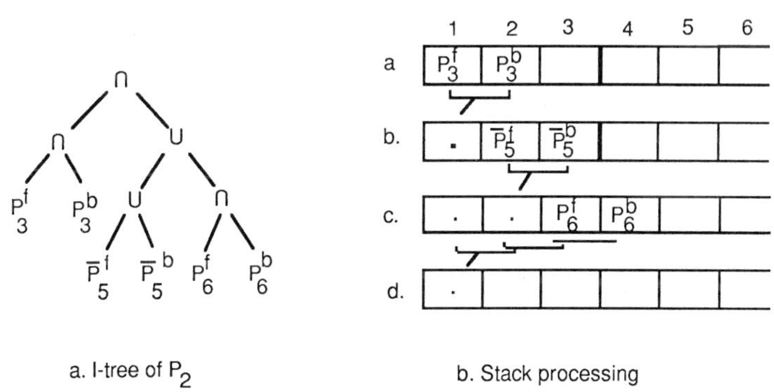

Figure 7.6. Classification of a point by a tree traversal.

It is convenient to see the recursive combine operation of the individual point-primitive classifications as a postorder traversal of the CSG tree that processes information with a stack. For instance, see figure 7.6 for the classification of a point on P_2^f.

Figure 7.6b shows the intermediate results of the depth comparisons and the combine operations for the classification of P_2^f, using its I-tree (figure 7.5b with $\overline{P_4}$ removed).

For the evaluation of a tree with a depth of *m*, a maximum of *m+1* positions may be needed for the stack (each stack position can be represented by one bit in the frame buffer). In this example, four stack positions are needed. However, in most rendering architectures the available buffer memory at each pixel is limited and thus not all classification results can be stored. In case not enough buffer memory is available for the standard procedure, the tree restructuring techniques can be used, ie. the tree is converted into linear trees which each require only three stack positions at a time, or into a sum-of-products form requiring only two stack positions at a time to render a product. As explained in 7.1, the conversion can also be simulated with a selective tree traversal. The selective tree traversal algorithm can be combined with the standard tree traversal, in the sense that processing of the primitives is minimized when enough stack memory is available for the tree evaluation, and memory use is minimized with the selective tree-traversal method (Jansen 1987).

7.3 Sum-of-products Rendering

The rendering algorithm for the sum-of-products form can also be derived from observing that the front faces of a product are a subset of the front faces of the primitives defining that product. A point on the boundary of a primitive in a product P will lie on the boundary of P containing that primitive only if it lies inside all the other primitives defining P.

The product rendering can thus be implemented by scan-converting the front faces of each primitive in a temporary buffer, and scan-converting the front and back faces of all other primitives in the product for comparison. Parts of the primitive that fail to pass one of the inside tests are discarded from further processing (see figure 7.7).

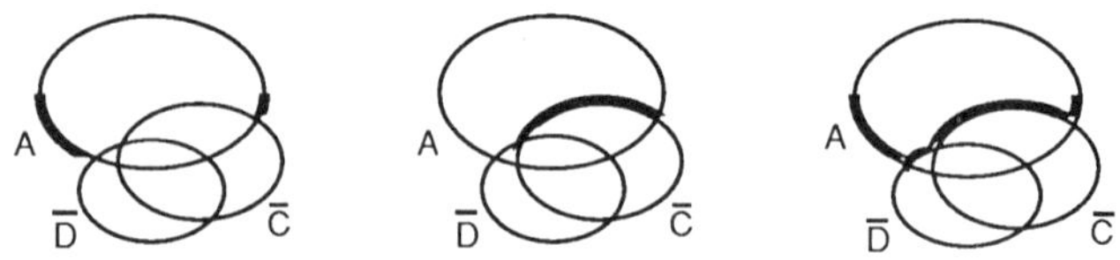

a. front of A in product   b. front of C in product   c. front of product

Figure 7.7. Front of A for product $A.\overline{C}.\overline{D}$ (a), front of C (b) and front of product (c).

The product expression thus acts as a clipping expression that successively cuts pieces of the primitive's front face as it is compared with the other primitives in the product. The part of the front face that is classified as 'in' the product (and consequently will lie on the boundary of the product, because the boundary of a primitive is either on the boundary of the product or outside of it) is written into the 'final' depth buffer using a minimum depth test to remove hidden and internal faces of the potentially overlapping products.

The complete algorithm is as follows:

- the CSG tree is converted into the sum-of-products form;

- for each product, each primitive is classified by comparing its front with the forward and backward facing boundaries of the other primitives in the product;
- the valid parts (pixels) are merged into the final depth buffer with a depth test.

Note that the amount of processing is exactly the same as for the algorithm of 7.2, except that now all the primitives in one product are processed before passing to the next product. In the earlier version one primitive was tested against all the primitives of the products it belongs to.

The algorithm can be extended to process non-convex primitives (Goldfeather et al 1989).

7.4 Trickle Algorithm

The redundancy of the product rendering algorithms becomes apparent when we consider that each primitive may appear in several products, and that each primitive is compared with all other primitives in these products. A new version of the product rendering algorithm, the *trickle* algorithm (Epstein et al 1989) makes the rendering of a product quadratic only to the number of negative primitives, at the cost of using one extra depth buffer. The basic idea of the trickle algorithm is to calculate the forward facing boundary of a product directly, instead of calculating the individual contributions of the primitives. The overall strategy, however, is the same: conversion into sum-of-products form and merging each front into a final buffer. In the following, we will discuss how a front of a product is calculated.

The first step of the algorithm is to calculate a good tentative front. First observe that negative primitives can only subtract from and not add to the product. For a tentative front, it is thus sufficient to calculate the front of only the *positive* primitives. Second, observe that a point on the front should be inside all the positive primitives. This is only guaranteed if we take the *maximum* of the nearest fronts of the positive primitives. Figure 7.8a shows the first front for product $A\,\overline{C}\,\overline{D}$.

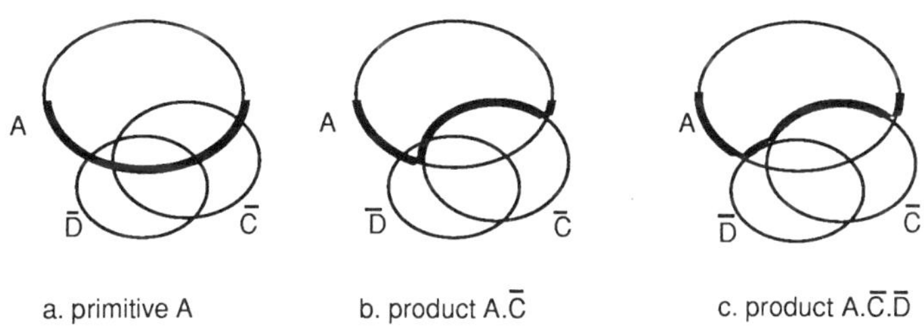

Figure 7.8. Rendering of a product, first tentative front (a), and subsequent modifications (b) and (c).

The second step is to correct the front. If the front is intersected by a negative primitive, it does not lie on the product. The correction operation is based on the idea that if a portion of the front is outside one of the primitives, then we replace that portion of the front by the front of that primitive, if it lies behind the tentative front (because any point in between is invalid anyhow). If the front of the primitive is not behind the current tentative front, then the front is invalidated and should not be used in the final merge operation. Because negative primitives and cavities may overlap, the newly created front of the product has to be tested against all the other (negative and non-convex) primitives again to check for additional subtractions. This procedure must be repeated until no further changes occur (the resulting front is no longer contained in any of the negative primitives or any of the cavities of the non-convex primitives).

The successive modifications to the front are shown in figure 7.8b and 7.8c. The algorithm is given in figure 7.9.

```
procedure sum_of_products_rendering; { trickle version }
{
X_z^f, X_i^f     depth and intensity of front of primitive X
ZBUF, ZB_1, ZB_2 final and temporary depth buffers
IBUF, IB_1, IB_2     final and temporary frame buffers
E  enable bit
k+     total number of cavities in the positive primitives
k-  total number of negative primitives plus the number of cavities in the negative primitives
}
( ZBUF , IBUF ) ← (max_depth, background_color);
for each product do
    ZB_1 ← min_depth; { initialize front of product }
    for each positive primitive X do
        ZB_2 ← max_depth;
        for each front face of X where ( X_z^f < ZB_2 ) do
            ( ZB_2 , IB_2 ) ← ( X_z^f , X_i^f ); { find front of prim.}
        where ( ZB_2 > ZB_1 ) do ( ZB_1 , IB_1 ) ← ( ZB_2 , IB_2 ); {tentative front of product}
    repeat (k+ + k-) times { test-and-push phase }
        for each primitive X do ( ZB_2 , IB_2, E ) ← (max_depth, background_color, 'set' );
        for each face of X
            where ( X_z > ZB_1 ) and ( X_z < ZB_2 ) do ( ZB_2 , IB_2, E ) ← ( X_z^f, X_i^f, 'set' );
        where ( E = 'set' ) do ( ZB_1 , IB_1 ) ← ( ZB_2 , IB_2 ); { move front profile }
    where ( ZF < ZBUF ) do ( ZBUF , IBUF ) ← ( ZB_1 , IB_1); { final merge}
```

Figure 7.9. Trickle algorithm.

First a tentative front of the product is generated which is the maximum of the minimum depth values of the primitives (in case a primitive is non-convex, it can have more than one front). Then the fronts and backs of the primitives are scanned and compared to ZB_1 to compute, at each pixel, the first surface behind ZB_1. This surface is stored in ZB_2. If the surface is a front surface, the enable bit E is set; if it is a back surface, then the bit is cleared. After processing the surfaces of a primitive, ZB_2 is copied for the enabled pixels into ZB_1. Note that ZB_2 is initialized to *max_depth* and E is set, so, if there is no face of the primitive, then the front is set to *max_depth*, effectively disabling the front for the final summing operation. Finally, the product's front profile is merged into the summing buffer with a depth test. The net effect is that pixels in the previously computed sum with depth values larger than those of valid corresponding pixels in the product are overwritten by the product's pixels.

If it cannot be detected that additional subtractions are not needed, then the complexity of the algorithm is quadratic for the number of negative primitives in a product. In general, however, the number of scan-conversions can be reduced when negative primitives can be separated into smaller sets, in such a way that most primitives in one set are disjoint from most primitives in the other set. If n negative primitives can be clustered into m clusters of disjoint primitives, then the number of scan-conversions is equal to $m(n-1)+1$ times the average number of scan-conversions for a cluster.

The CSG product rendering algorithm described above may be implemented with minor changes on existing depth-buffer hardware (depth-buffer compare and conditional depth-buffer copy). For logic-enhanced frame buffer systems (Fuchs et al 1985) and other advanced rendering architectures, the implementation is straightforward and only requires two extra depth values and one enable bit to be located in the pixel memory.

8. Conclusions

In recent years, considerable improvements have been made in the design and display of solid models. Powerful conceptual tools have been developed that allow the designer to express his ideas in terms not related to coordinates, control points, surfaces and volumes, but to more functional entities, and that allow him to manipulate and modify these concepts, and still see at the same time the materialization of his ideas as a real object, and with the realism and interactivity made possible by real-time CSG display techniques. The direct manipulation paradigm allows the designer to manipulate graphical representations of concepts that react to his messages and commands in an object-oriented sense, give him the capability to manipulate abstract semantic and symbolic information, and still give him the feeling of manipulating real life objects. Research will continue in these areas, and will be directed towards incorporation of intelligence in the design process, in particular the use of techniques based on geometric reasoning.

In the area of display techniques there is a growing interest in high-quality rendering that will cover radiosity shading and texture mapping. The complexity of these display techniques, however, will hamper the development of specialized hardware. Research on advanced workstation architectures in the direction of homogeneous and heterogeneous multi-processors will continue.

References

Aldefeld B. (1983) On automatic recognition of 3D structures from 2D representations. Computer-Aided Design 15(2): 59-64

Ando H., Susuki H., and Kimura F. (1989) A geometric reasoning system for mechanical product design. In: Proceedings CAPE '89, Kimura F., and Rolstadås A. (eds), Elsevier Science Publishers, Amsterdam, pp 131-140

Arbab F., and Wing J.M. (1985) Geometric reasoning: a new paradigm for processing geometric information. Report TR-85-33, CS dept. USC, Los Angeles

Arvo J., and Kirk D. (1989) A survey of ray tracing acceleration techniques. In: An Introduction to Ray Tracing, Glassner A.S. (ed), Academic Press, New York, pp 201-262

Atherton P.R. (1983) A scan-line hidden surface removal procedure for constructive solid geometry. Computer Graphics 17(3): 73-82

Barr A.H. (1984) Global and local deformations of solid primitives. Computer Graphics 18(3): 21-30

Barr A.H. (1986) Ray tracing deformed surfaces. Computer Graphics 20(4): 287-296

Baumgart B.G. (1975) A polyhedron representation for computer vision. In: AFIPS Proceedings National Computer Conference 44, AFIPS Press, Arlington, pp 589-596

Beeker E. (1986) Smoothing of shapes designed with free-form surfaces. Computer-Aided Design 18(4): 224-232

Böhm W. (1980) Inserting new knots into B-spline curves. Computer-Aided Design 12(4): 199-201

Bronsvoort W.F., van Wijk J.J., and Jansen F.W. (1984) Two methods for improving the efficiency of ray casting in solid modelling. Computer-Aided Design 16(1): 51-55

Bronsvoort W.F., and Klok F. (1985) Ray tracing generalized cylinders. ACM Transactions on Graphics 4(4): 291-303 (corrigendum ibid 6(3): 238-239)

Bronsvoort W.F. (1986) Techniques for reducing Boolean evaluation time in CSG scan-line algorithms. Computer-Aided Design 18(10): 533-538

Bronsvoort W.F. (1987) An algorithm for visible-line and visible-surface display of CSG models. The Visual Computer 3(4): 176-185

Bronsvoort W.F., and Garnaat H. (1989) Incremental display of CSG models using local updating. Computer-Aided Design 21(4): 221-231

Bronsvoort W.F., van Nieuwenhuizen P.R., and Post F.H. (1989) Display of profiled sweep objects. The Visual Computer 5(3): 147-157

Casale M.S., and Stanton E.L. (1985) An overview of analytic solid modeling. IEEE Computer Graphics and Applications 5(2): 45-56

Casale M.S. (1987) Free-form solid modeling with trimmed surface patches. IEEE Computer Graphics and Applications 7(1): 33-43

Catmull E.E. (1974) A Subdivision Algorithm for Computer Display of Curved Surfaces. Thesis, Report UTEC-CSc-74-133, Computer Science Department, University of Utah

Chiyokura H. (1988) Solid Modelling with Designbase: Theory and Implementation. Addison-Wesley, Singapore

Chung W.L. (1984) A new method of view synthesis for solid modelling. In: Proceedings CAD '84, Wexler J. (ed), Butterworths, Guildford, pp 470-480

Cohen E., Lyche T., and Riesenfeld R.F. (1980) Discrete B-splines and subdivision techniques in computer-aided geometric design and computer graphics. Computer Graphics and Image Processing 14(2): 87-111

Cook R.L. (1989) Stochastic sampling and distributed ray tracing. In: An Introduction to Ray Tracing, Glassner A.S. (ed), Academic Press, New York, pp 161-199

Coquillart S. (1987) A control-point-based sweeping technique. IEEE Computer Graphics and Applications 7(11): 36-45

Courter S.M., and Brewer J.A. (1986) Automated conversion of curvilinear wire frame models to surface boundary models: a topological approach. Computer Graphics 20(4): 171-178

Crocker G.A. (1987) Screen-area coherence for interactive scanline display algorithms. IEEE Computer Graphics and Applications 7(9): 10-17

van Emmerik M. (1988) A system for graphical interaction on parametrized models. In: Proceedings Eurographics '88, Duce D.A., and Jancene P. (eds), North-Holland, Amsterdam, pp 233-242

van Emmerik M. (1989) Graphical interaction on procedural object descriptions. In: Theory and Practice of Geometric Modeling, Springer-Verlag, Berlin, pp 469-482

van Emmerik M., and Jansen F.W. (1989) User interface for feature modeling. In: Proceedings CAPE '89, Kimura F., and Rolstadås A. (eds), Elsevier Science Publishers, Amsterdam, pp 625-632

van Emmerik M. (1990) A system for interactive graphical modeling with 3D constraints. In: Proceedings CG International '90, Springer-Verlag, Berlin

Epstein D.A., Jansen F.W., and Rossignac J.R. (1989) Z-buffer rendering from CSG: the trickle algorithm. IBM Research Report RC 15182, IBM Research Yorktown Heights, New York

Farin G. (1988) Curves and Surfaces for Computer Aided Geometric Design: a Practical Guide. Academic Press, Boston

Farouki R.T. (1985) Exact offset procedures for simple solids. Computer Aided Geometric Design 2(4): 257-279

Farouki R.T. (1987) Graphical methods for surface differential geometry. In: The Mathematics of Surfaces II, Proceedings 2nd Conference on the Mathematics of Surfaces, Martin R.R. (ed), Clarendon Press, Oxford, pp 363-385

Faux I.D., and Pratt M.J. (1979) Computational Geometry for Design and Manufacture. Ellis Horwood, Chichester

Filip D.J., and Ball T.W. (1989) Procedurally representing lofted surfaces. IEEE Computer Graphics and Applications 9(6): 27-33

Fournier A., and Wesley M.A. (1983) Bending polyhedral objects. Computer-Aided Design 15(2): 79-87

Fournier A., and Fussell D. (1988) On the power of the frame buffer. ACM Transactions on Graphics 7(2): 103-128

Freeman-Benson B.N., Maloney J., and Borning A. (1990) An incremental constraint solver. Communications of the ACM 33(1): 54-63

Fuchs H., Goldfeather J., Hultquist J.P., Spach S., Austin J.D., Brooks Jr. F.P., Eyles J.G., and Poulton J. (1985) Fast spheres, shadows, textures, transparencies, and image enhancements in Pixel-planes. Computer Graphics 19(3): 111-120

Fujimoto A., Tanaka T., and Iwata K. (1986) ARTS: accelerated ray-tracing system. IEEE Computer Graphics and Applications 6(4): 16-26

Gero J.S. (1989) Knowledge-based computer-aided design. In: Proceedings CAPE '89, Kimura F., and Rolstadås A. (eds), Elsevier Science Publishers, Amsterdam, pp 13-20

Glassner A.S. (1984) Space subdivision for fast ray tracing. IEEE Computer Graphics and Applications 4(10): 15-22

Glassner A.S. (ed) (1989) An Introduction to Ray Tracing. Academic Press, New York

Goldfeather J., Hultquist J.P.M., and Fuchs H. (1986) Fast constructive solid geometry display in the Pixel-Powers graphics system. Computer Graphics 20(4): 107-116

Goldfeather J., Molnar S., Turk G., and Fuchs H. (1989) Near real-time CSG rendering using tree normalization and geometric pruning. IEEE Computer Graphics and Applications 9(3): 20-28

Gossard D.C., and Lin V. (1983) Representation of part families through variational geometry. In: Advances in CAD/CAM, Proceedings 5th PROLAMAT Conference, Ellis T.M.R., and Semenkov O.I. (eds), North-Holland, Amsterdam, pp 47-53

Hall R. (1989) Illumination and Color in Computer Generated Imagery. Springer-Verlag, New York

Hanrahan P. (1983) Ray tracing algebraic surfaces. Computer Graphics 17(3): 83-90

Hearn D., and Baker M.P. (1986) Computer Graphics. Prentice-Hall, Englewood Cliffs

Ho Bin (1986) Inputting constructive solid geometry representations directly from 2D orthographic engineering drawings. Computer-Aided Design 18(3): 147-155

Hoffmann C.M., Hopcroft J.E., and Karasick M.S. (1989) Robust set operations on polyhedral solids. IEEE Computer Graphics and Applications 9(6): 50-59

Holmström L. (1987) Piecewise quadric blending of implicitly defined surfaces. Computer-Aided Geometric Design 4(3): 171-189

Jansen F.W. (1986) A pixel-parallel hidden surface algorithm for constructive solid geometry. In: Proceedings Eurographics '86, Requicha A.A.G. (ed), North-Holland, Amsterdam, pp 29-40

Jansen F.W. (1987) CSG hidden surface algorithms for VLSI hardware systems. In: Advances in Graphics Hardware I, Strasser W. (ed), Springer-Verlag, Berlin, pp 75-82

Jansen F.W., and Sutherland R.J. (1987) Display of solid models with a multi-processor system. In: Proceedings Eurographics '87, Maréchal G. (ed), North-Holland, Amsterdam, pp 377-387

Jared G., and Stroud I. (1983) Local operators in the BUILD system. In: Advances in CAD/CAM, Proceedings 5th PROLAMAT Conference, Ellis T.M.R., and Semenkov O.I. (eds), North-Holland, Amsterdam, pp 55-64

Joy K.I., and Bhetanabhotla M.N. (1986) Ray tracing parametric surface patches utilizing numerical techniques and ray coherence. Computer Graphics 20(4): 279-285

Kajiya J.T. (1982) Ray tracing parametric patches. Computer Graphics 16(3): 245-254

Kajiya J.T. (1983) New techniques for ray tracing procedurally defined objects. Computer Graphics 17(3): 91-102; also in: ACM Transactions on Graphics 2(3): 161-181

Kapur D., and Mundy J.L. (eds) (1989) Geometric Reasoning. Proceedings of an International Workshop on Geometric Reasoning at Oxford University 1986, MIT Press

Kay T.L., and Kajiya J.T. (1986) Ray tracing complex scenes. Computer Graphics 20(4): 269-278

Laidlaw D.H., Trumbore W.B., and Hughes J.F. (1986) Constructive solid geometry for polyhedral objects. Computer Graphics 20(4): 161-170

Lane J.M., Carpenter L.C., Whitted T., and Blinn J.F. (1980) Scan line methods for displaying parametrically defined surfaces. Communications of the ACM 23(1): 23-34

Lee Y.T., and Requicha A.A.G. (1982) Algorithms for computing the volume and other integral properties of solids. Communications of the ACM 25(9): 635-650

Lequette R. (1988) Automatic construction of curvilinear solids from wire frame views. Computer-Aided Design 20(4): 171-180

Mäntylä M. (1983) Set operations of GWB. Computer Graphics Forum 2(2/3): 122-134

Mäntylä M., and Tamminen M. (1983) Localized set operations for solid modeling. Computer Graphics 17(3): 279-288

Mäntylä M. (1986) Boolean operations of 2-manifolds through vertex neighborhood classification. ACM Transactions on Graphics 5(1): 1-29

Mäntylä M. (1988) An Introduction to Solid Modeling. Computer Science Press, Rockville

Middleditch A.E., and Sears K.H. (1985) Blend surfaces for set theoretic volume modelling systems. Computer Graphics 19(3): 161-170

Miller J.R. (1987) Geometric approaches to nonplanar quadric surface intersection curves. ACM Transactions on Graphics 6(4): 274-307

Miller J.R. (1988) Analysis of quadric-surface-based solid models. IEEE Computer Graphics and Applications 8(1): 28-42

Mortenson M.E. (1985) Geometric Modeling. John Wiley, New York

Myers B.A. (1988) A taxonomy of window manager user interfaces. IEEE Computer Graphics and Applications 8(5): 65-84

Nasri A.H. (1987) Polyhedral subdivision methods for free-form surfaces. ACM Transactions on Graphics 6(1): 29-73

Navazo I., Fontdecaba J., and Brunet P. (1987) Extended octtrees, between CSG trees and boundary representations. In: Proceedings Eurographics '87, Maréchal G. (ed), North-Holland, Amsterdam, pp 239-247

Newell R.G., and Parden G. (1983) Parametric design in the Medusa system. In: Proceedings CAPE '83 Conference, Warman E.A. (ed), North-Holland, Amsterdam, pp 667-677

Okino N., Kakazu Y., and Morimoto M. (1984) Extended depth-buffer algorithms for hidden-surface visualization. IEEE Computer Graphics and Applications 4(5): 79-88

van Overveld C.W.A.M. (1989) Application of a perspective cursor as a 3D locator device. Computer-Aided Design 21(10): 619-629

Painter J., and Sloan K. (1989) Antialiased ray tracing by adaptive progressive refinement. Computer Graphics 23(3): 281-288

Piegl L. (1989a) Geometric method of intersecting natural quadrics represented in trimmed surface form. Computer-Aided Design 21(4): 201-212

Piegl L. (1989b) Modifying the shape of rational B-splines. Part 1: curves. Computer-Aided Design 21(8): 509-518

Piegl L. (1989c) Modifying the shape of rational B-splines. Part 2: surfaces. Computer-Aided Design 21(9): 538-546

Post F.H., and Klok F. (1986) Deformations of sweep objects in solid modelling. In: Proceedings Eurographics '86, Requicha A.A.G. (ed), North-Holland, Amsterdam, pp 103-114

Pueyo X., and Brunet P. (1987) A parametric-space-based scan-line algorithm for rendering bicubic surfaces. IEEE Computer Graphics and Applications 7(11): 17-25

Pueyo X., and Mendoza J.C. (1987) A new scan line algorithm for the rendering of CSG trees. In: Proceedings Eurographics '87, Maréchal G. (ed), North-Holland, Amsterdam, pp 347-361

Requicha A.A.G. (1980) Representations for rigid solids: theory, methods and systems. ACM Computing Surveys 12(4): 437-464

Requicha A.A.G., and Voelcker H.B. (1985) Boolean operations in solid modeling: boundary evaluation and merging algorithms. Proceedings IEEE 73(1): 30-44

Rossignac J.R., and Requicha A.A.G. (1984) Constant-radius blending in solid modeling. Computers in Mechanical Engineering 3(1): 65-73

Rossignac J.R. (1986) Constraints in constructive solid geometry. In: Proceedings Workshop on Interactive 3D Graphics, ACM Press, pp 93-110

Rossignac J.R., and Requicha A.A.G. (1986a) Offsetting operations in solid modelling. Computer Aided Geometric Design 3(2): 129-148

Rossignac J.R., and Requicha A.A.G. (1986b) Depth-buffering display techniques for constructive solid geometry. IEEE Computer Graphics and Applications 6(9): 29-39

Rossignac J.R., and Voelcker H.B. (1986) Active zones in constructive solid geometry for redundancy and interference detection. IBM Research Report RC 11991, IBM Research Yorktown Heights, New York. Also as: Rossignac J.R., and Voelcker H.B. (1989) Active zones in CSG for accelerating boundary evaluation, redundancy elimination, interference detection, and shading algorithms. ACM Transactions on Graphics 8(1): 51-87

Roth S.D. (1982) Ray casting for modeling solids. Computer Graphics and Image Processing 18(2): 109-144

Rubin S.M., and Whitted T. (1980) A three-dimensional representation for fast rendering of complex scenes. Computer Graphics 14(3): 110-116

Sakurai H., and Gossard D.C. (1983) Solid model input through orthographic views. Computer Graphics 17(3): 243-252

Sato H., Ishii M., Sato K., Ikesaka M., Ishihata H., Kakimoto M., Hirota K., and Inoue K. (1985) Fast image generation of constructive solid geometry using a cellular array processor. Computer Graphics 19(3): 95-102

Sederberg T.W., and Parry S.R. (1986) Free-form deformation of solid geometric models. Computer Graphics 20(4): 151-160

Sederberg T.W., and Zundel A.K. (1989) Scan line display of algebraic surfaces. Computer Graphics 23(3): 147-156

Segal M., and Séquin C.H. (1988) Partitioning polyhedral objects into nonintersecting parts. IEEE Computer Graphics and Applications 8(1): 53-67

Shimada K., Numao M., Masuda H., and Kawabe S. (1989) Constraint-based object description for product modeling. In: Proceedings CAPE '89, Kimura F., and Rolstadås A. (eds), Elsevier Science Publishers, Amsterdam, pp 95-106

Shneiderman B. (1983) Direct manipulation: a step beyond programming languages. IEEE Computer 16(8): 57-69

Sillion F., and Puech C. (1989) A general two-pass method integrating specular and diffuse reflection. Computer Graphics 23(3): 335-344

Takala T. (1984) User interface management system with geometric modelling capabilities: a CAD system's framework. IEEE Computer Graphics and Applications 5(4): 42-50

Thomas A.L. (1983) Geometric modelling and display primitives towards specialised hardware. Computer Graphics 17(3): 299-310

Tiller W. (1983) Rational B-splines for curve and surface representation. IEEE Computer Graphics and Applications 3(6): 61-69

Tilove R.B., Requicha A.A.G., and Hopkins M.R. (1984) Efficient editing of solid models by exploiting structural and spatial locality. Computer Aided Geometric Design 1(3): 227-239

Wallace J.R., Cohen M.F., and Greenberg D.P. (1987) A two-pass solution to the rendering equation: a synthesis of ray tracing and radiosity methods. Computer Graphics 21(4): 311-320

Watson D.F. (1981) Computing the n-dimensional Delaunay tessellation with application to Voronoi polytopes. The Computer Journal 24(2): 167-172

Wesley M.A., and Markowsky G. (1980) Fleshing out wire frames. IBM Journal of Research and Development 24(5): 582-597

Wesley M.A., and Markowsky G. (1981) Fleshing out projections. IBM Journal of Research and Development 25(6): 934-954

Whitted T. (1980) An improved illumination model for shaded display. Communications of the ACM 23(6): 343-349

Wilson P. R. (1987) A short history of CAD data transfer standards. IEEE Computer Graphics and Applications 7(6): 64-67

van Wijk J.J. (1984a) Ray tracing objects defined by sweeping planar cubic splines. ACM Transactions on Graphics 3(3): 223-237

van Wijk J.J. (1984b) Ray tracing objects defined by sweeping a sphere. In: Proceedings Eurographics '84, Bø K., and Tucker H.A. (eds), North-Holland, Amsterdam, pp 73-82

van Wijk J.J. (1986a) SML: a solid modelling language. Computer-Aided Design 18(8): 443-449

van Wijk J.J. (1986b) On new types of solid models and their visualization with ray tracing. Doctoral thesis, Delft University of Technology, Delft University Press, Delft

Woodward C.D. (1986) Methods for cross-sectional design of B-spline surfaces. In: Proceedings Eurographics '86, Requicha A.A.G. (ed), North-Holland, Amsterdam, pp 129-142

Woodwark J.R., and Quinlan K.M. (1982) Reducing the effect of complexity on volume model evaluation. Computer-Aided Design 14(2): 89-95

Woodwark J.R. (1987) Blends in geometric modelling. In: The Mathematics of Surfaces II, Proceedings 2nd Conference on the Mathematics of Surfaces, Martin R.R. (ed), Clarendon Press, Oxford, pp 255-297

Woodwark J.R. (ed) (1989) Geometric Reasoning. Proceedings of a Workshop held at IBM UK Scientific Centre 1986, Clarendon Press, Oxford

State of the Art in Image Synthesis

Michael F. Cohen and James S. Painter

1. Introduction

Image Synthesis is not a new idea. Human have been creating pictures of non-existent worlds for as long as they have had the capacity to imagine them. These efforts have ranged from cave drawings to fantastically rendered scenes of great complexity. They have depicted scenes of great horror in the paintings of Hironymous Bosch, to the impossible worlds of M. C. Escher.

The invention of the camera made it possible to quickly capture and create highly realistic images, however, the camera is only able to record a scene which already exists. Artists are not restricted in this way, but it takes a great deal of skill to create a realistic image of an imaginary scene. The advent of the computer, and the image synthesis techniques described in these notes, bring the ability to create realistic images to a much wider group.

Creating a realistic synthetic image on a computer requires two steps:

(1) describing the geometry of the environment to be rendered and the material properties of the objects which make up the environment, and

(2) simulating the propagation of light through the synthetic environment and displaying the results of the simulation.

The technology is not yet capable of creating images as fantastic as those of Bosch and Escher, but the shortcomings can probably be placed primarily in the first task, that of describing the environment to the computer. The focus of this tutorial will be on the second part of the problem, that of simulating and displaying the interaction of light in the synthetic environment.

1.1 Why?

There are many reasons one might want to create realistic synthetic images. In general, the primary purpose is for communication; to present an idea, to describe an imaginary world. Beyond the obvious artistic significance are many real world problems which can be greatly aided by the use of image synthesis. These include architecture in which the architect wants to take their client on a "walk" through a yet to built building, or a mechanical engineer who is trying to create a complex model and needs the visual cues presented by a realistic rendering to understand and communicate the shape of an object. Finally, realistic imaging can play a role in presenting images of objects which cannot be seen in the scale of the world we live in. These might include images of molecules or galaxies.

1.2 Realism

This course will focus on creating *realistic* images, and thus it is appropriate to try to define what we will mean by realism. Simply put, if we are successful, the synthetic image will be indistinguishable from the real object we are trying to create an image of. A number of constraints, however, make this goal unattainable. We will restrict ourselves to images displayed on a Cathode Ray Tube (CRT), which immediately limits the colors and dynamic range available to us. The fact that the CRT sits in an environment in which the ambient illumination is out of our control also limits our ability to reproduce the visual sensation one would get looking at the real object. Never-the-less, one can make intuitive judgements about the success of various methods given these constraints.

It is often mentioned in the context of "scientific visualization" that realism is not the goal, but rather communication of *abstract* ideas. This is undoubtedly true, however, it should be noted that abstraction begins with reality. We communicate abstract ideas through transformation from recognizable objects. This is obvious in the case of renderings of molecules as a series of spheres. Although this is not what a molecule really "looks" like, the realistic shading of the spheres provides the visual cues about shape, which in turn provide the insight into the actual structure of the molecule.

1.3 History

The roots of computer graphics can be traced back as far as the 1950's, however, Ivan Sutherland's "Sketchpad" project in the 1960's in recognized as the first major project which brought the potential of using computer graphics into focus. For the next ten years, graphics displays presented only line drawings but were impressive for their ability to perform perspective transformations of numerically defined objects. Realism only became an issue with the ability to display solid color images on a raster display screen in the 1970's. Gouraud and Phong devised algorithms (in wide use today in the hardware of current workstations) to model the smoothly varying shading of light across objects. More sophisticated local reflection models have been suggested and demonstrated by Blinn, Cook, and others to produce realistic looking images of materials ranging from plastic to metal. These models only dealt with *local* effects of light reflection from a single surface as opposed to the *global* effects of one object on another. This includes shadowing and interreflection between objects.

The decade of the 1980's saw the development of global algorithms capable of handling most or all of the propagation of light through complex environments. Two global illumination algorithms, Ray Tracing, introduced by Turner Whitted, and Radiosity, introduced by Cindy Goral, have produced the most striking results. Each of these algorithms will be discussed in some detail in the following sections, and their advantages and limitations will be outlined. Recent developments have brought these two algorithms closer together and have made the distinctions less important.

A common concern in all image synthesis algorithms is the need to discretize a continuous environment and image into a finite number of sample points. In general, the primary distinction which can be made between ray tracing and radiosity is whether the discretization of the environment is made based on the image plane (view dependent) or on the objects in the environment themselves (view independent). Many hybrid schemes have been discussed in the past few years and have been demonstrated to combine the best features of each.

The choice of algorithm for a particular application is dependent on many parameters. These include:

- the complexity of the environment,
- the types of materials one wishes to display
- the types and number of light sources
- the need for fidelity to the actual scene (the realism)
- the types of objects, e.g. polygonal vs. sculpted surfaces
- the computational resources available
- the type of computational resources, e.g. parallel vs. serial computation
- etc....

Although this course's main focus is on the algorithms for realistic image synthesis, we will begin with a short discussion of the human visual system, how it affects the development of display devices, and how these two technologies, biological and electronic, influence image synthesis strategies. This will be followed by a discussion of the problems presented by discretizing a continuous phenomenon, i.e. aliasing. We will then continue with a discussion of local reflection models since they lie at the heart of any global algorithm. The global rendering algorithms mentioned above will then be described in some detail. Finally we will try to take a quick view of the future and make some predictions about what is in store for us in the 1990's.

I. Human Perception, Image Discretization, and Local Illumination

2. Human Perception, CRTs, and Color Science

This section of the course will provide a very brief introduction to some of the problems related to displaying a color image on a CRT. In particular, we will need to understand a little bit about how our visual system works, and how a Cathode Ray Tube (CRT) works and why it is designed the way it is. Hopefully, this will provide some understanding for selecting color values when trying to display an image. A more complete treatment of these subjects can be found in [Meyer, 1986], [Meyer , 1988]. (Note: figures in this section are based on figures from [Meyer, 1986]).

2.1 The CRT

A *raster* image is one which is made up of a series of discrete points. The most common raster device is probably the television and its video raster tube or CRT. The main components of the CRT are one or more electron guns, electromagnets for focusing and directing the beams of electrons streaming from the guns, a shadow mask, and a phosphor coated screen (Figure 2.1). Color monitors have three electron guns which emit a quantity of electrons dependent on the electrical energy directed at the gun. The electrons are focused into a beam and directed at a point on the screen.

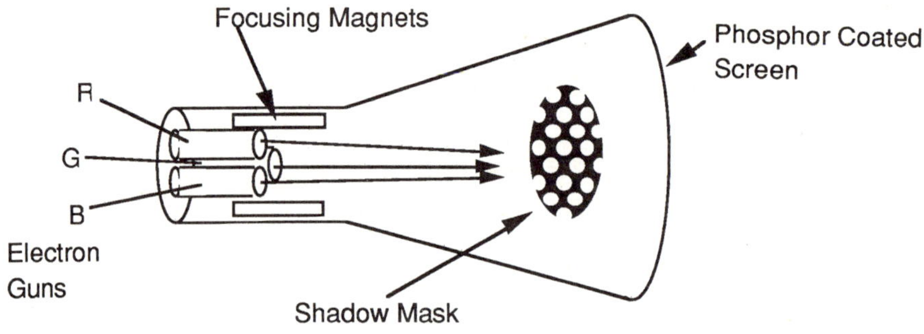

Figure 2.1: Cathode Ray Tube

The front surface of the screen is coated with phosphor dots which glow either Red, Green, or Blue when excited by an electron beam. A triangle of Red, Green, and Blue phosphors are simultaneously excited by the three guns to produce the range of colors we see. To prevent the wrong electron gun from exciting a particular phosphor, a shadow mask consisting of a series of holes allows only one gun's beam to hit the red phosphors, one to hit the green, and one to hit the blue phosphors (Figure 2.2). The beams are guided by a set of magnets to sweep across the surface of the screen at very high rates, allowing the entire screen to be re-illuminated every 1/30 of a second.

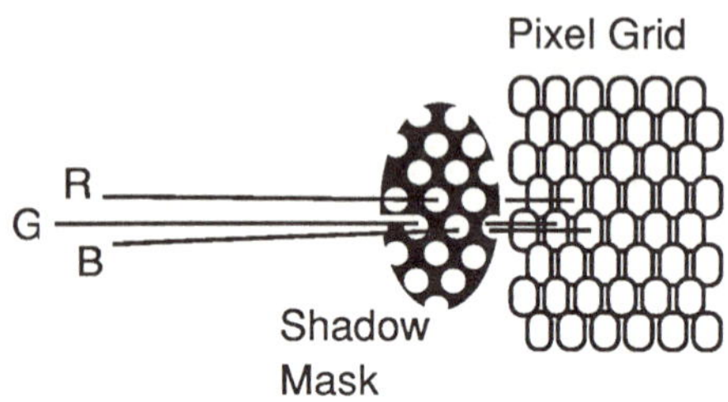

Figure 2.2: Shadow Mask

2.2 Image Discretization

If one begins with a continuous image and wants to display such an image on a CRT, there are three types of discretization which must be dealt with. First, the screen is made up of a finite number of discrete picture elements, or *pixels*. The problems presented by this spatial discretization are discussed in some detail in the next section. The second type of discretization involves the discrete amount of time (1/30 second) that a single image exists on the screen. This temporal discretization or *refresh* time is selected to be just below the frequency at which we would notice a flickering of the image. Finally, the third discretization, intensity discretization, is a result of the finite number of intensity values which can be displayed at a single pixel. To produce color images, each pixel is further divided into Red, Green, and Blue (RGB) phosphors, each of which independently are capable of some number of discrete intensities. The problem of selecting RGB phosphor values to represent real world colors is the primary subject of this section of the tutorial.

2.3 Light and Vision

To understand why there are three types of phosphors and how we can reproduce most colors with them, we need to look at our own visual system. An initial observation is that our eyes are sensitive to only a very small band of wavelengths within the total electro-magnetic energy spectrum which ranges from long radio waves to short x-rays. The visible range, light, is approximately from 380 to 770 nanometers in wavelength.

Each individual wavelength in the visible range produces a *spectral* color (i.e. those found in the rainbow). Different combinations of energy across the visible spectrum produce the range of color sensations we experience.

2.4 Hue, Saturation, and Brightness

People have little difficulty categorizing color according to its *Hue*, *Saturation*, and *Brightness*. Hue describes what we generally think of as the primary characteristic of a color, e.g. red, blue, yellow, turquoise, etc. Saturation characterizes the color's purity, or its difference from the *achromatic* grays ranging from black to white. Brightness, as the name indicates, denotes the intensity of the color. These dimensions are often thought of as describing a cylinder in which the central axis corresponds to brightness with the achromatic colors lying along the axis. Saturation is measured by the distance outward from the axis, and Hue varies as one moves about the axis. Other coordinate systems are also in use.

One should not jump to the conclusion that color sensation can be directly measured from the spectral energy distribution of the light. Many environmental factors influence our perception of an individual color sample. Never-the-less, we will ignore these effects for the time being, while understanding that any model we adopt to translate from spectral energy to phosphor illumination is limited.

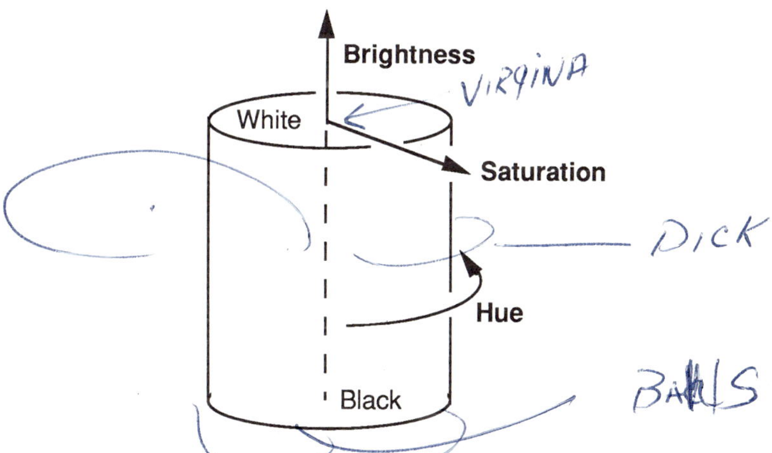

Figure 2.3: Hue, Saturation, Brightness

2.5 Some Color Matching Experiments

2.5.1 Metamers

Without understanding the full mechanics of vision we can perform some experiments and make observations. Imagine a setup in which a panel is placed in front of a viewer and is divided into two regions.

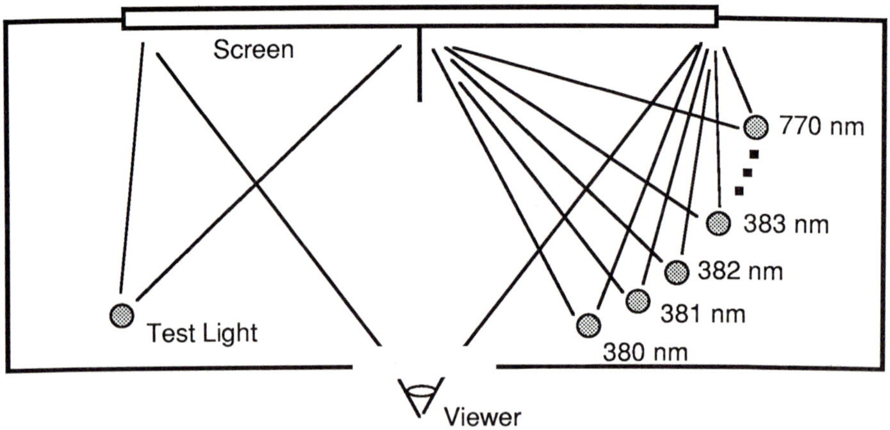

Figure 2.4: Color Matching Experiment with Single Wavelength Sources.

The first region is illuminated by a test source with some unknown energy spectrum. The second region is illuminated by a series of single wavelength sources ranging across the visible spectrum. Each spectral source can be individually modulated. If we adjust these sources to reproduce the spectrum of the test source on the other side, not surprisingly the viewer will report that the two regions appear the same. A more surprising result is that there are many other (an infinite number) of very different combinations which will also produce the identical color sensation. These different combinations are called *metamers*. A question come to mind: How many sources are needed to be able to create all or most color sensations?

2.5.2 Tristimulus Values

Lets consider a second experiment. This time we will place a test source on one side and ask a viewer to try to reproduce the sensation by combinations of only three spectral sources on the other side. We will select a low (l), medium (m), and high (h) wavelength. Quite amazingly, most test sources can be matched by adjusting only the three somewhat arbitrarily selected adjustable sources. It is this fact which makes color reproduction possible.

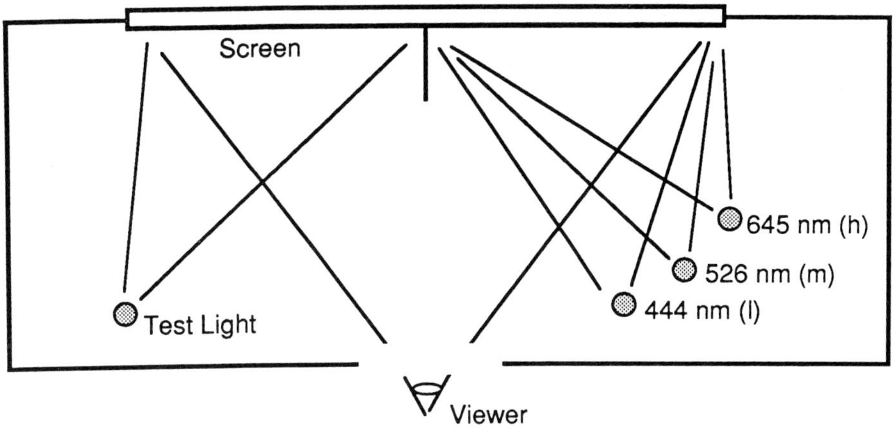

Figure 2.5: Tristimulus Color Matching Experiment.

In the experiment above, if the test light is a single spectral source, however, combinations of the three adjustable sources cannot create a match. If the viewer is allowed to "cheat" by moving one of the adjustable sources to the test light side, a match can then be made. This can be thought of as setting one of the three sources to a negative value. By plotting the amounts (both positive and negative) of *l*, *m*, and *h* needed to match each spectral source a set of *matching functions* can be generated.

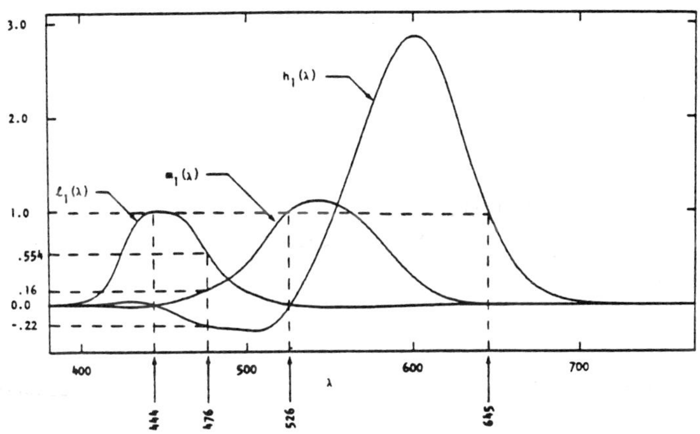

Figure 2.6: Color Matching Functions

These should not be confused with spectral energy distributions! They are three functions from which we can read off how much of these three particular sources we need to create the same sensation as that of any single wavelength source. The matching functions can be plotted in a space defined by *l*, *m*, and *h* axes.

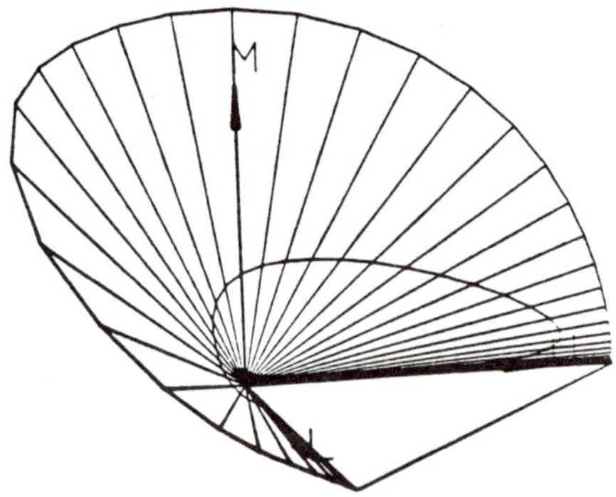

Figure 2.7: Cone of Realizable Color

The spectral colors lie along the edge of the cone, with all possible colors, i.e. combinations of spectral values, lying within this *cone of realizable color*.

Can this result be generalized to three other sources which may not be single spectral sources? Yes. In other words, we can use the results from the matching experiments to tell us how much of any sources we need to create the color sensation given by any single source.

First, it is quite easy to determine the amounts of the original three (*l, m, h*) spectral sources from above needed to reproduce each of three new sources. Lets call them *L*, *M*, and *H*. Since *L*, (or *M* or *H*), is simply a linear combination of single spectral sources as given by its spectral energy distribution, the specific combination of *l*, *m*, and *h* is found by integrating the product of *L*'s spectral energy distribution with the matching functions. Thus any three general light sources are simply linear combinations of the matching functions, i. e.

$$\begin{bmatrix} a_1 & a_2 & a_3 \\ b_1 & b_2 & b_3 \\ c_1 & c_2 & c_3 \end{bmatrix} \begin{bmatrix} l \\ m \\ h \end{bmatrix} = \begin{bmatrix} L \\ M \\ H \end{bmatrix}$$

where the a's, b's, and c's can be determined directly from the spectral energy distribution of the L, M, and H sources and the matching functions. In fact, any three linear combinations of the original matching functions provide a new set of functions which define a new set of axes on which we can plot the spectrum and cone of realizable color. One such set represents the C.I.E. XYZ tristimulus functions, which were selected in such a way to have the Y axis correspond to brightness, and also to have the entire cone lie in the positive octant.

Finally, we are ready to determine how to produce the same color sensation as any spectral energy distribution from any set of three sources. We can plug in the $l\lambda$, $m\lambda$, and $h\lambda$ for any wavelength, λ, from the matching functions into the above equation to get the energy needed for a single wavelength of the distribution we desire. We can simulate the full distribution by simply repeating this process across the spectrum and integrating.

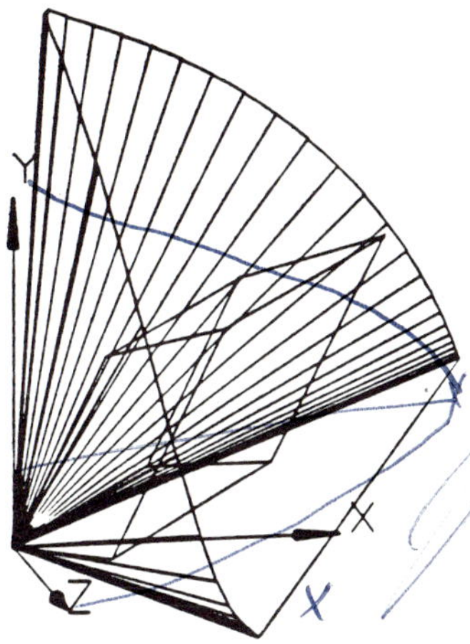

Figure 2.8: RGB Gamut and Cone of Realizable Color in CIE XYZ Space

2.6 Red, Green, and Blue

Does this mean we can get any color from our RGB color monitor? NO! Unfortunately, if we plug in the RGB distributions for the *L*, *M*, and *H* above, we will end up with negative values for some distributions we want to create. In addition, the dynamic range of intensities available to us on a CRT limit the scale of brightnesses we can reproduce. The limited RGB range is plotted inside the XYZ cone in the above figure. Never-the-less, we now have a means to determine the best RGB for any combination and to understand the approximations we need to make for colors we cannot reproduce on the CRT.

2.6.1 A Lesson

If you begin with R, G, and B, as your parameters for defining color in the real world, you have already eliminated many colors which exist. (On the other hand, you don't have to understand what is written in the above section!) Better color spaces exist for use in computation of the illumination model. These include the C.I.E. XYZ color space or alternatively selection of some number of discrete wavelength values [Meyer, 1988]. You are encouraged to look at the references listed at the end of the section for a more complete explanation of color science, as well as for many practical matters related to color reproduction.

2.7 The Human Visual System

You may have been wondering by now why we are able to trick our brains into seeing the same color sensation from two very different spectral energy distributions. Without going into any detail, our eyes have two main components, the lens which focuses incoming light and the retina which receives the light at the back of the eye. The retina contains a series of receptors scattered over its surface which send signals via a network of neurons to the brain.

It is believed that we have only three distinct type of receptors, which each have different sensitivity distributions across the visible spectrum. (Tests of color blind persons indicate that they are usually deficient in one of the three receptor types.) Thus, as long as the spectral distribution of the light stimulus multiplied by the sensitivity distribution of the sensors produces the same three signals to the brain, we cannot tell them apart.

3. Spatial Discretization and Anti-Aliasing

3.1 The Problem

Images are represented discretely in raster computer graphics. Raster computer graphics display devices represent an image as a *raster*, a two dimensional array of color values. The raster is mapped to the continuous plane of the display screen by the display hardware. The display hardware reconstructs a continuous image function from the discrete samples given in the raster.

The input to a realistic image synthesis program (i.e., a renderer) is a scene description, describing the geometric and optical properties of the objects in the desired scene, along with information describing a virtual camera: position, direction, and field of view. The desired output is an image displayed on a computer display that appears to an observer to be a photograph of the input scene.

The image function defined indirectly by the input to the renderer, is defined over a continuous domain, the image plane. On the other hand, the final output of the renderer is a two dimensional array of color values representing the color at each pixel of the display. The renderer must bridge the gap between the continuous representation of the image function given as input and the discrete representation it must output. In general this transformation from a continuous representation to a discrete one will not be lossless. The visual artifacts that can result from this change of representation are called *spatial aliasing* artifacts and the methods used to avoid them are called *anti-aliasing* methods.

One way to span the gap from continuous to discrete is to sample the image function at the center of each pixel. This method results in many spatial aliasing defects. The most obvious defects are at edges of high contrast in the image function, for example silhouette edges between objects and the background. These sharp boundaries will appear jagged instead of smooth. Small objects may disappear completely if they fall entirely between sample points. Moiré patterns will occur when a regular pattern in the image function beats against the regular lattice of the discrete image plane.

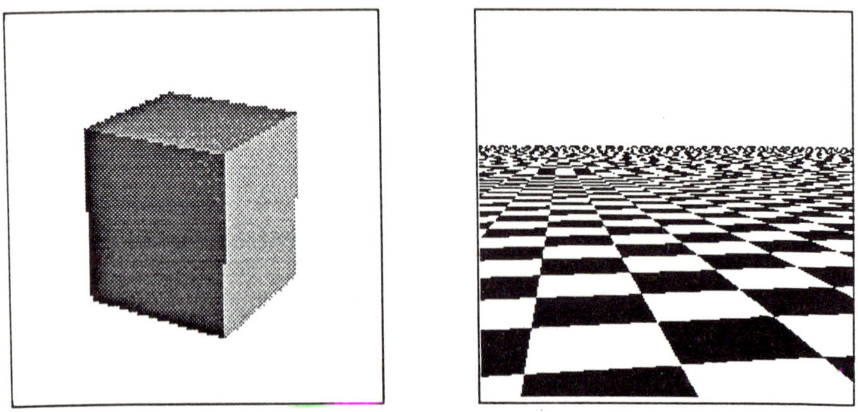

Figure 3.1: Examples of Spatial Aliasing Artifacts

These defects are the result of regular sampling of a signal containing high frequency detail, e.g. sharp edges and rapidly fluctuating intensities. High frequency detail can not be captured in the discrete sampled signal; there simply aren't enough samples to capture the behavior of the signal if it is fluctuating too rapidly. The *sampling theorem* states this in more precise terms: A function which is sampled at a sample interval of Δ can be reconstructed perfectly from the sample values if, and only if, the function has energy only in frequencies below $1/(2\Delta)$ (called the Nyquist frequency). We must have at least two sample points per cycle of the highest frequency in the input signal if we are to reproduce the original signal perfectly. Any energy in frequencies above the Nyquist frequency is mapped by the sampling process to a lower frequency, hence the term aliasing.

3.2 Examples:

To gain insight into the process of sampling and reconstruction, we will examine three one dimensional examples. The first example illustrates that perfect reconstruction is possible if the sample rate is sufficiently high. The second example illustrates what can go wrong if an insufficient sample rate is used. The final example shows that even when the conditions of the sampling theorem are satisfied, perfect reconstruction may not be achieved if an inadequate reconstruction filter is used.

In order to understand the process of sampling it is useful to examine both the spatial domain and the frequency domain representations of the signals. The frequency domain representation shows the magnitude of the signal at each frequency.

3.2.1 Perfect Sampling and Reconstruction

Figure 3.2 shows the process of sampling and reconstruction of a properly band-limited signal. All signals are discretized to 128 points.

The first row shows the original signal to be sampled. For this example, we have chosen a sum of sine waves. The highest frequency represented is 0.3125 cycles per pixel (5 cycles over the displayed range of [-8,8]). Notice that the frequency domain representation of the signal is non-zero only on a finite region [-0.3125,0.3125], *i.e.* the signal is band-limited with no frequencies above 0.3125 cycles per pixel.

The second row shows the sites at which sampling is to occur. This is represented discretely as a comb function, a set of equally spaced impulses corresponding to the sample sites. Notice that the frequency domain representation is also a comb function with impulses spaced at one cycle/pixel.

The third row shows the result of sampling the original signal. This is simply the product, in the spatial domain, of the original signal with the sampling comb. The value of the original signal is retained at each sample site. Elsewhere, the sampled signal is zero. Notice that in the frequency domain, the effect has been to replicate the frequency spectrum of the original signal, placing the shifted copies at intervals of 1 cycle per pixel. This is true for any signal when sampled on a regular grid and can be seen from the frequency convolution theorem, which states that multiplication of two signals in the spatial domain is equivalent to convolution in the frequency domain. Convolution[1] with a comb function results in replication and shifting of the frequency spectrum, one copy over each impulse in the comb.

The fourth row shows the spatial and frequency domain representations of a high quality reconstruction filter, a windowed sinc function. Notice in the frequency domain representation that the filter is a near perfect low pass filter, passing with little attenuation those frequencies in the range [-0.5,0.5] cycles per pixel and fully attenuating frequencies outside this range.

The fifth row shows the result of convolving the reconstruction filter with the sampled signal. The effect in the frequency domain, by a result known as the convolution theorem, is simply to take the product of the filter frequency spectrum with the sampled signal spectrum. This allows exactly one copy of the frequency spectrum of original signal to be retained, restoring the original signal spectrum.

3.2.2 Insufficient Sample Rate

What can go wrong in the process of sampling and reconstructing a signal? Consider the case where the sample rate is below the Nyquist frequency for the signal. Figure 3.3 shows an example of this case. Notice that the frequency domain representation of the signal contains frequencies outside the range [-0.5,0.5] cycles per pixel.

When the signal is sampled, the replication of the frequency spectrum evident in the frequency domain results in an overlap between adjacent copies of the spectrum. The frequency spectrum of the original signal is lost in these areas of overlap. Even reconstruction with a perfect reconstruction filter cannot hope to recover the original signal.

The high frequency component of original signal has been lost in the resulting signal. Moreover, a new lower frequency component, not in the original signal, has been introduce. This effect, high frequency components "aliased" as lower frequency components, motivates the use of the term *aliasing*.

3.2.3 Poor Reconstruction Filter

A sufficiently high sample rate does not guarantee perfect reconstruction of the original signal. The spectral properties of the filter are critical as well. Figure 3.4 shows the effect of a poor reconstruction filter. The sample signal used in Figure 3.4 is identical to the signal used in Figure 3.2. The reconstruction filter used here is a simple *box* filter, a filter commonly used in computer graphics. The box filter is 1 inside its range of support and zero elsewhere.

The frequency domain representation of the filter shows that a box filter is far from perfect. The ideal filter passes all frequencies in the range [-0.5,0.5] cycles per pixel without attenuation and fully attenuates frequencies outside this range. This allows exactly one of the copies of the original signal spectrum to be recovered. The box filter significantly attenuates much of the signal spectrum which should be allowed to pass, yet lets much of the high frequencies outside

---

[1] Convolution amounts to a local averaging or smoothing operator and is performed by passing one function over another and at each point integrating the product of the first function with the value of the second:

$$f(x) * g(x) = \int_{-\infty}^{\infty} f(x')g(x-x')dx'$$

this range slip through. The effect is excessive blurring of the signal, due to the attenuation of the signal in the pass band, and distortion of the signal, due to the high frequencies of the shifted replicas of the original signal leaking through.

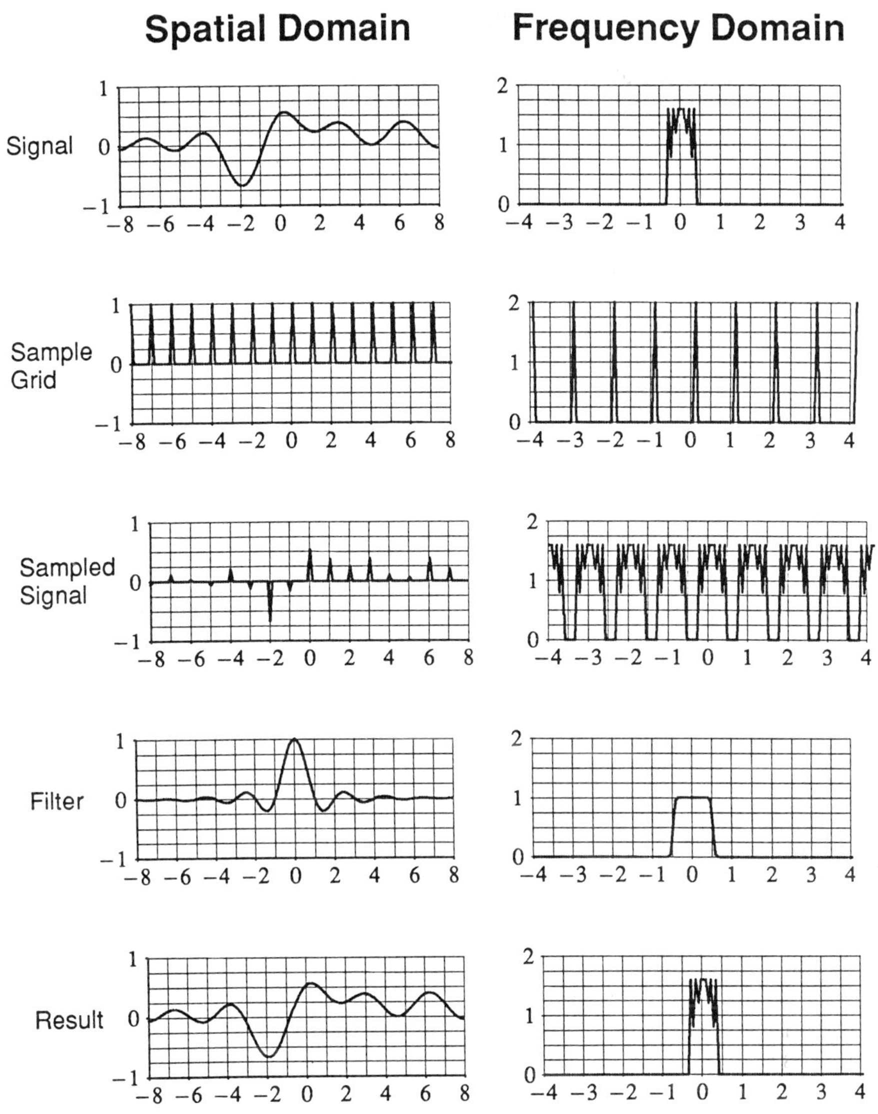

Figure 3.2: Results of Regular Sampling and Reconstruction of a Properly Bandlimited Signal.

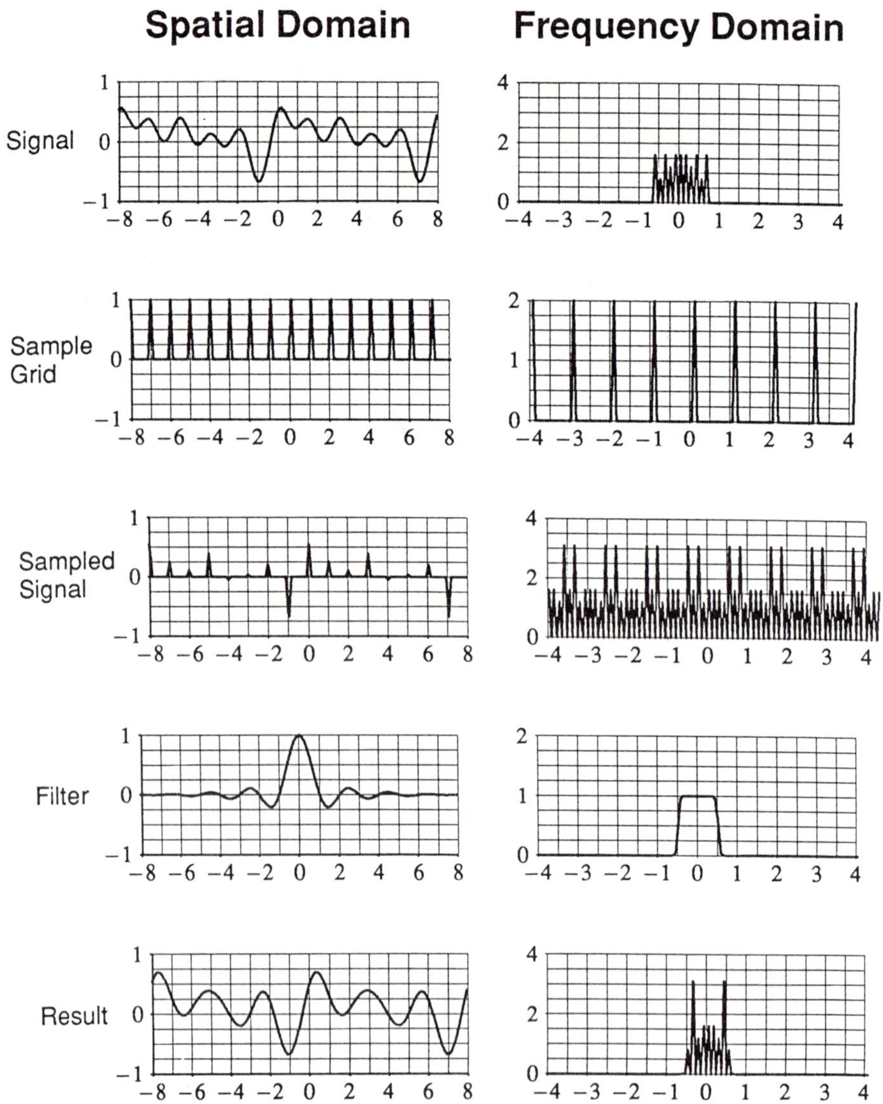

Figure 3.3: Results of Regular Sampling and Reconstruction of a Signal with Frequencies above the Nyquist Frequency.

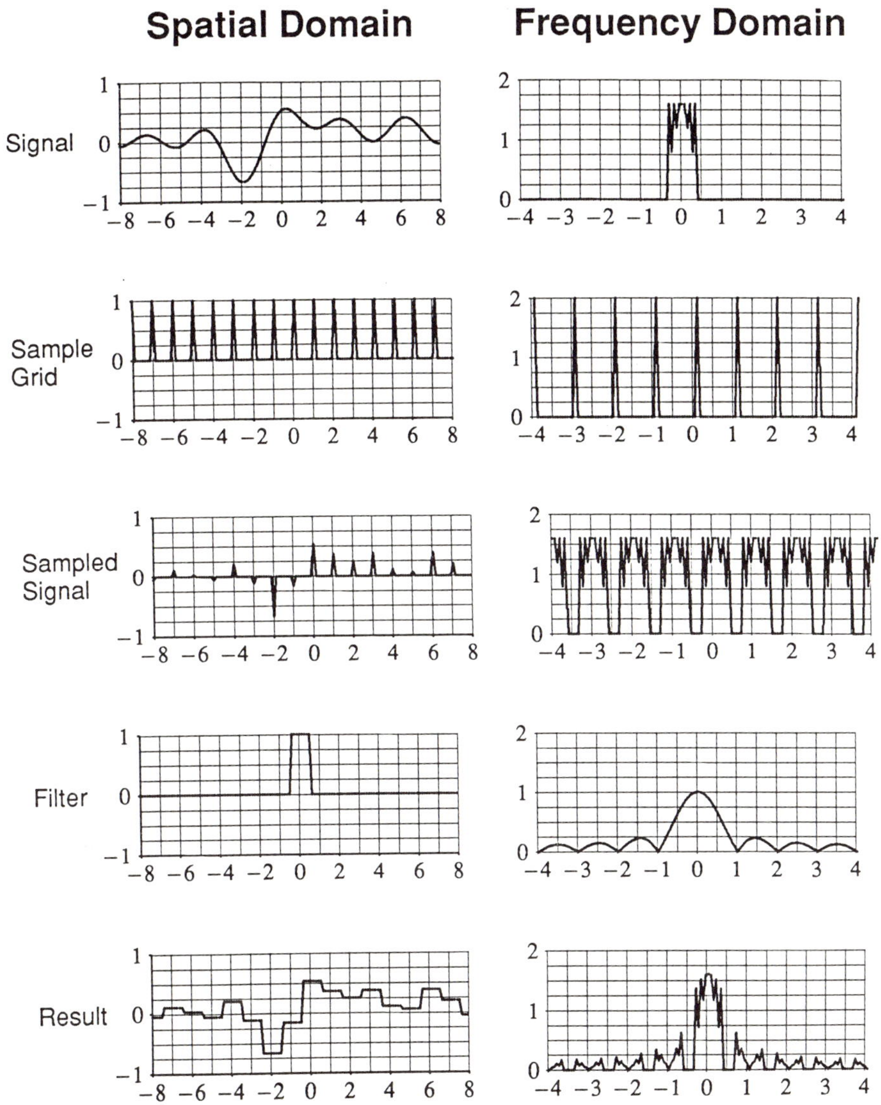

Figure 3.4: Results of Regular Sampling and Reconstruction of a Properly Bandlimited Signal using an Inadequate Reconstruction Filter.

3.3 Solutions

There are two standard signal processing solutions to the aliasing problem. The first is simply to raise the sample rate to the point that the conditions for perfect reconstruction, given by the sampling theorem, are met. This is possible if the signal spectrum is known in advance of sampling and there are no constraints on the sample rate. When this is not possible, the alternative solution is to low pass filter the signal before sampling to insure that the sampled signal has no frequencies above the Nyquist frequency. Filtering before sampling changes the signal to be sampled so that the conditions for perfect reconstruction are met. Of course, the signal that will be perfectly reconstructed is not the original signal, but instead, the filtered signal. The high frequency information was lost in the filtering process. But at least it didn't “fold over”, aliasing itself as a lower frequency. This was avoided by removing it before the signal spectrum was replicated by sampling.

3.3.1 Why Not Use the Signal Processing Solutions?

The standard signal processing solutions to alias avoidance are not directly applicable to many image synthesis algorithms.

In general, the image function that arises from a scene description is not band limited. Discontinuities in the image function occur at boundaries between objects and silhouette edges. These discontinuities cause the frequency spectrum of the image function to be unlimited, that is, there is some energy at all frequencies, no matter how high. The spectral characteristic of a step edge can be observed in the box filter shown in the fourth row of Figure 3.4.

High spatial frequencies may also arise from texture patterns on the surface of objects in the scene. When texture is compressed into a small area of the image plane by perspective projection, very high frequencies are produced.

Since we can't, in general, put a bound on the frequency spectrum of the image function, we can never set a sample rate high enough to ensure that no aliasing will occur. Nevertheless, this technique, called *super sampling*, is useful and is a common technique in computer graphics. Images can be computed at a higher resolution than is ultimately desired, averaged (e.g. low pass filtered), and reduced to the final desired resolution. While it doesn't eliminate all aliasing artifacts, it certainly can decrease the amount of aliased high frequency energy that slips through in the sampling process.

This leaves the option of pre-filtering. Prefiltering is accomplished by convolving the image function with a low pass filter before sampling. This convolution can be thought of as a moving average of the image function with weights provided by the filter function. Since this convolution occurs before sampling, it must convolve continuous signals rather than discrete ones. This makes the formula for convolution an integral rather than a sum.

The convolution integral can be solved by analytic means if both the image and filter functions are represented explicitly in a form that is conducive to integration, polynomials for example. Unfortunately, the image function is rarely represented explicitly. Instead, we often have a procedural definition that provides a method of evaluation at point samples, a ray tracing algorithm for example. But to accomplish pre-filtering, we need to be able to convolve the image function with a filter, that is, take weighted averages over areas in the image plane.This is very difficult to do directly since we don't have an explicit representation of the image function.

A third alternative is stochastic sampling [Cook, 1986]. The convolution integral can be evaluated approximately at the center of each pixel by numerical integration. The image function is sampled at many irregularly spaced sites in the domain of integration. The results are weighted by the corresponding values of the filter function and combined to yield an approximation to the convolution integral. Stochastic sampling will still generate errors if the image function contains frequencies above the Nyquist limit. But the errors appear as noise in the image function rather than coherent errors, like jagged edges. The human visual system is more willing to ignore noise than it is willing to ignore coherent errors.

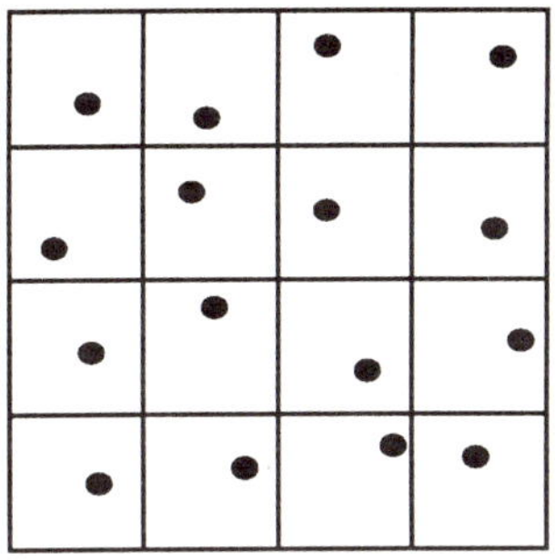

Figure 3.5: A Jittered Sampling Pattern.

One way to generate a stochastic sampling pattern is by *jittering* a regular sampling pattern. We start with a regular sampling pattern and add noise to each of the x and y locations of the sample sites. Think of a pixel being split into a number of subcells. A sample is placed in each subcell, uniformly distributed over the cell (See Figure 3.5). Other stochastic sampling patterns have also been considered [Dippé, 1985], [Cook, 1986], [Mitchell, 1987].

If the resolution of the display device is N by N, we must solve N^2 integration problems, one for each output pixel. Each problem could be solved independently by a Monte Carlo numerical integration technique. However, the integration problems are not entirely independent. Each involves evaluation of the integrand, and therefore of the image function, at many points in the domain of integration and the domains of integration overlap. If evaluation of the image function is a dominant cost, as it is in ray tracing for example, the evaluated samples should be shared between pixels so avoid additional expense.

Regular sampling allows incremental techniques to be used to step between sampling points. This is the principle behind Bresenham's line drawing algorithm. Unfortunately, incremental techniques are not possible with stochastic sampling since the sample spacing is nonuniform.

3.4 Temporal Aliasing

We have focused our attention here on spatial discretization and spatial aliasing. In animation, the same problems arise when discretizing time. Animation sequences are discrete in time, with a new frame being displayed at regular intervals, typically at 30 frames a second. We must take care that the scene being rendered isn't changing too quickly over time to be sure that temporal aliasing artifacts are not produced. Rapidly changing scenes must be low passed filtered over time, producing motion blur, to avoid temporal aliasing defects [Cook *et al.*, 1984].

4. Local Reflection Models

At this point, we have spent most of our time talking about what makes up an image, how we see color, and how we can display an image on a CRT, once we know what the image we want looks like. We have not begun yet to talk about how to construct that image from a physical description of an imaginary environment.

The problem we are presented with is to simulate the light propagation within the environment. More specifically, we are interested in the light which eventually passes through an imaginary screen and into the *eye* .

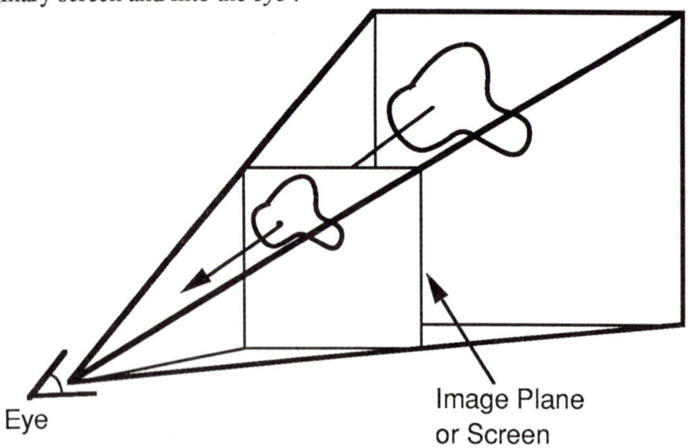

Figure 4.1: Projection onto Image Plane

If we can determine the light passing through each point of this screen, determine an appropriate RGB combination to represent a small region of the screen (using the lessons from the last two sections) and display this at the corresponding pixel on a CRT then we are finished.

The problem of simulating light propagation in an environment can be broken down into two sub problems. The first, the main topic of this section, is to model the interaction of a single *ray* of light with a single surface[1] . This is the local reflection problem[2] . The second topic, that of modeling global, inter-surface effects is the topic of the following three sections.

Let's consider a ray of light which is incident on some surface. Some portion of the ray's energy may be reflected back into the environment, some may be transmitted through the

---

1 We will generally ignore effects of reflection and absorption of light which occurs within participating media, e.g. the air.

2 Although the word reflection is used, it is meant to encompass both the reflection from and transmission through a surface.

surface, and finally, the remainder of the light is absorbed and leaves the system in some other form. Our problem, given the physical characteristics of the surface, and the direction from which the light arrives, is to determine the distribution of the reflected and transmitted light.

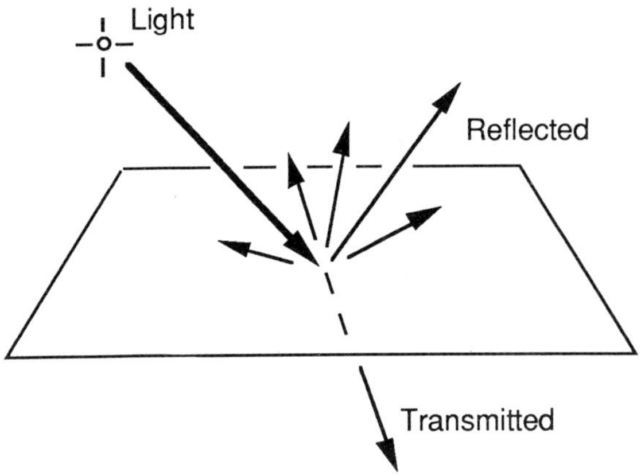

Figure 4.2: Reflection and Transmission of Light

4.1 Energy vs. Intensity

Before beginning a discussion of light reflection we should define a couple of terms. Light is a form of *energy* and thus the terms light and energy are often used interchangeably. Energy is a unit of power per unit time, however, when we discuss energy leaving a surface we normally consider the energy flux, or energy per unit area. Finally, most introductions to the topic talk about *intensity* which is usually what we mean when we discuss the brightness of what we see. Intensity is energy per unit projected area per unit solid angle.

In simple terms, if we think about the sphere of directions around us, the intensity we see in a particular direction is proportional to the amount of energy arriving from that direction per unit time.

4.2 Empirical Models

4.2.1 Lambertian Diffuse Reflection

The simplest type of reflection is Lambertian diffuse, the type of reflection which characterizes a dull surface. In this model, the energy of the ray (after some fraction is absorbed), is scattered back into the environment with equal intensity in all directions.

The amount of energy reflected per unit area is proportional to the cosine of the angle between the normal to the surface at that point and the direction to the light source.

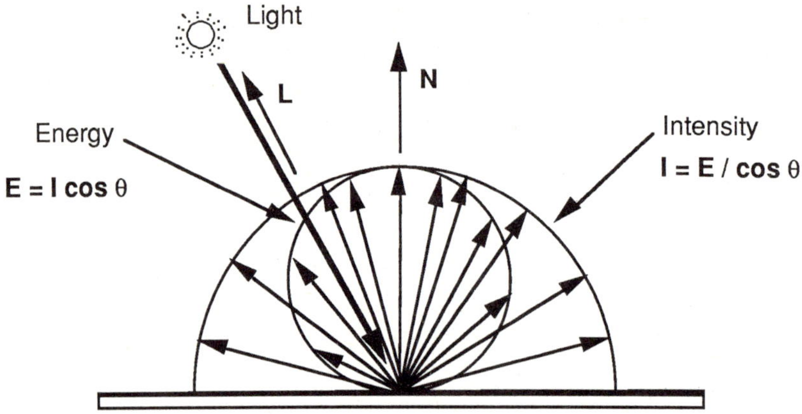

Figure 4.3: Lambertian Diffuse Reflection Energy vs. Intensity

Lambertian reflection can be written:

$$I_d = I_i K_d \cos \theta$$

where: I_i is the intensity of the light source,
K_d is a constant of reflection dependent on the surface material, and
θ is the angle between the incident light and the surface normal.

This can be rewritten as:

$$I_d = I_i K_d (L \cdot N)$$

where: L is a unit vector in the direction of the light source, and
N is a unit normal vector.

Although the intensity is equal in all directions, the energy reflected in all directions is not. This is the difference between energy and intensity. Intensity is energy per unit projected area and projected area is inversely proportional to the cosine of the angle off the normal. Energy, therefore, is reflected from the surface in quantities proportional to the cosine. Thus, the intensity the viewer sees reflected off a diffuse surface is independent of viewer position, while energy is not.

4.2.2 Specular Reflection

Specularity refers to that portion of the reflection due to the shininess of the surface. In contrast to diffuse reflection, specular reflection is highly dependent on the relationship between the direction to the light source and to the viewer.

The simplest specular reflection model is mirror specular. As the name implies, this would be the reflection from a perfect mirror. A ray of incident light is reflected back as a single ray in a direction, the *mirror direction* (R), which is exactly opposite the normal from the incident direction.

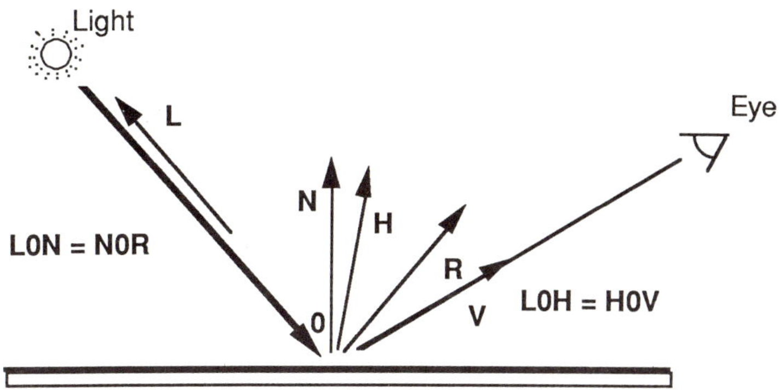

Figure 4.4: Unit Vectors

More complex specular reflection occurs at surfaces which are shiny but not mirrorlike. In this case the specular reflection is scattered in some way about the mirror direction.

4.2.2.1 The Phong Model

Phong suggested an empirical model for specular reflection in which the intensity of specular reflection is proportional to the cosine, raised to some power, of the angle between the mirror direction (R) and viewer direction (V).

$$I_s = I_i K_s (R \cdot V)^n$$

where: K_s is a constant representing the fraction of energy reflected specularly, a function of the surface properties,
R is a unit vector in the mirror direction,
V is a unit vector in the viewer direction, and
n is the specular exponent, again a function of the surface properties.

The power (n), is a material property of the surface. Small values of n denote a not very shiny surface, while large values denote a very shiny surface. At the limits, one returns to a Lambertian diffuse reflectance (n = 0), and a mirrored surface (n = infinite).

A minor variation which is more computationally efficient was introduced by Blinn. Here the vectors R and V are replaced by N and H which lies midway between L and V.

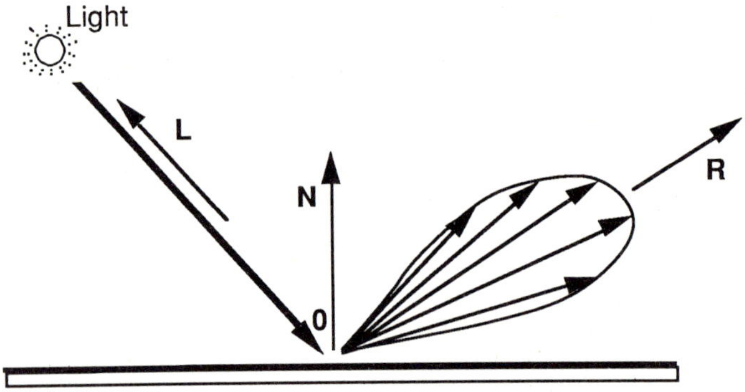

Figure 4.5: Specular Reflection

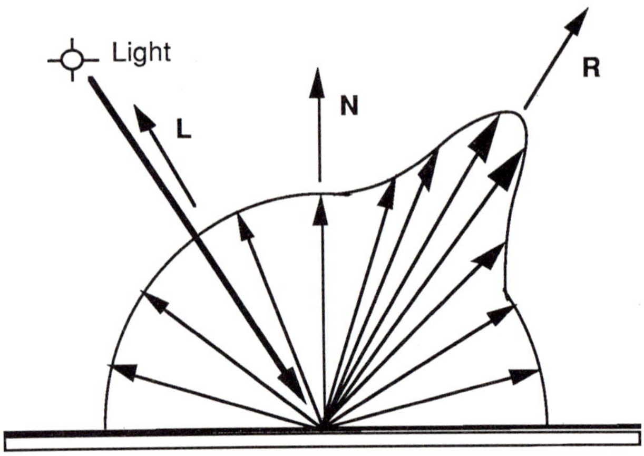

Figure 4.6: Diffuse + Specular

4.2.3 The Ambient Term

Finally there is a third term, *the ambient term*, which is added to most local reflection models. Since all the models above deal only with light arriving directly from a light source, a simple global term is added to account for any light which may arrive from other directions through indirect routes. If we assume that this light source arrives equally from all directions, then we can simply add a constant term, K_a, times the ambient intensity, I_a.

4.2.4 Transmission

Not all of the light that arrives at a surface will be either reflected or absorbed. Some portion may also be transmitted through the surface in the case of transparent, or semi-transparent materials. The transmission itself may be diffuse (e.g. frosted glass) or specular (e.g. clear glass). We will simply state that some portion, K_t, of the incident Illumination will be transmitted.

4.2.5 Total Illumination

We can now sum the above terms to determine a total illumination based on an empirical model for local reflectance (ignoring transmission).

$$I_{total} = I_a K_a + I_i K_d (N \cdot L) + I_i K_s (R \cdot V)^n$$

4.2.5.1 Color

You may have noticed that there has been no mention of color above. It can be assumed that there is no wavelength dependence in most cases (except for florescent materials). Thus, the above equation must be repeated for each color band of interest. The material property associated with this aspect is termed the reflectance and is usually denoted by ρ. Thus for some wavelength λ,

$$I_\lambda = \left(I_{a\lambda} K_a + I_{i\lambda} K_d (N \cdot L)\right) \rho_{d\lambda} + \left(I_{i\lambda} K_s (R \cdot V)^n\right) \rho_{s\lambda}$$

4.3 Physically Based Models

We have presented the above models for local illumination without discussing the physical nature of the surface except to define a number of empirical constants to plug into the equations to get a variety of effects. If we look a closely at surfaces in the real world we will find that even flat surfaces are made up of a large number of small imperfections. Looking closer, in particular at plastics, we might find that the material is in fact a composite.

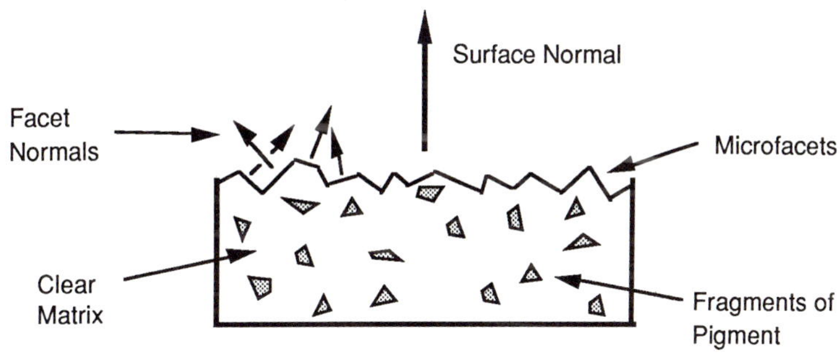

Figure 4.7: Microfacets

In this microscopic view of a the surface of a piece of plastic we can see that although the average normal is straight up, the surface actually has a large number small facets, each with its own normal. It is this microstructure which produces the of scattering of light we see from real materials. The smoother the surface, (the more horizontal and smaller the facets), the more mirrorlike the reflection. In addition, we can see the potential for two types of reflection, surface reflection from the microfacets, and scattering from the pigment fragments after some of the light penetrates the surface. The scattering from the pigment is typically diffuse and takes on the color of the pigment, while the surface scattering is specular in nature and carries the color of the light source.

A model of specular reflection based on the existence of microfacets was described by Cook and Torrance. Their specular term is given by:

$$R_s = \frac{F\,D\,G}{\pi\,(N \cdot V)\,(N \cdot L)}$$

D is a term describing the distribution of the microfacets on the surface. A number of functions have been suggested for this term. Cook and Torrance used:

$$D = \frac{1}{m^2 \cos^4 \alpha} \exp\left[-\frac{\tan^2 \alpha}{m^2}\right]$$

where: α is the angle between N and H
and m is the root mean square slope of the microfacets
If m = 0 then D = 0 and the surface is a perfect mirror.

The (N•V) in the denominator can be understood if one considers viewing a surface from a glancing angle. From this angle most of the facets which are visible must have normals near the H direction and thus provide a higher shine. This effect can easily be seen by positioning ones eye near the surface of a table and observing the increase in the surface's mirrorlike quality.

The G term is a geometric term which describes the shadowing of one facet by another. Thus just as placing the eye near the surface removes some facets from view, placing the light near the surface shadows some facets from the light. Without deriving the term further, it is given by:

$$G = \min\left(1, \frac{2(N{\bullet}H)(N{\bullet}V)}{(V{\bullet}H)}, \frac{2(N{\bullet}H)(N{\bullet}L)}{(V{\bullet}H)}\right)$$

Finally, F, is a fresnel term which accounts for the fact that as the light approaches a glancing angle the color of the specular reflection approaches that of the light rather than the surface color. This term is dependent on material properties such as its *refractive index*, η. Again there are more than one derivation for F, the form used by Cook and Torrance is given by:

$$F = \frac{1}{2}\frac{(g-c)^2}{(g+c)^2}\left[1 + \frac{(c\,(g+c) - 1)^2}{(c\,(g-c) + 1)^2}\right]$$

where c is equal to (V•H)
and g^2 is equal to $\eta^2 + c^2 - 1$

at normal incidence this reduces to:

$$F = \frac{(\eta - 1)^2}{(\eta + 1)^2}$$

The fresnel term is wavelength dependent due to the index of refraction term. Values for this term can be found in various sources.

4.4 In Summary

From the very brief introduction to local illumination models above it can be seen that one is free to choose between very simple and quite complex models. Clearly as the model complexity increases, so will the computation cost. The choice of model is highly dependent on the application for which the image is being created. The simple Phong model is now standardly built into hardware in many workstations, and thus provides a very fast and easy solution for most problem domains. It has been said that "you can simulate any material with the simple Phong model, that is, so long as it is plastic".

II. Global Illumination Models

The remainder of this tutorial will concentrate on global illumination models and the algorithmic problems associated with computing such models for complex environments. Global illumination models deal with inter-object effects such as one object shadowing another, one object seen through another, i.e. transparency, or one object reflecting light to another and in effect becoming a light source on its own.

We will concentrate on two algorithmic approaches, *ray tracing* and *radiosity*. Each model has advantages and disadvantages depending on the complexity of the environment and the type of application which requires a realistic image.

5. Ray Tracing

This section describes the ray tracing rendering method. We will examine the basic method, look at techniques to speed it up, and discuss extensions that can be used to improve the lighting model.

5.1 Basic Algorithm

Shadows, reflections and refractions are phenomena that not captured in the local reflection models. Whitted suggested that these illumination effects could be modeled by explicitly tracing light rays around in the scene [Whitted, 1980].

Ray tracing rendering methods use the principles of ray optics to estimate the image function at sample points in the image plane domain. The basic idea is to trace rays of light around in the scene to determine the intensity of light which reaches the eye from points in the scene. Because most of the light rays emanating from a light source never reach the eye, rays are generally traced backwards, from the eye.

The classic algorithm, illustrated in Figure 5.1, is as follows: At each sample point in the image plane, a ray (called a primary ray) is cast from the eye point, through the image plane and out into the world. The first intersection point of the ray with an object in the scene is identified. If the ray strikes an object then several new rays are cast. A shadow ray is cast from the point of intersection towards each light source to determine whether the source directly illuminates the object. If it does, the contribution to the ray intensity is computed based on the diffuse and specular reflection properties of the object and the intensity of the light source. Reflection and transmission rays are traced recursively. The reflection ray is cast in the reflection direction, as determined by the surface normal at the intersection point. The transmitted ray is cast in the direction determined by the surface normal and the refractive index. In general a tree of rays is cast at each sample point, as is illustrated in Figure 5.2. The resulting intensities from the reflected or transmitted rays are summed with the direct illumination term. The recursive ray tracing algorithm can account for only one diffuse scattering along the ray path from the eye to the light source. This is accounted for by the shadow ray and is the first scattering, from the point of view of the light source. An ambient term is normally included as a coarse approximation for the missing global illumination effects of multiple diffuse interreflections.

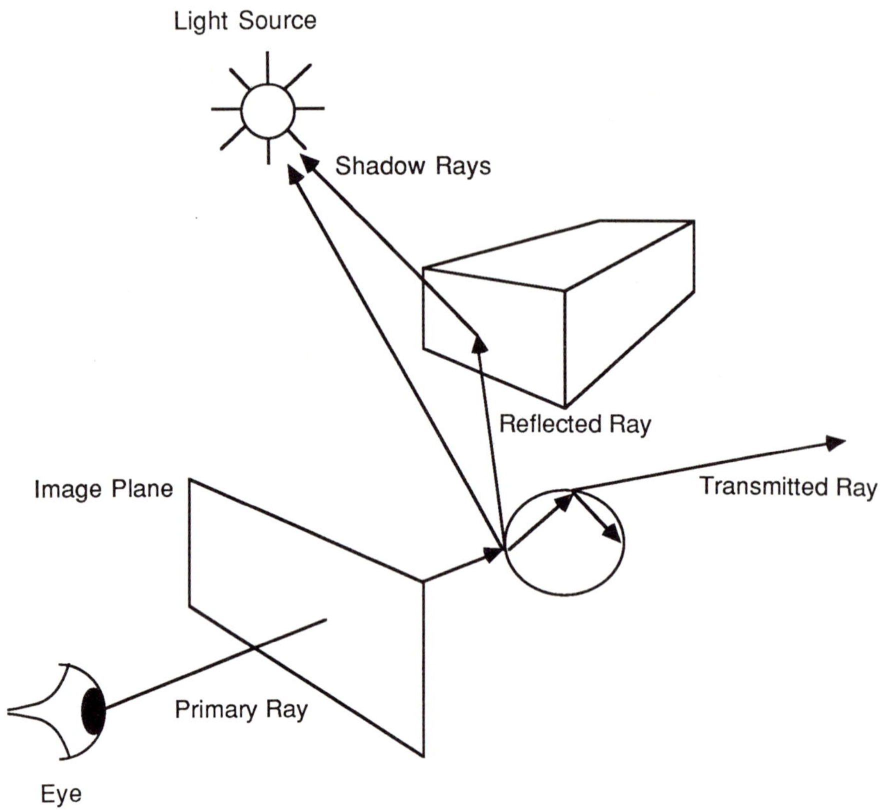

Figure 5.1: Ray Tracing Schematic

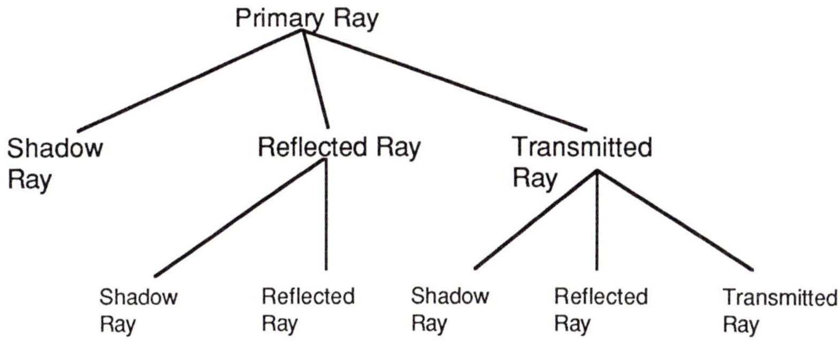

Figure 5.2: Ray Tree

5.1.1 Stopping the Recursion

When do we stop this recursive ray casting process? We will certainly stop when a ray leaves the scene or hits a non-specular surface. We can also stop when the contribution from a ray after a series of scatterings has been attenuated enough that its effect can be considered negligible [Hall and Greenberg, 1983]. We may also want to have a fixed maximum depth on the recursion tree.

5.1.2 Primitives

Ray tracing can handle a wide variety of geometric primitives. The fundamental operation that each primitive must support is ray-object intersection. This operation may be performed in the local coordinate system of the ray (in which case we transform the ray to the objects coordinate system) or in the world coordinate system. Some common primitives used in ray tracing are:

- Polygons
  Find the intersection of the ray with the plane of the polygon. Then find whether the intersection point lies inside the polygon.

- Implicit Surfaces
  Substitute the ray equation into the implicit surface equation. Solve for any positive roots. For low degree surfaces, *e.g.* quadrics: spheres, cones, cylinders, the roots can be found by straight forward analytic methods. Implicit surfaces of degree higher than 4 will require a numerical root finding method [Hanrahan, 1983], [Blinn, 1982], [Kalra and Barr, 1989].

- Parametric Patches
  One method is to implicitize the patch and use the methods for (high degree) implicit surfaces [Kajiya, 1982], [Sederberg and Anderson, 1984],. An alternative method uses a multivariate rootfinder [Toth, 1985].

- Construct Solid Geometry
  CSG operations (union,intersection,difference) allow compound objects to be built up from simpler primitives. The ray is intersected with each object in the CSG tree yielding a set of spans along the ray. The CSG operation can be applied to the set of spans yielding the closest intersection point [Roth, 1982].

5.2 Efficiency

Ray tracing is a computationally intensive process. Each primary ray may lead to many recursive rays being cast. Each ray cast must be tested against the objects in the scene to locate the nearest object that it intersects. This ray--object intersection test is a bottleneck in ray tracing based renderers. The most effective way to speed up a ray tracer is to reduce the number of ray--object intersection tests. This can be accomplished by either reducing the number of rays casts or by reducing the number of objects tested for each ray. Let's consider the latter first:

5.2.1 A Simple Method

How does one go about locating the nearest object intersection for a ray? A simple, albeit slow, approach is to test the ray against every object in the scene, retaining only the closest intersection. A complex scene may have thousands of primitives and a high resolution image will require hundreds of thousands of primary rays, each possibly generating many recursively rays. The simple approach will clearly be impractical for complex scenes since it requires every ray to be tested against every object.

5.2.2 Object Partitioning — Bounding Volumes

Bounding volumes reduce the number of ray--object intersections by providing a method for quickly ruling out objects which have no chance of intersecting the ray. Each object in the scene is enclosed by another simpler object, a *bounding volume*. If the ray doesn't intersect the bounding volume, the object need not be considered further since the ray can't possibly intersect anything in the enclosed volume. This technique will avoid many ray--object intersection. The cost is the addition of the ray--bounding volume intersection tests.

Clusters of objects can be grouped together with a bounding volume around the entire group. Here, a single ray--bounding volume test may rule out an entire group of objects. This idea can be carried further, creating a single bounding volume for several nearby object clusters. By grouping objects hierarchically and placing a bounding volume at each node of the hierarchy tree, we can avoid the majority of the ray-bounding volume tests that would be required if we were to test the bounding volumes of each object independently.

Obviously, if this is to be a win, the ray--bounding volume test should be particularly fast and the bounding volumes should be a fairly tight fit to the enclosed objects. These two goals are in conflict with each other in general, so they must be balanced against each other in selecting the form for a bounding volume. Rubin and Whitted chose rectangular solids, deformed under an affine map [Rubin and Whitted, 1980]. Kay and Kajiya use parallelopipeds constructed from a set of plane normals [Kay and Kajiya, 1986]. Each normal results in a "bounding slab" — two planes perpendicular to the normal that bound the given object. The intersection of the set of bounding slabs yields the bounding parallelopiped. Objects can be bound arbitrarily tightly by increasing the number of plane normals and hence the number of faces in the parallelopipeds. The cost of the ray--bounding volume intersection is fairly low: two subtracts, two multiplies and a comparison for each slab contributing to the bounding volume.

Figure 5.3 shows a schematic diagram of the bounding volume method applied to a sample scene. Each object has a bounding box. The six small spheres are grouped in pairs to produce second level bounding boxes: {3,4}, {5,6}, {7,8}. The three pairs are clustered further to produce another hierarchical bounding box.

The primary ray must initially test 3 top level bounding volumes: for object 1, object 2 and for the cluster of small spheres. Since the ray intersects the box for object 2, a ray-object intersection test must be performed with object 2. The ray also intersects the box for the cluster of spheres so the second layer of bounding boxes for the cluster must be tested. The ray crosses the bounding volumes for the pairs {5,6} and {7,8} so each of the bounding volumes inside must be tested as well. Finally, the ray is tested against objects 6 and 7 and the intersection with object 7 is found.

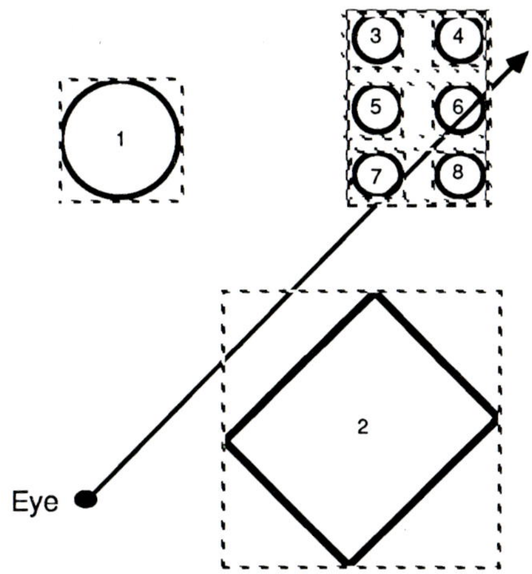

Figure 5.3: Bounding Volumes

5.2.3 Spatial Partitioning

An alternative set of techniques partitions space rather than objects. The basic idea behind all the methods is to partition the scene space into a set of cells. A preprocessing step constructs, for each cell, the list of objects it contains. When a ray is cast it need only be tested against the set of objects contained in the cells that it intersects. These method have the benefit that objects are tested in approximately the order that they occur along the ray. When a cell is found with an object that intersects the ray, processing can stop, for no cell further away can possibly contain an object with a closer intersection point. The methods have the disadvantage that an object may appear in more than one cell and therefore a ray may be tested against a particular object more than once.

5.2.3.1 Octrees

Glassner considered the use of an octree for partitioning space [Glassner, 1984]. Octrees can be used to subdivide space adaptively. A box is placed around the entire space of interest for the scene bounding all objects in the scene and the eye point. The bounding box is then subdivided into eight sub-boxes by splitting it in to two halves in each of the three Cartesian planes. Each time a set of sub-boxes is created we determine which of the objects in the parent cell should be passed down to the new child cells. A sub-box is subdivided further if it contains more than a certain number of objects (*e.g.* three) as long as the subdivision depth doesn't exceed a preset limit The maximum depth constraint is necessary because certain object geometries could otherwise result in infinite depth octrees.

Figure 5.4 shows a schematic diagram the octree spatial subdivision method applied to the sample scene used in Figure 5.3 above. The primary ray steps through the cells of the octree, first testing object 2, then object 1, then objects 2,7, and 8. No further tests are needed since we can be certain that object 7 is the closest intersection.

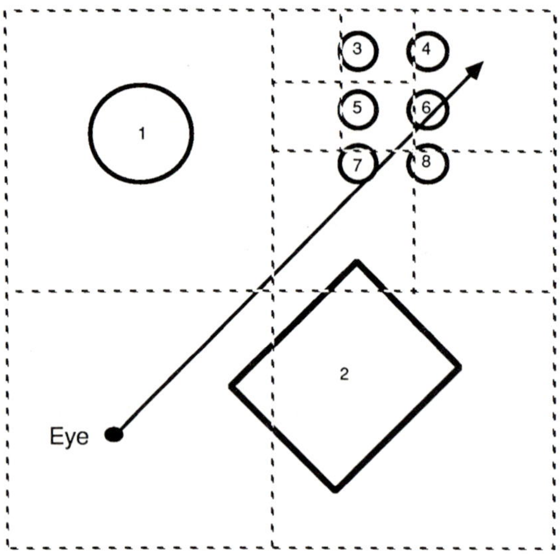

Figure 5.4: Octree Spatial Subdivision

5.2.3.2 Spatial Enumeration

Another method of subdividing space is based on uniform subdivision [Fujimoto, 1986]. Instead of subdividing space adaptively, as is done with the octree, space is subdivided by a uniform three dimensional grid. As in the octree method, each grid cell contains a list of the objects it contains. This method does not adapt to the data as the octree method does, but it has the advantage that the regular structure of the grid can be exploited to speed up traversal. A ray can be traced through the grid by an incremental algorithm that executes quickly.

Figure 5.5 shows a schematic diagram the octree spatial subdivision method applied to the sample scene used above. The primary ray steps through the cells, first testing object 2, then object 1, then objects 2,7, and 8. No further tests are needed since we can be certain that object 7 is the closest intersection.

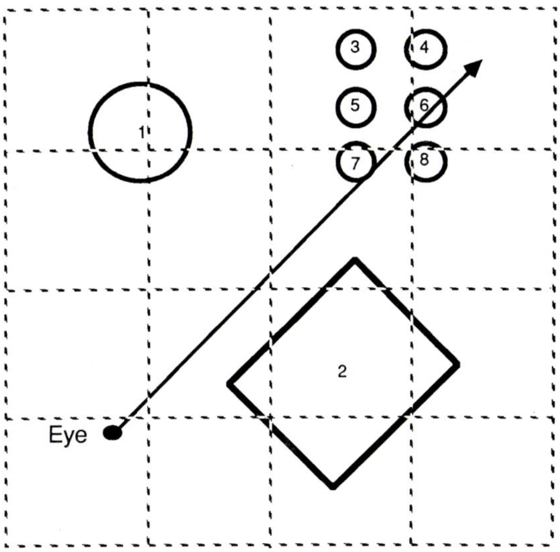

Figure 5.5: Spatial Enumeration

5.2.4 Ray Classification

Arvo and Kirk subdivide the five-dimensional ray space rather than the three dimensional object space [Arvo and Kirk, 1987]. A ray can be considered as a element in a five dimensional space given by its base point and two direction angles. If we partition this space into cells, we have grouped together rays that have nearby base points and similar directions. If the five-dimensional space is subdivided finely enough, there will be a fairly small "candidate set" of objects which can be seen from the rays within each cell. These are the only objects that need to be tested for the ray.

Arvo and Kirk describe the lazy subdivision of a five-dimensional tree which is used to sort ray queries and return small candidate sets for actual ray intersection testing. Objects can be sorted within the candidate sets allowing them to be tested in approximately nearest first order. That allows the list to be truncated early when an intersection is found under certain circumstances.

5.2.5 Anti Aliasing

Ray tracing is a point sampling technique and hence it is prone to aliasing artifacts. We would like to be able to prefilter the image function before sampling, but it is impractical to do so since it is never represented explicitly, only as the ray tracing procedure that can produce a color value at a point in the image plane. If we must sample we would like to do so in a way that will minimize the artifacts that will appear as a result of the sampling.

One technique is to *super sample*, casting several primary rays for each pixel and combining their results in a weighted average. If we sample at regular intervals within each pixel, alias artifacts still abound. The classic example is an infinite ground plane covered with a checkerboard texture pattern. The texture detail is compressed into a smaller and smaller area as the horizon is reached. A regular sampling pattern, even if much denser than one sample per pixel, will beat against the texture pattern yielding Moirè patterns. On the other hand, if the sampling pattern we use is *stochastic*, visible aliasing artifacts can be minimized. Stochastic sampling converts the aliasing energy into noise rather than coherent errors [Cook, 1986], [Dippé and Wold, 1985], [Mitchell, 1987].

Adaptive sampling can reduce the cost of anti aliasing by concentrating samples where they are needed most [Whitted, 1980], [Lee *et al.*, 1985], [Dippé, 1985], [Kajiya, 1986]. In general, not every pixel needs to be super sampled. Samples should be concentrated in the areas with the greatest amount of local variation. Local image variation can be estimated based on the samples seen so far.

Adaptive stochastic ray tracers which share samples between pixels can produce anti aliased images with only a modest increase in the number of samples required per pixel [Painter and Sloan, 1989] [Mitchell, 1987]. In areas of the image where the image function is nearly constant the sample rate can be less than one sample per pixel. However, if the minimum sample rate is too large there is the danger that small objects in the scene may be completely missed.

5.3 Distributed Ray Tracing

The classic ray tracing algorithm is unable to render "fuzzy" phenomena such as penumbras, fuzzy reflections, translucency, depth of field and motion blur. Shadows, reflections and refractions are unnaturally sharp. Cook, Porter and Carpenter suggested that fuzzy effects could be rendered by distributing the ray directions according to an appropriate probability distribution [Cook, Porter and Carpenter, 1984]. Shadow rays are distributed according to an illumination function for each light source producing penumbra effects. Reflection rays are distributed according to a reflectance function allowing for soft, blurred reflections instead of only mirrored reflections. This method is known as distributed ray tracing. Distributed ray tracing effectively evaluates a complex lighting integral by a Monte Carlo integration technique.

Each of the following effects can be simulated by distributing sample rays over an appropriate domain:

- Depth of Field
  Use a lens with a finite aperture and distribute rays over lens area.
- Gloss, Fuzzy Reflection
  Distribute rays over the solid angle of the specular reflection function.
- Translucency
  Distribute rays over the solid angle of the specular transmission function.
- Motion Blur
  Distribute rays over time.
- Penumbras
  Distribute shadow rays over the area of the light source.
- Indirect Lighting, Radiosity
  Distribute rays over the entire hemisphere over each intersection point. This is likely to require a tremendous number of rays because we must sample over such a large domain.
- Spectral Integration
  Many lighting effects have a spectral dependency that can not be accurately captured using only a few color bands. These effects can be captured by distributing rays over the wavelengths in the visible light spectrum.

5.4 The Rendering Equation

The distributed ray tracing algorithm is still unable to correctly model global, diffuse reflection (the "ambient" term) because the cost of distributing rays over the entire hemisphere is just too great. We are still limited to a single diffuse scattering from the light source, possible followed by one or more specular reflections or transmissions.

Just what is the physics we are trying to simulate when we attempt realistic image synthesis and what equation(s) is it governed by? Kajiya's "Rendering Equation" paper describes a complete illumination equation based on earlier work in radiative heat-transfer [Kajiya,1986]. An equivalent formulation can be found in [Immel, 1986].

The Rendering Equation is:

$$I(x,x') = g(x,x')\left[\varepsilon(x,x') + \int_S \rho(x,x',x'')I(x',x'')dx''\right]$$

where:

x,x',x''	are points in the scene.
$I(x,x')$	measures the energy of radiation passing from point x' to point x".
$g(x,x')$	is a "geometry" term. It is zero if x and x' are not visible to each other, and $1/r^2$ otherwise.
$\varepsilon(x,x')$	is the emittance term which measures the energy emitted by x' reaching x.
$\rho(x,x',x'')$	is the scattering term which measures the intensity of energy scattered by x', which originated at x" and terminated at x.

Kajiya showed how this equation could be solved by rewriting it as a series:

$$I = g\varepsilon + gMg\varepsilon + gMgMg\varepsilon + g(Mg)^3\varepsilon \;\cdots$$

M is the integral operator given in the rendering equation above.

The series has a nice interpretation: the first term corresponds to direct illumination from a light source, the second term corresponds to light reaching x after one bounce, and so on. Reminds you of ray tracing, doesn't it?

5.4.1 Path Tracing

Kajiya presented a Monte Carlo method for evaluating the rendering equation above using Markov chains. In essence, a set of transition probabilities is assigned determining the selection of the x primes, $(x',x'',x''',\cdots)$. A sample from this Markov chain is taken, and the integrand of each term in the series, is evaluated at a single point. Terms are weighted according to the transition probabilities of the Markov chain. The expected value can be shown to be an unbiased estimator for the value of the integral. The integral can be estimated by taking many samples and averaging the results. Kajiya calls this method path tracing.

How does path tracing differ from conventional distributed ray tracing? The standard ray tracing algorithm generates a full ray tree for each primary ray. Path tracing, instead, follows a single path from the eye out into the world. When a choice needs to be made between several new ray directions, the choice is made probabilistically, using the reflection function as a distribution function. A shadow ray is always cast towards know light sources however.

Path tracing clearly cuts down enormously the number of recursive rays shot for a single primary ray. On the other hand, the primary rays produce much noisier results since two primary rays at the same location in the image plane can produce very different results depending on what path they happen to take through the ray tree. Kajiya reported sample rates in the range of 40-64 primary rays per pixel to achieve an acceptable noise level.

5.5 Summary

5.5.1 What Ray Tracing Can Do:

Ray tracing easily supports a wide variety of geometric primitives, from polygons through surface patches and implicit surfaces. The critical requirement is to be able to write a ray-object intersection function. Ray tracing is conceptually straightforward. A basic ray tracer can be written easily in a few thousand lines of code, though it can be much harder to write a full featured, efficient ray tracer. Ray tracing can model "sharp" (*i.e.* specular) optical phenomena such as mirror reflection and transparency quite well.

5.5.2 What Ray Tracing Can't Do:

The classic ray tracing algorithm can't model "soft" optical phenomena such as penumbra (soft edged shadows) and fuzzy reflections. Everything is "sharp" in a ray traced image — much more so than the real world. Distributed ray tracing improves the situation greatly but still has difficulty handling indirect lighting through several diffuse interreflections. Kajiya's Monte Carlo evaluation method for the rendering equation solves these problems but is prone to noise. Achieving a reasonable noise level seems to require a great number of samples, making the technique impractical at present.

6. Radiosity

Radiosity takes a very different approach to solving the global illumination problem than was taken by the ray tracing algorithms. In particular, the radiosity method was formulated to try to capture the diffuse interreflection of light which is simply approximated by a constant ambient term in a ray tracing algorithm. In many environments, particularly interiors, this is a major part of the total illumination and is not well modeled as a constant.

The radiosity method was first developed in the context of heat transfer and a more complete description of the underlying theory can be found in most radiative heat transfer texts [Seigal and Howell, 1981] [Sparrow, 1963] [Sparrow, 1978]. It was introduced in the context of image synthesis by Goral et al [Goral et al., 1984].

We will begin the discussion by assuming all surfaces are Lambertian diffuse reflectors or emitters.

6.1 The Radiosity Equation

The underlying assumption of Lambertian Diffuse reflection allows a single nondirectional intensity value per wavelength band to describe the light leaving a surface. As indicated earlier, the constant intensity distribution should not be confused with the energy distribution which is proportional to the cosine of the angle off of the surface normal (Figure 4.3).

Without loss of generality we can also restrict ourselves to a monochromatic description of the light. Exceptions to this will be pointed out where relevant.

We will begin by defining some terms:

Radiosity: (***B***) The basic quantity we want to compute for each surface. Energy per unit area per unit time.

Emission: (***E***) Energy which the surface emits itself, as in the case of a light source. Also energy per unit area per unit time.

Reflectivity: (ρ) A number between 0 and 1 which indicates the fraction of light which is reflected from a surface.
Absorption = 1 - reflectivity. Unitless.

Form-factor: (***F***) The fraction of the light leaving one surface which arrives at another. Also between 0 and 1 and also unitless.

This gives us all the terms we need to derive the radiosity of a single differential area, dA_i. The intensity of a differential surface area depends on any light which it emits directly plus light which is reflected. This reflected light depends on the light leaving every other surface in the environment. Some fraction of the leaving leaving every other surface may arrive at the surface in question and be reflected back into the environment. This fraction depends on the form-factor between the surfaces and the reflectivity of the differential area. Putting this together results in the interrelationship:

$$B_{dA_i} dA_i = E_{dA_i} dA_i + \rho_{dA_i} \int_j B_{dA_j} F_{dA_j\text{-}dA_i} dA_j$$

where:
B_{dA_i} = Radiosity of differential area dA_i
dA_i = Differential Area i
E_{dA_i} = Emission of differential area dA_i
ρ_{dA_i} = Reflectivity of differential area dA_i
$F_{dA_j\text{-}dA_i}$ = Formfactor from dA_j to dA_i
= fraction of energy leaving dA_j arriving at dA_i

6.1.1 Discretization

Since we cannot hope to find a separate radiosity for each differential area, the problem must be made finite by discretizing the surfaces of the environment. By subdividing the environment into discrete areas or *patches*, the integral equation above can be recast as the summation:

$$B_{A_i} A_i = E_{A_i} A_i + \rho_{A_i} \Sigma_j B_{A_j} F_{A_j - A_i} A_j$$

An assumption is made in this formulation that the radiosity and emission do not vary over the patch area.

6.1.2 Reciprocity

If one were to switch the roles of equally sized emitters and receivers, the fraction of the energy emitted by one and received by the other would be identical to the fraction of energy going the other way. This fact is independent of any reflecting or absorbing surfaces in between. Thus, a *reciprocity* relationship exists between formfactors. The formfactor between area *i* and area *j* are simply related by the ratio of their areas.

$$F_{A_i - A_j} A_i = F_{A_j - A_i} A_j$$

thus:

$$F_{A_i - A_j} = F_{A_j - A_i} A_j / A_i$$

Therefore the summation above can be divided through by A_i to yield the basic radiosity relationship for finite area patches.

$$B_{A_i} = E_{A_i} + \rho_{A_i} \sum_j B_{A_j} F_{A_i - A_j}$$

6.2 Matrix Formulation and Solution

If the environment is divided into *N* finite patches, this results in *N* equations of the form above. These can be rewritten in matrix form:

$$\begin{bmatrix} 1 & -\rho F_{1,2} & -\rho F_{1,3} & \cdots & -\rho F_{1,N-1} & -\rho F_{1,N} \\ -\rho F_{2,1} & 1 & -\rho F_{2,3} & \cdots & -\rho F_{2,N-1} & -\rho F_{2,N} \\ \bullet & \bullet & \bullet & \bullet & \bullet & \bullet \\ \bullet & \bullet & \bullet & \bullet & \bullet & \bullet \\ -\rho F_{N-1,1} & -\rho F_{N-1,2} & -\rho F_{N-1,3} & \cdots & 1 & -\rho F_{N-1,N} \\ -\rho F_{N,1} & -\rho F_{N,2} & -\rho F_{N,3} & \cdots & -\rho F_{N,N-1} & 1 \end{bmatrix} \begin{bmatrix} B_1 \\ B_2 \\ \bullet \\ \bullet \\ B_{N-1} \\ B_N \end{bmatrix} = \begin{bmatrix} E_1 \\ E_2 \\ \bullet \\ \bullet \\ E_{N-1} \\ E_N \end{bmatrix}$$

This set of linear equations can be solved with most linear equation solvers, however it should be noted that special properties of this matrix allow more efficient solutions.

In particular, since the sum of the formfactors across a row are, by definition, equal to unity, and the reflectivity is less than one, the matrix is strictly *diagonally dominant.* This means that an iterative Gauss-Siedel solution method is guaranteed to converge to a solution [Horn, 1975].

Each step in the Gauss-Siedel process involves a vector multiplication of a row in the matrix with the current guess at the radiosity solution. If the initial guess is set to be the emission values, then each step can be thought of as projecting the illumination of the current guess onto a patch, resulting in an updated estimate for that patch. This solution process can be greatly enhanced through reordering as will be described in a later section.

The reflectivity value is typically defined for a discrete number of color bands (e.g. red, green, and blue), thus the matrix must be formed and solved for each such band. Note that the formfactors remain constant, as they are solely a function of geometry.

6.3 The Formfactor

The formfactor between patches defines the fraction of energy (light) leaving a patch which arrives at the other. The formfactor has proven to be the most computationally expensive part of the radiosity computation for complex environments. The formfactor is purely a function of the geometric relationship between patches, and thus does not depend on viewer position or reflectivity attributes (color) of the surfaces. This is an important aspect of the radiosity method in that it allows rapid changes to viewing and attribute parameters.

6.3.1 The Formfactor Equation

Between differential areas, the formfactor depends on the distance between them, *r*, and their orientation towards one another, q_i and q_j. The formfactor follows the familiar $1/r^2$ drop off as the distance between patches grows. The formfactor is also proportional to the projected area of one patch as seen from the other and thus is related to the *cosine* of the angle between the patch normal and the line connecting them. In other words, the formfactor is proportional to the *solid angle* subtended by one patch centered at the the other. This relationship can be expressed:

$$F_{dA_i - dA_j} = \frac{\cos\theta_i \cos\theta_j}{\pi r^2} dA_j$$

The formfactor between patches can be found by integrating over *area j* and taking the area average over *area i.* Thus, the formfactor can be expressed as a double area integral over the two patches.

$$F_{A_i - A_j} = \frac{1}{A_i} \int_{A_i} \int_{A_j} \frac{\cos\theta_i \cos\theta_j}{\pi r^2} dA_j dA_i$$

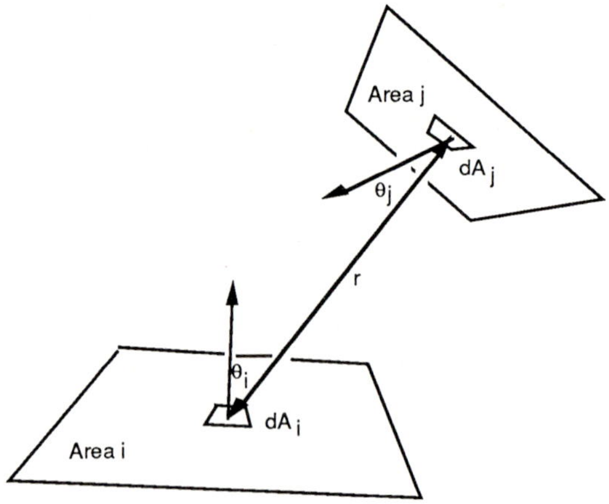

Figure 6.1: Geometric Interpretation of the Individual Terms

In general, there is no analytical solution for this integral equation. However, a set of formulae for specific patch shapes and orientations can be found in the appendix of a number of radiative heat transfer texts. For more complex shapes and relationships, a number of numeric and analog approaches have been developed.

6.3.2 Nusselt's Analog

An analog approach has been developed which although not directly useful for image synthesis, does provide a starting point for development of algorithmic techniques. The inner integral in the above integral equation represents the formfactor from a differential area to a finite patch. This quantity can be determined by surrounding the area with an imaginary hemisphere oriented about the differential area's normal. A finite patch can then be radially projected onto the hemisphere and from the hemisphere, orthogonally down onto the base of the hemisphere. The fraction of the base area covered by this projection will be equal to the formfactor.

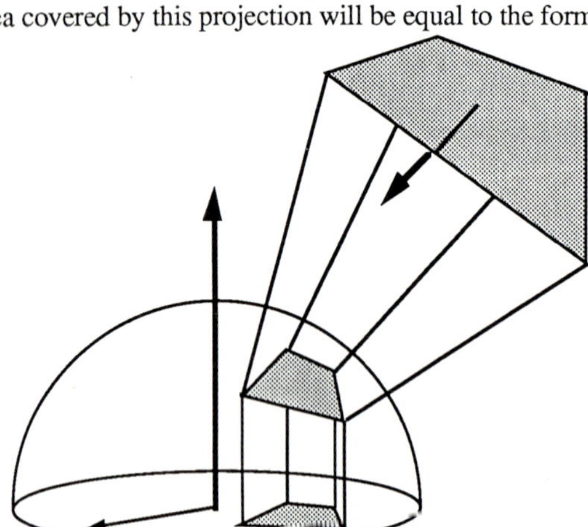

Figure 6.2: The Nusselt Analog

Why does this work?

The projection onto the hemisphere accounts for the $\cos\theta_j$ term as well as the $1/r^2$ The projection down onto the base accounts for the $\cos\theta_j$ term, and the π in the denominator is the area of a unit circle. This analog can be (and has been) performed photographically on real models using a fisheye lens and manually measuring the area covered on the resulting photograph.

6.3.3 Contour Integral

A numerical approach to solving the integral can be found by converting the double area integral into a double contour integral using Stokes Theorem [Sparrow, 1978] [Goral et al., 1984]. Unfortunately this method is still computationally expensive and does not lend itself readily to complex environments containing hidden surfaces since intervening surfaces in essence change the apparent contour of a patch. It may, however, be useful in circumstances in which the approximations made by numerical methods outlined below become too large. This was pointed out and used by Baum et al [Baum et al, 1989].

6.3.4 The Hemi-cube

The Nusselt analog illustrates the fact that any patch which covers the same projected area on the hemisphere has the same formfactor (since it occupies the same solid angle). From this observation, it can be seen that any intermediate surface can be used to project the patches onto without changing the formfactor value of the corresponding projection.

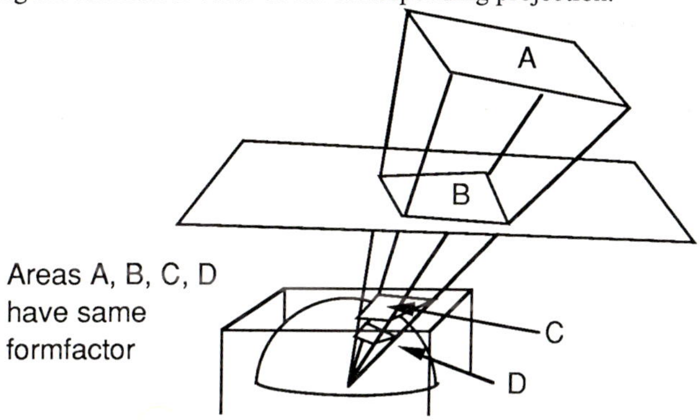

Figure 6.3: Areas with Equal Form Factors

This leads to the use of a *Hemi-cube* [Cohen and Greenberg, 1985], rather than a hemisphere. A hemi-cube (half of a cube) is placed around a differential area with the sides subdivided into small grid cells. Each grid cell defines a particular direction and solid angle, thus a specific *delta form factor* can be associated with each of these grid cells based on its size and orientation. Although the formfactor of the grid cells are independent of the size of the imaginary hemi-cube, it is easiest to think of it as a unit hemi-cube similar to the unit hemisphere above.

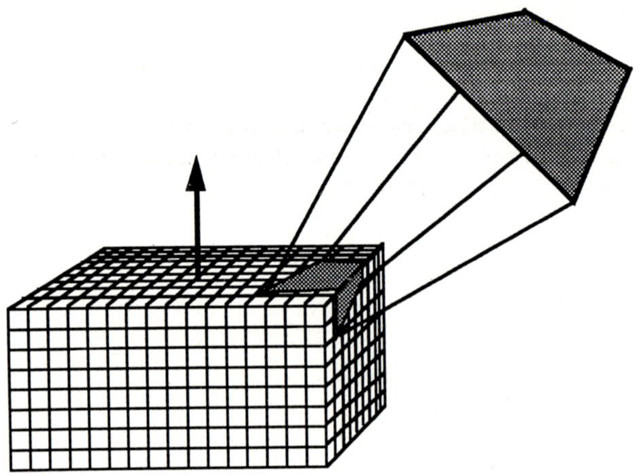

Figure 6.4: The Hemi-cube

Each face simply represents a 90° viewing frustum, although the sides represent only half this frustum since the bottom half is obscured. This type of frustum is well known in computer graphics, thus all the technology which has been developed for projecting environments within a frustum can be taken advantage of. The patches can be projected onto the five hemi-cube surfaces and the hidden surfaces determined using standard scanline Z-buffer techniques. Rather than recording a surface intensity at each grid cell, an ID referring to the projected patch is saved. The hidden surface algorithms are now embedded in silicon on many graphics workstations, thus hardware assistance is available.

Once the total environment has been projected, the ID contained in each grid cell represents the patch visible in that direction. The formfactor to each patch is determined simply by summing the precomputed delta formfactors for each grid cell containing the patch's ID.

$$F_{ij} = \sum_{q} \Delta F_{qj}$$

where: q represents delta grid cells covered by patch j.

6.3.4.1 Problems with the Hemi-cube

Because the hemi-cube divides the hemisphere into discrete regularly spaced small solid angles, a number of aliasing problems may occur. Very small patches may ``fall between the cracks''. Others may be sampled by only one or two grid cells causing accuracy problems when determining the formfactors. This often results in a quilt-like pattern of illumination due to the coherence of the errors because of the regular grid of the hemi-cube beats against the grid of the patches. These problems can be ameliorated to some extent by increasing the hemi-cube resolution but eventually other methods are necessary as the environment complexity increases.

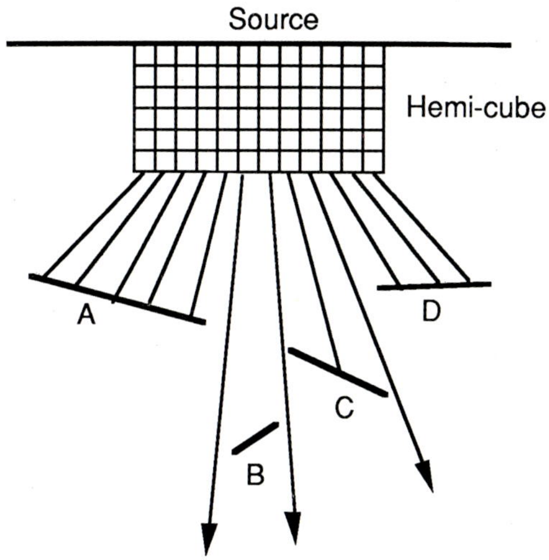

Figure 6.5: Hemi-cube Aliasing

6.3.5 Ray Tracing Formfactors

Ray tracing from a differential area outwards to sample the environment is an attractive alternative. Two such method are described in the SIGGRAPH 89 Proceedings [Wallace et al, 1989] [Sillion and Puech, 1989]. They differ primarily with respect to how the sample directions are selected. Although one does not get the type of coherence as in a scan line method used with the hemi-cube, ray tracing does not have to suffer from the aliasing problems which a regular sampling creates.

What we would like to do is replace the visibility sampling which takes place in the hemi-cube algorithm with a set of rays between pairs of patches. We are not restricted to distribute these rays in a regular pattern so long as we are able to determine a delta form-factor for each ray. As will be discussed in the next section, the final rendering requires radiosity values at the <u>vertices</u> of the patches. This leads to a simple decision to cast a ray from each patch to each other patch vertex.

The form-factor now takes on a slightly different form since we are computing a form-factor from an area to a differential area at each vertex:

$$dF_{A_i - dA_j} = dA_i \frac{\cos\theta_i \cos\theta_j}{\pi r^2 + A_2}$$

This form allows for a solution of the radiosity values directly at the vertices. The details of this method and another alternative to ray tracing form-factors can be found in the SIGGRAPH 89 in papers by Wallace et al [Wallace et al., 1989] and by Sillion et al [Sillion and Puech, 1989].

6.4 Data Representations and Rendering

The result of the radiosity computation is a set of radiosity values for the patches. Rendering an image from these values involves selecting an eye point and other viewing parameters. The patches can then be displayed as polygons in screen space. To create a continuous shading across patches, the patch values must be interpolated to the vertices of the patch, unless a direct method such as ray tracing form-factors is used.

With the radiosity values residing with the vertices, the patches can be displayed as Gouraud shaded polygons through software or by utilizing the hardware shading and hidden surface capabilities of current workstations. In a workstation environment, reasonably complex environments of 5-10K patches can be displayed in subsecond time allowing dynamic walkthroughs simply by varying the view position and orientation. This is in sharp contrast to ray tracing methods which are inherently view dependent. Lighting or reflectivity parameters can also be changed quickly since the form-factors are purely geometric quantities.

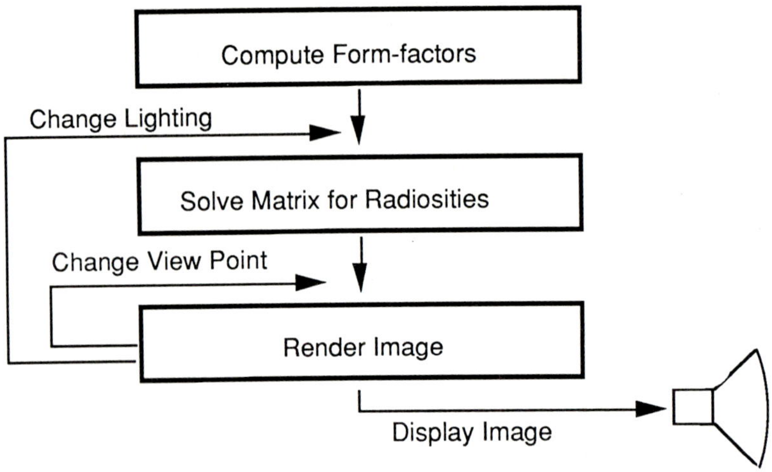

Figure 6.6: Radiosity Pipeline

6.5 Adaptive Subdivision of the Environment

An assumption was made throughout the discussion above that the radiosity of a patch was continuous across its surface. This is adequate for areas in which the radiosity varies very little (i.e. has a low *gradient*), or if the patches are very small. Unfortunately, high gradients occur in many places, particularly at shadow boundaries and making the patches small enough to capture this would make the $O(N^2)$ formfactor computation prohibitive.

6.5.1 Patches and Elements

These problems can be overcome by adopting a two level hierarchy to the subdivision of the environment [Cohen et al, 1986]. The assumptions that patches act as a reflecting *light source* with constant shading is adequate for large areas with a few exceptions. On the other hand one would like more detailed information about the *received* illumination to accurately display the radiosity gradients. Thus each patch can be further subdivided into smaller *elements* .

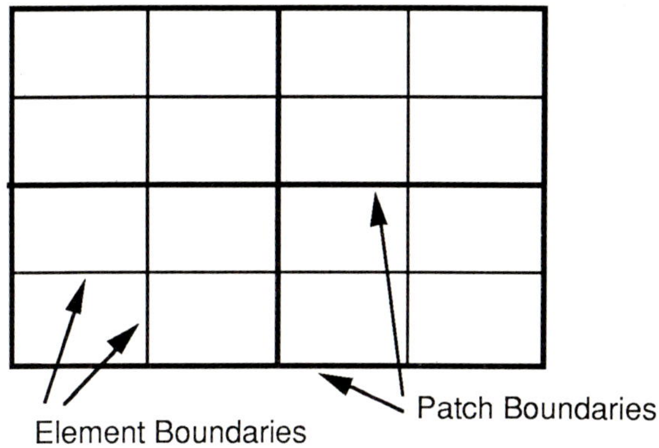

Figure 6.7: Patches and Elements

Each element, or better yet each element vertex can act as an individual receiver of light and can have its own radiosity value associated with it. The patch radiosity is simply the area average of the element radiosities. (The use of the term element may be read as an element vertex. The area associated with a vertex is such that the sum of the vertex-areas within a patch sum to the area of the patch.)

A formfactor is now required from each element (or vertex) to each patch. The radiosity equations now become:

$$B_e = E_e + \rho_e \Sigma_j B_j F_{ej}$$

where:

B_e = Radiosity of element e
E_e = Emission of element e
ρdA_i = Reflectivity of element e
F_{ej} = Formfactor from element e to patch j

The patch radiosity is simply the area average over its elements:

$$B_i = \Sigma_{e_i} B_e A_e / A_i$$

and the patch to patch formfactor is simply:

$$F_{ij} = \Sigma_{e_i} F_{ej} A_e / A_i$$

where:
the summation is over those elements e (or vertices) which are part of patch i.

6.5.2 Element (or Vertex) Radiosity Solution

The solution process now consists of 5 steps:

- Determine element to patch formfactors
- Sum formfactors to determine patch to patch formfactors
- Solve for patch radiosities
- Determine element radiosities directly from patch radiosities
- Display elements

6.5.3 Adaptive Subdivision

This creates more accurate formfactors between patches and allows the matrix solution process to stay small. At the same time the high gradients can be found and displayed within patch boundaries. The number of patches can remain small while the subdivision of elements can adapt to the gradients found within the environment.

Once the patch radiosities are determined and a set of element radiosities have been derived from them, high radiosity gradients within patches can be found by examining neighboring elements. These elements can be further subdivided into new smaller elements. The only new computation which is necessary are the small number of new element to patch formfactors. Since the patches remain unchanged their radiosity solution is still valid and can be used to directly determine the new element radiosities.

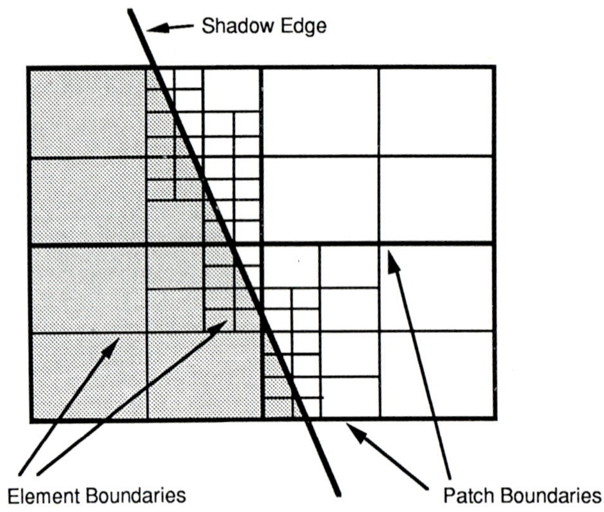

Figure 6.8: Adaptive Subdivision

This process can continue to iterate to any desired level. Intermediate images can be generated since they contain information for the whole environment.

6.6 Progressive Refinement

There are still a number of limitations inherent in the algorithms described above. The radiosity method as outlined above is still of an exponential order, O(NM), where N = number of patches, and M = the number of elements or element vertices. This is due to the fact that all of the form-factors have to be computed before the matrix solution can begin.

A more appealing algorithmic approach would be to compute only a single row of form-factors, compute a single step in the solution and display results as the solution process continues. This *progressive refinement approach* is described in detail in [Cohen et al, 1988] and is briefly outlined here.

By examining the Gauss Seidel iterative matrix solution we can discover a different way to approach the problem. Each row of the matrix represents the effect of all patches on the patch represented at that row. Each step in the standard solution multiplies this row by the current guess for the radiosity solution vector to determine a new single new radiosity value. This new value is then included in the current solution vector when proceeding to the next row, and so on.

6.6.1 Shooting vs. Gathering

In essence this process *gathers in* the light from all patches to determine a new radiosity for one patch.

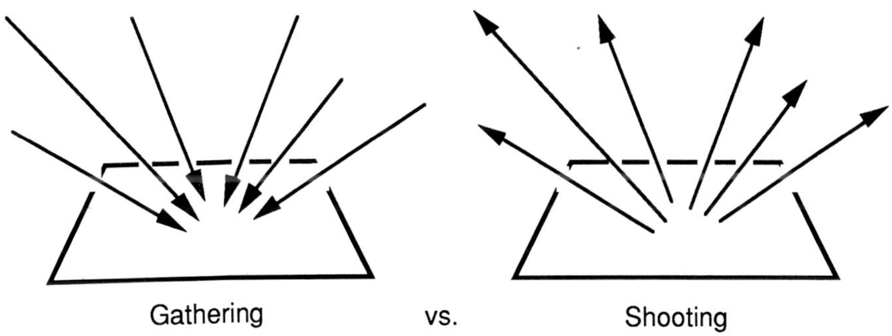

Figure 6.9

The iterative step is given by:

$$\text{New } B_i = B_i + \rho_i \Sigma B_j F_{ij}$$

We can achieve our progressive refinement goal by converting the row of form-factors to a column. Since we know from the reciprocity principle that $F_{ij} A_i = F_{ji} A_j$ then we can turn the row of F_{ij}'s into the column of F_{ji}'s given the areas of the patches. This allows us now to select one patch and *shoot the light* to all other patches. This new iterative step is given by:

$$\text{For all j: New } B_j = B_j + \rho_j B_i F_{ji}$$

6.6.2 Sorting by Unshot Radiosity

Selecting the patch to shoot next is of great importance. Clearly the patch with most energy (B_iA_i) will have the greatest effect on the solution by shooting its energy. Thus, after each iteration, selecting the patch with the maximum *unshot energy* is selected for the next iteration. Unshot energy is used since we do not want to reshoot energy which has already been distributed to the environment. It is possible that a patch will receive significant new energy after it has been selected. This new energy will then be considered for future iterations.

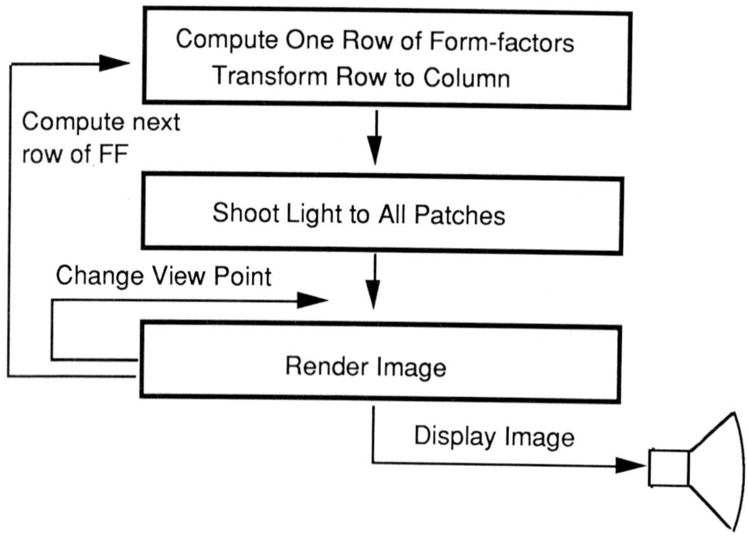

Figure 6.10: Progressive Refinement

In practice, it has been found that the progressive refinement algorithm produces an image almost as accurate as the complete solution after only a small fraction of the rows of form-factors have been computed. This represents a significant savings over the original algorithm.

6.7 Combining Radiosity and Ray Tracing

An assumption was made at the very beginning of this section that all surfaces exhibited diffuse reflection and emission. The restrictions on light sources is easily dealt with, however, the reflecting surfaces present more difficulty. The major difficulty lies in the fact that specular surfaces do not allow us to represent their intensity by a single value since the intensity varies depending on direction. If we try to extend the matrix solution techniques by discretizing the directions we quickly get an intractable problem [Immel et al, 1986]. For example, if we have 1000 patches discretized into 1000 direction we have 1,000,000 unknowns and 10^{12} form-factor coefficients!

6.7.1 Four Mechanisms of Light Transport

A better solution is to combine the best aspects of ray tracing and radiosity [Wallace, et al, 1987]. Once we accept a local reflection model which separates diffuse and specular reflection we can identify four mechanisms of light transport.

1	Diffuse	->	Diffuse
2	Diffuse	->	Specular
3	Specular	->	Diffuse
4	Specular	->	Specular

Clearly, radiosity is designed to handle the first case. Ray tracing is able to account for diffuse to specular as in the visibility of one surface in another shiny surface. By creating a recursive tree of rays, ray tracing also accounts for the specular to specular reflection. Unfortunately, neither method directly accounts for the third case in which light bounces of a specular surface onto a diffuse one. Some methods have been suggested to handle this with varying degrees of success. These include "The Rendering Equation" by Kajiya [Kajiya, 1986] and "Backward Ray Tracing" by Arvo [Arvo, 1986].

6.7.2 A Two Pass Solution

The solution to combining ray tracing and radiosity as outlined by Wallace et al involves performing a two pass solution. The first is a standard *view-independent* radiosity solution for diffuse interreflection. This is followed by a *view-dependent* solution for the specular component only via ray tracing. The ray tracing algorithm does not have to perform any shadow ray testing when encountering a diffuse surface since this process was previously carried out to determine the local lighting model. The radiosity solution can simply be picked off, given the location of the ray intersection.

6.8 A Summary of the Radiosity Algorithm

This brief pass through the radiosity method and the algorithms which have been developed should provide an outline for studying the method in greater detail. The references provided at the end of these notes can fill in the missing details in most cases.

It should be clear from the above discussion that the radiosity method provides many advantages over earlier methods in some cases. In particular when dealing with diffuse environments, the radiosity method provides a means to achieve a high level of realism very quickly and provides the added benefit of allowing dynamic walkthroughs due to its view independence.

It should be equally clear that it does not provide answers for all applications, and that hybrid methods are perhaps the best route when a general and complete global illumination model is required. The exact nature of such methods remains a research topic.

7. Conclusion

We hope the above sections have provided enough inspiration to dig further into the literature on realistic image synthesis. The field is now only a decade old and there is no definitive single source for information. Many questions still remain about how best to unify the algorithms presented above and maintain generality and efficiency. A number of the algorithms are just now appearing in products, so we will have to wait to see how they are accepted and used in real applications.

A considerable amount of time was spent in this tutorial to stress the importance of understanding the complete scope of the problem presented by image synthesis. This includes the need to understand the human visual system and the role it plays in this process. Although we restricted ourselves to creating images on a CRT, there is a need to understand similar problems when moving to a reflective print medium and to film. A good solution to the global illumination can be destroyed by a poor transition to a viewable medium.

The exciting part of the process is just beginning. As these tools become more widely available, the artist, architect, and engineer will be free to create more complex models and environments. The ability to create images of these models will make them available for all to learn from and enjoy.

References

[Amanatides, 1984] John Amanatides. Ray Tracing with Cones. *Computer Graphics (SIGGRAPH '84 Proceedings)*, 18(3):129–135, July 1984.

[Amantides, 1987] J. Amantides. A Fast Voxel Traversal Algorithm for Ray Tracing. In *Proceedings of Eurographics'87*, 1987.

[Appel, 1968] Arthur Appel. Some Techniques for Shading Machine Renderings of Solids. *AFIPS 1968 Spring Joint Computer Conf.*, 32:37–45, 1968.

[Arvo and Kirk, 1987] James Arvo and David Kirk. Fast Ray Tracing by Ray Classification. *Computer Graphics (SIGGRAPH '87 Proceedings)*, 21(3):55–64, July 1987.

[Baum *et al.*, 1986] Daniel R. Baum, John R. Wallace, Michael F. Cohen, and Donald P. Greenberg. The Back-Buffer Algorithm: An Extension of the Radiosity Method to Dynamic Environments. *The Visual Computer*, 2(5):298–308, September 1986.

[Baum *et al.*, 1989] Daniel R. Baum, Holly E. Rushmeier, and James M. Winget. Improving Radiosity Solutions Through the Use of Analytically Determined Form-Factors. In *Proceedings of SIGGRAPH'89 (Boston, Mass., July 31–Aug 4, 1989)*, volume 23. ACM, July 1989.

[Blinn, 1977] Jim F. Blinn. Models of Light Reflection for Computer Synthesized Pictures. In *Proceedings of SIGGRAPH'77 (1977)*, volume 11, pages 192–198. ACM, Fall 1977.

[Blinn, 1982] James F. Blinn. A Generalization of Algebraic Surface Drawing. *ACM Trans. on Graphics*, 1(3):235–256, July 1982.

[Blinn, 1989] Jim Blinn. Return of the Jaggy. *IEEE Computer Graphics and Applications*, 9(2):82–89, March 1989.

[Bouville, 1985] Christian Bouville. Bounding Ellipsoids for Ray-Fractal Intersection. *Computer Graphics (SIGGRAPH '85 Proceedings)*, 19(3):45–52, July 1985.

[Bracewell, 1978] R. Bracewell. *The Fourier Transform and Its Applications*. McGraw-Hill, New York, second edition, 1978.

[Bronsvoort *et al.*, 1984] Willem F. Bronsvoort, Jarke J. van Wijk, and Frederik W. Jansen. Two Methods for Improving the Efficiency of Ray Casting in Solid Modeling. *Computer-Aided Design*, 16(1), January 1984.

[Bui-Tuong, 1975] Phong Bui-Tuong. Illumination for Computer-Generated Pictures. *Communications of the ACM*, 18(6):311–317, June 1975.

[Chen, 1989] Shenchang Eric Chen. A Progressive Radiosity Method and its Implementation in a Distributed Processing Environment. Master's thesis, Program of Computer Graphics, Cornell University, Ithaca, NY, January 1989.

[Cleary and Wyvill, 1987] John G. Cleary and Geoff Wyvill. An Analysis of an Algorithm for Fast Ray-Tracing using Uniform Space Subdivision. Research Report 87/264/12, Department of Computer Science, University of Calgary, Canada, 1987.

[Cohen and Greenberg, 1985] Michael F. Cohen and Donald P. Greenberg. A Radiosity Solution for Complex Environments. In *Proceedings of SIGGRAPH'85 (San Francisco, California, July 22–26, 1985)*, volume 19, pages 31–40. ACM, July 1985.

[Cohen *et al.*, 1986] Michael F. Cohen, Donald P. Greenberg, David S. Immel, and Philip J. Brock. An Efficient Radiosity Approach for Realistic Image Synthesis. *IEEE Computer Graphics and Applications*, 6(2):26–35, March 1986.

[Cohen *et al.*, 1988] Michael F. Cohen, Shenchang Eric Chen, John R. Wallace, and Donald P. Greenberg. A Progressive Refinement Approach to Fast Radiosity Image Generation. In *Proceedings of SIGGRAPH'88 (Atlanta, Georgia, August 1–5, 1988)*, pages 75–84. ACM, August 1988.

[Cook and Torrance, 1981] Robert L. Cook and Kenneth E. Torrance. A Reflectance Model for Computer Graphics. In *Proceedings of SIGGRAPH'81 (Dallas, Texas, August 3–7, 1981)*, volume 15, pages 307–316. ACM, August 1981.

[Cook *et al.*, 1984] Robert L. Cook, Thomas Porter, and Loren Carpenter. Distributed Ray Tracing. *Computer Graphics (SIGGRAPH '84 Proceedings)*, 18(3):137–145, July 1984.

[Cook, 1986] Robert L. Cook. Stochastic Sampling in Computer Graphics. *ACM Transactions on Graphics*, 5(1):51–72, January 1986.

[Crow, 1977] Frank C. Crow. The Aliasing Problem in Computer-Generated Shaded Images. *Communications of the ACM*, 20(11):799–805, November 1977.

[Dippé and Swensen, 1984] Mark E. Dippé and John Swensen. An Adaptive Subdivision Algorithm and Parallel Architecture for Realistic Image Synthesis. *Computer Graphics (SIGGRAPH '84 Proceedings)*, 18(3):149–158, July 1984.

[Dippé and Wold, 1985] M.A.Z. Dippé and E.H. Wold. Antialiasing Through Stochastic Sampling. *Computer Graphics (SIGGRAPH '85 Proceedings)*, 19(3):69–78, July 1985.

[du Montcel and Nicolas, 1985] B. Tezenas du Montcel and A. Nicolas. An Illumination Model for Ray-Tracing. In *Eurographics '85*, September 1985.

[Foley and van Dam, 1982] James D. Foley and Andries van Dam. *Fundamentals of Interactive Computer Graphics.* Addison Wesley, Reading, Massachusetts, 1982.

[Fujimoto *et al.*, 1986] Akira Fujimoto, Takayuki Tanaka, and Kansei Iwata. ARTS: Accelerated Ray-Tracing System. *IEEE Computer Graphics and Applications*, 6(4):16–26, April 1986.

[Fujimoto, 1985] Akira Fujimoto. Accelerated Ray Tracing. In *Computer Graphics: Visual Technology and Art*, pages 41–65. Springer Verlag, Tokyo, 1985.

[Glassner, 1984] Andrew S. Glassner. Space Subdivision for Fast Ray Tracing. *IEEE Computer Graphics and Applications*, 4(10):15–22, October 1984.

[Glassner, 1987] Andrew Glassner. Spacetime Ray Tracing for Animation. Introduction to Ray Tracing (SIGGRAPH'87 course notes #13, Anaheim, California, July 27–31, 1987), July 1987.

[Glassner, 1988] Andrew S. Glassner. Spacetime Ray Tracing for Animation. *IEEE Computer Graphics and Applications*, 8(2):60–70, March 1988.

[Glassner, 1989] Andrew S. Glassner. *Ray Tracing.* Academic Press, 1989.

[Goldsmith and Salmon, 1987] Jeffrey Goldsmith and John Salmon. Automatic Creation of Object Hierarchies for Ray Tracing. *IEEE Computer Graphics and Applications*, 7(5):14–20, May 1987.

[Goral *et al.*, 1984] Cindy M. Goral, Kenneth E. Torrance, and Donald P. Greenberg. Modeling the Interaction of Light Between Diffuse Surfaces. In *Proceedings of SIGGRAPH'84 (Minneapolis, Minnesota, July 23–27, 1984)*, volume 18, pages 213–222. ACM, July 1984.

[Gouraud, 1971] H. Gouraud. Continuous Shading of Curved Surfaces. *IEEE Transactions on Computers*, C-20(6):623–628, June 1971.

[Haines and Greenberg, 1986] Eric A. Haines and Donald P. Greenberg. The Light buffer: a Shadow Testing Accelerator. *IEEE Computer Graphics and Applications*, 6(9):6–16, September 1986.

[Haines, 1987] Eric Haines. A Proposal for Standard Graphics Environments. *IEEE Computer Graphics and Applications*, 7(11):3–5, November 1987.

[Hall and Greenberg, 1983] Roy A. Hall and Donald P. Greenberg. A Testbed for Realistic Image Synthesis. *IEEE Computer Graphics and Applications*, 3(8):10–20, November 1983.

[Hall, 1989] Roy Hall. *Illumination and Color in Computer Generated Imagery.* Springer-Verlag, New York, N.Y., 1989.

[Hanrahan, 1983] Pat Hanrahan. Ray Tracing Algebraic Surfaces. *Computer Graphics (SIGGRAPH '83 Proceedings)*, 17(3):83–90, July 1983.

[Hanrahan, 1986] Pat Hanrahan. Using Caching and Breadth-First Search to Speed Up Ray-Tracing, May 1986.

[Heckbert and Hanrahan, 1984] Paul S. Heckbert and Pat Hanrahan. Beam Tracing Polygonal Objects. *Computer Graphics (SIGGRAPH '84 Proceedings)*, 18(3):119–127, July 1984.

[Heckbert, 1986] Paul S. Heckbert. Filtering By Repeated Integration. *Computer Graphics (SIGGRAPH '86 Proceedings)*, 20(4):315–321, August 1986.

[Immel *et al.*, 1986] David S. Immel, Michael F. Cohen, and Donald P. Greenberg. A Radiosity Method for Non-Diffuse Environments. In *Proceedings of SIGGRAPH'86 (Dallas, Texas, August 18–22, 1986)*, volume 20, pages 133–142. ACM, August 1986.

[Jansen, 1986] Frederik Jansen. Data Structures for Ray Tracing. In L. R. A. Kessener, F. J. Peters, and M. P. L. van Lierop, editors, *Data Structures for Raster Graphics*, pages 57–73. Springer-Verlag, New York, 1986.

[Kajiya and Herzen, 1984] James T. Kajiya and Brian P. Von Herzen. Ray Tracing Volume Densities. *Computer Graphics (SIGGRAPH '84 Proceedings)*, 18(3):165–174, July 1984.

[Kajiya, 1982] James T. Kajiya. Ray Tracing Parametric Patches. *Computer Graphics (SIGGRAPH '82 Proceedings)*, 16(3):245–254, July 1982.

[Kajiya, 1983] James T. Kajiya. New Techniques for Ray Tracing Procedurally Defined Objects. *ACM Trans. on Graphics*, 2(3):161–181, July 1983.

[Kajiya, 1986] J.T. Kajiya. The Rendering Equation. *Computer Graphics (SIGGRAPH '86 Proceedings)*, 20(4):143–150, August 1986.

[Kajiya, 1988] James T. Kajiya. An Overview and Comparison of Rendering Methods. *ACM SIGGRAPH Course Notes*, 10:249–264, 1988.

[Kalra and Barr, 1989] Devendra Kalra and Alan H. Barr. Guaranteed Ray Intersections with Implicit Surfaces. *Computer Graphics (SIGGRAPH '89 Proceedings)*, 23(3):281–287, July 1989.

[Kaplan, 1985] Michael R. Kaplan. Space-Tracing, A Constant Time Ray-Tracer. SIGGRAPH '85 State of the Art in Image Synthesis seminar notes, July 1985.

[Kay and Greenberg, 1979] Douglas S. Kay and Donald P. Greenberg. Transparency for Computer Synthesized Images. *Computer Graphics (SIGGRAPH '79 Proceedings)*, 13(2):158–164, August 1979.

[Kay and Kajiya, 1986] Timothy L. Kay and James T. Kajiya. Ray Tracing Complex Scenes. *Computer Graphics (SIGGRAPH '86 Proceedings)*, 20(4):269–278, August 1986.

[Lee *et al.*, 1985] M.E. Lee, R.A. Redner, and S.P. Uselton. Statistically Optimized Sampling for Distributed Ray Tracing. *Computer Graphics (SIGGRAPH '85 Proceedings)*, 19(3):61–67, July 1985.

[Meyer and Greenberg, 1980] Gary W. Meyer and Donald P. Greenberg. Perceptual Color Spaces for Computer Graphics. *Computer Graphics*, 14(3):254–261, 1980.

[Meyer *et al.*, 1986] Gary W. Meyer, Holly E. Rushmeier, Michael F. Cohen, Donald P. Greenberg, and Kenneth E. Torrance. An Experimental Evaluation of Computer Graphics Imagery. *ACM Transactions on Graphics*, 5(1):30–50, January 1986.

[Meyer, 1986] Gary W. Meyer. Tutorial on Color Science. *The Visual Computer*, 2:278–290, 1986.

[Meyer, 1988] Gary W. Meyer. Wavelength Selection for Synthetic Image Generation. *ComputerVision, Graphics, and Image Processing*, 41:57–79, 1988.

[Mitchell, 1987] D.P. Mitchell. Generating Antialiased Images at Low Sampling Densities. *Computer Graphics (SIGGRAPH '87 Proceedings)*, 21(3):65–69, July 1987.

[Moravec, 1981] Hans P. Moravec. 3D Graphics and the Wave Theory. *Computer Graphics (SIGGRAPH '81 Proceedings)*, 15(3):289–296, August 1981.

[Nishita and Nakamae, 1985] Tomoyuki Nishita and Eihachiro Nakamae. Continuous Tone Representation of Three-Dimensional Objects Taking Account of Shadows and Interreflections. In *Proceedings of SIGGRAPH'85 (San Francisco, California, July 22–26, 1985)*, volume 19, pages 23–30. ACM, July 1985.

[Painter and Sloan, 1989] James S. Painter and Kenneth Sloan. Antialiased Raytracing by Adaptive Progressive Refinement. *Computer Graphics (SIGGRAPH '89 Proceedings)*, 23(3):281–287, July 1989.

[Phong, 1975] Bui-Tuong Phong. Illumination for Computer-Generated Pictures. *Communications of the ACM*, 18(6):311–317, June 1975.

[Porter and Duff, 1984] Thomas Porter and Tom Duff. Compositing Digital Images. *Computer Graphics (SIGGRAPH '84 Proceedings)*, 18(3):253–259, July 1984.

[Roth, 1982] Scott D. Roth. Ray Casting for Modeling Solids. *Computer Graphics and Image Processing*, 18(2):109–144, February 1982.

[Rubin and Whitted, 1980] Steve M. Rubin and Turner Whitted. A Three-Dimensional Representation for Fast Rendering of Complex Scenes. *Computer Graphics (SIGGRAPH '80 Proceedings)*, 14(3):110–116, July 1980.

[Rushmeier and Torrance, 1987] Holly E. Rushmeier and Kenneth E. Torrance. The Zonal Method for Calculating Light Intensities in the Presence of a Participating Mediuim. In *Proceedings of SIGGRAPH'87 (Anaheim, California, July 27–31, 1987)*, volume 21, pages 293–302. ACM, July 1987.

[Rushmeier, 1988] Holly E. Rushmeier. *Realistic Image Synthesis for Scenes with Radiatively Participating Media*. PhD thesis, Cornell University, June 1988.

[Sederberg and Anderson, 1984] Thomas W. Sederberg and David C. Anderson. Ray Tracing of Steiner Patches. *Computer Graphics (SIGGRAPH '84 Proceedings)*, 18(3):159–164, July 1984.

[Shannon, 1949] Claude E. Shannon. Communications in the Presence of Noise. *Proc. IRE*, 37(1):10–21, January 1949.

[Shao *et al.*, 1988] Min-Zhi Shao, Qun-Sheng Peng, and You-Dong Liang. A New Radiosity Approach by Procedural Refinements for Realistic Image Synthesis. In *Proceedings of SIGGRAPH'88 (Atlanta, Georgia, August 1–5, 1988)*, pages 93–102. ACM, August 1988.

[Shinya *et al.*, 1987] Mikio Shinya, Tokiichiro Takahashi, and Seiichiro Naito. Principles and Applications of Pencil Tracing. In *Proceedings of SIGGRAPH'87 (Anaheim, California, July 27–31, 1987)*, volume 21, pages 45–54. ACM, July 1987.

[Siegel and Howeol, 1981] Robert Siegel and John R. Howeol. *Thermal Radiation Heat Transfer*. Hemisphere Publishing Corp., Washington DC., 1981.

[Sillion and Puech, 1989] Francois Sillion and Claude Puech. A General Two-Pass Method Integrating Specular and Diffuse Reflection. In *Proceedings of SIGGRAPH'89 (Boston, Mass., July 31–Aug 4, 1989)*, volume 23. ACM, July 1989.

[Sparrow, 1963] E. M. Sparrow. A New and Simpler Formulation for Radiative Angle Factors. *Transactions of the ASME, Journal of Heat Transfer*, 85(2):81–88, 1963.

[Speer *et al.*, 1985] L. Richard Speer, Tony D. DeRose, and Brian A. Barsky. A Theoretical and Empirical Analysis of Coherent Ray-Tracing. In *Graphics Interface '85*, May 1985.

[Toth, 1985] Daniel L. Toth. On Ray Tracing Parametric Surfaces. *Computer Graphics (SIGGRAPH '85 Proceedings)*, 19(3):171–179, July 1985.

[van Wijk, 1984] Jarke J. van Wijk. Ray Tracing Objects Defined by Sweeping Planar Cubic Splines. *ACM Transactions on Graphics*, 3(3):223–237, July 1984.

[Wallace *et al.*, 1987] John R. Wallace, Michael F. Cohen, and Donald P. Greenberg. A Two-Pass Solution to the Rendering Equation: A Synthesis of Ray Tracing and Radiosity Methods. In *Proceedings of SIGGRAPH'87 (Anaheim, California, July 27–31, 1987)*, volume 21, pages 311–320. ACM, July 1987.

[Wallace *et al.*, 1989] John R. Wallace, Kells A. Elmquist, and Eric A. Haines. A Ray Tracing Algorithm for Progressive Radiosity. In *Proceedings of SIGGRAPH'89 (Boston, Mass., July 31–Aug 4, 1989)*, volume 23. ACM, July 1989.

[Ward *et al.*, 1988] Gregory J. Ward, Francis M. Rubinstein, and Clear Robert D. A Ray Tracing Solution for Diffuse Interreflection. In *Proceedings of SIGGRAPH'88 (Atlanta, Georgia, August 1–5, 1988)*, pages 85–92. ACM, August 1988.

[Watt, 1989] Alan Watt. *Fundamentals of Three-Dimaensional Computer Graphics.* Addison-Wesley, Wokingham, England, 1989.

[Weghorst *et al.*, 1984] Hank Weghorst, Gary Hooper, and Donald P. Greenberg. Improved Computational Methods for Ray Tracing. *ACM Trans. on Graphics*, 3(1):52–69, January 1984.

[Whitted, 1980] T.J. Whitted. An Improved Illumination Model for Shaded Display. *Communications of the ACM*, 23(6):343–349, June 1980.

[Wyvill *et al.*, 1986] Geoff Wyvill, Tosiyasu L. Kunii, and Yasuto Shirai. Space Division for Ray Tracing in CSG. *IEEE Computer Graphics and Applications*, 6(4):28–34, April 1986.

Parallel Computing for Graphics

Franklin C. Crow

Apple Advanced Technology Group

Cupertino, California

Abstract

The cost in computing cycles for state-of-the-art imagery continues to rise exponentially. Fortunately, so does the cost-effectiveness of state-of-the-art computer processors. However, that leaves us continually several orders of magnitude short on processing power if we wish to make state-of-the-art images in real-time or even interactive time. An obvious answer to this dilemma lies in parallel processing. As massively parallel supercomputers become reality and promise a future including massively parallel everyday computers, it is no longer a silly exercise to consider how to use thousands or even millions of processors in computer graphics.

Many algorithms from traditional computer graphics lend themselves to parallel implementation. However, there are many ways in which the remaining algorithms can prevent a system from realizing the potential of a massively parallel computing resource. Many parallel architectures for graphics have been proposed and a few have even been available commercially in the past few years. A close look at these architectures usually reveals underlying assumptions about the nature of computations for graphics which may not always prove true.

Keywords

Parallel architectures, Parallel rendering algorithms, SIMD, MIMD, texture, visible surface algorithms, shading.

Introduction

Choosing a computational base for doing computer graphics is not getting simpler. In addition to networked workstation computers of various sorts, a wide variety of special-purpose graphics processors, more general-purpose vector machines, multiprocessors, and general-purpose supercomputers are now commercially available. An even wider variety of computational bases have been promised or proposed, suggesting that the choices will be even more varied in the future.

Historically, use of concurrency in graphics systems has been the province of special-purpose hardware, chiefly that used in the flight simulator business. However, it has always seemed clear that more general-purpose massively parallel processors could easily be applied to computer graphics.

As more potent computing resources have become widely available, it has been discovered that, by squandering processor cycles, spectacular imagery comes relatively easily. The result is that it has become acceptable, even fashionable in some circles, to make images which require immense computing resources. Furthermore, the resulting images demonstrate that orders of magnitude more time could be used effectively in improving the realism and richness of the images.

This following section traces the growth of computing power devoted to graphics as seen in example images from the literature whose execution times are known. Recent growth in workstation computing power is compared to motivate the use of parallelism. Current choices for a computational base are examined and the promise of current trends in chip technology explored. A brief taxonomy of parallel architectures is offered, followed by a survey of ways in which parallelism has been applied to graphics and a look at existing parallel architectures applied to graphics.

The Growth of "Instructions Per Image"

For almost twenty years, it has been customary to appear at an annual conference (Siggraph is the most obvious example) proudly displaying an image which probes some new avenue of realism and nearly always sets new standards for profligacy in heavy use of computing cycles. A look at a collection of representative images from our two-decade vantage point is both interesting in itself and instructive.

The first obvious example of this sort is the introduction of highlights to enhance the appearance of smoothly curving surfaces. In 1973 the author, along with Bui Tuong Phong made the image shown in figure 1 [1]. The image was computed on a DEC PDP-10 with the KA-10 processor in ten minutes. Actually, since the image had to be recorded on the fly on film using a precision CRT, three passes were required to produce the color image (frame buffers were not yet available). However, the single-pass time makes a more legitimate comparison with later images. Assuming that a KA-10 processor was worth about 0.25 million instructions per second (MIPS), the image required roughly 150 million instructions to produce.

In 1976 Blinn and Newell introduced environmental reflections and produced wonderful images of teapots with texture and reflected windows and doors [2]. These images took roughly 25 minutes on a DEC PDP-11/45 using a frame buffer for display. Making a rough assumption of 0.33 MIPS for the 11/45, Blinn and Newell's image cost around 500 million instructions.

In 1979 Whitted introduced a unified method for refraction and reflection through ray tracing [3]. His images, of glass balls, textured balls and simple tabletop scenes took from 44 to 122 minutes. Fortunately, he made his images on a DEC VAX 11/780 which became the most popular machine for state-of-the-art graphics for several years. The VAX 11/780 is generally used as a standard of comparison at 1 MIPS. Therefore Whitted's images required from 2.6 to 7.3 billion instructions.

Figure 1: Phong shaded glass, University of Utah - 1973

The consistent use of the VAX 11/780 for several years required increasing levels of patience as ever more expensive images were made. One of the author's graduate students, Robert Conley, made the image in figure 2 in 1982. He used partially adaptive supersampling to make anti-aliased ray traced images. The example shown took 4 hours, or about 14.4 billion instructions.

Professor Don Greenberg's students at Cornell University made a number of images of richly textured ray traced scenes in the mid 80s as part of an ongoing quest for photo-realism. Some particularly nice images made in 1986 [4] initially took roughly 12 hours on VAX 11/780, 43 billion instructions.

Simultaneously with their advanced work in ray tracing, Prof. Greenberg's students were developing techniques for capturing subtle lighting effects due to diffuse reflection, which they call "radiosity". A relatively simple example image including a few tables, chairs and a table lamp took 208 minutes on a VAX 11/780 or 12.5 billion instructions.

Unfortunately, the VAX 11/780 has passed out of favor and much faster machines are now generally in use making comparisons more difficult. Jim Kajiya and his colleagues at the California Institute of Technology have been championing the "teraflop club" for those working towards images which use a trillion (floating point) instructions or more. Kajiya himself took a major step in this direction with an image showing caustics (the refracted image of the light source) in the shadows of transparent objects [5]. This image took 20 hours to compute on an IBM 3081. We have estimated this as about 50 billion instructions.

Figure 2: Ray tracing by Robert Conley, Ohio State U. - 1981

More recently, Kajiya, with his student Tim Kay, published a paper on fur [6] including an image containing a single teddy bear. This image required roughly 25 hours of IBM 3090 CPU time, estimated as 250 billion instructions or so, which were actually computed in parallel distributed over four 3090 processors.

These figures are summarized on a semilog graph in figure 3. From this it is easy to see that this rather small, but perhaps representative, sample shows the log of instructions used for each of these images is roughly linear over time. Note that the instruction count estimates could stray by factors of 2 or 3 without upsetting that conclusion. Therefore, we can conclude that the expense of state-of-the art images is increasing exponentially. Fortunately the cost-effectiveness of computing hardware is also increasing roughly exponentially.

The line in the lower right portion of figure 3 shows the prediction given by "Joy's Law". Bill Joy, of Sun Workstations Inc. has been promoting the idea that state-of-the-art workstation processors have been doubling in speed every year starting with a base of 1 MIPS in 1984. This says that currently (1990) there should be processors capable of 64 MIPS, and indeed there are.

One is led by this evidence to the conclusion that state-of-the-art imagery computed on state-of-the-art processors is doomed to remain over 5 orders of magnitude short of real-time (more than 20 frames per second) for the foreseeable future. However, there are mitigating forces acting against this conclusion.

First, we have seen a repeating pattern recently in the field of computer graphics. (1) a new technique for improved realism is developed. (2) the technique proves to be extraordinarily expensive. (3) the conferences for the next few years are replete with papers on how to improve the performance of the technique. Examples can be found in surface texturing, radiosity, and most noticeably, ray-tracing.

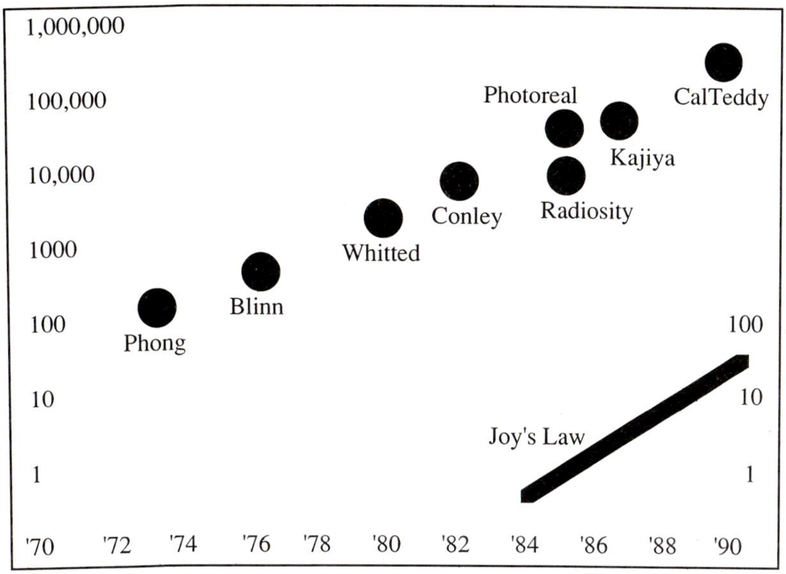

Figure 3: Semilog graph of year vs. instruction count and mips

Second, graphics hardware continues to shadow state-of-the-art rendering. Eventually, a popular technique will be offered in a hardware accelerator. However there is often a lag of a decade or more for commercially available hardware. Furthermore, the technique must be popular enough to justify the considerable expense of developing the hardware.

Lastly, as should be obvious from the subject of these writings, multiple processors can be used to compute images more rapidly. The advantage posed by multiple processor approaches is scalability, the chance to choose your execution speed by the level of resources devoted to the computation.

There is a set of thresholds of practicality in computer graphics. There is abundant anecdotal evidence that fanatics are willing to devote days or even weeks to producing a single significant image. However, to make imagery practical, a general rule of thumb has been that an image should be produced every 3-6 minutes. That allows 10-20 frames per hour, or 3-8 seconds of animation overnight. The "practical" level requires that design work can be done using fully rendered imagery for feedback and that short snippets of animation can be viewed on a daily basis.

Further levels of practicality are reached when images can be made in "interactive time" and in "real-time". Interactive time requires that images be made quickly enough to hold the attention of the person creating them. The nanocentury (about 3 seconds) is sometimes used as a definition for the threshold of interactivity. Real-time is usually meant to be the rate necessary to cause adjacent images in an animation to fuse in the eye of the observer. This is around 20 frames a second. However, existing standards for television and other media may require specific frame rates higher than that. Furthermore, subtler effects such as "ghosting", caused by the latent images of recent frames imposed over the current one, may dictate even higher rates. On the other hand, ghosting can usually be removed by using motion blur.

The preceding gives an interestingly even set of steps. The level of practicality requires 2-3 orders of magnitude speedup from the limits of graduate student patience. Interactivity requires a 2 order of magnitude improvement over practicality. The threshold of real-time lies 2 orders of magnitude below the threshold of interactivity. Every couple of orders of magnitude speedup makes an important shift in the utility of the imagery.

There appears to be no end to the computational power that can be expended in pursuing ever-increasing realism. Proposals for algorithms which would require much greater resources than we use today have been published [7, 8]. Furthermore, the models from which images are made today are still vastly short of the detail needed to approach the richness of natural images [9]. Our techniques for modeling and rendering surface texture and complicated surfaces such as fur, forests, or clouds are still woefully primitive. Computer graphics offers a sink capable of swallowing all the computing cycles one can afford as far into the future as we can see.

A Look at Commercial Approaches to Increased Power

Inevitably the most cost-effective way to render images is with an architecture dedicated to the purpose. If all one wants is images of a few thousand polygons using only bilinear smooth shading, the solution is at hand. Workstations with special hardware are available for a few tens of thousands of dollars from a number of sources which can smoothly animate such images. More expensive graphics workstations now offer increasingly advanced shading hardware including features such as highlights and surface texturing.

The drawback in special-purpose hardware, of course, is that if more elaborate imagery is desired than the hardware provides, you must wait much, much longer, since the general-purpose workstation processor must do the job by itself. An equally expensive machine which provides a better general-purpose processor instead of the special hardware cannot be expected to deliver the simpler imagery nearly as rapidly. However, the compensating advantage is that the greater general-purpose power of the machine may be brought to bear on a wider variety of styles of imagery.

The current economics of hardware make the most cost-effective general-purpose system, in terms of MIPS per dollar, that which can be made from a small number of commodity chips sold in the millions. Thus the computational component (processor and memory) of machines based on, say, the M68000 family or i80x86 family is very inexpensive for the power provided.

Why not just use a flotilla of standard workstation computers for all computing then? If you have 1000 images to compute by next week and everything has been worked out so that it can all run automatically, then that may be the right choice. On the other hand, if you are trying to develop an image and need feedback, or you are trying to interact with the imagery, then you may be limited to representations so simplistic as to be useless.

Furthermore, workstations come with a separate chassis, power supply, network connection, etc., and even a keyboard and display, for each processor. Clearly, a machine with many processors could be packaged more inexpensively. However, in a personal survey, this author found a wide selection of parallel machines ranging from roughly 1.5 to 10 thousand dollars per 32-bit processor or equivalent. These figures bracket the roughly 5 thousand dollar cost of a minimal low-end workstation with a standard 32-bit processor. The claimed cost per MIPS of the machines surveyed varies, but stays within half an order of magnitude. Unfortunately, multiprocessor machines are not yet made in the high volume which brings out the cost advantages of denser packaging.

If general-purpose computing power is needed at all costs, the fastest available scalar processors are the supercomputers. However, it is still unusual to find a Cray or similar machine used for interactive graphics. On the other hand, the need for supercomputer power for interactive graphics has spawned a new generation of "crayola" [10-13] computers designed to mix a bit of supercomputer technology (e.g.. floating point vector pipelines, scoreboarding) with powerful graphics I/O. These machines fill a niche and drive the level of the practical up to an order of magnitude higher for well-matched applications.

Another developing class of computers are the "massively parallel" machines. These include: (1) a specialized frame buffer architecture with a a quarter million single-bit processors, one per pixel [14], (2) a general-purpose computer with up to 64k bit-serial processors intimately connected in a cleverly designed network and driven by a single instruction stream [15], (3) a machine with hundreds of 32-bit processors, each running its own program, communicating over a multi-stage network to shared memory modules [16], and (4) a handful of different architectures with up to a thousand or more 32-bit processors communicating over networks with multiple connections per processor (supplied by NCube,

Meiko, and Intel Scientific Systems). However, despite all this effort, there is, at the moment, no way to get more than about 3 orders of magnitude more speed over a standard workstation just by spending more money.

Power to be expected from unavoidable technological improvements

Twenty-five years ago, in the mid sixties, the fastest scalar computers available ran at about 10 MIPS [17]. Just over a decade later the Cray 1 [18] was running nearly an order of magnitude faster. However, after a decade and a half, today's supercomputers have yet to achieve the next order of magnitude speedup in scalar speed. The billion-instruction-per-second processor isn't available yet, although there are plans for it. By comparison, today's high-volume single-chip processors have exceeded the 10 MIPS of the fastest computers of the mid sixties and are doubling in speed every year.

We are already hearing reports of processors targeted for workstation use which have exceeded the scalar performance of the Cray-1 on certain problems. There seems to be no obstacle to the arrival of the 100 MIPS workstation in the next few years. Furthermore, Joy's Law predicts a billion-instruction-per-second processor in the mid 90s. However, such laws inevitably fail sooner or later.

Commercial parallel machines are offering up to 3 orders of magnitude potential speedup through parallelism. Moreover, reports of real problems attaining very close to 3 orders of magnitude speedup on such machines are beginning to surface. Proposed machines with serious chances of actually being built are intended to involve over a hundred thousand 32-bit processors [19-21].

There seem to be no good technical reasons (ignoring organizational and economic issues) why a million-processor machine won't be realized within the decade. Therefore, there is the strong possibility that the raw computational power needed to surpass today's most ambitious images in real-time will be available. Whether that power can be harnessed to the task of generating images quickly enough is a more complicated question.

Parallel Architectures

There are many ways to cause more than one operation to take place simultaneously. Today's processors usually overlap the fetching of one instruction with the execution of the previous one, for example. Supercomputers have used such pipelining techniques to compute floating point operations on vectors for 2 decades. Predictions of faster commodity processors generally assume increasingly heavy use of pipelining techniques. However, instructions in general-purpose computers are too simple to allow speedups of more than 2 or 3 from pipelining alone.

To get orders of magnitude speedup, massive parallelism involving multiple streams will be necessary. What architectures are capable of providing this? In the simplest terms, the architectures can be divided into three groups: (1) Single Instruction stream Multiple Data stream (SIMD) machines [22], in which all processors execute the same instruction on differing data in lock-step, (2) Multiple Instruction stream Multiple Data stream (MIMD) machines in which all processors share access to a global memory, and (3) MIMD machines or groups of machines in which processors communicate by sending messages to each other over interprocessor links. The last two types actually represent a continuum of architectures ranging over the amount of globally shared state in the system.

SIMD machines have a long history as massively parallel architectures. Experimental machines such as Illiac IV [23], MPP [24], and most recently, Pixel Planes [14] have demonstrated increasing numbers of active processing elements. Moreover, such machines are commercially available from Thinking Machines [15] and MasPar.

Two reasons are usually given for pursuing SIMD designs. (1) A SIMD architecture provides more computational power for a given cost in any given technology because the instruction fetch and decode hardware need not be replicated for each processor. However, realizing this advantage in competition with high-volume commodity processors may be impossible. (2) SIMD machines are conceptually easier to program since all processors are doing the same thing. Furthermore, since the state of the machine changes in lock-step, debugging is relatively easy.

The difficulty with SIMD processors is that for many algorithms it is very difficult to keep all processors doing useful work all the time. Processor utilization may be low enough to offset any cost advantage due to the shared instruction unit. The difficulty arises from the fact that in order to execute conditional code, all processors failing the condition must go idle while those who satisfied the condition execute the appropriate code, and vice versa.

Fortunately, many of the operations in computer graphics can be done without conditional instructions in which the condition varies across the processors. 3-d vector and matrix operations supporting transforms and some shading have this characteristic.

In MIMD machines each processor operates independently. However, there are vastly different ways in which to use the processors. The concept of task granularity is a useful way to rank different usage styles.

Large grain parallelism is characterized by large tasks which run using little or no communication with other tasks. Each computing element might compute a separate frame from an animation, for example. Fine grain parallelism is characterized by very small tasks and much higher rates of inter-task communication. A computing element might, as its task, input a vector, transform it, then pass the result to another computing element.

The spectrum of MIMD architectures useful for graphics spans a wide range of examples. The following is a list of architectural examples ranging from those useful for coarser grained parallelism to those useful for finer grained parallelism:

(1) mainframe computers connected by wide area networks,

(2) workstations connected by local area nets,

(3) multicomputers consisting of processors each with its own memory, communicating over multiple serial links, and

(4) multiprocessors consisting of processors communicating through shared memory.

At the finest end of the granularity spectrum are numerous experimental and proposed architectures such as dataflow machines, neural networks, multiple functional unit machines, etc. These machines are designed for parallel execution at the machine instruction level. They are intended either to translate existing algorithms automatically or to use completely new programming techniques.

There remains controversy over whether shared-memory or message-passing is the right path to take in MIMD architectures. There are a few examples of each kind available commercially. In general the message-passing architectures are more scalable. They can be expanded more easily to larger configurations. The shared-memory architectures in their pure form (in which all processors may access all memory) are forced to either provide access to shared memory over a common bus as in the Sequent Balance architecture, or must provide a complicated switching mechanism limited to a fixed maximum size and not easily expanded beyond that size [16]. There will undoubtedly be hybrid machines in which not all memory is shared by all processors, but memory is generally available as a more flexible resource than currently found in message passing systems. As it stands currently, algorithms intended to scale beyond a few hundred MIMD processors must assume a message passing architecture

Granularity is a useful concept in terms of parallel algorithms as well as parallel architectures. A fine grained task might accumulate surface data for a single pixel, doing depth comparisons and other operations to determine its color. A coarse grained task might do the entire rendering task for a section of the image, or generate all the pixels for a given object.

Thinking simplistically, one might want to organize the computing tasks by one or more of the following items:

(1) pixel or group of pixels,

(2) vertex or control point,

(3) polygon,

(4) patch,

(5) object or subobject, or

(6) frame or subimage.

The lack of pixel-to-pixel coherence in the typical ray-tracing algorithm and the simplicity of its implementation has made it a popular early application for massively parallel architectures. It is relatively easy to broadcast the description of a simple scene and accompanying ray tracing program to a large collection of processors, then have each processor compute a pixel or group of pixels [25]. At the other end of the spectrum it has been easy to use a collection of computers, preferably networked, to compute individual frames for an animation [26].

To a large extent, these examples span the range of grain sizes for applications of parallel rendering, the individual pixel (or subpixel sample) being the smallest computable unit and the single image (or contiguous group of images) being the largest.

It is interesting that the simplest implementations of parallel rendering lie at these extremes. In both cases, all computing units use identical programs and scene descriptions, only a few input parameters need be varied from unit to unit. This simplicity has its costs, however. If the unit of computation is an entire frame, then the first frame is completed no more quickly with many computing units than with one. If the unit of computation is just a pixel or group of pixels, you would expect to get the first frame much more quickly. However, each pixel must be computed more or less independently of its neighbors, preventing use of efficient display algorithms.

To compute each pixel completely independently, each process must execute with access to the entire scene description. Therefore, either all processors must have the scene stored in their memories (limiting the complexity of the scene) or the data must be in a shared memory (limiting the number of independently-executing processors). In practice this has meant that ray-tracing images may be finished in minutes instead of hours, but not in real-time.

Other simplistic approaches have adapted scan line algorithms to compute scanlines or groups of scanlines independently [27,28] or have broken the image into slices [29]. Machines have also been proposed and built to operate on a polygon or rectangle at a time [30-33].

Another longstanding method has been to use pipelining on a fairly standard sequence of tasks. (1) input data delivered to the head of the pipeline, (2) vertices transformed, (3) polygons clipped to the image limits, (4) polygons scan converted, and (5) scan segments shaded. This is especially true in hardware designs where these tasks are overlapped and pipelines are replicated for higher performance [34-36].

There is clearly a wide range of choices for mapping the computer graphics onto multiple processors. Ideally, once the process is broken down to small enough tasks, a standard algorithm (which may someday be considered part of any parallel operating system) may manage distribution of the tasks to processors and forwarding of the results to succeeding tasks. Under such a system, performance should be primarily a matter of how many processors are available. Partitioning algorithms into such tasks and finding algorithms which thrive under such partitioning are current challenges.

Parallel computations on subimages

Where each node in a system is large and fast enough to run the whole rendering process quickly, simple division of the image and distribution over a number of independent processors running the same code is a strategy worth considering. This is especially true at the moment, since (1) operating system support for many small tasks is lacking and (2) the shape models making up the scene are relatively simple, meaning that the bulk of the computation goes into scan conversion and shading.

Given a few dozen processors and a million-pixel image, each processor must produce on the order of ten thousand pixels. For optimum load-balancing, a given processor's pixels should be interleaved with the others as shown in figure 4. If the pixels are not interleaved, unevenly distributed detail will cause unevenly distributed computation. Note that computing the images shown in figures 1 and 2 would leave processors assigned to some areas of the image with little to do.

p0	p1	p2	p3	p0	p1	p2	p3
p3	p0	p1	p2	p3	p0	p1	p2
p2	p3	p0	p1	p2	p3	p0	p1
p1	p2	p3	p0	p1	p2	p3	p0
p0	p1	p2	p3	p0	p1	p2	p3
p3	p0	p1	p2	p3	p0	p1	p2
p2	p3	p0	p1	p2	p3	p0	p1
p1	p2	p3	p0	p1	p2	p3	p0

p0	p0	p0	p0	p1	p1	p1	p1
p0	p0	p0	p0	p1	p1	p1	p1
p0	p0	p0	p0	p1	p1	p1	p1
p0	p0	p0	p0	p1	p1	p1	p1
p2	p2	p2	p2	p3	p3	p3	p3
p2	p2	p2	p2	p3	p3	p3	p3
p2	p2	p2	p2	p3	p3	p3	p3
p2	p2	p2	p2	p3	p3	p3	p3

Figure 4: Interleaved (l) and non-interleaved (r) pixel processor mappings

On the other hand, efficient implementation of proper Anti-aliasing frequently involves sharing computed color values between neighboring pixels. For example, when ray-tracing, Anti-aliasing is often implemented by calculating multiple rays per pixel. The best results are obtained by a weighted average of all rays over an area which overlaps neighboring pixels by at least one-half. Therefore, each pixel must be able to use its neighbor's ray values or be stuck with doing 4 times as much work.

Also, most faster rendering algorithms make use of area coherence, reducing the calculation for each pixel to incremental changes from the shade of its neighbor. It is considerably more efficient, in such cases to scan convert 100 pixel polygons than 10 pixel polygons. Therefore, having each processor operate on a contiguous set of pixels is preferable. For larger polygons or more elaborate shading, however, this argument holds little weight.

It is possible to balance the processor loads when dividing into subimages with contiguous sets of pixels. An analysis of the scene is required to determine the average amount of work needed in each area. Having done this, the image can be adaptively divided based on the analysis. However, this imposes a limit due to the speed with which controlling processors can analyze the image and parcel out subimages.

Another approach is to divide the image into much smaller cells and parcel out cells to processors as they need work. This maintains the advantages of area coherence while balancing the load as long as the cell size is small enough. However, too small a cell size loses the advantages of coherency.

Another argument against having each processor execute the whole rendering process is that many operations will have to be replicated in each processor. Transformations and clipping to remove items falling outside the field of view are two obvious examples. In the face of much more complicated scene descriptions, parallelizing by subdividing the image looks like a bad choice. When a scene is described by millions of small details, the memory of a single processor will be inadequate to store all of it. Furthermore, since only a few pixels will be produced by each surface element (polygon, patch ,etc.), the percentage of the effort going into scan conversion and shading will be reduced. It will be necessary to carefully parcel out the work of the entire rendering pipeline.

One further complication arises out of texture mapping. Texture maps use a great deal of storage. Furthermore, a scene may require a number of different textures. Replicated storage of several texture maps in every processor's memory is at worst, impossible, at best, wasteful. Storing the texture maps centrally or in a smaller number of distributed locations brings on algorithmic complexity which was heretofore avoided and imposes a substantial interprocessor communication overhead.

In summary, parallelizing by subdividing the image makes sense where the scene description is simple, the bulk of the computation is centered on operations concerning pixels (scan conversion and shading), and only limited communication is required between neighboring pixels or subimages. It is not a good idea for very complicated imagery or cases where large amounts of shared data are used.

Currently active parallel architectures

There are now a number of proven parallel processors, some commercially available. Each has its strengths and limits as a rendering engine. The following is an attempt to survey some available machines and a few interesting research projects with respect to their potential utility for computer graphics.

Flight Simulator Architectures

Visual simulators for flight training are still available for those equipped to pay for them. They are still highly specialized machines costing millions of dollars and therefore not of great interest to the majority of the graphics community. Historically, these machines have been built with special-purpose circuitry in order to wring all the speed possible out of the hardware. This has put them in a position where they are often not able to take advantage of the most cost-effective technologies because of the extensive redesign required.

Nonetheless, these machines have been the very essence of parallelism applied to graphics. Initially they were primarily pipelined hardware units: one did coordinate transforms, the next did clipping, the next scan converted polygons, etc. As customer demands grew with the increasing sophistication of non-real-time graphics, vendors had to supply shadows, Anti-aliasing, texture, etc. In general, the techniques used for visual flight simulators are considered proprietary and there is little published about them. However, Schachter [28] did manage to get enough material together for a book on the subject.

There is a cursory description of the architecture of the CT5 from Evans and Sutherland [34]. The CT5 was an aggressively new architecture for its time. It was an early indication of a realization of the value of commodity chips and it made strategic use of frame buffer technology. Earlier designs had been based on producing the image in scanline order, requiring a fixed maximum number of edges per scan line because of the number of registers available to store them. Instead of sorting polygons to scan order, a depth-ordered sort was used for the CT5.

A frame buffer memory was enhanced with a "mask memory" which kept track of what part of a pixel had been covered by polygons written to the frame buffer. This same concept is now reaching the workstation market (see below). Polygons were converted to pixels in parallel by hardware units, each of which dealt with a fixed size array of pixels. Instead of converting directly to pixels, however, subpixels are produced. These are then summed under a weighting filter two pixels wide to give a proper anti-aliased value for the displayed pixel. The filtering operations required numerous arithmetic. The author was told at the time that the CT5 contained around 1100 multiplier chips.

The very closely proscribed purpose of visual systems for flight simulators has allowed them to be quite inflexible. They cannot be considered useful for anything for which they were not initially intended. However, more recent proposals for visual systems for flight simulators have tended to move toward greater use of commodity parts and more programmability. In fact, graphics workstations are now able to take on the task for lower-quality applications [37].

Current Graphics Workstations

Recent high-end workstations from Silicon Graphics Inc. [38] have internal architectures reminiscent of the flight simulator world. However, the higher volume in the workstation market allows them to use a much shorter product cycle and the competitive nature of the market forces them to.

Scan conversion in current Silicon Graphics workstations is done by an expanding tree of hardware. (1) A polygon processor decomposes polygons into vertically oriented trapezoids. (2) Edge processors iterate along the top and bottom edges of the trapezoids, incrementing x, y, z, red, green, blue and alpha (blending or coverage) values. (3) At each step of the incrementation top and bottom value vectors are passed to a "span" processor which expands the pixel column represented thereby. There are five span processors, used cyclically, each one handles every fifth column of pixels. (4) Each span processor drives a group of four "Image Engines™", 20 in all, each of which manages one twentieth of the pixels in the frame buffer. The Image Engines are interleaved over the image shown on the display. Each pixel can have 96 bits, 32 for each of two rgb+alpha images, 32 for depth, and 4 each for overlay and window tag.

Image engines compute simple operations, such as clear, overwrite, conditional overwrite on depth comparison, and blended overwrite on depth comparison. The last operation uses the alpha values to compute a linear blend of the source and destination colors if the source depth is on the desired side of the destination depth.

While the Image Engines write to the frame buffer's video random access memory (VRAM), the 5 processors in the display subsystem read from the VRAM to refresh the display. The display systems reads all pixel bits except for the 24 depth bits. The various overlay and window tag bits are used to make decisions such as which bank of pixels to display, whether to pass the pixels straight through to the display or to use the 12-bit input lookup tables, and how to use the lookup tables, if they are selected.

Recent enhancements to this architecture [39] extend its capabilities to texturing and also a number of non-real-time effects made possible by an accumulation buffer. Texturing is handled by the span processors which now have the additional responsibility for looking up a texture value in a 256 x 256 x 32 bit table and modifying the incrementally computed rgba vector. Apparently, texture coordinates are incremented along with the xyz and rgba vectors.

The accumulation buffer allows successive images to be summed, offering various interesting effects at slower frame rates. Apparently the blending arithmetic capabilities of the Image Engines are used to accomplish this. The accumulation technique can be used to implement anti-aliasing by making several images with slightly offset pixel positions. This makes each pixel an average of several offset samples, making it more likely that multiple surfaces in a single pixel will be properly represented. Motion blur can be implemented similarly by increasing the frame rate for an animation to, say, 150 frames per second then accumulating five frames before loading the result to a frame recorder. Depth of field, can be simulated by slightly pivoting the scene around the center of focus in several directions while accumulating, thereby blurring everything very far distant from the pivot point.

The "crayola" graphics personal supercomputer manufacturers, Stellar and Ardent (now merged as Stardent), both tried to decentralize graphics to some extent by moving part of the job into general-purpose hardware. For example, the Ardent machine moved calculations for transformations and other floating point work from a special-purpose unit back to the vector processing hardware needed for other scientific computations. That move meant that the earlier stages of the traditional graphics pipeline were then under the control of conventional software.

The Stellar machine [40] took a somewhat more extreme position. Only pixel-level graphics was centralized. Access to the frame buffer was through a set of "pixel buffer" registers, each 512 bits long (16 32-bit pixels). Values stored in one of these registers could be stored in or read from arbitrary positions in the frame buffer and combined with frame buffer values for standard raster op functions. All standard pixel-moving operations were controlled by bits in a "drawing state" register. More complicated graphics operations were done by processors not intimately connected with the frame buffer and, therefore, available for other purposes as well.

As in the Ardent, the vector processing unit was used for transformation, clipping, and lighting calculations. In addition, however, a rendering processor does scan conversion. The unique thing about the machine is that all these operations are done using the high-bandwidth primary memory system of the machine. Virtual frame buffers are allocated out of primary memory space and can therefore be any size up to 216 x 216 pixels. There is no penalty for doing graphics which isn't on its way directly to the frame buffer. This general notion meets our general notion of scalability. There is no fundamental reason not to have as many vector processors and rendering processors as one would like. All that is needed is enough bandwidth to get things to and from memory and to the frame buffer when ready for display.

AT&T Pixel Machine

AT&T's DSP32 floating point signal processing chip inspired a distributed frame buffer architecture quickly commercialized by a team at Bell Laboratories [41]. The machine consists of a front-end configurable pipeline of 9 or 18 of the processors, each independently programmed. This in turn feeds an array of 16 to 80 back-end pixel processors which are hardwired to interleaved subsets of the pixels in a frame buffer. Pixel processors may communicate with their 4 neighboring processors, allowing messages to be passed across the array.

The DSP32 is intended for small compute-intensive tasks. Therefore, the first-generation chip used in the Pixel Machine addresses only 64k bytes of memory. Each processor in the machine has a dedicated 36 kilobyte memory, 4k bytes of which is on-chip. The frame buffer is implemented as 256 x 256 32-bit words per processor. The words are interpreted by the display system as 4 bytes: red, green, blue and alpha (a blending, or coverage, value). In addition another 256 x 256 word memory supplies a 32-bit word intended as a floating point depth value for each pixel.

In typical usage, tasks are sent from the host computer to the head of the pipeline. Each processor does its part of the job and passes the results to the next processor in line. At the end of the pipeline the output is broadcast to all pixel processors. Each one then carries out the appropriate calculations on its subset of the pixels. Meanwhile the display refresh processor, called the "pixel funnel" is reading, in parallel, a pixel from each of the 256 x 256 frame buffer pieces and using them to fill a contiguous chunk of scanline. This organization enforces a rigid interleaved pixel distribution over the memory. Advantages and disadvantages of this organization were addressed above. It should be noted that, by using the interprocessor communication paths, the memory can be "de-interleaved". Of course what is seen on the display will then be incorrect, but computations which require adjacency can be carried out and the memory "re-interleaved'.

For today's imagery, this is a successful architecture. It is limited by its dedicated architecture to algorithms which can be distributed across the image pixels; but that is a large class of algorithms. The system is well-balanced for situations in which most of the processing is associated with pixels rather than surface elements. However, the system is not expandable to greater numbers of processors and the limited amount of memory per processor restricts the complexity of algorithms which can be run on it. On the other hand, code and data overlays are possible by reloading the pixel processor array from the host bus, if absolute speed is not the primary goal.

Pixel Planes 4

When one hears "massively parallel" and "computer graphics" in the same sentence the usual first reaction is to think in terms of a processor per pixel. That is a large part of the architectural notion behind the Pixel Planes project at the University of North Carolina.

Pixel Planes is an ongoing project name. Pixel Planes 4 and earlier were conceived as some dedicated memory (72 bits in PP IV) and part of a one-bit processor. The processing is done in a tree organization which calculates a linear equation as calculation moves down the tree. The parameters A, B and C are delivered to the input stream and $F(x,y) = Ax + By + C$ is computed for every pixel [42].

Clearly the whole calculation of F need not be done at every processor. For example, The calculation Ax + C is needed but once per column and By but once per row. Calculations are done bit serially. Therefore By is calculated by flowing the bits of B through circuits which add delayed copies of B to the developing sum depending on whether the corresponding bits of y are set or not. One such circuit is needed for the most significant bit of y, two circuits for the next bit, 4 for the next, etc. Finally, an adder for each scanline acts on the least significant bit of y, shifting the incoming sum to the left by delaying it for a cycle, then adding in B if y is odd and passing it through unchanged if y is even. By is then broadcast to all pixels on row y where adders sum the similarly calculated values for Ax and then add C.

Additional control paths allow the result of the linear expression to be compared with a stored value at each pixel, enabling depth comparisons. Also, a disable bit allows the pixel to ignore cycles until it is reset. With a total of 72 bits of storage for each pixel, quite a number of interesting algorithms are possible. While the initial intent was to do the scan conversion, depth comparisons and smooth shading for convex polygons, many additional schemes have been hatched. Algorithms for shadows, texture, transparency, and sphere-like shading have been proposed, as well as various methods for image processing [14].

Straightforward polygonal scenes are generated by calculating the linear equation describing each edge of a convex polygon. All pixels are enabled, then each polygon edge equation is passed to the evaluation tree. Pixels with negative results can assume that they are outside the polygon and set their disable flags until the next polygon. Each successive edge disables more pixels until, after the final edge, only the pixels inside the polygon remain active.

To ensure that only visible pixels are shaded, the equation describing the plane of the polygon is then evaluated. Each of the active pixels compares the result with its currently stored depth value and disables itself if the new value is larger. Finally, the remaining active pixels can be sent a constant value for red, green and blue, or additional plane equations can be used to calculate linearly varying shading for smoother surfaces.

Pixel Planes 5

The latest machine to carry the name Pixel Planes [43] is under construction at this writing. It represents a distinct departure from the earlier machines in that it is not a SIMD machine. It makes use of a number of SIMD arrays similar to the previous generation but each one has only 128 x 128 pixels. The previous Pixel Planes implementation was usually limited by the front-end computer. To address that problem, the new machine will have a collection of general-purpose processors for transformations, calculating expression parameters for the SIMD arrays, and other tasks. All these computing elements will be connected to a frame buffer and a host workstation on a ring network.

The SIMD rendering arrays will compute the quadratic expression, Ax + By + C + Dx2 + Exy + Fy2, in a manner similar to that described for Pixel Planes 4 above. However the quadratic function will allow expanded operations involving curved surfaces and enhanced shading. In addition the speed of the processors is improved and each processor has 208 bits of memory instead of 72. Furthermore, a "backing store" of 4k bits per pixel will be provided for quick access to larger amounts of memory.

The projects goals include (a) 1 million z-buffered, Phong-shaded, 100 pixel (average) triangles per second, (b) enough generality to support volume rendering, CSG rendering, radiosity, and other ideas yet to come, and (c) a 1280 x 1024 display driven at over 60 frames per second with an update rate greater than 20 frames per second, and (d) containable in a workstation cabinet with no unusual power requirements.

To meet those goals, the configuration under construction includes (a) 8-10 SIMD rendering arrays, (b) an 8-channel token ring with a total bandwidth of 160Mwds per second, (c) enough Intel i860 computing units to achieve an aggregate computing rate of several hundred million floating point operations per second (MFLOPS).

This project represents the mature vision of a number of researchers who have worked long and hard, plus the wisdom of every advisor who could be cornered. It is quite complicated but has a good chance to meet its goals.

Connection Machine and MasPar

The Connection Machine has a very large number of very slow bit-serial processors which must execute in lock-step [15, 44, 45]. Therefore it is at its best when the problem can be divided into at least tens of thousands of identical tasks. For complicated environments with at least tens of thousands of surface elements, it promises to be quite successful. However, so far it appears poorly matched for interactive or real-time image rendering.

Current-model Connection Machines (the CM2) come with up to 64k processors, all of which are cleverly connected by a network giving the appearance of a 16-dimensional hypercube. Therefore a message from any processor can reach any other processor in no more than 16 steps. Furthermore, the entire processor array can exchange messages in a single operation. This makes for very interesting modes of programming, since it is easy to rearrange the data in the machine between stages of a computation.

A floating point option for the Connection Machine provides a commodity floating point processor for every 32 processors. The floating point chip is time-sliced among its set of 32 processors to complete an instruction. The total computational power available with this option is considerable.

Since computation must cease while messages are routed, and routing is relatively slow, message routing is often seen by Connection Machine programmers as something to be avoided. However, by not overlapping the two functions the programming model for the machine is kept simple, one of its selling points. If routing can be restricted to a grid, then the number of routing steps may be reduced to one, considerably shortening the routing time. Since many problems can be treated this way, 2d mesh routing is a frequently-used speedup.

Two options provide increased I/O bandwidth: The DataVault and the high resolution graphics display. The DataVault attaches to an I/O controller. Each I/O controller transfers 256 bits in parallel in or out of the machine at a bandwidth of 40 megabytes per second. There can be up to 8 controllers for a maximum aggregate bandwidth of 320 megabytes per second.

The DataVault is an array of 39 disk drives, providing 32 bits in parallel with single-bit error correction. In addition, three spares are available for switching in to replace a failed drive. Using the error correction circuitry, the data on the failed drive can be reconstructed on its replacement, a process referred to as "healing." The aggregate bandwidth of the disk system matches that of the I/O port, 40 megabytes per second. A single DataVault can fill the entire memory of a 16k processor CM-2 (128 MBytes) in under 4 seconds. Up to 8 DataVaults may be attached to a system.

The high resolution graphics display circumvents the I/O controller, attaching directly to the backplane where it can command up to 128 megabytes (1 gigabit) per second. This feeds a 2 megapixel frame buffer memory with 28 planes. The frame buffer refreshes a 1280 by 1024 pixel display at 60Hz. The refresh processor also provides pan and zoom operations over the nearly two screensful of frame buffer memory.

Processors in the CM2 are grouped 16 to a chip with only a single input-output line. An I/O controller, or the display, connects to 256 of these wires, one 4k bank of processors. Therefore a bit from each processor gets out to the display in 16 cycles, the display getting 1k bits from every 16k processors each cycle. Bits can be shoved toward the display at a rate of 1 gigabit per second, or about 30 frames per second. However, that leaves no time for computing. Attempts at extremely simple dynamic display updates (e.g. computing a checkerboard) yielded update rates of several frames per second.

A competitor to the Connection Machine is now available from a company called MasPar. Using a later technology, they are able to claim better price/performance ratios and they also offer smaller machines with as little as 1k processors, designed to be used in an ordinary office environment. On the other hand, their largest configuration is only 16k processors. They claim performance up to 30k MIPS and 1.5k MFLOPS as against claims of up to 6k MIPS and 10k MFLOPS for the CM2. However, MasPar does not yet offer a display (it is listed as a "future" product in their literature). Furthermore, there is rumored to be a CM3 in the offing.

Osaka Links-1

Perhaps the first massively parallel MIMD machine used for graphics, certainly the first one devoted to graphics, was the 256-processor Links-1 built at Osaka University [46]. The machine was used to produce a great deal of animation at Osaka. It was so successful that a copy was built for a commercial animation house to use.

Each processing unit consisted of five boards: (1) a control unit consisting of a Z8001, 8k bytes of read-only memory, 256k bytes of read/write memory and extensive I/O connections for debugging, etc., (2) an arithmetic processing unit consisting of an i8086 coupled with an i8087, again with 256k bytes of memory, (3) a board containing a megabyte of memory, (4) a board devoted to I/O with a parallel port to disk, and (5) a 256k byte board strictly for exchanging data between neighboring processors.

The processing units were given tasks by a root computer. When pixels were ready to be displayed, a collection device would be notified. It then fetched the pixels over a bus structure for delivery to a display system. A videotape unit was attached to the system under control of the root computer to capture frames for animation.

The exchange memories made implementing pipelined schemes very easy. A typical use of the machine (ray tracing) involved the root computer broadcasting the code to be executed and perhaps the scene data to all the processing units. The root computer would then distribute rays to be evaluated to those processing units which were designated pipeline heads. Those units would then do their part of the calculation and pass their results on to the next unit in the pipe, presumably through an exchange memory. A pipeline might consist of (1) a process which finds all the objects pierced by a ray and sorts them in depth, (2) a process which then finds the exact point of ray intersection for relevant surfaces and verifies the closest one, (3) a shading process which takes the surface-ray intersection and calculates the shade for the corresponding pixel. The last stage in the pipeline then notified the collection device to pick up the pixel for display.

Images produced on the machine generally took on the order of a minute or more, so the update bandwidth to the display was not a problem. The Osaka group published figures indicating a 30-fold speedup over the single processor time when using 64 processors. Links-1 was certainly a monumental effort .

Meiko Computing Surface

The Computing Surface is an MIMD machine made of an array of Inmos transputers. Each computer has 4 links to other computers. A ray-tracing program often shown by Meiko runs the same program at each processor (homogeneous code). However the array allows much wider possibilities in that each processor can run different code (heterogeneous code). For example, the array could be organized into multiple interlocking pipelined data streams for transforming, shading and scan converting.

The fact that Meiko chooses to use homogeneous code points up the difficulty of optimizing use of such an array with heterogeneous code. It could be a delightful challenge, but mapping a rendering algorithm optimally to a given array size will be difficult. The data flow must be carefully mapped onto the processor interconnection since only 4 direct links to another processor are available to each processor.

Even more difficult will be the problem of designing a general scheme which will scale over different size arrays. On the other hand, assuming adequate bandwidth to the frame buffer, there is a great deal of potential. The ultimate limitation in this architecture may lie in the relatively low interconnection level.

To get a message across a large Computing Surface requires that it be passed from processor to processor in several stages. At each stage a processor must interpret the destination of the message and pass it along the next link. Meiko offers an electronically reconfigurable interconnect which allows the links to be assembled in any way which can be supported by 4 connections to each processor or less. Clearly this architecture is not optimum for large broadcast or collection scenarios or for remapping parameters randomly across the network. However for directed graph connections supporting lots of pipelined activity with modest levels of fan-in and fan-out, it works quite well.

Meiko offers a display board which consists of a transputer with 4 links to the 2d mesh, a modest-sized frame buffer and display refresh circuitry. A single display board is not sufficient to support real-time graphics of non-trivial imagery. However, two or four display boards may be connected to support larger displays, double-buffering, and higher bandwidth to the main processor array. A high-speed output bus snaking through the processor array has been proposed as a means for driving real-time graphics, an interesting possibility.

Hypercubes: Intel Scientific and NCube

Two U.S. companies (Intel Scientific, NCube) have offered MIMD systems using the n-dimensional hypercube interconnect based on the Cosmic Cube [47]. A binary n-cube has 2n processors interconnected so that any processor can route a message to any other in n steps. Similarly, each processor has n routing connections. Thus a 3-cube would be exactly equivalent to a cube. Eight processors (vertices) would each have three connections (edges) and any processor could be reached by traversing no more than three connections (figure 5). Hypercubes have the disadvantage that they are not easily extended. Increasing the size means doubling the number of processing elements and incrementing the number of connections to each one.

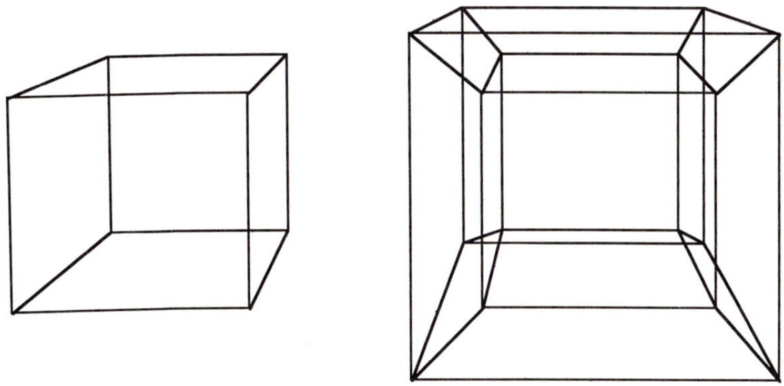

Figure 5: Hypercubes of 3 and 4 dimensions

Given routing support in the operating system, messages should be sent equally easily to any processor. However each connection involves processor involvement as in the Computing Surface. The advantage here is that the connectivity is higher and thus the maximum number of steps lower.

The NCube machine [48] was beautifully packaged. Using a custom processor with built-in serial links and memory control, a processing node consisted of only 7 chips, the processor and 6 memory chips (512kByte, error-correcting). Each node had power roughly equivalent to a VAX 11/780. The high-density processor board consisted of 64 processing nodes, an amazing amount of processing power in a small space. The maximum configuration provided a total of 1024 processors.

A graphics option for the NCube machine provided a board including 16 processing nodes each with an additional memory acting as a subset of the scanlines of a frame buffer. Display refresh circuitry maintained an 8-bit per pixel display. There was a total of 2 MBytes of display memory allowing for double buffering and frame update rates of 30 frames per second. Each processing node had links to the others so that pixels and other data could be transferred. Although a promising graphics architecture, the author has not seen it in use.

NCube now offers a second generation machine with a more powerful processor and a maximum of 8192 processors. Maximum performance is claimed to b 60k MIPS and 27k MFLOPS. Packaging has been improved by putting the processing nodes on daughter boards so that they may be replaced in the field. Daughter boards have either a processor and 10 memory chips (64 to a mother board) or a processor and 39 memory chips (32 to a mother board). Thus a processors can command from 1 to 16 MBytes.

Intel Scientific offered a first-generation hypercube based on the i80286 processor with a maximum size of 128 processing nodes. They have subsequently produced a second-generation machine, using the 80386 chip and better routing technology. Messages are now routed over the interconnection network without the processors having to be involved in directing messages across intermediate nodes. A small pile of programmable logic serves the message routing function.

An third generation machine, a project called Touchstone, is being developed currently. This machine uses the i860 processor. A Gamma prototype has been delivered using the second generation routing hardware and comprising 128 processing nodes. A Delta prototype is targeted for late 1991. It will have 2k processors and be capable of 100-150k MFLOPS. The routing system will go to a 2d mesh-style interconnect consisting of high-speed data highways with direct source to destination connections.

BBN Butterfly and Monarch

The BBN Butterfly used a multistage crossbar net (figure 6) to allow access from any of up to 256 processors (M68020+M68881 each) to any of up to 256 memory modules (4 MBytes each). Interprocessor communication was done by leaving messages in shared memory. Each processor had its own local memory which was more quickly accessible and therefore generally the source of instructions and local data.

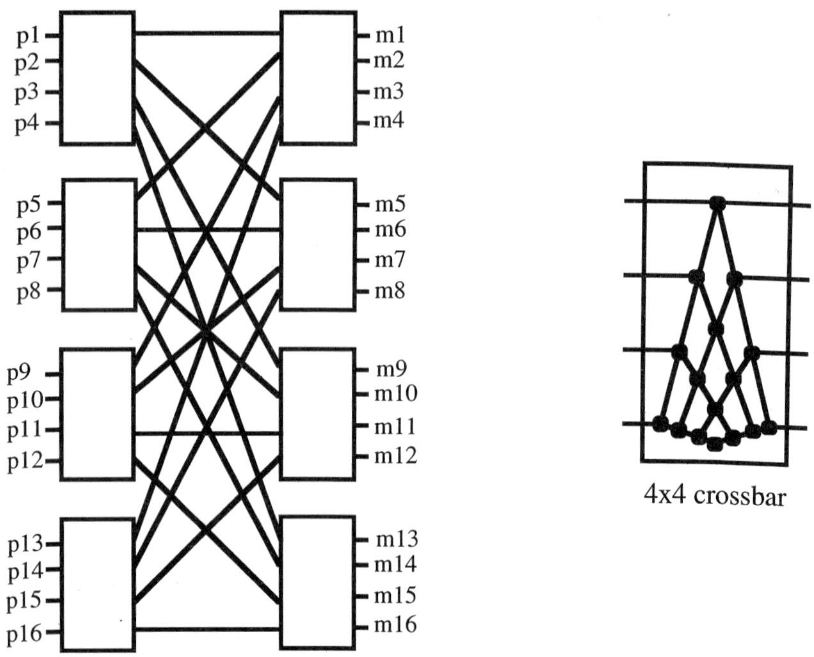

Figure 6: Multistage processor-memory network

The Butterfly, which required an additional routing stage to double the number of processors, was less easily extended than the Computing Surface, but more configurable than the hypercubes. Since any memory could be made available to any processor at the cost of a small network reconfiguration, large amounts of data could be passed very easily in a manner similar to that used in Links-1. The fact that results had to be passed through shared memory increases memory contention. However, that was claimed to have not been a serious problem [16].

The Butterfly has been supplanted by a newer machine called the TC2000. The new machine can have up to 512 processors and is based on the Motorola 88000 RISC processor. Meanwhile the BBN design team is working on a newer architecture called Monarch [49]. Monarch has lofty goals of up to 64k processors with uniform access to up to 64k MBytes of memory. A maximum configuration would be theoretically capable of 384k MIPS and 128k MFLOPS. Currently, the project is awaiting a sponsor.

Local-Area Networks

The limitation on local networks is clearly in the speed of the network. Everything must travel over the same path. Fiber optic networks promise adequate bandwidth for transmitting images in real time. A 1 gigabit/second path can handle up to 40 million 24-bit pixels per second while real-time video-resolution images require only 10 million pixels per second. Currently, the technology to get messages on and off the network is not quite up to the speeds the optical fibers can handle. However, this is an area of rapid development.

The limit on performance of such a net would then lie in the bandwidth of the frame buffer's connection to the network and on the level of interprocess communication. Subdividing the job so that each processor produces a subimage pretty much independently, the limit would appear to lie in the number of processors which can be attached to the net.

Getting back to reality, current local area networks typically offer 10 megabits per second. This will remain the major limitation for the immediate future.

In Summary

The SIMD (lock-step execution) machines such as Pixelplanes and the Connection Machine are successful partially because they are easy to program. They provide orders of magnitude more processors than other existing machines. However, they offer very little power per processor and often very low processor utilization.

Existing MIMD (independently executing) machines offer orders of magnitude greater power per processor but orders of magnitude fewer processors.

Roughly equivalent performance (within an order of magnitude) has been demonstrated for simple ray tracing using homogeneous code.

There appear to be substantial untapped possibilities for MIMD machines using heterogeneous code. However, the operating system support needed to ease the task of loading and controlling a complex program is still relatively primitive. Arranging a hundred processors and code segments by hand will not be a welcome chore. Arranging thousands by hand may be effectively impossible. Massively parallel MIMD machines will not achieve their potential until better programming environments emerge.

Conclusion

This is an exciting time for those interested in parallel algorithms. New architectures are becoming commercially available at a rapid pace and there will clearly be more innovation in the near future. Just about every machine introduced does something very well (otherwise they wouldn't have been developed). However, no parallel machine yet matches the universal applicability of the traditional Von Neumann uniprocessor.

Most newly introduced machines are too expensive for interactive (personal computer) applications. However, that will change. The basic cost of producing and packaging a substantial parallel machine could be quite low if the volume were high enough. Volume at that level, however, requires widely available parallel systems software and applications support.

As interest in these new architectures builds, the systems and applications software which can make them useful to a wider community will be developed. No one can deny the benefits of inexpensive, very powerful machines when it comes to extending the use of rich, dynamic computer imagery. Furthermore, computer imagery has a history of showing to best advantage the improvements afforded by better machinery. Hopefully, early use of computer graphics on developing technology will help accelerate the widespread acceptance of parallel hardware.

References

1. Bui-Tuong Phong, "Illumination for Computer Generated Images", Communications of the ACM, 18, 6, June 1975, pp. 311-317.

2. James F. Blinn and Martin E. Newell, "Texture and Reflection in Computer Generated Images", Communications of the ACM, 19, 10, October 1976, pp. 542-547.

3. Turner Whitted, "An Improved Illumination Model for Shaded Display", Communications of the ACM, 23, 6, June 1980, pp. 343-349.

4. Eric A. Haines and Donald P. Greenberg, "The Light Buffer: A Shadow-Testing Accelerator", IEEE Computer Graphics and Applications, 6, 9, September 1986, pp. 6-16.

5. James T. Kajiya. ``The Rendering Equation," Computer Graphics (Siggraph '86) 20 4. August 1986, pp. 143-150.

6. James T. Kajiya, Timothy L. Kay. ``Rendering Fur with Three Dimensional Textures," Computer Graphics (Siggraph '89) 23 3. August 1989, pp. 271-280.

7. Hans P. Moravec "3D Graphics and the Wave Theory", Proc. Siggraph '81, Computer Graphics, 15, 3, August 1981.

8. Peter Kochevar, PhD. Dissertation, Cornell University, Ithaca, New York, 1990.

9. John M. Snyder and Alan H. Barr, "Ray Tracing Complex Models Containing Surface Tesselations", Proc. Siggraph '87, Computer Graphics, 21, 3 (July 1987), pp. 119-128.

10. Lawrence Curran, "Surprise! Apollo Unveils a 'Desktop' Supercomputer", Electronics, 61, 5, March 3, 1988, pp. 69-70.

11. Jonah McLeod, "Ardent Launches First 'Supercomputer on a Desk'", Electronics, 61, 5, March 3, 1988, pp. 65-68.

12. C. Methias, "Stellar Personal Supercomputer", Proceedings 33rd IEEE Computer Society International Conference (Spring COMPCON 88), February 1988.

13. Rick Rashid, Chair, "Supercomputer Graphics Workstations - The Advent of the Crayola", Panel Session at IEEE 2nd Conference on Computer Workstations, Santa Clara, CA, March 1988.

14. Henry Fuchs, et al, "Fast spheres, shadows, textures, transparencies and image enhancements in Pixel-planes", Proc. Siggraph '85, Computer Graphics, 19, 3, July 1985, pp. 111-120.

15. "Connection Machine Model CM-2 Technical Summary", Tech. Report HA87-4, Thinking Machines Corp., April 1987.

16. Randall Rettberg. and Robert Thomas, "Contention is no Obstacle to Shared Memory Multiprocessing", Communications of the ACM, 29, 12, Dec 1986., pp. 1202-1212

17. James E. Thornton, "Parallel Operation in the Control Data 6600", AFIPS Proceedings of the Fall Joint Computer Conference, 26, pt. 2, 1964, pp. 33-40.

18. Richard M. Russell, "The CRAY-1 Computer System", Communications of the ACM, 21, 1, Jan 1978, pp. 63-72

19. Abhiram G. Ranade, Sandeep N. Bhatt and S. Lennart Johnsson, "The Fluent Abstract Machine", TR-573, Dept. Computer Science, Yale U., January 1988.

20. G. F. Pfister, W. C. Brantley, D. A. George, S. L. Harvey, W. J. Kleinfelder, K.P.McAuliffe, E. A. Melton, V.A. Norton, and J. Weiss, "The IBM Research Parallel Processor Prototype (RP3): Introduction and Architecture", in Proceedings of International Conference on Parallel Processing, pp. 764-771, 1985.

21. A. Gottlieb, R. Grishman, C. Kruskal, K. McAuliffe, L. Rudolph, and M. Snir. The NYU Ultracomputer - Designing an MIMD Shared Memory Parallel Computer, IEEE Transactions on Computers, C-32:175-189, February 1983.

22. M. J. Flynn, "Very High-Speed Computing Systems", Proc. of the IEEE, 54, 1966, pp. 1901-1909.

23. D. L. Slotnick, "The Fastest Computer", Scientific American, Feb. 1971, pp. 76-87.

24. Kenneth E. Batcher, Design of a massively parallel processor, IEEE Trans. on Computers, C-29, 9 (Sept. 1980), pp. 836-840

25. Franklin C. Crow, Gary Demos, Jim Hardy, John McLaughlin, and Karl Sims, "3D Image Synthesis on the Connection Machine", In: (P. M. Dew, R. A. Earnshaw, T. R. Heywood Eds.) Parallel Processing for Computer Vision and Display, Addison-Wesley, 1989, pp. 254-269

26. Midnight Movie Group (contact: Michael Sciulli), Apollo Computer Co., "Fair Play", ACM Siggraph '87 Film and Video Show, July 1987.

27. Michael R. Kaplan and Donald P. Greenberg, Parallel Processing Techniques for Hidden Surface Removal, Proc. Siggraph '79, Computer Graphics, 13, 2, August 1979, pp. 300-307.

28. Bruce J. Schachter, Computer Image Generation, John Wiley & Sons, New York, 1983.

29. Franklin C. Crow, "Experiences in Distributed Execution: A Report on Work in Progress", ACM Siggraph '86 Course Notes #15, August 1986.

30. Rodney S. Rougelot, "The General Electric Computer Color TV Display", in M. Faiman and J. Nievergelt, Eds., Pertinent Concepts in Computer Graphics, University of Illinois Press, Urbana, 1969.

31. Ivan E. Sutherland, Robert F. Sproull, and Robert A. Schumaker, A Characterization of Ten Hidden-Surface Algorithms, Computing Surveys, 6, 1, March 1974, pp. 1-55

32. Bart Locanthi, Object-Oriented Raster Displays, Proc. Caltech Conference on Very Large Scale Integration, January 1979, pp. 215-225.

33. Daniel S. Whelan, A Rectangular Area Filling Display Architecture, Proc. Siggraph '82, Computer Graphics, 16, 3, July 1982, pp. 147-154.

34. R. A. Schumaker, "A New Visual System Architecture", Proceedings, 2nd Interservice/Industry Training Equipment Conference, 1980, pp. 94-101.

35. James H. Clark, "The Geometry Engine: A VLSI Geometry System for Graphics", Proc. Siggraph '82, Computer Graphics, 16, 3, July 1982, pp. 127-133.

36. John G. Torborg, "A parallel Processor Architecture for Graphics Arithmetic Operations", Proc. Siggraph '87, Computer Graphics, 21, 3 (July 1987), pp. 197-204.

37. Michael J. Zyda, Robert B. McGhee, Ron S. Ross, Douglas B. Smith, and Dale G. Streyle, "Flight Simulators for Under $100,000", IEEE Computer Graphics and Applications, 6, 1, January 1988, pp. 19-27.

38. Kurt Akeley and Tom Jermoluk, "High-Performance Polygon Rendering", Proc. Siggraph '88, Computer Graphics, 22, 4, August 1988, pp. 239-246.

39. Paul Haeberli and Kurt Akeley, "The Accumulation Buffer: Hardware Support for High-Quality Rendering", Proc. Siggraph '90, Computer Graphics, 24, 3, August 1990.

40. Brian Apgar, Bret Bersack, and Abraham Mammen, "A Display System for the Stellar™ Graphics Supercomputer Model GS1000™", Proc. Siggraph '88, Computer Graphics, 22, 4, (August 1988), pp. 255-262.

41. Michael Potmesil and Eric M. Hoffert, "The Pixel Machine: A Parallel Image Computer", Proc. Siggraph '89, Computer Graphics, 23, 3 (August 1989), pp. 69-78.

42. Henry Fuchs, et al, "Developing PixelPlanes: A Smart Memory-Based Raster Graphics System", Proc. Conf. on Advanced Research in VLSI, 1982, pp. 137-146 (also in: Selected Reprints on VLSI Technologies and Computer Graphics, (H. Fuchs, Ed.)., IEEE Computer Society Press. 1983, pp 371-380).

43. Henry Fuchs, et al, "Pixel Planes 5: A Heterogeneous Multiprocessor Graphics System Using Processor Enhanced Memories", Proc. Siggraph '89, Computer Graphics, 23, 3, July 1989, pp. 79-88.

44. W. Daniel Hillis, The Connection Machine, The MIT Press, 1985.

45. W. Daniel Hillis, and Guy L. Steele, Jr., Data parallel algorithms, Communications of the ACM, 29, 12, December 1986, pp. 1170-1183

46. Hitoshi Nishimura, Hiroshi Ohno, Toru Kawata, Isao Shirakawa, and Koichi Omura, "Links-1: A Parallel Pipelined Multimicrocomputer for Image Creation", Proc. Ninth Symposium on Computer Architecture, ComputerArchitecture News, 11, 3, June 1983, pp. 387-394.

47. Charles L. Seitz, "The Cosmic Cube", Communications of the ACM, 28, 1, January 1985, pp. 22-33.

48. John P. Hayes, Trevor Mudge, Quentin F. Scott, Stephen Colley, and John Palmer, "A Microprocessor-based Hypercube Supercomputer", IEEE Micro, 6, 5, October 1986, pp. 6-17.

49. Randall Rettberg. William R. Crowther, Phillip P Carvey, and Raymond S. Tomlinson, "The Monarch Parallel Processor Hardware Design", IEEE Computer, 23, 4, April 1990., pp. 18-3

Computer Vision

T.S. Huang

1. Introduction

Researchers in computer vision aim to make computers to do some of the things which the human visual system can do. Perhaps the major thing is the understanding of three-dimensional (3D) time-varying scenes. There are many applications: Inspection and quality control, monitoring and surveillance, navigation of mobile robots, etc. It is fair to say that computer scene understanding is still in a primitive state; most problems are unsolved. This makes computer vision a very challenging field to work in.

Researchers with an artificial intelligence or psychology background are very much interested in the interrelationship between computer vision and human vision, while researchers with an engineering background are mainly interested in getting the job done. This paper is written from the engineering viewpoint. Furthermore, the several detailed examples we shall give are the work of our own lab. Thus, the reader is forewarned that this is a rather biased account of computer vision.

From an engineering viewpoint, the goal of computer vision is to build automated systems capable of analyzing and understanding 3D and possibly time-varying scenes. The input to such systems are typically two-dimensional (2D) images taken for example by television cameras, although sometimes direct range sensors are also used. There are three levels of tasks in computer vision systems. (i) Level 1 (lowest): Reconstruction—to recover 3D information, both geometrical (shape) and photometric (texture), from the sensed data. (ii) Level 2 (middle): Recognition—to detect and identify objects. (iii) Level 3 (highest): Understanding—to figure out what is going on in the (possibly time-varying) scene. In this paper, we shall touch on all these three levels.

The organization of this paper is as follows. Section 2 discusses object representation which serves as a prelude to section 3 on reconstruction, where various methods are briefly reviewed. Section 4 gives three examples of object recognition. The major aspects of time-varying scene analysis and understanding are discussed in section 5, followed by a detailed example in section 6.

It is to be noted that one common theme in many computer vision algorithms is matching. Throughout this paper, a number of matching techniques will be described.

2. Representation

Representation is a central issue in object recognition and scene understanding. In this section, we shall concentrate on the representation of 3D geometry (3D shape of an object, spatial relationship between objects), and only mention very briefly the representation of the photometric aspects (texture) of objects. There are two main classes of 3D shape representation methods: surface and volume. The spatial relationships between objects can be represented by relational graphs (structures).

The desirable features of a representation are: It should be easy to construct (from sensed data), easy to update, easy to utilize (for particular applications such as object recognition), and efficient to store.

2.1 Surface Representation

In the simplest case, the surface of the object is approximated by planar patches. Then the representation can be stored as: A list of face labels, a list of edge labels, a list of vertex labels, pointers from faces to edges, and pointers from edges to vertices. The faces and edges are characterized by equations, and the vertices by their 3D coordinates, all with respect to some reference coordinate system.

For better approximations, curved patches can be used. Then the equations for the patches and the bounding edges are more complicated.

2.2 Volume Representation

Assume an object is contained in a cubic universe. Each of the three sides of the cube is quantized to N intervals. Then the cube contains N^3 cells (called voxels). We put a "1" in a cell if it is inside the object, and "0" otherwise. Then, a straightforward representation of the object is the 3D array of N^3 bits. This brute-force method is too inefficient in terms of storage.

A more efficient representation is the octree. Let $N = 2^n$. The octree representation is obtained by recursively subdividing the cubic space into octants. A $2^d \times 2^d \times 2^d$, $1 \leq d \leq n$, octant is divided into eight $2^{d-1} \times 2^{d-1} \times 2^{d-1}$ smaller octants if the unit cubes contained in the octant are not entirely 1's (BLACK) or entirely 0's (WHITE). The same process continues recursively until the octant (suboctant) contains unit cubes of a single value. Each octant generated in the process is assigned a label, from 0 to 7. *Figure 1* shows a common way of labeling the octants.

The results of the recursive subdivision process is represented by a tree of degree 8 whose nodes are either leaves or have eight children. Thus, the tree is called an octree. Each node of the tree is given the same label as that assigned to its corresponding octant. The root node of the resulting tree represents the entire space. Leaf nodes represent octants containing unit cubes of the same value and are marked BLACK or WHITE accordingly, and nonleaf nodes are called internal nodes and are marked GRAY. The resulting octree is a condensed tree. Normally, WHITE nodes of the octree are omitted for compactness. *Figure 2* contains an example object and its corresponding octree representation. For a survey of techniques for the construction and manipulation of octrees, see [1].

2.3 Generalized Cylinders [2]

A cylinder is the volume swept out by translating an arbitrary cross-section along a straight line. This may be generalized by sweeping along a space curve (called the spine) instead of a straight line, and by changing the cross-section (according to some "sweeping function") as it is swept. The resulting volume, called a generalized cylinder, is characterized by the spine and the sweeping function.

2.4 Constructive Solid Geometry [3]

The constructive solid geometry (CSG) representation of an object is a binary tree whose nonterminal nodes represent set operators (union, difference, intersection, and complement) and whose terminal nodes represent primitive solids. One can think of the object as a number of primitive solids grouped together by the set operations. The primitive solids of CSG are typically simple convex objects such as blocks, cylinders, cones, and spheres.

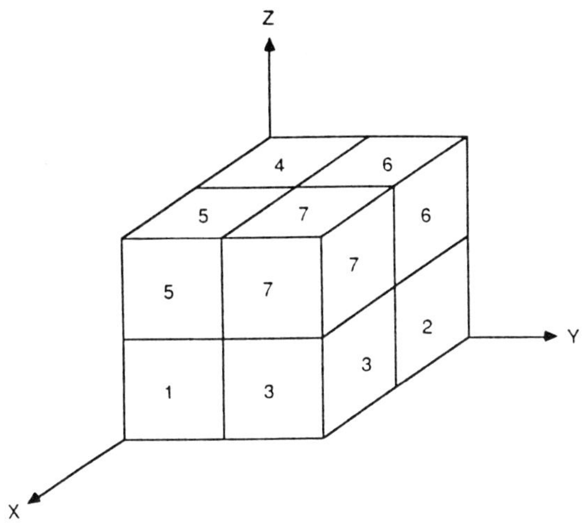

Fig. 1. Labels of the octants of a cube (octant 0 not shown).

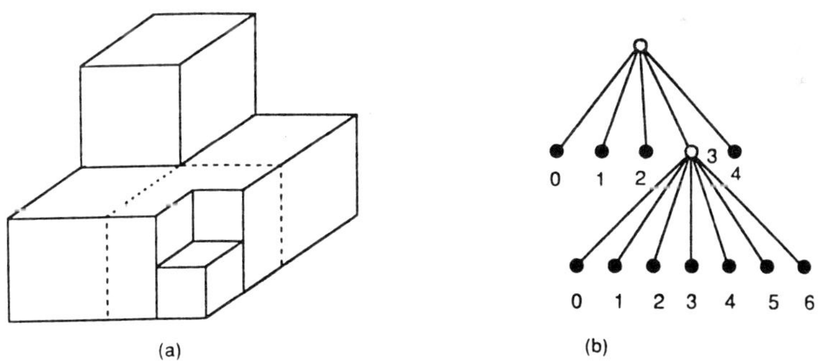

Fig. 2. (a) An example object, and (b) its octree representation.

2.5 Relational Structures [4]

To describe the relationships (spatial or otherwise) between objects, a relational graph is often used. The nodes of the graph represent the objects, and the arcs or branches linking the nodes represent relationships. For example, the relationships can be: To the right of, behind, etc. (from a particular viewpoint). More generally, one can allow relationships among more than two objects. E.g. A and B are symmetrical with respect to C.

2.6 Reflectance Function

Most work on object representation in computer vision has been on the geometrical aspects. Relatively little has been done on the photometric aspects of object representation. Horn was among the first to investigate the photometric aspects of computer vision in his work on shape from shading [5]. Generally, each point on the object surface is characterized by a reflectance function, $r(\Theta_1, \Theta_2, \Phi_1, \Phi_2, \lambda)$, where (Θ_1, Θ_2) specifies the direction of the incident light with respect to the surface normal, (Φ_1, Φ_2) specifies the viewing direction, and λ is the wavelength of the illumination. As one can see, there are too many variables to do analysis with, unless simplifying assumptions (such as the surface is Lambertian) can be made.

More recently, interesting work has been done on color [6] and polarization [7].

3. Reconstruction

By reconstruction, we mean the determination of the 3D coordinates of points on the object surface and some of the reflectance properties. Again, most work in computer vision has been on the geometrical aspects.

3.1 Laser Range Finders

This is the most direct way of obtaining ranges of points on an object surface. A laser beam hits a surface point, and the reflected light is caught by a sensor. The range of the point is determined by either the time-of-flight or the phase shift of the beam. By scanning the laser beam, one can obtain a range map.

A recent example is the ERIM laser scanner which uses the phase-shift method. It gives a 256 x 256 range map as well as several bands of intensity images in about 2 seconds. The maximum range is about 32 feet, and the accuracy about ± 0.5 feet.

3.2 Structured Illumination [8]

The 3D shape of an object surface can be deterrmined from a single 2D image of it, if a regular structure (such as a line array or a square grid) is projected on it. For example, if a square grid is projected on a plane (in 3D), then the images of the grid lines are still straight lines, and from the skewness of the grid, one can determine the orientation of the plane.

3.3 Laser Illuminated Triangulation

The method involves a laser and a camera. The geometry of the setup is known. The laser beam illuminates a spot on the object surface. An image of the surface is taken, and the 2D coordinates of the image of the spot are measured. Then, by triangulation, the 3D coordinates of the point are determined. By changing the direction of the laser beam, one can obtain 3D coordinates of different points on the surface.

3.4 Passive Stereo

This is the classical technique of photogrammetry [9]. While the methods in sections 3.1–3.3 are "active" in the sense that the illumination is controlled, this method is "passive"—the illumination is natural. Two images of an object are taken from different viewpoints. Then: (i) corresponding points are found between the two images. (ii) for each corresponding pair, the 3D coordinates of the point are determined by triangulation. The first step, that of finding correspondences, is extremely difficult. Typically, for each point in one of the images, one aims to find the corresponding point in the other image. This is usually done by some sort of cross-correlation. In computer vision, seminal work in stereo was done by Marr [10].

Usually, it is not possible to find point correspondences in some regions of the images (e.g., where the intensity is almost uniform). Thus, 3D surface fitting (interpolation) is necessary [11].

3.5 Shape from X

The most difficult problem in reconstruction is to extract 3D information of an object from a single 2D image. The pioneering work is that of Horn [5], who investigated the problem of shape from shading, i.e., to extract surface orientation information of an object from a 2D intensity image of it. Equations can be written, relating the normal direction at a 3D surface point and the observed intensity of the corresponding image point, which involve the reflectance function at the 3D point and the illumination parameters. The difficulty is that there are too many unknown variables, making the problem basically underdetermined.

Witkin [12] was the first to investigate the recovery of surface orientation from texture. If we assume that the surface texture is actually isotropic in 3D, then from the anisotropicity of the observed image texture, the surface orientation in 3D may be deduced. For example, we can estimate the orientation of a planar lawn relative to the camera geometry from the local density variation of the grass in the image.

Kanade [13] was the first to investigate the recovery of surface orientation from 2D shapes in the image. If we can assume that the 3D object has certain symmetry, then surface orientation may be recovered from the skew symmetry of the image. For example, if we can assume that an observed 2D ellipse is the perspective view of a circle in 3D, then the orientation of the circle may be determined.

More recently, interesting work has been done using color [6] and polarization [7].

4. Object Recognition

The problem is to recognize a 3D object from one (or sometimes several) 2D views of it. By recognition, one usually means to classify the object into one of a set of prescribed classes. In an easy case, all objects belonging to the same class look almost exactly the same, and the number of classes is small. In a harder case, the number of classes is very large—e.g., in fingerprint identification. In the hardest case, the classes are generic, i.e., objects in the same class may look very different—e.g., to recognize a "chair."

The main approach to recognition of a 3D object from a single 2D view is as follows. We have a 3D model for each class. The observed 2D view of the unknown object is compared with many 2D views generated from the 3D models of candidate classes. The best match determines the class. In practice, a major problem is how to reduce the search space (the number of candidate classes, and the number of 2D views from each 3D model) by using a priori information, heuristics, etc. For example, in vehicle classification, to detect and count the number of wheels can help to limit the number of candidate classes. Thus, if there are more than two wheels in the side view of a vehicle, it cannot be a sedan.

A general way of reducing the number of 2D views of a 3D model (which one has to generate and compare with the 2D view of the unknown object) is the concept of aspect graph [14,15,16]. An aspect graph enumerates all possible "qualitative" aspects an object may assume. We partition the viewing space into regions such that viewpoints within the same region give 2D views of the object which are "qualitatively" similar. A change in "quality" occurs only when the viewpoint crosses a region boundary. Thus, it is necessary to compare the 2D view of the unknown object with only one typical 2D view from each region. Of course, for a given application one has to define precisely what is meant by "quality." And the definition of quality will obviously influence the matching criterion. E.g., if the 3D object is a polyhedron, then the "quality" of a 2D view could be the numbers of faces, edges, and vertices.

We shall now give three examples of object recognition systems.

4.1 Airplane Recognition Using Silhouettes [17]

The problem is to classify an unknown 3D airplane into one of six possible classes, based on a single 2D silhouette of the airplane obtained from an unknown view angle. *Fig. 3* shows four such 2D silhouettes. The approach is a brute-force one, without the use of aspect graphs.

The system stores 143 2D views (silhouettes) of each of the six 3D airplanes. These are generated from CAD models of the airplanes. One set of these 143 silhouettes is shown in *Fig. 4*. The 2d silhouette of the unknown airplane is compared with each of the 6×143 silhouettes. The comparison is done by calculating the squared-error between the Fourier series coefficient sets of the silhouettes. Note that when the match is found, we also get the orientation of the airplane. Extensive experiments showed that a recognition accuracy of above 95% could be achieved.

4.2 Airplane Recognition Using Relational Graphs [18]

The experiment to be described is on the recognition of airplanes from a top view. Thus it is a 2D object recognition problem. However, the method can be extended to 3D, as we shall discuss later. The problem is to detect airplanes from an aerial photograph of an airfield. There are only two classes: airplanes, and nonairplanes. However, the class of airplanes is generic, since we are not looking for any particular airplane type (e.g., Boeing 747).

Because of the generic nature of the airplane class, a flexible model is needed. We use the relational graph approach. The top view of an airplane is characterized by the relationships between its 8 main edge segments. Three relations are used *(Fig. 5)*: Antiparallel, collinear, and adjacent. Note that an edge element has a sense attached to it. The convention is that if we look along the direction of the arrow, the right side has higher intensity than the left in the intensity image of the airplane. In *Fig. 6*, we have the 8 edge segments of our generic airplane and its relational graph model. Each node represents one of the edge segments.

The input to the system is an aerial photo which may or may not contain airplanes. The first step is to extract long straight edge segments. For a particular input image, *Fig. 7* shows these edge elements. The second step is to construct a relational graph for this edge map by examing for each edge pair whether one or more of the 3 relations

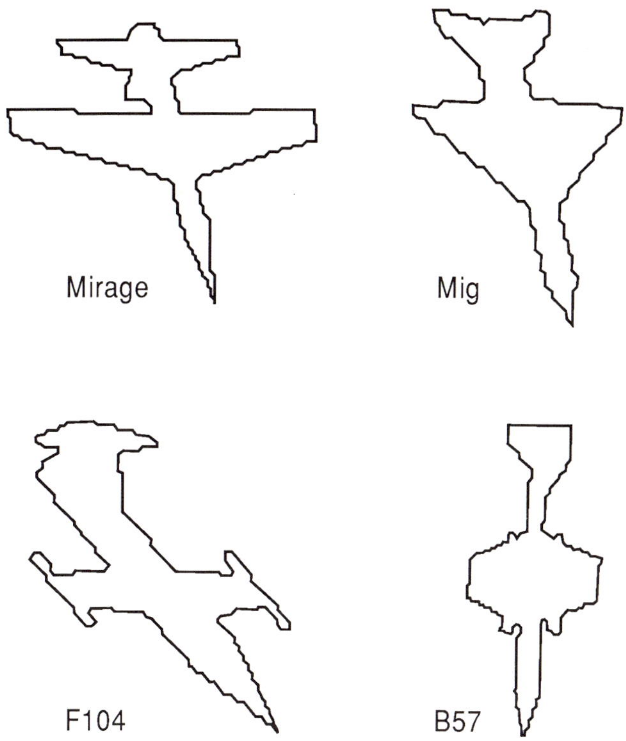

Fig. 3. Typical 2D silhouettes of 3D airplanes.

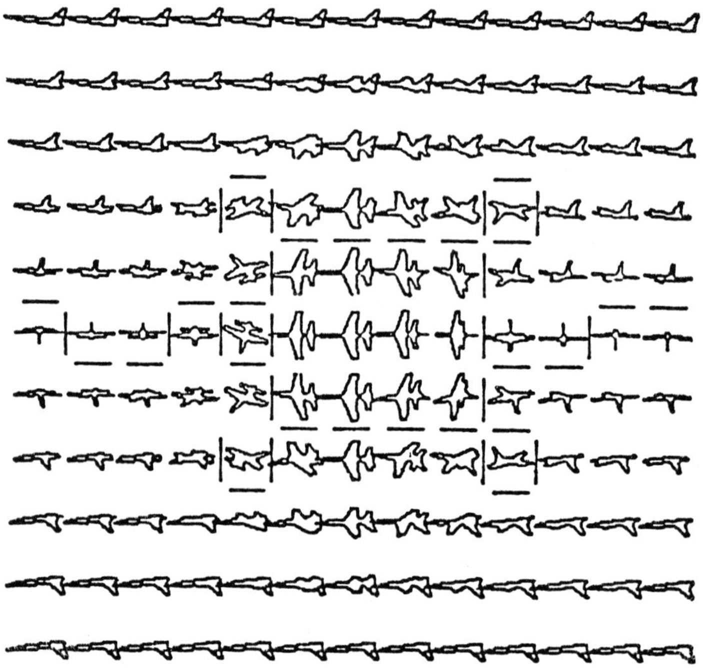

Fig. 4. A dictionary of 2D silhouettes of a 3D airplane from different viewpoints.

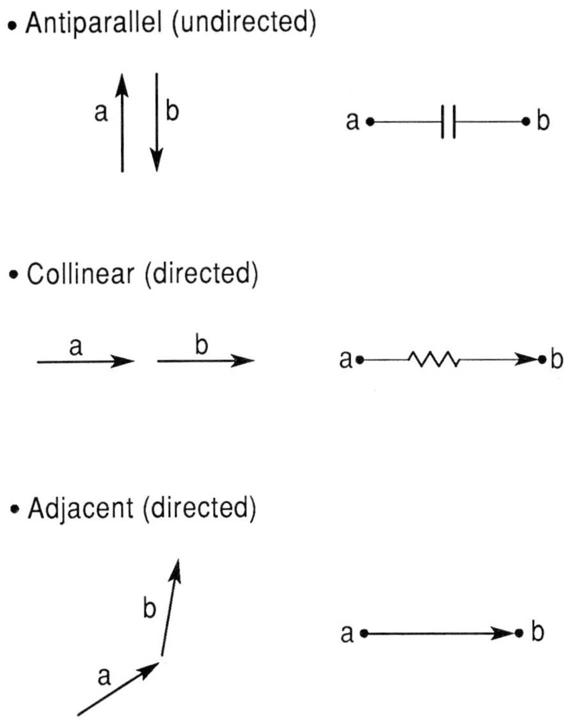

Fig. 5. Three types of relations.

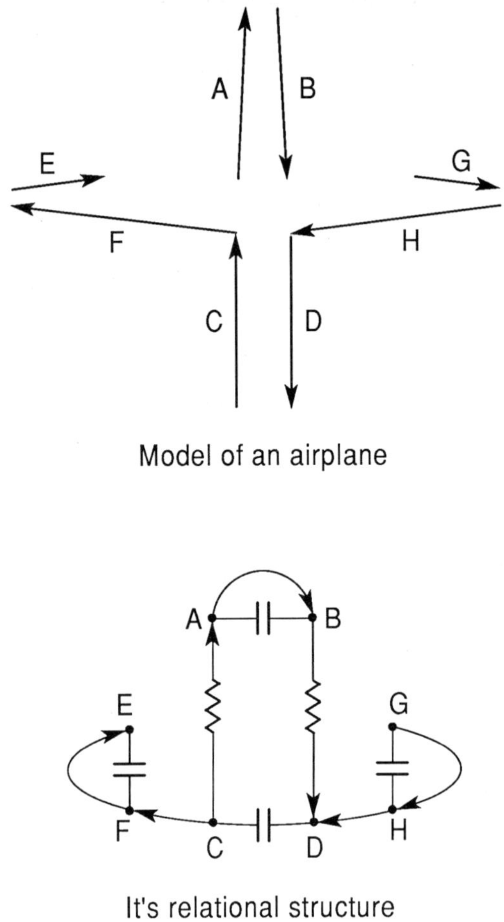

Fig. 6. Edge-model for a generic airplane and its relational graph.

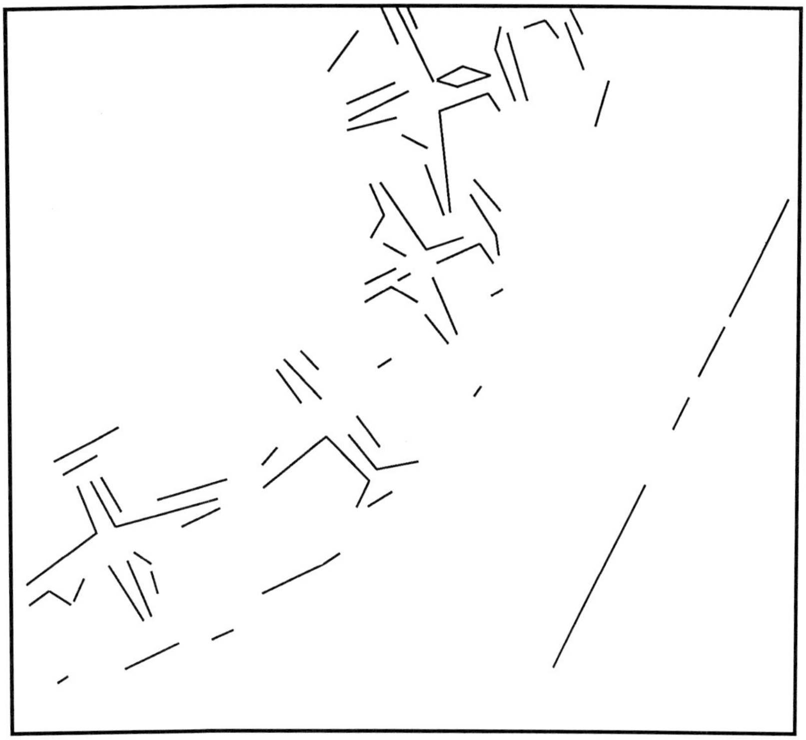

Fig. 7. Significant edge segments in an aerial image.

hold. Finally, we do a maximal matching between this large relational graph and the small model graph. In this particular example, all four airplanes are detected.

The method described above can be extended to 3D object recognition by using aspect graphs. Take the problem of 3D airplane recognition. We need to divide the viewing space into regions such that within each region, a single relational graph model suffices. We will probably use more than three relations. Further work needs to be done to find efficient ways of obtaining the aspect graph.

4.3 ACRONYM [19]

The most extensive work on recognition of 3D objects from 2D images is embodied in the ACRONYM system. The system uses a prediction-verification process that uses the image to make predictions about the object and verifies that the image could in fact have been arisen from an object that satisfies the resulting set of constraints. Generalized cylinders are use for 3D object models.

5. Dynamic Scene Analysis and Understanding

A major problem in computer vision is the analysis and understanding of dynamic scenes [20]. The goal is to build an autonomous system which will look at a dynamic scene and come up with a description of the unfolding events. Such a system can conveniently be thought of as comprising two modules. The first module extracts from the observed raw data (e.g., an image sequence taken by a TV camera), low and intermediate level features such as 3D shapes and motion parameters of objects in the scene. Then the second module arrives at a symbolic description of the dynamic scene by high- level reasoning based on the low/intermediate level features as well as other a priori information about the scene.

In Section 5.1, we give some examples of dynamic scene analysis systems and point out that one of the major obstacles in constructing such a system lies in the first module. Specifically, the problem of estimating 3D motion and structure remains a challenge to researchers in computer vision.

In Section 5.2, we give an overview of one of the approaches to motion estimation—using feature correspondences, and summarize some of the difficulties.

5.1 Event Description and Identification

For truly 3D scenes a complete dynamic scene-analysis system is hard to construct. The main problem is that the low/intermediate-level features the high-level module needs for its reasoning may be very difficult, if not impossible, to extract from the raw data. In fact, the low/intermediate-level module will probably need help from high-level reasoning to improve its performance. Some impressive examples of high-level modules are [21,22,23]. Reference [22] describes a system that observes traffic scenes and produces natural-language descriptions of them. In particular, the system will recognize and verbalize interesting occurrences (events) in the scene—e.g., one car is overtaking another. Reference [23] describes an expert system for event identification. The applications considered are simple assembly-line tasks. However, in both systems the low/intermediate-level features needed by the high-level modules are furnished at least in part by human operators.

To convey the flavor of typical high-level modules, the results in [23] will now be briefly described.

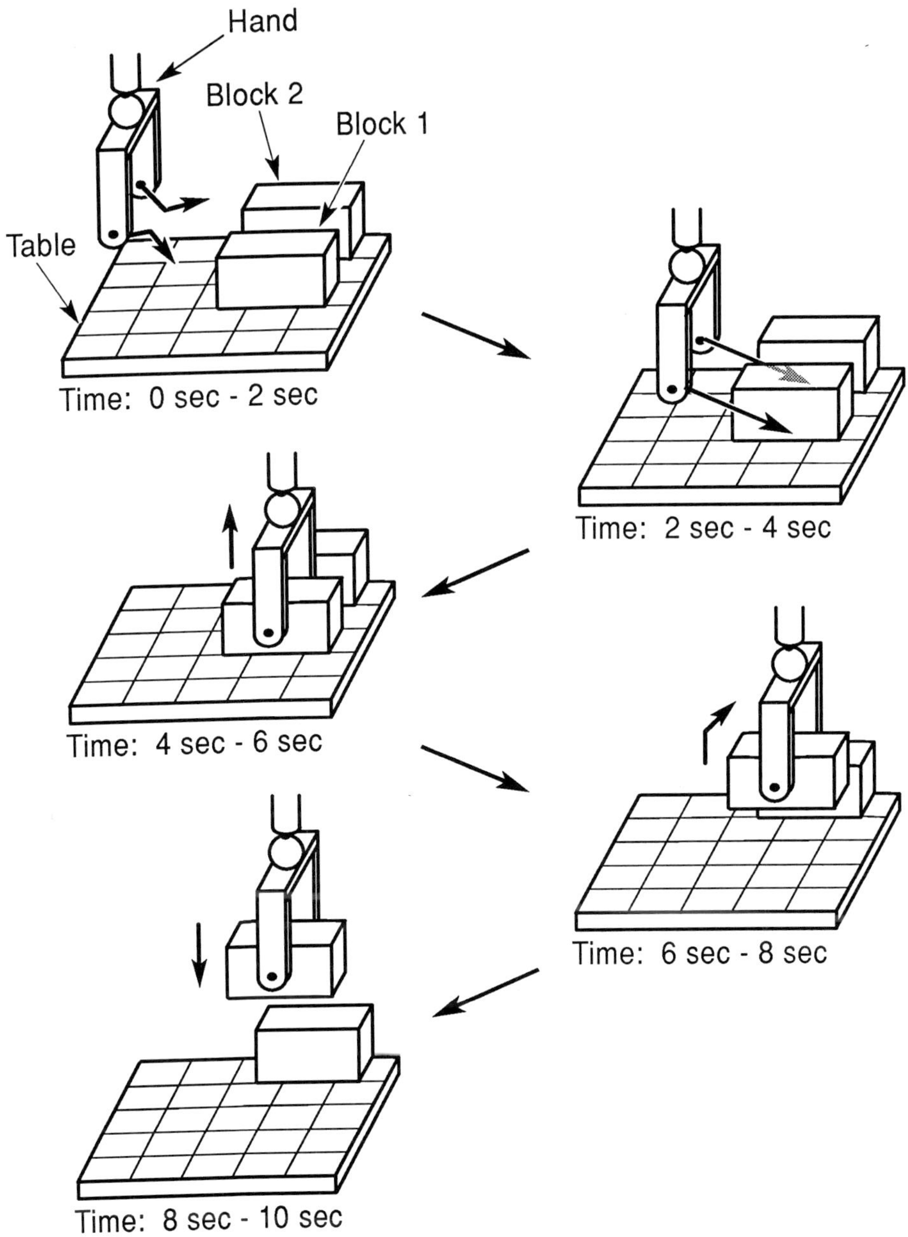

Fig. 8. Sequence of actions for the example.

This work presents a formal mechanism for specifying the steady and time-varying characteristics of a large class of physical events. The rules which embody these specifications are then used to identify occurrences of particular events in a changing scene, starting from low-level data such as the positions and orientations of objects as they vary over time. In this manner, a high-level description of changes occurring in a scene is formed.

This mechanism has been implemented as a package which runs in the Interlisp environment on a VAX 11/780 computer. A knowledge base has been constructed for the application of this system in a simplified assembly-line context, including robot arms, bolts, nuts and other simple objects, and events such as transportation of objects in different manners, stacking objects, fastening objects together with bolts, etc.

The process of recognizing physical events occurs at such a low level in humans that much of its inherent complexity in hidden from view. When this process is duplicated computationally, this complexity becomes apparent. Some of the finer points which must be dealt with include the following:

(a) Time-related parts of an event. Many events contain parts or sub-events which may or may not be required to fit together in a particular manner in time. All instances of these events must nevertheless be recognized.
(b) Parts of wholes. If a hand is seen to be grasping an object, for example, it is necessary to have some idea of whether or not that object is part of a larger object. If so, then the event should be taken in a more general sense of the hand grasping the larger object, and so forth.
(c) Avoiding redundancy. If a simple event is found to occur (for example, a hand carrying an object) then if later a higher level event is found which contains the first event as a component (for example, stacking that object on another object) the first event should be excluded from a final description of changes in the scene, as a statement that the latter event has occurred is sufficient.

Figure 8 illustrates the sequence of actions for a particular example involving a robot arm and two blocks. The robot hand first makes a false grasping motion at BLOCK1 followed by an actual grasping of the object, a lifting of the object and a setting down of the object on top of BLOCK2.

Input to the implemented system, however, is provided at a level which is considerably less refined than the verbal description above. The input file contains only data which falls into one of the following three categories.

(1) Static attributes and relationships of objects. This includes dimensions of objects and relationships of parts of an object to the whole (e.g. the parts of the robot hand). All composite objects are represented using constructive geometry based on simple objects such as spheres, cylinders and blocks.
(2) Time-varying positions and orientations of objects. These are input as graphs of values over time. For positions, each object is traced along the "world" coordinate axes "X," "Y," and "Z." For orientations, each object is associated with zero to three "object axes." Spheres have no object axes, cylinders have one. Components relating vectors along these axes to the world axes "X," "Y" and "Z," comprise the input for orientations of objects.
(3) Simple spatial relationships of the objects For this example these include notions of "betweenness" (one object directly between two others), touching (or more precisely, very close proximity), and support (when one object touches a part of another which faces downwards).

Given input of the form described above, the resulting description of changes occurring in the scene as produced by the implemented package is as follows:

(HAND1 IS PICKING BLOCK1 UP FROM TIME 0 TO TIME 6)
(HAND1 IS GRASPING BLOCK1 FROM TIME 2 TO TIME 4)
(HAND1 IS HOLDING BLOCK1 FROM TIME 4 TO TIME 6)
(HAND1 IS STACKING BLOCK1 ON BLOCK2 FROM TIME 6 TO TIME 9)
(HAND1 IS HOLDING BLOCK1 FROM TIME 9 TO TIME 10)

(This high-level description should be contrasted with the low-level description in the input file, which is some 550 lines long.)

A number of observations can be made about this resultant description. First of all, the implemented package has correctly identified the major events occurring in the example. Of equal importance however, it has also attached reasonable boundaries in time to these events. Secondly, although the system must identify many lower-level events in the course of finding the high-level events, only the top-most events are included in the final description. For instance, HAND1 is holding BLOCK1 from time 4 to time 10, but for those times at which a higher-level event occurs which explains the holding (e.g. stacking), the event of holding is not mentioned.

Without going into details, we mention very briefly that the implemented system can be seen as the integration of three parts: a knowledge base of rules for determining the occurrences of particular events, an interpreter for evaluating these rules, and a supervisory program which forms a high-level description of changes in a scene from the input low-level description by a process of successive refinement.

It should be emphasized that this work does not consider the very difficult problem of how to extract the input information needed for the implemented system from raw image data.

5.2 Motion Estimation

5.2.1 Two-View Motion Estimation

Generally, a scene contains a number of objects moving differently. To detect and tract these objects and to estimate and predict the motion of each of them are formidable tasks indeed. In fact, to date even the following simplest motion estimation problem has not been solved satisfactorily: Given two time-sequential images (perspective views) of a single rigid object, estimate its equivalent rotation and translation from the first time instant to the second. In this section, we shall review results pertaining to this "two-view" motion estimation problem, and point out some of the difficulties.

Several approaches to motion estimation have been proposed and studied [24]. Here we shall look at only one of them: the approach of using feature correspondences. We first state the problem more precisely.

The basic geometry of the problem is sketched in *Fig. 9*. The object- space coordinates are denoted by lowercase letters, and the image-space coordinates by uppercase letters. Let the two perspective views (central projections) be taken at t_1 and t_2, respectively, and $t_1 < t_2$. The coordinates at t_2 are primed, and the coordinates at t_1 are unprimed. Specifically, consider a particular physical point on the surface of a rigid body in the scene. Let (x,y,z) be the object-space coordinates of P at time t_1, (x', y', z') the object-space coordinates of P at time t_2, (X,Y) the image-space coordinates of P at time t_1, (X', Y') the image-space coordinates of P at time t_2, and

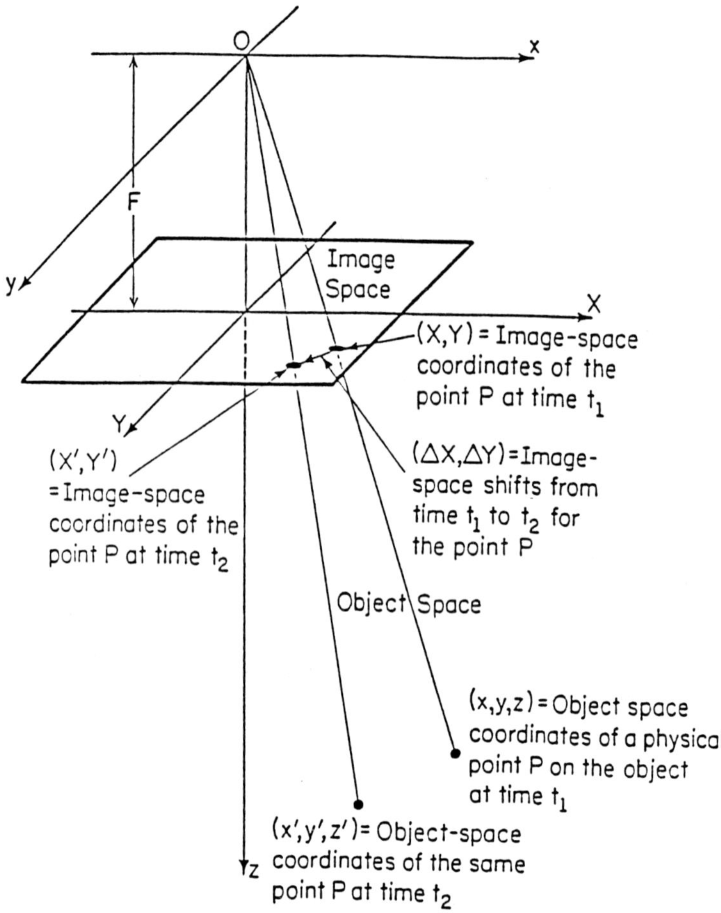

Fig. 9. Basic imaging geometry for motion analysis.

$$\Delta X \triangleq X' - X, \ \Delta Y \triangleq Y' - Y \tag{1}$$

the image-space shifts (or displacements) of P from t_1 to t_2.

It is well known from kinematics that the object coordinates of P at time instants t_1 and t_2 are related by

$$\begin{bmatrix} x' \\ y' \\ z' \end{bmatrix} = R \begin{bmatrix} x \\ y \\ z \end{bmatrix} + T = \begin{bmatrix} r_{11} & r_{12} & r_{13} \\ r_{21} & r_{22} & r_{23} \\ r_{31} & r_{32} & r_{33} \end{bmatrix} \begin{bmatrix} x \\ y \\ z \end{bmatrix} + \begin{bmatrix} \Delta x \\ \Delta y \\ \Delta z \end{bmatrix} \tag{2}$$

where R represents a rotation and T a translation. To make the representation unique the rotation is specified around an axis passing through the origin of our coordinate system. Let $n = (n_1, n_2, n_3)$ be a unit vector along the axis of rotation, and Θ be the angle of rotation from t_1 to t_2. Then the elements of R can be expressed in terms of n_1, n_2, n_3, and Θ. Since $n_1^2 + n_2^2 + n_3^2 = 1$, there are six motion parameters we have to determine: n_1, n_2, Θ, Δx, Δy, Δz. However, from the two perspective views, it is impossible to determine the magnitude of the translation, i.e., if the object size and position as well as the translation are scaled by the same factor, one gets exactly the same two image frames. One can therefore determine the translation to only within a scale factor.

To summarize, our problem is: Given two image frames at t_1 and t_2, find the motion parameters T (to within a scale factor) and R. As shown below, the equations relating the motion parameters to the image-point coordinates inevitably involve the ranges (z-coordinates) of the object points. Therefore, in determining the motion parameters, one also determines the ranges of the observed objects points. It will be seen that the translation vector T and the object point ranges can be determined to within a positive global scale factor. The value of this scale factor could be found if the magnitude of T or the absolute range of any observed object point is known.

5.2.2 Using Point Correspondences

Consider a two-stage method to solve the posed problem. In the first stage, one finds point correspondences in the two perspective views (images). A point correspondence is a pair of image coordinates (X_i, Y_i), (X_i', Y_i') which are images at t_1 and t_2, respectively, of the same physical point on the object. Then, in the second stage, one determines the motion parameters from these image coordinates by solving a set of equations.

(a) Finding point correspondences. In order to be able to find point correspondences, the images must contain points that are distinctive in some sense. For example, images of man-made objects often contain sharp corners which are relatively easy to extract [25]. More generally, image points where the local gray-level variations (defined in some way) are maximum can be used [26].

In any case, in each of the two images a large number of distinctive points are extracted. Then one tries to match the two point patterns in the two images using spatial structures of the patterns [27]. The matching will be successful only if the amount of rotation (Θ) is relatively small (so that the perspective distortion is small). For example, in [25], good matching results are obtained if $\Theta < 5°$. This restriction may be relaxed if there is some a priori information about the object [28].

It can readily appreciated that this first stage is by far the more difficult of the two stages in the method. No algorithm exists which works well for a large variety of images. For many images, no existing algorithms work.

(b) Nonlinear algorithm. From *Fig. 9* and *Eq. (2)*, we get

$$X' = \frac{(r_{11}X + r_{12}Y + r_{13})z + \Delta x}{(r_{31}X + r_{32}Y + r_{33})z + \Delta z}$$

$$Y' = \frac{(r_{21}X + r_{22}Y + r_{23})z + \Delta y}{(r_{31}X + r_{32}Y + r_{33})z + \Delta z} \tag{3}$$

where r_{ij}'s can be expressed in terms of n_1, n_2, n_3, and Θ. Eliminating z from *Eq. (3)*, we get

$$(\Delta x - X'\Delta z)\ \{Y'(r_{31}X + r_{32}Y + r_{33}) - (r_{21}X + r_{22}Y + r_{23})\}$$

$$= (\Delta y - Y'\Delta z)\ \{X'(r_{31}X + r_{32}Y + r_{33}) - (r_{11}X + r_{12}X + r_{13})\} \tag{4}$$

Eq. (4) is nonlinear in the 6 unknowns: Δx, Δy, Δz, n_1, n_2, Θ. Also, it is homogeneous in Δx, Δy, Δz. Therefore, as mentioned earlier, one can only hope to find T to within a scale factor. After finding T (to within a scale factor) and R, one can find z_i for each observed point to within the same scale factor using *Eq. (3)*.

To fix ideas, let the translation sought after be the unit translation vector

$$\hat{T} = (\Delta\hat{x}, \Delta\hat{y}, \Delta\hat{z}) \triangleq \frac{1}{\sqrt{\Delta x^2 + \Delta y^2 + \Delta z^2}}\, T \tag{5}$$

Then, *Eq. (4)* can be considered as a nonlinear equation in the five unknowns: $\Delta\hat{x}$, $\Delta\hat{y}$, n_1, n_2, Θ. Thus, with 5-point correspondence, there are five equations with five unknowns. Well-known iterative techniques can then be used to find solutions. In practice, because of noise in the image data, one tries to find more than 5 point correspondences and seek a least-squares solution.

(c) Linear algorithm. It turns out that by introduction of appropriate intermediate variables (which are functions of the motion parameters), *Eq. (4)* becomes linear [29,30]. If we define

$$E = \begin{bmatrix} e_1 & e_2 & e_3 \\ e_4 & e_5 & e_6 \\ e_7 & e_8 & e_9 \end{bmatrix} = GR \tag{6}$$

where

$$G = \begin{bmatrix} 0 & -\Delta\hat{z} & \Delta\hat{y} \\ \Delta\hat{z} & 0 & -\Delta\hat{x} \\ -\Delta\hat{y} & \Delta\hat{x} & 0 \end{bmatrix} \text{ (skewsymmetric)} \tag{7}$$

$\hat{T} = (\Delta\hat{x}, \Delta\hat{y}, \Delta\hat{z})$ is the unit translation vector defined in *Eq. (5)*, and R is the orthonormal rotation matrix. Then *Eq. (4)* becomes

$$[X' \; Y' \; 1] \, E \begin{bmatrix} X \\ Y \\ 1 \end{bmatrix} = 0 \tag{8}$$

which is linear and homogeneous in the nine new unknowns: $e_1, e_2, \ldots, e_9$.

The algorithm consists of two steps:

Step 1—From 8 or more point correspondences determine E to within an unknown scale factor k.
Step 2—Decompose kE to obtain R and $\hat{T}$.

Step 1 is relatively simple: it amounts to finding the least-squares solution of a set of linear equations (8). Step 2 is more complicated, and will not be discussed here. The reader is referred to Ref. [7] for several algorithms. It can be shown [31] that, except for degenerate cases, 8 or more point correspondences yield a unique solution for R and T.

5.2.3 Using Straight Line Correspondences

In the presence of image noise and/or due to the spatial sampling, the coordinates of feature points cannot be determined accurately. This may make the estimation of motion parameters unreliable. Usually, it is easier to detect and determine the location of straight edges than feature points. Therefore, the question arises: Can one estimate 3D motion parameters by using straight line correspondences?

(a) Finding line correspondences. Images of man-made objects often contain straight edges. These straight edges can be detected using edge point detectors (such as the Sobel operator) followed by Hough transform. One can first detect straight edges in both image frames and then uses structural information to match the two straight-line patterns. The algorithm of Cheng and Huang [18] can be used to do the matching if the motion from t_1 and t_2 is small. Alternative algorithms include Faugeras, et. al. [32]

(b) Nonlinear algorithm (over 3 views). By a straight-line correspondence over two frames, one knows the equations in the image plane at t_1 and t_2 of a 3D line on the object:

$$\text{At} \quad t_1 : \alpha X + \beta Y = 1; \tag{9}$$

$$\text{At} \quad t_2 : \alpha' X + \beta' Y = 1; \tag{10}$$

where $(\alpha, \beta) \longleftrightarrow (\alpha', \beta')$. Note that one does not assume any point correspondences on the two lines. Unfortunately, a little reflection convinces one that no matter how many straight- line correspondences we know over two frames, it is impossible to determine R and T uniquely.

With straight-line correspondences over three image frames (at $t_1 < t_2 < t_3$), it is possible to determine the motion parameters R_{12}, T_{12} (from t_1 to t_2) and R_{23}, $\hat{T}_{23}$ (from t_2 to t_3). An equation involving R_{12} and R_{23} can be obtained. Let the equations in the image plane at t_1, t_2, and t_3, of a 3D straight-line be given by *Eqs. (9), (10)* and

$$\text{(11)} \qquad \text{At} \quad t_3 : \alpha''X + \beta''Y = 1$$

Then it can be shown that [33]

$$\text{(12)} \qquad q' \cdot (R_{12}q \times R_{23}^{-1}q'') = 0$$

where

$$q = (\alpha, \beta, -1)$$
$$q' = (\alpha', \beta', -1) \text{ and}$$
$$q'' = (\alpha'', \beta'', -1)$$

Here a 3-element array is considered as either a vector or a column matrix from context.

Eq. (12) is nonlinear in the six unknown motion parameters (three from each rotation matrix). With 6 or more straight-line correspondences over 3 views, we can solve these nonlinear equations by least-squares. It is easy to show that once the rotations are found, the translation vectors can be obtained by solving linear equations.

(c) Linear algorithm (over 3 views). Linear algorithms exist which require 13 or more straight line correspondences over 3 views [34,35]. Similar to the point case, a set of 27 intermediate variables are defined which are elements of:

$$\text{(13a)} \qquad F \triangleq T_{13}R_{12}^{(1)t} - R_{13}^{(1)}T_{12}^{t}$$

$$\text{(13b)} \qquad G \triangleq T_{13}R_{12}^{(2)t} - R_{13}^{(2)}T_{12}^{t}$$

$$\text{(13c)} \qquad H \triangleq T_{13}R_{12}^{(3)t} - R_{13}^{(3)}T_{12}^{t}$$

where $R_{ij}^{(k)}$ denotes the kth column of R_{ij} and the superscript "t" denotes matrix transposition. These intermediate unknowns can be obtained to within a global scale factor from solving linear equations. Then, the rotation and translation parameters are determined from them. The readers are referred to [34,35] for details.

5.3 Remarks

One of the most difficult parts of dynamic scene analysis is motion/structure estimation. The problems of multiple moving objects [36,37], motion prediction [38], and nonrigid objects [39] have been studied only slightly. Even the simplest problem of two-view (and three-view) motion estimation of a single rigid object has not been resolved satisfactorily, mainly because of two interrelated factors:

(i) For many real-world images, it is extremely difficult to extract and locate features (points, lines) reliably and accurately, and to match them over two or three views.

(ii) Existing algorithms for determining the motion parameters from feature correspondences are sensitive to errors in the image coordinates of the features. The dependence of estimation errors on feature configurations and motion parameter values are not well understood [40].

6. Estimating 3D Vehicle Motion in an Outdoor Scene from Stereo Image Sequences

Motion estimation has evolved into a major research area in computer vision during the last decade. Many algorithms have been proposed. However, most algorithms have been applied to only computer synthesized data, a few to images of indoor scenes, and very few to images of outdoor scenes. And among the last category, we have not found results which are based on data obtained with careful camera calibration and which are compared with carefully calculated ground-truth.

To remedy this situation, we have created, jointly with the U. S. Army Engineer Topographic Laboratory (AI Center) and Purdue University (Photogrammetry Group), a set of image data base which are well calibrated and with ground-truth. The data base consists of stereo image sequences of an outdoor scene containing moving vehicles with a stationary background. The purpose of this section is to give some experimental results of applying motion estimation algorithms to an image sequence from this data base. There is only one moving vehicle, a truck, in the scene, and we aim to estimate its motion in 3D.

In Section 5.2, we described motion estimation algorithms based on monocular image sequences, and commented on the difficulties. With stereo image sequences, the situation is somewhat better. We have applied both monocular and binocular algorithms to the data, but shall present only the binocular results here.

Motion estimation methods using feature correspondences consist of two steps: (i) Extract and match features over several images. (ii) Determine the motion parameters from feature correspondences. Both these steps are addressed in this section.

The image data we use are difficult in the sense that the range to baseline ratio ($\approx 10:1$) and the range to focal length ratio ($\approx 900:1$) are both large. The question we have tried to answer is: Could existing algorithms with modifications give reasonable motion estimation results? As we shall see, the answer is a qualified yes.

6.1 Image Data Base

Reference [41] describes the details of the image set and calibration methods. The imaging setup consisted of two A.M.I./ Bronica SQ-Am 70mm metric cameras with 40mm nominal focal length and 50mm $\times$ 50mm usable image frame size. The two cameras were aligned so that: i) the film planes lay in the same plane, ii) the optical axes were parallel and the plane containing them was parallel to the ground and iii) the baseline between the cameras was approximately 3 meters. *Figure 10* shows the relationship between the cameras and the object coordinate system.

The experiment reported in the present paper was performed on a sequence of 24 stereo image pairs taken at consecutive time instants of an U. W. Army 10-ton truck in a parking lot, asphalt surfaced, with trees and one building as the background. The path of the truck was approximately a circular arc. *Figure 11* shows the top view of the actual relationship between the cameras, the truck trajectory and the object coordinate system. The images were digitized to 4096 $\times$ 4096 pixels (pixelsize = 13μm) using a PDS Microdensitometer at U. S. Army Engineer Topographic Laboratories. *Figure 12* presents two typical digitized stereo image pairs at t_7 and t_{15}.

For the experimental work reported in this paper, the original digitized images were sub-sampled to 2048 $\times$ 2048 pixels. Then, a region of 512 $\times$ 512 pixels around the truck on each sub-sampled image was segmented out and used as the input for the experimental work.

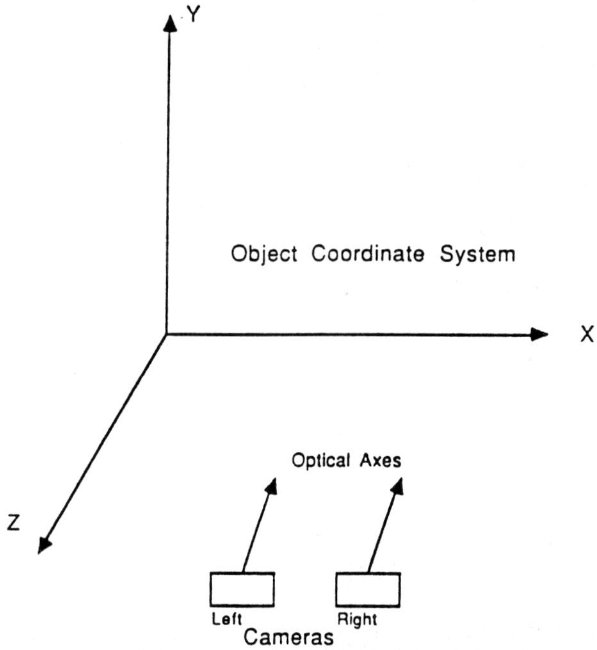

Fig. 10. Relationship between camera locations and object coordinate system.

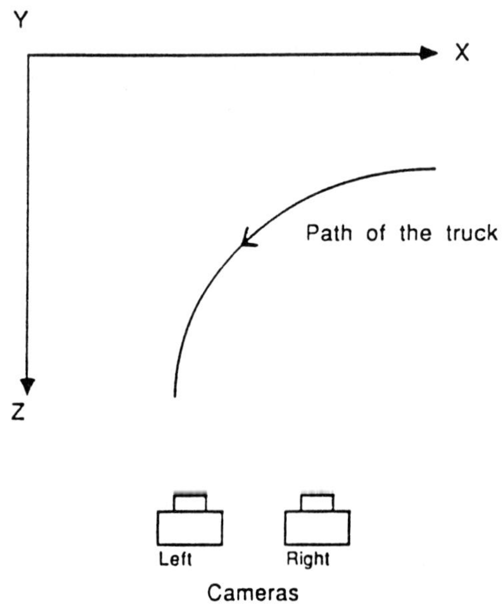

Fig. 11. Top view of experimental set up.

Left

Right

(a) Time instant 7

Left

Right

(b) Time instant 15

Fig. 12. Two typical digitized stereo image pairs.

6.2 Motion Estimation Using 3D Point Correspondences

In this section, we present the process of motion estimation using 3D point correspondences [42]. The process consists of four stages: (1) Determination of point correspondences on two stereo image pairs, (2) Correction of distortions in image coordinates, (3) Derivation of 3D point coordinates from 2D correspondences, and (4) Estimation of motion parameters based on the 3D point correspondences. We shall give a brief description of each stage.

6.2.1 Point Matching

In the first stage, we employ the 4-way matching algorithm suggested in [43] to obtain matched point pairs in two stereo image pairs at two consecutive time instant (t_i and t_{i+1}). The algorithm has two steps which are extracting features and matching. The features used in this algorithm are edge points that extracted by locating zero crossings of an image. In the matching step, there are three procedures which are i) stereo matching, ii) time matching, and iii) elimination of multiple matches. The basic evidences exploited in these procedures to obtain unambiguous match point pairs are the normalized correlation coefficient and zero crossing patterns [44]. To obtain 2D point correspondences, we apply this 4-way matching algorithm to the involved images and the results are two sets of unambiguous stereo matched point pairs in the image coordinates at time instants t_i and t_{i+1}.

6.2.2 Correction of Distortions

Since the image sequence used in this paper was obtained from optical cameras, the images were corrupted by the two major distortions of film and lens. The distortion of film is caused by the unstable nature of the acetate base of the commercial film while the distortion of lens is due to aberrations. These two distortions on the image coordinates have to be corrected before any process, such as derivation of 3D coordinates, can be applied to the matched points. Therefore, after the matching process, the next stage is correction of distortions in the image coordinates. We use the method described in [41,42] to perform the required corrections. The method consists of two steps which are i) use of bilinear transform for the correction of film distortion and ii) use of lens distortion formulas for the correction of lens distortion. These two steps are applied to all the points obtained in the matching process. The results are the corrected image coordinates (in mm) that can be used in the 3D coordinates derivation stage.

6.2.3 3D Coordinates

Having corrected the distortions in the image coordinates, the next stage is to derive 3D coordinates from the corrected 2D position. The procedure used to compute 3D coordinates is photogrammetric intersection with collinearity equation modification described in [41,42]. It involves solving a system of non-linear equations and the main idea can be stated as follows : Given the exterior orientation of the imaging cameras, the 3D coordinates of a point which appears on two or more overlapping images taken from two or more distinct exposure stations can be computed from image coordinates of the point. In this approach, the minimum number of images required is two; therefore, a pair of stereo images is enough for calculating 3D coordinates of all the interest points on the images. The result of this procedure is a list of 3D coordinates. For the motion estimation algorithm used in our work, it requires two such lists of 3D coordinates (X,Y,Z) that correspond to each other at two different time instants (t_i and

t_{i+1}); however, due to data noise, the majority of these 3D coordinates do not represent a consistent rigid structure that is suitable for estimating the motion parameters between two different time instants. If all the 3D coordinates are used as the input for motion estimation, the result, in general, does not give a meaningful interpretation of the object motion. Moreover, two corresponding sets of 3D coordinates at two different time instants that spread evenly across the rigid object are required for an accurate motion estimation result. Therefore, in order to alleviate these two problems, we use the technique suggested in [42] to select the best 3D point sets for motion estimation. This technique uses two constraints, (1) rigidity between different time instants and (2) uniform point distribution across the object on the image, to accomplish such kind of selection. In conclusion, after the application of all the procedures described above, we may have more than one 3D point sets between t_i and t_{i+1} as suitable inputs for motion estimation.

6.2.4 Motion Estimation

At this stage, we have 3D point sets that correspond to each other at two different time instants, i.e. p_i and p_i'; $i = 1, 2, \ldots, N$ (p_i and p_i' are 3×1 column matrices). A typical set contains around 10 points. Based on these 3D point correspondences, the motion equation is :

$$p_i' = Rp_i + T + N_i \tag{14}$$

where R is a 3×3 rotation matrix, T is a translation vector (3×1 column matrix), N_i is a noise vector. In this equation, we assume that the rotation is around an axis passing through the origin.

The task is to find R and T to minimize:

$$\Sigma^2 = \sum_{i=1}^{N} \| p_i' - (Rp_i + T) \|^2 \tag{15}$$

It was shown in [45] that we can decouple the determination of rotation and translation. Consequently, *Eq. (15)* can be simplified as follows:

$$\Sigma^2 = \sum_{i-1}^{N} \| q_i^t - Rq_i \|^2 \tag{16}$$

where

$$p' \triangleq \frac{1}{N} \sum_{i=1}^{N} p_i'$$

$$p \triangleq \frac{1}{N} \sum_{i=1}^{N} p_i$$

$$q_i \triangleq p_i - p$$

$$q' \triangleq p_i' - p'$$

Therefore, the original least-square problem is reduced to two parts:

1. Find R to minimize Σ^2 in *Eq. (16)*.
2. Calculate the translation T by $T = p' - \hat{R}p$ and the centroid translation T_c as $p' - p$.

For calculating R (estimated rotation matrix), the algorithm using quaternions $q = [w_1, w_2, w_3, s]$ suggested in [46] is employed. From the minimum quaternion $q_{min} = [w_{m1}, w_{m2}, w_{m3}, s_m]$, the rotation angle is given by $\alpha = 2\cos^{-1} s_m$ and the rotation axis $(\hat{\eta}_1, \hat{\eta}_2, \hat{\eta}_3)$ can be obtained from:

$$(\hat{\eta}_1, \hat{\eta}_2, \hat{\eta}_3) = \left(\frac{\omega_{m1}}{\sin\frac{\alpha}{2}}, \frac{\omega_{m2}}{\sin\frac{\alpha}{2}}, \frac{\omega_{m3}}{\sin\frac{\alpha}{2}}\right) \tag{17}$$

Moreover, the rotation matrix R corresponding to the minimum quaternion q_{min} is given by

$$R = \left(I + (1 - \cos\alpha)W^{o^2} + \sin\alpha W^o\right)^T \tag{18}$$

where

$$W^o = \begin{bmatrix} 0 & \omega_{m3} & -\omega_{m2} \\ -\omega_{m3} & 0 & \omega_{m1} \\ \omega_{m2} & -\omega_{m1} & 0 \end{bmatrix} \tag{19}$$

Since the translation T is the result of the motion parameters formulation and may not represent an actual physical translation, the centroid translation T_c provides a more realistic translation representation of the rigid object.

In this paper, the 4-way matching algorithm discussed in Section 6.2.1 is used to extract corresponding feature points among two stereo image pairs at two consecutive time instants (t_i, t_{i+1}); for every two stereo image pairs, there are usually more than one 3D point set that are suitable for motion estimation after the selection of 3D point sets. Hence, the motion estimation algorithm is applied to each selected 3–D point set and a list of motion parameters, i.e. (R, T) between t_i and t_{i+1}, is obtained. Among these estimated parameters (R, T) in the list, the (R, T) with the smallest mean squared error according to *Eq. (15)* is regarded as the motion of the rigid object between t_i and t_{i+1}.

6.3 Experimental Results

We now report the results of our motion estimation method (using 3D correspondences) on eight sets of stereo image pairs, each at two consecutive time instants (t_i and t_{i+1}). These eight sets of images are *time7–8, time8–9, time9–10, time10–11, time11–12, time12–13, time13–14* and *time14–15*. The matching algorithm is applied to all these image sets to obtain the matched point pairs. *Figure 13* serves as an example and depicts the matched results of the image set *time10–11*.

The procedures of the other stages discussed, which include image distortions correction, 3D coordinates calculation and selection and motion parameters computation, are applied to the matched points of the eight sets of stereo image pairs (*time7–8, time8–9, time9–10, time10–11, time11–12, time12–13, time13–14 and time14–15*). The estimated motion parameters of the eight sets of stereo image pairs are tabulated in *Table 1*. We also show the estimated motion parameters with hand picked point correspondences (their Y coordinates in 3D are set to zero) of the same eight sets (except *time8–9* and *time9–10*) of stereo image pairs in *Table 2*. In this case, the image coordinates were

Left Right

(a) Time instant 10

Left Right

(b) Time instant 11

Fig. 13. Matched points of time 10–11.

Table 1 Estimated motion parameters of the eight sets of stereo image pairs

File	Rotation Axis $\hat{\eta}$			Angle α	Translation of Centroid T_c			Translation T		
	$\hat{\eta}_1$	$\hat{\eta}_2$	$\hat{\eta}_3$	Deg	X (mm)	Y (mm)	Z (mm)	X (mm)	Y (mm)	Z (mm)
time7-8	-0.1361	0.9906	0.0111	6.17	-931.42	2.20	537.36	-3838.67	-436.00	4004.03
time8-9	-0.0709	0.9949	0.0721	3.74	-989.33	-10.00	478.26	-2773.00	-293.17	2632.98
time9-10	-0.0024	0.9992	-0.0402	5.08	-791.31	-1.33	857.38	-3328.95	102.23	3584.18
time10-11	0.0219	0.9993	-0.0315	8.00	-738.31	-9.09	585.13	-4782.79	216.75	4931.64
time11-12	0.0925	0.9949	-0.0401	4.82	-807.26	-11.76	414.51	-3271.42	321.40	2992.77
time12-13	0.0973	0.9931	-0.0655	6.13	-587.12	3.93	900.55	-3838.46	526.85	3996.81
time13-14	-0.0764	0.9970	-0.0091	5.72	-523.02	-18.46	830.93	-3741.30	-239.98	3607.94
time14-15	0.0137	0.9997	-0.0213	5.45	-544.22	-15.87	778.34	-3587.09	81.81	3406.88

File	Centroid Location					
	First Time Instant			Second Time Instant		
	X (mm)	Y (mm)	Z (mm)	X (mm)	Y (mm)	Z (mm)
time7-8	30800.79	1359.37	28982.32	29869.36	1361.57	29519.68
time8-9	32250.00	820.86	28638.72	31260.67	810.85	29116.98
time9-10	29458.82	850.34	29929.25	28667.52	849.01	30786.63
time10-11	29107.22	946.57	31096.31	28368.90	937.47	31681.45
time11-12	29676.63	1614.34	30642.84	28869.37	1602.58	31057.35
time12-13	27570.88	1297.05	32032.10	26983.76	1300.98	32932.64
time13-14	26119.52	1626.20	33661.80	25596.50	1607.74	34492.73
time14-15	26126.05	1105.97	33280.53	25581.83	1090.09	34058.86

Table 2 Ground-truth for motion estimation

File	Rotation Axis $\hat{\eta}$			Angle α	Translation of Centroid T_c			Translation T		
Y = 0.00	$\hat{\eta}_1$	$\hat{\eta}_2$	$\hat{\eta}_3$	Deg	X (mm)	Y (mm)	Z (mm)	X (mm)	Y (mm)	Z (mm)
time7-8	0.00	1.00	0.00	5.23	-945.41	0.00	286.88	-3475.65	0.00	3424.76
time8-9	N/A	N/A	N/A	N/A	N/A	N/A	N/A	N/A	N/A	N/A
time9-10	N/A	N/A	N/A	N/A	N/A	N/A	N/A	N/A	N/A	N/A
time10-11	0.00	1.00	0.00	5.91	-743.04	0.00	642.98	-3787.28	0.00	3798.66
time11-12	0.00	1.00	0.00	4.53	-642.27	0.00	757.66	-3089.39	0.00	3056.09
time12-13	0.00	1.00	0.00	5.48	-590.79	0.00	745.81	-3602.12	0.00	3491.67
time13-14	0.00	1.00	0.00	4.50	-562.40	0.00	792.53	-3082.15	0.00	3016.54
time14-15	0.00	1.00	0.00	5.87	-459.67	0.00	864.27	-3796.00	0.00	3751.46

File	Centroid Location					
	First Time Instant			Second Time Instant		
	X (mm)	Y (mm)	Z (mm)	X (mm)	Y (mm)	Z (mm)
time7-8	33118.53	1870.43	29294.37	32173.12	1857.75	29581.25
time8-9	N/A	N/A	N/A	N/A	N/A	N/A
time9-10	N/A	N/A	N/A	N/A	N/A	N/A
time10-11	29070.00	1691.23	31089.63	28326.97	1676.94	31732.61
time11-12	27820.65	1378.55	32072.48	27178.38	1363.90	32830.14
time12-13	27178.38	1363.90	32830.14	26587.59	1353.31	33575.95
time13-14	27028.42	1652.20	33162.03	26466.02	1641.12	33954.57
time14-15	26466.02	1641.12	33954.57	26006.35	1636.42	34818.84

Table 3 Error of rotation axis

File	Difference in Rotation Axis $\Delta\hat{\eta}$			Angle γ
	$\Delta\hat{\eta}_1$	$\Delta\hat{\eta}_2$	$\Delta\hat{\eta}_3$	Deg
time7-8	0.1361	0.0094	-0.0111	7.86
time8-9	N/A	N/A	N/A	N/A
time9-10	N/A	N/A	N/A	N/A
time10-11	-0.0219	0.0007	0.0315	2.20
time11-12	-0.0925	0.0051	0.0401	5.79
time12-13	-0.0973	0.0069	0.0655	6.74
time13-14	0.0764	0.0030	0.0091	4.41
time14-15	-0.0137	0.0003	0.0213	1.45

Table 4 Error of rotation angle

File	Rotation Angle α (Deg)		Difference (Deg)
	Ground-truth	Estimated	$\|\Delta\alpha\|$
time7-8	5.23	6.17	0.94
time8-9	N/A	3.74	N/A
time9-10	N/A	5.08	N/A
time10-11	5.91	8.00	2.09
time11-12	4.53	4.82	0.29
time12-13	5.48	6.13	0.65
time13-14	4.50	5.72	1.22
time14-15	5.87	5.45	0.42

Table 5 Error of centroid translation

File	Difference in Translation of Centroid ΔT_c			Error	Angle γ
	$\Delta X(mm)$	$\Delta Y(mm)$	$\Delta Z(mm)$	%	Deg
time7-8	-13.99	-2.20	-250.48	8.84	13.10
time8-9	N/A	N/A	N/A	N/A	N/A
time9-10	N/A	N/A	N/A	N/A	N/A
time10-11	-4.73	9.09	57.85	4.12	2.53
time11-12	164.99	11.76	343.15	8.63	22.54
time12-13	-3.67	-3.93	154.74	13.00	5.29
time13-14	-39.38	18.46	-38.40	1.05	3.35
time14-15	84.55	15.87	85.93	2.97	7.02

Table 6 Error of translation

File	Difference in Translation ΔT			Error	Angle γ
	$\Delta X(mm)$	$\Delta Y(mm)$	$\Delta Z(mm)$	%	Deg
time7-8	363.02	436.00	-579.27	14.03	4.78
time8-9	N/A	N/A	N/A	N/A	N/A
time9-10	N/A	N/A	N/A	N/A	N/A
time10-11	995.51	-216.75	-1132.98	28.14	1.97
time11-12	182.03	-321.40	63.32	2.30	4.71
time12-13	236.34	-526.85	-505.14	10.96	5.80
time13-14	659.15	239.98	-591.40	20.65	2.68
time14-15	-208.91	-81.81	344.58	7.29	1.48

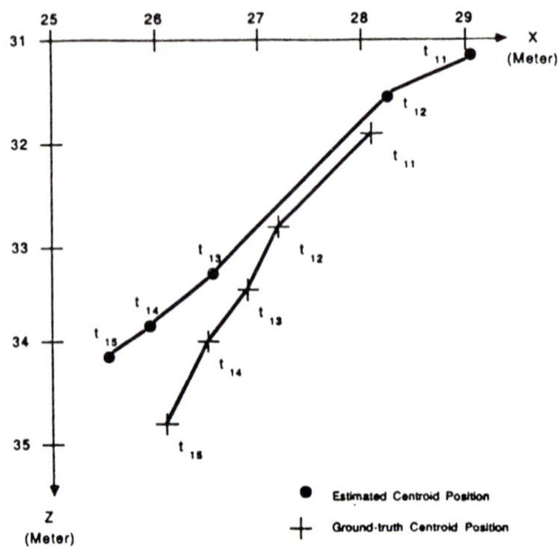

Fig. 14. Centroid positions on x-z plane between t_{11} and t_{15}.

read off the original photographs (transparencies) before digitization using an optical comparator [41] to very high accuracy. Thus, the numbers in *Table 2* are considered as ground-truth. According to Section 6.1, the truck was moving in a circular arc on a horizontal surface (the parking lot), which is the X–Z plane with respect to the ground coordinates; therefore, the truck should have a motion with $\hat{\eta} = (0.0, 1.0, 0.0)$ as the axis of rotation and zero Y-component in both translation of centroid T_c and translation T. These constraints were explicitly used in obtaining the ground truth.

In both *Table 1* and *Table 2*, the first column presents the rotation axis $(\hat{\eta}_1, \hat{\eta}_2, \hat{\eta}_3)$ and the second column is for rotation angle in degrees. The third column shows the translation of centroid T_c and the fourth column contains the translation T. For our comparison, the error E between two translation vectors $(\vec{V}, \vec{V}_{gt})$ is defined as $E = \left|\frac{\|\vec{V}_{gt}\| - \|\vec{V}\|}{\|\vec{V}_{gt}\|}\right|$ and the angle between them is given by $\gamma = \cos^{-1} \frac{\vec{V}_{gt} \cdot \vec{V}}{\|\vec{V}_{gt}\| \, \|\vec{V}\|}$. *Table 3* shows the comparison between the estimated results (*Table 1*) and the ground truth (*Table 2*). To summarize the comparison:

1. For the rotation axis $(\hat{\eta}_1, \hat{\eta}_2, \hat{\eta}_3)$, the angle between the two axes (the estimated and the ground truth) has an average value $\bar{\gamma} = 4.74°$ with standard deviation $\sigma_\gamma = 2.32°$.
2. For the rotation angle α, the average absolute error $|\bar{E}_\alpha|$ is 0.9350° with standard deviation $\sigma_\alpha = 0.6025°$.
3. For the translation of centroid T_c, the average error $\bar{E}_{T_c}$ is 6.44% with standard deviation $\sigma_{T_c} = 4.08\%$. For the angle γ between the two centroid translation vectors (the estimated and the ground truth), the average value $\bar{\gamma}$ is 8.97° with standard deviation $\sigma_\gamma = 6.97°$.
4. For the translation T, the average error $\bar{E}_T$ is 13.90% with standard deviation $\sigma_T = 8.52\%$. For the angle γ between the two translation vectors (the estimated and the ground truth), the average value $\bar{\gamma}$ is 3.57° with standard deviation $\sigma_\gamma = 1.61°$.

For a visual comparison, we plot in *Figure 14* the projections on the X–Z plane of the ground-truth and estimated centroid locations at the various time instants.

6.4 Discussion

From the experimental results, we observe that the rotation estimation is reasonable. The average relative error in the rotation angle is around 20%; and if we discount the worst estimate (*time10–11*), around 10%. This agrees well with the error range analysis for quantization. However, the estimation of centroid locations and translations is grossly in error. The comparison of estimated centroid locations with ground truth (*Figure 12*) indicates that the errors in centroid locations are around 1m in both the Z and X directions.

Assume the camera calibration and the ground-truth calculation were perfect. Then the only error would be due to image sampling (spatial quantization). From the geometry of the imaging setup it can be readily calculated that an uncertainty of 1 pixel in the right and left images of a stereo pair will cause an uncertainty of around 3m in the Z coordinate of the 3D point location obtained by triangulation. Since the centroid location is the average of 4 to 11 3D points, the uncertainty (in Z) should be reduced. Thus the 1m errors we obtained are expected.

However, the ideal uncertainty in the X-direction is very small, on the order of 0.1m. The fact that we obtained errors of around 1m can perhaps be explained at least partially by noting that the centroid location is actually "floating". To calculate the ground-truth, 4 target points on the truck were picked by eye. The centroid locations of the ground-truth are the centroids of these 4 or a subset of 3 of these 4 points (depending on which points are visible in the images). At each time instant, the group of 4 to 11 points used for motion estimation most likely do not coincide or include the 4 target points. Thus the centroid locations will be different. Since the truck length is 6m, a 1m difference in centroid location is not unreasonable.

References

1. Chen, H.H., Huang, T.S.: A Survey of Construction and Manipulation of Octrees. Computer Vision, Graphics, and Image Processing (CVGIP) *43*, 409–431 (1988)
2. Agin, G.J., Binford, T.O.: Computer Analysis of Curved Objects. Proc. Int. Joint Conf. on Artificial Intelligence (IJCAI), 1973, pp. 629–640
3. Requicha, A.A.G.: Representations of Rigid Solids. ACM Computing Surveys *12*, 437–464 (1980)
4. Barrow, H.G.: Popplestone, R.J.: Relational Descriptions in Picture Processing. In B. Meltzer, D. Michie (eds.): Machine Intelligence, 6. Edinburgh Univ. Press, Edinburgh 1971
5. Horn, B.K.P.: Robot Vision. McGraw-Hill, 1986
6. Lee, H.C.: Method for Computing the Scene-Illuminant Chromaticity from Specular Highlights. Jour. Optical Society of America A (JOSA A) *3* (10), 1694–1699 (Oct. 1986)
7. Wolff, L.B.: Shape from Photometric Flow Fields. Proc. SPIE, Optics, Illumination, and Image Sensing for Machine Vision, III, Cambridge, MA, Nov. 1988 *1005*, pp. 206–213
8. Will, P.M., Pennington, K.S.: Grid Coding: A Preprocessing Technique for Robot and Machine Vision. Artificial Intelligence *2*, 319–329 (Winter 1971)
9. Moffitt, F.H., Mikhail, E.M.: Photogrammetry, 3rd ed. Harper & Row, 1980
10. Marr, D.: Vision. W.H. Freeman, 1982
11. Grimson, W.E.L.: An Implementation of a Computational Theory of Visual Surface Interpolation. Computer Vision, Graphics, and Image Processing (CVGIP) *22* (1), 39–69 (April 1983)
12. Witkin, A.P.: Recovering Surface Shape and Orientation from Texture. Artificial Intelligence *17*, 17–45 (1981)
13. Kanade, T.: Recovery of the 3D Shape of an Object from a Single View. Artificial Intelligence *17*, 409–460 (1981)
14. Koenderink, J.J.,van Doorn, A.J.: The Internal Representation of Solid Shape with Respect to Vision. Biological Cybernetics *32*, 211–216 (1979)
15. Eggert, D., Bowyer, K.: Computing the Orthographic Projection Aspect Graph of Solids of Revolution. Proc. IEEE Workshop on Interpretation of 3D Scenes, Austin, TX, Nov. 1989, pp. 102–108
16. Ponce, J., Kriegman, D.J.: On Recognizing and Positioning Curved 3D Objects from Image Contours. Proc. IEEE Workshop on Interpretation of 3D Scenes, Austin, TX, Nov. 1989
17. Wallace, T.P., Mitchell, O.R.: Analysis of 3D Movement Using Fourier Descriptors. IEEE Trans. on PAMI *2* (6), 583–588 (Nov. 1980)
18. Cheng, J.K., Huang, T.S.: Image Registration by Matching Relational Structures. Pattern Recognition *17* (1), 149–160 (1984)
19. Brooks, R.A.: Model-Based 3D Interpretation of 2D Images. Proc. 7th Int. Joint Conf. on Artificial Intelligence (IJCAI), 1981, pp. 619–624
20. Huang, T.S. (ed.): Image Sequence Processing and Dynamic Scene Analysis. Springer-Verlag, Heidelberg 1983
21. O'Rourke, J., Badler, N.: Model-Based Image Analysis of Human Motion Using Constraint Propagation. IEEE Trans. PAMI *2*, 522–536 (1980)
22. Neumann, B.: Natural Language Description of Time-Varying Scenes. Bericht nr. 105, FBI-HH-B-105/84. Fachberich Informatik, Univ. Hamburg, W. Germany, Aug. 1984
23. Borchardt, G.C.: A Computer Model for the Representation and Identification of Physical Events. Tech. Rep. T-142. Coordinated Science Laboratory, Univ. of Illinois, Urbana, IL, May 1984
24. Huang, T.S.: Motion Analysis. In S. Shapiro (ed.): Artificial Intelligence Encylopedia. Wiley, 1987, pp.620–632
25. Fang, J.Q., Huang, T.S.: A Corner Finding Algorithm for Image Analysis and Registration. Proc. AAAI-82, Pittsburgh, PA, Aug. 18–20, 1982, pp. 46–49
26. Moravec, H.P.: Obstacle Avoidance and Navigation in the Real World by a Seeing Robot Rover. Ph.D. dissertation, Stanford Univ., Stanford, CA, Sept. 1980
27. Fang, J.Q., Huang, T.S.: Some Experiments on Estimating the 3D Motion Parameters of a Rigid Body from Two Consecutive Image Frames. IEEE Trans. on PAMI *6* (5), 547–555 (Sept. 1984)

28. Gu, W.K., Yang, J.Y., Huang, T.S.: Matching Perspective Views of a 3D Object Using Composite Circuits. Proc. 7th ICPR, July 30–Aug. 2, 1984
29. Longuet-Higgins, H.C.: A Computer Program for Reconstructing a Scene from Two Projections. Nature *293*, 133–135 (Sept. 1981)
30. Tsai, R.Y., Huang, T.S.: Uniqueness and Estimation of 3D Motion Parameters of Rigid Bodies with Curved Surfaces. IEEE Trans. PAMI *6* (1), 13-27 (1984)
31. Longuet-Higgins, H.C.: The Reconstruction of a Scene from Two Projections-Configurations that Defeat the 8-Point Algorithm. Proc. 1st Conf. Artificial Intelligence Applications, Denver, CO, Dec. 5–7, 1984, pp. 395–397
32. Faugeras, O.D., Lustman, F., Toscasi, G.: Motion and Structure from Motion from Points and Lines. Proc. 1st Int. Conf. Computer Vision, London, England, June 8–11, 1987
33. Liu, Y.C., Huang, T.S.: Estimation of Rigid Body Motion Using Straight-Line Correspondences. Proceedings of IEEE Workshop on Motion: Representation and Analysis, Kiawah Island, SC, May 7–9, 1986, pp. 47–52
34. Spaetsakis, M.E., Aloimonos, J.: Closed Form Solution to the Structure from Motion Problem from Line Correspondences. Tech. Rept. CAR-TR-374. Center for Automation Research, Univ. of Maryland, March 1987
35. Liu, Y.C., Huang, T.S.: A Linear Algorithm for Motion Estimation Using Straight Line Correspondences. Tech. Note ISP-309. Coordinated Science Laboratory, Univ. of Illinois, Urbana, IL, April 15, 1987
36. Chen, H.H., Huang, T.S.: Multiple Object Motion Determination by Matching 3D Points. Pattern Recognition, (Dec. 1987)
37. Chen, H.H., Huang, T.S.: Multiple Object Motion Estimation by Matching 3D Line Segments. Tech. Note ISP-120. Coordinated Science Laboratory, Univ. of Illinois, Urbana, IL, Dec. 15, 1986
38. Huang, T.S., Weng, J., Ahuja, N.: 3D Motion from Image Sequences: Modeling, Understanding, and Prediction. Proceedings of IEEE Workshop on Motion: Representation and Analysis, Kiawah Island, SC, May 7–9, 1986, pp. 125–130
39. Chen, S.S.: Shape and Correspondence of Nonrigid Objects. In T.S. Huang (ed.): Advances in Computer Vision and Image Processing, Vol. 3. JAI Press, 1987
40. Weng, J., Huang, T.S., Ahuja, N.: Error Analysis of Linear Algorithm for Motion Estimation. Proc. 1st Int. Conf. Computer Vision, London, England, June 8–11, 1987
41. Mikhail, E.M., Paderes, F.C.: Photogrammetric Series of Moving Vehicle. Scientific Services Program DAAL03-86-D-0001 (0683), CAI-RI, U.S. Army ETL, Fort Belvoir, VA, Nov. 1988
42. Leung, M.K., Huang, T.S.: Estimating 3D Vehicle Motion in an Outdoor Scene Using Stereo Image Sequences. Tech. Rep. ISP-1010. Coordinated Science Laboratory, Univ. of Illinois, Urbana, IL, Apr., 1990
43. Leung, M.K., Choudhary, A.N., Patel, J.H., Huang, T.S.: Point Matching in a Time Sequence of Stereo Image Pairs and its Parallel Implementation on a Multiprocessor. IEEE Workshop on Visual Motion, Irvine, CA, Mar. 1989
44. Kim, Y.C., Aggarwal, J.K.: Finding Range from Stereo Images. IEEE Conf. Computer Vision and Pattern Recognition, San Francisco, CA, June 1985
45. Huang, T.S., Blostein, S.D., Margerum, E.A.: Least-Squares Estimation from 3D Point Correspondences. IEEE Conf. Computer Vision and Pattern Recognition, Miami Beach, FL, June 1986
46. Faugeras, O.D., Hebert, M.: A 3D Recognition and Positioning Algorithm Using Geometrical Matching Between Primitive Surfaces. Int. Joint Conf. Artificial Intelligence, Karlshrue, West Germany, Aug. 1983

Acknowledgement

The preparation of this paper was supported by National Science Foundation Grant IRI-89-08255.

3D Volume Visualization

Arie Kaufman

1. Introduction

Three-dimensional volume visualization is a method that allows one to observe and manipulate 3D volumetric data. Many objects and natural phenomena in our spatial and temporal surroundings and in computational models are 3D volumes of data. Unlike traditional techniques, which represent 3D objects in terms of surfaces and edges approximated by polygons and lines, volume data are 3D entities that have information also inside them. They might not consist of surfaces and edges entirely. Three-dimensional volume visualization is concerned with the representation, manipulation, and rendering of the volume data. The volume visualization method allows one to peer inside the volumetric objects to view that which is not ordinarily viewable, and further to probe into the voluminous and complex structures and their dynamics to comprehend that which is not ordinarily comprehensible.

This chapter opens a window to the emerging field of volume visualization, its terminology, techniques, relevant technologies, and the associated applications. It is a tutorial organized in two introductory sections followed by six technical sections on volume representation, viewing algorithms, shading techniques, 3D discrete space, architectures for volume visualization, and applications of volume visualization. The chapter is appended with a comprehensive bibliography.

Volume visualization is a rapidly growing field of computer graphics and imaging. It is emerging as a key field of computer science, with an array of techniques, a novel technology, a new nomenclature, a band of experts, and substantial challenges. The techniques provide mechanisms to reveal and explore the inner or unseen structures of volumetric data, and allow visual insight into opaque or complex data sets. Volume visualization as a technology brings a revolution to computer graphics and promises important breakthroughs in the applications of volume visualization. Just as raster graphics in the seventies superseded vector graphics for visualizing surfaces, volume visualization is now superseding raster graphics for handling and visualizing volumes. Furthermore, just as raster graphics has been dominant for rendering both surfaces and lines, volume visualization coupled with the progress in hardware will liberate computer graphics from the limitations of 2D raster graphics and will prevail in the nineties for rendering volumes as well as surfaces and lines.

Volume visualization is related to visualization in scientific computing and has been identified by the Visualization in Scientific Computing (ViSC) report [127] as "an emerging visualization environment." This 1987 report claims that software and hardware for volume graphics and imaging are still rudimentary. Nevertheless, the technology, the tools, and the environment of volume visualization are available today to scientists and engineers in scientific discoveries, in engineering tasks, in provoking of insights, and in communicating of the new knowledge.

The field of volume visualization can be traced back to the mid-70's, when the use of volumetric data, particularly in 3D medical imaging, was first reported. In the late 1980's, the field matured with several breakthroughs and seminal projects, most of which are reported in this tutorial. Out of the interest and enthusiasm of the cohort of experts and the perplexed users of volume visualization has sprung a series of workshops and tutorials devoted to the topics of volumetric data, the associated visualization techniques, and the related applications. One was the *Chapel Hill Workshop on Volume Visualization* which was held in May of 1989. The proceedings of the workshop [176] could serve as complementary material to this tutorial. The workshop focused on software toolkits and environments [47, 80, 159, 180], algorithms [54, 69, 169], applications [73, 75], data classification [113, 153], and system implementations [121, 181].

Inspired by this workshop, Pacific Interfaces, in cooperation with ACM SIGGRAPH, produced a comprehensive video review of "Volume Visualization – State of the Art" [67], which may serve as an excellent source of information on the field. The second workshop on volume visualization was held in San Diego, California, in December of 1990. Other conferences in 1990 that include papers or tutorials on volume visualization are the Conference on Biomedical Computing in Atlanta, Georgia (May 1989), ACM SIGGRAPH in Dallas, Texas (August 1990), EUROGRAPHICS '90 in Montreux, Switzerland (September 1990), and IEEE Visualization '90 in San Francisco, California (October 1990).

A special issue on Visualization in Scientific Computing of *Computer* includes several articles reporting on various aspects of volume visualization [31, 43, 61, 68, 107, 124, 138, 151]. Also, *Computer & Graphics* devoted its April 1989 issue to the subject of "3D Voxel-Based Graphics" [46, 79, 85, 108], and the February 1990 issue of *The Visual Computer* is a special issue on "Volume Visualization" [28, 38, 71, 94, 118, 179]. In addition, IEEE Press recently published a tutorial titled "Volume Visualization" [86]. The proliferation of conferences and literature on volume visualization demonstrates that this area is rapidly developing into a major computer technology of the 1990's.

2. Terminology

Volume visualization encompasses both multi-dimensional image synthesis and multi-dimensional image processing. It provides for the analysis and understanding of volumetric experimental or scanned data (primarily 3D), for the synthesis of volumetric objects by a computer model, for interaction, transformation, and manipulation of the data, and for producing images from these complex data sets.

A consensus has not been reached yet on the nomenclature of volume visualization. Nevertheless, we attempt to capture the basic jargon for volume visualization in Figure 1, which depicts the taxonomy and data flow for volume visualization. The primary source of volume data is empirical. The data is generated either by a 3D or 2D sampling device or by a computer model that produces discrete sampling points of a real or simulated object or phenomenon, usually as a sequence of cross-sectional scans. These data sets can be processed and filtered by 2D (or 3D) image processing techniques and then can be *3D reconstructed* into a 3D volume data set by stacking the cross-sections and interpolating between them. A volumetric object is typically represented as a large 3D grid of *voxels* (unit volume elements or cells). Each voxel has a numeric value (or values) associated with it, which represents some measurable properties of a small cube of the real objects. The 3D volume data set within *3D discrete/digital voxel space* is commonly stored in a *cubic frame buffer (CFB)* which is a 3D array of voxels – a *3D raster.*

An alternative source of volume data is by *3D scan-converting (voxelizing)* a *3D continuous geometric model*, commonly represented as a *display list* of geometrically- or parametrically-defined polygons or surfaces. A 3D scan-conversion (voxelization) algorithm generates a set of voxels which "best" approximates the synthetic model within the discrete voxel space. These 3D scan-conversion algorithms bridge the gap between traditional computer graphic modeling and volume visualization. The digital synthetic model may be intermixed with the sampled data set to form a *hybrid voxel model* [53, 97, 119].

In order to visualize the volume data set, the volume primitives are projected or reduced into *discrete pixel space* and stored as a *raster image* in a *frame buffer.* This process, which is termed as *volume rendering* (or *discrete volume visualization*), involves both the viewing (i.e., projection) and the shading stages.

Alternatively, the volume data can first be converted into geometric primitives in a process called *iso-contouring*, *iso-surfacing*, *surface extraction*, *surface tracking*, or *border following* (see also Section 4). Then, the geometric primitives are rendered to the screen by a process called *surface rendering* (or *continuous volume visualization*). This process again involves both the viewing and the shading stages. Surface rendering is thus an indirect technique for visualizing volume primitives by first converting them into an intermediate surface primitive and then employing conventional computer graphics techniques to render them to the screen. Volume rendering, on the other hand, is a direct display of the volume primitives without any intermediate conversion of the volume data to surface primitives.

Figure 2 presents the volume visualization pipeline. The first phase of the pipeline is the data acquisition phase. The sources of volume data are either sampled data of real objects or simulated data generated by a computer model. Sampled data are generated by 2D, 3D, or multi-dimensional scanners or sensors that measure the real object and usually produce a sequence of 2D cross-sections or slices of the object.

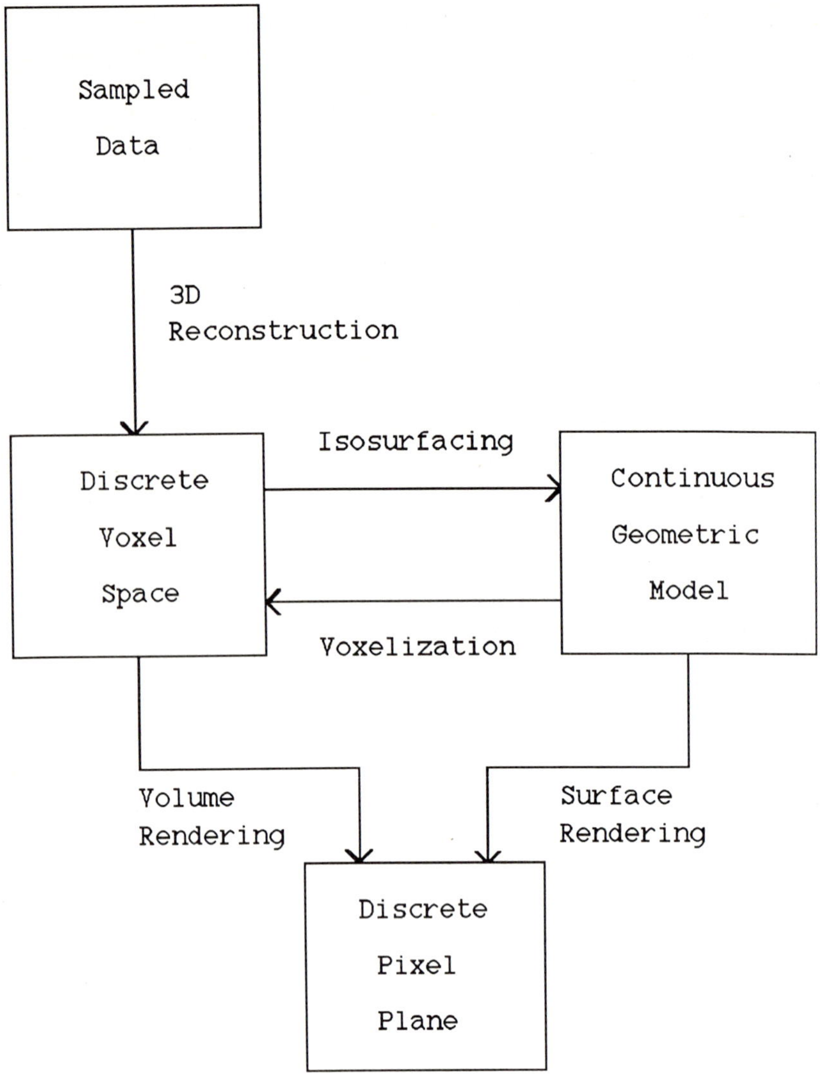

Figure 1: Taxonomy of Volume Visualization

For example, a real human organ sampled experimentally with medical scanners, like Computed Tomography (CT) [12], Magnetic Resonance Imaging (MRI) [70], or ultrasonography, are represented as a series of slices through the sampled organ. Similarly, a biological cell can be sampled by physically slicing it into very thin specimens and then using an electron microscope (EM) to sample each slice, by focusing on successive depth planes of a 3D specimen using a light microscope and then performing optical sectioning which eliminates the out-of-focus data from the images [1], or by sampling a 3D specimen with a confocal microscope.

Simulated data are generated by a computer running a mathematical model. The data produced is either a scalar, a vector, or a tensor field of the 3D spatial grid or a sequence of 2D planar slices. Examples of such computer modeling can be seen in fluid dynamics [124, 159], earth science [68], and molecular graphics [54].

The next stage of the pipeline is the enhancement of the original data. This stage may change the data by enhancing and enriching it into a more informative, filtered, uniform, and possibly less voluminous form. The details of the numerous and matured image processing techniques that can be used here are beyond the scope of this paper.

The next stage is the reconstruction of the 3D voxel model. The enhanced images are stacked together, and the missing data between the slices are estimated by an interpolation process. A linear interpolation between adjacent slices is typically used with adequate results. Numerous trilinear, sophisticated non-linear interpolations, or even shape-based interpolations (e.g., [144]), are available and can be used for a superior reconstructed 3D voxel image.

Another mechanism for generating 3D voxel images is a pipeline stage that voxelizes or 3D scan-converts a geometric model into a 3D voxel image [27, 90, 96, 99]. This process is further discussed in Section 7.

Once the 3D voxel image has been reconstructed and/or voxelized, it is then enhanced using 3D image processing techniques and operators (e.g., [184]) to prepare for the manipulation and mapping stages. The manipulation stage includes geometric transformations, domain transformations, or *voxblt* manipulations (a generalization of 2D bitblt operations) [87]. The mapping stage maps the 3D voxel data into geometric/display primitives. Specifically, the volume data may be mapped into surface primitives by a surface extraction step for visualization using surface rendering. Volume representation is further discussed in Section 4 (also see [174]), and surface extraction is briefly introduced in Sections 4 and 7.

Once the display primitives are generated, they are projected to form a 2D screen image. The projection algorithm is heavily dependent upon the display primitive generated by the mapping stage. Conventional viewing algorithms and geometry engines can be exploited for displaying conventional geometric primitives, typically using surface rendering. However, when volume primitives are displayed directly, a special volume viewing algorithm should be employed. Volume viewing algorithms are described in Section 5.

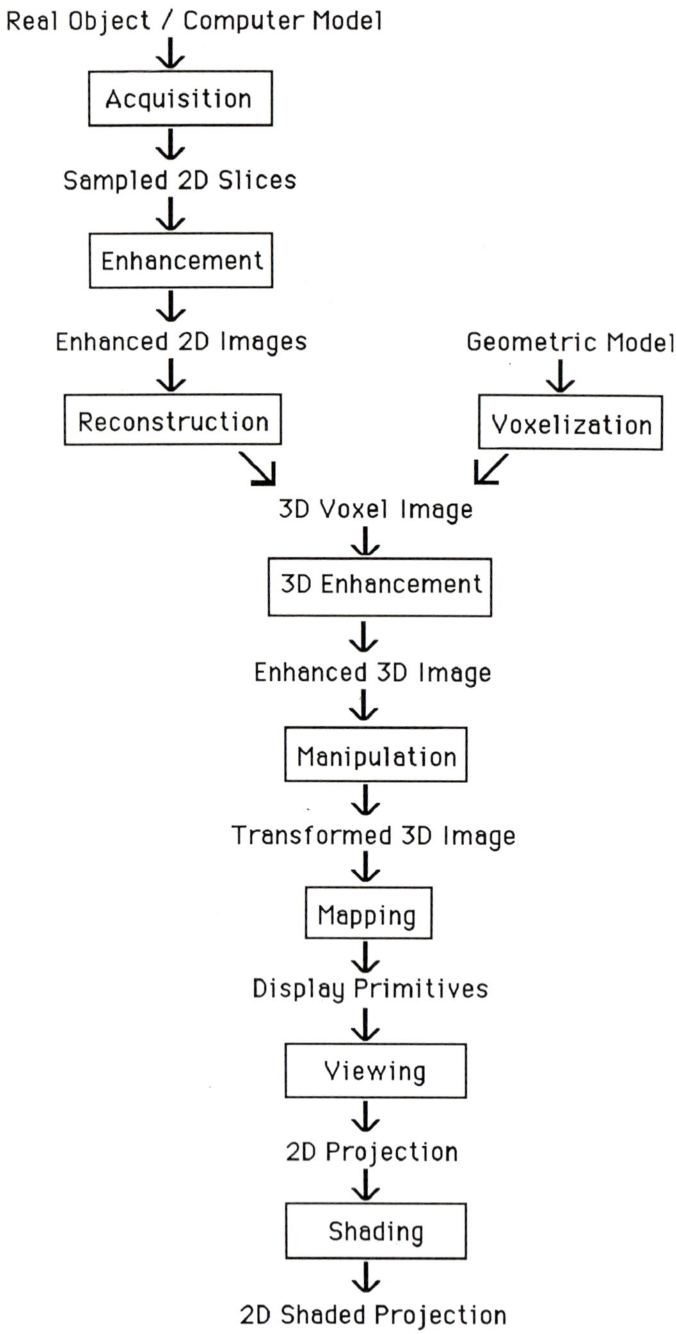

Figure 2: Volume Visualization Pipeline

The final stage of the volume visualization pipeline is the shading of the 2D projection. Again, the conventional shading technique can be used when geometric primitives have been selected as the display primitives. Otherwise, a special discrete shading technique should be used, in which the displayed surface gradient is recovered from the volume data itself. Discrete shading techniques are discussed in Section 6.

3. Representation

This section focuses on the data structures and data representations for volumetric objects. Volume data are 3D entities that have information inside them. They might not consist of surfaces and edges at all. A volumetric object is typically represented as a large 3D grid of voxels. A voxel is the 3D counterpart of the 2D pixel. Each voxel is a quantum unit of volume and has a numeric value or values associated with it, representing some measurable properties or independent variables (e.g., color, opacity, density, material, coverage proportion, refractive index, normal vector, velocity, strength, deformation, time) of the real objects. Voxels are obtained from discrete samples of a real object or synthesized by a computer model. A voxel is commonly represented as a unit cube centered at a discrete address in 3D space, and the aggregate of voxels tessellating the volume forms the volumetric data set.

The voxels are derived from discrete samples of the physical phenomenon as in medical imaging, or may be synthesized by a computer model as in computational fluid dynamics. Both the physical phenomenon and the computer model may generate 3D or multi-dimensional lattices of scalar, vector, or tensor fields, where the lattice is either regular (even), rectilinear, or general (random or deformed) [159]. A tensor field of rank zero is actually a scalar field in which every voxel has a single value (magnitude). A tensor field of rank one is a vector field in which each voxel has a value as well as a direction.

Regardless of the origin of the data set, it can be stored, manipulated, and displayed using a variety of representation and display primitives. Figure 3 displays the possible mappings from 3D volume data to a variety of display primitives (see also [162, 174]). The display primitives range from zero-dimensional points or particles; one-dimensional curves, lines, vectors, ribbons, or contours; two-dimensional polygon meshes, curved surfaces, pixel maps, or iso-surfaces; to three-dimensional volume cells or voxels. Although volume visualization focuses on the latter primitive, the volume visualizer may capitalize on the advantages of the more traditional, lower-dimensional primitives to represent and visualize the various aspects of the same data set. For example, the volume visualizer may intermix a point cloud that provides "see-through" viewing, with flat ribbons that demonstrate flow and twist, together with several iso-surface layers as NURBS, where the outer layers are rendered translucent. All of this is embedded within a 3D voxel raster showing internal object information on oblique cuts.

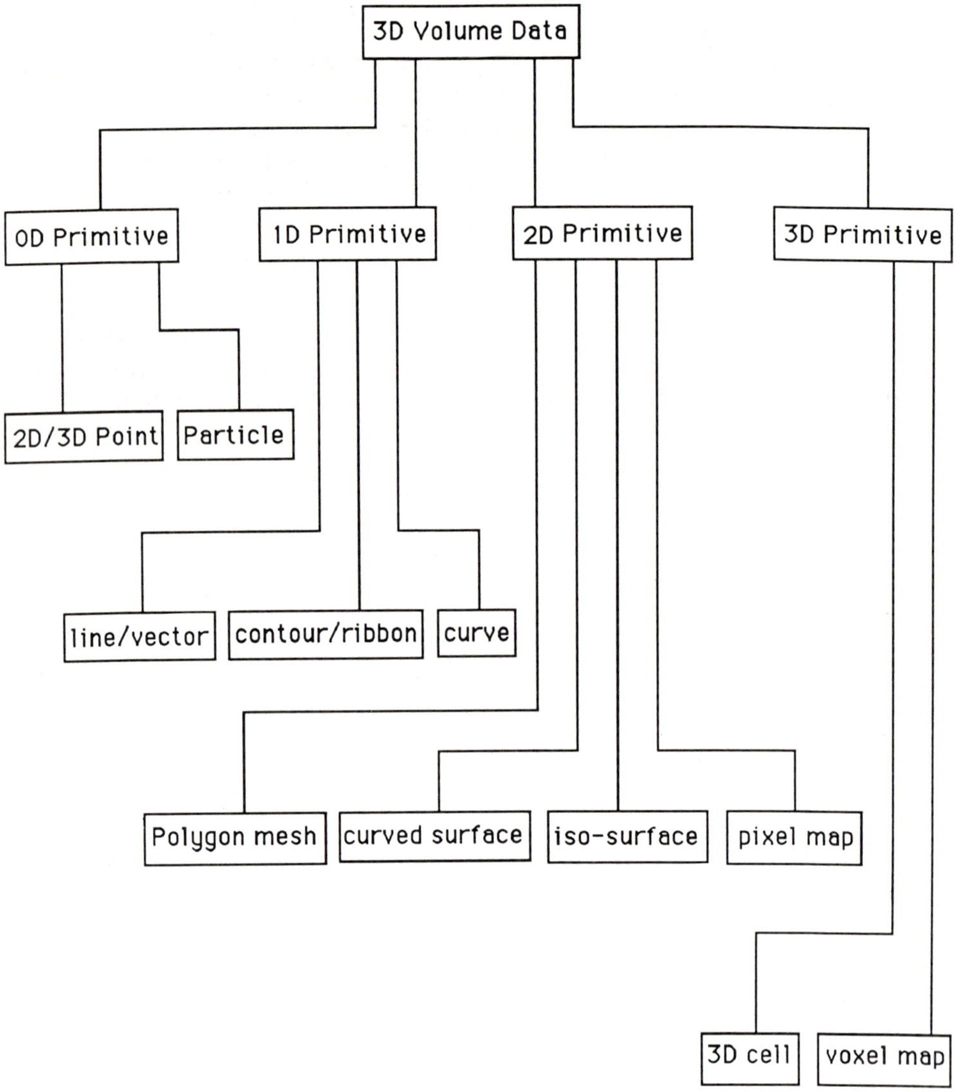

Figure 3: Display Primitives Used for Volume Visualization

The choice of the type of display primitive is closely related to whether volume rendering, surface rendering, or a hybrid rendering is used [53, 97, 119]. The display primitive is also associated with the reconstruction process used to form the 3D model. Typically, the missing data is interpolated by constructing an imaginary approximated surface that does not necessarily pass through the original sampled points. One reconstruction technique represents the 3D image as a stack of 2D contours [134]. The contours are traced interactively with the support of an edge detector [73]. A stack of contours can be converted into a surface representation applying one of the numerous triangulation techniques (e.g., [4, 15, 24, 38, 45, 58, 103, 163, 185]).

An alternative approach is to directly extract the display primitive from the volume itself. This includes the cuberille model in which the exterior rectilinear faces of all the volume voxels are used to form a polygon (square) mesh [23, 66], a fine polygon mesh generated, for example, by the marching cubes algorithm [125], a cloud of points generated by the dividing cubes algorithm [26], by a surface tracking algorithm [6, 55, 170], or by applying a 3D filter [136, 184].

There is a large number of data structures that are used to represent the volume data set, which are closely related to the display primitive employed. Those include spatial enumeration using a full voxel matrix (either binary or a color/grayscale array), a sparse matrix, or a flat matrix, cell decomposition as in octrees [32, 78, 156, 183], constructive solid geometry, a run-length encoding (e.g., [148]), surfaces of the objects, primitive instancing, sweep methods, a chain code for each region in each slice (e.g., [39]), and boundary models.

4. Viewing

Volume visualization also refers to the image presentation that captures the contents of the voxels on the surface and inside the volume being visualized by projecting them onto the 2D display. This section surveys the various algorithms which create a 2D projection from the 3D volumetric data set. A volume viewing algorithm generates a 2D pixel map representing a projection image along the specified viewing direction of the 3D voxel map.

The volume viewing algorithms are classified according to three categories: (1) whether the algorithm operates in 3D voxel space where voxels are examined to determine which pixels are influenced (termed *voxel order*), in 2D pixel space where each pixel is examined to determine which voxels influence it (termed *pixel order*), or in both 3D voxel space and 2D pixel space (termed *hybrid*); (2) whether the voxel value is represented by either a binary or a graded (non-binary, multi-valued, percentage, mixture) value, where the multi-value function may be classified as representing either partial coverage, variable densities, or graded opacities and where the binary field is a result of applying a binary classification function to the volume data (which might be in color or gray scale); and (3) whether the traversal for voxel visibility is performed back-to-front (BTF), where voxels closer to the observer overwrite those that are further to the back ("painters' algorithm"), or front-to-back (FTB), where voxels are traversed in increasing distance order until the pixel value is determined.

These categories lead to a classification of viewing algorithms for volume data, which is shown in Table 1 (cf. [117]). Based on these categories a vocabulary of volume rendering has been established. For example, *binary volume rendering,* and *graded/percentage volume rendering* are terms that are used. The special case of rendering by combining graded opacities is termed *volume compositing.*

The pioneering work in medical volume visualization in the 1970's introduced the rather simple binary field, in which a threshold is applied to the 3D volume data to produce a binary array of ones for one class (e.g., opaque voxels, bony material) and zeros for another class (e.g., transparent voxels, soft tissue, air). Tuy and Tuy

Table 1: Classification of Volume Viewing Algorithms

	Voxel Value	
	Binary	*Graded*
Algorithm		
Pixel-Based (FTB)	Tuy & Tuy 1984	Levoy 1988 Upson & Keeler 1988 Kaufman & Bakalash 1988 Hoehne et al. 1989 Sabella 1988
Voxel-Based	Frieder et al. 1985 (BTF) Gordon & Reynolds 1985 (FTB) Meagher 1982 (BTF) Goldwasser 1984 (BTF)	Westover 1989 (FTB/BTF)
Hybrid	Herman & Liu 1979 {cuberille} Reynolds et al. 1987 (FTB) Meagher 1982 (FTB)	Drebin et al. 1988 (BTF) Upson & Keeler 1988 (FTB) Kaufman et al. 1990 (FTB)

[171] present a binary pixel order technique in which rays are cast into the 3D volume data set and each ray stops when an object is encountered. Pixel order ray casting is inherently front-to-back. The quality of the ray cast 2D image, which suffers from aliasing, can be improved either by resampling, higher order interpolation (e.g., [42, 81]), or by various shading techniques (to be discussed in Section 6).

An alternative to pixel order is the voxel order technique. The front-to-back paradigm has been used in binary voxel order by Gordon and Reynolds [56]. The back-to-front paradigm has been used in binary voxel order by Meagher [132] and by Frieder, Gordon, and Reynolds [40]. This technique has been implemented in Goldwasser's Voxel processor [52].

The cuberille method is a binary hybrid method [66]. The voxel image is traversed yielding a set of square faces, six for each opaque voxel, and then the visible faces are displayed using a pixel order Z-buffer algorithm. Another binary hybrid method has been used by Reynolds, Gordon, and Chen [148]. They have used the front-to-back technique for objects presented in voxel run-length encoding, and a *dynamic screen* which is a run-length encoding of the black pixels of each scan-line. The algorithm merges a voxel run-length linked list along with a linked list of the dynamic screen. Meagher [131] has also used a hybrid front-to-back approach to generate images of octree based images. The octree is traversed recursively into a quadtree representing the screen.

The use of non-binary field has been reported by many researchers [21, 30, 126, 139, 146, 147, 154]. More appropriate projects to volumetric graded fields are on clouds [13], non-homogeneous media [81], and 3D texture [82]. These projects have inspired a similar approach in volume viewing and rendering.

A pixel order approach for graded field has been adopted by Levoy [120]. He employs ray casting and computes colors and opacities directly from the scalar value of each voxel. A simplified ray casting version of this is used in the Cube architecture [98] for orthographic projection. Upson and Keeler [173] present two algorithms. One is a ray casting image order algorithms with high order interpolation. The other is a hybrid cell-by-cell model in which the volume cells are processed front-to-back in the voxel order, and for each scanline color opacity integration is performed. Unlike previous techniques, Sabella [155] suggests a ray casting pixel order approach, but the volume field is characterized as a varying density emitter of tiny particles.

Westover's splatting technique [180] operates solely in voxel space. The technique maps each voxel to a 2D footprint that covers multiple pixels using blending lookup tables.

The approach taken by Pixar [33] is a hybrid voxel/pixel order. It first estimates the voxel's composition, and thus its color and partial opacity, by the percentage of each material present in the voxel. The viewing algorithm transforms by scanline order (with possible resampling) so that the final image lies along the front face of the viewing pyramid and then projects back-to-front while blending with the projection formed by previous slices. Similar hybrid approaches that employ a front-to-back strategy are among the mechanisms for volume rendering in the Cube architecture [98]. Specifically, the volume is first transformed [87] so that it can then be viewed orthographically using ray casting. Another hybrid mechanism is an extension of the Cube viewing architecture, which accommodates arbitrary parallel and perspective projections [88]. Projections are performed by retrieving a plane of projection rays, and then, employing three additional buffers, the plane is aligned for conflict-free retrieval of projection rays.

5. Discrete Shading

Another stage in the volume visualization pipeline is the shading, termed *discrete shading* or *volumetric shading*, of the projected volume. This section introduces the various techniques for discrete shading. The ultimate goal in shading is to provide a 2D image that is practically indistinguishable from a photograph of the real object, while retaining all the minute details of the original data which might be of great scientific or medical value. Unlike shading of geometric objects where the normals are calculated directly from the geometric information, in discrete shading the normals have to be recovered from the volume data. Discrete shading techniques are concerned with this issue.

An attempt to use the visible voxel faces as a polygon mesh with *block (constant) shading* creates a displeasing checkerboard effect, which is accentuated by the fact that the visible faces of the same voxel are orthogonal. However, a variation of this technique used in earlier methods of discrete shading [23, 66] ameliorates the problem of artificial edges by de-emphasizing the dependency on the incident angle. Alternatively, the mesh of faces can be shaded by the well-known Gouraud or Phong shading [37].

Another simple shading technique is *distance-only (depth-only) shading* [52, 63, 178]. The color of a surface varies only as a function of the distance between the observer and the surface point, ignoring the surface normal. Although this technique smooths out any sampling noise, it suppresses edges, discontinuities, and the minute details that are essential, especially in applications such as medical imaging.

A computationally simple discrete shading technique is *contextual shading* [63]. In this technique the face normal is estimated (and stored with the face) based on the relative orientation of the face and its adjacent faces. The initial implementation [63], called *image based contextual shading*, uses a weighted code for each face, while the *normal-based contextual shading* [23] assigns to each neighbor one of three possible orientation codes (-1, 0, 1) relative to the center face. The primary advantage of normal-based contextual shading is that the 25 possible shading values can be precomputed and stored in an intensity look-up table for fast retrieval. In spite of the coarse granularity of the estimated normal vector, the quality of the contextual shaded images is relatively impressive [23].

Gordon and Reynolds [56] introduce the image-based *gradient shading.* This technique, also referred to as "distance gradient shading," was first published by Horn [74]. It accepts as input a pixel image and its depth buffer. The gradient value is obtained from the immediate discrete neighborhood of the point. The x derivative, for example, is estimated from either the forward (right), the backward (left), or the central differences of the depth values of the two immediate neighbors of the center point along the x direction. A main drawback of this technique is its sensitivity to discretization and sampling artifacts. Tam and Davis [165] propose a normal-averaging method which would take into account a larger neighborhood and thus better estimates the normal.

Bright and Laflin [19] describe two methods to improve the depth gradient shading technique. The first would improve the gradient resolution by examining variable neighborhoods of depth values. The second method would smooth the gradient variance by interpolating the gradients of the two adjacent neighborhoods. The results are smoother objects, but with higher computation costs.

Cohen et al. [28, 91] describe a *congradient shading* technique which, like normal-based contextual shading, defines the surface orientation as one of a finite set of neighborhood codes and, consequently, can employ a look-up table. However, instead of defining the orientation of a voxel face relative to its adjoint faces by a sign function, the congradient technique computes the gradient in a way similar to the gradient shading method. Thus, no additional memory is required to store the neighboring code with each voxel face. The technique has been designed in real-time hardware as part of the Cube architecture prototype [98]. In spite of its simplicity, the results are practically indistinguishable from images generated by conventional techniques.

Unlike the previous techniques, which are appropriate solely for binary voxel fields, the technique of *gray level shading,* also called *density gradient shading* [72], is suitable for graded and multi-value voxel data. This technique uses the value of the voxels rather than their distance or location to estimate the gradient of the density value corresponding to the surface inclination. In other words, the gradient indicates the direction in which the density values change most rapidly. This method, due to the high resolution range of the gray scale, produces a smooth shading of high quality and has been widely used in 3D medical imaging [25, 26, 72, 95, 157, 160, 180] and in volume compositing [120]. Density gradient shading, however, has inferior results for binary voxel data and for thin objects (but see [120, 142]).

Another method which computes the normal, based on the densities, is the *local surface interpolation* [179]. A biquadratic surface is approximated for each voxel based on a $3 \times 3 \times 3$ neighborhood. Obviously, this method is time consuming, but for a biquadratic object it offers an accurate location of the surface as well as its normal estimation.

6. 3D Discrete Space

Both the synthesis and analysis of voxel models require a substantial mathematical and theoretical foundation. This section provides a brief introduction to the field of 3D discrete space, its topology, and the use of 3D discrete topology in the development of surface extraction and 3D scan-conversion (voxelization) algorithms. Many theoretical studies have been conducted to characterize the 3D discrete space whose primary goal has been to devise a framework for discrete space that is a close analog of continuous space. In such a case the discrete space is labeled as well-behaved.

In order to support the 3D discrete space framework, a nomenclature and a theory of 3D discrete topology have been developed. These include issues such as 6-, 18- and 26-neighbors, connectivity, paths, metrics, etc. These terms are generalizations of those used in 2D discrete topology [141, 152, 162]. Each voxel (x,y,z) in discrete 3D space has three kinds of *neighbors*:

(1) six *face neighbors*: $(x \pm 1, y, z)$, $(x, y \pm 1, z)$, and $(x, y, z \pm 1)$;

(2) twelve *edge neighbors*: $(x \pm 1, y \pm 1, z)$, $(x \pm 1, y, z \pm 1)$, and $(x, y \pm 1, z \pm 1)$; and

(3) eight *corner (verlex) neighbors*: $(x \pm 1, y \pm 1, z \pm 1)$.

We further define the six face neighbors as *6-neighbors.* The combination of the six face and twelve edge neighbors is defined as *18-neighbors,* while that of all three kinds of neighbors is defined as *26-neighbors.* A *6-connected path* is a sequence of voxels where consecutive pairs are from the same class (e.g., black, opaque, bone) and are 6-neighbors. The *18-* and *26-connected paths* are similarly defined. A *6-connected tunnel* is a path of 6-connected transparent voxels through a surface or a volume. Similarly, an *18-connected tunnel* and a *26-connected tunnel* are defined.

In surfacing rendering where the object surface is first extracted, the discrete surface to be extracted, is characterized and determined based on the desired connectivity and classification of the object. Liu [123] pioneered studying the definition and detection of 3D surfaces in 3D digital images. He defines a surface as a *connected* set of voxel faces detected by a gradient operator. More elaborated results have been reported by Morgenthaler and Rosenfeld [136], Zucker and Hummel [184], Herman and Liu [62], and Cappelletti and Rosenfeld [20]. Frieder et al. [41] describe a region-based voxel classification by thresholding, where the surface of an object is the set of all voxel faces shared by the object (which is a connected component of opaque voxels satisfying a certain connectivity relation) and a connected component of transparent voxels. The surface is extracted by recursively tracking a connected component of boundary faces starting from a given seed on the boundary [7, 55, 160].

A different approach considers the surface as being made up of voxels rather than voxel faces [104-106, 111, 145, 152]. The motivation of this approach is to generalize the 2D discrete space theory to 3D, primarily in the topological sense (e.g., [108-111, 168]).

A particular interest in well-behaved spaces is related to 3D scan-conversion (voxelization) algorithms. A voxelization algorithm generates from a geometric representation of an object, a connected set of voxels in 3D voxel space, that "best" represents or approximates the object. The generated digital representation has to conform to fidelity and connectivity requirements. For example, a digital surface formed by a voxelization process might have a certain "thickness", characterized by the absence of tunnels of certain connectivity. In other words, the thickness of the surface determines which connectivity type of the projection rays that may or may not penetrate it.

Kaufman pioneered the study of voxelization algorithms [99]. Such an algorithm approximates the continuous geometric object by a set of voxels in discrete space. Synthetic objects in 3D discrete space are classified based on their connectivity for 1D objects (i.e., curves), absence of tunnels of certain connectivity for 2D objects (i.e., surfaces), and absence of cavities for 3D objects (i.e., solids). For each 3D geometric object and desired connectivity or thickness, a voxelization algorithm has to be devised [27, 83, 90, 96, 99, 135]. For example, for linear objects (lines, polygons, polyhedra) either a 3D Bresenham-like algorithm or a scan-line algorithm is utilized [90]. For cubic polynomial objects (curves, surfaces, volumes) a third order DDA of forward differences is used [96], while for algebraic spatial curves intersecting surfaces can be employed [135]. For quadratic objects an adaptation of Bresenham's [17, 99] or Van Aken and Novak's [27, 177] circle algorithm is used. The algorithms for scan-converting polyhedra, spheres, and volumes write a whole run of voxels in parallel to the cubic frame buffer, exploiting a special parallel organization of the cubic frame buffer [98].

Voxel-based representation is emerging as a key representation for applications that employ synthetic models. These include computer aided design (e.g., solid modeling, finite elements, material stress patterns), simulation and animation (e.g., flight simulation), and scientific visualization (e.g., astrophysical simulation, fluid flow). Although the voxel representation is more effective for empirical imagery, it also has a significant utility in synthetic 3D graphics or in applications merging empirical and synthetic images [53, 97, 119] (see Figure 7). For example, in surgical planning and radiation therapy planning, the sampled volume data need to be visualized, manipulated, and analyzed along with objects such as osteotomy surfaces, surgical cuts, prosthetic devices, grafts, scalpels, injection needles, isodose surfaces, and radiation beams, which may not be available in digital form. Consequently, there is a real need for a mechanism to input a geometric model into volume visualization systems. The primary advantage of this approach is that voxel-based manipulation and rendering is independent of the scene complexity. This is due to the fact that voxelization is performed only once, followed by a separate rendering process that can be repeated again and again. Furthermore, attributes such as texture can be assigned once to the voxel representation, thus eliminate the need to repeat texture mapping during the rendering process.

7. Special-Purpose Architectures

Volume images are huge 3D matrices of the order of giga bits for moderate spatial resolution, with voxel granularity as fine as that of the pixel. This places new demands on graphic systems for more memory, faster computing and communications, and new breeds of processing and display. About a decade ago, the notion that computers or special-purpose hardware could be efficiently used for volume processing of 512^3 resolution or higher was merely a dream. Nowadays, with the rapid progress of parallel processing and microelectronics (especially in memory compactness), the dream is being brought closer to reality. This section introduces some innovative special-purpose hardware architecture for volume visualization: the GODPA/Voxel processor, the 3DP^4 architecture, the Cube architecture, the PARCUM architecture, and the Insight system. A comparison of their organization, capabilities, and performance can be found in [93, 102].

GODPA [52], which was designed for medical applications, is a derivative of the Voxel Processor [48, 49, 51]. Unlike the Voxel Processor, GODPA is capable of displaying many independently controllable objects. GODPA is a hierarchical pipelined hardware organization, in which the 256-cube voxel memory is divided into 64 symmetric equal sub-cubes, each processed by a separate concurrent processing element. The Voxel architecture has been used as the underlying architecture for a physician workstation [48, 50]. A prototype system of 64^3 voxels, 4-bit each, has been implemented, at a 16 frames per second image update rate. The full-scale VLSI system of 256^3 voxels is estimated to have an update rate of 20-30 frames per second.

Two projects have been proposed in Japan. One is a prototype system SCOPE [172], and the other system, which is very similar to GODPA, is the 3DP^4 architecture [140]. 3DP^4 has been simulated in software. A 256^3 hardware implementation is estimated to generate up to 10 frames/second.

The *Cube architecture* [98] is a versatile volume visualization system which handles both empirical and synthetic objects. The Cube architecture is centered around a full cubic frame buffer of voxels. In order to cope with the huge quantity of voxels and still perform in real time, two special features were incorporated within the architecture; a unique skewed memory organization which permits the retrieval and storage of voxels in parallel [89], and a multiple-write bus with massively parallel processing which speeds up the viewing process [98]. There are three processors that access the cubic frame buffer to input synthetic [83, 96, 99] and sampled volume data, to manipulate the volume images [87], and to view the volume images from an arbitrary direction [88] and render them [28]. They all exploit the parallel processing of an entire or partial beam of voxels to achieve real-time performance [84]. Two small scale prototypes of the architecture have been realized in hardware (printed circuit design and VLSI design) and have been operating in true real-time [88], faster than the alternative voxel systems. Currently, a 256^3 resolution VLSI-based prototype is being fabricated and is estimated to operate in true real time [10]. A 3D workstation environment has also been designed around the Cube architecture, [100] employing 3D input devices for a variety of applications (e.g., [9, 95]). Figures 4-7 were captured from the Cube workstation screen.

In the PARCUM system [76, 77] the memory cube is divided into 4^3 macro voxels, each of which is 4^3 voxels, one bit each. The read access fetches a macro voxel that is sorted in an output dataword. Two hardware implementations for the projection process are proposed: a surface detection technique with ray following using a binary rate multiplier, and an analytical approach using matrix multiplication.

Insight [130], developed by Phoenix Data Systems mainly for solid modeling and medical applications, combines hardware and software for octree encoded images [132]. It can display complex objects at a near real-time rate [133].

Several general-purpose systems, like the Ardent Titan [16, 60], the AT&T Pixel Machine [143], the HP Turbo SRX [164], the Pixar machine [22, 33, 75, 113, 116, 158], the Pixel-Plane [35, 44, 121], the Silicon Graphics 4D [2, 3], the Stellar GS2000 [5, 47, 161, 175], and the Sun TAAC-1 [8, 34, 80, 128], provide some software support for volume visualization, relying on partial hardware support of geometry and pixel manipulations.

8. Applications

This section describes various applications of volume visualization. Three-dimensional medical imaging (e.g., computed tomography, magnetic resonance imaging, positron emission tomography, and ultrasonography) has been the primary application of volume visualization and a driving force in the development of this field (e.g., [9, 18, 36, 43, 64, 65, 95, 112, 137, 150, 166, 178], see Figures 6 and 7). Primary medical applications include clinical diagnosis [29], orthopedic diagnosis [50], surgical planning [14, 18, 178], reconstructive and corrective surgery [57, 149], radiation therapy planning [14, 129], medical education [18], and medical research [11, 167].

Voxel representation is very effective for the traditional applications that employ empirical 3D voxel imagery, such as medical imaging, where the acquired data is already in a volumetric form. These applications include: biology (e.g., confocal microscopy [101, 115], see Figure 4), geoscience (e.g., seismic measurements [122, 155, 182]), industry (e.g., industrial inspection [114]), meteorology [59, 68, 173], molecular systems (e.g., electron density maps [53]), and 3D image processing (e.g., time varying 2D images), where the acquired data is in the form of a voxel image.

Volume visualization has a great potential beyond its original goal to observe internal human organs. It is also effective for new model-based volumetric applications like computer aided design (e.g., solid modeling [92] (see Figure 5), finite elements, material stress patterns), simulation and animation (e.g., flight simulation),

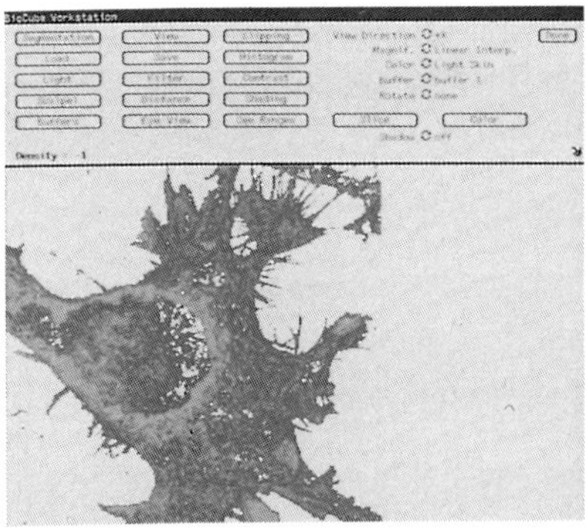

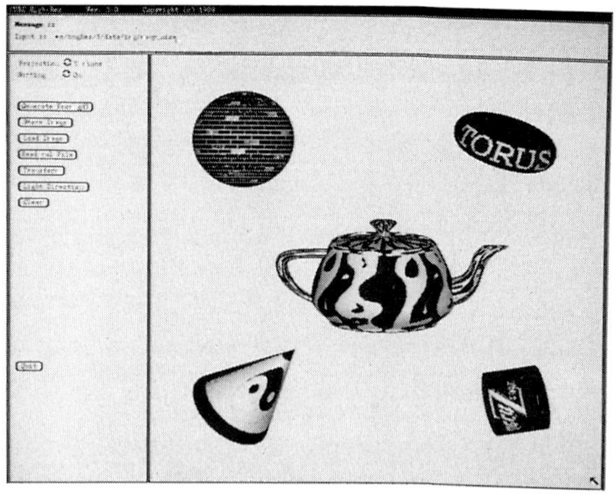

Figure 4 (left): 3D volume rendering of 256^3 cell cytoskeleton reconstructed from confocal microscope data.

Figure 5 (right): 512^3 voxelized and texture mapped geometric objects.

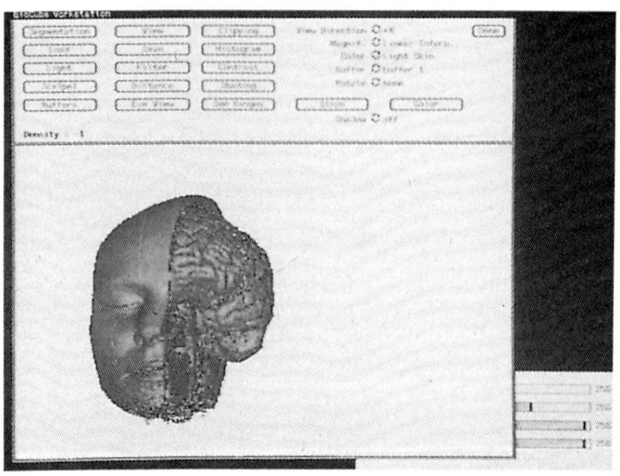

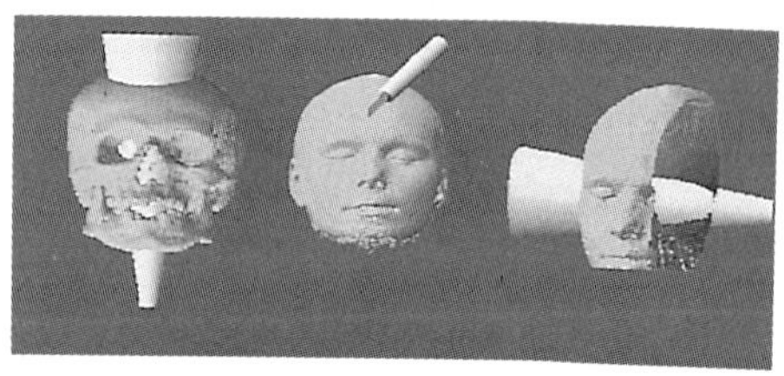

Figure 6 (left): 3D volume rendering of a 256^3 head with half the brain segmented and exposed.

Figure 7 (right): 3D volume rendering of heads reconstructed from MRI and CT slices intermixed with voxelized objects.

and scientific visualization (e.g., astrophysical simulation, fluid flow [159, 173]). With the advent of 3D scan-conversion algorithms, which form a bridge between geometric models and volume representation, the new model-based applications become commonplace.

The ViSC report [127] predicted that "in the future animated and interactive presentation and analysis of volume imagery will play a central role in medical imaging, geoscience, astrophysics, computational fluid dynamics, and finite element analysis, as well as many other scientific and engineering fields of research". A special issue on Visualization in Scientific Computing of *Computer* [138] includes several articles reporting on various applications of volume visualization, such as earth sciences [68], flows and flames [61, 124], and 3D medical imaging [43]. Furthermore, the paper on scientific visualization at five large research laboratories [151] illustrates applications to gas jets, quantum physics, neutron transport, cell biology, the greenhouse effect, astrophysics, aerodynamics, oceanography, molecular modeling, underwater acoustics and radar.

Volume visualization has recently emerged as a key to research and development of computer graphics. Volume visualization is a technical reality today and is imperative for tomorrow. The progress in volume visualization and computer development, coupled with the desire to reveal the inner structures of volumetric data sets, guarantees that volume visualization will develop into a dominant field in computer graphics and its associated applications.

Acknowledgement

This work was supported by the National Science Foundation under grants MIP-8805130 and IRI-9008109, and grants from Hughes Aircraft Company, Hewlett Packard, and Silicon Graphics. I wish to thank the many students of mine who have worked on 3D volume visualization, 3D scan-conversion algorithms, and the Cube project. Among them, special thanks are due to R. Bakalash, D. Cohen, and R. Yagel.

9. References

1. Agard, D. A., "Optical Sectioning Microscopy", *Annual Review of Biophysics and Bioengineering,* **13**, (1984), 191-219.

2. Akeley, K. and Jermoluk, T., "High-Performance Polygon Rendering", *Computer Graphics,* **22**, 4 (August 1988), 239-246.

3. Akeley, K., "The Silicon Graphics 4D/240GTX Superworkstation", *IEEE Computer Graphics & Applications,* **9**, 7 (July 1989), 71-83.

4. Anjyo, K. T., Usami, Y. and Kawashima, Y., "A Practical Method of Constructing Surface in Three-Dimensional Digitized Space", *The Visual Computer,* **3**, 1 (1987), 4-12.

5. Apgar, B., Bersack, B. and Mammen, A., "A Display System for the Stellar Graphics Supercomputer Model GS1000", *Computer Graphics,* **22**, 4 (August 1988), 255-262.

6. Artzy, E., Freider, G. and Herman, G. T., "The Theory, Design, Implementation and Evaluation of a Three Dimensional Surface Detection Algorithm", *Computer Graphics and Image Processing,* **15**, 1 (January 1981), 1-24.

7. Artzy, E., Frieder, G. and Herman, G. T., "The Theory, Design, Implementation and Evaluation of a Three-Dimensional Surface Detection Algorithm", *Computer Graphics and Image Processing,* **15**, 1 (January 1981), 1-24.

8. Austin, J. D. and Van Hook, T., "Medical Image Processing on an Enhanced Workstation", *Proceedings of SPIE, Medical Imaging II: Image Data Management and Display,* **914**, Part B (February 1988), 1317-1324.

9. Bakalash, R. and Kaufman, A., "MediCube: a 3D Medical Imaging Architecture", *Computers & Graphics,* **13**, 2 (1989), 151-157.

10. Bakalash, R., Kaufman, A. and Xu, Z., "Cube-3: Building a Full Scale VLSI-Based Volume Visualization System", *5th EG Workshop on Graphics Hardware,* Lausanne, Switzerland, September 1990.

11. Barillot, C., Gibaud, B., Scarabin, J. and Coatrieux, J., "3D Reconstruction of Cerebral Blood Vessels", *IEEE Computer Graphics and Applications,* **5**, 12 (December 1985), 13-19.

12. Bates, R. H., Garden, K. L. and Peters, T. M., "Overview of Computerized Tomography with Emphasis on Future Developments", *Proc. of the IEEE,* **71**, 3 (March 1983), 356-372.

13. Blinn, J. F., "Light Reflection Functions for Simulation for Clouds and Dusty Surfaces", *Computer Graphics,* **16**, 3 (July 1982), 21-29.

14. Bloch, P. and Udupa, J. K., "Application of Computerized Tomography to Radiation Therapy and Surgical Planning", *Proceedings of the IEEE,* **71**, 3 (March 1983), 351-355.

15. Boissonnat, J. D., "Shape Reconstruction from Planar Cross Sections", *Computer Vision, Graphics and Image Processing,* **44**, 1 (October 1988), 1-29.

16. Borden, V. S., "Graphics Processing on a Graphics Supercomputer", *IEEE Computer Graphics & Applications,* **9**, 7 (July 1989), 56-62.

17. Bresenham, J. E., "A Linear Algorithm for Incremental Digital Display of Circular Arcs", *Communications of the ACM,* **20**, 2 (February 1977), 100-106.

18. Brewster, L. J., Trivedi, S. S., Tuy, H. K. and Udupa, J. K., "Interactive Surgical Planning", *IEEE Computer Graphics and Applications,* **4**, 3 (March 1984), 31-40.

19. Bright, S. and Laflin, S., "Shading of Solid Voxel Models", *Computer Graphics Forum,* **5**, 2 (June 1986), 131-138.

20. Butland, J., Leach, A. R., Cappelletti, J. D. and Rosenfeld, A., "Three-Dimensional Boundary Following", *Computer Vision, Graphics, and Image Processing*, **48**, 1 (October 1989), 80-92.

21. Catmull, E., "A Subdivision Algorithm for Computer Display of Curved Surfaces", PhD Thesis, University of Utah UTEC-CSc-74-133, December 1974.

22. Chen, H., Sedat, J. W. and Agard, D. A., "Manipulation, Display, and Analysis of Three Dimensional Biological Images", in *The Handbook of Biological Confocal Microscopy, The Confocal Microscopy Workshop*, The Electron Microscopy Society of America, San Antonio, TX, August 1989, 127-135.

23. Chen, L., Herman, G. T., Reynolds, R. A. and Udupa, J. K., "Surface Shading in the Cuberille Environment", *IEEE Computer Graphics and Applications*, **5**, 12 (December 1985), 33-43.

24. Christiansen, H. N. and Sederberg, T. W., "Conversion of Complex Contour Line Definitions into Polygonal Element Meshes", *Computer Graphics*, **12**, 3 (August 1978), 187-192.

25. Chuang, K. S. and Udupa, J. K., "Boundary Detection in Grey Level Scenes", *Proceedings of NCGA'89 Conference*, **I**, (April 1989), 112-117.

26. Cline, H. E., Lorensen, W. E., Ludke, S., Crawford, C. R. and Teeter, B. C., "Two Algorithms for the Three-Dimensional Reconstruction of Tomograms", *Medical Physics*, **15**, 3 (May/June 1988), 320-327.

27. Cohen, D. and Kaufman, A., "3D Scan Conversion Algorithms for Linear and Quadratic Objects", in *Volume Visualization*, A. Kaufman, (ed.), IEEE Computer Society Press Tutorial, 1990, 280-301.

28. Cohen, D., Kaufman, A., Bakalash, R. and Bergman, S., "Real-Time Discrete Shading", *The Visual Computer*, **6**, 1 (February 1990), 16-27.

29. Cook, L. T., Dwyer III, S. J., Batnitzky, S. and Lee, K. R., "A Three-Dimensional Display System for Diagnostic Imaging Applications", *IEEE Computer Graphics and Applications*, **3**, 5 (August 1983), 13-19.

30. Csuri, C., Hackathorn, R., Parent, R., Carlson, W. and Howard, M., "Towards an Interactive High Visual Complexity Animation System", *Computer Graphics*, **13**, 2 (August 1979), 289-299.

31. DeFanti, T. A., Brown, M. D. and McCormick, B. H., "Visualization: Expanding Scientific and Engineering Research Opportunities", *IEEE Computer*, **22**, 8 (August 1989), 12-25.

32. Doctor, L. J. and Torborg, J. G., "Display Techniques for Octree-Encoded Objects", *IEEE Computer Graphics and Applications*, July 1981, 29-38.

33. Drebin, R. A., Carpenter, L. and Hanrahan, P., "Volume Rendering", *Computer Graphics*, **22**, 4 (August 1988), 64-75.

34. England, N., "Development of the TAAC-1", *Sun Technology*, **1**, 1 (Winter 1988), 34-41.

35. Eyles, J., Austin, J., Fuchs, H., Greer, T. and Poulton, J., "Pixel-Planes 4: A Summary", in *Advances in Computer Graphics Hardware II*, Eurographics Seminars, 1988, 183-208.

36. Farrell, E. J., Yang, W. C. and Zappulla, R. A., "Animated 3D CT Imaging", *IEEE Computer Graphics and Applications*, **5**, 12 (December 1985), 26-32.

37. Foley, J. D. and van Dam, A., *Fundamentals of Interactive Computer Graphics*, Addison-Wesley, Reading, MA, 1982.

38. Frederick, C. and Schwartz, E. L., "Brain Peeling: Viewing the Inside of a Laminar 3D Solid", *The Visual Computer*, **6**, 1 (February 1990), 37-49.

39. Freeman, H., "Computer Processing of Line-Drawing Images", *ACM Computing Surveys*, **6**, 1 (March 1974), 57-97.

40. Frieder, G., Gordon, D. and Reynolds, R. A., "Back-to-Front Display of Voxel-Based Objects", *IEEE Computer Graphics and Applications*, **5**, 1 (January 1985), 52-60.

41. Frieder, G., Herman, G. T., Meyer, C. and Udupa, J., "Large Software Problems for Small Computers: An Example from Medical Imaging", *IEEE Software*, **2**, 5 (September 1985), 36-47.

42. Fuchs, H., Levoy, M., Pizer, S. M. and Rosenman, J. G., "Interactive Visualization and Manipulation of 3-D Medical Image Data", *Proceedings of NCGA'89 Conference*, **I**, (April 1989), 118-131.

43. Fuchs, H., Levoy, M. and Pizer, S. M., "Interactive Visualization of 3D Medical Data", *IEEE Computer*, **22**, 8 (August 1989), 46-51.

44. Fuchs, H., Poulton, J., Eyles, J., Greer, T., Goldfeather, J., Ellsworth, D., Molnar, S., Turk, G., Tebbs, B. and Israel, L., "Pixel-Planes 5: A Heterogeneous Multiprocessor Graphic System Using Processor-Enhanced Memories", *Computer Graphics*, **23**, 3 (July 1989), 79-88.

45. Fuchs, H., Kedem, Z. M. and Uselton, S. P., "Optimal Surface Reconstruction from Planar Contours", *Communications of the ACM*, **20**, 10 (October 1977), 693-702.

46. Geist, D. and Vannier, M. W., "PC-Based 3-D Reconstruction of Medical Images", *Computers & Graphics*, **13**, 2 (1989), 135-144.

47. Gelberg, L., Kamins, D. and Vroom, J., "VEX: A Volume Exploratorium. An Integrated Toolkit for Interactive Volume Visualization", *Proceedings of the Chapel Hill Workshop on Volume Visualization*, Chapel Hill, NC, May 1989, 21-26.

48. Goldwasser, S. M., Reynolds, R. A., Talton, D. A. and Walsh, E. S., "High Performance Graphics Processors for Medical Imaging Applications", in *Parallel Processing for Computer Vision and Display*, P. M. Dew, R. A. Earnshaw and T. R. Heywood, (eds.), Addison Wesley, 1989, 461-470.

49. Goldwasser, S. M. and Reynolds, R. A., "An Architecture for the Real-Time Display of Three Dimensional Objects", *Proceedings International Conference on Parallel Processing*, Bellaire, Michigan, August 1983, 269-274.

50. Goldwasser, S. M., Reynolds, R. A., Bapty, T., Baraff, D., Summers, J., Talton, D. A. and Walsh, E., "Physician's Workstation with Real-Time Performance", *IEEE Computer Graphics and Applications*, **5**, 12 (December 1985), 44-57.

51. Goldwasser, S. M. and Reynolds, R. A., "Real-Time Display and Manipulation of 3-D Medical Objects: The Voxel Processor Architecture", *Computer Vision, Graphics and Image Processing*, **39**, 1 (July 1987), 1-27.

52. Goldwasser, S. M., "A Generalized Object Display Processor Architecture", *IEEE Computer Graphics and Applications*, **4**, 10 (October 1984), 43-55.

53. Goodsell, D. S., Mian, S. and Olson, A. J., "Rendering of Volumetric Data in Molecular Systems", *Journal of Molecular Graphics*, **7**, (March 1989), 41-47.

54. Goodsell, D. S. and Olson, A. S., "Molecular Applications of Volume Rendering and 3-D Texture Maps", *Proceedings of the Chapel Hill Workshop on Volume Visualization*, Chapel Hill, NC, May 1989, 27-32.

55. Gordon, D. and Udupa, J. K., "Fast Surface Tracking in Three-Dimensional Binary Images", *Computer Vision, Graphics and Image Processing*, **45**, 2 (February 1989), 196-214.

56. Gordon, D. and Reynolds, R. A., "Image Space Shading of 3-Dimensional Objects", *Computer Graphics and Image Processing*, **29**, 3 (March 1985), 361-376.

57. Granholm, J. W., Robertson, D. D., Walker, P. S. and Nelson, P. C., "Computer Design of Custom Femoral Stem Prostheses", *IEEE Computer Graphics and Analysis*, **7**, 2 (February 1987), 26-34.

58. Greenberg, D. P., Wu, S. C. and Abel, J. F., "An Interactive Computer Graphics Approach to Surface Representation", *Communications of the ACM*, **20**, 10 (October 1977), 703-712.

59. Grotjahn, R. and Chervin, R., "Animated Graphics in Meteorological Research and Presentation", *Bulletin of American Meteorological Society*, **65**, (1984), 1201-1208.

60. Hagenmaier, T. D. C. F., Miranker, G. S., Rubinstein, J. J., Worley, W. S. J., "The Titan Graphic Supercomputer Architecture", *Computer*, **21**, 9 (September 1988), 13-29.

61. Helman, J. and Hesselink, L., "Representation and Display of Vector Field Topology in Fluid Flow Data Sets", *IEEE Computer*, **22**, 8 (August 1989), 27-36.

62. Herman, G. T. and Liu, H. K., "Dynamic Boundary Surface Detection", *Computer Graphics and Image Processing*, **7**, (1978), 130-138.

63. Herman, G. T. and Udupa, J. K., "Display of Three Dimensional Discrete Surfaces", *Proceedings of SPIE*, **273**, (1981), 90-97.

64. Herman, G. T., "Special Issue on Computerized Tomography", *Proceedings of the IEEE*, **71**, (1983), .

65. Herman, G. T. and Udupa, J. K., "Display of 3D Digital Images: Computational Foundations and Medical Applications", *IEEE Computer Graphics and Applications*, **3**, 5 (August 1983), 39-46.

66. Herman, G. T. and Liu, H. K., "Three-Dimensional Display of Human Organs from Computed Tomograms", *Computer Graphics and Image Processing*, **9**, 1 (January 1979), 1-21.

67. Herr, L., *Volume Visualization - State of the Art*, ACM SIGGRAPH Video Review, Issue 44, 1989.

68. Hibbard, W. and Santek, D., "Visualizing Large Data Sets in the Earth Sciences", *IEEE Computer*, **22**, 8 (August 1989), 53-57.

69. Hibbard, W. and Santek, D., "Interactivity is the Key", in *Proceedings of the Chapel Hill Workshop on Volume Visualization*, C. Upson, (ed.), University of North Carolina at Chapel Hill, Chapel Hill, NC, May 1989, 39-44.

70. Hinshaw, W. S. and Lent, A. H., "An Introduction to NMR Imaging: From the Bloch Equation to the Imaging Equation", *Proc. of the IEEE*, **71**, 3 (March 1983), 338-350.

71. Hoehne, K. H., Bomans, M., Pommert, A., Riemer, M., Schiers, C., Tiede, U. and Wiebecke, G., "3D-Visualization of Tomographic Volume Data Using the Generalized Voxel Model", *The Visual Computer*, **6**, 1 (February 1990), 28-37.

72. Hoehne, K. H. and Bernstein, R., "Shading 3D-Images from CT Using Gray-Level Gradients", *IEEE Transactions on Medical Imaging*, **MI-5**, 1 (March 1986), 45-47.

73. Hoehne, K. H., Bomans, M., Pommert, A., Riemer, M., Schiers, C., Tiede, U. and Wiebecke, G., "3D-Visualization of Tomographic Volume Data Using the Generalized Voxel Model", in *Proceedings of the Chapel Hill Workshop on Volume Visualization*, C. Upson, (ed.), University of North Carolina at Chapel Hill, Chapel Hill, NC, May 1989, 51-58.

74. Horn, B. K. P., "Hill Shading and the Reflection Map", *Geo-Processing*, **2**, (1982), 65-146, Elsevier Scientific Publishing.

75. Hu, X., Tan, K. K., Levin, D. N., Galhotra, S. G., Pelizzari, C. A., Chen, G. T. Y., Beck, R. N., Chen, C. T. and Cooper, M. D., "Volumetric Rendering of Multimodality, Multivariable Medical Imaging Data", *Proceedings of the Chapel Hill Workshop on Volume Visualization*, Chapel Hill, NC, May 1989, 45-50.

76. Jackel, D. and Strasser, W., "Reconstructing Solids from Tomographic Scans - The PARCUM II System", in *Advances in Computer Graphics Hardware II*, A. A. M. Kuijk and W. Strasser, (eds.), Springer-Verlag, Berlin, 1988, 209-227.

77. Jackel, D., "The Graphics PARCUM System: A 3D Memory Based Computer Architecture for Processing and Display of Solid Models", *Computer Graphics Forum*, **4**, 1 (January 1985), 21-32.

78. Jackins, C. and Tanimoto, S. L., "Octrees and Their Use in Representing Three-Dimensional Objects", *Computer Graphics & Image Processing*, **14**, 3 (Nov. 1980), 249-270.

79. Jense, G. J. and Huijsmans, D. P., "Interactive Voxel-Based Graphics for 3D Reconstruction of Biological Structures", *Computers & Graphics*, **13**, 2 (1989), 145-150.

80. Johnson, E. R. and Mosher, C. E., "Integration of Volume Rendering and Geometric Graphics", *Proceedings of the Chapel Hill Workshop on Volume Visualization*, Chapel Hill, NC, May 1989, 1-8.

81. Kajiya, J. T. and Von Herzen, B. P., "Ray Tracing Volume Densities", *Computer Graphics*, **18**, 3 (July 1984), 165-174.

82. Kajiya, J. T. and Kay, T. L., "Rendering Fur with Three Dimensional Textures", *Computer Graphics*, **23**, 3 (July 1989), 271-280.

83. Kaufman, A., "Efficient Algorithms for 3D Scan-Converting Polygons", *Computers & Graphics*, **12**, 2 (1988), 213-219.

84. Kaufman, A. and Bakalash, R., "Parallel Processing for 3D Voxel-Based Graphics", in *Parallel Processing for Computer Vision and Display*, P. M. Dew, R. A. Earnshaw and T. R. Heywood, (eds.), Addison-Wesley, 1989, 471-478.

85. Kaufman, A., "Guest Editor's Introduction: 3D Voxel-Based Graphics", *Computers & Graphics*, **13**, 2 (1989), 133-134.

86. Kaufman, A., *Volume Visualization*, IEEE Press, 1990.

87. Kaufman, A., "The voxblt Engine: A Voxel Frame Buffer Processor", in *Advances in Graphics Hardware III*, A. A. M. Kuijk and W. Strasser, (eds.), Springer-Verlag, Berlin, 1990.

88. Kaufman, A., Bakalash, R. and Cohen, D., "Viewing and Rendering Processor for a Volume Visualization System", in *Advances in Graphics Hardware IV*, R. L. Grimsdale and W. Strasser, (eds.), Springer-Verlag, Berlin, 1990.

89. Kaufman, A., "Memory Organization for a Cubic Frame Buffer", *Proceedings EUROGRAPHICS'86*, Lisbon, Portugal, August 1986, 93-100.

90. Kaufman, A., "An Algorithm for 3D Scan-Conversion of Polygons", *Proceedings of EUROGRAPHICS'87 Conference*, Amsterdam, The Netherlands, August 1987, 197-208.

91. Kaufman, A., Bakalash, R., Bergman, S. and Cohen, D., "Real-Time Shading for 3-D Frame Buffer", *Proceedings of the Eighth Conference on CAD/CAM and Robotics*, Tel-Aviv, December 1986, 6.2.4.1-11.

92. Kaufman, A., "Voxel-Based Solid Modeling", *Proc. International Conference on CAD/CAM and AMT*, Jerusalem, Israel, December 1989, 1.1.3-1-3.

93. Kaufman, A., Bakalash, R., Cohen, D. and Yagel, R., "Architectures for Volume Rendering - A Survey", *IEEE Engineering in Medicine and Biology*, December 1990.

94. Kaufman, A., "Editorial: Volume Visualization", *Visual Computer*, **6**, 1 (February 1990), 1.

95. Kaufman, A. and Bakalash, R., "The CUBE System as a 3D Medical Workstation", *Proceedings of SPIE, '89 Symposium on 3D Visualization of Scientific Data*, Los Angeles, CA, January 1989, 189-194.

96. Kaufman, A., "Efficient Algorithms for 3D Scan-Conversion of Parametric Curves, Surfaces, and Volumes", *Computer Graphics*, **21**, 4 (July 1987), 171-179.

97. Kaufman, A., Yagel, R. and Cohen, D., "Intermixing Surface and Volume Rendering", in *3D Imaging in Medicine: Algorithms, Systems, Applications*, K. H. Hoehne, H. Fuchs and S. M. Pizer, (eds.), Travemunde, West Germany, June 1990, 217-227.

98. Kaufman, A. and Bakalash, R., "Memory and Processing Architecture for 3D Voxel-Based Imagery", *IEEE Computer Graphics and Applications*, **8**, 6 (November 1988), 10-23.

99. Kaufman, A. and Shimony, E., "3D Scan-Conversion Algorithms for Voxel-Based Graphics", *Proceedings ACM Workshop on Interactive 3D Graphics*, Chapel Hill, NC, October 1986, 45-75.

100. Kaufman, A., "The CUBE Workstation - a 3D Voxel-Based Graphics Environment", *The Visual Computer*, **4**, 4 (October 1988), 210-221.

101. Kaufman, A., Yagel, R., Bakalash, R. and Spector, I., "Volume Visualization in Cell Biology", *Proceedings Visualization '90*, San Francisco, CA, October 1990, 161-167.

102. Kaufman, A., "Voxel-Based Architectures for Three-Dimensional Graphics", *Proceedings IFIP'86*, Dublin, Ireland, September 1986, 361-366.

103. Keppel, E., "Approximating Complex Surfaces by Triangulation of Contour Lines", *IBM Journal of Research and Development*, **19**, 1 (January 1975), 2-11.

104. Kim, C. E., "Three-Dimensional Digital Line Segments", *IEEE Transactions on Pattern Analysis and Machine Intelligence*, **PAMI-5**, 2 (March 1983), 231-234.

105. Kim, C. E. and Rosenfeld, A., "Convex Digital Solids", *IEEE Transactions on Pattern Analysis and Machine Intelligence*, **PAMI-4**, 6 (November 1982), 612-618.

106. Kim, C. E., "Three-Dimensional Digital Planes", *IEEE Transactions on Pattern Analysis and Machine Intelligence*, **PAMI-6**, 5 (September 1984), 639-645.

107. Kluksdahl, N., Kriman, A. and Ferry, D., "The Role of Visualization in the Simulation of quantum Electronic Transport in Semiconductors", *IEEE Computer*, **22**, 8 (August 1989), 60-67.

108. Kong, T. Y., "A Digital Fundamental Group", *Computers & Graphics*, **13**, 2 (1989), 159-166.

109. Kong, T. Y. and Rosenfeld, A., "Digital Topology: Introduction and Survey", *Computer Vision, Graphics and Image Processing*, **48**, 3 (December 1989), 357-393.

110. Kong, T. Y. and Roscoe, A. W., "A Continuous Analog of Axiomatized Digital Surfaces", *Computer Vision, Graphics and Image Processing*, **29**, 1 (January 1985), 60-86.

111. Kong, T. Y. and Roscoe, A. W., "A Theory of Binary Digital Pictures", *Computer Vision, Graphics and Image Processing*, **32**, 2 (November 1985), 221-243.

112. Kramer, D. A., Kaufman, L., Guzman, R. J. and Hawryszko, C., "A General Algorithm for Oblique Image Reconstruction", *IEEE Computer Graphics and Applications*, **10**, 2 (March 1990), 62-65.

113. Kraske, W. F., George III, F. W. and Halls, J. M., "Morphological Description in 3D Volumetric Biomedical Visualization", *Proceedings of the Chapel Hill Workshop on Volume Visualization*, Chapel Hill, NC, May 1989, 59-66.

114. Kruger, R. P. and Cannon, T. M., "The Application of Computerized Tomography, Boundary Detection, and Shaded Graphics Reconstruction to Industrial Inspection", *Materials Evaluation*, **36**, (April 1978), 75-80.

115. Leith, A., Marko, M. and Parsons, D., "Computer Graphics for Cellular Reconstruction", *IEEE Computer Graphics and Applications*, **9**, 5 (September 1989), 16-23.

116. Levinthal, A. and Porter, T., "Chap - A SIMD Graphic Processor", *Computer Graphics*, **18**, 3 (July 1984), 77-82.

117. Levoy, M., "Introduction to Viewing Algorithms", in *Volume Visualization*, A. Kaufman, (ed.), IEEE Press, 1990.

118. Levoy, M., "Volume Rendering by Adaptive Refinement", *The Visual Computer*, **6**, 1 (February 1990), 2-7.

119. Levoy, M., "A Hybrid Ray Tracer for Rendering Polygon and Volume Data", *IEEE Computer Graphics & Applications*, **10**, 3 (March 1990), 33-40.

120. Levoy, M., "Display of Surfaces from Volume Data", *IEEE Computer Graphics and Applications*, **8**, 5 (May 1988), 29-37.

121. Levoy, M., "Design for Real-Time High-Quality Volume Rendering Workstation", *Proceedings of the Chapel Hill Workshop on Volume Visualization*, Chapel Hill, NC, May 1989, 85-92.

122. Lin, C. and Cohen, M. H., "Quantitative Methods for Microgeometric Modeling", *Journal of Applied Physics*, **53**, (1982), 4152-4165.

123. Liu, H. K., "Two- and Three-Dimensional Boundary Detection", *Computer Graphics and Image Processing*, **6**, (1977), 123-134.

124. Long, M. B., Lyons, K. and Lam, J. K., "Acquisition and Representation of 2D and 3D Data from Turbulent Flows and Flames", *IEEE Computer*, **22**, 8 (August 1989), 39-45.

125. Lorensen, W. E. and Cline, H. E., "Marching Cubes: A High Resolution 3D Surface Construction Algorithm", *Computer Graphics*, **21**, 4 (July 1987), 163-169.

126. Max, N. L., "Atmospheric Illumination and Shadows", *Computer Graphics*, **20**, 4 (August 1986), 117-124.

127. McCormick, B. H., DeFanti, T. A. and Brown, M. D., "Visualization in Scientific Computing", *Computer Graphics*, **21**, 6 (November 1987), .

128. McMillan, D., Johnson, R. and Mosher, C., "Volume Rendering on the TAAC-1", *Sun Technology*, **2**, 4 (Autumn 1989), 52-58.

129. McShan, D. L., Silverman, A., Lanza, D. M., Reinstein, L. E. and Glicksman, A. S., "A Computerized Three-Dimensional Treatment Planning System Utilizing Interactive Color Graphics", *British Journal of Radiology*, **52**, 6 (June 1979), 478-481.

130. Meagher, D. J., "Applying Solids Processing Methods to Medical Planning", *Proceedings NCGA'85 Conference*, Dallas, TX, April 1985, 101-109.

131. Meagher, D., "Efficient Synthetic Image Generation of Arbitrary 3-D Objects", *Proceedings of IEEE Computer Society Conference on Pattern Recognition and Image Processing*, June 1982.

132. Meagher, D. J., "Geometric Modeling Using Octree Encoding", *Computer Graphics and Image Processing*, **19**, 2 (June 1982), 129-147.

133. Meagher, D. J., "Interactive Solids Processing for Medical Analysis and Planning", *Proceedings NCGA'84 Conference*, Anaheim, CA, May 1984, 96-106.

134. Mohan, R., Barset, G., Brewster, L. J., Chui, C. S., Kutcher, G. J., Laughlin, J. S. and Fuks, Z., "A Comprehensive Three-Dimensional Radiation Treatment Planning System", *International Journal of Radiation Oncology Biological Physics*, **15**, (August 1988), 481-495.

135. Mokrzycki, W., "Algorithms of Discretization of Algebraic Spatial Curves on Homogeneous Cubical Grids", *Computers & Graphics*, **12**, 3/4 (1988), 477-487.

136. Morgenthaler, D. G. and Rosenfeld, A., "Multidimensional Edge Detection by Hypersurface Fitting", *IEEE Transactions on Pattern Analysis and Machine Intelligence*, **PAMI-3**, 4 (July 1981), 483-486.

137. Ney, D. R., Fishman, E. K., Magid, D. and Drebin, A., "Volumetric Rendering of Computed Tomography Data: Principles and Techniques", *IEEE Computer Graphics & Applications*, **10**, 3 (March 1990), 24-32.

138. Nielson, G. M., "Guest Editor's Introduction: Visualization in Scientific Computing", *IEEE Computer*, **22**, 8 (August 1989), 10-11.

139. Nishita, T., Miyawaki, Y. and Nakamae, E., "A Shading Model for Atmospheric Scattering Considering Luminous Intensity Distribution of Light Sources", *Computer Graphics*, **21**, 4 (July 1987), 303-310.

140. Ohashi, T., Uchiki, T. and Tokoro, M., "A Three-Dimensional Shaded Display Method for Voxel-Based Representation", *Proceedings EUROGRAPHICS '85*, Nice, France, September 1985, 221-232.

141. Pavlidis, T., *Algorithms for Graphics and Image Processing*, Computer Science Press, 1982.

142. Pommert, A., Tiede, U., Wiebecke, G. and Hoehne, K. H., "Image Quality in Voxel-Based Surface Shading", *Proceedings of the International Symposium on Computer Assisted Radiology, CAR'89*, Berlin, West Germany, 1989, 737-741.

143. Potmesil, M. and Hoffert, E. M., "The Pixel Machine: A Parallel Image Computer", *Computer Graphics*, **23**, 3 (July 1989), 69-78.

144. Raya, S. P. and Udupa, J. K., "Shape-Based Interpolation of Multidimensional Objects", *IEEE Transactions on Medical Imaging*, **9**, 1 (March 1990), 32-42.

145. Reed, G. M. and Rosenfeld, A., "Recognition of Surfaces in Three-Dimensional Digital Images", *Information and Control*, 1982, 108-120.

146. Reeves, W. T., "Particle Systems - A Technique for Modeling a Class of Fuzzy Objects", *ACM Transactions on Graphics*, **2**, 2 (April 1983), 91-108.

147. Reeves, W. T. and Blau, R., "Approximate and Probabilistic Algorithms for Shading and Rendering Structured Particle Systems", *Computer Graphics*, **19**, 3 (July 1985), 313-322.

148. Reynolds, R. A., Gordon, D. and Chen, L. S., "A Dynamic Screen Technique for Shaded Graphic Display of Slice-Represented Objects", *Computer Vision, Graphics and Image Processing*, **38**, 3 (June 1987), 275-298.

149. Rhodes, M. L., Kuo, Y. and Rothman, S. L. G., "An Application of Computer Graphics and Networks to Anatomic Model and Prosthesis Manufacturing", *IEEE Computer Graphics and Applications*, **7**, 2 (February 1987), 12-25.

150. Rhodes, M., "Computer Graphics in Medicine", *IEEE Computer Graphics and Applications*, **10**, 2 (March 1990), 20-23.

151. Rosenblum, L., "Scientific Visualization at Research Laboratories", *IEEE Computer*, **22**, 8 (August 1989), 68-69.

152. Rosenfeld, A., "Three-Dimensional Digital Topology", *Information and Control*, **50**, 2 (August 1981), 119-127.

153. Rossignac, J. R., "Considerations on the Interactive Rendering of Four-Dimensional Volumes", *Proceedings of the Chapel Hill Workshop on Volume Visualization*, Chapel Hill, NC, May 1989, 67-76.

154. Rubin, S. M. and Whitted, T., "A 3-Dimensional Represetation for Fast Rendering of Complex Scenes", *Computer Graphics*, **14**, 3 (July 1980), 110-116.

155. Sabella, P., "A Rendering Algorithm for Visualizing 3D Scalar Fields", *Computer Graphics*, **22**, 4 (August 1988), 51-58.

156. Samet, H. and Webber, R. E., "Hierarchical Data Structures and Algorithms for Computer Graphics, Part II: Applications", *IEEE Computer Graphics and Applications*, **8**, 7 (July 1988), 59-75.

157. Schlusselberg, D. S., Smith, K. and Woodward, D. J., "Three-Dimensional Display of Medical Image Volumes", *Proceedings of NCGA'86 Conference*, **III**, (May 1986), 114-123.

158. Schreiter, D. and Zimmerman, J. B., "Evaluation of 3D Voxel Rendering Algorithms for Real-Time Interaction on a SIMD Graphic Processor", *Proceedings of SPIE, Medical Imaging II: Image Data Management and Display*, **914**, Part B (February 1988), 1291-1298.

159. Shirley, P. and Neeman, H., "Volume Visualization at the Center for Supercomputing Research and Development", *Proceedings of the Chapel Hill Workshop on Volume Visualization*, Chapel Hill, NC, May 1989, 17-20.

160. Sobierajski, L., Cohen, D., Kaufman, A., Yagel, R. and Acker, D., "Trimmed Voxel Lists for Interactive Surgical Planning", Tech. Rep. 90.05.22, SUNY Stony Brook, May 1990. (Submitted).

161. Sporer, M., Moss, F. H. and Mathias, C. J., "An Introduction to the Architecture of the Stellar Graphic Supercomputer", *Proceedings of the Thirty-Third IEEE Computer Society International Conference*, San Francisco, CA, March 1988, 464-467.

162. Srihari, S. N., "Representation of Three-Dimensional Digital Images", *ACM Computing Surveys*, **4**, 13 (December 1981), 399-424.

163. Sunguroff, A. and Greenberg, D., "Computer Generated Images for Medical Application", *Computer Graphics*, **12**, 3 (August 1978), 196-202.

164. Swanson, R. W. and Thayer, L. J., "A Fast Shaded Polygon Renderer", *Computer Graphics*, **20**, 4 (August 1986), 95-101.

165. Tam, Y. W. and Davis, W. A., "Display of 3D Medical Images", *Proceedings of Graphics Interface'88*, Edmonton, Alberta, June 1988, 78-86.

166. Tiede, U., Hoehne, K. H., Bomans, M., Pommert, A., Riemer, M. and Wiebecke, G., "Investigation of Medical 3D-Rendering Algorithms", *IEEE Computer Graphics & Applications*, **10**, 3 (March 1990), 41-53.

167. Toga, A. W. and Arnicar, T. L., "Image Analysis of Brain Physiology", *IEEE Computer Graphics and Applications*, **5**, 12 (December 1985), 20-25.

168. Toriwaki, J., Yokoi, S., Yonekura, T. and Fukumura, T., "Topological Properties and Topology-Preserving Transformation of a Three-Dimensional Binary Picture", *Proceedings of the 6th International Conference on Pattern Recognition*, **IEEE82CH1801-0**, (1982), 414-419.

169. Torson, J. M., "Interactive Image Cube Visualization and Analysis", *Proceedings of the Chapel Hill Workshop on Volume Visualization*, Chapel Hill, NC, May 1989, 33-36.

170. Trivedi, S. S., Herman, G. T. and Udupa, J. K., "Segmentation into Three Classes Using Gradients", *IEEE Transactions on Medical Imaging*, **MI-5**, 2 (June 1986), 116-119.

171. Tuy, H. K. and Tuy, L. T., "Direct 2-D Display of 3-D Objects", *IEEE Computer Graphics and Applications*, **4**, 10 (October 1984), 29-33.

172. Uchiki, T. and Tokoro, M., "SCOPE: Solid and Colored Object Projection Environment", *Transaction of the Institute of Electronics and Communication Engineers of Japan*, **68-D**, 4 (April 1985), 741-748, (in Japanese).

173. Upson, C. and Keeler, M., "V-BUFFER: Visible Volume Rendering", *Computer Graphics*, **22**, 4 (August 1988), 59-64.

174. Upson, C. and Kerlick, D., "Volumetric Visualization Techniques", in *Two and Three Dimensional Visualization Workshop, ACM SIGGRAPH'89 Course Notes*, vol. 13, Boston, MA, August 1989, 1-86.

175. Upson, C., Faulhaber, Jr., T., Kamins, D., Laidlaw, D., Schlegel, D., Vroom, J., Gurwitz, R. and van Dam, A., "The Application Visualization System: A Computational Environment for Scientific Visualization", *IEEE Computer Graphics and Applications*, **9**, 4 (July 1989), 30-42.

176. Upson, C., in *Proceedings of the Chapel Hill Workshop on Volume Visualization*, University of North Carolina at Chapel Hill, Chapel Hill, NC, May 1989, edited proceedings.

177. Van Aken, J. R. and Novak, M., "Curve-Drawing Algorithms for Raster Displays", *ACM Trans. on Graphics*, **4**, 2 (April 1985), 147-169.

178. Vannier, M. W., Marsh, J. L. and Warren, J. O., "Three Dimensional Computer Graphics for Craniofacial Surgical Planning and Evaluation", *Computer Graphics*, **17**, 3 (July 1983), 263-273.

179. Webber, R. E., "Ray Tracing Voxel Based Data via Biquadratic Local Surface Interpolation", *The Visual Computer*, **6**, 1 (February 1990), 8-15.

180. Westover, L., "Interactive Volume Rendering", *Proceedings of the Chapel Hill Workshop on Volume Visualization*, Chapel Hill, NC, May 1989, 9-16.

181. Wixson, S. E., "True Volume Visualization of Medical Data", *Proceedings of the Chapel Hill Workshop on Volume Visualization*, Chapel Hill, NC, May 1989, 77-84.

182. Wolfe, R. H. and Liu, C. N., "Interactive Visualization of 3D Seismic Data: A Volumetric Method", *IEEE Computer Graphics and Applications*, **8**, 7 (July 1988), 24-30.

183. Yamaguchi, K., Kunii, T. L., Fujimura, K. and Toriya, H., "Octree Related Data Structures and Algorithms", *IEEE Computer Graphics & Applications*, **4**, 1 (January 1984), 53-59.

184. Zucker, S. W. and Hummel, R. A., "A Three-Dimensional Edge Operator", *IEEE Transactions on Pattern Analysis and Machine Intelligence*, **PAMI-3**, 3 (May 1981), 324-331.

185. Zyda, M. J., Jones, A. R. and Hogan, P. G., "Surface Construction from Plane Contours", *Computers & Graphics*, **11**, 4 (1987), 393-408.

Introduction to Digital Image Processing *

Murat Kunt

1. Generalities

Along with sounds, images are one of the most important means human beings use to communicate with each other. Recent efforts enlarge this communication even to machines. Image processing is the ensemble of methods which make this operation possible, simplier, more efficient and more pleasant. This is an important aid for man who can satisfies his curiosity and the requirement associated with them. Aren't we all conscious of the joy we have for example to find the picture which freezed a happy event in the past.

Image processing is multidimensional signal processing. The representation of the luminance l of the picture is a function of the coordinates x and y of the plane is made with a two-dimensional signal $l(x,y)$. An image sequence such as that of the television for example is represented by a three-dimensional signal $l(x,y,t)$ where t represents time.

The processing of the signals could be made by optical means or by digital means. In the first case, signals and systems are essentially analog, whereas in the second case they are digital. Here, we limit ourselves exclusively to digital processing. This implies the digitization of signals to be compatible with digital processing.

In this section, we give a brief overview, first on the history of the image processing which allows us to define major activity areas nowadays classical. The multidisciplinary aspect of image processing is emphasized by placing it with regards to other areas. The variety of processing that could be imagined is also discussed. Finally, the main application areas as well as problems related to the computation problems are presented.

1.2 Historical Notes

The first image processing by technical means goes as back as to eighteenth century at the time of pioneers of photography. The comparison between the first results of exposure of silver nitrate to light and those we obtain today with films and cameras available on the

---

* This chapter has previously been published in the book "Traitement de l'information", Presses Polytechniques Romandes - 1990

market show the progress accomplished in this area. Electronic made its apparition in image processing towards the end of 19th century, when the Nipkow disc in 1884 allowed the transcription of an image into an electrical signal. From amelioration to perfection, one came to television in 1941. Techniques based on photography, optics and analog electronics made up what is called analog image processing.

By associating to each little elementary surface of a few square millimetre of an image, a number which represents the luminance of this region, it is possible to transform the image into a set of numbers. Section 2 gives the detail of this operation. Even if this set of numbers may be quite large (hundreds of thousands), it remains acceptable for processing by computer. This was the start of digital image processing, with a development parallel to that of computers and for the time being with no visible or previsible sign of saturation.

If the computer offers a large flexibility challenging the imagination, it conserves a disadvantage which becomes progressively apparent. Many of the processings, specially those which are relatively complex cannot be done rapidly. This is the contradiction still not solved which should be accompanied with a compromise between the flexibility and the speed of the processing. The increase of one leads necessarily to the decrease of the other. However, researchers try to push the limits of this compromise everyday a little further with new technologies and architectures for processing systems.

The first digital processing on images aimed at the simulation of image transmission systems such as television or telefax. The large number of symbols necessary to represent an image in digital form opened rapidly the way to important research work still of great importance today to reduce this number. This is the area called redundancy reduction or image compression. At the beginning, digital images were relatively small (about 256x256). Although the available channel capacity increased quite constantly, it was not enoug to stop the activity on redundancy reduction. To obtain images with better definition, the size has been increased and applications have been diversified to require in term even larger channels. This process still continues today with the high definition television.

Another area of digital processing which has received the particular attention is that of the classical signal processing generalized to two and three dimensions specially in filtering. Even if the study of linear systems and filtered design have reached a certain saturation level, the introduction of non linear systems and processings and neural networks are an important and attractive activity.

The improvement of the quality of a degraded image or the modification of an image to improve its subjective appearance concerns the third important area of image processing. This is an area called *restoration and enhancement* .

Over these three historical areas are added today a large number of processing which makes digital image processing a very important scientific and technical area in full expansion. As an example, one can consider the contour extraction image segmentation and texture analysis.

1.3 Diversity of Processing

Image processing calls a number of important disciplines. Signal theory, system theory, numerical analysis, statistics, information theory, neurophysiology and psychophysics, optics, electronics and computer science, to mention the main ones. This situation is summarized in figure 1. We can see image processing as a continuation of digital signal processing and as a prerequisite to pattern recognition, scene analysis and artificial intelligence (Figure 2). These rich relations with various areas are responsible of the very large diversity of processing one can implement digitally on images. Certain salesmen of image processing systems or image processing software say that these are limited only by the imagination of the user! To illustrate this diversity, here are some examples :

- improve the quality of a blurred image
- improve the contrast of an image
- filter out disturbances in an image
- compress the number of samples of an image by a ratio of hundred to one or more and of an image sequence such as digital TV by a ratio of thousand to one or more
- recognize and count bacteries in microscopic preparations
- recognize fingerprints, signatures
- authentify bank notes
- detect intrusions in uncontrolled areas
- detect sickness in x-ray pictures
- help the pilots and drivers to train
- conduct a vehicle without driver
- monitor the quality of products in production lines
- monitor machines tools to prevent accidents
- help robots to see , etc..

This kind of list increases in time with progress made in the means and the methods and the appearance of new applications.

1.4 Applications

A characteristic of image processing which is both important and rich is its interdisciplinary aspect as it was mentioned. We can find applications in various areas such as telecommunications (TV, video, transmission, storage, teleconferencing, integrated services, ISDN, publicity), the medicine (x-rays, tomography, ultra sounds, microscopy, electronic files and remote diagnosis), industry (robotics, quality monitoring, security), meteorology, earth resources, architecture, printing industry, military, etc. The list is long and becomes even longer every day.

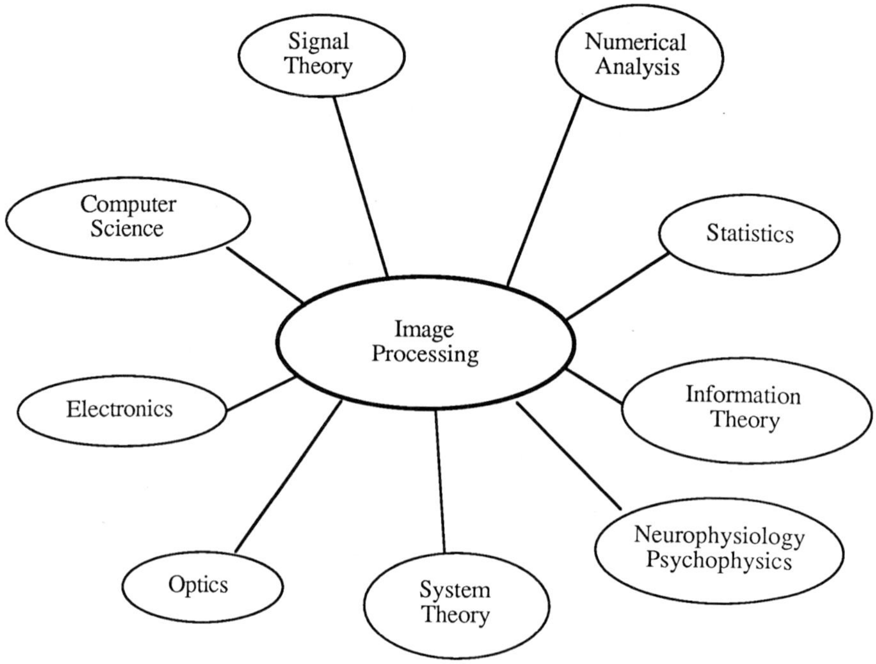

Fig. 1: Relationships between image processing and other areas

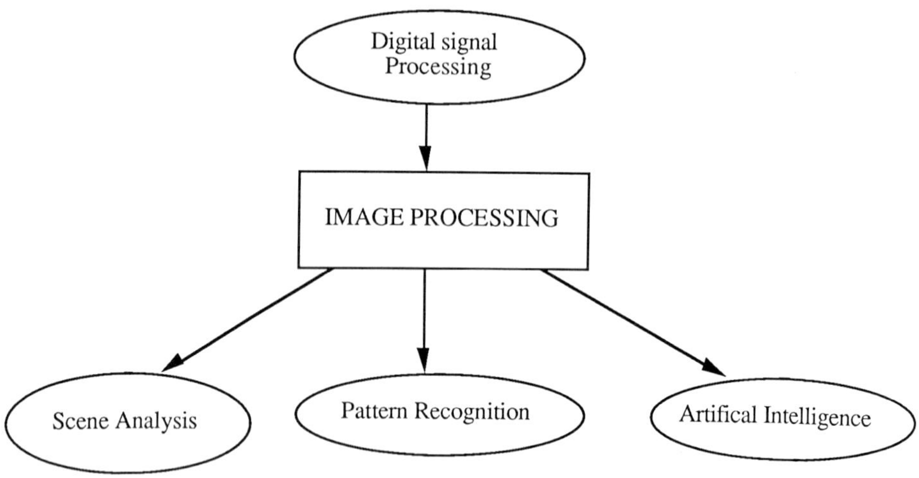

Fig. 2: Situation of image processing.

The main difficulty in the realization of an application is the lack of a universal processing which can solve all the possible problems. For example, a method to detect a sickness in a x-ray image cannot be used to monitor quality in printing. Accordingly, each particular application requires a study for itself. This is then using a plethor of basic methods. One has to choose specific methods suitable to solve the problem and apply them in the right order. This selection is mainly based on personal experience. That is why it is difficult to find the right collection of methods right away. It is often necessary to simulate several possibilities and compare performances before the final choice.

1.5 Computational Means

In computational means, image processing relies almost entirely on digital electronics. Some exceptions concern certain applications where one can also use optical means. However, one should notice that the problem related to computational means in image processing is not definitely solved and probably will never be solved. The reasons are multiple. Processing methods are renewed constantly. The same is true for the applications and for the new possibilities the technology offers us. The applications we think frozen change the requirements. On such a moving area, one can only find temporary solutions.

The processing could be implemented with three types of systems : entirely hardwired (electronic VLSI) semi-hardwired semi-programed (systems based on microprocessors or specialized processors) and systems fully programmed. Whatever the type, the speed in execution is only obtained by increasing the parallelism. In modern processing systems, one introduces hierarchy in addition to parallelism as well. This poses an important architectural problem which is still open. Unfortunately, there is no a unique architecture which is convenient in all the circumstances. As this was the case for the selection of methods, the optimum architecture needs to be studied for each case. However, if the rates achievable with the programmable conventional system (mini or micro-computer) are acceptable, the requirements of many applications could be satisfied without being completely optimum.

In this chapter, we shall discuss the main basic methods for digital image processing. Furthermore, we will restrict ourselves to the case of static images, namely photographies. In the next two sections, we will discuss the digitization of an image. This is done using the sampling and the quantization. Elementary two-dimensional signals and linear processing systems are discussed next. The two-dimensional Fourier transform is then introduced as well as its discrete version necessary for digital computation. Finally, the two-dimensional pre-processing and filtering techniques as well as image enhancement are presented at the end.

2. Two-dimensional Sampling

2.1 Ideal Sampling

Let $x_a(u,v)$ be an analog two-dimensional function representing an image and $X_a(f,g)$ its Fourier transform defined by:

$$X_a(f,g) = \int_{-\infty}^{+\infty}\int_{-\infty}^{+\infty} x_a(u,v)e^{-j2\pi(fu+gv)}du\,dv \tag{1}$$

The sampling of the function $x_a(u,v)$ is realised by taking periodically samples along the direction of the u and v axes. The digital signal is denoted by :

$$x(k\Delta u, l\Delta v) = x(k,l) = x_a(u,v)\big|_{u=k\Delta u,\ v=l\Delta v} \tag{2}$$

where Δu and Δv are the sampling periods along the axes u and v respectively. In order to recover the analog function from its samples $x(k,l)$, Δu and Δv must satisfy certain conditions. These are consequences of the two-dimensional sampling theorem.

2.2 Two-dimensional Sampling Theorem

An analog signal $x_a(u,v)$ limited in frequencies to F and G (cycles by unit distance) can exactly be recovered from its samples if and only if these samples are obtained with sampling periods Δu and Δv less or equal to $1/2F$ and to $1/2G$ respectively.

2.3 Demonstration

The sampled version $x_e(u,v)$ of the analog signal may be viewed as the product of $x_a(u,v)$ and of a double periodical Dirac pulses $e(u,v)$:

$$x_e(u,v) = x_a(u,v)e(u,v) \tag{3}$$

with

$$e(u,v) = \sum_{k=-\infty}^{+\infty}\sum_{l=-\infty}^{+\infty} \delta(u-k\Delta u, v-l\Delta v) \tag{4}$$

To the simple product (3) in the spatial domain, corresponds in the frequency domain the following convolution :

$$X_e(f,g) = X_a(f,g)**E(f,g)$$

$$= \int_{-\infty}^{+\infty} \int_{-\infty}^{+\infty} X_a(f',g')E(f-f',g-g')\mathrm{d}f'\mathrm{d}g' \quad (5)$$

We can show that :

$$E(f,g) = \frac{1}{\Delta u \Delta v} \sum_{m=-\infty}^{+\infty} \sum_{n=-\infty}^{+\infty} \delta(f-\frac{m}{\Delta u}, g-\frac{n}{\Delta v}) \quad (6)$$

By taking into account the property is of the convolution with Dirac impulse :

$$Y(\alpha,\beta)**\delta(\alpha-a,\beta-b) = \int_{-\infty}^{+\infty} \int_{-\infty}^{+\infty} Y(\alpha',b')\delta(\alpha-\alpha',\beta-\beta')\mathrm{d}\alpha'\mathrm{d}\beta' = Y(\alpha-a,\beta-b) \quad (7)$$

We can rewrite equation (6) in the following form

$$X_e(f,g) = \frac{1}{\Delta u \Delta v} \sum_{m=-\infty}^{+\infty} \sum_{n=-\infty}^{+\infty} X_a(f-\frac{m}{\Delta u}, g-\frac{n}{\Delta v}) \quad (8)$$

The function $X_e(f,g)$ is obtained by periodical repetition in both directions with periods $1/\Delta u$ and $1/\Delta u$ of the Fourier transform $X_a(f,g)$. These operations are summarized in Fig. 3. In fact, this function $X_e(f,g)$ is the two-dimensional Fourier transform $X(f,g)$ of the digital signal in the sense of the definition (2).

Two-dimensional sampling leads to a double succession of secondary spectrums in both directions proportional to the main spectrum $X_a(f,g)$. We can recover the analog signal $x_a\ (u, v)$ only if the secondary spectra could be eliminated without modifying the main $X_a(f,g)$ spectrum. This operation, realized in principle with a low-pass filter, it is possible only if $X_a(f,g)$ is zero for frequencies greater than $F = 1/2\Delta u$ along the f axis and greater than $G = 1/2\Delta v$ along the g axis:

$$X_a(f,g) = 0 \quad \text{for } f > F = 1/2\Delta u \text{ and } g > G = 1/2\Delta v \quad (9)$$

If this condition is not satisfied, secondary spectra overlap with the main spectrum.

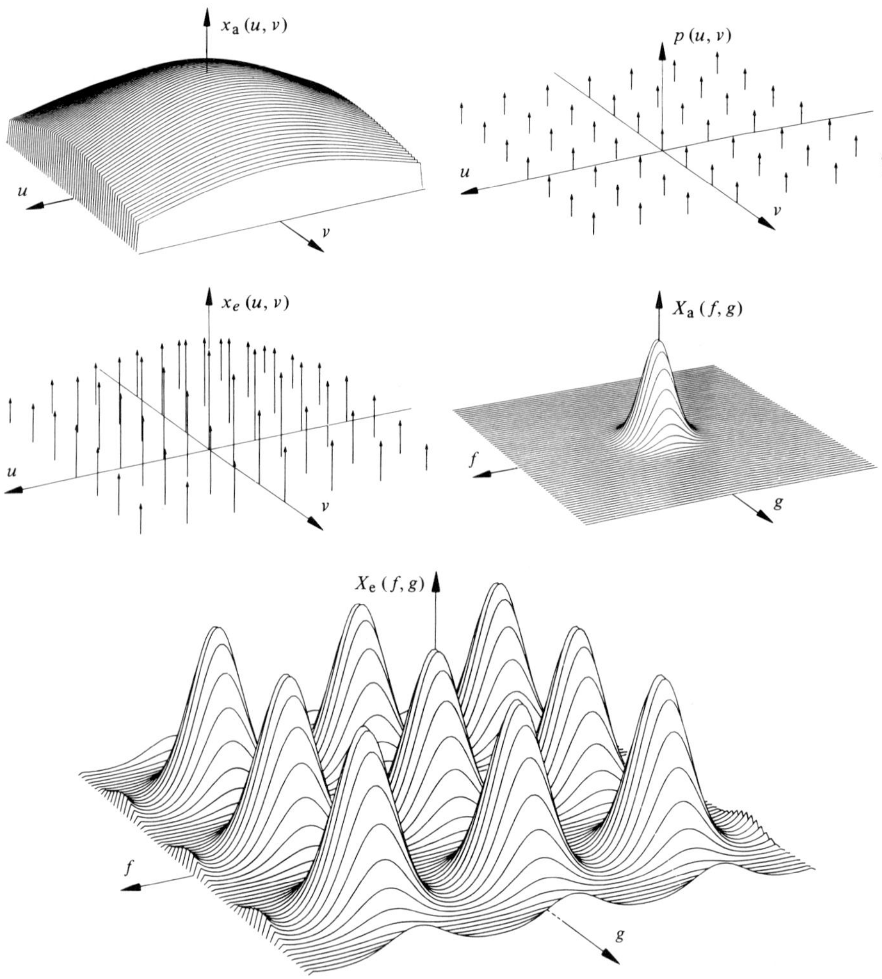

Fig. 3: Illustrating the two-dimensional sampling

2.4 Overlapping Errors

The secondary spectra overlap the main spectrum $X_a(f,g)$ in the case where the conditions i (9) are not satisfied. In this case, even if one can recover the main part of $X_a(f,g)$ with rectangular ideal low-pass filter, the output signal of this filter will be a distorted version of the analog signal $x_a(u,v)$. Figure 4 shows the case overlapping spectra.

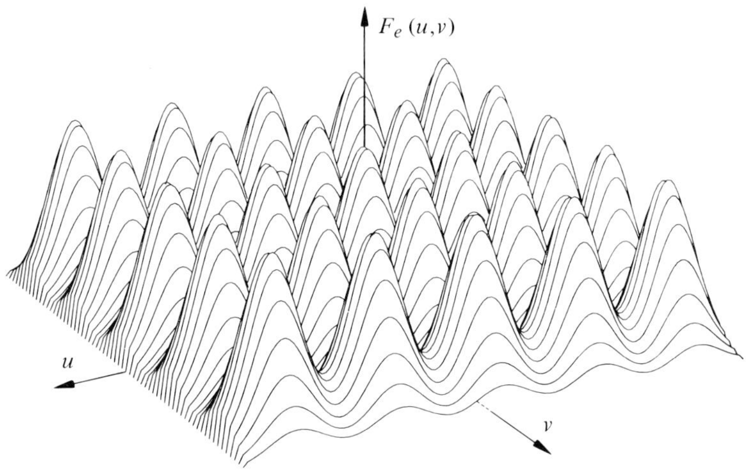

Fig. 4: Two-dimensional sampling with overlapping spectras

These considerations are purely theoretical. They are even more difficult to implement than in the one-dimensional case. A first difficulty is in the measure of $X_a(f,g)$ given the corresponding image $x_a(u,v)$ appropriate methods or instruments, we can only make more or less coarse estimations of the spectral extent of $X_a(f,g)$. Then, almost always, we should take into account the reconstitution. Processed images are generally aimed at the human observer. Since digital processings are often long and complex, one prefers not to make them heavier by incorporating reconstitution filters. Thus, we try to exploit the integrating effect of the eye and the physical support of the image. In this case, one should choose a sampling period (the same on both directions) slightly smaller than the separation power of the eye (about one minute of arc). For example, for printed documents observed at a viewing distance of 30 cm, one should use a sampling size of about 0,1 mm. It should be noticed that since the resolving power of the eye depends on the viewing distance, for a giving sample size, the visual effect will vary if the viewing distance is modified. Figure 5 shows a portion of an original text in real size and its digital reproduction after two-dimensional sampling with a period of 0,2 mm in both directions. The sampling effect is better emphasized on the corresponding enlargements (Fig. 6).

The overlapping of the spectra may lead to Moiré figures if an image which contains a series of narrow lines is undersampled. Let us consider for example an image where there is a series of black lines on white background alternating with the special frequency f_r. In case of undersampling, the reconstructed image after low-pass filtering will show another series of lines in a different direction and with a different spacial frequency.This is shown in figure 7.

One can rewrite the preceeding development for the three-dimensional signal $x_a(u,v,w)$ This is the case of an image sequence as in the TV for example. The result will be the same. The non-respect of sampling theorem in this case will lead to aberrations that a physic or mechanic teacher may not like at all. The scene of the car which the progress in one direction and its wheels turning in the opposite directions as the car was going backwords is the most known one.

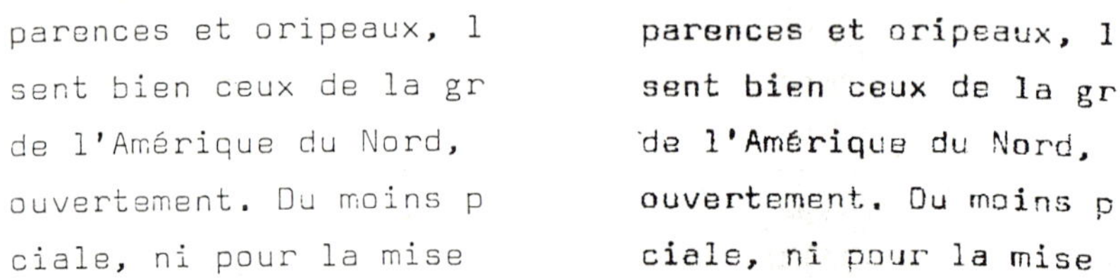

(a) (b)

Fig. 5: Effect of sampling: (a) original image (b) reconstructed image

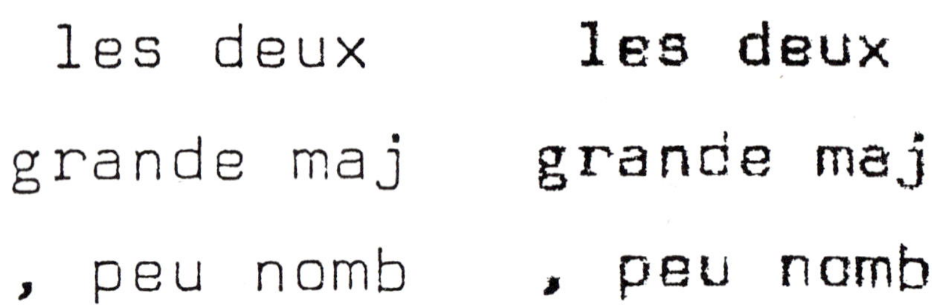

(a) (b)

Fig. 6: Effect of sampling with enlargment (a) original image (b) reconstructed image

2.5 Prefiltering in Sampling

The sampling system analyses a given image $x_a(u,v)$ with a light beam concentrated on a given point of the image. The amount of light reflected or transmitted at that point is a measure of its luminance. Because of the imperfections of the optical system, this beam is never concentrated on a single point. The measured light is in fact a mean value integrated over every small region around a point. Let's call $y_a(u,v)$ the function representing the shape of the aperture of the beam. The measured luminance at a given point (u_0,v_0) is giving by :

$$l_a(u_0,v_0) = \int\int x_a(\alpha,\beta) y_a(u_0-\alpha, v_0-\beta) d\alpha d\beta \quad (10)$$

where the double integral is computed over a small area S representing the aperture of the function $y_a(u,v)$. At this convolution in the image domain corresponds in the frequency domain the simple product :

$$L_a(f,g) = X_a(f,g)\, Y_a(f,g) \quad (11)$$

where $L_a(f,g)$, $X_a(f,g)$ and $Y_a(f,g)$ are the two-dimensional Fourier transform of signals $l_a(u,v)$,$x_a(u,v)$ et $y_a(u,v)$ respectively [in the sense of the definition (1)]. The real luminance is thus filtered by a filter whose characteristics are give in $Y_a(f,g)$.

For commonly used beam shapes, $Y_a(g, f)$ is generally the frequency response of a low-pass filter. If the beam is wide, the area S of the function Y_a (g,f) is large. Than Y_a (g,f) becomes relatively severe low-pass filter. Main aperture shapes $Y_a(u,v)$ and their frequency responses are represented in figure 8.

2.6 Sampling Rasters

For practical reasons related to the realizations of image acquisition and reconstitution equipments, the two-dimensional sampling is almost always made according to a rectangular or a square cartesian grid. In this grid the coordinates of sampling points are even by the couple $(k\Delta u, l\Delta v)$ with respect to the origin $k = l = 0$. For a given square grid, we have obviously $\Delta u = \Delta v$. A given point in this grid is surrounded by eight points. Half of this points in the diagonal directions are at a distance $\Delta u\sqrt{2}$ from the centre, whereas the other half of the points are at a distance Δu . In certain applications requiring the measurement of length and areas by the ordinated string of a number of points, the existence of two different distances in neighbourhoods creates complications. Some weighting methods are needed to take into account these different distances.

Another possibility for sampling is the use of an hexagonal grid. In this case, each point has six neighbours at equal distance. This type of grid has been used with the appropriate operators in pattern recognition in biological images [2]. A grid which is similar to the hexagonal grid could be obtained from a cartesian grid by shifting even numbered or odd numbered lines by $\Delta u /2$.

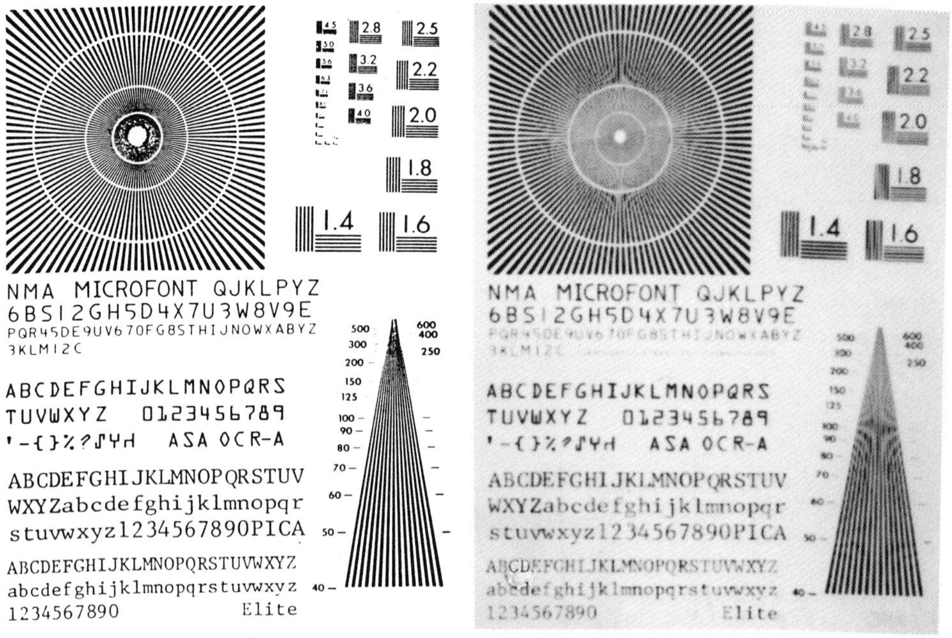

Fig. 7: Moiré figures

The sampling grid could be very large. For example, to reproduce a photography of passport size without distorsion, one needs about 200 x 300 points. For the same photographic quality over a postcard, we need 600 x 900. For x-ray films of large dimensions 10'000 x 10'000 is the appropriate size. The TV, for example, produce every 25th of a second a matrix of about 300 x 300 points. Since at each point, we associate a sample (the numerical value of luminance) the total number of samples required to represent a digital image is always very large. The next step in digitalization is quantization.

3. Quantization

3.1 Important Parameters

The operation which follows the sampling is the quantization of the luminance. The latter varies in a continuous manner between two limits, which determine its dynamic range. The quantification is the subdivision of this dynamic range into a finite number of intervals and attributing to all the values of a given interval a single luminance value. The problems related to this operation are to find the dynamic range and determine

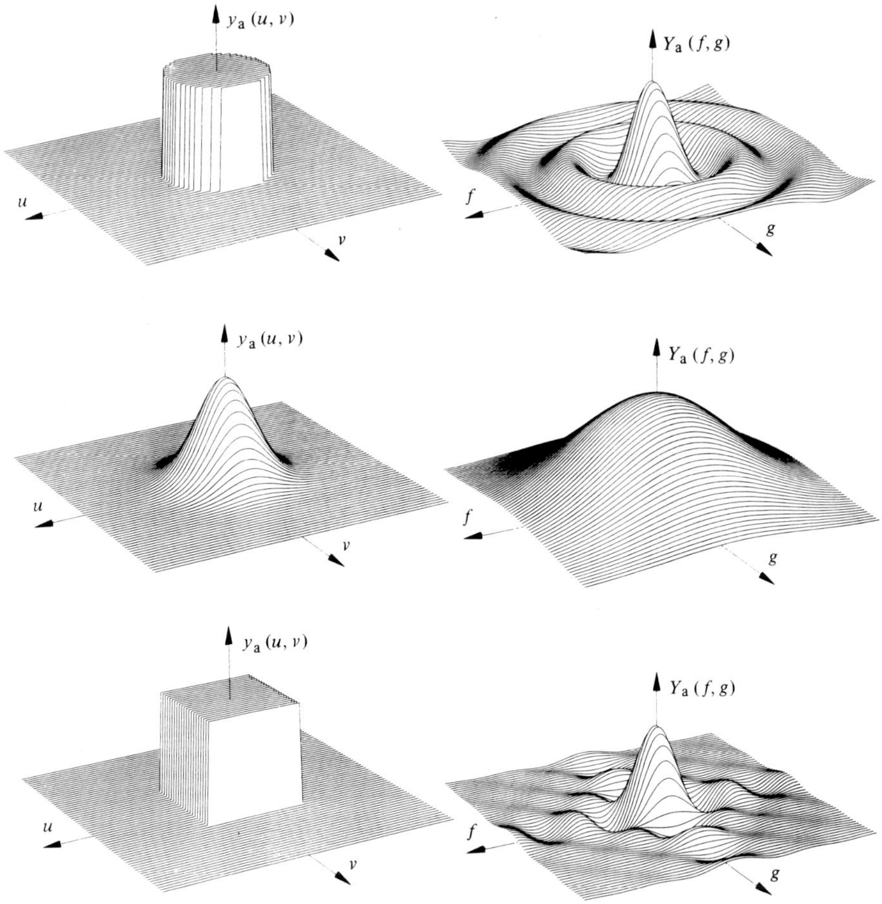

Fig. 8: Beam aperture shapes and their transform

how many intervals one needs to cover this range and how to distribute them.

The solution of these problems depends on two important factors. The first one is the physical support on which the quantized image is reproduced. This is an objective criteria related to the photometric qualities or properties of the support. The second is the eye, the human visual system of the observer. This is a subjective factor since two observers don't see a giving image in the same way.

3.2 Dynamic Range of the Support

Images are reproduced on well-known supports such as photographic film, photographic paper or a screen. These supports are characterized by photometric units related to their absorbence α, reflectence ρ and transmittance τ. Whatever the selected support, there are limits to the degree of darkness or brightness one can put on them. Let us consider the case of a photographic paper on which we want to reproduce a quantized image. It will be characterized mainly by its reflectance. The highest reflectance value τ_1 will be obtained when this paper is developed without being exposed to light. In contrast, the smallest reflectance will be obtained when this paper is exposed to light at saturation level. The dynamic range of this paper is giving by the difference τ_1 - τ_2. It is common to express this dynamic range in unity of optical density units.

$$D = d_{\rho_1} - d_{\rho_2} = -(\log_{10}\rho_1 - \log_{10}\rho_2) \tag{12}$$

It is the value of D which we should divide into a number of intervals. To establish the dynamic range of a support, one thus need to know the reflectance or the transmittance without exposure and with exposure to saturation.

3.3 The Smallest Visible Luminance Interval

The smallest visible interval is by definition, the smallest light difference we can still see. If it is known, one can perform the quantization without having any visible difference between the original image and quantized image. The difference between these two images is called quantization noise. In this case it will be invisible.

The oldest determination of the smallest visible luminance difference is made with the Weber-Fechner experiment. In this experiment, a visual field is uniform luminance l is divided into two areas along a straight line. The possibility is offered to the observer to change the luminance of one of the areas by a small amount Δl. The observer does not see any variation until Δl reach a certain non zero value. In addition, by repeating this experience for several values of luminance, one notice that the report or the ratio $\Delta l \,/\, l$ is constant.

$$\frac{\Delta l}{l} = C_w \tag{13}$$

This is the Weber-Fechner law. It is valid over a very wide range of luminance going from 1 to 1000 nits. In this luminance interval, the constant C_w vary from one observer to another. This is the subjective aspect we mentioned previously. However, this variation is between 0,01 and 0,02 for a large number of observers. To find the number of quantization intervals it is thus sufficient to divide the dynamic range by the constant C_w by making sure that they are expressed with the same units. The smallest perceivable luminance C_w given by equation (13) is expressed in percentage. In order to convert it into optical density units one needs to consider the term $1 + C_w$. This allows to avoid negative densities by translating to the origin the logarithmic curve to point 1 over the horizontal axis. The smallest perceivable luminance interval C_W, expressed in optical density units is thus $\log_{10}(1 + C_w)$. The number of quantization levels N_q is then given by :

$$N_q = \frac{D}{\log_{10}(1 + C_w)} = \frac{(\log_{10}\rho_2 - \log_{10}\rho_1)}{\log_{10}(1 + C_w)} \qquad (14)$$

To compute this value, one needs to know the dynamic range and select reasonable value for C_w if one cannot repeat easily Weber-Fechner experiment.

3.4 Example

To illustrate the quantization and the use of equation (14) let us consider the example of a photographic film of dynamic range $D = 2$ optical density unit. This kind of film is very often used in amateur photography. With an average value of $C_w = 0{,}015$ one has :

$$N_q = \frac{2}{\log_{10}(1.015)} = 309.3$$

Or, N_q represents a number of intervals, it should be an integer number, we can round it to $N_q = 309$ or to $N_q = 310$.

Usually, the luminance of a sample is represented by a binary word. The parameter of practical importance is the number of bits in this word. To obtain it ,one need to look for the power of 2 closest to N_q by larger values and take its logarithm in base 2. In the case of our example, the power of 2 is 9, $2^9 = 512$. The number of bits is $B_q = \log_2 512 = 9$.

If we consider a severe observer with $C_w = 0.01$, we have :

$$N_q = \frac{2}{\log_{10}(1.01)} = 462.8$$

The same number of bits is sufficient in this case.

If we consider the other extreme case with $C_w = 0.02$, we have :

$$N_q = \frac{2}{\log_{10}(1.02)} = 232.5$$

In this case, it is sufficient to use binary words of $B_q = 8$ bits.

3.5 Comments

Several remarks are in order. First, the Weber-Fechner experiment is a little too simple. There is no real image which looks like the union of two uniformly illuminated regions. For simplicity, one realizes an experiment which does not correspond to reality. If we measure the ratio $\Delta l / l$ as a function of the luminance l_0 of the surrounding, one can notice that it remains constant over a much smaller scale than 1000 units as mentioned previously. A target which can be used in such an experiment is shown in figure 9.

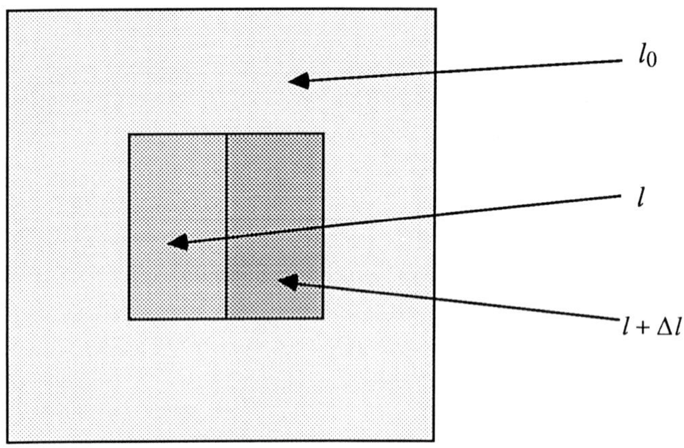

Fig. 9: Contrast sensitivity measurement target

With such a target, one emphasizes the importance of luminance l_0 of the surrounding. If this is very large with respect to the central square, the latter appears as black whatever its luminance. In the opposite case, the central square appears as white. It may even appear like a light source instead of an illuminated surface, when the difference between l_0 and l is very large.

By comparing these two experiments one can draw the following conclusions. In the first experiment, that of Weber-Fechner, there is a dynamic range of about 4 orders of magnitude to guarantee a constant C_w. This is the case when our visual field is complete, namely when we are looking at a landscape on a summer day. Such a condition is almost fulfilled when one projects a film in a dark movie room or movie theatre. In the second experiment, the presence of a surrounding luminance l_0 over an important area of the visual field implies a compression of the dynamic range. This is what happens when we watch the TV screen. The TV screen does not occupy our entire vision field. Under such conditions, the dynamic range must be compressed to give the illusion of well contrasted images.

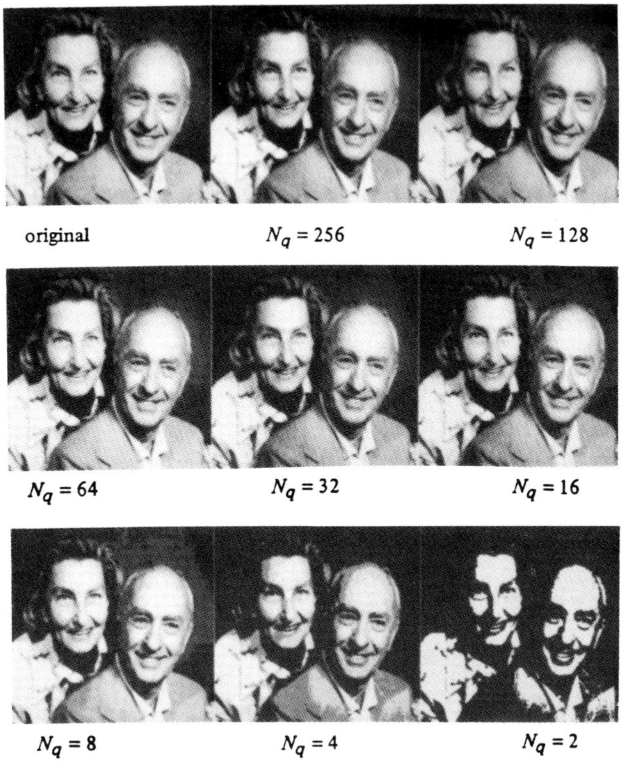

Fig. 10: A digital image and its quantized version

In cases where one cannot satisfy the number of levels given by equation (14), the quantization noise become visible. It is important to examine its appearance. In regions of an image where the luminance varies slowly as a function of the position (low spatial frequency areas) the quantization will create a constant level of luminance. Between two of such areas, there will be a jump from onc level to another whereas the original luminance varies continuously. These jumps when they become visible create in general artificial contours in the image. They can be very disturbing, depending on the case they may create artificial shapes or objects which do not exist in the original image. Figure 10 shows an original image on the upper left part and quantized versions with 256, 128, 64, 32, 16, 8, 4 and 2 levels. Even these results are affected by serious distorsions due to the printing process, artificial contours are visible for example (on the front) even on the image quantized with 64 levels.

The number of levels given by equation (14) concerns all the samples. In practice, it is interesting to use the same number of levels, in other words the same number of bits, for each sample. However, an image by its nature is non stationary. Certain regions are of low spatial frequency whereas some others are of high spatial frequency. It appears that our visual system is less sensitive to the quantization noise in the high spatial frequency areas. This is a consequence of the second experiment we discussed previously. Consequently, specially on a theoretical level, an efficient use of the number of quantization bits should be made by adapting the member of levels to the local spatial frequency of the image.

3.6 Quantization Laws

The number of levels given by equation (14) guarantees us the invisibility of the quantization noise whatever the luminance value. The width of the intervals distributed over the dynamic range is the same. In this case one talks about linear quantization, since the law between the original luminance and quantized luminance is a linear law, piecewise constant (Fig.11).

Such a law gives an identical importance to all the regions of the dynamic range. A quantized image is often addressed to an observer. One can thus use quantization laws better adapted to the property of our visual system. Indeed, equation (13) indicates non linear sensitivity of our visual system. Since the ratio $\Delta l \,/\, l$ is constant, the increment Δl is much smaller for small value of the luminance. In other words, our visual system is more sensitive to small variation of luminance in the dark areas than in the white areas. This is the reason why the popular saying claims that we see better in the dark than in the light. The error not to commit is to integrate equation (13). Indeed, one can interpret the ratio $\Delta l \,/\, l$ as the elementary luminance Δb. By integration, one obtains :

$$b = c_1 \log l + c_2 \qquad (15)$$

This is a simple relation relating the apparent luminosity b to the effective luminance l with c_1 and c_2 as constant. Because of this relation, one always claims that the eye is logarithmic.This is true only approximatively. In fact, recent experimental results indicate another law of the type :

$$b = c_3\, l^{\zeta} \qquad (16)$$

where the exponent depends on the surrounding visual field and the adaptation state of the eye. It varies from 0.3 for a dark neighbouring field without adaptation till 3 for very clear visual fields.

What preceding shows that a linear quantization law does not make efficient use of the quantization levels. Useless levels are spent in the high values of luminance towards white. One can use a non linear quantization law with more smaller levels towards black and wider levels towards white. Figure 12 shows an image quantized with 16 levels with linear and logarithmic laws.

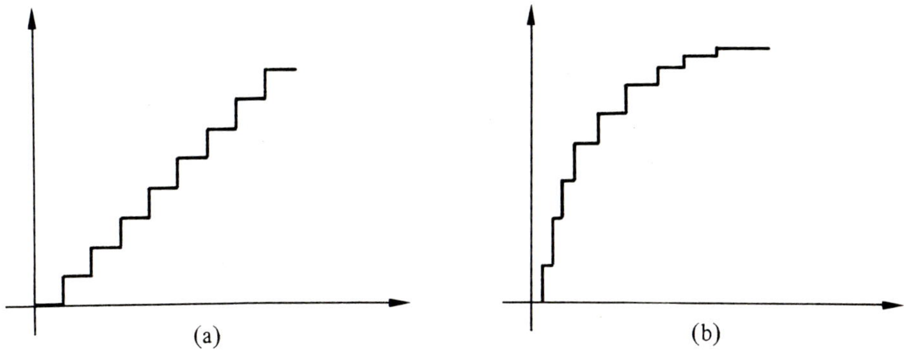

Fig. 11: Quantization laws (a) linear, (b) non linear

3.7 Optimal Quantization

In the preceeding paragraph, the quantization has been discussed in an intuitive manner. In this paragraph, we will develop the optimal quantization with a higher degree of rigor. When one quantizes the samples of a signal $x_e(k,l)$, one compares the value of each sample to a decision level. All the samples whose value fall between two successive decision levels, take the same quantized value defined by a reconstruction level. This operation is shown at figure 13, where decision and reconstruction levels are defined.

Let x be the value of a sample $x_e(k,l)$ restricted to the dynamic range D and x_q its quantized version. If :

$$d_i \leq x < d_{i+1} \tag{17}$$

then

$$x_q = r_i \tag{18}$$

The problem of optimal quantization consists in finding the levels d_i and r_i in order to minimize the error between the sampled signal and quantized signal.

(a) (b)

Fig. 12: A sampled image quantized with 16 levels with (a) a linear law, (b) a non-linear law

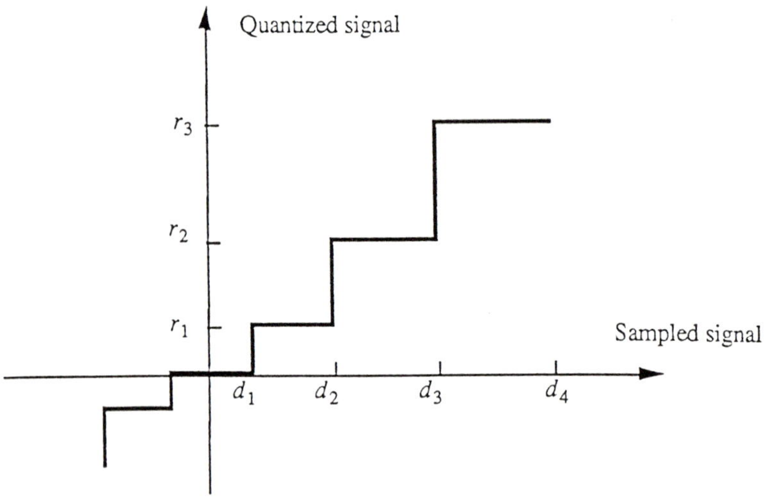

Fig. 13: Decision levels and reconstruction

The error criterion is of primary importance since the results depend from it. Unfortunately, there is no criterion which suits analytical computations while following fairly the subjective judgement of the human visual system. For the needs of an analytical computation one always selects the mean quadratic error since it is easy to manipulate in equations. However, its correlation with the subjective judgement is very weak to say the least.

Let then $p_x(x)$ be the probability density of the signal $x_e(k,l)$ with:

$$\int_D p_x(x)\,\mathrm{d}x = 1 \tag{19}$$

where D is the dynamic range of the signal.

The mean quadratic error is given by :

$$\varepsilon = \mathrm{E}\left[(x - x_q)^2\right] = \int_D (x - x_q)^2 \, p_x(x) \, \mathrm{d}x \tag{20}$$

taking into account equation (18), one has :

$$\varepsilon = \sum_{i=0}^{N_q - 1} \int_{d_i}^{d_{i+1}} (x - r_i)^2 \, p_x(x) \, \mathrm{d}x \tag{21}$$

To find the optimal position of levels d_i and r_i, one should derive ε with respect to these variables and equate to zero the result . One has :

$$\frac{\partial \varepsilon}{\partial d_i} = (d_i - r_i)^2 p_x(d_i) - (d_i - r_{i-1})^2 p_x(d_i) = 0 \tag{22}$$

$$\frac{\partial \varepsilon}{\partial r_i} = 2 \int_{d_i}^{d_i + 1} (x - r_i) p_x(x) \, \mathrm{d}x = 0 \tag{23}$$

for : $i = 0, \ldots, N_q - 1$

After simplification of the system of equations, we have :

$$r_i = 2d_i - r_{i-1} \tag{24}$$

$$r_i = \frac{\int_{d_i}^{d_{i+1}} x \, p_x(x) \, \mathrm{d}x}{\int_{d_i}^{d_{i+1}} p_x(x) \, \mathrm{d}x} \tag{25}$$

These equations could be solved recursively for a given probability density $p_x(x)$. These are used so often, even in other areas that there are tables [3] giving the optimal levels for usual distributions such as Gaussian distribution, Rayleigh distribution or exponential distribution.

The direct solution to equations (24) and (25) can be obtained if one can choose a number of quantization levels N_q sufficiently large. In this case one can admit, in a first approximation that the probability density is constant over each quantization band. Thus equation (21) becomes :

$$\varepsilon = \sum_{i=0}^{N_q - 1} p_x(r_i) \int_{d_i}^{d_{i+1}} (x - r_i)^2 \, dx$$

$$\varepsilon = \frac{1}{3} \sum_{i=0}^{N_q - 1} p_x(r_i) \left[(d_{i+1} - r_i)^3 - (d_i - r_i)^3 \right] \quad (26)$$

The optimal position of levels r_i between d_i and d_{i+1} is obtained by minimising ε with respect to r_i :

$$\frac{\partial \varepsilon}{\partial r_i} = 0 \quad (27)$$

the solution is:

$$r_i = \frac{d_i + d_{i+1}}{2} \quad (28)$$

Thus, the optimal position of the reconstruction levels is the middle of each decision interval. By substituting equation (28) in (26) one obtains :

$$\varepsilon = \frac{1}{2} \sum_{i=0}^{N_q - 1} p_x(r_i) \, (d_{i+1} - d_i)^3 \quad (29)$$

One should minimize by using Lagrange multipliers to find the values d_i. For certain distributions, there are purely numerical solutions.

3.8 Linear Quantization after Transformation

It is possible to implement the non linear quantization by using a non linear transformation and a linear quantization. The transformed signal is quantized linearly with equally spaced decision and reconstruction levels. Then, the inverse non linear transformation provides the quantized version of the original signal. These operations are summarized in figure 14.

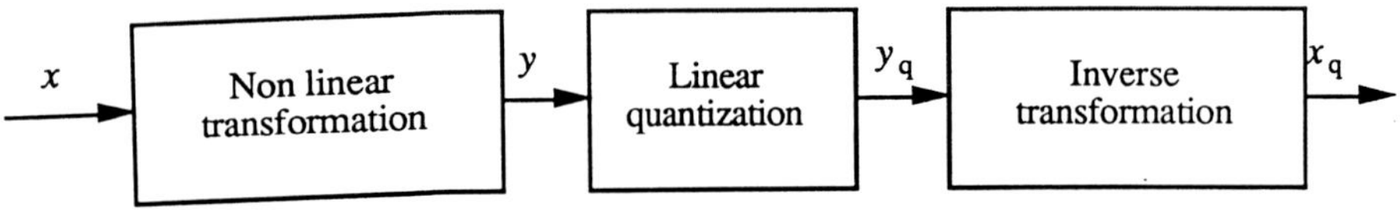

Fig. 14: Linear quantization with transformation

The signal $y(k,l)$ at the output of a non linear transformer is given by :

$$y(k,l) = T[x(k,l)] \tag{30}$$

where the transformation T [.] is chosen in such a way to force the probality density of the signal $y(k,l)$ to be uniform. It is obtained by the principle of equivalence in probability :

$$p_x(x)\,\mathrm{d}x = p_y(y)\mathrm{d}y \tag{31}$$

by setting $p_y(y) = 1$.

If the signal $x(k,l)$ has zero mean, the transformation needed is given by :

$$T[x] = \int_{-\infty}^{x} p_x(u)\,\mathrm{d}u - \frac{1}{2} \tag{32}$$

If the signal has a mean different from zero, one can use an intermediary signal by taking away the mean value. This relation shows that the transformation required is nothing else than the repartition function of the distribution $p_x(x)$. Once this is known, the direct transformation as well as the inverse transformation, can be computed. For example, for a gaussian distribution :

$$p_x(x) = \frac{1}{\sqrt{2\pi\sigma^2}} \exp(-\frac{x^2}{2\sigma^2}) \tag{33}$$

the direct transformation is given by :

$$y = T\,[x] = \frac{1}{2}\,\mathrm{erf}(\frac{x}{\sqrt{2}\sigma}) \tag{34}$$

with :

$$\mathrm{erf}(u) = \frac{2}{\sqrt{\pi}} \int_0^u \exp(-v^2)\mathrm{d}v \tag{35}$$

The inverse transformation is given by :

$$x_q = \sqrt{2}\sigma\, \mathrm{erf}^{-1}(2y_q) \tag{36}$$

For other distributions, equivalent relations of the direct and inverse transformations could be obtained starting from equation (31).

3.9 Vector Quantization

The quantization which we discussed in the preceeding paragraphs is implemented sequentially by quantizing samples one by one. Each sample is thus viewed as a scalar.

To reduce the quantization error (or the quantization noise), it is possible to quantize and reconstruct simultaneously a series of samples by grouping them into a vector. In this case, one talks about vector quantization. The principle is the following.

A vector x is defined with an ensemble of samples to be quantized $x(k,l)$:

$$\mathbf{x} = \{x(1,1),\, x(1,2),\, x(1,3),\, ...,\, x(2,1), x(2,2),\, ...,\, x(N,N)\} \tag{37}$$

where N is the size of a square region representing a small area of a digital image . The global image will be represented by an ensemble of vectors of this type. Since the image is supposed to be unknown, these vectors are random vectors characterized by a joint probability density function $p_x(\mathbf{x})$. The vector given by equation (37) has thus $M = N^2$ components. It is represented in a vector space of M dimensions. The vector quantization consists in subdividing the space into N_q decision regions D_i, with i = 1, ..., N_q and to represent all the vectors whose extremity falls within D_i by a reconstruction vector $\mathbf{r}_i = \mathbf{x}_q$. This definition is the generalisation of the scalar quantization we discussed previously into a M dimensional space. For the mathematical formulation one assumes that the joint probability function $p_x(\mathbf{x})$ of the vector $\mathbf{x}$ is known. This hypothesis is almost never valid in practice.

The quadratic quantization error for a vector $\mathbf{x}$ is given by :

$$\varepsilon = \|\mathbf{x} - \mathbf{x}_q\|^2 = \sum_{j=1}^{M} (x_j - x_{qj})^2 \tag{38}$$

where x_j are the components of the vector $\mathbf{x}$. This simplified notation replaces that of equation (37). The mean quadratic error is the expected value of the preceeding result :

$$\varepsilon = \mathrm{E}\left[\varepsilon\right] = \sum_{i=1}^{N_q} \int_{D_i} \mathrm{Tr}\left[(\mathbf{x} - \mathbf{r}_i)\,(\mathbf{x} - \mathbf{r}_i)^{\mathrm{T}}\right] p_x(\mathbf{x})\, \mathrm{d}\mathbf{x} \tag{39}$$

where the superscript T represents the transpose vector and whereTr[.] is the trace of the matrix. The optimum reconstruction vectors can be obtained for giving decisions regions D_i by driving ε with respect to the vectors $\mathbf{r}_i$ and by equating the result to zero. One has :

$$\frac{\partial \varepsilon}{\partial \mathbf{r}_i} = \int_{D_i} (\mathbf{x} - \mathbf{r}_i)\, p_x(\mathbf{x})\, d\mathbf{x} = 0 \tag{40}$$

After some algebraic manipulation, we obtain :

$$\mathbf{r}_i = \frac{\int_{D_i} \mathbf{x} p_x(\mathbf{x})\, d\mathbf{x}}{\int_{D_i} p_x(\mathbf{x})\, d\mathbf{x}} \tag{41}$$

This relation is the conditional mathematical expectation of **x** knowing that **x** is in region D_i. It is reduced to equation (25) in the case of scalar quantization.

As indicated previously, to find the optimal reconstruction vectors, it is necessary to know the joint probability density $p_x(\mathbf{x})$. This information is rarely available. In addition, the evaluation of equation (41) in the general case is difficult. That is why it is necessary to introduce simplifications to the general formulation of the vector quantization.

The first simplification consists to quantize each component of the vector **x** separately but by expressing the reconstruction vectors $\mathbf{r}_i$ as a function of regions D_i. In such a case if the components of the vector **x** are independent from each other the vector quantization in a N_q dimensional space is reduced to N_q scalar quantization. If the components are correlated, the problem remains difficult to solve without other simplifications.

Another way to avoid the difficulties is nowadays very popular. It is based on the following. In the set of vectors to quantize, one chooses a subset that can be used as a learning set to determine the mean error of quantization with vectors $\mathbf{r}_i$ and regions D_i well adapted to this data. The adaptation is made iteratively in the following way. The ensemble of vectors $\mathbf{r}_i$ used for the learning is called the dictionary. A first dictionary and the regions D_i are chosen more or less arbitrarily or by scalar quantization of the component. One checks to see if the quantization error which results from this is acceptable. If this is the case, the quantization is performed. If not, in each region D_i one compute the barycenter (or the centre of gravity) of the vector **x** which has been quantized by the first dictionary. One requantizes these vectors with the new dictionary obtained by the center of gravities computed previously. This is equivalent to renewing the dictionary. This requantization is carried out very often with the nearest neighbour rule. It is this rule which determines the new regions D_i. Regions obtained by this rule are called

Voronoi regions or *Dirichlet* cells. The quantization error is computed again. In case of satisfactory results the quantization is achieved. If not, one iterates again to compute the centre of gravities. At each step, quantization error can only decrease or remain unchanged.

This method has several variations. The choice of the first dictionary and its volume offers interesting possibilities. One can use a random dictionary or a small dictionary that is enlarged progressively. One can also make the method more complex by introducing feedbacks. This allows us to go from the memoryless case discussed previously where each vector is quantized without knowing what happened to the preceeding vectors to the case with memory. These variations are subject of much work in the area of data compression or image coding. They can also be applied to speech coding. Their interest is in the structure they offer well-adapted for VLSI integration.

3.10 Quantization of the Colour

A colour image can be represented by its red, green or blue components or by reversible linear or non linear transformation of these components. A coarse approach will be to quantize separately these components.

In this case, the determination of reconstruction and decision levels is made according to what we have discussed in paragraphs 3.1. until 3.7. However, in such an approach the properties of our visual system are used only superficially.

Our visual system has a non linear response for various components of the light spectrum. To take this into account in quantization, it is preferable to transform separately the three stimuli according to paragraph 3.8. It is well known that our visual system is more sensitive in green, averagely sensitive in blue, and less sensitive in red. The quantization levels may be assigned according to such a base.

Figure 15 shows a general colour quantization system. In this system, the colour transformation (linear or non linear) produces three other components α, b and γ which are quantized. During this quantization the colour space is subdivided into regions. A unique colour is assigned to all the vectors of a given region. Here, the vector quantization could be used very advantageously. In case of complexity, each component could be quantized scalarly within its dynamic range. After quantization, the inverse transformation allows us to obtain the three quantized stimuli.

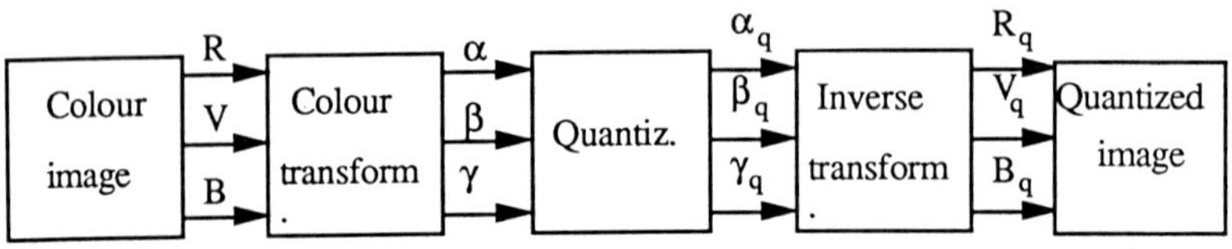

Fig. 15: Colour image quantization

4. Signal and Linear Systems

4.1 Introduction

The two preceeding sections were devoted to sampling and to quantization. After these operations, one obtains a digital image represented by $x(k,l)$. This function takes on discrete values in the dynamic range as a function of integer independent variables k and l of the image plane. The size of an image should be limited for its manipulation. The digital version of this size is the variation area of variables k and l. This is called the extent of the image. For certain two-dimensional signals, very interesting from a theoritical point of view, but which does not correspond to a physical image, the extent may be infinite.

In this section, we discuss elementary two-dimensional signals as well as linear processings systems. Certain important notions related to these systems will be discussed in the following sections.

4.2 Notation and Elementary Signals

A two-dimensional signals $x(k,l)$ of finite extent is represented by a rectangular matrix :

$$x(k,l) = \mathbf{X} = \begin{pmatrix} x(k_1,l_1)\ x(k_1,l_2) & \ldots\ldots & x(k_1,l_L) \\ x(k_2,l_1) & & \\ \cdot & & \\ x(k_K,l_1)\ x(k_K,l_2) & \ldots\ldots & x(k_K,l_L) \end{pmatrix} \tag{42}$$

The size of the image is determined by the integers K and L. Let us consider now a few simple signals.

The two-dimensional unit impulse is defined by :

$$d(k,l) = \begin{cases} 1 & \text{for } k = l = 0 \\ 0 & \text{everywhere else} \end{cases} \tag{43}$$

The two-dimensional step function is defined by :

$$\varepsilon(k,l) = \begin{cases} 1 & \text{for } k \geq 0 \text{ and } l \geq 0 \\ 0 & \text{everywhere else} \end{cases} \tag{44}$$

The two-dimensional rectangular signal is defined by :

$$\text{rect}_{K,L}(k,l) = \begin{cases} 1 & \text{for } 0 \le k \le K-1 \text{ and } 0 \le l \le L-1 \\ 0 & \text{everywhere else} \end{cases} \tag{45}$$

A two-dimensional signal is called separable if it can be written as :

$$x(k,l) = x_1(k)\, x_2(l) \tag{46}$$

For example, the rectangular signal given by equation (45) is a separable signal.

$$\text{rect}_{K,L}(k,l) = \text{rect}_K(k)\, \text{rect}_L(l) \tag{47}$$

4.3 Two-dimensional Correlation

The two-dimensional intercorrelation function is a measure of the similarity between two signals $x(k,l)$ et $y(k,l)$. In mathematical terms it is given by :

$$\varphi_{xy}(k,l) = \sum_{k'=-\infty}^{+\infty} \sum_{l'=-\infty}^{+\infty} x(k',l')\, y(k'+k, l'+l) \tag{48}$$

For signals at least one of which is of finite extent. Since $\varphi_{xy}(k,l)$ is a measure of similarity between $x(k,l)$ and $y(k,l)$, it reaches its maximum for a couple of values k and l, when the similarity is the greatest.

In image analysis, the correlation function allows to detect the presence of a given object in the image. For example, if $x(k,l)$ represents the image and $y(k,l)$ that of the object we are looking for, the position of the maximum cross-correlation will indicate the position of the object in the image $x(k,l)$. The value of this maximum could be a measure of the confidence one can have in that decision. If this value is absolute maximum, as this is the case in autocorrelation function of $y(k,l)$ at the origin, then they certainly could be admitted. However, the cross-correlation (48) is very sensitive to orientation. For the preceeding analysis to be valid, it is necessary that the object in $x(k,l)$ and in $y(k,l)$ has the same orientation. If this is not the case, we should repeat the cross correlation measurement for all the possible orientations by reorienting the reference $y(k,l)$ before each measure. This operation could be very time consuming and complex in computation.

If the two signals $x(k,l)$ and $y(k,l)$ are identical, then the signal $j_{xy}(k,l)$ is called two-dimensional autocorrelation function. It reaches its maximum at the origin $k = l = 0$ since a signal is most similar to itself when both versions overlap exactly.

The various steps in the evaluation of equation (48) can be listed as follows :

- The signal $y(k',l')$ is translated in the plane $k'l'$ at a point (k,l);
- The product $x(k',l')\,y(k'+k\,,l'+l)$ is computed sample by sample for all the values k' and l' on the intersection of the expend of the two signals ;
- the values thus obtained are accumulated to obtain one sample of the signal $\varphi_{xy}(k,l)$.

These steps are repeated for other values of k and l. At the next section, we will discuss another method called indirect method, to compute the correlation function using the Fourier transform.

In what preceeds, we have admitted that one of the two signals has a finite extent.

This is rarely the case for random signals. For stationary random signals the cross-correlation function is given by the following expectation

$$\varphi_{xy}(k,l) = \mathrm{E}\left[x(k',l')\,y(k'+k,l'+l)\right] \tag{49}$$

Let us recall that the stationarity hypothesis allows to be independent from any shift in the image plane. If in addition one can admit the ergodicity hypothesis which allows the identification of averages with space averages, one can write :

$$\varphi_{xy}(k,l) = \overline{x(k',l')\,y(k'+k,l'+l)} \tag{50}$$

where the upper bar represents the mean value along the variables k' and l'. The auto-covarience function of a stationary and ergodic random signal is defined by :

$$\gamma_x(k,l) = \mathrm{E}\left[\left(x(k',l') - m_x\right)\left(x(k'+k,l'+l) - m_x\right)\right] \tag{51}$$

$$= \overline{\left(x(k',l') - m_x\right)\left(x(k'+k,l'+l) - m_x\right)}$$

where m_x is the mean value of the signal

By comparing equations (50) and (51) one can show that

$$\varphi_x(k,l) = \gamma_x(k,l) - m_x^2 \tag{52}$$

the normalized autocovariance function is defined by :

$$\rho_x(k,l) = \frac{\gamma_x(k,l)}{\gamma_x(0,0)} = \frac{1}{\sigma_x^2}\gamma_x(k,l) \tag{53}$$

where σ_x^2 is the variance of the signal $x(k,l)$. The maximum value of this function is unity. It is reached at the origin. Thus we have :

$$\rho_x(0,0) = 1 \tag{54}$$

One can easily show that autocorrelation, autocovariance and normalized autocovariance functions are even functions for each of the variables k and l. These functions allow, with the Fourier transform, the establishment of the frequency description of two-dimensional random signals .

4.4 Two-dimensional Digital Systems

A two-dimensional digital system characterized by an operator S, acts on an input signal or excitation $x(k,l)$, to produce at its output another signal $y(k,l)$ which is the response of the system to that excitation. This operation is represented by :

$$y(k,l) = S\,[x(k,l)] \tag{55}$$

Different classes of systems are defined using constraints one can impose on the operator S. If equation (55) is one-to-one the same excitation produces always the same response. A large number of systems we shall use will be of this type.

If the application represented by equation (55) is many to one, the system may have the same response to several different excitations. A system which computes the mean value of the signal is such a system. Many different signals may have the same mean value.

We will exclude one-to-many types systems which may give different responses to the same excitation.

The very important class of digital systems is that of linear systems. They are characterized by the superposition principle which is the constraint posed on the operator S. One has :

$$S\left[a_1 x_1(k,l) + a_2 x_2(k,l)\right] = a_1 S\left[x_1(k,l)\right] + a_2 S\left[x_2(k,l)\right] \tag{56}$$

where a_1 and a_2 are two constants. This relation indicates that a linear system processes a linear combination of excitations as if they were processed separately and then combined. The importance of linear systems relies on the fact that they are relatively easy to analyze and to characterize leading thus to powerful and elegant mathematical representations. For this reason, they are also used in the study of complex systems where the linearity is realized only approximatively. One should underline however that the processing one can implement on real images with linear systems are very limited and often do not perform well. The application area of image processing is enlarged by the use of non linear systems. In that context, linear systems can be used as prerequisite.

4.5. Two-dimensional Convolution

Linear systems are entirely represented by their response to the unit impulse. Indeed by expressing the input signal using unit in pulses (43), we have :

$$x(k,l) = \sum_{k'=-\infty}^{+\infty} \sum_{l'=-\infty}^{+\infty} x(k',l')\, d(k-k',l-l') \tag{57}$$

By substituting equation (57) in (55) and taking into account equation (56), one obtains

$$y(k,l) = \sum_{k'=-\infty}^{t\infty} \sum_{l'=-\infty}^{T\infty} x(k',l')\, S\left[d(k-k',l-l')\right] \tag{58}$$

If $g(k,l,k',l')$ represents the response of the systems to the excitation $d(k-k',l-l')$, one has :

$$y(k,l) = \sum_{k'=-\infty}^{+\infty} \sum_{l'=-\infty}^{+\infty} x(k',l')\, g(k,l,k',l') \tag{59}$$

A sub-class of linear systems plays an important role in image processing. This is a class of shift-invariant linear systems. Let $y(k,l)$ be the response to $x(k,l)$. A linear system is called shift-invariant if the response to the translated excitation $x(k-k_0, l-l_0)$ and $y(k-k_0, l-l_0)$ where k_0 and l_0 are two integral numbers. For shift-invariant linear systems equation (59) takes the following particular form :

$$y(k,l) = \sum_{k'=-\infty}^{+\infty} \sum_{l'=-\infty}^{+\infty} x(k',l')\, g(k-k',l-l') \tag{60}$$

$$y(k,l) = x(k,l) ** g(k,l) = g(k,l) ** x(k,l)$$

This relation is called two-dimensional convolution. It is commutative. One can easily show that it is also assocative and distributive.

$$x(k,l) ** [y(k,l) ** z(k,l)] = [x(k,l) ** y(k,l)] ** z(k,l) \tag{61}$$

$$x(k,l) ** [y(k,l) + z(k,l)] = x(k,l) ** y(k,l) + x(k,l) ** z(k,l) \tag{62}$$

By using equation (61), one can show that the cascade of two shift-invariant systems with impulse responses $g_1(k,l)$ and $g_2(k,l)$ is equivalent to a global shift-invariant linear system whose impulse response $g(k,l)$ is given by :

$$g(k,l) = g_1(k,l) ** g_2(k,l) = g_2(k,l) ** g_1(k,l) \tag{63}$$

By using equation (62), one can show that putting in parallel two shift-invariant systems with impulse responses $g_1(k,l)$ and $g_2(k,l)$ is equivalent to a global shift-invariant systems whose impulse response is the sum of the invidual impulse responses.

The comparison between equations (48) and (60) shows a certain similarity between convolution and cross-correlation function. Indeed we have :

$$\varphi_{xy}(k,l) = x(-k,-l) ** y(k,l) \tag{64}$$

Observing equation (60), one can list different steps and operations involved in the direct computation of two-dimensional convolution.

- the impulse response is flipped over around the origin to obtain $g(-k',-l')$
- then it is shifted to a point (k,l);
- the product $x(k',l')g(k-k',l-l')$ is computed sample by sample for all the values of k and l.
- the values thus obtained are accumulated to obtain one value of the output $y(k,l)$.

The last three steps are repeated as many times as necessary. One can interpret this computation as the shift of the matrix or mask **G** made up with the samples of the impulse response as that given by equation (42), over the matrix **X** of the impulse signal. At each position of **G**, the corresponding elements or entries intercepted by the mask are multiplied two by two and added together. In the next section, another method called the indirect method using the Fourrier transform will be described.

If the impulse response is separable, the computation of a two-dimensional convolution is decomposed into a series of one-dimensional convolutions computed on the lines of the matrix (42) followed by another series of onedimensional convolutions computed on the columns of the same matrix. By equation (46), we have :

$$g(k,l) = g_1(k)\, g_2(l) \tag{65}$$

By substituting this result into (60), one obtains :

$$y_1(k,l-l') = \sum_{k'=-\infty}^{+\infty} g_1(k')x(k-k',l-l') \tag{66}$$

$$y(k,l) = \sum_{l'=-\infty}^{+\infty} g_2(l')\, y_1(k,l-l') \tag{67}$$

This decomposition may allow to decrease memory space necessary to the computation.

4.6 The Two-dimensional z Transform

The two-dimensional *z tranform* of a signal $x(k,l)$ is defined by :

$$X(z_1,z_1) = \sum_{k=-\infty}^{+\infty} \sum_{l=-\infty}^{+\infty} x(k,l)\, z_1^{-k} z_2^{-l} \tag{68}$$

where z_1 and z_2 are two complex variables .

For this transformation to exist, it is necessary that the series (68) converges. This is equivalent to saying that the following condition must be satisfied

$$\sum_{k=-\infty}^{+\infty} \sum_{l=-\infty}^{+\infty} \left| x(k,l)\, z_1^{-k} z_2^{-l} \right| < \infty \tag{69}$$

The ensemble of values z_1 and z_2 for which this condition is fulfiled defines the convergence regions of $X(z_1,z_2)$.

The inverse transform is obtained by generalizing results of the one dimensional case by using the Cauchy theorem. It is given by :

$$x(k,l) = \frac{1}{(2\pi j)^2} \oint_{c_1} \oint_{c_2} X(z_1,z_2)\, z_1^{k-1} z_2^{l-1} dz_1 dz_2 \tag{70}$$

where c_1 and c_2 are two closed contours around the origin of the plane z_1 z_2 and included in the convergence region of $X(z_1,z_2)$. In contrast to the one-dimensional case, it is in general difficult to determine the convergence region and the integration contours c_1 and c_2. The exceptional case is that of finite extend signals such as one given by equation (42). In such a case, provided that all the samples of the signal are finite, this z transform converges everywhere in the planes z_1 and z_2, except maybe at the origin $z_1 = z_2 = 0$ or for z_1 and z_2 going to infinity depending on the position of the signal in the plane (k,l).

An important class of two-dimensional z transform is that of separable transform :

$$X(z_1,z_2) = X_1(z_1)\, X_2(z_2) \tag{71}$$

A z transform is separable if the correspondant signal is separable The z transform of a signal $x(k,l)$ translated to k_0, l_0 is given by :

$$Y(z_1,z_2) = z_1^{-k_0} z_2^{-l_0} X(z_1,z_2) \tag{72}$$

where $Y(z_1,z_2)$ is the z transform of the shifted signal $y(k,l) = x(k - k_0, l - l_0)$.

The z transform of the both parts of equation (60) leads to a very important result which is the bases of twodimensional linear filtering. We have :

$$Y(z_1,z_2) = G(z_1,z_2)\, X(z_1,z_2) \tag{73}$$

where $Y(z_1,z_2)$,$G(z_1,z_2)$ and $X(z_1,z_2)$ are the z tranform of the response $y(k,l)$, of the impulse response $g(k,l)$ and of the excitation $x(k,l)$ respectively. The z transform $G(z_1,z_2)$ is called the *tranfer function* of the corresponding linear shift-invariant system. It determines the modifications that the input signal receives from the system. With respect to ideal modifications difficult to implement the transfer function is very often approximated by the ratio of two two-dimensional polynomials.

$$G(z_1,z_2) = \frac{\sum_{k''=0}^{K_2} \sum_{l''=0}^{L_2} b_{k''l''} z_1^{-k''} z_2^{-l''}}{\sum_{k'=0}^{K_1} \sum_{l'=0}^{L_1} a_{k'l'} z_1^{-k'} z_2^{-l'}} \tag{74}$$

By substituting this equation in (73) and by computing the inverse transform of both members of the result using (72) one obtains:

$$\sum_{k'=0}^{K_1} \sum_{l'=0}^{L_1} a_{k'l'}\, y(k-k', l-l') = \sum_{k''=0}^{K_2} \sum_{l''=0}^{L_2} b_{k''l''}\, x(k-k'', l-l'') \tag{75}$$

This equation is called the two-dimensional difference equation with constant coefficients. The system is entirely characterized by the symbol of coefficients $\{a_{k'l'}\}$ and $\{b_{k''l''}\}$.

Remember that equation (75) has been obtained for a shift-invariant system. That is why the coefficients $\{a_{k'l'}\}$ and $\{b_{k''l''}\}$ are constant. If shift-invariance is not realized, then the coefficients vary as a function of the variables k and l.

The implementation of a difference equation of the type (75) requires an ensemble of $(K_1 + 1)\ (L_1 + 1) + k_2 + 1)\ (L_2 + 1)$ initial conditions. The recursions implied by the double summations are at the origin of some algorithmic problems which are discussed in the next paragraph.

4.7 Implementation of the Difference Equation

In equation (75), one can set without loss of generality, $a_{00} = 1$ and solve it with respect to $y(k,l)$. We have :

$$y(k,l) = \sum_{k''=0}^{K_2} \sum_{l''=0}^{L_2} b_{k''l''}\, x(k-k'', l-l'') - \sum_{k'=1}^{K_1} \sum_{l'=1}^{L_1} a_{k'l'}\, y(k-k', l-l') \tag{76}$$

This equation can only be computed if the values of k and l are incremented. To examine the situation, let us consider the ensemble of coefficients $\{a_{k'l'}\}$ and $\{b_{k''l''}\}$. Each group of coefficients may be represented as a matrix or a masque. For example, for $K_1 = L_1 = K_2 = L_2 = 3$, we have :

$$\mathbf{A} = \begin{pmatrix} a_{30} & a_{20} & a_{10} & \\ a_{31} & a_{21} & a_{11} & a_{01} \\ a_{32} & a_{22} & a_{12} & a_{02} \\ a_{33} & a_{23} & a_{13} & a_{03} \end{pmatrix} \text{ and } \mathbf{B} = \begin{pmatrix} b_{30} & b_{20} & b_{10} & b_{00} \\ b_{31} & b_{21} & b_{11} & b_{01} \\ b_{32} & b_{22} & b_{12} & b_{02} \\ b_{33} & b_{23} & b_{13} & b_{03} \end{pmatrix} \tag{77}$$

The absence of element in matrix **A** in the upper right corner is to be noticed which is the result of the double sums over k' and l' in (76) strarting at 1 and not at 0. The evaluation of equation (76) can be made in the following manner :

1) We shift the matrix **B** over the matrix **X** of the impulse signal at a position (k,l), and compute the two by two product of the elements in correspondence and accumulate them.

2) To repeat similar operations with the matrix **A** placed at the same position (k,l) and the matrix **Y** of the output signal.

3) The result is the difference between the numbers obtained and two previous steps.

4) The preceeding steps are repeated for other values of (k, l).

The preceeding computation can be computed at a position (k,l) if and only if the matrix **A** covers samples of the output signal which is already computed. This explains the conditions posed previously over the variation of variables k and l and rises the question of initial conditions. To compute equation (76) recursively, it is necessary that the output be zero for $k<0$ and $l<0$.

By shifting the empty entry in the matrix at other corners, upper left, lower right or lower left, one can establish other conditions of recursion. Each of these cases pose the conditions on incrementing or dicrementing the variables k and l during the computation. The four possible positions of the empty entry correspond to four quadrants of the plane (k,l). That is why this type of implementation is called *implementation by quadrant.* It is also possible to develop implementation by half-plane by algebraic manipulations of the difference equation.

4.8 Stability

The stability is a constraint of great pratical importance that we should impose to the system. By definition, a system is said to be stable if its response to an excitation with bounded dynamic range is also with a bounded dynamic range. The necessary and sufficient condition for a system to be stable is the following.

$$T = \sum_{k=-\infty}^{+\infty} \sum_{=-\infty}^{+\infty} |g(k,l)| < \infty \qquad (78)$$

Indeed if the excitation $x\ (k,l)$ has a bounded dynamic range, we have $|x(k,l)| < A$ for all the values of k and of l, where A is a positive finite number. The magnitude of the response is then given by :

$$|y(k,l)| = \left| \sum_{k'=-\infty}^{+\infty} \sum_{l'=-\infty}^{+\infty} g(k',l')x(k-k', l-l') \right| \le A \sum_{k'=-\infty}^{+\infty} \sum_{l'=-\infty}^{+\infty} |g(k',l')| \qquad (79)$$

Thus if the condition (78) is fulfilled, the system is stable. The necessity of this condition may be shown with the following particular signal :

$$x(k,l) = \begin{cases} +1 \text{ if } g(-k,-l) \ge 0 \\ -1 \text{ if } g(-k,-l) \le 0 \end{cases} \qquad (80)$$

The dynamic range of the signal is bounded. The output signal of the system at the origin $k = l = 0$ is given by :

$$y(0,0) = \sum_{k'=-\infty}^{+\infty} \sum_{l'=-\infty}^{+\infty} g(k',l')x(-k',-l') = \sum_{k'=-\infty}^{+\infty} \sum_{l'=-\infty}^{+\infty} |g(k',l')| = T \tag{81}$$

Consequently, the dynamic range of the response is not finite if the condition (78) is not fulfilled.

This theorem could be transposed by z transform to the complex domain z_1, z_2. The necessary and sufficient condition for a system to be stable is that the polynomial at the denominator of the transfer function (74) is not equal to zero for $|z_1| \leq 1$ and $|z_2| \leq 1$:

$$A(z_1,z_2) = \sum_{k'=0}^{K_1} \sum_{l'=0}^{L_1} a_{k'l'} z_1^{-k'} z_2^{-l'} \neq 0 \quad \text{for } |z_1| \leq 1 \text{ and } |z_2| \leq 1 \tag{82}$$

The verification of this condition is complex. It has been transposed by Huang in the following way. A system is stable if and only if :

1) the image of the unit circle c_1 of the plane z_1, modified to exclude singularities do not fall by the application $A(z_1, z_2) = 0$ inside the unite circle c_2 defined by $|z_2| = 1$;

2) no point inside the unit circle c_1 can go to the point $z2 = 0$ by the same application $A(z1, z2) = 0$ can go to the point $z2 = 0$.

5. Two-dimensional Fourier Transform

5.1 Definition and Properties

The two-dimensional Fourier transform of a digital signal $x(k,l)$ is defined by :

$$X(f,g) = \sum_{k=-\infty}^{+\infty} \sum_{l=-\infty}^{+\infty} x(k,l)\, e^{-j2\pi(fk+gl)} \tag{83}$$

where f and g are two continuous real variables representing two special frequencies corresponding to the directions k and l. This transform exists if the right-hand side of equation (83) is finite, in other words if the series converges. The sufficient condition for the convergence of the series is the following :

$$\sum_{k=-\infty}^{+\infty} \sum_{l=-\infty}^{+\infty} |x(k,l)| < \infty \tag{84}$$

If this condition is fulfilled, then the series converges absolutely towards continuous complex functions of f and g.

The Fourier transform defined by (83) is doubly periodical in f and in g of period unity. Indeed we have :

$$X(f+1,g+1) = \sum_{k=-\infty}^{+\infty} \sum_{l=-\infty}^{+\infty} x(k,l)\, e^{-j2\pi[(f+1)k + (g+1)l]}$$

$$= \sum_{k=-\infty}^{+\infty} \sum_{l=-\infty}^{+\infty} x(k,l)\, e^{-j2\pi(fk + gl)}\, e^{-j2\pi(k+l)} = X(f,g) \tag{85}$$

Because of this double periodicity, any domain of unit surface in the plane (f,g) is sufficient to describe the function $X(f,g)$ entirely. One usually uses the domain :

$$-1/2 \leq f \leq 1/2 \text{ and } -1/2 \leq g \leq 1/2 \tag{86}$$

called *principal* or *main* domain.

One can interpret equation (83) as the expansion into classical Fourier series of a two-dimensional periodical function. The samples of the signal $x(k,l)$ may be obtained from the transform $X(f,g)$ by the following relation :

$$x(k,l) = \int_{-1/2}^{1/2} \int_{-1/2}^{1/2} X(f,g)\, e^{j2\pi(fk + gl)} df\, dg \tag{87}$$

This is the inverse Fourier transform for two-dimensional digital signals.

In general, the Fourier transform is a complex function :

$$X(f,g) = \mathrm{Re}[X(f,g)] + j\, \mathrm{Im}[X(f,g)] \tag{88}$$

For a real signal, the real and imaginary parts of $X(f,g)$ are respectively given by :

$$\mathrm{Re}\left[X(f,g)\right] = \sum_{k=-\infty}^{+\infty} \sum_{l=-\infty}^{+\infty} x(k,l) \cos\left[2\pi(fk + gl)\right] \tag{89}$$

and

$$\mathrm{Im}[X(f,g)] = \sum_{k=-\infty}^{+\infty} \sum_{l=-\infty}^{+\infty} x(k,l) \sin[2\pi(fk + gl)] \tag{90}$$

Equation (88) may also be written in the following form :

$$X(f,g) = |X(f,g)| \exp\{\mathrm{j} \arg[X(f,g)] \} \tag{91}$$

The magnitude $|X(f,g)|$ is called the *two-dimensional magnitude spectrum*. It expresses the frequential repartition in the plane (f,g) of the amplitude of the signal. Let us mention that in this case the notion of frequency is associated to a spatial evolution in the plane (k,l) of the image.

The term $\theta_x(f,g) = \arg[X(f,g)]$ is called the *two-dimensional phase spectrum*. It expresses the frequential repartition in the plane (f,g) of the phase of the signal.

The term $|X(f,g)|^2$ is the *energy spectrum.*

5.2 Examples

Let us consider the computation of the Fourier transform of the unit sample $d(k,l)$. By applying the definition (83), we obtain easily :

$$X(f,g) = \sum_{k=-\infty}^{+\infty} \sum_{l=-\infty}^{+\infty} d(k,l)\, e^{-j2\pi(fk + gl)} = \sum_{k=0}^{0} \sum_{l=0}^{0} 1 = 1$$

The magnitude spectrum and the energy spectrum are thus constant whatever the value of the frequencies f and g. The phase spectrum is identically zero.

As a second example, let us consider the rectangular signal (45):

$$\mathrm{rect}_{K,L}(k,l) = \begin{cases} 1 & \text{for } 0 \le k \le K-1 \text{ and } 0 \le l \le L-1 \\ 0 & \text{everywhere else} \end{cases}$$

Using the definition (83), we have :

$$X(f,g) = \sum_{k=-K/2}^{K/2-1} \sum_{l=-L/2}^{L/2-1} e^{-j2\pi fk}\, e^{-j2\pi gl} = \sum_{k=-K/2}^{K/2-1} e^{-j2\pi fk} \sum_{l=-L/2}^{L/2-1} e^{-j2\pi gl}$$

$$= e^{-j2\pi fK} e^{-j2\pi gL} \sum_{k'=0}^{K-1} \sum_{l'=0}^{L-1} e^{-j2\pi fk'}\, e^{-j2\pi gl'}$$

$$= e^{j\pi(fK + gL)} \frac{1 - e^{-j2\pi fK}}{1 - e^{-j2\pi f}} \frac{1 - e^{-j2\pi gL}}{1 - e^{-j2\pi g}}$$

$$= e^{j\pi(f + g)} \frac{\sin(\pi fK)}{\sin(\pi f)} \frac{\sin(\pi gL)}{\sin(\pi g)}$$

The magnitude of this function is shown in figure 16 for $K = L = 6$.

5.3 Correlation and Convolution through Fourier Transform

In the previous section, while listing the steps of computation for the correlation and the convolution, an indirect method has been announced, based on the Fourier transform. It is obtained simply by computing the Fourier transform of both members of equations (48) and (60). In the case of correlation, we have :

$$\Phi_{xy}(f,g) = \sum_{k=-\infty}^{+\infty} \sum_{l=-\infty}^{+\infty} \varphi_{xy}(k,l)\, e^{-j2\pi(fk + gl)}$$

$$= \sum_{k=-\infty}^{+\infty} \sum_{l=-\infty}^{+\infty} \sum_{k'=-\infty}^{+\infty} \sum_{l'=-\infty}^{+\infty} x(k',l')y(k' + k, l' + l)\, e^{-j2\pi(fk + gl)} \tag{92}$$

With the following change of variables $u = k' + k$ and $v = l' + l$, we have:

$$\Phi_{xy}(f,g) = \left[\sum_{k'=-\infty}^{+\infty} \sum_{l'=-\infty}^{+\infty} x(k',l')\, e^{j2\pi(fk' + gl')} \right] \left[\sum_{u=-\infty}^{+\infty} \sum_{v=-\infty}^{+\infty} y(u,v)\, e^{-j2\pi(fu + gv)} \right]$$

$$\Phi_{xy}(f,g) = X^*(f,g)\, Y(f,g) \tag{93}$$

The cross-correlation function is obtained by computing the inverse Fourier transform $\Phi_{xy}(f,g)$. In the preceeding development, we have admitted that signals $x(k,l)$ and $y(k,l)$ were real.

In the case of convolution, similarly to the previous calculations, we have :

$$Y(f,g) = G(f,g)\, X(f,g) \tag{94}$$

The Fourier transform $G(f,g)$ of the impulse response is called *the two-dimensional frequency response* of the corresponding system.

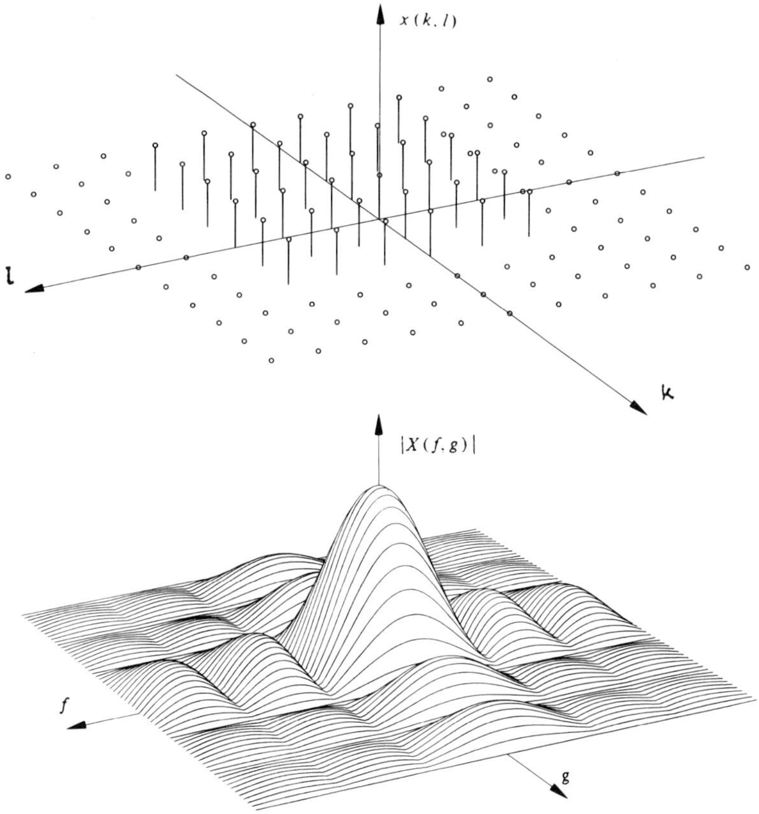

Fig. 16: Fourier transform of a rectangular signal

5.4 Two-dimensional Discrete Fourier Transform (TDFT)

We were able to compute preceeding examples because the signals we have selected lend themselves to an analytical computation. For two-dimensional signals more complex or for digital data obtained by sampling and quantizing an analog scene, it is not possible to compute the Fourier transform analytically. It is therefore necessary to use numerical calculation in which we use the two-dimensional discrete Fourier transform.

In the practical use of equations (83) and (87) there are two difficulties. The first is that f and g are analog variables which we cannot manipulate in a digital processing system. The second difficulty is due to the infinite number of samples of the signals $x(k,l)$ which is impossible to process in practice. One can overcome these difficulties by replacing the analog variables by discrete variables and by limiting in the plane (k,l)

the extend of the signal. However, we have to be careful to the consequences of these simple solutions.

In the principal domain (86), we replace the continuous variables f and g by the discrete variables m and n by posing :

$$f = m\Delta f \text{ and } g = n\,\Delta g \text{ with } \quad \Delta f = 1/M \text{ and } \Delta g = 1/N \tag{95}$$

where M and N are two integers. The substitution (95) is equivalent to the representation of the Fourier transform by MN samples in the main domain. Equation (87) takes the following form :

$$x(k,l) \cong \frac{1}{MN} \sum_{m=-M/2}^{M/2-1} \sum_{n=-N/2}^{N/2-1} X(m,n) \exp\left[j2\pi(\frac{mk}{M} + \frac{nl}{N}) \right] \tag{96}$$

One can remark that the right-hand side of this equation is periodical in k of period M and in l of period N. Thus, the approximation in equation (96) becomes an equality if the extend of the signal $x(k,l)$ is limited to a rectangular domain of dimension M x N. In this case, one can extract $x(k,l)$ exactly from any given period of the right-hand side of equation (96). We have then :

$$x(k,l) = \frac{1}{MN} \sum_{m=-M/2}^{M/2-1} \sum_{n=-N/2}^{N/2-1} X(m,n) \exp\left[j2\pi(\frac{mk}{M} + \frac{nl}{N}) \right] \tag{97}$$

with

$$k_0 \leq k \leq k_0 + M - 1 \text{ and } l_0 \leq l \leq l_0 + N - 1 \tag{98}$$

By taking into account the relation (95), one can write the Fourier transform of a signal whose extend is limited to the domain (98) in the following way :

$$X(m,n) = \sum_{k=k_0}^{k_0+M-1} \sum_{l=l_0}^{l_0+N-1} x(k,l) \exp\left[-j2\pi(\frac{mk}{M} + \frac{nl}{N}) \right] \tag{99}$$

Equations (97) and (99) define the *two-dimensional discrete Fourier transform* (TDFT) for a finite extend signal.

5.5 Matrix Form of the TDFT

For the establishment of computational algorithms, for the theoretical studies and for all the cases where the detail of the serial formalism is not necessary, it is very useful to transform equations (97) and (99) into matrix form. The kernel of this transformation is given by :

$$\exp\left[\pm j2\pi(\frac{mk}{M}+\frac{nl}{N})\right] = \exp\left[\pm j2\pi(\frac{mk}{M})\right] \exp\left[\pm j2\pi(\frac{nl}{N})\right] \tag{100}$$

It is separable. Thus, one can express the TDFT using the one-dimensional discrete Fourier transform. This latter is well known, efficiently computable thanks to a fast computational algorithm called fast Fourier transform.

The extend of the signal $x(k,l)$ in the plane (k,l) and the extend of the transform $X(m,n)$ in the plane (m,n) are limited to the ensembles of M x N numerical values or samples. We can thus represent the signal and its transform by two matrixes.

Let $\mathbf{x}$ and $\mathbf{X}$ be the matrices corresponding respectively to the signal and to its transform. Each exponential in the right-hand side of equation (100) is the kernel of the one-dimensional discrete Fourier transform. The matrixes of these transformations can be denoted by $\mathbf{F}_M$ and $\mathbf{F}_N$ respectively. The matrix form of equation (99) is thus :

$$\mathbf{X} = \mathbf{F}_N \ \mathbf{x} \ \mathbf{F}_M{}^{\mathrm{H}} \tag{101}$$

where the exponent H represents the hermitian transpose.
The inverse transform is given by :

$$\mathbf{x} = \mathbf{F}_N{}^{-1} \ \mathbf{X} \ (\mathbf{F}_M{}^{-1})^{\mathrm{H}} \tag{102}$$

6. Filtering and Preprocessing

6.1 Preliminary Remarks

The action of a linear two-dimensional shift invariant system may be viewed as filtering. As we have seen by equation (94), a linear system modifies the frequential distribution of the components of the input signal to produce the output signal. If such a system is implemented with arithmetic operations with finite precision, it is called *digital filter*. The processing which corresponds to this is called *digital filtering*. This section is a summary of the principles and two-dimensional digital filtering methods.

The mathematical tools of filtering have been developped in preceeding sections. They are briefly recalled here.

In the spatial frequency domain, the action of the filter is controlled by equation (94):

$$Y(f,g) = G(f,g)\, X(f,g) \tag{103}$$

The particular form of the frequential response used $G(f,g)$ determines the attenuations or the amplifications of the components at various frequencies f and g.

In the signal domain, the equivalent relation is :

$$y(k,l) = \sum_{k'=-\infty}^{+\infty} \sum_{l'=-\infty}^{+\infty} x(k',l')\, g(k-k',l-l') \qquad (104)$$

The z transform of both sides of this equation leads to :

$$Y(z_1,z_2) = G(z_1,z_2)\, X(z_1,z_2) \qquad (105)$$

In the case where the transfer function $G(z_1,z_2)$ can be written as a quotient of two two-dimensional polynomials, the input and output signals are related by the following difference equation :

$$\sum_{k'=0}^{K_1} \sum_{l'=0}^{L_1} a_{k'l'}\, y(k-k',l-l') = \sum_{k''=0}^{K_2} \sum_{l''=0}^{L_2} b_{k''l''}\, x(k-k'',l-l'') \qquad (106)$$

Equations (103) to (106) are the mathematical tools for basic two-dimensional digital filtering.

The goal in digital filtering is to design a shift invariant linear system which possesses the desired frequency response $G_d(f,g)$ and which allows itself to a practical implementation. Because of this last constraint, one can obtain the ideal frequency response only in an approximative way. It is necessary that the system be stable, recursible and that only finite a number of arithmetic operation with limited precision is involved.

The extend of the impulse response $g(k,l)$ is of primary importance. The methods used change depending if this extend is finite or infinite. For example, it is impossible in practice to use the convolution (104). One should use an equation of the type (106) where the number of operations is finite. That is why the filters are classified in two categories depending on the extend of their impulse response : *finite extend impulse responses* filters abbreviated as FIR and *infinite extend impulse response* filters, abbreviated as IIR.

6.2 FIR Filters Design

The majority of digital two-dimensional FIR filters design results from the generalization into two dimensions of one-dimensional methods. They are briefly summarized herewith without re-developing detailed formalism shown elsewhere.

A first method obtained by generalization from one-dimensional case is the *frequency sampling method*. Starting with a continuous two-dimensional function that we consider as the ideal frequency response $G_i(f,g)$, we collect a finite number of samples which are assigned to the coefficients $G(m,n)$ of the two-dimensional discrete Fourier transform, given by equation (99). If the inverse transform computed with these coefficients, the impulse response obtained $g(k,l)$ may be that of a FIR filter. However, the frequency response of this filter will be identical to the ideal frequency response only at the sampling frequencies. For all other frequencies, its behaviour will be very different than that of $G_i(f,g)$. That's why the coefficients $G(m,n)$ which are over the transition bands are considered as parameters. Their value is adjusted by optimization methods (for example linear programming) by minimizing the error between $G_i(f,g)$ and the effective frequency response of the filter. The disadvantage of this method is its computation time.

Another method obtained by generalization of one-dimensional case is the *limitation of the extend* by a window function. Very often, the frequency response of the ideal filter $G_i(f,g)$ contains rapid transition between passing-bands and stop-bands. The corresponding impulse response $g_i(k,l)$, by inverse Fourier transform, is necessarily of infinite extend. It cannot thus be assigned to a FIR filter which requires a finite extend. The ideal response is then multiplied by a window function to limit the extend.

$$g(k,l) = g_i(k,l)\, w(k,l) \qquad (107)$$

where $w(k,l)$ is the window function. The real frequency response $G(f,g)$ is given by :

$$G(f,g) = G_i(f,g) ** W(f,g) \qquad (108)$$

where $W(f,g)$ is the Fourier transform of the window function. The problem is to find the window $w(k,l)$ which minimizes the distance between $G_i(f,g)$ and $G(f,g)$. It is now well-established that if $u(k)$ is a good one-dimensional window function, then

$$w(k,l) = u(\sqrt{k^2 + l^2}) \qquad (109)$$

is a good two-dimensional window function with circular symmetry. This method is easy to apply and allows to design large variety of FIR filters.

An appropriate change of variable may transform a one-dimensional filter into a two-dimensional filter. This method requires a one-dimensional filter whose impulse response should be sufficiently long but whose design doesn't create any problem. The computations involved are not very complex and the resulting two-dimensional filter may be optimized if the one-dimensional filter is also optimized. For example, the following change of variables :

$$\cos f_1 = \mathrm{A} \cos f + \mathrm{B} \cos g + \mathrm{C} \cos f \cos g + \mathrm{D} \qquad (110)$$

transforms a one-dimensional FIR filter $G(f_1)$ of odd length and zero phase into a two-dimensional filter with quadrantal symmetry. This change of variable produces in the two-dimensional frequency plane (f,g)

a contour for each value of one-dimensional frequency f_1. Along this contour, the frequency response of the two-dimensional filter is constant and equal to that of the one-dimensional filter at f_1. The problem is to find the values of the parameters A,B,C and D which allow to obtain the contours approximating the desired frequency response. The implementation of this technique is very fast, even for large extend filters, for example 30 x 30.

The change of variable (110) may be generalized in the following way :

$$\cos f_1 = \sum_{p=0}^{P} \sum_{q=0}^{Q} u(p,q) \cos pf \cos qg \tag{111}$$

It allows to design a much wider set of FIR filters. One can also free one from the constraint of quadrantal symmetry with the following change of variable which exploits symmetries and antisymmetries :

$$\cos f_1 = \mathrm{A} + \mathrm{B} \cos f + \mathrm{C} \cos g + (\mathrm{D} + \mathrm{E}) \cos f \cos g - (\mathrm{D} - \mathrm{E}) \sin f \sin g \tag{112}$$

It is also possible to design a two-dimensional filter starting from one-dimensional filters. The most simple case is that of a separable frequency response :

$$G(f,g) = G_1(f) G_2(g) \tag{113}$$

where $G_1(f)$ and $G_2(g)$ may be obtained by one of the one-dimensional designed methods. In case where the separation (113) is not valid, one can approximate the desired response by a separable response. The gain in computation time of this technique compensates often the approximation error between non separable ideal response and a separable practical response. One-dimensional filters are designed more efficiently than two-dimensional filters.

Let us mention finally the optimization technique in the minimum sense or Chebychev sense. The general idea consists in varying a certain number of samples of the frequency response in order to satisfy a given specification on the real frequency response. However, these methods are very complex and require an important computation time. Their use can only be justified in the case of small extend (in the order of 5 x 5).

6.3 IIR Filter Design

A IIR filter is implemented using a difference equation of type (106). To design a IIR filter, one should obtain coefficients of this equation. One possibility consists in transforming a one-dimensional analog filter into a two-dimensional digital filter, similarly to what is done in the one-dimensional case. Let us consider a one-dimensional analog filter $G(s)$. One can view it as a two-dimensional analog filter which varies only in one dimension if we write :

$$G(s_1,s_2) = G(s_1) \quad (114)$$

One can implement a rotation of β radians in the (s_1, s_2) plane to define a new axes system in a plane (s'_1, s'_2) using the following transformation :

$$s_1 = s'_1\cos\beta + s'_2\sin\beta$$

$$s_2 = s'_2\cos\beta - s'_1\sin\beta \quad (115)$$

Finally, one applies a bilinear transformation (103) to variables s'_1 and s'_2. One obtains :

$$s'_1 = c\frac{1 - z_1}{1 + z_1} \quad and \quad s'_2 = c\frac{1 - z_2}{1 + z_2} \quad (116)$$

where c is a constant. Serial organization of several one-dimensional filters, which were rotated different ways, can lead to various two-dimensional filters.

As in the case of FIR filters, one can use optimization techniques. These computer aided methods lead to filters which have the following characteristics : the resulting filter is optimized, it may serve as a reference for other sub optimal methods, and it is quite suitable for a VLSI implementation and there is no special constraint on the specifications. One possibility is to realize such a filter as a product of the first order and second order filter responses. The stability can be checked at each step of the synthesis by using simple inequalities relating partial filters coefficients.

7. Enhancement and Restoration of Images

7.1 Definitions

The quality of an image may be degraded when it changes its support (reproduction, transmission, storage, redundancy reduction, etc.). An image may also be of poor quality at its birth because of bad tuning of the acquisition system. The ensemble of methods developed to compensate the known or estimated degradations in order to re-establish the initial quality of the image is called *image restoration.*

The ensemble of methods which change the appearance of an image in a way to make it more suitable for a human observer or for a machine to extract a certain information more easily is called *enhancement.*

Unfortunaltey, sometimes enhancement and restoration are notions which are confused in the literature.

7.2 Comments

To judge the modifications or the "improvements" an image has received, one should have a quality criteria. But, the image quality depends heavily on the goal. For example, the quality of a television image cannot be judged the same way as that of a radiograph. Although many efforts have been spent on this, there is still no criteria which is sufficiently versatile and relatively simple for mathematical treatments and satisfactory for the subjective judgement of the visual system.

A large part of image restoration methods have been developed as a function of an objective criteria, such as the mean square error, the mean absolute error or the maximum absolute error. Unfortunately, these criteria do not follow the subjective judgement of the visual system. In each specific case, one should use an appropriate criteria as a function of the goal to be obtained.

7.3 General Image Restoration Problem

The detailed analysis of degraded images one can often encounter shows that the most common degradations may be represented by the model of a linear shift-invariant system. Thus, the degraded image $y(k,l)$ is represented by :

$$y(k,l) = \sum_{k'=-\infty}^{+\infty} \sum_{l'=-\infty}^{+\infty} g(k',l')x(k-k', l-l') + b(k,l) \tag{117}$$

where $x(k,l)$ is the ideal image, $g(k,l)$ is the impulse response of the degradation and $b(k,l)$ is the additive noise which is characteristic of the degradation system. The block-diagram of the model (117) is represented at figure 17.

One can establish and study more complex models than (117) by introducing for example a multiplicative noise in addition to the additive noise. Such a noise characterizes in photography the film grain and can be brought to an additive noise using the homomorphic model.

The restoration problem is the following : given the degraded image $y(k,l)$ and some possible a priori information, how to obtain the ideal image $x(k,l)$ or, at least, how to come as closest as possible? The problem is the determination of the impulse response $g(k,l)$. For other methods, $g(k,l)$ can be determined, either from the physical phenomenon which produces the degradation, or from the degraded image by itself. In the last case, one should know a priori that certain regions of the degraded image correspond to a single point, to a lign or to other simple geometric figures of the ideal image.

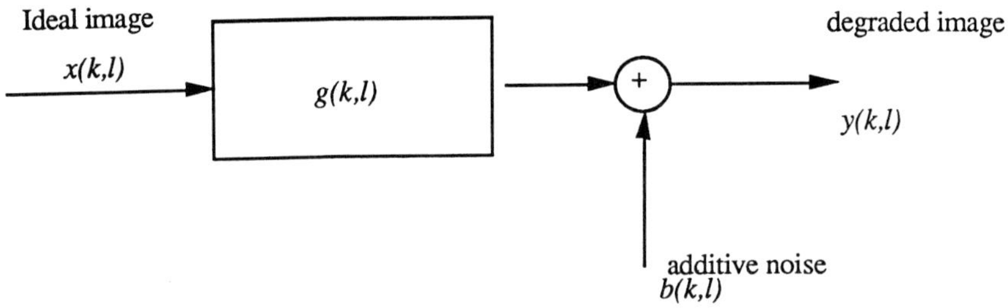

Fig. 17: Block diagram of image degradation model

7.4 Modelling Degradations

To solve the restoration problem in certain particular cases, it is useful to model the main degradations such as camera motion, blurred image with bad focusing and atmospheric turbulences.

Let us consider picture taking with exposure over T units of time, during which there is a uniform motion in the horizontal direction of the type $k = \alpha n$ where n represents time. By assuming the obturator opens and closes instantaneously, a point of the image, situated at the opening at a given place will be displaced in the horizontal direction at a distance αT. In the context of the relation (117), the impluse response is consequently given by :

$$g_c(k,l) = \sum_{m=-\infty}^{+\infty} d(m - \frac{\alpha T}{2}, l) - d(m + \frac{\alpha T}{2}, l) \qquad (118)$$

where $d(k,l)$ is the two-dimensional unit sample (43). A motion in any other direction can easily be expressed by rotating the coordinated axes.

Still in the same context of the model (117), a bad focusing can be approximately represented by a constant and non zero function over a circular area. This approximation is deduced from optical laws. One has thus :

$$g_m(k,l) = \begin{cases} 1 & \text{for } k^2 + l^2 \leq a^2 \\ 0 & \text{for } k^2 + l^2 > a^2 \end{cases} \qquad (119)$$

where the paramater a is a measure of how bad is the focusing.

The last type of degradation one encounters often is that caused by atmospheric turbulences (the change in the refraction index). This degradation is represented, according to physical laws, by a two-dimensional gaussian function :

$$g_a(k,l) = \exp\left[-b\,(k^2+l^2)\right] \tag{120}$$

7.5 Restoration by Inverse Filtering

Let us consider first the convolution model (117), without the additive noise, in other words with $b(k,l) = 0$. In this case, the two-dimensional Fourier transform of both sides leads to :

$$Y(f,g) = G(f,g)\,X\,(f,g) \tag{121}$$

In the discrete case, we have :

$$Y(m,n) = G(m,n)\,X(m,n) \tag{122}$$

Knowing $y(k,l)$ and $g(k,l)$, one can compute $Y(m,n)$ and $G(m,n)$ using the two-dimensional fast Fourier transform. Thus :

$$X(m,n) = \frac{Y(m,n)}{G(m,n)} \tag{123}$$

This is the classical problem of deconvolution by inverse filtering. The degraded image is filtered by a filter whose frequency response is $1/G(m,n)$. The inverse transform of the relation (123) gives the image needed.

However, a certain number of problems rise in the use of the relation (123). In the frequency domain, $G(m,n)$ may be zero. It is also possible that, for the same values of m and n, $Y(m,n)$ and $G(m,n)$ be simultaneously zero, leading thus to an indetermined situation. This shows that, despite the simplicity of the relations (121) and (123), one can obtain the ideal image $x(k,l)$ only in an approximated way, by using tricks to avoid discontinuity and indeterminations.

In the presence of noise, the Fourier transform leads to :

$$X(m,n) = \frac{Y(m,n) - B(m,n)}{G(m,n)} \tag{124}$$

For small values of $G(m,n)$, the ratio $B(m,n)\,/G(m,n)$ may be large and may influence in a non negligible way the transform $X(m,n)$.

In practice, one evaluates the relation (124) only at frequences (m,n) where the signal-to-noise ratio is high. Thus, the frequency response of the inverse filter is not $1/G(m,n)$, but another function of m and of n. In general, the response $G(m,n)$ is of the type low frequency. In order to avoid the influence of noise at other frequences, one often use a restoration filter whose response is :

$$G'(m,n) = \begin{cases} 1/G(m,n) & \text{for } m^2+n^2 \leq o^2 \\ 1 & \text{for } m^2+n^2 > o^2 \end{cases} \tag{125}$$

where o is a radial frequency beyond which the noise is dominant.

7.6 Restoration by Mean Squares

The inverse filtering, as discussed, leads to a number of practical problems, which can be overcome by tricks more or less arbitrary. Another way to solve the restoration problem consists in looking for an estimate $\hat{x}(k,l)$ of the ideal image $x(k,l)$, in order to minimize a difference measure. A measure which is quite practical mathematically, but unsatisfactory for the subjective judgement, is the mean square error. The filter which minimizes the mean square error is :

$$\varepsilon^2 = \mathrm{E}\left[(x(k,l) - \hat{x}(k,l))^2\right] \tag{126}$$

in the statistical sense, called the Wiener filter. The restoration method using the Wiener filter is called mean square restoration.

The frequency response of the Wiener filter will not be established here, due to its very specialized nature. A detailed description may be found in the literature. This response is of the following form :

$$G_w(m,n) = \frac{G^*(m,n)\Phi_x(m,n)}{|G(m,n)|^2\Phi_x(m,n) + \Phi_B(m,n)} \tag{127}$$

where $\Phi_x(m,n)$ and $\Phi_B(m,n)$ are respectively the power spectrum density of the ideal image and of the noise. Equation (127) is established with the hypothesis of statistical independance between the noise and the ideal image. One can notice that without noise ($\Phi_B(m,n) = 0$), the Wiener filter is identical to the inverse filter.

The a priori knowledge required for this method is that the impulse reponse of the degradation $g(k,l)$ and the power spectrum density (or autocorrelation functions) of the noise and of the image are known.

7.7 Constrained Mean Square Restoration

One can eliminate the necessity to know a priori the power spectrum density or the correlation functions of the previous method, by developing an optimization problem under constraint. The constraint one can use is that the residual signal [see relation (117)]

$$z(k,l) = y(k,l) - \sum_{k'}\sum_{l'} g(k',l')x(k-k',l-l') \tag{128}$$

has the same second order moment as the noise $b(k,l)$

$$\sum_k\sum_l z^2(k,l) = \sum_k\sum_l b^2(k,l) = \varepsilon \tag{129}$$

Because of the inherent correlation, the function $x(k,l)$ does not vary much from one point to the next. One can thus minimize a measure of the smoothness related to a second derivated of the type :

$$\sum_k\sum_l \left[x(k-1,l) + x(k,l-1) + x(k+1,l) + x(k,l+1) - 4x(k,l)\right]^2 \tag{130}$$

The restoration problem is thus to find a signal $x(k,l)$ which minimizes the quantity (130) still satisfying the constraint (129). The solution of this problem is relatively long and complex. It will be omitted in this text. The frequency response of the restoration filter is of the type :

$$G_H(m,n) = \frac{G^*(m,n)}{|G(m,n)|^2 + \lambda|C(m,n)|^2} \tag{131}$$

where $C(m,n)$ is the Fourier transform of the extended Laplacian operator deduced from equation (130) and λ a parameter obtained iteratively to satisfy (129).

7.8 Image Restoration by Homomorphic Processing

Here we consider the degraded image as that given by the model (117), but in the case where there is no noise ($b(k,l) = 0$). The degradation may be, for example, one of the three degradations modelled with relations (118)-(120). We have thus :

$$y(k,l) = x(k,l) ** g(k,l) \tag{132}$$

The complex logarithm applied to the Fourier transform of both sides of this equation leads to :

$$\ln[Y(f,g)] = \ln[X(f,g)] + \ln[G(f,g)] \tag{133}$$

To find the image $x(k,l)$, one should estimate one way or another $G(f,g)$ and subtract its complex logarithm to that of $Y(f,g)$ in (133). A possible method is the use of equation (133) for several degraded images by the same degrading system and then to compute the mean of both sides of this equation over this ensemble of images. With a sufficient number of degraded images, each containing a signal $x(k,l)$ relatively different from the others, the right-hand side will converge towards ln $[G(f,g)]$ within a constant value. This procedure, known as *statistical filtering,* is unfortunately not applicable as it is, because it is very difficult to find several images degraded by the same degradation system. One can overcome this difficulty by dividing the image supposed to be N x N a square into I subimages of size K x K, with :

$$M \leq K \leq N \tag{134}$$

where M is the extend of the impulse response of the degradation. We assume that it is smaller than that of the subimages. For each subimage, we have an approximate relationship of the type :

$$y_i(k,l) \approx g(k,l) ** x_i(k,l) \qquad \text{with } i = 1, ..., I \tag{135}$$

The signals $y_i(k,l)$ may be viewed as the product of the image $y(k,l)$ by window functions $w_i(k,l)$ of identical form. We have thus :

$$y_i(k,l) = w_i(k,l)\, y(k,l) = w_i(k,l) \left[g(k,l) ** x(k,l)\right] \tag{136}$$

If the function $w_i(k,l)$ is almost constant over the extend of $g(k,l)$, we have :

$$y_i(k,l) \approx \left[w_i(k,l) x(k,l)\right] ** g(k,l) = x_i(k,l) ** g(k,l) \tag{137}$$

If the function $w_i(k,l)$ is not rectangular, an overlapping of the subimages should be considered to avoid block effects. For example, for a Hanning window, a half overlap of each subimage is necessary. In this case, equation (135) may be viewed as a periodical convolution. The complex logarithm of the two-dimensional Fourier transform of both sides of equation (137) leads to :

$$\ln[Y_i(f,g)] \approx \ln[X_i(f,g)] + \ln[G(f,g)] \tag{138}$$

By using the definition of the complex logarithm :

$$\ln[z] = \ln|z| + j \arg(z) \tag{139}$$

one can deduce from equation (138) the following results :

$$\ln|Y_i(f,g)| \approx \ln|X_i(f,g)| + \ln|G(f,g)| \tag{140}$$

$$\arg\left[Y_i(f,g)\right] \approx \arg\left[X_i(f,g)\right] + \arg\left[G(f,g)\right] \tag{141}$$

The average over I section of equation (140) leads to :

$$\frac{1}{I}\sum_{i=1}^{I}\ln\left|Y_i(f,g)\right| \approx \frac{1}{I}\sum_{i=1}^{I}\ln\left|X_i(f,g)\right| + \ln\left|G(f,g)\right| \tag{142}$$

The first term of the right-hand side of this equation is the estimation of the half of logarithmic power spectrum density of the original image. It changes very little from one image to another. Thus, one can compute a prototype spectral density over a clear image, having statistical characteristics similar to those of the image we want to restore. We have :

$$\frac{1}{I}\sum_{i=1}^{I}\ln\left|X_i(f,g)\right| = \ln\left|X(f,g)\right| \tag{143}$$

By combining equations (142) and (143) we obtain :

$$\ln\left|G(f,g)\right| \approx \frac{1}{I}\sum_{i=1}^{I}\ln\left|Y_i(f,g)\right| - \ln\left|X(f,g)\right| \tag{144}$$

or

$$G(f,g) \approx \exp\left[\frac{1}{I}\sum_{i=1}^{I}\ln\left|Y_i(f,g)\right| - \ln\left|X(f,g)\right|\right] \tag{145}$$

This relation allows to obtain the magnitude of the harmonic response of the degradation system as a function of the logarithmic spectrum of the image to be restored and of the prototype spectrum $X(f,g)$ measured on a clear image.

Unfortunately, one cannot use statistical filters for equation (141) since the sum of the principal determinations of the phase is not equal to the principal determination of the sum. One possibility is the use of the two-dimensional cepstrum (Fourier transform of the logarithm of the magnitude of the Fourier transform) to estimate the zeros of the function $G(f,g)$ and thus, to generate the appropriate phase 0 or π depending on the sign of certain lobes of $G(f,g)$. If for example the degradation is caused by the camera motion, $g_c(k,l)$ is a rectangle of width αT. The harmonic response corresponding is of the type :

$$G_c(f,g) = \alpha T \frac{\sin \pi\alpha T f}{\pi\alpha T f} \tag{146}$$

and has zeros at integer multiples of $1/\alpha T$. The logarithm of its magnitude will have picks periodically at period $1/\alpha T$ with a magnitude going to $-\infty$. The Fourier transform of such a function will have consequently an important pick at a distance αT of the origin, in a direction corresponding to the direction of the camera motion. The cepstrum of an image took with a bad focus is of the same type, but with a circular symmetry in the distribution of the picks. The distribution and the position of these picks allow to differentiate an image with bad focusing from an image took with a camera motion. The cepstrum of an image degraded by atmospheric turbulences does not have such characteristic picks which is in fact a characteristic by itself. Consequently, it is possible to design a method which looks in the cepstrum, the distribution and the position of possible picks, first to determine the type of degradation and then the phase of the corresponding harmonic response.

Figure 18 shows three images degraded respectively by bad focusing, by camera motion and by atmospheric turbulences.

The results obtained using the method we described are represented on the same figure. The improvement obtained is quite visible. The contours of the building are much sharper, the text in the advertisement of Hilton hotel is readable. Though the text in the third image is not readable, the improvement is appreciable. The deteriorations we observe in the results come not from the method itself, but from its implementation with a small number of samples. It is useful to be reminded that these results are obtained without any a priori information on the perturbations.

Fig. 18: Image restoration by homomorphic processing

7.9 Enhancement by Grey Scale Modification

In the reproduction from a monochromatic image, one should in principle conserve the same grey scale. Figure 19 shows an ideal input-output relation. It is possible that, due to imperfect techniques in the optic or in the sensitive surface, the ideal law is not respected over the entire image. In such a case, luminances are weighted differently depending on the position of the corresponding sample. We have then an image of the type :

$$y\,(k,l) = p(k,l)\,x(k,l) \tag{147}$$

where $x(k,l)$ is the ideal image and $p(k,l)$ is the weighting function. The latter may be determined by calibration of the system using a uniform illumination. The ideal image is then simply given by :

$$x(k,l) = y(k,l)\ /\ p(k,l) \tag{148}$$

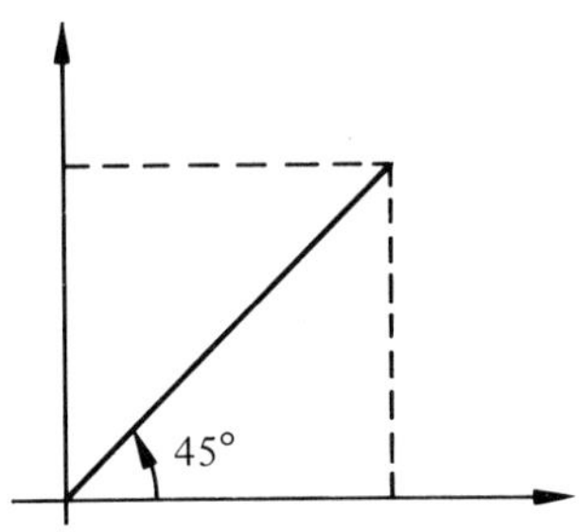

Fig. 19: Ideal input-output relationship

Another grey scale modification consists in changing the input-output law the same way for each sample, in order to improve the contrast. The contrast improvement allows often to emphasize better certain details of the image, which accelerates observation and interpretation. The general problem, in this case, is posed in the following way. We have an image $x(k,l)$ having a dynamic range within the interval $[x_1, x_2]$. We want to produce an image $y\,(k,l)$ over another support whose dynamic range is within the interval $[y_1, y_2]$, by changing the grey level repartition. It is a one-to-one mapping of the interval $[x_1, x_2]$ over the interval $[y_1, y_2]$ (fig. 20). One can in principle use any monotonic function $y = f(x)$ to emphasize or deemphasize certain portions of the interval $[x_1, x_2]$.

The contrast increase is obtained generally with functions $y = f(x)$ in the shape of an "s". Such a curve allows to compress large areas towards black and white.

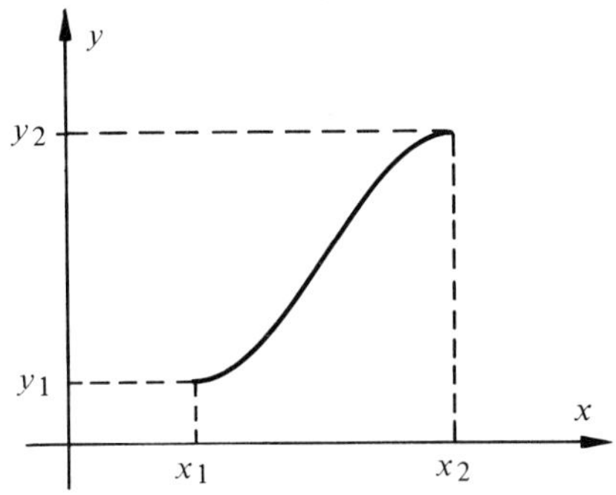

Fig. 20: Input-output relationship

7.10 Enhancement by Histogram Modification

Let us assume that digital image $x(k,l)$ is in its canonical form, in other words a set of N x N numerical values, each quantified with a given number of levels. Let p_i be the number of samples having the value i (i = 1, ..., Q). A function which is very useful in image processing is the representation of p_i as a function of the index i. This function is called *the histogram* of the image. To diminish the quantization error, to compare two images obtained under different illuminations, or to measure certain properties over an image, one often modify the corresponding histogram. Generally, one looks to make the histogram uniform to give equal weight to all the grey levels. This has the consequence of increasing sensively the contrast. Indeed, by making the histogram uniform, we force samples at dense levels to occupy other levels less dense. Thus, in these regions, the grey scale is enlarged. This enlargement is compensated by a compression in the less dense areas.

Histogram uniformisation is equivalent to the establishment of a relationship of the type $y = f(x)$ where y represents the modified image $y(k,l)$. For this, we have to consider the discrete version of the equivalence condition in probability which is given by :

$$p(y)\ \mathrm{d}y = p(x)\ \mathrm{d}x \tag{149}$$

Let $\Delta^i x$, $\Delta^i y$ be the corresponding interval at level i and p_{ix}, p_{iy} the number of samples in these intervals. The discrete version of equation (149) is :

$$p_{iy}\ \Delta^i y = p_{ix}\ \Delta^i x \tag{150}$$

Since we want to have p_{iy} constant whatever i, the repartition of the levels along y is simply given by :

$$\Delta^{i}y = p_{ix}\, \Delta^{i}x / C \quad \text{with } C = p_{iy} = N^2 / Q \tag{151}$$

An example of histogram uniformisation is shown in figure 21.

7.11 Enhancement by Unsharp Masking Filtering

Enhancement by unsharp masking filtering consists simply in adding to the original image the difference between this image and a low-pass filtered version of this one. Originally, this is a photographic process in which one superpose to the original film a mask obtained by the superposition of the film and of its negative slightly defocused. The effect of this operation is to enhance the high spatial frequencies, in other words to increase the contrast.

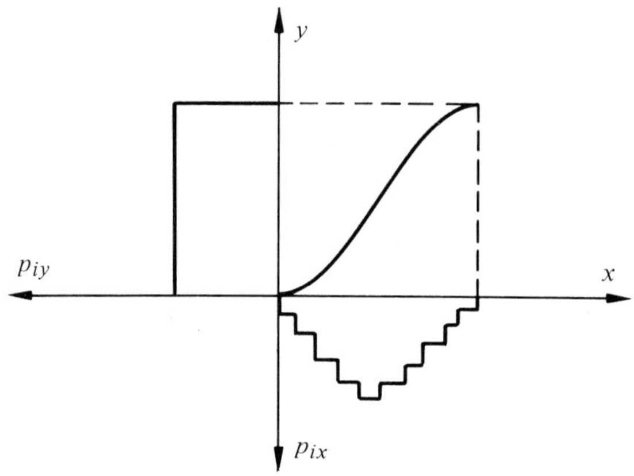

Fig. 21: Histogram uniformization

For the simplicity of the representation, we illustrate this method in the one-dimensional case, by considering an image of the type $x(k,l) = \text{rect}_N(k)$ (fig. 22). The version $x'(k,l)$ slowly low-pass filtered of this signal is shown on the same figure. By adding the difference of these two signals $x(k,l)$, one obtains the result $y(k,l)$.

7.12 Enhancement by Filtering

Generally, one can improve the contrast of an image by linear high-pass filtering. Unsharp masking is a particular case as we discussed. Among the two-dimensional filters, one can mention the digital Laplacian. The enhanced image is obtained by the difference between the original image and its Laplacian. The advantage of the digital Laplacian comes from the

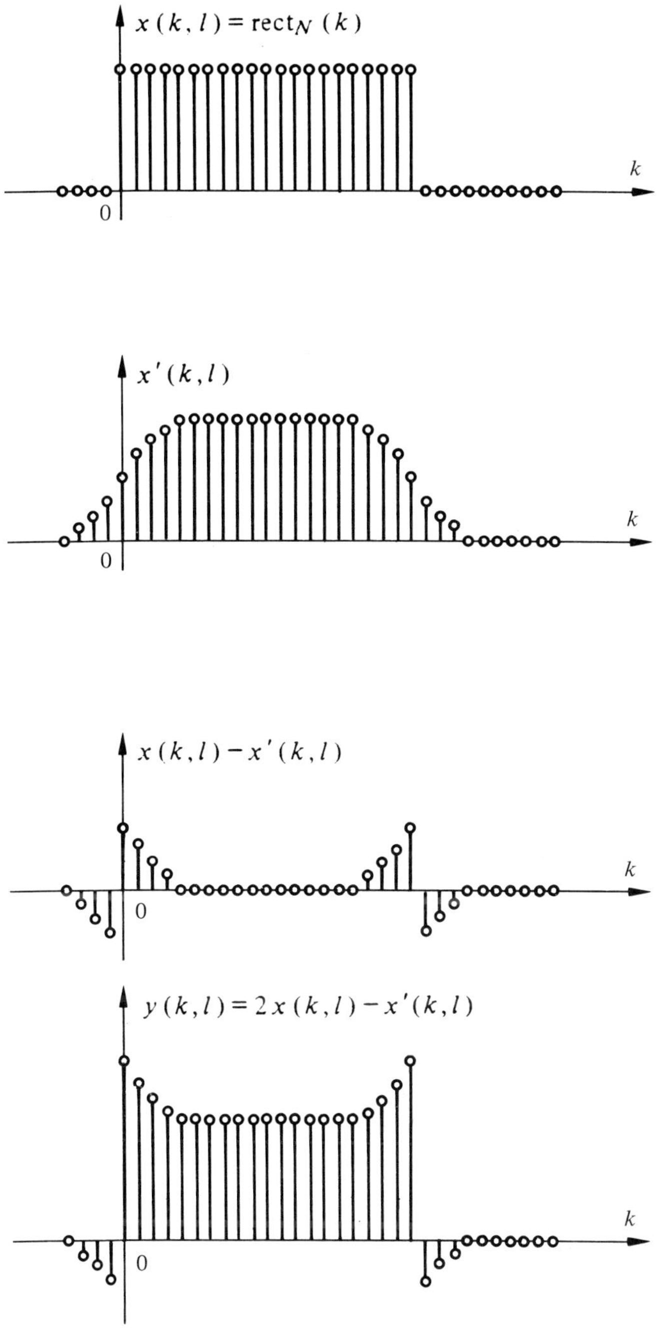

Fig. 22: Unsharp masking

7.12 Enhancement by Filtering

simplicity of its implementation. It is sufficient to implement the two-dimensional convolution of the image with the following matrix :

$$\Delta^2 = \begin{pmatrix} 0 & 1 & 0 \\ 1 & -4 & 1 \\ 0 & 1 & 0 \end{pmatrix} \tag{152}$$

In opposition to the contrast augmentation by high-pass filtering images that are disturbed by high-frequency noise, one can implement a low-pass filtering for enhancement. Even if one decreases the contrast by this operation, the image is enhanced by the attenuation of the noise.

7.13 Enhancement by Homomorphic Processing

An image is made by the reflection of the incident light of the objects. The structure of the luminance of this image can be divided into two parts. One is the amount of light used to illuminate the objects, and the other one is the reflection ability that have these objects to reflect incident light. These elementary parts which are two-dimensional signals are called respectively *illumination* $x_e(k,l)$ and *reflectance* $x_r(k,l)$. Physical laws determine the limits of their validation. Illumination is a finite positive quantity. The reflectance cannot go beyond unity and must be positive or zero. However, in practice it is impossible to find a material which reflects less than 1% of the incident light. We have thus :

$$0 < x_e(k,l) < \infty \tag{153}$$

$$0{,}01 \leq x_r(k,l) < 1 \tag{154}$$

These two components are related by the reflection law to form the luminance $x(k,l)$ of the image. This law is multiplicative, it is given by :

$$x(k,l) = x_e(k,l)x_r(k,l) \tag{155}$$

Since these two components are positive or zero, one can take the logarithm of both sides of the equation (155). We obtain :

$$\hat{x}(k,l) = \ln[x(k,l)] = \ln[x_e(k,l)] + \ln[x_r(k,l)] = \hat{x}_e(k,l) + \hat{x}_r(k,l) \tag{156}$$

One can thus process the signal (156) in a linear system. At the output of such a system, we have :

$$\hat{y}(k,l) = \hat{y}_e(k,l) + \hat{y}_r(k,l) \qquad (157)$$

where $\hat{y}_e(k,l)$ and $\hat{y}_r(k,l)$ are respectively the illumination and the reflectance after filtering. The luminance $y(k,l)$ processed by the non linear system is thus given by :

$$y(k,l) = \exp\left[\hat{y}(k,l)\right] = y_e(k,l)y_r(k,l) \qquad (158)$$

This equation indicates that the output luminance and its components are all positive provided that the linear sytsem which processes the signal (156) is real. This satisfies the physical constraints (153) and (154) for real images. The choice of the linear system depends on the properties of signals $\hat{x}_e(k,l)$ and $\hat{x}_r(k,l)$. The reflectance, which depends on the form of objects, on their contours and their textures, is essentially a high-frequency signal. In contrast, the illumination is a slowly varying signal, dominating mainly at low frequences. Even if the separation of these two components in the frequency domain is not very clear, a filtering may be implemented independent on both signals.

Illumination varies over the scene in a relatively large dynamic range. If we want to keep these images over a support, such as magnetic tape or transmit them through a transmission channel, it is necessary to decrease this dynamic range. However, its effect may decrease the subjective quality. In the other direction, enhancement consists in increasing the contrast increasing the compressed dynamic range. More precisely, the contrast is related to the rapid change of luminance over the contours of objects. It is thus related to the reflectance. To increase the contrast, we have to amplify the reflectance. The desired effect may be obtained with a filter whose frequency response is isotropic (circular symmetry). One can thus express the function of radial frequency $f_r = (f^2 + g^2)^{1/2}$. The form of the function $G(f_r)$ is represented at figure 23. The usual values of parameters a and b in this case are respectively 0.5 and 2.

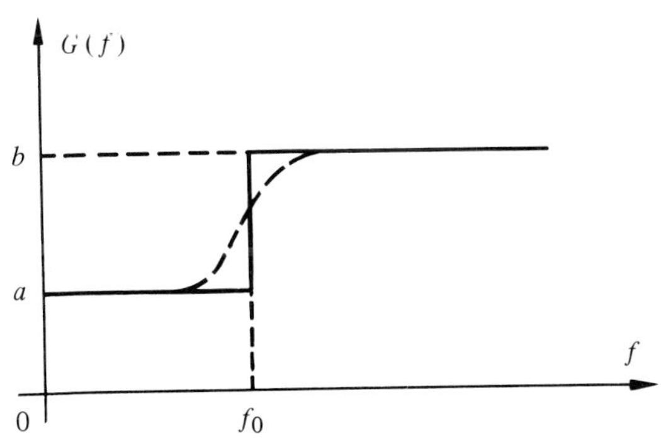

Fig. 23: Radial frequency response for enhancement

Two original images and their reproduction after processing with a = 0.5 and b = 2 are represented at figure 24. One can notice that a lot of details in the shadowed parts are enhanced.

8. Conclusions

This chapter is devoted to the basic methods of image processing. The first two sections concern respectively the sampling and the quantization of two-dimensional signals. Even if one can establish a two-dimensional sampling theorem to fix the rules of the game on the theoretical side, often the choice of the sampling is based on the resolving power of the eye. The overlapping effects of spectrums lead to visual phenomenas that are easy to identify. The quantization is also discussed on the theoretical and practical sides. Vectorial quantization which is presently a very fashionable method to code speech and images is also discussed along with colour signals.

The next section introduces the elementary notions of signals and systems in two dimensions. The convolution, the z transform and the correlation functions are introduced, as well as difference equations. Then, we study in detail the two-dimensional Fourier transform and its discrete version.

Digital filtering, filter design and their use as preprocessing are presented at the next section. Even if the notions corresponding in one dimension can easily be generalized to the two-dimensional case, some specific techniques are also indicated.

Finally, the last section discusses two sets of methods for restoration and enhancement of images. The restoration concerns the improvement of the quality of an image which is degraded with a bad manipulation, whereas the enhancement changes the appearence of an image in a way so that information can be extracted subjectively easily.

The ensemble of the methods discussed in this chapter are the fundamentals of classical digital image processing.

Fig. 24: Two original images and their enhanced version

X and PEX Programming

Spencer W. Thomas

1. Introduction

The X window system version 11 (X11)[1] is an increasingly popular "standard" window system for bit-mapped workstation displays. It is interesting that this standard was designed and implemented by a small group of people at the Massachusetts Institute of Technology (MIT), and pioneered several new concepts; rather than being a codification of existing practice by a large committee, as are most standards. X[1] owes its popularity, in part, to the free distribution of its source code, and to the fact that it runs on a wide assortment of hardware, ranging from the IBM-PC and the Apple Macintosh up to the newest, fastest, and most expensive "graphics super-workstations." It has been adopted as the standard window system by many hardware vendors, and is available as an alternative on other systems.

X was designed to provide display management and graphics for two-dimensional graphics applications. While the designers realized the importance of three-dimensional graphics, they lacked the expertise and resources to develop a corresponding set of 3-D graphics operations. This task was left to be done later, by people knowledgeable in the area. A group (the X3D committee) was quickly formed, and it issued the PEX (PHIGS[2] Extension to X) specification[2; 3]. PEX is an *extension* to X that is designed to support three-dimensional graphics in general, and PHIGS and PHIGS PLUS[3] in particular. There are now several proprietary implementations of PEX available, and a public implementation will be available soon (projected for January, 1991).

This tutorial will provide a basic grounding in the design goals, concepts, and principles underlying both X and PEX, and an introduction to programming using these systems. It will concentrate on concepts and features, since it is impossible to teach all the details of even one of these systems in a tutorial of this length, and a listing of details without any underlying principles does not advance understanding. The X programming sections will rely heavily on dissection of sample programs. As the application programmer interface (API) for PEX is exactly PHIGS PLUS, only the unique aspects of using PEX will be discussed here.

After finishing this tutorial, the student should have a good understanding of how X applications are put together, and, with a good reference in hand, will be ready to write programs.

---

1. Note that the proper forms of reference are "X window system" and "X". As the designers put it, "it's a *window system* named X, not a *system* named X *windows*."
2. PHIGS = Programmer's Hierarchical Interactive Graphics System is an international standard for writing three-dimensional interactive graphics programs. PHIGS specifies simple geometric elements, transformations, and color.
3. PHIGS PLUS = PHIGS Plus Lumière Und Shading is a proposed standard that adds several features to PHIGS. Among these are additional graphics primitives including spline curves and surfaces, lighting and shading information, data mapping, and hidden surface removal.

2. X Overview

2.1 Features

X provides a high-performance, high-level interface to do display management and graphics on a bit-mapped workstation or terminal. The performance of applications using X should be almost as good as if the application were running "stand-alone" with direct access to the display hardware. An application communicates with the server in relatively high-level concepts – dealing with graphics primitives such as text, lines, arcs, and polygons, with attributes such as font, color, fill pattern, line width, and dash pattern. For the most part, the application is insulated from dealing with how to set the individual pixels. The X server makes sure that drawing actions in independent windows do not interfere with each other, and handles allocation of all shared resources, such as the screen area, colormaps, and fonts. In addition, the X server handles all user input, dispatching each input event to the appropriate application and window. Thus, the X application programmer can, for the most part, pretend that the application will be running as the only user of a single, powerful graphics display.

The architecture of the X window system is based on a *client-server* model. The display is controlled by the *X server*[4], while application programs, or *clients*, make *requests* of the server to perform various graphics and window manipulation operations.

The X window system was designed to be as device independent as possible. The application programmer can remain blissfully ignorant of most of the substantive differences between different graphics hardware. In particular, all the hardware interface details are completely hidden. Certain differences are visible: color versus black and white, the number of colors available, and the size of the screen are the most noticeable. If an application does not use color, and does not require an overly large window, the visible differences between displays can be ignored.

A significant difference between X and almost all other window systems is its *network transparency*. An X application need not be running on the computer to which the display is physically connected. Indeed, the application need not even be aware that the display is on a different computer. All network connection and communication details are invisible to the programmer. The application can be on the same computer as the display, down the hall, across campus, or on the other side of the world. The only perceivable difference between these cases is a decrease in performance due to network latency. The X communication protocol is designed to minimize this performance reduction, but cannot totally eliminate it.

One of the overriding goals of the X designers was that X should always provide mechanisms, and never prescribe policy. Following this goal led to a tremendously flexible system; however, this has both positive and negative aspects. Almost any style of user interface and display management can be implemented on top of the mechanisms defined by X, but the application programmer must be prepared to deal with the different policies that may be imposed by different users. This flexibility is probably the largest source of complexity in X programs. As one of the designers expressed it, "We give you lots of rope, it's up to you to hang yourself with it."

Display, network, computer, and language independence are accomplished by precisely defining two things: a client-server communication protocol, and the

4. In general, a *server* provides and controls access to a *resource*. In this case, the resource is the display hardware and input devices.

drawing semantics of each of the input and output operations. Any program on any machine can communicate with the X server, as long as it "speaks" the protocol correctly. And, because of the precise semantic specification, the application programmer knows exactly what will appear on the screen, no matter what display hardware is used.

2.2 Design Requirements and Principles

This section will take a closer look at the design requirements and principles that guided the development of X11. Most of these arose from the designers' experience with earlier versions of X (most notably, X version 10) and other windowing systems.

Transportability. The system should be implementable on a variety of displays. Features that are unique to a particular display type should be eliminated or generalized. Conversely, an attempt should be made to support most features of most display hardware. If a particular feature is not supported, a vendor will have less motivation to adopt X, or may be tempted to make a non-standard extension to support that feature. While strict semantic definitions of output operations allow the application to precisely control the appearance of the display, some implementation dependent flexibility should also be allowed for efficiency's sake.

Device independent applications. Applications should be device independent. This can be accomplished in two ways. Many graphics standards achieve "device independence" by providing a large library of "inquiry" functions. A truly device independent application becomes so only by adapting its behavior, sometimes severely, in response to the results obtained from these inquiries. This method puts a very heavy load on the application programmer to correctly deal with all possible combinations of device features. X takes a different approach. Except where device differences absolutely cannot be hidden, an application program should work essentially identically on all displays, without change, and without adapting its behavior to the display. The place where differences between devices are most apparent is in color handling. Even so, applications that make simple uses of color, perhaps using just a few colors to distinguish different user interface components, can pretty much ignore display differences and still work correctly.

Network transparency. The X designers were determined that applications should be able to run locally or remotely with no change, and with no need to be aware of the difference. There are several aspects to this transparency. First, a number of communication protocols must be supported; X currently supports communication via Unix-domain sockets, System V streams, TCP, and DECNET. As the application and X server may be running on different computers, some attention must be paid to differences in byte ordering. In X11, the server accepts connections with either byte order and automatically converts all incoming and outgoing data if its internal byte order differs from that of the CPU on which the application program is running.

Multiple, concurrent applications. X is designed to be used in a multi-processing environment, and must be able to share the display among several concurrently running applications. Therefore, it should be able to correctly interleave output from multiple sources to multiple windows, or even from multiple sources to a single window. Additionally, X must dispatch input events to the applications that have requested them, based on the window in which each input takes place. No application should be able to inadvertently affect the correct functioning of another, but X should provide means for applications to communicate and act cooperatively.

Application and management interfaces. Users should be able to use their preferred styles of application and window management interface. X should not force any particular style of interaction on the user or application writer. In particular, X provides functionality and "hooks" for use by a separate *window manager* application.

Overlapping windows. X supports multiple overlapping windows, with output and input possible to a window that is obscured or partly obscured. This is a good example of providing *mechanism, not policy*. A user who prefers a window management policy that prohibits overlapping windows (such a window manager is usually called a *tiling* window manager) is free to implement such a policy. If X prohibited overlapping windows, then users who did not want a tiling window manager would be out of luck. Besides, even when using a tiling window manager, there would still be some windows, such as menus, that overlap other windows temporarily.

Hierarchy of resizable windows. Windows are arranged in a hierarchy rooted at a single window that covers the entire screen (the *root* window). In this, X differs from many other window systems that allow windows only at the top level, and make applications responsible for any window subdivision (e.g., Macintosh or Apollo DM). Since applications usually require window-like subdivisions of their top-level windows, it makes sense to have the window system provide this functionality directly using subwindows. This frees the application from such onerous tasks as clipping and input event dispatching, at little increased cost to the X server. Windows are considered a cheap resource in X, and some applications create hundreds of windows to implement user interface components such as "push buttons" and menus.

High performance, high quality text, graphics and images. X should provide the best performance possible on the given display hardware while minimizing delays caused by the network connection. In addition, the text, graphics, and images drawn by X should be of the highest possible quality. To help meet this end, the X protocol specification precisely defines the drawing semantics of each operation; so that, for example, an application will be able to predict exactly which pixels will be affected by a line drawn from (100,100) to (157, 308) with a line width of 2 and dashes with a length of 10 and spacing of 5 pixels. Or, when a connected sequence of line segments of width 1 is drawn, each pixel affected by the operation will be touched exactly once. This guarantees that pixel operations such as XOR will work as expected. These precise operations are not inexpensive, however, and the designers provided an "escape hatch" to allow a server to draw in the fastest way possible by specifying a width of 0 for lines and arcs. Width 0 lines do not have to follow the precise pixel coloring semantics, so it is not possible to predict exactly which pixels will be affected, and some pixels may be touched more than once.

Extensible. Finally, the designers realized that they could not possibly implement or even predict everything that someone would want to do with his or her window system. An example of this, mentioned above, is three-dimensional graphics. Instead, a method for adding *extensions* to the basic X server was provided. Extensions have been designed to accommodate such functionality as 3-D graphics, video, and sound, or to add other output types such as Bézier curves.

2.3 Basic Elements and Concepts

Client-server model. As mentioned above, X has an architecture based on the client-server model. The server is a program running the computer to which the display is

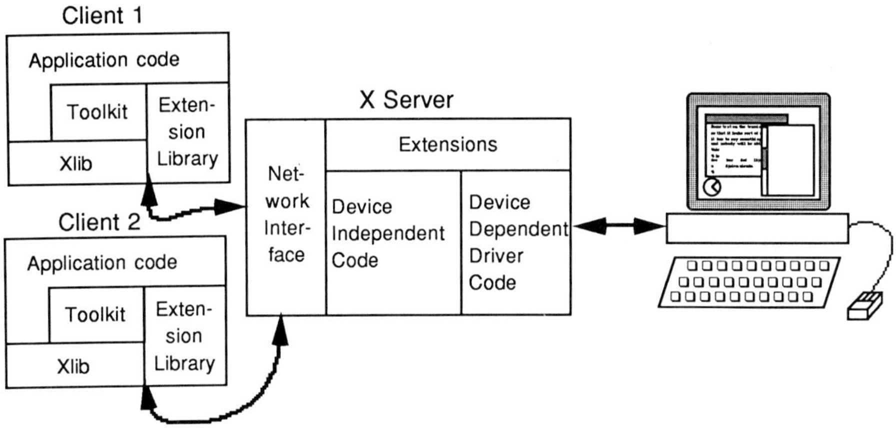

Fig. 1. X window system architecture.

connected. All device dependent code is contained in the server. The server is responsible for dealing with the display and its attached keyboard and mouse.

To draw on the display, a client (application program) must first establish a *connection* to the server. It will create one or more windows, and then draw in them. A client communicates with the server by sending it *requests*. Responses from the server are either *replies* to client requests or *events* indicating user input, errors, or other external (to the client) events. For programs written in the C language, this is done via calls to a library known as *Xlib*[5]. Most Xlib functions map one-to-one with X protocol requests. The library also hides the network-dependent details of establishing and maintaining a connection with the X server. The overall architecture is illustrated in Figure 1.

Communication between clients and the server uses the *X Protocol*[4; 5]. The protocol is device and computer independent. In particular, the protocol definition explicitly deals with the issue of byte ordering, that different computers order the bytes within an integer either with the high byte first or with the low byte first. When a connection is established, the server determines the client's byte order, and will then automatically translate all communications on that connection into that byte order.

An important feature of the X protocol is that it has been designed to operate *asynchronously*. The only requests that need an immediate reply are those that ask for information that only the server has. Asynchrony aids overall system performance, as a client does not need to wait after sending most requests, and can proceed with further computation.

Displays and screens. The terms *display* and *screen* are given specific meanings by X. A *display* corresponds to all the resources controlled by a single server, and has at least one screen, a keyboard, and a mouse. A *screen* corresponds to a single physical or logical display screen. For example, the Sun CG4 graphics board supports both a monochrome binary mode and a color mode. While these are logically independent, they both correspond to a single physical monitor. The user can switch be-

5. Other languages may provide linkage for Xlib, or they may provide their own interfaces to the X server. For example, there is a package in Common Lisp, analogous to Xlib, called CLX, that provides an object-oriented interface to X.

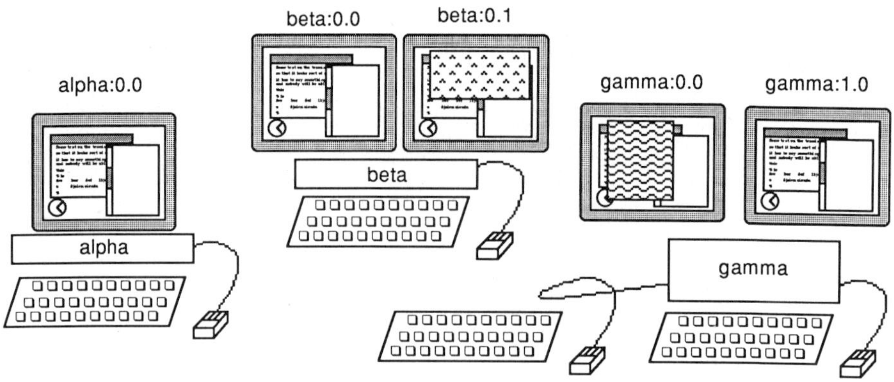

Fig. 2 Several displays and screens.

tween modes in software. The X server for the CG4 treats each mode as a separate screen, but both screens are driven by a single server (since there is only a single keyboard and mouse) and therefore are screens of a single display. Figure 2 shows several computers, their attached screens and the corresponding display and screen designations. Host alpha has the usual configuration: a single display with a single screen. Host beta has two physical screens attached, but only a single keyboard and mouse, so it has a single display with two screens. Finally, host gamma has two physical screens, each with its own keyboard and mouse, and therefore has two displays, each with a single screen.

The figure also illustrates the display and screen naming and numbering system. A display name is of the form *host:server.screen*. The *host* portion specifies the network address of the machine on which the server is running. If the server is on the same machine as the client, the host portion may be empty. A single colon indicates that the server connection should be made using the TCP network protocols; a double colon (*host::server.screen*) indicates a connection via DECNET. The *server* portion chooses a specific server on that host[6]. The optional *screen* portion of the display name, if present, indicates the default screen for new windows. The client is free to create windows on any screen of the display. The display name is used by the Xlib routine `XOpenDisplay` to establish the initial connection to the X server.

Windows. A window is a rectangular region of the screen[7] that in many ways acts as a miniature screen. A window may be any size, even larger than the screen, and windows may overlap each other. Additionally, any window may contain any number of subsidiary windows, so that the complete collection of windows on a particular screen form a hierarchy. The root of this hierarchy is called, appropriately, the *root window*. Windows at the first level of the hierarchy (children of the root) are usually called *top level* windows, and each will typically belong to a different application although, (some applications may have multiple top level windows). This hierarchy is illustrated in Figure 3. At the left is a view of the screen with several windows, and on the right is a drawing of the hierarchy.

An important aspect of the hierarchy is the *stacking order*. The stacking order determines which windows are completely visible, and which are obscured by other

6. Note that most X documentation calls this number the "display number". The term "server" is used here to try to minimize the confusion between a physical display and an X server.
7. Release 4 of X includes an extension for non-rectangular windows.

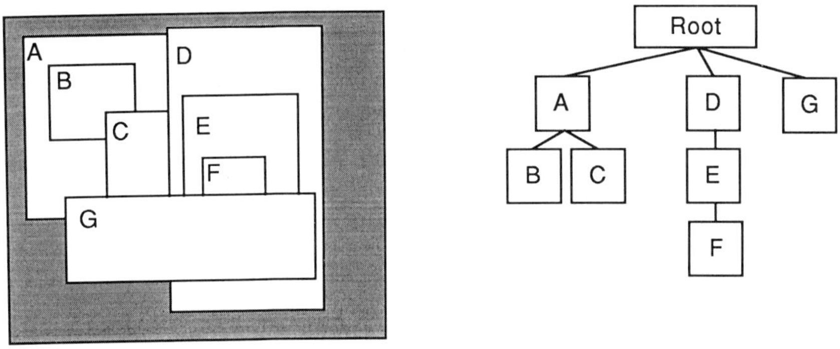

Fig. 3 Window hierarchy.

windows. In the figure, the stacking order is indicated by the left to right order of the elements of the hierarchy; the elements to the left are at the bottom of the stack. Note that a child of one window can never obscure a window that is not its sibling or a child of a sibling. E.g., while C can obscure B, C will never be able to obscure D, E, or F. However, A could obscure D, E, and F if the stacking order were changed.

Windows have a number of characteristics. The most important of these are probably its position and size. The position of a window is specified in the coordinate system of its parent window, and gives the position of the window's origin with respect to the parent. Unless it is changed by an application, the origin of a window's coordinate system is in the upper left corner of the window, as shown in Figure 4. The X coordinate increases from left to right, and the Y coordinate increases from top to bottom. Coordinates are always integers, and are measured in pixels. Every window has a border surrounding the area defined by its origin, width, and height.

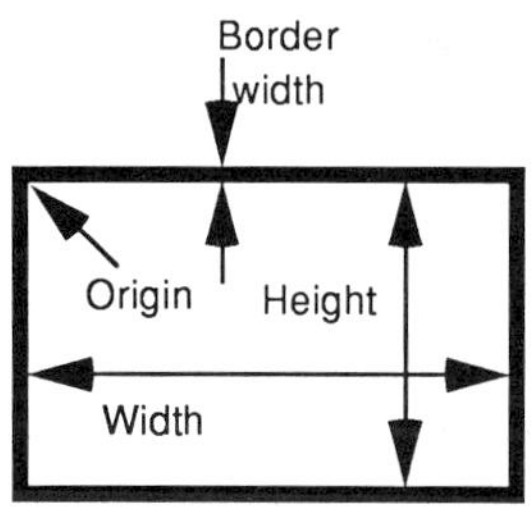

Fig. 4 Window coordinates.

A window may be either visible or invisible. In order to be visible, a window must be *mapped*, and all of its ancestors must be mapped. An unmapped window still has a position, width, height, etc., but it is not shown on the screen, nor can it receive input. When a top level window is mapped, the window manager has a chance to determine its initial placement and size, usually by asking the user to place it. This means that the initial mapping of a top level window can be indefinitely delayed, and an application should not assume that anything drawn in the window is visible until it has received notification that the window has actually been mapped to the screen. Normally an application will wait for the first *expose* event (see below) before drawing in a window.

Window management. All window systems provide some way of moving the windows around on the screen. Some, such as the Macintosh, require the application program to move its own windows. Others, such as the Apollo DM, have a built in *window manager* that lets the user move, resize, iconify, and kill windows. In keeping with the "mechanism, not policy" principle, the X server does not include a window manager. Instead, it provides functions that are needed for a separate application to act as a window manager. This way, the user can choose the style of window management she prefers. An X window manager is primarily responsible for

- Initial placement of (top level) windows,
- Moving, resizing, and restacking windows,
- Installing colormaps at client request, and
- Possibly controlling which (top level) window receives keyboard input,

and otherwise managing the limited screen resources according to the user's directions.

Clients are required to defer to the window manager in these matters.[8] For example, if the window manager, perhaps at the request of the user, makes a client's window too small for proper functioning of the client, the client may not make the window bigger, but could instead display a message, "Make me bigger." At the same time, clients are expected to run properly when there is no window manager present. Thus, although they may be ignored by the window manager, clients should always specify reasonable default values for initial window size and position, in case there is no window manager.

Events are communications from the server to the client. They may be generated by user input, by a change in the configuration of the windows on the screen, by another client, or to report an error in a client request. Most types of events are generated only if a client has specifically indicated interest in them. Events usually have an associated window, and an event may be said to be "sent to a window". For keyboard and mouse related events, this window is usually (but not always) the window containing the cursor.

User generated events are generated by the keyboard and mouse. Whenever the user presses or releases a key on the keyboard, a *keypress* or *keyrelease* event will be generated. Other events are generated if a mouse button is pressed or released (*buttonpress* and *buttonrelease*), or if the mouse is moved (*motion*). If the mouse moves into or out of a window, an *enter* or *leave* event results. A keyboard or mouse event *propagates* up the window hierarchy until it reaches the smallest enclosing window that has indicated interest in (*selected for*) that type of event.

Other events are not the direct result of a user action, and may therefore be classed as system-generated. The most important of these is the *expose* event. An expose event is sent to a window when a previously obscured portion of that window becomes visible. All X applications are expected to select for and respond to expose events by redrawing the correct contents of the exposed region of the window. A *configure* event is sent to a window when it has been moved, resized or restacked. An application usually responds to a resize event by redrawing the contents of the window to fit the new window size.

A client may request that all keyboard input be delivered to a particular window, regardless of the cursor position. The window receiving keyboard input is said to have the keyboard *focus*. *Focus in* and *focus out* events are sent when a window gains or loses the focus. These events can be generated as a result of the user moving the mouse, or because the window manager has explicitly set the keyboard focus.

An *error* is also a type of event. The asynchronous nature of the X protocol means that the client does not wait to see if each request has succeeded. Thus, the error will

8. A cardinal commandment for X applications is "Thou shalt not fight with the window manager over window size or placement."

be unexpected by the client, and is best sent as an event. Because it is difficult to debug a program when errors are not reported at the point that caused them, the X library provides a facility for synchronous behavior, for a large performance hit.

Graphics. X provides a variety of graphical forms and attributes. Graphics primitives include:

- *Lines*, including wide lines, dashed lines, and connected lines with a variety of join and cap styles. A variety of line types are illustrated to the right.
- *Rectangles*, either outlined or filled.
- *Circles*, *ovals*, and *arcs*, hollow or filled. Arcs can be filled as wedges or as closed by the chord segment. Several examples are shown to the right.

- *Text*. X uses "bitmap" fonts for efficiency. Both 8 bit per character (for Western languages) and 16 bit per character (for Chinese-type writing systems) text are supported.
- *Pixmaps* and *bitmaps*. A *pixmap* is similar to a window, but is not displayed on the screen, nor is it susceptible to being obscured. All X drawing operations operate on pixmaps just as they do on window. The term *drawable* encompasses both windows and pixmaps. A pixmap may be copied into a drawable or vice-versa. Pixmaps may be used for "double buffering," to store images or icons to be drawn quickly at various locations on the screen, or as *tiling* patterns for window backgrounds and borders and to fill graphics primitives. A *bitmap* is a pixmap that has only one bit per pixel. Bitmaps are most commonly used as stipple patterns or clipping masks.
- *Images*. An *XImage* is a data structure defined by Xlib that provides a client counterpart to a pixmap. Pixels in XImages may be manipulated directly by the client, and an XImage may be written to a drawable or read from a drawable. The distinction between an XImage and a pixmap is that a pixmap is stored in the X server, and an XImage is stored in the client.

The appearance of the graphics primitives may be modified by a number of attributes. These include:

- *Color*. X supports several color models, ranging from binary black and white to mapped pseudo-color to full color with up to 32 bits per pixel. Most applications can ignore the actual color representation by using pixel values obtained from the X server. A color allocation request, given a color defined in terms of its red, green, and blue components, returns the pixel value corresponding to the closest available hardware color. On a black and white display, this value will be either 0 or 1. On a pseudo-color display, it will be a colormap index (assuming the colormap was not yet full). And, on a full color display, it will contain the RGB values packed into a single 32 bit quantity. In any case, the application that wants to color a rectangle red can ask the server for the pixel value representing "red" and then use that pixel value, without needing to know anything about the actual color capabilities of the display.
  Foreground and background colors may be specified. Most graphics requests draw using the foreground color, though some use both.
- *Line width, style, cap style,* and *join style*. These affect the appearance of lines, as illustrated above. Lines with a width greater than zero have an appearance that

is precisely defined by the X protocol specification, and are therefore significantly more expensive to draw than lines with zero width.

- *Fill style*, *rule*, and *pattern*. Some objects, such as rectangles or ovals, may be filled. These attributes specify whether they are filled, and if so, how. Tiled fill uses the data in a pixmap directly to fill the area. Stippled fill uses a bitmap together with the foreground and background colors (background is used only for opaque stipple) to define a fill pattern.
- *Text font*. The X server uses bitmapped fonts; see below for more detail.
- *Clip mask*. This is a bitmap that can be used to clip drawing to arbitrary areas. Only those pixels corresponding to a 1 bit in the clip mask will be modified during drawing operations.

All drawing is affected by a "raster op" function. Conceptually, one can think of drawing in X as copying pixels from a source raster to a destination raster through a mask. The mask is defined as the set of pixels that would be colored by the particular primitive. The source pixel value and the destination pixel value can be combined using one of 16 logical functions, commonly known as "raster ops." The most commonly used functions are *copy*, *invert*, and *XOR*. The copy function sets the destination pixel to be equal to the source pixel. The invert function just logically negates the destination pixel value. This is typically only useful on a binary or true color display, as inverting an arbitrary color index value will usually result in a totally unrelated color.

The XOR (exclusive or) function, if used carefully, can be used on both black and white and color displays. On a black and white display, XOR is usually used to get reversible drawing by switching black and white where the primitive is drawn. Drawing the same primitive again with XOR switches black and white again, returning the image to its previous state. In color, one must be more careful. To exchange two colors with pixel values A and B, one would draw using XOR with a source (foreground) color (pixel) value of (A XOR B) and a background pixel value of 0. Where the destination pixel originally has a value of A, the resulting pixel value will be (A XOR (A XOR B)) = ((A XOR A) XOR B) = B. Similarly, an original pixel value of B will result in a pixel value of A after drawing. Unfortunately, pixels with values other than A or B will have unpredictable colors after the drawing operation. XOR drawing in color is still completely reversible regardless of the original pixel value.

3. X Internals

A short discussion of how X is put together is presented here. This should aid you to better use the X window system by providing some understanding of its internal workings.

3.1 Data Types and Resources

The X server defines several data types which are visible to the user as *resources*. A resource is a data structure owned by the server, created on behalf of a client, and which a client may query and modify via X protocol requests. The client has a *resource ID* by which it refers to the resource. A resource ID is created by the client[9] and transmitted to the server as part of the request that creates the resource. This

9. The server allocates a range of resource ID values when the connection is established and tells the client. Thus, each client creates distinct resource IDs, with no chance of inter-client conflicts (unless a client allocates more than 2^{20} resources).

eliminates the need for a *round-trip* communication with the server. If the resource creation fails, the server will send an error event to the client. A resource ID uniquely identifies the resource out of all resources created by all clients. Any client may use a resource, if it has the resource's ID.

The most important resources provided by the X server are

- *Drawables*, comprising windows and pixmaps.
- *Fonts*. A font is loaded by the server in response to a request from a client. A font naming scheme allows the client to request a font on the basis of criteria such as the font family name, the size in pixels or the size in points, the "font foundry" that produced it, the style (plain, bold, italics, etc.) and so on. For example, the font name "*-*-helvetica-medium-r-*-*-*-180-*-*-*-*-iso8859-1" refers to an 18.0 point Helvetica font, not bold, not italic, and from the ISO Latin-1 character set.
- *Cursors*. The cursor indicates the mouse position on the screen, and consists of a shape bitmap, a mask bitmap, and a pair of colors. A distinguished point in the cursor is known as the "hot spot," and is always placed at the mouse position. A cursor is usually created by selecting a "character" from the cursor font.
- *Graphics Contexts*. Most drawing operations require a number of attributes to be specified. Rather than specifying them explicitly with each request, X uses a resource known as a *graphics context* to save values of all the relevant attributes. Then, a drawing request need only contain the resource ID of the desired graphics context. Any number of different graphics contexts may be created, each with a different collection of attribute values, or a single graphics context may be modified each time an attribute change is needed.[10]

So that the X server can most effectively handle multiple concurrent connections, no state (such as a "current window") is maintained for each connection. Thus, any operation that affects or uses a resource must explicitly specify the resource ID. This appears to be a necessary trade-off between a slight increase in communication cost and a great increase in server complexity.

3.2 The X Protocol

The X Protocol is the official definition of the X window system. Any system that properly implements the protocol can be called an X server. It is designed to communicate all the information needed to run a window system over an asynchronous, stream-like, 8 bit communication channel. The protocol definition not only includes byte-by-byte (and bit-by-bit) definitions of the communication protocol, but also defines the exact semantics of each request.

As was mentioned above, the protocol is carefully designed to be machine-independent. Only 8, 16, and 32 bit integer quantities are transmitted, and the server reorders the bytes in each packet if necessary.

In order to operate efficiently, the protocol is designed to work over an asynchronous communication channel. Both requests and replies (and events and errors) are generally buffered by the client. Xlib buffers outgoing requests until one of four things happens: the buffer fills up, a request is sent that requires an immediate reply, the application tries to read an event and the event queue (see below) is empty, or the application explicitly "flushes" the buffer by calling `XFlush`.

10. There seems to be no consensus on which approach is better. To some extent it depends on the particular X implementation and hardware.

Input events are queued by Xlib until the application tries to read them with XNextEvent. A number of functions are available to inspect the queue and discard unwanted events. For example, it is easy for an application requesting *motion* (mouse moved) events to get overwhelmed by a flood of events. Using a routine like XCheckTypedEvent, it can quickly discard all but the most recent event.

4. X Programming

Programming the X window system will be approached through dissection and analysis of several programs. These are:

- A Hello program that displays the string "Hello, World" in a window.
- A second version of this program is interactive. Clicking the mouse in the window will cause the string "Hello" to be drawn at the cursor position.
- A version of Hello using the Motif toolkit. This program, called Goodbye, displays the string "Goodbye, World!" in a window. Clicking the mouse on the window will cause the program to exit.
- A very simple graphics editor using the Motif toolkit. The user can create an image from straight lines and circular arcs.
- The implementation of a "display list" widget for the graphics editor.

Complete listings of these programs will be made available.

4.1 Xlib Programming

First, we will look at a program that uses only the Xlib calls. While any X application can be programmed using just Xlib, there are many code sections that will vary little from one application to the next, and which are tedious to write. The X toolkits provide a higher level interface that hides many of the repetitive details from the application programmer. Therefore, we will move quickly to programs using a toolkit. Even when using a toolkit, most application-specific drawing is done using Xlib calls, so it is important to learn Xlib first.

An X application has a stereotyped program structure. First, the program initializes the connection to the X server. Next, it creates any windows it will use, and sets up for the main interaction loop. The windows are then mapped to the screen. Finally, the program enters an *event loop*, reading and processing events from the X server. One of the first events received will be an expose event. Not until this event is received should the application draw anything in the corresponding window.

We will now look at the program hello.c. Any X program must start by including several header files that define the X data structures, macros, functions, and symbols. The file Xlib.h defines (almost) all the interface information for the X library.

```
#include <X11/Xlib.h>
```

XUtil.h has some other useful definitions. Rather than enumerating them and trying to remember them, it is probably easier just to always include the file.

```
#include <X11/Xutil.h>
```

Finally, Xos.h hides some operating system dependencies, to provide a more portable environment.

```
#include <X11/Xos.h>
```

Next, our program defines some implementation constants and some global variables to simplify the use of values that are needed throughout the program.

```
#define FONTNAME        "fixed"          /* Name of font to use. */
#define WINSIZE         250              /* How big to make the window. */
#define WINNAME         "Hello"          /* Window has to have a name. */
#define HELLO           "Hello, World!"
```

```
/* It's easier for this program if all these are global. */
Display          *dpy;              /* Display pointer. */
int              screen;
Window           win;               /* Our single window. */
XFontStruct      *font_info;
GC               gc;                /* Necessary for drawing. */
int              win_width, win_height;
```

Establishing a Connection. At this point, we are ready to look at how the program initializes itself and opens a connection to the X server. Most X programs accept a common set of command line arguments that specify the display to use, the default window *geometry* (size and placement), colors to be used, etc. This simple program does not; we will ignore the command line until we look at using the X toolkit, which takes care of parsing the common command line arguments. This program gets the name of the display from the `DISPLAY` environment variable.

```
main( argc, argv )
int argc;
char **argv;
{
    /*
     * We really should parse the command line, for arguments such as
     *          -display display-spec
     * and      -geometry geometry-spec
     */

    /* Open the X display. Use the DISPLAY environment variable. */
    dpy = XOpenDisplay( NULL );
    if ( dpy == NULL ) {
        fprintf( stderr, "hello: can't open display %s\n",
                 XDisplayName( NULL ) );
        exit( 1 );
    }
```

After opening the connection, save the number of the default screen for later use.

```
    screen = DefaultScreen( dpy );
```

Setting up Windows. The next task is to create and set up any windows the program will use. Hello uses a single window, which is created and mapped in the subroutine `create_win`. (The two parameters will be discussed below.)

```
    create_win( argc, argv );
...
create_win( argc, argv )
int argc;
char **argv;
{
    int x, y, width, height, border_width;
    unsigned long background_pix, border_pix;
```

The minimal information needed to create a window is its size, position, the width of its border, and the color of the window background and border. The default size of our window is fixed, but we will compute its position to center it on the screen. The border width and colors must also be chosen.

```
    width = WINSIZE;
    height = WINSIZE;
    x = (DisplayWidth( dpy, screen ) - width) / 2;
    y = (DisplayHeight( dpy, screen ) - height) / 2;
    border_width = 3;

    /* Make background white, border black. */
    background_pix = WhitePixel( dpy, screen );
    border_pix = BlackPixel( dpy, screen );
```

Note that BlackPixel and WhitePixel are *not* constants. They depend on the display and screen. Even among binary black and white displays, some use 0 as black, while others use 1 for black. Next, a call to XCreateSimpleWindow creates the window.

```
win = XCreateSimpleWindow( dpy, RootWindow( dpy, screen ),
                           x, y, width, height, border_width,
                           border_pix, background_pix );
```

It would do no good to check the return value for errors, as the window resource ID is generated by the client. In fact, due to the output buffering that Xlib does, the request has probably not yet been sent to the server. The next step is to select the input events that should be delivered for the window. Finally, after dealing with some window manager-related issues (see below), we can map the window.

```
XSelectInput( dpy, win, ExposureMask | StructureNotifyMask |
              KeyPressMask | ButtonPressMask );

XMapWindow( dpy, win );
```

Responding to Events. After creating the window, and doing a little more initialization (described below), the program enters an infinite loop reading and responding to events. The procedure `main_event_loop` takes care of this. It consists of an infinite loop containing a call to `XNextEvent` to read an event and a switch statement based on the event type.

```
main_event_loop()
{
     XEvent ev;

     for (;;) {
          XNextEvent( dpy, &ev );
          switch( ev.type ) { ...
```

One of the first events the program receives will be an *expose* event indicating that the window has been mapped and is now visible. The program should draw nothing until it gets this event. The server may send multiple expose events in response to a single action, if that action caused several rectangular areas to be uncovered at once. The application can choose to respond to these multiple events in several ways.

- The simplest and slowest is to redraw everything after reading each event. This can also leave the wrong image if a drawing function such as XOR is used.
- Each expose event specifies the rectangle that was exposed. The application could redraw just the contents of that rectangle. This is probably a good approach only if redrawing a sub-rectangle of the window is significantly faster than redrawing the whole window.
- Expose events have a count field that indicates the number of exposures resulting from the same action that are yet to come. The application can ignore events with a non-zero count and redraw the whole window when the event with a zero count is received, or it can accumulate the rectangles into a region and then redraw using the region as a clip mask.
- As a variation, the application can accumulate all expose events that are pending in the event queue. This may be the best option, particularly since on some occasions the server can generate two expose events in a row, both with zero counts. It is still worthwhile to check the count of the last event read with this technique, as a non-zero value indicates that some events are still pending.

```
case Expose:
     while ( XCheckTypedEvent( dpy, Expose, &ev ) )
          ;
     if ( ev.xexpose.count == 0 )
          draw();
     break;
```

If the user resizes the window using a window manager, a *configureNotify* event will be delivered. This event will always be followed by an expose event, so all that is needed is to note the new size. The window size is stored in a pair of global variables that the `draw` routine will use. The size is initialized in `create_win`.

```
/* (In create_win)  Initialize global window size. */
win_width = width;
win_height = height;
... /* In main_event_loop */
    case ConfigureNotify:
        /* Window has been resized.  Get new width and height. */
        win_width = ev.xconfigure.width;
        win_height = ev.xconfigure.height;
        break;
```

Hello will exit if the user presses a mouse button or a key on the keyboard while the pointer is in the window (or if the window has the keyboard focus). This event processing is particularly simple, as we act merely on reception of the event, and need not be concerned with its contents. All X resources allocated by the client are automatically released by the server when the client exits, so there is no need to explicitly free them.

```
    case ButtonPress:
        /* Does the same as KeyPress. */
    case KeyPress:
        /* On any key or button press, exit the program. */
        exit( 0 );
```

Finally, any application that uses the keyboard must be ready to deal with *MappingNotify* event. This event informs that application that the mapping of the keys on the keyboard to character strings has changed. The following lines should be included in every X event loop.

```
    case MappingNotify:
        XRefreshKeyboardMapping( &ev ); /* Incantation. */
        break;
```

Graphics. We now come to what most would consider the "meat" of the program – drawing the image in the window. In this case, the image is a simple text string "Hello, World!" drawn in the center of the window in the "fixed" font. Before drawing, we must first load the font and get its resource ID. The procedure `load_font` is called after creating the window and before entering the event loop.

```
load_font()
{
    font_info = XLoadQueryFont( dpy, FONTNAME );
    if ( font_info == NULL ) {
        fprintf( stderr, "hello: Can't load font %s\n", FONTNAME );
        exit( 1 );
    }
```

Besides loading the desired font, `load_font` also creates a GC for drawing. The GC uses the font just loaded and also specifies the foreground color. It is important to set the foreground color here, in case the default value would result in drawing with white on a white background.

```
    unsigned long gcv_mask = 0;
    XGCValues gcv;
    ...
    gc = XCreateGC( dpy, win, gcv_mask, &gcv );
    XSetFont( dpy, gc, font_info->fid );
    XSetForeground( dpy, gc, BlackPixel( dpy, screen ) );
}
```

The procedure `draw` computes the appropriate positioning to center the text string in the window and draws it. The centering arithmetic is only a little tricky. Horizontal centering is straightforward – the X position is just the center of the window less one-half the string length in pixels. Centering vertically is a little more difficult, as the Y position of a string specifies the position of the baseline. Two values, ascent and descent, measure the distance from the baseline to the top and bottom, respectively, of the character box. Thus, the height of the box is the sum of the ascent and descent values. To center the string vertically, the top of the character box is placed at one half the font height above the center of the window, and then the ascent value is added to find the Y position of the baseline.

```
draw()
{
    int len, text_width, text_height, x, y;

    len = strlen( HELLO );
    text_width = XTextWidth( font_info, HELLO, len );
    text_height = font_info->max_bounds.ascent +
                  font_info->max_bounds.descent;

    x = (win_width - text_width) / 2;
    y = (win_height - text_height) / 2 + font_info->max_bounds.ascent;

    /* Now draw it. */
    XDrawString( dpy, win, gc, x, y, HELLO, len );
}
```

Communication with a Window Manager. Finally, to cooperate properly with a window manager, our program must attach a set of window manager related properties to the window. These *standard properties* include hints regarding the desired size and minimum and maximum sizes of the window, the window name, and the command line of the application. This last provides the window manager a way to restart the application if it should be interrupted, or to restore the state of a session the next time the user logs in. A few lines of code added to `create_win` after the window has been created, but before it is mapped, accomplish this. (Recall that the program parameters `argc` and `argv` were passed as arguments to `create_win`.)

```
XSizeHints size_hints;
char *win_name, *icon_name;
Pixmap icon_pixmap;
...
/* Tell the window manager our preferred size information. */
size_hints.flags = PPosition | PSize | PMinSize;
size_hints.x = x;
size_hints.y = y;
size_hints.width = width;
size_hints.height = height;
size_hints.min_width = 100; /* Big enough for string? */
size_hints.min_height = 20; /* String will fit vertically. */

win_name = WINNAME;
icon_name = WINNAME;          /* Window and icon have same name. */

icon_pixmap = 0;              /* No icon pixmap. */

/* Set window manager properties (before mapping window!) */
XSetStandardProperties( dpy, win, win_name, icon_name, icon_pixmap,
                        argv, argc, &size_hints );
```

Results. Figure 5 shows two screen dumps of the hello program in operation. The windows are "decorated" with a title bar and frame by the Motif window manager, mwm. The first image, on the left, shows the initial 250x250 window with the string centered. The second image, on the right, shows the window after it has been resized to make it smaller. Note that the string is still centered.

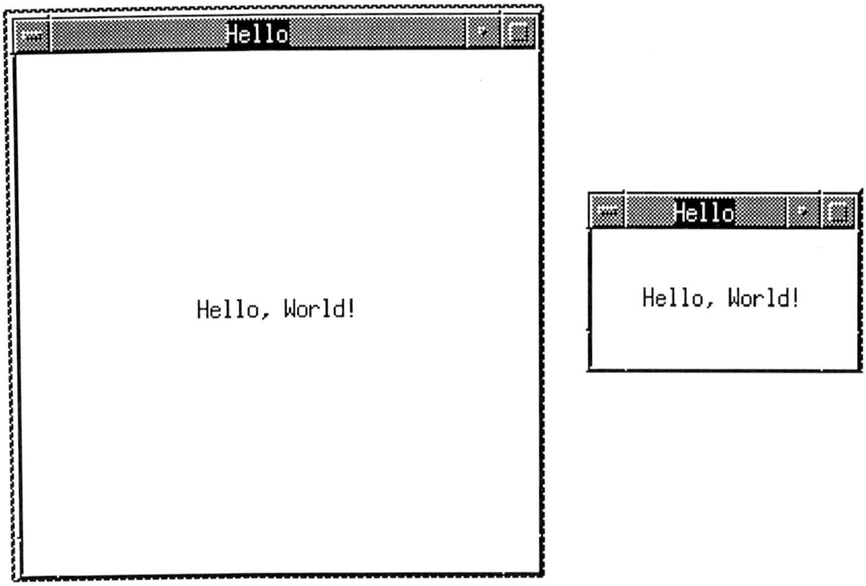

Fig. 5 Hello results.

More interaction. While the Hello program illustrates many of the issues involved in writing an X program, it is pretty boring. Before moving on to using the X toolkit, we will first enhance Hello to place a message in the window at the points where the user clicks the mouse button. This requires only a few small changes to the original program. The first change is to draw a string upon receipt of a *ButtonPress* event.

```
#define HELLO1          "Hello!"
...
        case ButtonPress:
            /* Button presses draw a message at the mouse position. */
            XDrawString( dpy, win, gc, ev.xbutton.x, ev.xbutton.y,
                         HELLO1, strlen( HELLO1 ) );
            break;
```

This works fine until we partially cover the window and then uncover it (see Figure 6). All the Hello! messages that were covered disappear. X does not maintain the contents of a window, but instead relies on the application to regenerate them when necessary. Our program does not do this. A *display list* is required to remember the positions of all the messages. For this program, the display list is simple – it is just an array containing the (x,y) position of the messages. It is declared as a global variable and is filled by the *ButtonPress* case.

```
/* A list of all message positions, for refresh. */
#define MAXHELLO        1000
XPoint hello_list[MAXHELLO];
int nhello = 0;
...
        case ButtonPress:
            ...
            hello_list[nhello].x = ev.xbutton.x;
            hello_list[nhello].y = ev.xbutton.y;
            nhello++;  /* Should check against MAXHELLO? */
            ...
```

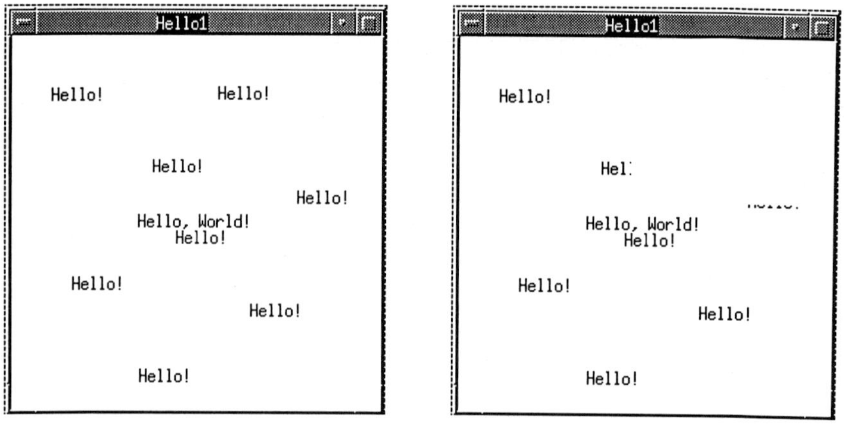

Fig. 6 Hello1 program showing expose problem.

The display list is used by the `draw` routine when it redraws the window contents after an *expose* event.

```
        /* Also draw all the user messages. */
        len = strlen( HELLO1 );

        for ( i = 0; i < nhello; i++ )
             XDrawString( dpy, win, gc, hello_list[i].x, hello_list[i].y,
                          HELLO1, len );
}
```

One last unrelated change requires that the user type the character 'q' in order to exit the program. This is more complex than one might think. A *KeyPress* event does not contain the ASCII code of the key that was pressed, as many keys (function keys, for example) do not correspond to an ASCII character. The event contains a key code, a server-dependent value indicating the key that was pressed. This can be translate to a *KeySym*, a server-independent representation of the key that was pressed, or directly to a string of ASCII characters, if the key has such a representation. Two Xlib functions provide these translations: `XLookupKeysym` and `XLookupString`. Since we are looking for a keystroke, we will use the former.

```
#include <X11/keysym.h>
     KeySym key;
     ...
          case KeyPress:
               key = XLookupKeysym( &ev.xkey, 0 );
               if ( key == XK_q )
                   exit( 0 );
```

4.2 X Toolkit Programming

Our first two X programs were pretty easy, if a little longer than we might have expected for a "Hello, World!" program. Unfortunately, programming user interaction sequences that are only somewhat more complicated than these is a dauntingly complex task. Consider, for example, allowing the user to type in a string for the message. The program would have to handle any correction and control keys (backspace, tab, return), and would also have to provide echo as the string was typed. The toolkit was developed to simplify the programming necessary to create user interfaces. As we will see, the Hello program is significantly shorter when the toolkit is used, and has significant additional functionality.

A toolkit provides user interface components, called *widgets*, event dispatching, and user control over the appearance and actions of the widgets, plus functions for assembling these into a complete user interface. It hides the implementation details, providing a clean, uniform application programmer's interface.

Toolkit Basics. The toolkit is actually composed of two major parts, the *intrinsics* and the *widgets*. The basic software architecture is illustrated in Figure 7. The intrinsics are support functions that provide basic support for event dispatching, resource value binding, and the basic object-oriented widget model. Widgets are individual user interface components, such as push buttons, or menus, or scrollbars. Each widget is an individual X window with associated data and procedures that display or otherwise act on that data.

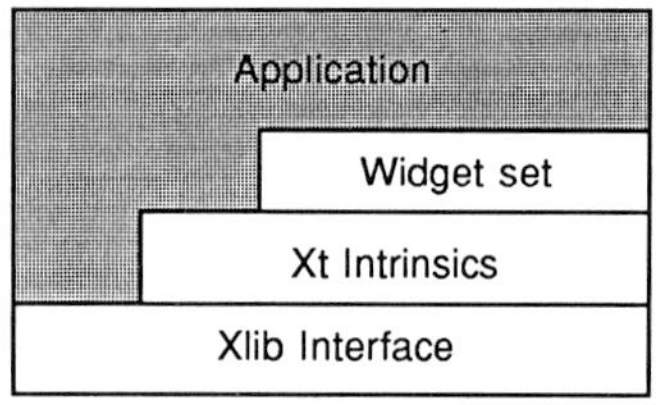

Fig. 7 X Toolkit architecture.

Widget definitions are organized into a "class" hierarchy. The use of an object-oriented approach allows a widget definition to inherit behavior and appearance from its superclass, and can greatly simplify the implementation and use of the toolkit. At the root of the hierarchy is a *Core* widget type. Figure 8 shows part of the class hierarchy of "Athena widgets." For example, the *Label* widget type is a subclass of *Simple*, which is a subclass of *Core*, and the *Command* (push button) widget type is a subclass of *Label*. A *Label* displays a text string centered in a window. The *Command* widget inherits this appearance, and adds a new behavior: When the user clicks the mouse button on a *Command* widget, it invokes an application defined *callback* procedure. The implementation of *Command* is greatly simplified because it inherits most of its definition from *Label*.

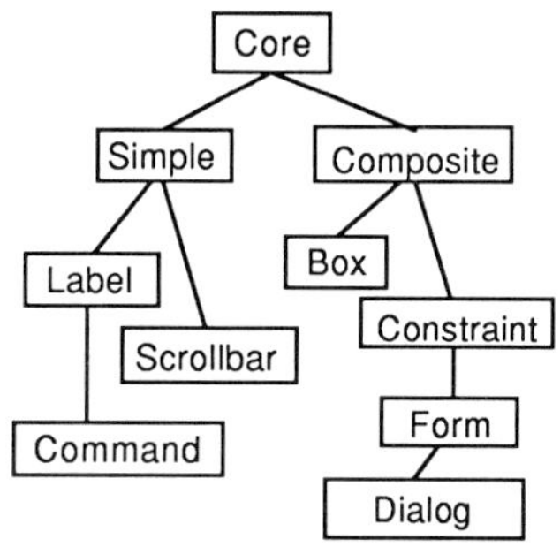

Fig. 8 Partial Athena Widget class hierarchy

Widget instances are composed hierarchically. Just as windows may have subwindows, composite widgets may have subwidgets. A widget *manages* its subwidgets, and may modify their positions and sizes as conditions change (e.g., if the user resizes the top-level window). The root of the hierarchy is a *shell* widget. A shell widget is designed to interact properly with a window manager, and manages its single child by forcing it to change size as the window manager changes the size of the shell.

The behavior and appearance of a widget can be configured by changing the values assigned to named variables of the widget, referred to as *resources*. Note that this is a distinct use of the term *resource*, and has nothing to do with the use of this term in the X protocol. Resource values may be hard-coded by the application, or may come from a set of application defaults, or may be specified by the user. The collection of resource names and values is referred to as the resource database. The resource database is maintained and modified by the toolkit intrinsics.

A resource name is of the form *application.object.subobject...attribute*. The object-subobject hierarchy corresponds exactly to the widget hierarchy. The *application* element refers to the top level shell. Each element of this list may refer to a particular instance of a widget or attribute or to a general class of widgets or attributes. For example, the resource specification "goodbye.quit.foreground" refers to the foreground color of the quit button of the goodbye application, while the specification "Demo.PushButton.Foreground" refers to all colors that are classed as foreground (which may include, e.g., highlight colors) of all PushButton widgets in all applications in the class Demo. Classes and instances may be intermixed. Additionally, it is not necessary to explicitly specify the entire hierarchy. For example, the specification "goodbye*Foreground" refers to all foreground class colors of all objects in the goodbye application. There is a complex set of rules for determining which of a collection of overlapping specifications will apply to a particular attribute of a particular widget instance. Basically, the most precise specification "wins". Instances are more precise than classes, and "." is more precise than "*".

Resources provide a tremendously powerful way for the end-user to affect the configuration of a toolkit-based application. Generally, the application writer should hard-code only those resource values that are critical to program function. The other resources should be given default values in an application defaults file.[11] This gives the user the most control over the application configuration. For example, if the label strings used in push buttons are specified in the application defaults file, the application may easily be changed to a different language, without recompiling it.

Using Widgets. Probably the easiest way to understand the effect of using the toolkit is to look at a small example. For this example, we recast Hello, and call it Goodbye. Several new header files must be included to get definitions for the toolkit data structures and functions. The examples will use the *Motif* toolkit from the Open Software Foundation. The file `Xm.h` is required to get the basic Motif-related definitions. The file `PushB.h` defines the push button widget.

```
#include <Xm/Xm.h>
#include <Xm/PushB.h>
```

The toolkit is initialized, and a connection opened to the X server by calling `XtInitialize`. In addition, `XtInitialize` parses the command line, looking for the standard X command arguments. Those that are found are used to modify the resource database. Arguments that are recognized are removed from the argument list, so that the application may do its own argument parsing after `XtInitialize` returns. Rules for parsing additional, application specific arguments may also be passed to `XtInitialize`. This program does not have any such arguments.

```
Widget top;

top = XtInitialize( "goodbye", "Demo", NULL, 0, &argc, argv );
```

The next step is to define the widget hierarchy. This application has only a single widget, a push button, which is a child of the top level shell. In this case, the string displayed in the push button is hard-coded into the program. Motif uses "composite strings" that have better support for non-European languages than ordinary ASCII strings. A consequence of this is that a conversion function must be called to change an ASCII string to a composite string for use by the widget.

The toolkit uses an `Arg` structure to set or retrieve resource values. An `Arg` is just a name and value pair. The macro XtSetArg sets the given arg structure to the string and value arguments. The sequence `XtSetArg(arg[n],...);n++;` is an idiom of toolkit programing.

11. Usually, on Unix, a file named the same as the application is searched for in the directory /usr/lib/X11/app-defaults.

```
int n;
Arg arg[10];
...
n = 0;
XtSetArg( arg[n], XmNlabelString,
          XmStringCreate( "Goodbye, World!",
                          XmSTRING_DEFAULT_CHARSET ) );
n++;
pushb = XtCreateManagedWidget( "quit", xmPushButtonWidgetClass,
                               top, arg, n );
```

A push button has an "activate callback" function associated with it. A callback function is called by the widget when some particular event or set of events occurs. The activate callback of a push button is called when the user presses and then releases the mouse button with the cursor in the push button widget window.[12] A callback function has three arguments, the widget invoking the callback, a pointer supplied by the application when it set up the callback, and a pointer to widget-specific data associated with the callback. The Motif toolkit defines a structure for the *call data*. It always includes at least two things: an integer "reason" for the callback, and a pointer to the event that eventually invoked the callback.

```
static void
do_quit( w, client_data, call_data )
Widget w;                     /* All arguments unused by this function. */
caddr_t client_data, call_data;
{
    exit( 0 );
}
...
    XtAddCallback( pushb, XmNactivateCallback, do_quit, NULL );
```

In order for a widget to show up on the screen, it must be *realized* and mapped. A widget that has been realized has an associated X window. Most widgets are automatically mapped when they are realized, according to the setting of the resource mappedWhenManaged. By default this is true, so realizing the top level widget will cause the entire hierarchy to be realized and mapped.

```
    XtRealizeWidget( top );
```

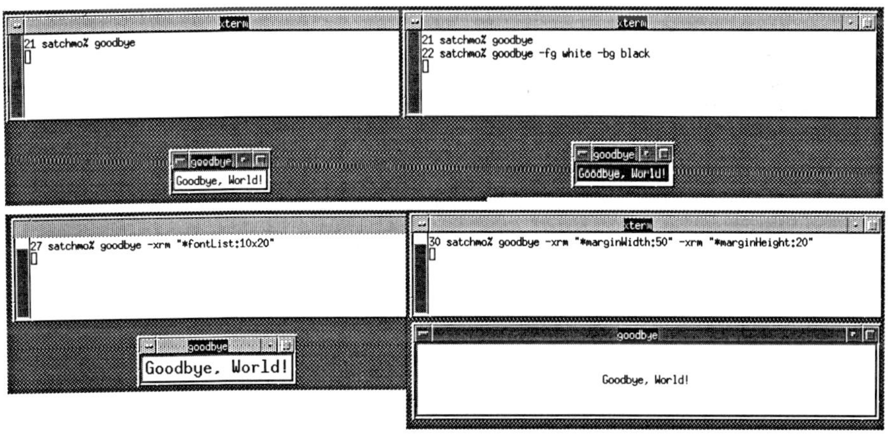

Fig. 9 Goodbye with different resource values.

---

12. The exact actions required to activate the push button may be affected to some extent by changing the *translations* for the widget. For example, a different mouse button could be used.

Fig. 10 Screen dump of line-edit program.

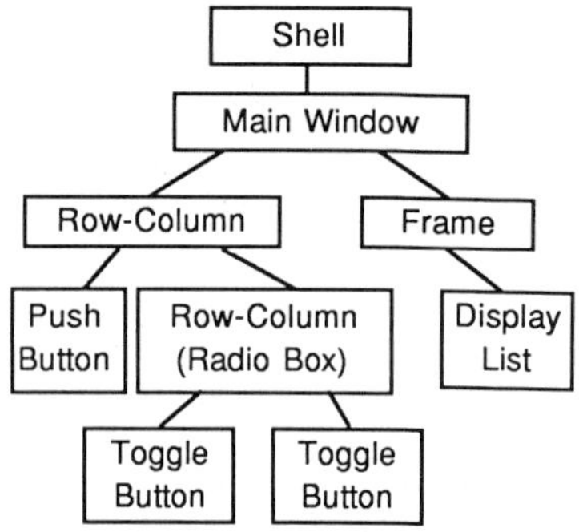

Fig. 11 Widget hierarchy of editor.

Finally, the program enters an event loop. The default event loop provided by the toolkit just reads events and dispatches each one. Options are available to also look for input availability on any stdio file descriptor, or to make a callback after a certain amount of time has elapsed. `XtMainLoop` does not return. To exit, the program must call `exit` or its equivalent directly.

```
XtMainLoop();
```

Some results are shown in Figure 9, with a variety of different resource values specified to change the coloring, the text font, and the widget size.

A Simple Drawing Editor. We will now consider the design of a simple drawing editor. The editor can create drawings made up of line segments and circular arcs. The user interactively shapes each line and arc by "dragging" it into position. No further editing functions are provided. The program uses an object-oriented approach, implemented in C. There are two graphic object types, line and arc, which inherit some behavior from a generic graphical object type. Figure 10 shows a "screen dump" of the program running. Besides the drawing area, there are three push buttons: a "Quit" button that does exactly that, and a linked pair of toggle buttons that choose between drawing lines and arcs. When one of the toggles is set, the other is cleared. A diagram of the physical widget hierarchy is shown in Figure 11. The top level shell contains a main window widget. The main window has a command area, occupied by the row-column widget, and a work area, occupied by a frame. The frame provides a visible border around the display list widget, which provides the drawing area. The row-column widget in the command area has two children. A push button lets the user quit the program, and another row-column widget, configured as a "radio box" contains a pair of toggle buttons.

The main window setup is simple. After creating the main window widget, its two children are created and registered as the command and work areas.

```
Widget main_w, cmd, work;

                /* Create main window.  Resource values default. */
main_w = XtCreateManagedWidget( "main", xmMainWindowWidgetClass,
                                 top, NULL, 0 );
                /* Create children */
cmd = setup_cmd( main_w );
work = setup_work( main_w );
                /* Register children as areas of main window */
XmMainWindowSetAreas( main_w, NULL, cmd, NULL, NULL, work );
```

The command area is somewhat more complex, but creating it is still straightforward.

```
static Widget setup_cmd( main_w )
Widget main_w;
{
    Widget row_c, pb, radio;
    int n = 0;                      /* For SetArg */
    Arg arg[10];                    /* ditto */
```

The children of the row column widget are arranged horizontally.

```
    SetArg( XmNorientation, XmHORIZONTAL );
    row_c = XtCreateManagedWidget( "command", xmRowColumnWidgetClass,
                                   main_w, arg, n );
```

The push button is labeled "Quit," and has an activation callback function. Again, the default label value should be read from an application defaults file instead of being hard coded into the program.

```
    n = 0;          /* Now create the push button. */
    SetArg( XmNlabelString,
            XmStringCreate( "Quit", XmSTRING_DEFAULT_CHARSET ) );
    pb = XtCreateManagedWidget( "quit", xmPushButtonWidgetClass,
                                row_c, arg, n );
    XtAddCallback( pb, XmNactivateCallback, do_quit, NULL );
```

The radio box is a special instance of a row-column widget. Rather than setting all the appropriate resource values by hand, we use a convenience function that does it for us. This function does not request that the parent manage the radio box, so we must explicitly call `XtManageChild`.

```
    n = 0;          /* And the radio box. */
    SetArg( XmNorientation, XmHORIZONTAL );
    radio = XmCreateRadioBox( row_c, "mode", arg, n );
    XtManageChild( radio );
```

Note that the toggle buttons are "gadgets" instead of widgets. A gadget is a widget without an associated window. It will generally be somewhat cheaper than a widget. The radio box requires that all its children be toggle button gadgets.

```
    n = 0;
    SetArg( XmNlabelString,
            XmStringCreate( "Lines", XmSTRING_DEFAULT_CHARSET ) );
    SetArg( XmNset, True );
    pb = XmCreateToggleButtonGadget( radio, "lines", arg, n );
    XtAddCallback( pb, XmNvalueChangedCallback, do_line, NULL );
    XtManageChild( pb );

    n = 0;
    SetArg( XmNlabelString,
            XmStringCreate( "Arcs", XmSTRING_DEFAULT_CHARSET ) );
    pb = XmCreateToggleButtonGadget( radio, "arcs", arg, n );
    XtAddCallback( pb, XmNvalueChangedCallback, do_arc, NULL );
    XtManageChild( pb );
    return row_c;
}
```

Finally, the work area consists of a display list widget inside a frame. The display list widget has been created especially for this program. We will look at its implementation later.

```
static Widget setup_work( main_w )
Widget main_w;
{
    Widget frame, work;
    int n = 0;                      /* For SetArg. */
    Arg arg[10];

    frame = XtCreateManagedWidget( "work-frame", xmFrameWidgetClass,
                                   main_w, arg, n );
```

```
                    /* Work area is a DList widget. */
    n = 0;          /* Use defaults */
    work = XtCreateManagedWidget( "work", dlistWidgetClass, frame,
                                  arg, n );
```

The display list widget has three callback functions. These are called when a mouse button is pressed, when the mouse is moved, and when a mouse button is released, respectively.

```
    XtAddCallback( work, XtNdownCallback, work_down, NULL );
    XtAddCallback( work, XtNtrackCallback, work_track, NULL );
    XtAddCallback( work, XtNupCallback, work_up, NULL );

    return frame;
}
```

Lines are drawn by pressing the mouse button in the drawing area, holding it down, and dragging out the line until the second endpoint is properly positioned. Arcs are more complicated. Pressing the mouse button and moving the mouse drags out a radius vector. When the mouse button is released and pressed again, the initial point of the arc is fixed. Motion of the mouse with the button down sets the angle subtended by the arc so that the second endpoint of the arc lies on the line through the arc center and the mouse position. The implementation of arcs and lines is object oriented. They share a set of methods for creating and drawing themselves. An initial mouse button press calls the work_down function. If there is no currently "active" object, one is created. Then the active object's `down` method is called.

```
static void work_down( w, client_data, event )
Widget w; caddr_t client_data; XEvent *event;
{
    if ( act_obj == NULL )
        act_obj = (*create_fn)();

    if ( act_obj )
        (*act_obj->ops->down)( act_obj, w, event );
}
```

The function pointer `create_fn` is set by the toggle button callback functions. For example, the callback function for the "lines" button assigns a pointer to the function `new_line_obj` to `create_fn` if the toggle is currently in the "set" state.

```
static void do_line( w, client_data, call_data )
Widget w;
caddr_t client_data;
XmToggleButtonCallbackStruct *call_data;
{
    if ( call_data->set )
        create_fn = (graf_obj_p_fn *)new_line_obj;
}
```

The function `work_track` calls the `track` method of the active object, if there is one. Note that `work_track` is called every time the mouse moves in the window, not just when the mouse button is pressed. This permits dragging of the arc radius to continue after the mouse button is released the first time.

The function `work_up` just calls the active object's `up` method. Usually, the `up` method will complete the process of creating the object, add it to the display list so it will continue to be displayed, and set the active object to NULL. In the case of the arc, the first call to the `up` method is ignored, as the arc requires two click-drag actions to completely define it.

We will take a brief look at the implementation of the line object. A line consists of the common object header and two point values. The object header has a pair of pointers for building doubly linked lists, a pointer to the function vector, and a tag value that makes the structure self-identifying.

```
typedef struct {
    graf_obj     *next, *prev;    /* List pointers. */
    graf_ops     *ops;            /* Operations vector. */
    int          tag;             /* Value LINE_TAG. */
    XPoint       start, end;      /* Endpoints of the line. */
} line_obj;
```

The line object subscribes to the default methods for down, track, and up events. The default down method just calls the `set_first` method, which is supposed to set the initial position of an object, and then draws the object using the XOR function, so that the drawing operation is reversible.

```
static void graf_obj_down( this, w, ev )
graf_obj *this;
Widget w;
XButtonEvent *ev;
{
    XPoint pt;
    extern GC xor_gc;

    pt.x = ev->x;
    pt.y = ev->y;
    (*this->ops->set_first)( this, pt );
    DListDraw( w, this, 1 );
}
```

The default `track` method erases the previous position of the object by redrawing it in XOR mode. It then calls the `set_next` method to update the object. Finally, it draws the object with its new shape.

```
static void graf_obj_track( this, w, ev )
graf_obj *this;
Widget w;
XMotionEvent *ev;
{
    XPoint pt;

    pt.x = ev->x;
    pt.y = ev->y;
    DListDraw( w, this, 1 );
    (*this->ops->set_next)( this, pt );
    DListDraw( w, this, 1 );
}
```

The default up method is the most complex of the three. It erases the object and updates it one last time. It then draws the object in Copy mode so that it is "permanently" drawn. Finally, it adds the object to the display list and sets the active object to NULL.

```
static void graf_obj_up( this, w, ev )
graf_obj *this;
Widget w;
XButtonEvent *ev;
{
    XPoint pt;
    extern graf_obj *act_obj;

    pt.x = ev->x;
    pt.y = ev->y;
    DListDraw( w, this, 1 );
    (*this->ops->set_next)( this, pt );
    DListDraw( w, this, 0 );

    DListAddObject( w, this );
    act_obj = NULL;
}
```

The remaining three methods are specific to the line object. The `set_first` method sets both start and end points to the position of the mouse.

```
static void line_obj_set_first( this, pt )
line_obj *this;
XPoint pt;
{
     this->start = pt;
     this->end = pt;
}
```

The `draw` method uses the Xlib routine `XDrawLine` to draw a line between the two endpoints. The drawing function is specified by the `gc` argument.

```
line_obj_draw( this, w, gc )
line_obj *this;
Widget w;
GC  gc;
{
     XDrawLine( XtDisplay( w ), XtWindow( w ), gc,
                this->start.x, this->start.y,
                this->end.x, this->end.y );
}
```

4.3 Creating Your Own Widgets

Finally, we will consider the implementation of the display list widget used in the line editor program. The display list widget is a simple drawing surface that supports callback functions to report mouse actions, and has an integral display list that it can use to regenerate the image when an expose event is received.

The code that implements a widget is stereotyped. There are certain functions that must be performed, and the interfaces for these functions must be identical to those for all other widgets. This is part of the cost of trying to do heavy object-oriented programming in a non-object-oriented language, such as C.

For our "DList" widget, the file "DList.h" defines the *private* part of the widget interface, including the actual data structure that stores the widget instance values. The file starts by including a couple of other headers that it requires.

```
#include "graf_obj.h"
#include "DList.h"
```

The header file must define two things: the class record, containing class variables, and the instance record, that contains instance variables. To support inheritance, each is composed of several parts, the parts belonging to the superclasses of this class, and this class's part. Most widgets have no private class variables, but the C compiler will not allow definition of a structure with no elements, so the class part has a dummy component.

```
/* DList class record. */
typedef struct { int empty; } DListClassPart;

typedef struct _DListClassRec {
     CoreClassPart        core_class;
     DListClassPart       dlist_class;
} DListClassRec;

/* New instance fields for the DList class. */
typedef struct {
     /* Resources. */
     Pixel                 foreground;      /* Foreground color. */
     XtCallbackList       down;             /* Called on button down. */
     XtCallbackList       track;            /* Called on motion. */
     XtCallbackList       up;               /* Called on button up. */
     Cursor                cursor;          /* Cursor to use. */
```

In addition to the resource values, most widgets have some private data, too. For our widget, we need a couple of graphics contexts and, of course, the display list. The original width and height are saved for use by the QueryGeometry method.

```
    /* Private data. */
    GC                     draw_gc, xor_gc;
    graf_obj               *d_list;         /* The display list */
    /* Original size for query_geometry method. */
    Dimension              orig_width, orig_height;
} DListPart;

/* Full instance record. */
typedef struct _DListRec {
    CorePart               core;
    DListPart              dlist;
} DListRec;
```

The public include file, "Dlist.h", defines any new resource names that the widget requires, and usually includes a comment listing the resources defined by the widget and their default values. Most importantly, however, it contains a reference to the widget's class record, which is required in order to create instances. Our file also includes declarations of some externally visible widget functions.

```
#define XtNdownCallback          "downCallback"
#define XtNtrackCallback         "trackCallback"
#define XtNupCallback            "upCallback"
#define XtNcursor                "cursor"

/* Function to add an object to the display list. */
extern void DListAddObject(); /* (w, graf_obj *obj) */
/* Function to clear the display list. */
extern void DListClear();
/* Function to draw an object.  xor_draw is 0 for normal drawing,
 * 1 to draw in XOR mode.
 */
extern void DListDraw();       /* (w, graf_obj *obj, Boolean xor_draw) */

/* Class record constants. */
extern WidgetClass dlistWidgetClass;
```

The file, "Dlist.c", contains initial values for the class record, some initialization information, and the code that implements the widget methods. We will start by defining the default resource values. An `XtResource` structure describes a resource by its name, its class name, its type, the size in bytes of the instance variable, the offset in bytes from the beginning of the instance record, the type of the initial value, and a pointer to the initial value. For example, here is the `XtResource` definition of the foreground color.

```
#define Offset(field)   XtOffset(DlistWidget, field)
...
  {XtNforeground, XtCForeground, XtRPixel, sizeof(Pixel),
            Offset(dlist.foreground), XtRString, "black"},
```

The initial value for the foreground color is given as a string. This works because the toolkit intrinsics contain a *converter* from string to pixel. Additional converters can be registered by an application if needed.

The mapping from input events to actions is specified by two tables, a *translations* specifier, and the *actions* table. The translations specifier is a string mapping arbitrary input actions or sequences of input actions to sequences of function calls. The actions table maps between the function names used in the translations string to actual function pointers. The translations specifier for our widget is simple; it maps each of the button down and up and mouse motion events to a function.

```
static char defaultTranslations[] =
    "<BtnDown>:    ButtonDown()\n\
     <BtnUp>:      ButtonUp()\n\
     <Motion>:     Move()\n";
static XtActionsRec actions[] = {
        {"ButtonDown",          ButtonDown},
        {"ButtonUp",            ButtonUp},
        {"Move",                Move},
        {NULL, NULL}
};
```

Next, the class record must be initialized. Many of its elements are function pointers to the object methods. There are also some variables that control the way in which the widget is handled by the intrinsics. The `compress_exposure` class variable, if true, tells the intrinsics to process all expose events in a sequence before calling the widget's expose method. Our widget requests compression of motion events, exposure events, and enter and leave events. Some values in the class record may be specified as `XtInherit`*Xxx*, to use the superclass method instead. Many methods are automatically chained, so that by the time the widget method is called, all the superclasses have already had their chance to process the method, too.

The *Initialize* method is called when a widget is first created, and should validate the resource values, since they may be specified by a malicious user, and should initialize any private instance variables. Ours saves the initial width and height, initializes the display list to empty, and gets graphics contexts for use in the drawing functions. The routine `XtGetGC` is provided by the toolkit intrinsics to promote sharing of graphics contexts among widgets. It returns a GC identifier corresponding to a GC with the requested values. If a matching GC has previously been allocated, it will be returned, otherwise a new GC will be created and returned. Thus, the widget should never modify the GC, as this may mess up other widgets. The foreground and background values for the XOR GC ensure that the foreground and background colors will be swapped when using this GC to draw with.

```
static void get_gcs( w )
DListWidget w;
{
    XGCValues gcValues;

    gcValues.foreground = w->dlist.foreground;
    gcValues.background = w->core.background_pixel;
    w->dlist.draw_gc = XtGetGC( w, GCForeground | GCBackground,
                                &gcValues);
    gcValues.foreground = w->dlist.foreground ^
                          w->core.background_pixel;
    gcValues.background = 0;
    gcValues.function = GXxor;
    w->dlist.xor_gc = XtGetGC( w, GCForeground | GCBackground |
                               GCFunction, &gcValues);
}

static void Initialize( request, new )
   Widget request;                /* what the client asked for */
   Widget new;                    /* what we're going to give him */
{
    DListWidget w = (DListWidget) new;

    get_gcs( w );
    w->dlist.d_list = NULL;
    w->dlist.orig_width = w->core.width;
    w->dlist.orig_height = w->core.height;
}
```

The `Realize` method creates the window. In our case, the only window attribute that needs to be set is the cursor (other attributes such as the background color, size, and position have already been set by the Core code).

```
static void Realize( gw, valueMask, attributes )
    Widget gw;
    Mask *valueMask;
    XSetWindowAttributes *attributes;
{
    DListWidget w = (DListWidget) gw;
    XGCValues gcValues;

    attributes->cursor = w->dlist.cursor;
    *valueMask |= CWCursor;

    XtCreateWindow( gw, InputOutput, (Visual *)CopyFromParent,
                    *valueMask, attributes );

    get_gcs( w );
}
```

The `SetValues` method is called when the application applies `XtSetValues` to the widget. It is given three widget pointers with the current state of the widget, the state if the requested changes are all made, and a widget that can be changed, if necessary, to reflect the desired final state. For example, when the label of a label widget is changed, the widget may need to compute a new size for itself, too. The `SetValues` method returns True if the changes require the widget to be redrawn. If the foreground or background values are changed, our widget needs to compute new GCs and redraw itself. If the cursor is being changed, it just changes the window's cursor.

```
static Boolean SetValues( current, request, desired )
    Widget current,              /* what I am */
           request,              /* what he wants me to be */
           desired;              /* what I will become */
{
    DListWidget w = (DListWidget) current;
    DListWidget rw = (DListWidget) request;
    DListWidget dw = (DListWidget) desired;
    Boolean redraw = FALSE;

    if (w->dlist.foreground != rw->dlist.foreground ||
        w->core.background_pixel != rw->core.background_pixel)
    {
        get_gcs( dw );
        redraw = TRUE;
    }

    if ( w->dlist.cursor != dw->dlist.cursor )
        XDefineCursor( XtDisplay(w), XtWindow(w), dw->dlist.cursor );

    return( redraw );
}
```

The `Redisplay` method redraws the contents of the window. In our case, it traverses the display list and redraws its contents. The third argument is the region that actually needs to be redrawn. We ignore this region, as we cannot effectively optimize our redraw using it, anyway. It doesn't matter, except for performance, whether this widget is redrawn several times, since the drawing is always done in Copy mode.

```
static void Redisplay( gw, event, region )
   Widget gw;
   XEvent *event;                  /* unused */
   Region region;
{
    DListWidget w = (DListWidget) gw;
    graf_obj *o;

    /* Traverse the display list and redraw everything. */
    for ( o = w->dlist.d_list; o != NULL; o = o->next )
        (*o->ops->draw)( o, w, w->dlist.draw_gc );
}
```

The `Resize` method is called whenever the widget is resized. It should recalculate any quantities that depend on the widget size. It should *not* call the redisplay method; an expose event will follow immediately. Ours does nothing.

The action functions are almost identical. The ButtonDown method will serve as an example. Since our widget does not do anything with input but pass it on to the application code, the only thing the action function must do is to build the `call_data` for the callback, and then call it. Our callbacks just pass the actual X event as the `call_data`.

```
static void ButtonDown( gw, event, params, num_params )
Widget gw;
XEvent *event;
String *params; Cardinal *num_params;       /* Unused. */
{
    XtCallCallbacks( gw, XtNtrackCallback, (caddr_t)event );
}
```

If there were parameters specified in the translations string, these will be passed as an array of strings in `params`, with the number of such parameters in `num_params`.

The DList widget also defines several globally visible functions to add an object to the display list, to clear the display list, and to draw an object either in Copy or XOR mode. There is at least one thing missing from this widget. It should define a `Destroy` method that calls `DlistClear` to free the contents of the display list when the widget is destroyed.

5. PEX Overview

PEX is a proposed extension to X to support 3-D graphics, and in particular, to support the PHIGS and PHIGS PLUS standards. The PEX architecture team produced a document describing the PEX protocol in detail, together with the expected semantics of each protocol request. With respect to the "PHIGS versus X" issues discussed below in section 5.3, PEX comes down squarely in the middle. The server may support a structure store, or it may require the application (client) to maintain it. The current PEX specification says nothing about input – it must be handled by channels outside the PEX protocol (i.e., through regular X input methods, possibly combined with PEX output requests). The server must handle pick processing, but the pick measure is supplied by the client. The specification also says nothing about the response to a window resize action, except to assume that it is handled via the standard X event mechanism (the application PHIGS library might intercept the resize event and recompute the workstation transformation). The PEX specification is still changing, partly in response to the evolving PHIGS PLUS proposed standard, and partly as a result of experience gained from building a few implementations.

5.1 PEX Design Goals

The goals of the PEX design were to

- Provide efficient support for PHIGS and the stable portions of PHIGS PLUS,
- Gracefully extend the capabilities of X, and
- Support a range of X platforms.

PEX serves as a foundation on which PHIGS, PHIGS PLUS and other graphics standards products could be built. It contains support for both display list and immediate mode graphics styles. It is an extension to the X protocol, and does not needlessly duplicate functionality already present in X. It should be possible to support PEX on a range of platforms, from a simple "bit-mapped" workstation to highly sophisticated 3-D graphics displays. An implementation should take advantage of the hardware wherever possible.

Some considerations that were explicitly not used in the design of PEX are

- PHIGS mapping,
- Total device independence, and
- Support for non-3D applications (e.g., image processing or document preparation).

PEX is not intended to be a one-for-one mapping of the PHIGS and PHIGS PLUS functions, but is intended to support both efficiently in the X window system. Functionality already present in X, or extensions being worked on by others (e.g., input extensions) are not duplicated here. In addition, PHIGS file operations (archiving, e.g.) are best performed by the client, so are not included in the protocol. PEX is not designed to provide total device independence (neither is PHIGS nor X); inquiry functions are provided to determine hardware limitations. It is possible to write highly portable applications using PEX.

5.2 PHIGS and PHIGS PLUS Overview

PHIGS was designed with the following goals in mind:

- A high degree of interactivity – the application should be able to update the display with as little work as possible.
- Conformability with application data base – the data structures used by PHIGS should resemble those used by the application.
- Fine modification granularity – it should be possible to make modifications to individual graphics primitives (rather than regenerating an entire segment, as is necessary in GKS).
- Real-time dynamics – on displays which support it.
- Geometric articulation – support simple rigid articulated models (e.g., a robot arm).
- 2D and 3D object representations – although PHIGS is primarily a 3D graphics standard, 2D objects should be represented and treated as such.
- Support high performance workstations.
- Compatibility with GKS where justified and possible.

Application areas addressed included

- Interactive design,
- Architecture,
- Molecular modeling,
- Picture layout,

- Process control, and
- Simulation.

Application areas that were explicitly not addressed included

- Realistic image synthesis,
- Paint systems,
- Image processing, and
- High quality text.

These requirements lead to the development of a standard that is based on a hierarchical graphical model, in which individual graphics elements can be modified. "Children" in the hierarchy inherit attributes and transformations from their "parents" (but can not affect the values of these attributes in the parent). This model was fashioned after the display lists of current high-performance graphics workstations, and the expectation that most application data could be easily expressed in this form.

The model can be viewed as a centralized data base (although it need not be implemented this way), any portion of which may be drawn on any open workstation. It has the form of an acyclic directed graph. The central component of the model, analogous to the GKS segment, is called a structure. A structure is a simple sequence of elements, each of which may be a graphics primitive, an attribute specification, a modeling transformation, an invocation of another structure, etc. An attribute specification affects all primitives following it in the structure, thus a primitive's attributes may be modified after it is inserted in the structure by editing the preceding attribute specifications.

A structure is displayed on a workstation by posting it to the workstation. A display process traverses the structure hierarchies posted to each workstation to draw them. Thus, structure creation and display are independent of each other (although, clearly, a structure cannot be displayed before it is created!) A structure may be edited simultaneously with display traversal.

PHIGS PLUS was proposed as an extension to PHIGS to support higher quality rendering, particularly lighting and shading operations. Enhancements over PHIGS include

- Support of "ultrahigh performance workstations,"
- Lighting and shading,
- Direct color support,
- New primitives,
- Extended primitives, and
- Traversal control.

Support for lighting and shading includes specification of light source positions and "with data" primitives which allow specification of normal vectors (per face or per vertex) and colors per vertex. Colors may be specified directly, in any one of a number of color models. This is makes sense for two reasons: many ultrahigh performance workstations allow direct color specification (by providing 24 or more bits per pixel), and colors must be translated to this form internally to do shading calculations, anyway.

The new and extended primitives are

- Polyline set 3 with data,
- Fill area (set) 3 with data,

- Extended cell array 3 (with direct color specification),
- Triangle strip 3 with data,
- Quadrilateral mesh 3 with data,
- Polyhedron 3 with data,
- Non-uniform B-spline (NURBS) curve and surface, and
- Parametric polynomial curve and surface.

The application can specify a "bounding box" in a structure (Set extent 3). When this is encountered, it sets two flags, a prune flag if the bounding box is entirely outside the display area, and a cull flag if the bounding box is smaller than a specified size. Then, a conditional structure execution element can be used to either execute or skip another structure depending on the state of the flags. This can be used to speed up rendering when a large portion of the data base is outside the view box, or to provide scale-dependent display.

5.3 PHIGS Versus X

To use PHIGS (or any graphics standard) in an X environment requires some cooperation between the two systems, and perhaps some degree of accommodation or modification of one or the other. For example, PHIGS draws on a *workstation*. In a non-windowed system, this will usually be the entire screen of the graphics display. This will not work if the display is under the control of the X server. The obvious mapping is for a PHIGS workstation to correspond to an X window. Then PHIGS can draw into the window just as any other X application does.

However, there are some subtle differences between a window and a physical screen. The most obvious is probably that a screen will never change size while the program is running. Most PHIGS applications assume that they can inquire the size of the workstation once, and then use that value for the duration of the run. If PHIGS is running in a window under X, the user can resize that window at any time. If the PHIGS device coordinates map straight onto the window coordinates, then either PHIGS will not use the whole window, if it was enlarged, or only a portion of the PHIGS display will be visible, if the window was made smaller. One solution might be to use pseudo device coordinates (e.g., zero to one), that are always mapped to the current window size.

A more serious problem is that PHIGS will be unable to use any special graphics hardware that is not supported by X. In particular, any 3-D graphics hardware will be completely unused. Why is this? X will not use it, because X is strictly a 2-D graphics system. PHIGS cannot use it directly, because it will interfere with the X display. Besides, if PHIGS uses the graphics hardware directly, then the application must run on that computer, and the network transparency provided by X will be lost.

There are basically two alternatives, then, for using PHIGS under X. The first is to have PHIGS treat X as if it were a two dimensional graphics device, and perform all the three dimensional processing in the application. If the actual display only has two dimensional graphics capabilities, then this may be satisfactory. There is still a potential problem, though. The amount of data sent to the server may be much larger than the data in the PHIGS structure store. How can this happen? Certain PHIGS PLUS primitives, particularly the parametric surfaces, generate a large number of sub-primitives (quadrilaterals or triangles) when they are evaluated for display. Also, if one of the interpolation modes is being used for PHIGS PLUS lighting and shading, it may be necessary to transmit each pixel individually, as the X server does not support color (nor normal vector!) interpolation over polygons.

The second alternative is to extend the X server to understand PHIGS and PHIGS PLUS primitives and actions. The extension can take advantage of any special graphics hardware that is present, and the communication overhead can be kept low. Furthermore, if the PHIGS structure store is placed in the X server, many applications will be able to function with very low overhead, after their data has been loaded into the structure store. Finally, the desired network transparency is retained.

Fortunately, the implementors of X (version 11) foresaw the need to extend the server in this way, and provided an extension mechanism. We will look at this in the next section.

There are still some other issues to consider before forging ahead with an extension. Probably the most important of these concerns the placement of the structure store. Should it lie in the application program or in the server? There are definite advantages to putting it in the server. If the display has high-performance 3-D hardware, it probably has a display list already. If the PHIGS structure store were not kept in the server, we would not be able to take advantage of the hardware display list. For many applications, communication overhead will be lower if the structure store is in the server.

However, this can make the server quite large, and may take up memory that would be better devoted to other server resources, such as windows. Also, unless the server is internally multi-threaded, if it must traverse the structure store itself, the rest of the display will "freeze" for the time it takes to do the traversal. On some displays, even the cursor will not move. If input from devices such as the mouse and keyboard is not handled expeditiously, some input may be lost, or (at the worst) the system may crash. The server needs to be robust, and should respond to requests from any source reasonably quickly. It should not be able to be monopolized for a long time by a single request.

Some applications may completely replace the contents of the store on each cycle (e.g., because they change the shape of a displayed surface each time it is displayed). For applications such as these, it would be better if they could just transmit the new data and have it displayed immediately; there is no point in saving it.

Another "should it be in the server?" question concerns the various processes associated with logical input devices. For best interaction, these should clearly be implemented in the server. However, mechanisms for dealing with input devices other than the mouse (or for treating the mouse as multiple logical devices) have not yet been developed for the X window system. Thus, it seems simpler to implement user interaction in the application code (presumably in a PHIGS library), even though it would be slower.

A final area of conflict between PHIGS and X concerns the treatment of color. PHIGS PLUS requires that, for best results, a large number of colors be available. However, the colormap on an X display is shared between all applications using the display. It is considered anti-social for a single application to take most of the colormap entries. PHIGS can allocate its own colormap, but then the colormap must be switched in when the PHIGS window is active and out when it is not. This will usually randomize the colors in all the other windows on the screen (one of which is probably a terminal window in which the PHIGS application is running) while the PHIGS window is selected. Unfortunately, there is no good answer to this problem on displays with a small (256 entries or less) colormap.

6. PEX Internals

This section presents a quick look at some of the internal details, on the basis that understanding a little about how it works makes it easier to understand how and when to most effectively use it.

6.1 The X Extension Mechanism

The X implementors provided a method by which the X server and protocol can be extended. To understand how this works, it is necessary to look a little more closely at the X protocol and server implementation. Each request from an application to the X server has a request type and a length. The length is there so that the server can decide when a complete request has been received, even if it knows nothing about the format of the contents. When it receives a request, a dispatching routine in the server looks at the request type, and calls the procedure that implements that request. Certain request types are designated as extension requests. A request of this type has a subtype that is meaningful to the particular extension that receives it. The server's main dispatch routine just passes the request to the extension's dispatching routine for further processing (see Figure 12).

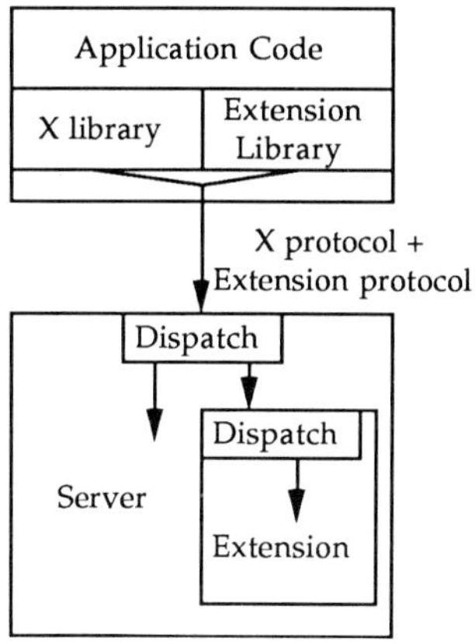

Fig. 12 X extension mechanism.

But how does the server know that the extension is there? The extension is loaded into the server in a system-dependent way (usually by recompiling the server). When the server starts up, it calls a routine `InitExtensions` that initializes each extension (usually by means of a line of code that calls the extension initialization procedure). This registers the extension with the server (passes a list of the extension entry points back to the server) and assigns it a request type. Once this has been done, an application program can inquire (by name) of the server whether a particular extension is installed, and get its extension request type if so.

Within the server, communication from the server to the extension is through one of the few procedures registered at initialization time (basically, the dispatch routines, a "shutdown" routine, and a few others). The interface between the extension and the server is similarly "thin". There are some server functions that the extension can call to manage resources (persistent data structures associated with a single application, such as PHIGS structures). The drawing interface between an extension and the server uses a data structure called the GC (graphics context). The GC contains the current set of graphics attributes and a list of procedures to call for various drawing operations. Thus, if requests to the extension can be translated into basic X drawing functions, the extension will fit cleanly into almost any X server.

If this is not the case, as it would be if the display had 3-D drawing hardware, then the extension must dig more deeply into the internals of the X server, and will be more dependent on implementation details of a single server. For example, the defined extension interface does not provide a way of getting the "clip list" for a window – this is the region of the window that is actually visible. Clearly, a PHIGS extension using 3-D hardware must know this information.

In any case, from the application's point of view, using an extension is simple. It obtains the extension request type from the server, then starts building and sending extension requests through the X Display connection. Normal X requests may be intermixed with extension requests with no problems. Figure 12 illustrates the request flow from the application program to the server and extension.

6.2 Data Types and Resources

PEX defines 9 new types of X resources. These are

Renderer – the PEX equivalent of the X GC. This data structure contains the current rendering state information, including lookup table IDs, highlight and invisibility filters, current structure access path, and pipeline context. A renderer is attached to a window or other drawable when a *Begin Rendering* request is executed.

Pipeline context – contains an instance of the attributes that affect the rendering pipeline. When rendering with a pipeline context, all values are (conceptually) saved when a structure is executed, and restored when it finishes. Elements of the pipeline context may be modified by attribute primitives during rendering, or by an explicit *Change Pipeline Context* request (if the pipeline context is being used for rendering, changes are deferred until the *End Rendering* request is executed).

Lookup table – supports all types of tables needed by PEX. A table contains zero or more entries of a given type. There is a table type for each PHIGS and PHIGS PLUS indexed attribute. During the process of rendering, indexed attributes may be obtained indirectly from the tables associated with the renderer. A single set of (overloaded) requests is provided for all lookup table manipulations.

Structure – supports the PHIGS structure store. A sequence of output commands may be stored in a structure for later rendering. Structures are linked together into a structure network by *Execute Structure* commands. A structure may be edited by inserting, deleting, and replacing individual structure elements.

Name set – a set of names. A name is represented as a 32 bit integer. Arbitrary strings can be mapped to names and back with the X atom mechanism.

Search context – defines constraints for searching a structure network. A search context defines a search position (a point in space), a distance, a starting and ending point in the structure network, and a filter. A search returns the path to the first element encountered which passes the filter, and which is within the given distance of the search position.

PHIGS workstation – encapsulates the necessary information to support a PHIGS (output) workstation. The PHIGS workstation is permanently bound to a particular window or pixmap, a set of lookup tables (one of each type), and filter name sets at the time it is created. A list of posted structure networks determines what will be drawn. The PHIGS workstation contains a superset of the capabilities found in a renderer. The difference is that the PHIGS workstation has additional "PHIGS policy" built in, while a renderer provides "mechanism, not policy."

Pick measure – contains information necessary for implementing pick devices. As in PHIGS, this is completely implementation dependent.

6.3 PEX Protocol

The PEX protocol encoding will be illustrated with two examples. The *Render Output Commands* request is a PEX request that specifies a renderer and contains a list of output commands, specified as

format:	FORMAT (see below)
rdr_id:	RENDERER_ID (a 32 bit integer)
cmds:	LISTofOUTPUT_CMD (a count followed by output commands)

The format specification contains two pieces of information: the floating point format (IEEE single precision, or DEC F), and the direct color format. Thus a single ROC request will contain only one type of floating point number and only one type of direct color.

Next, let us consider the *Fill Area Set 3D with Data* output command. Its specification is

shape:	SHAPE (an enumeration of convex, non-convex, etc.)
ignore_edges:	BOOLEAN
color_type:	COLOR_TYPE (indirect or direct)
facet_attributes:	BITMASK (specifying which facet attributes are present)
vert_attributes:	BITMASK
facets:	LISTofFACET

A FACET is

facet_data:	OPT_DATA
vertices:	LISTofVERTEX

An OPT_DATA is

color:	OPT_COLOR (a color if the appropriate bit is set in the facet_attributes, absent otherwise)
normal:	OPT_NORMAL (a 3D vector if present)
edges:	OPT_SWITCH (Off or on, for edge visibility, if present. If on, means that the edge starting at this vertex should be drawn.)

A VERTEX is

point:	COORD_3D
data:	OPT_DATA

This output command contains a variable length list of variable length lists of variably sized objects. It is not the most complex output command, either (I think that honor goes to the polyhedron, which has a list of fill area sets). The encoding and decoding routines must deal with this sort of variability, and also the underlying variability of floating point formats and color types.

6.4 Rendering Semantics

Structure traversal and rendering may occur solely in the client (via the *Render Output Commands* request), solely in the server (via the Render Network request), or in a mixed mode (either by intermixing the above two requests, or by including an *Execute Structure* output command in a *Render Output Commands* request). A *Begin Rendering* request must be issued before immediate mode rendering begins. This initializes the renderer state and associates it with a drawable, but does not clear the contents of the drawable. This must be done by a separate X request. An *End*

Rendering request indicates the end of a sequence of rendering requests. *Render Network* performs an implicit pair of *Begin/End Rendering* requests. Figure 13 illustrates the rendering process schematically. Structures may be stored in the client, and transmitted to the server each time they need to be drawn. Or, they may be stored in the server, where the renderer can grab them directly when a *Render Network* request is sent by the client.

Structures associated with a PHIGS workstation resource may be rendered by issuing one of the requests *Redraw All Structures* or *Update Workstation*, or by modifying a posted structure network when the workstation update mode is such that display regeneration occurs as a side effect.

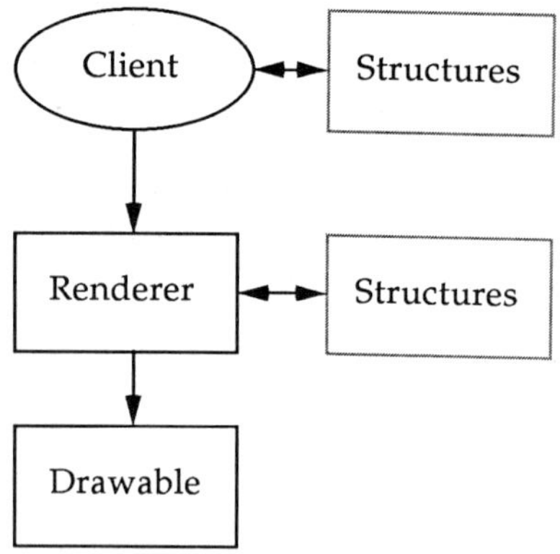

Fig. 13 Structures may be stored in the client or in the server.

7. Unique Aspects of PHIGS Programming with PEX

The application programmer interface for PEX is exactly that of PHIGS PLUS. Therefore, to a great extent, writing a PEX application is identical to writing a PHIGS application. PEX applications are unique in a couple of aspects. One is that in the PEX environment, a PHIGS workstation corresponds to an X window. Therefore, a PEX application may have to be slightly "X aware" to open the workstation. A second area of potential difference concerns input. The PEX protocol does not define any support for PHIGS input devices. Finally, as mentioned above, PHIGS workstations do not normally change size, nor do they receive expose events.

Vendors have taken different approaches to solve the problem of initially associating a PHIGS workstation with an X drawable. Two will be described here. One vendor has three PHIGS workstation types: XWindow, XPixmap, and XOutputOnlyWindow. Each can be customized by putting appropriate values in the X resource data base (toolkit-type resources), so that the user can specify default values for size, position, background color, etc. The connection id returned by OpenWorkstation is a structure containing a window and a display name.

Another scheme uses an extra routine to create a specific workstation type which is then passed to OpenWorkstation. The extra routine also uses the X resource data base to get default values for the workstation.

At least one other vendor is supplying PEX without a corresponding PHIGS implementation.

Several schemes have been proposed for mapping X input (typically using a mouse) onto the various devices and modes of PHIGS input. In most of these, the implementation uses a second process to asynchronously update the prompts and echos for the input values. This is necessary because, unlike X applications, a PHIGS application is not required to periodically check for input events. Thus, there is no guarantee that an input event can be responded to in a timely fashion by the application. It appears that this particular area of the PHIGS/X interface will continue to develop for some time yet, until a "most satisfactory" solution has been found.

Additionally, a "PEX aware" application can use Xlib or the toolkit for input, and completely ignore the PHIGS input options. A mixture of the two might work even better, the PHIGS input methods could be used where they were most appropriate, and the X input methods where the PHIGS facilities were not as capable (certainly the X toolkit provides a much more flexible set of user interaction capabilities than the stylized input facilities of PHIGS.)

There are a few options available for dealing with resize and expose events in a PEX implementation. One is to completely hide both. A resize event would merely change the internal mapping from a normalized device coordinate space to the X window so that the PHIGS workstation display continues to maximally fit the new size of the X window. An expose event would trigger an update workstation request. Both of these responses would be implemented internally to the application programmer's interface code. A second alternative provides an extension to PHIGS that allows the application to be notified when the workstation window has been resized or needs redisplay. The application may be able to make a more intelligent (from its point of view) response; one that takes into account application requirements.

8. Wrap up

Clearly, in a tutorial of this scope, it is not possible to give more than an introduction to using X, the X toolkits, and PEX. Understanding of the underlying principles has been emphasized, illustrated with some simple examples. There are many books dealing with X and toolkit programming now available. One of the most complete references is the O'Reilly series[5; 6; 7; 8; 9; 10]. There are currently 7 volumes[13] in this series, covering topics from the X protocol specification to programming using various widget sets. Other useful texts include Jones[11] on Xlib programming, and Young[12] on the use of the toolkit and Motif widget set. The X protocol and library are described by Scheifler, et al[4]. While this book is written by the implementors, I feel that its format is not as convenient as the O'Reilly Volumes 0 and 2, which cover basically the same material.

9. References

1. Scheifler, R., Gettys, J.: The X Window System. ACM Transactions on Graphics 5 (2), 79-109 (1986)
2. Rost, R.: PEX Protocol Specification,version 5.0., (1990).
3. Rost, R., Friedberg, J., Nishimoto, P.: PEX: A Network-Transparent 3D Graphics System. IEEE Computer Graphics and Applications 9 (4), 14-26 (1989).
4. Scheifler, R., Gettys, J., Newman, R.: X Window System. Digital Press (1988).
5. Nye, A.: X Protocol Reference Manual. O'Reilly & Associates, Inc., The X Window System Series, Vol. 0 (1989).
6. Nye, A.: Xlib Programming Manual. O'Reilly & Associates, Inc., The X Window System Series, Vol. 1 (1988).
7. Nye, A.: Xlib Reference Manual. O'Reilly & Associates, Inc., The X Window System Series, Vol. 2 (1988).
8. Nye, A.: X Window System User's Guide. O'Reilly & Associates, Inc., The X Window System Series, Vol. 3 (1989).
9. Nye, A., O'Reilly, T.: X Toolkit Intrinsics Programming Manual. O'Reilly & Associates, Inc., The X Window System Series, Vol. 4 (1990).
10. O'Reilly, T.: X Toolkit Intrinsics Reference Manual. O'Reilly & Associates, Inc., The X Window System Series, Vol. 5 (1990).
11. Jones, O.: Introduction to the X Window System. Prentice Hall, (1989).
12. Young, D.: X Window System Programming and Applications with Xt. Prentice Hall, (1989). Also OSF/Motif Edition, (1990).

---

13. The current volumes are numbers 0-5 and 7. Volume 6 will cover the use of the Motif widget set, and had not been published at the time of this writing.

IMAGE PROCESSING BY THE HUMAN VISUAL SYSTEM

Simon J. Thorpe*

1. INTRODUCTION

The processing power of the human visual system is truly awe-inspiring. Hundreds of millions of years of natural selection have led to the evolution of a visual system whose rapidity and accuracy is quite breathtaking. Images flashed on a screen can often be identified on the basis of only 100 to 150 ms of processing (see Thorpe & Imbert, 1989). Furthermore, the number of different objects and scenes that can be identified by the average human is probably well over 100,000. Such levels of performance make the processing capacities of current image processing technology look positively feeble. And the contrast between biological and artificial vision is made even more striking when one takes into account the fact that the components used by biological visual systems, namely neurons, are several orders of magnitude slower than the components used in current electronics : neurons typically operate with a maximum pulse rate of around 100 Hz, whereas even the humble PC uses components that operate with a clock rate of 10 MHz or more.

The performance advantage of biological visual systems is such that many computer vision specialists are looking towards such systems for inspiration. This tutorial is aimed at reviewing the current state of knowledge regarding image processing in human and animal visual systems. Particular attention will be paid to aspects of biological vision that could be used by researchers involved in the design of artificial visual systems.

2. THE SPEED OF VISUAL PROCESSING

Visual identification is so easy for humans that we often fail to realize just what a difficult task it is. Imagine flicking through a magazine full of photos. Even if the photos are of widely varying objects and scenes, we usually have no trouble in identifying what they are. We get the impression that we know what

* Supported by Grants from ESPRIT ("Mucom", 3149), MRT ("Sciences Cognitives"), and CNRS (ARI "Communication Multimédias")."

the stimulus is in just a fraction of a second, but it surprisingly difficult to get an accurate measure of how long the processing actually takes. The most obvious approach is simply to measure the time it takes people to name a picture of an object or scene. Typically, it takes about 750 msec to name an object. However, the time taken depends on the object in question - an apple, for example, can be named in 600 msec (Intraub, 1979), whereas less familiar objects, such as a xylophone can take as long as 1200 msec (Oldfield, 1966). The problem with such an approach is that we measure not only the time taken by the visual processing, but also the time needed to find the right word to describe the object and the time taken to generate the verbal response. We still need to know what proportion of the naming time is taken up by the visual processing per se.

Another possibility is to measure the *minimum presentation time* required for an object to be identified correctly. Such studies have shown that in most cases, a presentation lasting 10 to 15 msec is sufficient (Oldfield, 1965; Intraub, 1979) if the picture is followed by a blank field. But the problem in this case is that visual processing can continue afterwards, especially if we think of the visual system as some sort of pipeline processor.

Other psychological experiments have used *rapid serial visual presentation* techniques (or R.S.V.P. for short). In such experiments a series of say 16 colour images are presented one after the other. Subjects were instructed to press a button as soon as they saw a particular image (e.g. "A boat on a beach"), which could be situated anywhere in the sequence (Potter, 1975). In other experiments, the target was either specified by giving a category ("press when you see an animal") or a negative category ("press when you see something that you don't find in a house") (Intraub, 1980, 1981). Finally, Thorpe (1988, in preparation) used a procedure in which subjects actually had to identify two images presented one after the other. All these experiments have shown that with presentation times of 100 msec or so, identification is remarkably good.

Unfortunately, none of these psychological techniques actually enables us to directly measure processing time. To do this, we have to turn to neurophysiological experiments which actually determine how the cells that make up the visual system respond to visual inputs. In the last two decades, a number of researchers have started to analyze the visual response properties of individual neurons in different parts of the brain of awake behaving monkeys. Such studies have revealed that some neurons with quite complicated response properties can respond with remarkably short response latencies following the presentation of a visual stimulus, and this places clear limits on the time taken by visual processing.

For instance, in 1976, Edmund Rolls and his collaborators found neurons in a region known as the lateral hypothalamus which responded selectively to foods (e.g. a piece of banana, a peanut, a syringe filled with glucose solution etc) (Rolls, Burton and Mora, 1976). Remarkably, such neurons respond only 150 msec after the food was shown to the animal (Rolls, Sanghera and Roper-Hall, 1979). More recently, food selective visual responses have been found with even shorter latencies (around 120 msec) in a part of the frontal lobe known as the orbitofrontal cortex (Thorpe, Rolls and Maddison, 1983). The fact that such neurons appear to "know" whether a visual stimulus is food or not so soon after it has been presented implies that a great deal of visual processing has already been done by this time.

The same group of researchers reported a population of neurons in the anterior thalamus which showed highly characteristic responses during the performance of a visual recognition memory task (Rolls, Perrett, Caan and Wilson, 1982). These neurons had the remarkable property of responding selectively to familiar visual stimuli. If a novel visual stimulus (for instance a Coca-Cola bottle) was presented to the monkey, there was no response on the first presentation. However, if the same object was presented a second time, there was a large response from the neuron, even if the first and second presentations were separated in time by as much as 1 to 2 hours. Furthermore, these visual responses could be obtained with any visual stimulus - thus the same neuron could respond to faces, bunches of keys, pens and so on - the only essential characteristic was that the object should have been seen by the monkey shortly before. The shortness of the latency of some of these neurons was particularly remarkable - 130 msec in one case. Such data again implies that highly sophisticated visual processing must already have been done in this time.

Finally, other studies by Edmund Rolls, Dave Perrett and their colleagues have described a population of neurons in a part of the temporal lobe known as the superior temporal sulcus which have visual responses that are selective for faces and face features (Perrett, Rolls and Caan, 1982; Rolls, 1986; Perrett, Mistlin and Chitty, 1987). Similar neurons have also been reported in the temporal lobe of the sheep (Kendrick and Baldwin, 1987). The existence of such neurons implies a high level of visual processing, especially when one bears in mind the observation that some of these neurons can respond of a large range of sizes, colours and so on. Nevertheless, the latency with which such cells respond is typically in the range 100 to 140 msec. Interestingly, these results have been strengthened by the recent discovery of face-selective evoked potentials in humans (Jeffreys, 1988; Bötzel & Grüsser, 1989). These potentials, which can be recorded from electrodes attached to the subject's scalp, apparently only occur to stimuli that the subject himself considers as "face-like", and reach a peak around 150 to 180 msec after the stimulus was presented.

In conclusion, although it is remarkably difficult to directly measure the time taken by visual processing using behavioural methods, neurophysiological studies have demonstrated that sophisticated decisions such as whether an image contains food, a familiar stimulus or faces can be made after only 100-150 msec of processing. All such decisions are well beyond what can be currently achieved using even the most sophisticated computer vision systems - nobody knows how to build a machine capable of discriminating foods from non-foods, faces from non-faces or familiar from unfamiliar objects. Furthermore, the visual system is capable of identifying objects even when the viewing conditions vary greatly. For example, we have to be able to recognize the letter "A" irrespective of its position on the retina. The invariance of our perceptual responses despite changes in the size, position and orientation of the stimulus is again something that has not been succesfully dealt with in artificial vision systems.

Nevertheless, the human brain is an existence proof that such decisions can be made on the basis of only 100-150 msec of processing, despite the fact that the neurons with which the processing is done are themselves relatively slow. Thus the question arises of how does the visual system achieve this remarkable level of performance. Although an answer to this question is still a long way off, a great deal has been learnt about the mechanisms underlying visual processing in humans, and the aim of this tutorial is to try and review what is currently known about visual processing in human vision.

The next section will briefly introduce the main features of the anatomical organization of the visual system. This will further define the information processing problem that the visual system has to solve.

3. THE STRUCTURE OF THE VISUAL SYSTEM

The pattern of light falling on the retina is sampled by approximately 100 million photoreceptors - the rods and cones. The pattern of activity of these photoreceptors is processed in the retina via a network of bipolar, amacrine and horizontal cells before being transmitted to the brain by approximately 1 million ganglion cells whose axons form the optic nerve. Clearly, the retina must be performing some sort of sophisticated data compression algorithm in order to get through the information bottle-neck of the optic nerve, since, on average, there is only one optic nerve fibre for every 100 photoreceptors, although this ratio varies dramatically across the retina - indeed the ratio is more like one-to-one in the fovea - the part used for the most fine detailed analysis of the image.

The first structure in the central nervous system to receive the visual information arriving from the retina is the lateral geniculate nucleus, which also contains approximately 1 million cells. These cells in turn project to the first cortical visual area, the striate cortex, also known as area 17 or V1 (see Fig. 1). Here we see a massive expansion in the number of neurons available for processing visual inputs - there are something like 500 million neurons in V1 alone.

In addition to V1, it now appears that there are a large number of other cortical areas that are also involved in visual processing, but that, at least in the primate, most visual information has first to pass via V1. These other areas include V2, V3, MT, V4 and Inferotemporal cortex. Knowledge about the anatomical organization of these different extra-striate visual areas is advancing rapidly (For reviews see DeYoe and Van Essen, 1988; Maunsell and Newsome, 1987; Van Essen and Maunsell, 1983; Zeki and Shipp, 1988), and it is now generally accepted that different cortical visual areas are to some extent specialized for particular aspects of visual processing. For example, neurons in MT (Mid-temporal cortex) are known to be particularly sensitive to stimulus movement (Hildreth and Koch, 1987) and lesions to this area and an adjacent area known as MST have been reported to result in selective deficits in motion perception and pursuit eye movements (Newsome and Wurtz, 1988). In contrast, neurons in V4 have been shown by Zeki to be particularly important in colour processing (Zeki, 1980), an idea that would appear to be born out by the effects of lesions (Wild et al, 1986; but see Heywood and Cowey, 1988).

At a more global level, Mishkin and his co-workers have argued that a distinction can be made between two major cortical processing streams (Mishkin, Ungerleider and Macko, 1983). The first one, involving more ventral structures and leading ultimately to the inferotemporal cortex, is involved in the identification of visual objects. The second, involving the more dorsal areas and the parietal cortex, is suggested to be more important in analyzing the spatial configuration of visual space. Clearly, from the point of view of how visual identification occurs, it is the ventral path to the temporal lobe which is the most relevant. In a previous section we mentioned the face-selective neurons described by Perrett, Rolls and others in the superior temporal sulcus (part of the temporal lobe), whose visual responses have latencies which are typically in the range 100 to 140 msec. We can ask the question what is the shortest anatomical path by which such neurons can be activated? It would appear that in order to reach this part of inferotemporal cortex, the visual information would have to go through at least 3 intermediate cortical areas, namely V1, V2 and V4. This is because there is apparently no direct projection from V1 to V4, nor from V2 to IT.

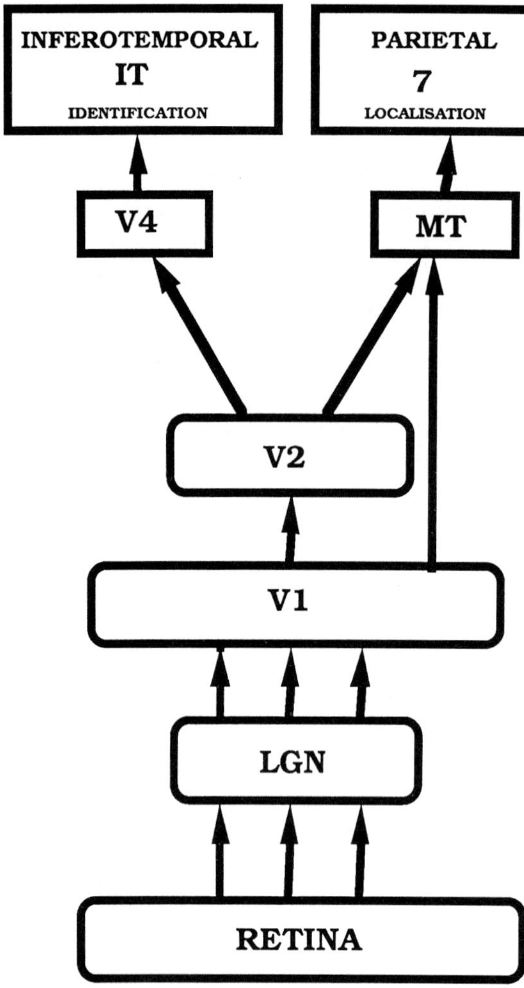

Fig. 1: Simplified diagram of the organization of the primate visual system.

Such anatomical features place additional constraints on the way in which information must be processed by the visual system. Jerry Feldman (1985) pointed out that humans are capable of making complex perceptual decisions in only a half-second or so. As the firing rate of cortical neurons is typically in the range 0 to 200 spikes per second, this results in what Feldman called the "100 step limit" - since only 100 sequential operations can be performed in such a time. However, if we restrict ourselves to the 100 or so msec taken by the visual processing, we find that the computational problem becomes even more acute. If we count up the number of processing layers between the photoreceptors of the retina and the face-selective responses of neurons in the temporal lobe, we find that there are probably at least 10 layers involved (De Yoe and van Essen, 1988; Zeki and Shipp, 1988; Bullier, 1983). Somehow using these 10 processing layers the visual system is able to compute the answers to questions like "is there a face present?". The intriguing problem facing those interested in biological vision, and which we will try to address in the following sections, is to know how it is that the human visual system can perform this feat. What are the operations being performed by these 10 or so layers of neuronal machinery between the photoreceptors and the temporal lobe? Could machines be built to do the same thing?

4. BASIC CONCEPTS

Before starting any detailed discussion of visual processing, it will be useful to introduce some fundamental concepts. The first point is that we will treat the visual system as a system for processing information. Starting with an input (a pattern of light on the retina) we want to finish up at the output with the identities and spatial relationships of the objects in the visual scene. In particular, we wish to know what the intermediate stages are between the input and output.

Most objects are identified on the basis of one of two basic characteristics. The first is their shape - cups, hammers, aeroplanes and chairs all have characteristic forms. A second major source of information comes from the surface properties of objects. These include colour, texture and smoothness. Granny smith apples are characteristically smooth, shiny and green. Lumps of coal are typically rough and black.

Thus, one might predict that the major aims of intermediate level vision should be to determine the shape and surface properties of objects in the image. But this assumes that we know where the objects are. Thus a second major problem is to segregate the image into its components. As those working in computer vision will testify, this is by no means a trivial problem.

Breaking up the image into objects and determining their shapes and surface properties is certainly a reasonable intermediate target, but what sorts of initial information do we have to work on? Essentially, it would appear that the visual system uses an initial stage of data compression in the retina, which removes much of the redundant data. Subsequently, separate systems are used to analyze aspects such as form (orientation of contours etc), movement, stereo, and colour. These processing modules provide the basic information for forming the intermediate level representations. Later sections of the course will look in greater detail at how particular types of visual information are handled at a high level, and how the visual system goes about recognizing particular patterns such as objects and faces.

One basic idea which will reappear at a number of points in the course is the idea of parallel architectures. Visual information processing is too fast to allow much time for sequential processing techniques to be applied. Instead, it would appear that a great deal depends on parallel processing. Ullman (1984) has proposed three different types of parallelism. The first, which he terms *spatial parallelism,* is where separate processors simultaneously perform the same operation but for separate parts of the image. This type of parallelism is particularly common in the retina. A second possibility is *functional parallelism* in which different processors each perform a different operation on the same bit of data. This is often used in the visual cortex, where different a range of neurons selective to different orientations are associated with each part of the retina. The third type of parallelism is *temporal,* and occurs in systems with several layers in which information flows through the system from layer to layer. Because of this, processors in lower layers can be performing a relatively elementary operation at the same time as higher level processors are operating on an earlier input. This type of "pipeline" arrangement, otherwise known as a feed-forward net seems to be characteristic of biological visual systems.

This also raises the important question of the relative importance of bottom-up and top-down influences in visual perception. To what extent can visual processing be viewed as the operation of a feed-forward pipeline operation? Is visual processing a relatively isolated module as Fodor (1983) has suggested?

Another approach which is becoming more and more prevalent is the use of "connectionist" models. The connectionist approach, developed during the 1980s by researchers such as Jerry Feldman, Dana Ballard, Geoff Hinton, Terry Sejnowski, James McClelland and Dave Rumelhart, is "neurally-inspired" in that they make use of large networks of relatively simple processing units, with properties similar to real neurons. In such systems, information is stored not so much at the nodes, but rather by the strengths of connections between the units. One of the major advantages of such models, apart from the fact that they are relatively plausible biologically, is their naturally parallel nature, and they are particularly well adapted to problems such as vision in which very large amounts of information have to be processed. Other advantages of such connectionist models is that they can allow cooperative and competitive processes to guide visual processing, and suggest ways of integrating information from a variety of sources.

Although many connectionist models are only relatively loosely tied to neurophysiological and anatomical constraints, the last few years has also seen the development of a large number of neural network models. In some cases, this has involved detailed modelling of the processing performed by real neuronal systems, and it seems likely that such work will provide increasing insights into the way in which information is processed in biological visual systems.

The remainder of the tutorial will be divided into a number of sections dealing with a range of specific problems. The first deals with the initial encoding steps which occur in the retina. Other sections deal with particular processing models, concerned with the processing of form (orientation and spatial frequency), movement, stereo and colour and lightness. The two sections that follow deal with the more general problems of segregating the image into its basic components, and determining the surface shape of objects in the visual field. The final sections deal with more specific domains of object, face and word processing.

5. INITIAL ENCODING

The essential task of early vision is to transform the basic information in the pattern of the light falling on the image into a form that can be used at later processing stages (Yellot, Wandell & Cornsweet, 1987; Dowling & Dubin, 1984; Julesz & Schumer, 1984). One important point is that in the human visual system, this requires a high level of data compression. There are some 100 million photoreceptors in each retina, and yet there are only 1 million nerve fibres running along the optic tract to the brain. One reason why this data compression is necessary is that our eyes have to be mobile, and if there were ten times as many fibres in the optic nerve, it would be much harder to make a visual system that could make saccadic eye movements to new targets of interest. But equally, it seems likely that a lot of the information contained in the activity of the photoreceptors is redundant and would not help in visual identification.

Another basic problem associated with data compression comes from the fact that the human visual system has to work with such an enormous range of possible light levels - there is an intensity difference between bright sunshine and the dimmest detectable light sources of some 10 billion to one. To cope with this the visual system uses a variety of strategies (see Barlow, 1982). One is to use two different sets of photoreceptors with different sensitivities. The cone system, composed of 3 main types of wave-length sensitive photoreceptors (sensitive to short, medium and long wavelength light) are relatively insensitive and require relatively high photopic light levels to operate. The rod system, which does not allow for colour sensitivity, is sensitive to substantially lower light levels.

Another trick is to only signal local differences in light level. Most retinal neurons have concentric receptive fields. They may be excited by light falling on a central region, but inhibited by light falling in the surrounding area (a so-called ON-center cell) (see Robson, 1975). Such cells respond poorly, if at all, to uniform patches of light, but respond vigorously to contrast borders. The well known Cornsweet-Craik-O'Brien illusion provides a good illustration of how poor the visual system is at signalling absolute light levels. Interestingly, the same approach is often used in machine vision systems. Often the original raw pixel data is convolved with an operator similar in shape to the receptive field of a retinal ganglion cell.

Another way of reducing the total amount of information that has to be sent to the brain for processing is by using non-homogeneous sampling of the image (Levick, 1987; Wässle, 1987). The density of photoreceptors in the central fovea is virtually as high as is physically possible. The receptors are packed very tightly in a hexagonal array (Shapley and Perry, 1986), and locally, there is actually one optic nerve fibre per receptor. However, as we move away from the fovea, receptor packing density drops rapidly, and the number of fibres per receptor drops away as well. Obviously, the human visual system makes up for this variation by having a highly precise eye movement control system which allows the highly accurate foveal retina to be directed towards points of interest.

Another remarkable fact about the way information is encoded in the retina is that in many situations, it can be shown that human observers can make judgments about stimuli which are finer that the separation between the elements of the photoreceptor array. For example, when asked to line up two line segments when using a Vernier measuring system, subjects can make judgments with a prevision of a few minutes of arc - closer than photoreceptor spacing in the fovea. This ability appears to depend on the fact that beyond the retina, there are actually several hundred cortical neurons involved in processing each retinal fibre leaving the fovea and that these neurons allow positions to be interpolated using the ratio of firing in the retinal output fibres.

We mentioned earlier the centre-surround organization of many neurons in the early stages of visual processing. Marr and Hildreth (1980) have argued that such Mexican-hat receptive field profiles may be used to calculate zero-crossings in the image - points where the intensity changes from above average to below average values. Attempts have been made to assess the plausibility of the zero-crossing detection algorithm in cortical neurons (Hochstein & Spitzer, 1984). More recently, it has been found by those working in computer vision that analyzing the zero-crossings in the image can be difficult. Another possibility is to determine the second derivative of the intensity function (the basic Mexican-hat operator can be used to determine the first-derivative of the intensity function). This second derivative possibility seems to have been independently suggested by both Watt (1988) and Richards (1988). As yet no-one has tested to see whether such second-derivative operators can be implemented in neuronal hardware.

One final insight that has been gained from examining the mechanisms of peripheral encoding comes from the discovery in the 1960s of separate classes of retinal projection cells. Some cells, typically referred to as X-type, are characterized by having small receptive fields, sustained responses and being relatively insensitive to moving stimuli. Another group, the Y-type cells, have larger receptive fields, transient responses and respond well to moving stimuli (see Levick, 1987 for a review). A number of authors have suggested that this dichotomy may reflect a fundamental difference between the neural pathways underlying spatial analysis (involving the high spatial resolution X-system) and motion processing based primarilly on the responses of Y-cells. As we shall see, it appears that this basic segregation of function at the level of the retina is carried on to higher levels of the visual system.

6. SPATIAL VISION : CONTOURS AND SPATIAL FREQUENCY

The ease with which human observers can interpret line drawings has led to the suggestion that one of first tasks of the visual system is to resume a complicated image as a set of simplified contours. Neurophysiological evidence supports this idea. Concentric receptive fields in the retina had been discovered in the early 1950s by workers such as Barlow and Kuffler. In the early 1960s, nobel prize winners David Hubel and Torsten Wiesel transformed our conceptions of visual analysis by reporting the existence of neurons in the visual cortex selectively responding to contours having particular orientations. Individual neurons in the striate cortex (known as V1 in the primate) respond best to contours at particular orientations and much less so, or not at all to orientations more than 20 or 30° to either side. Two types of cell were described. Simple cells had clearly segregated excitatory and inhibitory zones in their receptive fields and responded only to oriented contours in clearly defined positions in the visual field. Complex cells on the other hand would respond to oriented contours anywhere within a fairly large range of positions. They proposed a hierarchical model in which simple cell properties could be derived by having a row of cells with round concentric receptive fields converge on the same cell. By setting the threshold of the cell so that it responded best if all the excitatory inputs were activated it would be possible to account for the orientation selectivity of such cells. Subsequently, complex cell receptive fields could be produced by "ORing" together the outputs of a small number of simple cells with similar orienation preferences but with slightly different receptive field positions. Although they are some fairly clear experiments which argue against such a simple model (Ferster and Koch, 1987), the idea that increasingly abstract codes can be produced at successive stages in visual processing is one that seems as pertinent as ever.

Hubel and Wiesel also reported that the preferred orientation was found to change systematically by steps of about 10-15° between adjacent neurons leading to the idea of a topographic map for orientation superimposed on a more general retinotopic map. Until recently it was generally believed that perceived orientation is determined by the most active neurons in such an array of orientation tuned cells (e.g. Knudsen et al, 1987). However, recent experiments (reviewed by Thorpe, 1989) suggest that orientation may instead be encoded by the relative levels of firing in non-optimally activated cells.

Another feature of the cortical neurons described in Hubel and Wiesel's original studies is end stopping. Often, cells would be inhibited if a visual stimulus was too long. This phenomenon, apparently due to the presence of inhibitory zones in the receptive field could allow the neurons to detect the presence of corners in the image.

The findings of Hubel and Wiesel, together with other studies by Lettvin, Maturana, McCulloch and Pitts (1959) on neural coding in the retina of the frog were cornerstones of the so-called feature detector theory of perception. Neurons were seen as extracting primitive features from the image.

Later on, Campbell and Robson (1966) initiated the study of visual processing using sinusoidally modulated gratings of different spatial frequencies. Fourier had previously shown that any continuous function can be broken down into a set of sine-waves varying in amplitude, frequency and phase. The finding that cortical cells show selectivity to gratings of particular spatial frequencies led to the hypothesis that the visual system was carrying out a global Fourier analysis of the visual scene. There is even some evidence that spatial frequency tuned neurons are organized in topographic manner in the visual cortex, in a way analogous to the orientation columns found by Hubel and Wiesel (Tootell et al, 1981; see also Blasdel & Salama (1987), Grinwald et al (1987)). One advantage of such a scheme is that the essential structure of the fourier spectrum of an image is invariant with changes in stimulus size - thus resolving one of the serious problems that our visual systems have to cope with - namely, how to achieve size constancy.

Other evidence for both orientation and spatial frequency sensitive mechanisms came form psychophysical experiments investigating the effects of adaptation. Staring at a vertically oriented high spatial frequency grating selectively reduces your sensitivity to similar stimuli, and this has been used as evidence for tuned channels (Blakemore and Campbell, 1969).

For some time there was an ongoing battle between the "feature-creatures" and the "Fourier-freaks" - one group claiming that visual analysis involved the use of neurons responding to particular features (edges, corners etc.), the other claiming that vision involved a more global Fourier analysis (see Kulikowski and Kranda, 1987). However, nowadays it is felt that a more appropriate description of the analysis performed by the visual cortex is that it is more like a local Fourier analysis. Sakitt and Barlow (1982), and other workers such as DeValois and DeValois (1988) have proposed that for each part of the visual field, the visual cortex contains a relatively complete set of filters. Each filter is selective for a relatively small range of orientations and spatial frequencies. It appears that such a representational scheme is not only a very compact way of describing natural images, but may well constitute a very useful data base for further visual processing.

One other idea that has emerged recently is the idea that orientation tuned neurons and the like are not necessarily doing what we think they should. For example, Dobbins, Zucker and Cynader (1987) found that orientation selectivity was also a very useful way of extracting information about line curvature, and Lehky and Sejnowski (1988) used neural network modelling to show that orientation selective neurons could be used in the calculation of shape from shading (see later section).

A further topic of interest concerns the analysis of illusory contours, about which a great deal has been written. One very interesting finding was reported by Peterhans, von der Heydt and Baumgartner (1987) who reported that some neurons in the second cortical visual area of the primate (V2) could respond to such stimuli, whereas no such responses were seen in the neurons of V1. This again provides support for the idea of hierarchical extraction of more and more abstract features.

Many of the concepts that have emerged from the analysis of cortical processing of contours and spatial frequency have also appeared in the computer vision literature where pyramid processing algorithms have made much use of the sort of orientation and spatial frequency filtering techniques discussed here (see Grimson, 1987; Brady & Yuille, 1987; Zucker, 1987).

7. MOVEMENT

Many applications in machine vision involve the use of static images, but the fact is that biological vision systems are designed to be able to handle continuously changing inputs. Furthermore, it should be stressed that knowledge of the optic flow field can be extremely useful in segregating the image into its component parts. For instance, when one moves around in the environment, objects that are closer move relatively faster. This mechanism of motion parallax provides a way of not only grouping together the different bits of the same object, but also of estimating its distance from the observer (Rogers and Graham, 1979).

The importance of the optic flow field was stressed by Gibson (1950, 1966), and his suggestions have been extended by the work of a number of more recent authors. For instance, Koenderink (1985) pointed out that once you have calculated the optic flow field, the changes at each point in the retinal image can be decomposed into four components, a translation term, a rotation term, an expansion term and a deformation term. Each has its own particular points of interest. For example, the expansion term can be used to directly calculate the time to collision (T.T.C.) of an object. If the image of an object doubles in size in 5 seconds, it will impact in 2 x 5 = 10 seconds (Lee, 1980; Regan & Beverley, 1979). This is true irrespective of the actual distance or velocity of the object. Clearly such information could be very useful to people such as tennis players trying to determine how they should play a particular shot (McLeod, 1987).

Other useful information can be derived from the deformation component. Imagine a bird flying towards a plane surface at an angle. It was suggested by Gibson that the point of impact could be found simply by locating the centre of expansion, but it appears that this is only the case if the trajectory is perpendicular to the surface (see also Priest et al, 1988). However, Koenderink showed that the point of impact is characterized as being the point in the image where the deformation component is zero. The deformation component can also be used to derive the angle of orientation of a surface in space. Surprisingly, it appears that this trick has not be taken up by machine vision experts interested in guidance systems.

Other experiments by Gunnar Johannson (1975) have demonstrated the power of pure movement stimuli. If lights are attached to the joints of human subjects who are then filmed moving in the dark, it becomes immediately obvious on viewing the film that it is a person. One can even tell whether the person concerned is male or female - just on the basis of a few moving points.

So clearly knowledge of the optic flow field is potentially very useful, but how does the visual system go about calculating it? Braddick argued that motion detection mechanisms can be grouped into two types - short-range and long-range (see Burr & Ross, 1986, 1987). The short range mechanisms could depend on signals in the retina. Both Reichardt (1966, 1987) and Barlow (1965) have suggested simple neuronal circuits for calculating velocity which depend on the use of delay lines between adjacent elements in the retina. Recently, Koch and Poggio (1986; Poggio and Koch, 1987) have proposed that direction of motion could be calculated within the dendritic fields of neurons using so-called synaptic veto mechanisms. Marr and Ullman (1981) proposed that the temporal response properties of Y-type retinal neurons could also be used to determine the direction of motion locally, although this would not provide information about velocity.

However, not all motion detection can be done using such short range mechanisms. If two stimuli are presented successively at two different locations, we experience the phenomenon of apparent motion (Ullman, 1983; Nakayama, 1985), even when the spatial separation between the two stimuli is several degrees or more. Furthermore, where several targets are possible, there must be some sort of matching process between different potential stimuli, which implies that higher level processes are in operation (Ramachandran and Anstis, 1983, 1986; Shepard & Judd, 1976; Shepard & Zare, 1983).

Although movement selective neurons can be found in V1 of the primate (see Orban, 1984 for review), there is another cortical area, known as MT or V5, which appears to be particularly important for motion processing (Hildreth and Koch, 1987; Zeki, 1974). If a stimulus is presented which is composed of two gratings moving in different directions, neurons in V1 respond separately to the two components. In contrast, there are neurons in MT which respond to the movement the combined percept, which moves in a direction depending on the sum of the two component vectors (Movshon, 1986). Lesions to MT produce specific impairments in motion perception (Newsome and Wurtz, 1988) and this may be related to certain neuropsychological cases of cortical motion blindness (Zihl et al, 1983).

Many of the methods used by biological vision systems find parallels in the computer vision literature (Horn and Schunk, 1981; Hildreth, 1984; Lawton et al, 1987; Nagel, 1987). However, calculating the optic flow field by machines has proved a difficult problem to solve. One reason for this may be the fact that we are often forced to use video frames, sampled at a fixed 25 Hz frame rate. It may be that a more analog calculation in some sort of artificial retina may provide a more useful input to the system.

8. STEREO

One of the major goals of early visual processing is to derive the three-dimensional configuration of objects and surfaces in the visual field. A number of different aspects of the image can be useful, but one of the most important makes use of the fact that the view of the world through the left and right eyes are slightly different. As a result, there are small disparities between the retinal images of the two eyes, and these differences are used to calculate stereoscopic depth.

It was in 1967 that Barlow, Blakemore and Pettigrew first described neurons in V1 that are tuned to stimuli having particular retinal disparities. Some neurons "preferred" stimuli with zero disparity (located in the fixation plane), whereas others responded best to stimuli with either crossed or uncrossed disparities (corresponding to stimuli in front of or behind the fixation plane). More recent studies in the awake behaving monkey have confirmed the existence of three main neuronal types, namely, "near", "far" and "tuned" (Poggio and Poggio, 1984). It was suggested that such neurons could form the neural substrate for stereoscopic depth perception.

Differences in the positions of stimuli in the two eyes are not the only source of potential depth information. Blakemore and co-workers (1972) described another type of neuron responding best to stimuli with slightly different orientations in the two eyes. Such neurons could signal whether a line or surface was sloping towards or away from the subject.

Another potential cue comes from differences in the velocities of stimuli in the two eyes. If the image of a ball is seen by the left eye as moving to the right, and by the right eye as moving to the left, the inevitable conclusion is that the ball is going to hit you between the eyes! Regan and Beverley (1979) provided psychophysical evidence that the human visual system is sensitive to such "looming" movements, and neurophysiological experiments revealed the existence of a full range of neurons tuned to different combinations of velocity in the two eyes (Regan, Beverley and Cynader, 1979). Finally, there is some evidence that if stimuli arrive at the left and right eyes at slightly different times, this too can be used as a cue for depth (Gardner et al, 1985).

One major question concerns the level of the visual system at which stereoscopic analysis occurs. The introduction of the random dot stereogram technique by Julesz in the early 1960s demonstrated that monocular form vision was not necessary for stereoscopic vision to occur (see Julesz, 1971, 1986). This raises the question of the types of algorithms used. One of the first suggestions was made by Marr and Poggio (1976) who proposed that cooperative and competitive interactions between neurons coding different depths could be used to solve the so-called "correspondence problem". In such a scheme, each part of the visual field has a set of units coding different depths. Inhibitory connections between units coding different depths for the same part of the visual field can be used to implement the constraint that each point in the image normally has only one associated depth. In contrast, excitatory connections between units coding the same depth but for adjacent parts of the image can be used to implement the natural constraint that adjacent parts of the image tend to have similar depths. More recent algorithms have been developed both in natural and in computer vision (Marr & Poggio, 1979; Longuet-Higgins, 1981, 1986 Mayhew & Frisby, 1983; Mayhew & Longuet-Higgins, 1982; Kanade, 1981; Barrow & Tenenbaum, 1981; Barnard & Martin, 1982). One important principle is to assume that in the absence of other information one can interpolate the surface between points in the image with known depths (Grimson, 1982).

9. COLOUR AND LIGHTNESS

Another major task for early vision is to determine the surface properties of objects. In particular, many well known objects are characterized by their reflectance characteristics. For example, oranges are characterized by the fact that they reflect relatively large amounts of light in the middle portion of the wavelength spectrum, lumps of coal by the fact that they reflect very little light at any wavelength.

The problem is to know how to get at this information. It is simply not sufficient to measure the spectral composition of the light arriving at the eye from the object in question, because this depends not only on the surface properties of the object, but also the spectral composition of the illuminating source, the angle of illumination and the surface orientation of the object (see Richards, 1988). Nevertheless, it has been known for a long time that humans can make accurate judgments of relative reflectance, despite these confounding factors. This ability, termed colour constancy, is demonstrated by the fact that we will call a light green piece of paper light green, even when the illumination conditions change dramatically (see Hurvich and Jameson, 1989; Boynton, 1988; Mollon, 1982a,b).

But the first point to make is that the visual system does not calculate the spectral composition of the light. This is made clear by the fact that any light source can be matched by appropriate mixing of three separate wavelengths. This basic trichromacy of vision reflects the existence of three cone pigments, maximally sensitive to three different wavelengths. Information about the absolute levels of activation in these different systems is soon eliminated by the use of opponent mechanisms - retinal ganglion cells and cells later on in the visual system are typically excited by one type of cone and inhibited by another (DeValois and Jacobs, 1984). Thus in effect, the only information that the visual system has is the relative levels of excitation in the three pigments.

Edwin Land proposed that true colour could be calculated using relative lightness of surfaces in the image, and it could be that the opponent processes described in the last paragraph may enable this calculation to be performed. He proposed the "retinex" algorithm, which was able to predict reasonably accurately the perceived colour stimuli under a variety of lighting conditions (Land, 1977). More recently, a variety of colour algorithms have been developed, all with the aim of extracting surface colour properties (see Richards, 1988).

Zeki (1980) has recorded from neurons in a higher order visual area (V4) which seem to code the true colour of visual stimuli, unlike neurons in V1 which appear to have responses more directly determined by the wavelength composition of the stimuli. This may be related to the finding of cortical colour blindness in neuropsychological studies (Meadows, 1974).

The complexities of colour and lightness perception are such that parallel algorithms are likely to be of great benefit. Recently, attempts have been made to use connectionist type neural network models to investigate such possibilities (Sejnowski and Churchland, 1988; Hurlbert and Poggio, 1988; Grossberg, 1987a,b).

10. SEGREGATION

Real images can be very complex, and this complexity is one of the reasons why computer vision can be so difficult. One essential task is to be able to divide the image into its component sub-parts. Individual objects in a scene are likely to correspond to parts of the image where some property or properties remain roughly constant. We have already mentioned the visual processing of colour, movement and depth, but a further image characteristic which could be useful for segregation is texture (Voorhees and Poggio, 1986; Bergson and Adelman, 1988; Beck, 1981). Julesz has recently proposed that the visual system is sensitive to basic textural components which he called "textons" (Julesz, 1981,1984). Other neurophysiological evidence supports the existence of neuronal mechanisms specifically sensitive to textures even within V1 itself (Hammond, 1986).

In addition, it is often essential to be able to group together objects that go together (Hochberg, 1986). The work of the Gestalt psychologists in the first part of the 20th century revealed a number of natural laws of grouping - common fate, linearity and so on.

Of particular importance is the segregation between figure and ground (Weisstein and Wong, 1986, 1987). In many situations where the situation is ambiguous (the famous wine-glass/two faces figure for example) the figure and the ground can be seen to flip from one state to the other. Such phenomena suggest the existence of cooperative effects which could be explained in neural network terms, and some recent studies have looked at this possibility (Sejnowski and Hinton, 1987; Grossberg and Mingolla, 1987; Zucker, 1987). In particular, it seems that such grouping and segregation phenomena depend on neural interactions over relatively large spatial areas (see Allman et al, 1985; Frost and Nakayama, 1983; Egalhaaf et al, 1988).

11. SHAPE

Determining the shape of objects in the image is one of the most important stages in the process leading to their identification, and is the essential purpose of David Marr's 2.5D sketch (Marr, 1982). We have already looked at one source of information that can be useful for determining surface shape, namely stereoscopic vision. But there are many other useful cues.

Humans are remarkably efficient at making inferences about 3D structure on the basis of simple line drawings (Waltz, 1975; Kanade, 1981). A couple of contours are often all that are needed for defining a surface volume (see Richards, 1988). The efficiency of this process makes it seem all the more likely that one of the principal aims of early vision is to resume the image in the form of a sort of line drawing. One way in which lines can be used to infer three dimensional shape has been suggested by Barnard (1983). He pointed out that if three straight lines in a two-dimensional image converge towards the same point, it is highly likely that they all correspond to parallel lines in three-dimensional space. Other information comes from occluding edges which indicate that one object is in front of another. Such "tricks" may go a long way to explaining the ease with which humans can interpret 2D images.

Another important cue comes from motion parallax, and the deformation component of the optic flow field that we discussed briefly in the section on movement. Other work has also stressed the importance of movement in determining shape (Ullman, 1984; Todd, 1985; Hoffman and Bennet, 1986; Siegel and Andersen, 1988).

Texture can also be used as a source of information about surface shape. Many objects have regular surface patterns and by determining the overall orientation of the marks together with their size, one can often get a reasonable idea about their shape (Witkin, 1981; Stevens, 1981).

Finally, shading and highlighting have both been proposed as ways of determining shape (Ikeuchi and Horn, 1981; Ramachandran, 1987a,b). For example, Ramachandran found that people often assume illumination from above and interpret shaded images in very specific ways.

12. IDENTIFYING OBJECTS AND SCENES

In the previous sections on early and intermediate vision, we saw some of the steps involved in developing a detailed representation of the image. This intermediate representation makes explicit (a) the way the image can be decomposed into separate objects and surfaces, (b) the three-dimensional shape of these surfaces, and (c) their surface properties, such as colour, texture and so on. The next step for the visual system involves using this data base to identify the objects present in the image and to understand their spatial configuration.

How do we go from a description of the shape and surface properties of an object to its identity? We have already noted that visual processing is very fast (see section 2). It is also worth noting that the number of different objects and scenes that can be identified is remarkably high. Is it possible to say how many? Clearly, the overall figure should include familiar objects ("can-opener", "telephone", "hair-dryer" etc), animals and plants ("tiger", "carnation", "spider" etc.), geographical locations ("The empire state building", "Big Ben" etc.), signs ("MacDonalds", "Mercedes" etc), as well as faces ("Ronald Reagan", "Michael Jackson", etc.). Biederman (1987) estimated that we can name approximately 30,000 different objects. This estimate was based on a sample of the entries in Webster's dictionary, in which he counted the number of words that corresponded to objects which could be easily identified visually. Thus he counted penguin and ostrich, since they were clearly distinguishable, but not garden warbler, which, at least for him, was not sufficiently different from other types of bird.

Nevertheless, the value of 30,000 visually identifiable objects proposed by Biederman is certainly an underestimate, for two reasons in particular. Firstly, if instead of counting entries in a dictionary, you use a large encyclopedia, you will count not only simple words such as "chair", "hammer" and "ostrich", but also specific terms such as "Eiffel tower", "Mona Lisa" and "Adolf Hitler", which are also easy for most people to identify. Using the Encyclopedia Britannica, we have made such an estimation and found a value of 50 to 60,000 visually identifiable entries.

The second point is that even this value does not include all the objects and images that are part of the personal repertoire of every one of us, such as the faces of our family and friends, the school we attended when we were young, the sofa in our living room and so on. It is even harder to get a clear idea of the size of this number but it seems likely that the total number of objects and scenes that can be identified rapidly is well in excess of 100,000.

So psychological data leads us to the conclusion that with only 100 msec of presentation time, the human visual system can probably access any one of upwards of 100,000 different internal representations. It would appear inevitable that this rapid accessing of the identity of objects involves parallel access. One of the most plausible ways of understanding this is in terms of some form of connectionist model, somewhat like a semantic network, in which different hypotheses can be simultaneously tested.

Mishkin et al (1983) proposed that in the brain, there are two major cortical processing routes for visual analysis, both originating in V1. One pathway, the upper one, leads to the parietal cortex and appears to involved in the analysis of the spatial configuration of objects in space. The second pathway, extends through a variety of intermediate cortical areas (V2, V3, V4, etc.) before reaching the temporal lobe, and appears to be specialized for the identification objects. Lesions to the second cortical system result in problems in identifying objects, a condition known in the neuropsychological literature as visual agnosia (Humphreys and Riddoch, 1987, 1988). Sometimes these visual agnosias can be remarkably specific, being restricted to fruit and vegetables for example, or to inanimate objects (Warrington, 1982, Hart et al, 1985; Goodglass, 1980). This indicates a hitherto unexpected degree of modularity in the processing system.

The idea of modularity also appears to be involved in the case of two other classes of input that seem to call for specialised processing mechanisms - namely, faces and words. Biologically, faces are extremely important stimuli, and there is even some evidence for innate preferences for face stimuli in new-born babies. In addition, there is a clinical neuropsychological condition known as prosopagnosia where patients fail to identify faces, even though their ability to identify other categories of objects (foods, tools, means of transport) are basically intact (Damasio and Damasio, 1986; Bruyer, 1986).

Furthermore, we have already mentioned the neurophysiological evidence for the existence of neurons in a particular part of the monkey temporal lobe which respond selectively to faces (Perrett et al, 1987). As pointed out earlier, such neurons have also been reported in sheep (Kendrick and Baldwin, 1987), and there is even some preliminary evidence for face selective responses in the temporal lobe of humans (Heit et al, 1988). Some of these neurons are exquisitely sensitive to direction of gaze, responding maximally if the face is looking straight at the animal, but responding much less if the eyes are deviated by only 5-10° (Perrett et al, 1985).

Considerable work has gone into understanding the processes involved in face recognition (Bruce, 1988; Young and Ellis, 1987). One particularly interesting study by Rhodes et al (1987) showed that subjects could identify line drawings of faces more accurately if they were in the form of a caricature - that is to say with differences from some sort of prototypic "average" face accentuated. This leads to the possibility that faces are actually encoded in terms of the differences relative to some sort of norm.

The other type of stimulus that appears to involve specialised processing are words (see Carr, 1986). Again there is neuropsychological evidence that the ability to read can be selectively disrupted by cortical damage, leading to dyslexia or alexia. Some very recent studies have looked at the pattern of brain activation produced by single words in humans (Petersen et al, 1988), and the study by Heit et al (1988) also found evidence for single neuron responses in the temporal lobe that were selective for words.

Starting with the logogen theory (Morton, 1969), a number of models have been based on the idea that the human language system can be regarded as a sort of semantic net, with nodes corresponding to words, and with information stored in the connections between the nodes. In particular, McClelland and Rumelhart (1981) proposed an interactive-activation model of word identification which marked the start of the recent explosion of interest in connectionist models of cognition.

What do we know of the mechanisms underlying the recognition of complex stimulus such as objects, faces and words? Neurophysiological investigations have shown that as we move forward through the system, the receptive fields of the neurons become larger and larger, until in the inferotemporal cortex (the highest order cortical area specifically dealing with visual inputs), cells can respond to stimuli almost anywhere in the visual field (Gross, 1973). Furthermore, they also appear to become more selective - requiring more and more complex stimuli in order to be activated (Perrett et al, 1987; Desimone et al, 1985). In a part of the frontal cortex, which receives direct inputs from this area, neurons have been found which respond selectively to particular foods, and some even had bimodal responses, responding to either the sight or the taste of the same food (Thorpe et al, 1983). The idea that the visual system can be viewed as a set of hierarchically organized processing layers in which the units become increasingly more selective whilst losing their spatial specificity has been used in some neural network models of pattern recognition (for example, Fukushima, 1975, 1980, 1986).

Various suggestions have been made as to the representational schemes used for accessing object descriptions. Marr and Nishihara (1978) proposed that the objects could be described in terms of sets of generalized cylinders. Some evidence for this comes from the fact that easily recognizable animal figures can be produced with "pipe-cleaner" models (e.g. giraffe, dog, deer etc.). This would be one way of getting around the fundamental problem of object constancy, the fact that in general, we can identify objects from a variety of different angles of view (Humphreys and Quinlan, 1988), although many objects have "canonical perspective views" from which they are easiest to identify (Palmer et al, 1981). One suggestion is that during visual identification there is a very rapid process of normalization, in which the object is mentally rotated to a more prototypic view before identification can occur (Jolicoeur, 1985). Some authors have suggested an important distinction between object based and viewer based descriptions (Hinton and Parsons, 1981).

Another recent theory of object identification has been proposed by Irving Biederman (1987). He proposed that the visual system identifies objects by means of a set of something like 36 visual primitives, which he calls geons. Most objects can be defined using a relatively small number (5 to 10) such geons, and this would certainly simplify the task of matching features to object descriptions.

One major question concerns the so-called binding problem. How does the visual system know which features go together? Treisman and Gelade (1982) found that under certain conditions, subjects can mix up features - attributing inappropriate colours to letters for example - a phenomenon known as illusory conjunctions. A variety of experiments indicate that some sort of active attentional process is necessary in order to link features together (Treisman, 1986a,b; Ullman, 1984). Another recent possibility is that oscillatory neuronal activity in the visual cortex may act as some sort of indexing system (Gray and Singer, 1989). It seems likely that mechanisms involving attentional processes will prove essential for handling complex scenes, although the evidence suggests that the identification of many objects can be achieved without the need for such mechanisms.

13. CONCLUDING REMARKS

In this tutorial I have attempted to show that the speed with which the human visual system can process images poses a truly fascinating problem. How is it that after only 100 to 150 msec of processing the visual system is capable of making complex decisions such as "Can I eat it?", "Have I seen it before?" and "Is there a face present?". All these sorts of decisions, which seem so effortless to us, present problems which would completely overwhelm even the most sophisticated computer vision systems that we have so far been able to build. And yet each of us is making such decisions all the time, using 10 or more layers of rather slow neurons stacked one after the other. So what is the secret?

We have seen that as visual information flows through the various stages of the visual system, more and more sophisticated information is extracted. At the level of the retina, the image is convolved with a Mexican-hat type receptive field in order to simplify the information contained in the image. At an intermediate level a rich description of the image is developed in which information about contours, movement, stereo, colour and lightness is made explicit. Such information is used in various combinations to obtain information about the three-dimensional shapes and surface properties contained in an image. The ultimate stage of visual processing, probably involving neural structures such as the temporal lobe, uses these shape and surface characteristics to identify the objects contained in the scene.

If one idea can summarize why the human visual system works as well as it does it is probably that of massive parallelism. Unlike conventional computers, in which a single processor is used to analyse an image, the human visual system has literally billions, all of which can be simultaneously active. Different operations can be performed simultaneously on the same part of the image array (functional parallelism), and this can all be done at the same time for the whole image (spatial parallelism). Finally, the pipeline architecture of vision means that the visual system can process continuously changing inputs (temporal parallelism). Furthermore, it would appear that using such a massively parallel system means that the whole system can operate in a highly cooperative way that would be difficult if not impossible to achieve using more conventional computing techniques. The next decade or so will see whether researchers working in machine vision will be able to take advantage of the insights provided by the analysis of biological vision systems.

14. SUGGESTIONS FOR READING

A number of different books may be useful for those wishing further information on the topics dealt with in these tutorials. General books on visual perception include those by David Marr (1982), John Frisby (1979), Vicki Bruce & Patrick Green (1986), Martin Levine (1985) et Robert Baron (1987). The books edited by Braddick & Sleigh (1983), Rosenfeld (1986) and Schwab & Nusbaum (1986) all contain chapters resulting from interdisciplinary meetings on vision.

For books dealing more specifically with the neurophysiological mechanisms underlying visual perception the books by Spillman & Werner (1990), Barlow & Mollon (1982), Hubel (1988), Brown (1988) and Rose & Dobson (1986) are all useful. In addition, the chapters by Kaas (1987), Maunsell & Newsome (1987) and Marrocco (1986) are all good reviews. Finally, the reviews by Hubel (1982), Poggio (1984), Bishop (1984), Churchland & Sejnowski (1988), Schiller (1986) and Wise & Desimone (1988) are all to be recommended.

In psychology, I can recommend the books by Humphreys and Bruce (1989), Rock (1988), Sekular & Blake (1984), Spoehr & Lehmenkuhle (1984) and Wilding (1982). Another book dealing with other aspects of cognitive psychology is the textbook by Smyth et al (1987). There are also good review chapters by Atkinson et al (1982), Braddick & Atkinson (1982), Pinker (1984) Hochberg (1984, 1986, 1988) and Hoffman (1986). Details on the neuropsychological aspects of visual perception can be found in two books by Humphreys and Riddoch (1987, 1988) and in a recent review article by Kosslyn et al (1990).

Further material concerning computer vision can be found in Brady (1982), Richards & Ullman (1987), Ballard & Brown (1982), Fischler and Firschein (1988) and Winston (1975). Also useful are chapters by Barrow & Tenenbaum (1986), Stevens (1988) and Poggio (1986). For an introduction to the rapidly developing field of connectionist models the reader should consult the books by McClelland & Rumelhart (1986a, b), Hinton & Anderson (1981), Arbib & Hanson (1987), Anderson & Rosenfeld (1988) and Morris (1989). Other useful chapters can be found in Ballard et al (1983), Feldman (1986), Ballard (1986, 1987) and Sejnowski, Koch & Churchland (1988). More specific texts dealing with neural computing are the books by Wasserman (1989) and Simpson (1990).

15. BIBLIOGRAPHY

Allman J, Miezin F, McGuinness E, (1985). Stimulus specific responses from beyond the classical receptive field : Neurophysiological mechanisms for local-global comparisons in visual neurons. Ann. Rev. Neurosci. 8, 407-430.

Anderson JA, Rosenfeld E, (1988). Neurocomputing : Foundations of research. M.I.T. Press

Arbib MA, Hanson AR, (1987). Vision, brain and cooperative computation : An Overview. In Arbib MA & Hanson AR, (eds) Vision, brain and cooperative computation. M.I.T. Press, pp 1-86.

Atkinson RC, Herrnstein RJ, Lindzey G, Luce RD, (1988). Stevens' Handbook of experimental psychology. Second Edition. John Wiley

Ballard DH, Brown CM, (1982). Computer Vision. Eaglewood Cliffs

Ballard DH, (1986). Cortical connections and parallel processing : Structure and function. Behav. Brain Sci. 9, 67-120.

Ballard DH, (1987). Cortical connections and parallel processing : Structure and function. In Arbib MA & Hanson AR, (eds) Vision, brain and cooperative computation. M.I.T. Press, pp 563-621.

Ballard DH, Hinton GE, Sejnowski TJ, (1983). Parallel visual computation. Nature 306, 21-26.

Barlow HB, Mollon JD, (1982). The Senses. Cambridge University Press

Barlow HB, (1982). Physiology of the retina. In Barlow HB & Mollon JD, (eds) The Senses. Cambridge University Press, pp 102-113.

Barlow HB, Blakemore C, Pettigrew JD, (1967). The neural mechanism of binocular depth perception. J. Physiol. 193, 327.

Barnard ST, Martin AF, (1982). Computational stereo. Computing Surveys 14, 553-572.

Baron RJ, (1987). The cerebral computer : An introduction to the computational structure of the human brain. Lawrence Erlbaum

Barrow HG, Tenenbaum JM, (1981). Interpreting line drawings as three dimensional images. Artif. Intell. 17, 75-116.

Barrow HG, Tenenbaum JM, (1986). Computational approaches to vision. In Boff KR et al (eds), Handbook of Perception and Human Performance. Vol 2. Cognitive processes and John Wiley, Chap 38

Beck J, (1981). Textural segmentation. In Beck J, (ed). Organization and representation in perception. Lawrence Erlbaum (Hillsdale),

Bergen JR, Adelson EH, (1988). Early vision and texture perception. Nature 333, 363.

Biederman I, (1972). Perceiving real world scenes. Science 177, 77-80.

Biederman I, (1981). On the semantics of a glance at a scene. In Kubovy M & Pomerantz J, (eds) Perceptual organization. Lawrence Erlbaum (Hillsdale),

Biederman I, (1987). Recognition-by-components: A theory of human image understanding. Psychol. Rev. 94, 115-147.

Bishop PO, (1984). Processing of visual information within the retinostriate system. In Brookhart JM & Mountcastle VB, (eds) The nervous system. III. Sensory processes. American Physiological Soc., pp 341-424.

Blakemore C, Campbell FW (1969) On the existence of neurons in the human visual system selectively sensitive to the orientation and size of retinal images. Journal of Physiology, 203, 237-266.

Blakemore C, Fiorentini A, Maffei L, (1972). A second neural mechanism of binocular depth discrimination. J. Physiol. 226, 725-749.

Blasdel GG, Salama G, (1986). Voltage-sensitive dyes reveal a modular organization in monkey striate cortex. Nature 321, 579.

Botzel K & Grusser OJ (1989) Electric brain potentials evoked by pictures of faces and non-faces - a search for face-specific EEG potentials. Exp. Brain Research,77,349-360.

Boynton RM, (1988). Color vision. Ann. Rev. Psychol. 39, 69-100.

Braddick OJ, Atkinson J, (1982). Higher functions in vision. In Barlow HB & Mollon JD, (eds) The Senses. Cambridge University Press, pp 212-238.

Braddick OJ, Sleigh AC, (1983). Physical and biological processing of images. Series in Information Science, 11, Springer-Verlag

Brady M, Yuille A, (1987). An extremum principle for shape from contour. In Arbib MA & Hanson AR, (eds) Vision, brain and cooperative computation. M.I.T. Press, pp 329-360.

Brady M, (1982). Computational approaches to image understanding. Comput. Surveys 14, 3-71.
Brown JW (1988) Neurophysiology of Visual Perception. Hillsdale : Lawrence Erlbaum.
Bruce V, Green P (1982) Visual Perception: Physiology, Psychology and Ecology. Lawrence Erlbaum.
Bruyer R, (1988). Facial recognition. La Recherche 19, 774-783.
Bullier J, (1983). The maps of the brain. La Recherche 14, 1202-1215.
Burr D, Ross J, (1986). Visual processing of motion. Trends Neurosci. 9, 304.
Burr D, Ross J, (1987). Visual analysis during motion. In Arbib MA & Hanson AR, (eds) Vision, brain and cooperative computation. M.I.T. Press, pp 187-208.
Campbell FW, Robson JG (1968) Application of Fourier analysis to the visbility of gratings. J. Physiology, 197, 551-556.
Carr TH, (1986). Perceiving visual language. In Boff KR et al (eds), Handbook of Perception and Human Performance. Vol 2. Cognitive processes and John Wiley, Chap 29
Churchland PS, Sejnowski TJ, (1988). Perspectives on cognitive neuroscience. Science 242, 741-745.
Cowey A, (1979). Cortical maps and visual perception. The Grindley memorial lecture. Quart. J. Exp. Psychol. 31, 1-17.
Damasio AR, Damasio H, (1986). The anatomical substrate of prosopagnosia. In Bruyer R, (ed). The neuropsychology of face perception and facial expression. Lawrence Erlbaum, pp 31-38.
Desimone R, Schein SJ, Moran J, Ungerleider LG, (1985). Contour, color and shape analysis beyond the striate cortex. Vision Res. 25, 441-452.
DeValois RL, DeValois KK, (1988). Spatial vision. Oxford Psychology Series, 14, Oxford University Press
DeValois RL, Jacobs GH, (1984). Neural mechanisms of colour vision. In Brookhart JM & Mountcastle VB, (eds) The nervous system. III. Sensory processes. American Physiological Soc., pp 425-456.
DeYoe EA, Van Essen DC, (1988). Concurrent processing streams in monkey visual cortex. Trends Neurosci. 11, 219.
Dobbins A, Zucker SW, Cynader MS, (1987). Endstopped neurons in the visual cortex as a substrate for calculating curvature. Nature 329, 438.
Dowling JE, Dubin MW, (1984). The vertebrate retina. In Brookhart JM & Mountcastle VB, (eds) The nervous system. III. Sensory processes. American Physiological Soc., pp 317-340.
Egalhaaf M, Hausen K, Reichardt W, Wehrhahn C, (1988). Visual course control in flies relies on neuronal computation of object and background motion. Trends Neurosci. 11, 351-358.
Feldman JA (1985) Four frames suffice : A provisional model of vision and space. Behavioural and Brain Sciences, 8, 265-289.
Feldman JA, Ballard DH, (1982). Connectionist models and their properties. Cognitive Science 6, 205-254.
Feldman JA, (1986). Connectionist models and parallelism in high level vision. In Rosenfeld A, (ed). Human and Machine Vision. II. Academic Press, pp 86-108.
Feldman JA, (1987). A functional model of vision and space. In Arbib MA & Hanson AR, (eds) Vision, brain and cooperative computation. M.I.T. Press, pp 531-562.
Fester D, Koch C, (1987). Neuronal connections underlying orientation selectivity in cat visual cortex. Trends Neurosci. 10, 487.
Fischler MA & Firschein O (1987) Readings in Computer Vision : Issues, Problems, Principles and Paradigms. Morgan Kaufman.
Fodor J, (1983). The modularity of mind. Cambridge MA : MIT Press.
Fow PR, Miezin FM, Allman JM, Van Essen DC, Raichle ME, (1987). Retinotopic organization of human visual cortex mapped with positron-emission tomography. J. Neurosci. 7, 913-922.
Frisby J, (1980). Seeing : Illusion, brain and mind. Oxford University Press
Frost BJ, Nakayama K, (1983). Single visual neurons coding opposing motion independent of direction. Science 220, 744.
Frost BJ, (1985). Neural mechanisms for detecting object motion and figure-ground boundaries, contrasted with self-motion detecting systems. In Ingle DJ et al (eds), Brain mechanisms and spatial vision. Nijhoff (Holland), pp 415-450.
Fukushima K, (1975). Cognitron : A self-organizing multilayered neural network. Biol. Cybern. 20, 121-136.
Fukushima K, (1980). Neocognitron : A self-organizing neural network model for a mechanism of pattern recognition unaffected by shift in position. Biol. Cybern. 36, 193-202.

Fukushima K, (1986). A neural network model for selective attention in visual pattern recognition. Biol. Cybern. 55, 5-16.

Gardner JC, Douglas RM, Cynader MS, (1985). A time-based stereoscopic depth mechanism in the visual cortex. Brain Res. 327, 154-157.

Gibson JJ, (1950). The perception of the visual world. Houghton Mifflin

Gibson JJ, (1966). The senses considered as perceptual systems. Houghton Mifflin

Gilchrist AL, (1979). The perception of surface black and whites. Sci. Amer. 240, 112-124.

Goodglass H, (1980). Disorders of naming after brain damage. American Scientist 68, 647-655.

Gray CM, Singer W (1989) Stimulus-specific oscillations in orientation columns of cat visual cortex. Proc. National Academy of Sciences, 86, 1698-1702.

Gregory RL, (1970). The intelligent eye. Weidenfield & Nicholson

Grimson WEL, (1982). A computational theory of visual surface interpolation. Phil. Trans. Roy. Soc. Lond. B 298, 395.

Grinvald A, Lieke E, Frostig RD, Gilbert CD, Wiesel TN, (1986). Functional architecture of cortex revealed by optical imaging of intrinsic signals. Nature 324, 361.

Gross CG, (1973). Inferotemporal cortex and vision. Prog. Physiol. Psychol. 5, 77-123.

Grossberg S, Mingolla E, (1985). Neural dynamics of perceptual grouping : Textures, boundaries and emergent segmentations. Perception Psychophysics 38, 141-171.

Grossberg S, (1987). Cortical dynamics of three-dimensional form, color and brightness perception: I. Monocular theory. Percept. Psychophys. 41, 87-116.

Grossberg S, (1987). Cortical dynamics of three-dimensional form, color and brightness perception: II. Binocular theory. Percept. Psychophys. 41, 117-158.

Hammond P, (1986). Visual cortical processing : textural sensitivity and its implications for classical views. In Rose D & Dobson VG, (eds) Models of the visual cortex. John Wiley, pp 326-333.

Hart J, Berndt RS, Caramazza A, (1985). Category-specific naming deficit after cerebral infarction. Nature 316, 439-440.

Heit C, Smith ME, Halgren E, (1988). Neural coding of individual words and faces by the human hippocampus and amygdala. Nature 333, 773.

Hildreth EC, Koch C, (1987). The analysis of visual motion : From computational theory to neuronal mechanisms. Ann. Rev. Neurosci. 10, 477-534.

Hildreth EC, (1984). The computation of the velocity field. Proc Roy Soc Lond B 221, 189-220.

Hinton GE, Anderson JA, (1981). Parallel models of associative memory. Lawrence Erlbaum (Hillsdale)

Hinton GE, Parsons LM, (1988). Scene-based and viewer-centered representations for comparing shapes. Cognition 30, 1-36.

Hochberg J, (1984). Perception. In Brookhart JM & Mountcastle VB, (eds) The nervous system. III. Sensory processes. American Physiological Soc., pp 75-102.

Hochberg J, (1986). Representation of motion and space in video and cinematic displays. In Boff KR et al (eds), Handbook of Perception and Human Performance. Vol 1. Sensory processes and John Wiley, Chap 22

Hochberg J, (1988). Visual perception. In Atkinson RC et al (eds), Stevens' Handbook of experimental psychology. Second Edition. John Wiley, pp 195-276.

Hochstein S, Spitzer H, (1984). Zero-crossing detectors in primary visual cortex. Biol. Cybern. 51, 195-200.

Hoffman DD, Bennett BM, (1986). The computation of structure from fixed-axis motion : Rigid structure. Biol. Cybern. 54, 71-84.

Hoffman JE, (1986). The psychology of perception. In LeDoux JE & Hirst W, (eds) Mind and brain : Dialogues in cognitive neuroscience. Cambridge University Press, pp 7-32.

Horn BKP, Schunck BG, (1981). Determing optical flow. Artif. Intell. 17, 185-204.

Hubel DH, (1982). Exploration of the primary visual cortex, 1955-1978 : A review. Nature 299, 515-523.

Hubel DH, (1988). Eye, Brain and Vision. W.H. Freeman

Humpheys GW, Bruce V (1989) Visual Cognition. Lawrence Erlbaum Associates.

Humphreys GW, Quinlan PT, (1988). Normal and pathological processes in visual object constancy. In Humphreys GW & Riddoch MJ, (eds) Visual object processing : A cognitive neuropsychological perspective. Lawrence Erlbaum (Hillsdale), pp 43-106.

Humphreys GW, Riddoch MJ, (1987a). On telling your fruit from your vegetables: A consideration of category- specific deficits after brain damage. Trends Neurosci. 10, 145.
Humphreys GW, Riddoch MJ, (1987b). To see but not to see : A case study of visual agnosia. Lawrence Erlbaum
Humphreys GW, Riddoch MJ, (1988). Visual object processing : A cognitive neuropsychological perspective. Lawrence Erlbaum (Hillsdale)
Hurlbert AC, Poggio TA, (1988). Synthesizing a color algorithm from examples. Science 239, 482.
Ikeuchi K, Horn BKP, (1981). Numerical shape from shading and occuding boundaries. Artif. Intell. 17, 141-184.
Intraub H, (1980). Presentation rate and the representation of briefly glimpsed pictures in memory. J. Exp. Psychol. Hum. Learn. Mem. 6, 1-12.
Intraub H, (1981). Rapid conceptual identification of sequentially presented pictures. J. Exp. Psychol. Hum. Perc. Perf. 7, 604-610.
Jameson D, Hurvich LM (1989) Essay concerning color constancy. Annual Review of Psychology, 40, 1-22.
Johansson G, (1975). Visual motion perception. Sci. Amer. 232, 76-88.
Jolicoeur P, (1985). The time to name distorted natural objects. Memory Cognition 13, 289-303.
Julesz B, Schumer RA, (1981). Early visual perception. Ann. Rev. Psychol. 32, 575-627.
Julesz B, (1971). Foundations of cyclopean perception. University of Chicago Press
Julesz B, (1981). Textons, the elements of texture perception and their interactions. Nature 290, 91-97.
Julesz B, (1984). A brief outline of the texton theory of human vision. Trends Neurosci. 7, 41-44.
Julesz B, (1986). Stereoscopic vision. Vision Res. 26, 1601.
Kaas JH, (1987). The organization of neocortex in mammals : Implications for theories of brain function. Ann. Rev. Psychol. 38, 129-152.
Kanade T, (1981). Recovery of the three-dimensional shape of an object from a single view. Artif. Intell. 17, 409-460.
Kendrick KM, Baldwin BA (1987) Cells in temporal lobe of conscious sheep can respond preferentiallyh to the sight of faces. Science, 236, 448.
Knudsen EI, du Lac S, Esterley SD, (1987). Computational maps in the brain. Ann. Rev. Neurosci. 10, 41-66.
Koch C, Poggio T, (1986). The synaptic veto mechanism : Does it underlie direction and orientation selectivity in the visual cortex? In Rose D & Dobson VG, (eds) Models of the visual cortex. John Wiley, pp 408-419.
Koenderink JJ, (1985). Space, form and optical deformations. In Ingle DJ et al (eds), Brain mechanisms and spatial vision. Nijhoff (Holland), pp 31-58.
Kosslyn SM, Flynn RA, Amsterdam JA, Wang G (1990) Components in high-level vision: A cognitive neuroscience analysis and account of neurological syndromes. Cognition 34, 203-278.
Kulikowkski JJ, Kranda K, (1987). Image analysis performed by the visual system : Feature versus Fourier analysis and adaptable filtering. In Pettigrew JD et al (eds), Visual neuroscience. Cambridge University Press, pp 381-404.
Land EH, (1977). The retinex theory of colour vision. Sci. Amer. 237, 108-128.
Lawton D, Rieger J, Steenstrup M, (1987). Computational techniques in motion processing. In Arbib MA & Hanson AR, (eds) Vision, brain and cooperative computation. M.I.T. Press, pp 419-488.
Lee DN, (1980). The optic flow field : the foundation of vision. Phil. Trans. Roy. Soc. Lond. B 290, 169-179.
Lehky SR, Sejnowski T, (1988). Network model of shape-from-shading : neural function arises from both receptive and projective fields. Nature 333, 452.
Lettvin JY, Maturana HR, McCulloch WS, Pitts WH (1959) What the frog's eye tells the frog's brain. Proceedings of the IRE, 47, 1940-1951.
Levick WR, (1987). Sampling of information space by retinal ganglion cells. In Pettigrew JD et al (eds), Visual neuroscience. Cambridge University Press, pp 33-43.
Levine MD, (1985). Vision in man and machine. McGraw-Hill
Longuet-Higgins HC, (1981). A computer algorithm for reconstructing a scene from two projections. Nature 293, 133.
Longuet-Higgins HC, (1986). The reconstruction of a plane surface from two perspective projections. Proc. Roy. Soc. Lond. B 227, 388-410.
Marr D, Hildreth E (1980) Theory of edge detection. Proc. Royal Society of London, 207, 187-217.

Marr D, Nishihara HK, (1978). Representation and recognition of three-dimensional shapes. Proc. Roy. Soc. Lond. B 200, 269-294.
Marr D, Poggio T, (1976). Cooperative computation of stereo disparity. Proc. Roy. Soc. Lond. B 275, .
Marr D, Poggio T, (1979). A computational theory of human stereo vision. Proc. Roy. Soc. Lond. B 204, 301-328.
Marr D, Ullman S, (1981). Directional selectivity and its use in early visual processing. Proc. Roy. Soc. Lond. B 211, 151-180.
Marr D, Vaina L, (1982). Representation and recognition of the movements of shapes. Proc. Roy. Soc. Lond. B 214, 501-524.
Marr D, (1982). Vision. W.H. Freeman
Marr D, Hildreth E, (1980). Theory of edge detection. Proc. Roy. Soc. Lond. B 207, 187-217.
Marrocco RT, (1986). The neurobiology of perception. In LeDoux JE & Hirst W, (eds) Mind and brain : Dialogues in cognitive neuroscience. Cambridge University Press, pp 33-79.
Maunsell JHR, Newsome WT, (1987). Visual processing in monkey extrastriate cortex. Ann. Rev. Neurosci. 10, 363-402.
Mayhew JEW, Frisby JP, (1981). Psychophysical and computational studies towards a theory of human stereopsis. Artif. Intell. 17, 349-386.
Mayhew JEW, Longuet-Higgins HC, (1982). A computational model of binocular depth perception. Nature 297, 376.
McCarthy RA, Warrington EK, (1988). Evidence for modality-specific meaning systems in the brain. Nature 334, 428.
McClelland JL, Rumelhart DE, (1981). An interactive activation model of context effects in letter perception : Part 1. An account of basic findings. Psychological Review, 88, 375-407.
McClelland JL, Rumelhart DE, (1986). Parallel distributed processing : Explorations in the microstructure of cognition. Vol. 2. Psychological and biological models. MIT Press
McLeod P, (1987). Visual reaction time and high-speed ball games. Perception 16, 49-60.
Meadows JC, (1974). Disturbed perception of colours associated with localized cerebral lesions. Brain 97, 615-632.
Mishkin M, Ungerleider LG, Macko KA, (1983). Object vision and spatial vision: two cortical pathways. Trends Neurosci. 6, 414-416.
Mollon JD, (1982a). Colour vision and colour blindness. In Barlow HB & Mollon JD, (eds) The Senses. Cambridge University Press, pp 165-191.
Mollon JD, (1982b). Colour vision. Ann. Rev. Psychol. 33, 41-86.
Morris RGM (1989) Parallel distributing processing : Implications for Psychology and Neurobiology. Oxford : Oxford University Press.
Morton J (1979) Word recognition. In J Morton & J Marshall (eds). Psychololinguistics Series, 2, 107-156.
Movshon JA, Adelson EH, Gizzi MS & Newsome WT (1985) The analysis of moving visual patterns. Exp. Brain Res. Suppl.,11, 117-152.
Nagel HH, (1987). On the estimation of optical flow : Relations between different approaches and some new results. Artif. Intell. 33, 299-324.
Nakayama K, (1985). Biological motion processing. Vision Res. 25, 625.
Newsome WT, Wurtz RH, (1988). Probing visual cortical function with discrete chemical lesions. Trends Neurosci. 11, 394-399.
Oldfield RC, (1966). Things, words and the brain. Q. J. Exp. Psychol. 18, 340-353.
Orban GA, (1984). Neuronal operations in the visual cortex. Studies of Brain Function, 11, Springer-Verlag (Berlin)
Palmer S, Rosch E, Chase P, (1981). Canonical perspective and the perception of objects. In Long J & Baddeley A, (eds) Attention and Performance. IX. Lawrence Erlbaum (Hillsdale), pp 135-151.
Palmer SE, (1975). The effects of contextual scenes on the identification of objects. Memory Cognition 3, 519-526.
Perrett DI, Mistlin AJ, Chitty AJ, (1987). Visual neurons responsive to faces. Trends Neurosci. 10, 358.
Perrett DI, Rolls ET, Caan W, (1982). Visual neurons responsive to faces in the monkey temporal cortex. Exp. Brain Res. 467, 329-342.
Perrett DI, Rolls ET, Caan WC (1982) Visual neurons responsive to faces in the monkey temporal cortex. Experimental Brain Research, 467, 329-342.

Perrett DI, Smith PAJ, Potter DD, Mistlin AJ, Head AS (1985). Visual cells in the temporal cortex sensitive to face view and gaze direction. Proc. Roy. Soc. Lond. 223, 293-317.

Peterhans E, von der Heydt R, Baumgartner G, (1987). Neuronal responses to illusory contour stimuli reveal stages of visual cortical processing. In Pettigrew JD et al (eds), Visual neuroscience. Cambridge University Press, pp 343-351.

Petersen SE, Fox BT, Posner MI, Mintun M, Raichle ME, (1988). Positron emission tomographic studies of the cortical anatomy of single word processing. Nature 331, 585-589.

Pettigrew JD, (1987). The evolution of binocular vision. In Pettigrew JD et al (eds), Visual neuroscience. Cambridge University Press, pp 208-222.

Phillips CG, Zeki S, Barlow HB, (1984). Localization of function in the cerebral cortex: past, present and future. Brain 107, 327.

Pinker S, (1984). Visual cognition : An introduction. Cognition 18, 1-63.

Poggio GF, Poggio T, (1984). The analysis of stereopsis. Ann Rev. Neurosci. 7, 379-412.

Poggio T, Koch C, (1987). Synapses that compute motion. Sci. Amer. 256, 46-71.

Poggio T, (1984). Vision by man and machine. Sci. American 250, 106-117.

Poggio T, (1986). Early vision : From computational structure to algorithms and parallel hardware In Rosenfeld A, (ed). Human and Machine Vision. II. Academic Press, pp 190-206.

Poggio T, Gamble EB, Little JJ, (1988). Parallel integration of vision modules. Science 242, 436-439.

Posner MI, Petersen SE, Fox PT, Raichle ME, (1988). Localization of cognitive operations in the brain. Science 240, 1627-1631.

Potter MC, Faulconer BA, (1975). Time to understand pictures and words. Nature 253, 437-438.

Potter MC, (1975). Meaning in visual search. Science 187, 965-966.

Priest HF, Cutting JE, Torrey CC, Regan D, (1985). Visual flow and direction of locomotion. Science 227, 1063.

Ramachandran VS, Anstis SM, (1983). Perceptual organisation in moving patterns. Nature 304, 529-531.

Ramachandran VS, Anstis SM, (1986). The perception of apparent motion. Sci. Amer. 254, 102-109.

Ramachandran VS, (1988). Perceiving shape from shading. Sci. Amer. 259, 76-83.

Ramachandran VS, (1988). Perception of shape from shading. Nature 331, 163.

Regan D, Beverley KI, (1979). Visually guided locomotion : Psychophysical evidence for a neural mechanism sensitive to flow patterns. Science 205, 311-313.

Regan D, Beverley KI, (1981). How do we avoid confounding the direction we are looking and the direction we are moving. Science 215, 194.

Regan D, Beverley KIB, Cynader M, (1979). The visual perception of motion in depth. Sci. Amer. 241, 136-150.

Reichardt W, (1987). Evaluation of optical motion information by movement detectors. J. Comp. Physiol. A 161, 533-548.

Rhodes G, Brennan S, Carey S, (1987). Identification and ratings of caricatures : Implications for mental representation of faces. Cognitive Psychol. 19, 473-497.

Richards W (1988) Natural computation. MIT Press.

Richards W, Ullman S, (1987). Image understanding 1985-86. Ablex Publ. Corp. (Norwood)

Riddoch MJ, Humphreys GW, (1988). Picture naming. In Humphreys GW & Riddoch MJ, (eds) Visual object processing : A cognitive neuropsychological perspective. Lawrence Erlbaum (Hillsdale), pp 107-144.

Robinson DL, Petersen SE, (1986). The neurobiology of attention. In LeDoux JE & Hirst W, (eds) Mind and brain : Dialogues in cognitive neuroscience. Cambridge University Press, pp 142-171.

Robson JG, (1975). Receptive fields : Neural representations of the spatial and intensive attributes of the visual image. Handbook Perception 5, 81-112.

Rock I, (1984). Perception. W.H. Freeman (New York)

Rogers B, Graham M, (1979). Motion parallax as an independant cue for depth perception. Perception 8, 125-134.

Rolls ET, Burton MJ, Mora F (1976) Hypothalamic neuronal responses associated with the sight of food. Brain Research, 111, 53-66.

Rolls ET, Perrett DI, Caan AW, Wilson FAW, (1981). Neuronal responses related to visual recognition. Brain 105, 611-646.

Rolls ET, Sanghera MJ, Roper-Hall A (1979) The latency of activation of neurones in the lateral hypothalamus and substantia innominata during feeding in the monkey. Brain, 164, 121-135.

Rose D, Dobson VG, (1986). Models of the visual cortex. John Wiley

Rosenfeld A, (1986). Human and Machine Vision. II. Perspectives in Computing, 13, Academic Press
Rumelhart DE, McClelland JL, (1986). Parallel distributed processing: Explorations in the microstructure of cognition. Vol. 1. Foundations. MIT Press
Sakitt B, Barlow HB, (1982). A model for the economical coding of visual image in the cerebral cortex. Biol. Cybern. 43, 97-108.
Schiller PH, (1986). The central visual system. Vision Res. 26, 1351-1388.
Schwab EC, Nusbaum HC, (1986). Pattern recognition by humans and machines. Volume 2. Visual Perceptioin. Academic Press
Sejnowski TJ, Hinton GE, (1987). Separating figure from ground with a Boltzmann machine. In Arbib MA & Hanson AR, (eds) Vision, brain and cooperative computation. M.I.T. Press, pp 703-724.
Sejnowski TJ, Koch C, Churchland PS, (1988). Computational Neuroscience. Science 241, 1299-1306.
Sekular R, Blake R, (1984). Perception. New York : Knopf
Shapley R, Perry VH, (1986). Cat and monkey retinal cells and their visual functional roles. Trends Neurosci. 9, 229.
Shepard RN, Judd SA, (1976). Perceptual illusion of rotation of three-dimensional objects. Science 171, 701-703.
Shepard RN, Zare SL, (1983). Path guided apparent motion. Science 220, 632.
Siegel RA, Andersen RA, (1988). Perception of three-dimensional structure from motion in monkey and man. Nature 331, 259.
Simpson PK (1990) Artificial neural systems : Foundations, paradigms, applications and implementations. New York : Pergamon.
Smyth MM, Morris PE, Levy P, Ellis AW, (1987). Cognition in action. Lawrence Erlbaum
Spillman L, Werner JS (1990) Visual Perception : The Neurophysiological Foundations. San Diego : Academic Press.
Spoehr KT, Lehmkuhle SW, (1982). Visual information processing. W.H. Freeman (San Francisco)
Stevens KA, (1981). The information content of texture gradients. Biol. Cybern. 42, 95-105.
Stevens KA, (1988). Visual object processing from a computational perspective. In Humphreys GW & Riddoch MJ, (eds) Visual object processing : A cognitive neuropsychological perspective. Lawrence Erlbaum (Hillsdale), pp 17-42.
Thorpe S.J. & Imbert M. (1989) Biological constraints on connectionist modelling. In Pfeifer R (ed) "Connectionism in perspective". Amsterdam : Elsevier.
Thorpe S.J. & Pouget A. (1989) Coding of orientation by the visual cortex : Neural network modelling. In Pfeifer R (ed) "Connectionism in perspective". Amsterdam : Elsevier.
Thorpe S.J. (1988) Traitement de l'image chez l'homme. Techniques et Sciences Informatique, 7, 517-525.
Thorpe S.J. (1989) Coding of simple stimuli by the human visual system. In Kulikowski J.J. (ed.) "Seeing Contour and Colour", Oxford, Pergamon Press. pp 338-345.
Thorpe SJ, Rolls ET, Maddison SP, (1983). The orbitofrontal cortex : Neuronal activity in the behaving monkey. Exp. Brain Res. 49, 93-115.
Todd J, (1985). The analysis of three-dimensional structure from moving images. In Ingle DJ et al (eds), Brain mechanisms and spatial vision. Nijhoff (Holland), pp 73-94.
Tootell RBH, Silverman MS, DeValois RL, (1981). Spatial frequency columns in primary visual cortex. Science 214, 813.
Treisman A, (1986). Features and objects in visual processing. Sci. Amer. 255, 114-125.
Treisman A, (1986). Properties, parts and objects. In Boff KR et al (eds), Handbook of Perception and Human Performance. Vol 2. Cognitive processes and John Wiley, pp Chap 35
Treismen A & Gelade G (1980) A feature integration theory of attention. Cognitive Psychology, 12, 97-136.
Ullman S, (1983). The measurement of visual motion. Trends Neurosci. 6, 177.
Ullman S, (1984). Visual routines. Cognition 18, 97-159. Ullman S, (1986). Artificial intelligence and the neurosciences. Trends Neurosci. 9, 530.
Van Essen DC, Maunsell JHR, (1983). Hierarchical organization and functional streams in visual cortex. Trends Neuroscience 6, 370-375.
Voorhees H, Poggio T, (1988). Early vision and texture perception. Nature 333, 364.
Waltz D, (1975). Understanding line drawings of scenes with shadows. In Winston PH, (ed). The psychology of computer vision. Academic Press (New York), pp 19-91.
Warrington EK, (1982). Neuropsychological studies of object recognition. Phil. Trans. Roy. Soc. B 298, 15-33.

Wasserman PD (1989) Neural Computing : Theory and Practice. New York : Van Nostrand Reinhold.
Wässle H, (1987). Sampling of visual space by retinal ganglion cells. In Pettigrew JD et al (eds), Visual neuroscience. Cambridge University Press, pp 19-32.
Watt R, (1988). Visual processing : Computational psychophysical and cognitive research. Essays in Cognitive Psychology, Lawrence Erlbaum
Weisstein N, Wong E, (1986). Figure-ground organization and the spatial and temporal responses of the visual system. In Schwab EC & Nusbaum HC, (eds) Pattern recognition by humans and machines. Volume 2. Visual Perception. Academic Press, pp 31-64.
Weisstein N, Wong E, (1987). Figure-ground organization affects the early visual processing of information. In Arbib MA & Hanson AR, (eds) Vision, brain and cooperative computation. M.I.T. Press, pp 209-230.
Wilding JM, (1982). Perception : From sense to object. Hutchinson
Wilson HR, (1983). Psychophysical evidence for spatial channels. In Braddick OJ & Sleigh AC, (eds) Physical and biological processing of images. Springer-Verlag, pp 88-99.
Winston PH, (1975). The psychology of computer vision. Academic Press (New York)
Wise SP, Desimone R, (1988). Behavioral neurophysiology : Insights into seeing and grasping. Science 242, 736-740.
Witkin AP, (1981). Recovering surface shape and orientation from texture. Artif. Intell. 17, 17-46.
Yellot JI, Wandell BA, Cornsweet TN, (1984). The beginnings of visual perception : the retinal image and its initial encoding. In Brookhart JM & Mountcastle VB, (eds) The nervous system. III. Sensory processes. American Physiological Soc., pp 257-316.
Young AW & Ellis HD (1989) Handbook of research on face procesing. Amsterdam : North Holland.
Zeki S, Shipp S, (1988). The functional logic of cortical connections. Nature 335, 311-316.
Zeki S, (1980). The representation of colours in the cerebral cortex. Nature 284, 412-418.
Zihl J, von Cramon D, Mai N, (1983). Selective disturbance of movement vision after bilateral brain damage. Brain 106, 313-340.
Zucker SW, Hummel RA, (1986). Receptive fields and the representation of visual information. Human Neurobiol. 5, 121-128.
Zucker SW, (1987). The diversity of perceptual grouping. In Arbib MA & Hanson AR, (eds) Vision, brain and cooperative computation. M.I.T. Press, pp 231-262.

10

Intelligent CAD Systems

Tetsuo Tomiyama

1. Introduction

Computer Aided Design (CAD) systems are now indispensable in many industries, such as mechanical, aeronautical, electrical, automobile, architectural, and chemical industries. Particularly in mechanical engineering where geometrical information is dominant, CAD has become not optional but necessary. Recent advances of artificial intelligence (AI) and knowledge engineering technology have given a new direction for CAD, i.e., so-called intelligent CAD systems (ICAD). ICAD is advocated to be a promising approach to converting the designer's power to more essential and creative phases of design. However, unfortunately the state of the art is such that anything relevant to improving conventional CAD is called ICAD.

This tutorial paper aims at giving an extensive view that covers a wide range of issues discussed in ICAD research and identifying a way to a future CAD system that can truly be called ICAD. Chapter 2 gives a brief survey about research in CAD. Recent trends are analyzed and problems of current CAD systems are pointed out. Since designing activities and philosophy for CAD systems are completely dependent on the target area, those problems can be discussed only in a particular field. We take machine design as the subject area, because in many aspects a CAD system for machine design, being one of the most complicated software systems, has the strongest industrial impulses.

Chapter 3 proposes the concept of IIICAD (Intelligent Integrated Interactive CAD), and it is argued that we need a theoretical approach to develop IIICAD because design knowledge is considered complex. Design knowledge comprises knowledge about design objects and knowledge about design processes. Conventional CAD put emphasis more on representation of geometry than representation of design object knowledge and had absolutely no notion of design processes. Most of so-called expert systems for design do not stand on a theoretical foundation and in this sense they are *ad hoc*. It might be correct to say that expert systems technology is used just for implementational convenience. We believe that such an approach will eventually be beaten by the complexity of design knowledge and that we need a theoretical approach, instead.

Chapter 4 discusses theoretical and experimental approaches to understanding design and building a computable design process model. A design process model called the evolutionary model will be given computational interpretation. We will propose the concept of the metamodel as realization of mental models of the designers about the design object. Chapter 5 deals with an advanced approach to representing design objects. We will introduce qualitative physics to deal with so-called ontological knowledge that is indispensable for ICAD. We will also discuss that the metamodel concept is crucial as a central model of design objects. In order to implement the metamodel mechanism, qualitative physics plays a key role. Chapter 6 is a brief illustration of knowledge representation for IIICAD. In Chapter 7, the design knowledge representation language for IIICAD is described. A prototype implementation will also be demonstrated. Chapter 8 concludes the paper.

2. Trends in CAD Technology

2.1. Aspects of Design

In order to clarify the direction we should proceed, we try to understand the historical achievements of conventional CAD systems in Sections 2.2 and 2.3 and the problems in Section 2.4. Before doing this, we define three of aspects that design in common has; i.e., design is considered to consist of three components, *viz*., design activities, design object models, and design processes which are illustrated in Fig. 1 [5].

Activities include technological ones, such as drawing, sketching, calculating, retrieving information, problem solving, and writing documents, and organizational ones, such as planning, meeting, and negotiations. Depending on the domain there are varieties in models, but in mechanical engineering design most commonly used are a geometric model, an FEM model, a mathematical model, a rough skeleton model, etc. On the other hand, the design process is often classified from more organizational and technological viewpoints; i.e., the design process can be divided into conceptual, basic, detail, and production design processes.

2.2. Historical Overview

The history of CAD (Computer Aided Design) began with Sutherland's Sketchpad [109] and it has roughly three phases in its development.

- *1960's*: First generation experimental systems were developed, which resulted in a few industrially successful systems.
- *1970's*: Proliferation of two-dimensional turn-key systems into industries was observed.
- *1980's*: Three-dimensional systems became commercial. *Renaissance* of AI led to knowledge engineering of which applications could be found also in design and CAD.

The second phase was motivated by commercial (turn-key) two-dimensional drawing systems which were widely accepted by industries and, thus, successful from the point of view that they took over drawing boards. Research focused on three-dimensional solid modeling systems [75], free-form surface modeling, and CAD/CAM (Computer Aided Manufacturing) integration [36]. CAD in mechanical engineering is now in the third phase that has introduced three-dimensional (wire frame, surface, or solid) modeling systems with catch-phrases such as three-dimensional graphical presentation, CAD database, simulation, and CAE (Computer Aided Engineering).

Despite this popularity and commercial success, there are many deficiencies which have triggered research for a new generation CAD system [103]. For instance, since two-dimensional CAD systems support only the drawing activity, it is often articulated that CAD is not *Computer Aided Design* but *Computer Aided Drafting*. As CAD penetrated into design offices, we could observe a growing demand that information stored in CAD should be used

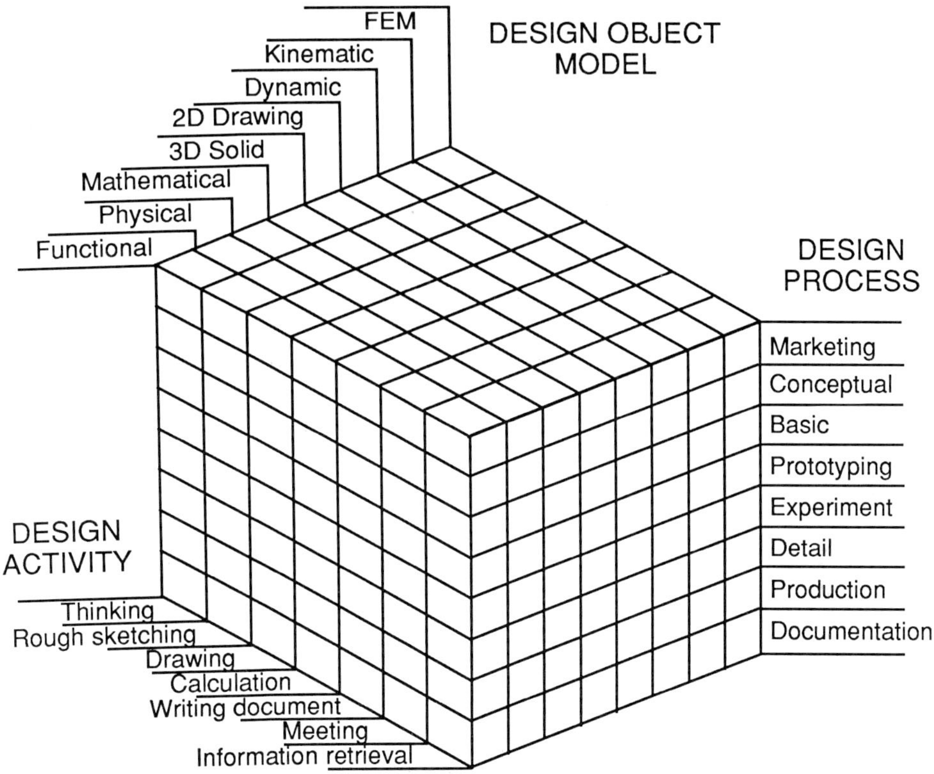

Fig. 1. Activities, models, and processes.

in various applications. Its good example is generation of CAM data and mesh data for an FEM (Finite Element Method) analysis from CAD data. Sutherland was mentioning the concept of constraint management even in the very beginning of the history of CAD [109]. This means that CAD has to have additional information, besides drawing data, to be used for other applications.

Three-dimensional systems were first considered to be innovative, revolutionary tools that could improve this situation, because they can deal with more realistic geometric representations. However, they once again turned out to be merely drawing tools for three-dimensional objects; they can convey more information than drawings, but only geometrical information of objects, leaving any other technical information behind. We can already find a considerable number of research directions towards future CAD systems to improve this situation. Needless to say, most of work owes much to recent advances of computer science and, among other things, AI.

2.3. Recent Trends

There seem to exist three distinctively different directions. One is that a future CAD system must be more *intelligent*, which is more appropriate for the name of intelligent CAD. In order to incorporate more domain knowledge and intelligence that are missing from conventional CAD, knowledge engineering technology that rose in 1980's looked most promising and influenced design and CAD[1] [4, 10, 45-48, 97, 104, 113, 114, 141-143]. These ideas led to concepts such as *intelligent CAD systems*, *knowledge based CAD systems*, and *expert systems for CAD*. This might be explained by the following reasons.

(1) Knowledge engineering, by definition, aims at use of knowledge about design in a more direct way for more complicated applications.

(2) Knowledge engineering makes it possible to integrate systems at higher semantical levels. It offers methods to describe models in a flexible and powerful way.

(3) Techniques developed in artificial intelligence (e.g., various inference techniques) can improve man-machine communication.

Early work began with applications of the so-called expert systems technology [101] to routine-type designs by extracting design knowledge (or design expertise) mostly in the form of rules [16, 28, 46, 70, 74, 115]. Most of these early systems formalized design as a process to combine pre-defined building blocks according to rules. This assumption might be appropriate to demonstrate applications of rule based systems to design. But, since there must exist *pre-defined* building blocks, it can be applicable only to so-called routine design. The design automation paradigm is an extreme of such formalization [139]. From the recognitions such as *designing as a problem solving process, designing as a decision making process,* and *designing as an optimization process,* we may implement an expert system which supports designers in the problem solving [46], decision making processes of designing [79], and optimization processes [1, 44]. The rest of designing processes might require intelligence and creativity, and hence will be difficult to support if not impossible. Thus, we implement an expert system which solves *overt* problems in a design process [11].

Use of advanced AI techniques can be classified into this direction as well. To summarize, it is a direction towards more built-in knowledge in the system both quantitatively and qualitatively. This direction includes qualitative reasoning [3, 32, 38, 61, 80, 81, 91], and feature based modeling [30, 83, 133] to add new problem solving abilities. Forbus recently proposed the concept of *intelligent computer-aided engineering* [43]. Especially in machine design, a design process can be sometimes regarded as a process to find the optimal solution under a number of constraints. Examples of this type of problem solving include constraint solving [34, 110] and geometric reasoning [6, 108, 134].

If we focus on various knowledge representation methods which may give a possibility to integrate descriptions, or at least, to allow flexible flow of information, we arrive at an idea of developing an integrated CAD framework based on knowledge engineering techniques [9, 85, 92, 116]. This type of intelligence, achieved by having more domain knowledge, further leads to the second direction of ICAD development, i.e., *integration* that the system must integrate design process, activities, subsystems, models, and eventually design knowledge. Product modeling [64] and its elaborated version, attribute modeling [82], try to model not only geometry but also any *formalizable attributes* in the same framework. If we need to take tolerances into consideration, we can incorporate information about it into the system by developing an an additional package for tolerances on top of nominal dimensions [65]. Concurrent engineering (or simultaneous engineering) [106] aims at bringing manufacturing knowledge into design. These directions should be interpreted as a way to implement more different types of knowledge but not more knowledge.

1. An interested reader may consult [105] for further bibliographical survey.

The third direction is that the system must be *interactive*, e.g., to allow the designer to explore more different design alternatives in a shorter time period. Virtual manufacturing [87] is an idea that the designer virtually creates and tests an artifact totally in a computer and, to do so, a *real-time* design/manufacturing simulation cycle is one of the key issues. Interactiveness of the system depends also on the user-friendliness of the user interface. From this point of view, *natural* representation of design knowledge is crucial [57]. By natural we mean that the system should understand the terminology of the domain and intentions of the designer. Natural language processing has invented many useful theories and technologies to understand the designers' intent. They can be applied to realize flexible and intelligent user interfaces [96]. In case of graphical interfaces, for example, graphical elements on the display should behave exactly as we expect. There is interesting work to deal with the semantics of graphical representations in this direction [90, 111].

2.4. Problems of Conventional CAD Systems

Let us consider problems of current CAD systems in order to draft out requirements for future ICAD [5].

(1) *CAD supports design processes only partially without integration.* The present trend in research is to integrate the system around models concerning products [64]. Integration of CAD, however, should have notions about design processes to deal with various different types of information other than geometry [125].

(2) *Conceptual design stages are not supported by CAD tools.* It is obvious that the so-called conceptual design stage should be supported by a certain type of CAD tool [116] which must at the same time contribute to the integration of CAD systems. Since the conceptual design stage is a highly intellectual process, this tool should be intelligent.

(3) *CAD supports few design activities.*

(4) *CAD cannot manage inaccurate, incomplete, inconsistent information.* Current CAD systems support, among other things, producing final drawings reasonably well, but there is virtually no support for conceptual design in which inaccurate, incomplete information is used.

(5) *Models are not integrated.* Integration of different models is significant in case of mechanical design which must deal with complicated structures. In the entire design process one object is represented in many models, such as a geometric model, a kinematic model, a dynamic model, etc., each of which is allowed to have different attributes.

(6) *Systems are not integrated.* Different systems use different data description schemata, which results in unnecessary confusion and interface problems. This may further imply that the real problem is the lack of integration of design knowledge.

(7) *CAD does not check errors.* CAD systems do not check semantical errors or mistakes of the designer. Sometimes, final outputs are so impressive that no one can detect such mistakes.

(8) *Data input is a problem.* The amount of (geometrical) input data for a CAD application is usually enormous, which results in errors, mistakes, and misunderstandings during man-machine communication regardless of the input device. The ultimate solution is that the system accepts substantially reduced but comprehensive, higher level data instead of raw data. This implies that the system needs to support already the very beginning of the design process, e.g., the conceptual design stage.

(9) *Terminology of the task domain cannot be understood.* Geometry-based CAD systems only understand geometry. In other words, conventional systems lack commonsense knowledge of the task domain (e.g. machine design) and they cannot understand the meanings of the designer's action and intention. This does not imply, however, that the use of natural language processing solves this problem.

(10) *CAD has only poor problem solving abilities.* Generally speaking, it is not quite common that a CAD system can answer strategic questions from the designer. If the system is able to make an appropriate suggestion for designer's queries, design work will become efficient.

3. The Concept of Intelligent CAD Systems

3.1. Intelligent Integrated Interactive CAD Systems

From the discussions in the previous chapter, the design requirements for a future CAD system can be summarized as follows.

(1) The system must cover the three aspects of design; i.e, it should support designers in the entire designing processes, using unified and integrated models with rich functions for various kinds of design activities.

(2) The system should be *integrated*; this includes

- integration of *subsystems*,
- integration of *design models* based on an integrated model description method,
- integration of *design processes* which means computerization of even very early design stages, and as its result,
- integration of *design knowledge*.

(3) The system should be *intelligent*; this includes

- *intelligent problem solving*: The system should be able to assist designers in solving design problems.
- *Intelligent support of designers*: The system should understand the task domain knowledge for more flexible man-machine communication and more powerful problem solving. This means it should be based on deeper models of machine but not so-called shallow knowledge [17, 73]. By deeper knowledge, we mean basic principle underlying the task domain
- *Intelligent interface*: The level of man-machine interaction should be high enough to provide more powerful abilities for consultation and error detection.

(4) The system should be *interactive*, so that

- the system should allow a design cycle to create and test an artifact totally in a computer in reasonably short turn-around time.
- The system should be interactive to increase the advantage of being intelligent and integrated.
- The system should directly interact on the level of meaning and intentions, not on a purely syntactical level.
- The system should provide the appropriate view on the design information, together with appropriate manipulation functions.

Based on these requirements, currently we are developing a prototype of ICAD, called IIICAD (Intelligent Integrated Interactive CAD) as an environment to easily install design knowledge [5, 9, 122]. The IIICAD project was first initiated at the Centre for Mathematics and Computer Science in Amsterdam by Bart Veth group in 1986 and now conducted also at the University of Tokyo and University of Amsterdam.

3.2. Architecture of Intelligent CAD Systems

In order to discuss the architecture of IIICAD, we first clarify the role of CAD in the design process. By doing so, the IIICAD architecture will be justified.

An important issue even in near future is that we still use CAD rather than DA (Design Automation). This means that CAD must have a *model* or descriptions about the design object which have maximum similarity to the designer's own image, and perform the best in computation and reasoning that can be expected by the present computer technology to answer questions about the model. The designer's own image about the design object might be called a *mental model* [58, 60], and it plays a crucial role in conceptual operations such as generating new concepts and performing simulations by a *thought experiment*.

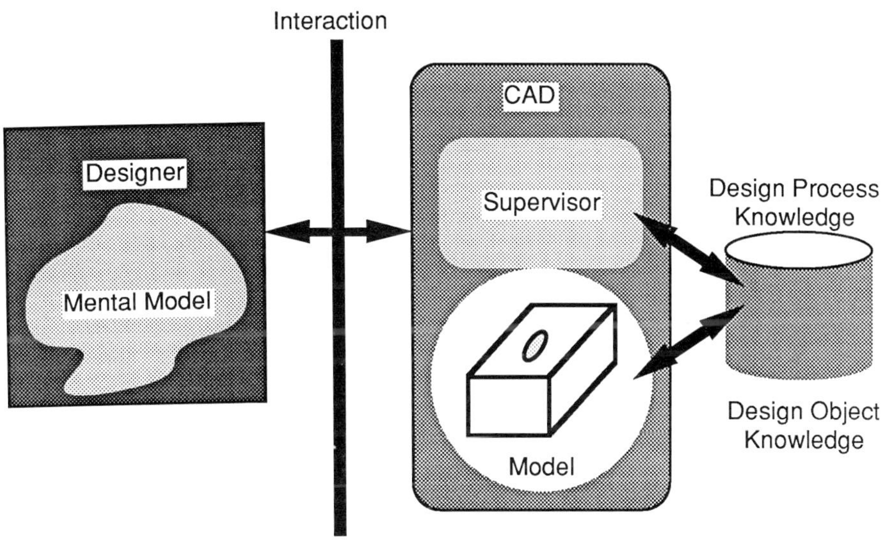

Fig. 2. CAD model.

At the same time, the system must have knowledge about the design process. This is achieved by explicit descriptions about the design process and a control mechanism to guide the designer. This means a future CAD system must be controlled by an *intelligent supervisor*. It can be justified by the absence of notions of design processes from conventional CAD systems. As shown in Fig. 2, these two components, i.e., the supervisor and models, will play a crucial role in the architecture of IIICAD. This CAD model in Fig. 2 can be once again elaborated and extended to an architecture shown in Fig. 3. The followings are the basic elements of IIICAD.

- *Supervisor* (SPV).
- *Integrated Data Description Schema* (IDDS) is a data (or even knowledge) description framework to integrate design knowledge written in *Integrated Data Description Language* (IDDL).
- *Intelligent User Interface* (IUI).
- *Application Program Interface* (API).
- *Applications*, such as geometric modeling systems, technological analysis systems, and expert systems.

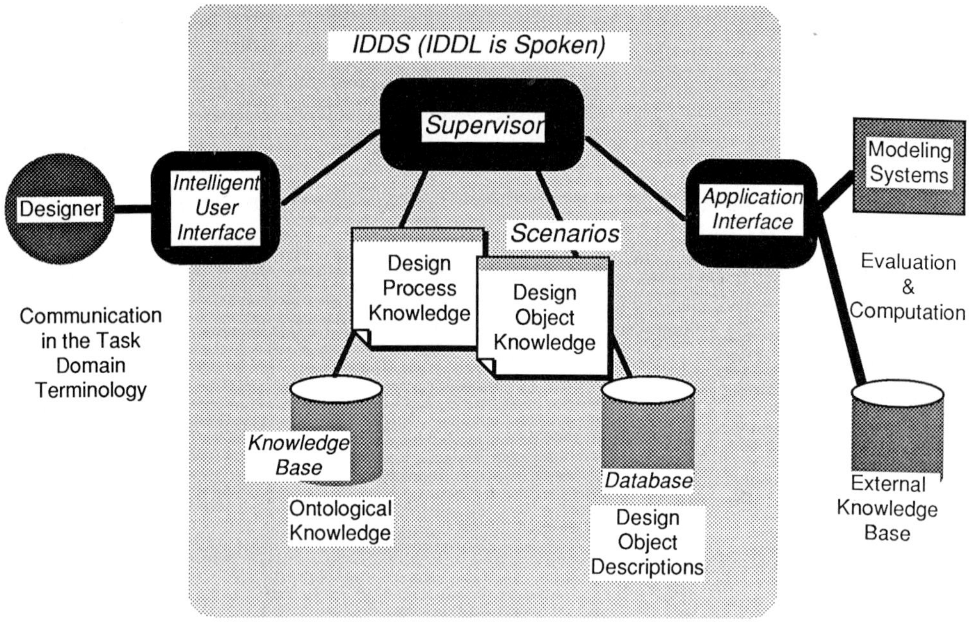

Fig. 3. The IIICAD architecture.

3.3. Theoretical Foundations for Intelligent CAD Systems

As the history of science shows, it is obvious that *ad hoc* approaches can only serve very limited problem areas but not problems in general. Since design is an intellectual activity resulting from human creativeness and the amount of skills needed for design is also large, the complexity of design knowledge is considered extremely high. Therefore, we need a sound theoretical basis to codify design knowledge [2, 9, 102]. Recent trends towards design theory and methodology also support this view [35, 41, 84, 140]. We do not think that all the problems of conventional CAD systems can be solved only by implementational techniques [29].

Thus, we must aim at building general and robust theories besides implementation technology to which the following items seem relevant;

be able to understand very difficult sentences, or you might be able to tackle slightly different language. This implies that, if you know a design methodology, you might be able to solve ill-structured problems or problems with similar structure but in a different domain. Sometimes such a methodology is a collection of episodes or lessons obtained from practices over years that must be helpful for particularly novice designers.

On the other hand, a design theory is a linguistic theory that is absolutely abstract and unnecessary to speak a language. Maybe we do not need to learn design theories, if the purpose is just to become a designer. However, if we want to construct e.g. a machine translation system, we definitely need a linguistic theory as well as the grammar. This means that we need a design theory to implement CAD systems and one of the problems of current research in engineering design methodology is that they are far from computer-implementable or computable theories [29, 62]. What we need is perhaps a method to describe design processes *logically*, so that we can trace design using computers [9].

According to Finger and Dixon [40], design process models can be categorized as follows.

(1) A *descriptive* design process model explains *how design is done* and its example is the work by Ullman and Dietterich [124] that studied mechanical design processes by protocol analysis.

(2) A *cognitive* design process model explains *the designer's behavior* and "describes the processes that underlie the set of behaviors that constitute a skill."

(3) A *prescriptive* design process model shows *how design must be done*. So-called design methodologies are its typical examples [55, 86, 94, 107].

(4) A *computable* design process model, on the other hand, "expresses a method by which a computer may accomplish a specified (design) task" and "generally is specific to a well-defined class of design problems." This type may include parametric design, configuration design, and other types of well-structured design problem solving.

4.2. General Design Theory

We have developed General Design Theory [117, 136] and its major achievements are the mathematical formulation of the design process and the justification of knowledge representation techniques in a certain situation. General Design Theory is a descriptive model that tries to explain how design is conceptually performed in terms of knowledge manipulation. In General Design Theory, a design process is regarded as a mapping from the function space onto the attribute space both of which are defined on the entity concept set. From this formalization based on axiomatic set theory, we can mathematically derive interesting theorems which can well explain a design process.

4.2.1. Design in Ideal Knowledge. We begin with three axioms, the entity concept set, and its topology to describe design knowledge.

Axiom 1 (Axiom of recognition)

Any entity can be recognized or described by attributes and/or other abstract concepts.

Axiom 2 (Axiom of correspondence)

The entity set S' and the set of entity concept (ideal) S have one-to-one correspondence.

Axiom 3 (Axiom of operation)

The set of abstract concept is a topology of the set of entity concept.

Here, we can introduce *ideal knowledge* which knows all of the elements of the entity set and that can describe each element by abstract concepts without ambiguity. The most

- knowledge engineering,
- computer graphics,
- geometric modeling,
- user interface management,
- database technology, and
- software engineering.

We propose here to build a *theory of CAD* [9] that comprises three subtheories, *viz*., a theory of design (processes), a theory of design objects, and a theory of knowledge. The first two are concerned with design itself and correspond to the two aspects of design, i.e., processes and models, while the last one is rather philosophical or metaphysical. The activity aspect of design can be included by the use of a wider range of design knowledge in different occasions. The theory of design objects is domain dependent, whereas the rest two are domain independent. Note that we must be able to build CAD for VLSI design, for example, by replacing theory of machines with theory of VLSI.

4. Theory of Design Processes

4.1. Design Theory and Methodology

Design objects, such as a machine part and a floor plan, can now be reasonably represented in computers owing to the virtue of geometric modeling. Compared with design objects, design processes are not well described nor even understood. In fact, IIICAD should support designers in wider range of design processes in an integrated way. This forces us to describe a design process, preferably, in a mathematical way, but we also realize we have no such method. Thus, theories of design processes are necessary;

(1) to clarify what design is,

(2) to formalize design processes, and

(3) to formalize design knowledge.

If we do not know what design is, we are obliged to use *ad hoc* approaches to building a CAD system which might be powerful in a particular field but not in general. At the same time, when we try to apply knowledge engineering techniques to CAD systems, we do not have a guide to formalize design knowledge so that these techniques can be used. This results in a hopeless trial-and-error search for the most appropriate knowledge representation technique. Therefore, the formalization of design processes and design knowledge (particularly, by mathematical means, such as logic) is extremely crucial.

Historically speaking, studies on engineering design resulted in design methodologies and typical examples of such efforts to theorize design can be found in the WDK publication series[2] (e.g. see [33, 54]). In this paper, we consider a design methodology as a description about how to design, while a design theory is an abstract theory about how design proceeds. There is a good analogy between design and language. In order to speak a foreign language, it might be useful to learn the grammer, which might not always necessary. For instance, if you are a native speaker of Portugues, perhaps you don't need to learn the Spanish grammer to speak it. However, if you have grammatical knowledge, there is one advantage; you might

2. Series editor: V. Hubka, ETH Zurich, CH-8092 Zurich, Switzerland. Publisher: Heurista, Postfach 102, CH-8028 Zurich, Switzerland.

significant result of having the ideal knowledge, which can be proved from those three axioms, is that design as a mapping from the function space to the attribute space immediately terminates when the specifications are described. (Since we perfectly know everything in the ideal knowledge, when we complete describing our specifications in terms of function the solution is obtained in terms of attributes.) This tells that design in the ideal knowledge is a mapping process from the function space to the attribute space without substantial computation required (see Fig. 4).

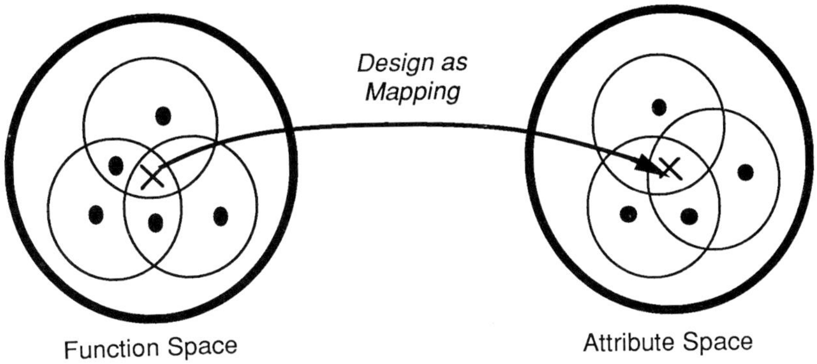

Fig. 4. Design process in the ideal knowledge.

4.2.2. Design in Real Knowledge. The situation in the ideal knowledge is not the case in the real design and we need to take the following characteristics into consideration:

(1) Design is not a simple mapping process but rather a stepwise refinement process where the designer seeks the solution satisfying constraints.

(2) The concept of function is difficult to formalize objectively, because it includes sense of value which can be different from person to person. Instead, we use *behavior* to deal with function.

(3) The ideal knowledge does not take physical constraints into consideration and it may produce design solutions such as permanent machines.

These restrictions are considered in the *real knowledge* in which design is regarded as a process that the designer builds the goal and tries to satisfy the specifications without violating physical constraints. In order to formalize the real knowledge, we first define a physical law as a description about the relationship between physical quantities of entities and the field and the concept of physical laws as one of the abstract concepts and formed when one looks at a physical phenomenon as manifestation of physical laws. Physical laws constraint entities in the real world; in other words any feasible entity must be explicable by physical rules. This fact can be proved as a theorem.

Theorem 1

The set of physical law concepts is a base of topology of the set of (feasible) entity concepts.

An interesting fact about the real knowledge is that we can prove finiteness or boundedness of our knowledge by having the following, a little bit too mathematical hypothesis.

Hypothesis

There exist finite subcoverings for any coverings of the set of feasible entity concepts made of sets chosen from the set of physical law concepts.

Basically, this hypothesis says that a feasible entity is explicable by not an infinite number but a finite number (as small as possible) of physical laws. From this hypothesis, we can prove an interesting theorem which explains that an attribute has a value, if it is possible at all to measure the distance.

4.2.3. Evolutionary Design Process Model. The next step is to formalize design processes in the real knowledge. For this purpose, the concept of *metamodels* is formally introduced, such that a metamodel is a finite set of attributes and the metamodel set is the set of all metamodels. If we choose the set of physical law concepts as the metamodel set, the entity as the limit of evolution is the design solution.

Theorem 2

If we choose concepts that can be explained by physical law concepts as the metamodel, we can describe the design specifications by the topology of metamodel, and there exists the design solution which is an element of this metamodel.

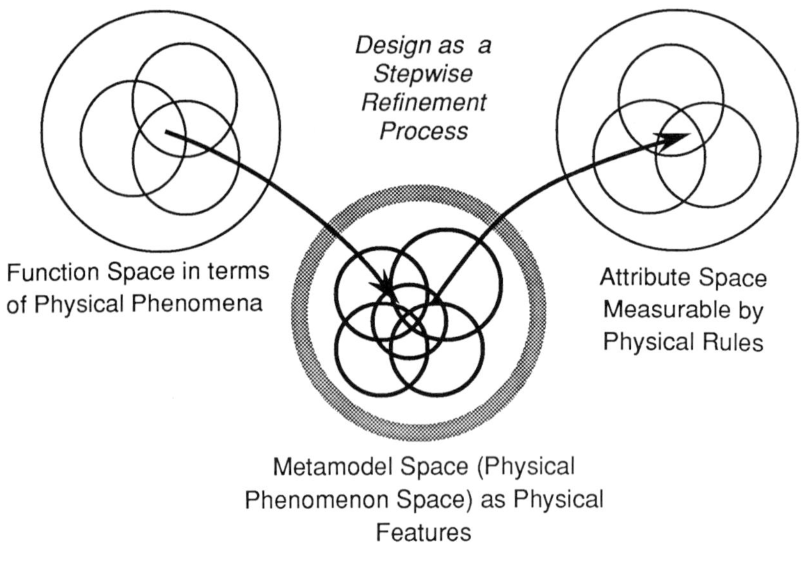

Fig. 5. Design process in the real knowledge.

Theorem 2 guarantees that we are able to design as far as specifications are given in terms of (physical) behaviors and solutions are described in terms of attributes that can be measured by physical laws. Furthermore, solutions contain only those can be realized physically; in other words we are not allowed to consider objects that contradict to physical laws. Figure 5 depicts a design process in the real knowledge in which we design, in fact, physical behaviors of the design object.

At the same time, the theorem indicates that a design process is a stepwise transformation process and solutions are obtained in a gradual refinement manner. In the ideal knowledge, design is a direct mapping process from the function space to the attribute space, while in the real knowledge, design is a stepwise, evolutionary transformation process.

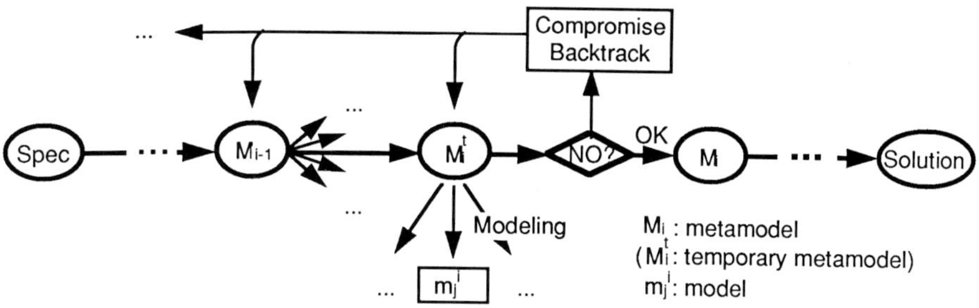

Fig. 6. The evolutionary design process model.

Figure 6 depicts this design process, which we call *evolutionary design process of metamodels*.

This model is a descriptive and maybe prescriptive model. The design object is stored in the central model, since models for various kinds of evaluation will be derived from this metamodel. There are many steps between the specification and the solution, and the metamodel is used as a place for designers to evolve design objects (in CAD terms as a working database). The metamodel can be a set of logical assertions and a model will be constructed from it using knowledge for evaluation. In this evolutionary design process model, design is treated as a sequence of unit processes, which is described as follows. The metamodel must have various information about not only design objects but also processes in order to perform those unit processes sequentially.

(a) The designer observes the current status of the metamodel and find what is decided next.

(b) She/He thinks around and generates candidate solutions for the given specifications.

(c) The designer evaluates their candidates using various models.

(d) She/He decides which candidate solution they adopt. Revising the metamodel means improvement of the design toward the final solution which satisfies the specifications. If there is no such solution, she/he must go back to and revise the current or older metamodel.

So far, we could theoretically formalize the concept of the metamodel based on General Design Theory. It has the following three meanings;

(1) as a central modeling mechanism to integrate models,

(2) as a mechanism to model physical phenomena (because metamodels must be explicable by physical laws), and

(3) as a working database for designers in the evolutionary design process model.

4.3. Design Experiment and a Cognitive Design Process Model

General Design Theory was developed as a descriptive model of design from a purely theoretical point of view. However, descriptive models do not necessarily justify the IIICAD architecture of ICAD nor derive the functional specifications for IDDL, the knowledge representation language for IIICAD. To do so, we need a computable design process model that should coincide, at least to some extent, with a cognitive model which explains actual design activities.

We began with what we call *design experiments* [112, 137, 138] to collect experimental data about design. It is a kind of psychological experiment in which designers are asked to design a mechanism from a given set of specifications. The whole designing session is recorded by a video tape recorder and a CAD-like drawing tool and analyzed by the protocol analysis method [37]. This experimental approach is also studied by e.g. Ullman *et al.* [124], Goel [49], and Baker *et al.* [8].

A cognitive model of design process could be derived from the results of design experiments. We could observe that a design process can be decomposed into small design cycles. Each design cycle has the following subprocesses.

(1) *Awareness of the problem* to pick up a problem by comparing the object under consideration and the specifications.

(2) *Suggestion* to suggest key concepts needed to solve the problem.

(3) *Development* to construct candidates for the problem from the key concepts using various types of design knowledge. When developing a candidate, if there is something unsolved, it becomes a new problem which is solved in another design cycle.

(4) *Evaluation* to evaluate the candidates in various ways, such as structural computation, simulation of behavior, and cost evaluation. If a problem is found as the result of evaluation, it also becomes a new problem to be solved in another design cycle.

(5) *Conclusion* to decide which candidate to adopt so as to modify the descriptions of the object.

Figure 7 illustrates the cognitive design process model. It has also a distinction between *action* and *object* levels. Object level activities are concerned with operations about the design object, while action level activities are more or less related to the design process. For example, deciding which problem to solve is an action level activity. This will be elaborated later in Section 4.5. Note that this cognitive design process model with five subdesign cycles is similar to the evolutionary design process model which also has four unit processes described in Section 4.2.3.

4.4. Logical Formalization of Design Processes

4.4.1. Design as a Deductive Reasoning Process. In describing design processes logically, it is reasonable to assume the following simple model as a first step;

$$S \cup K \vdash Ds$$

where S, K and Ds are a set of formulae that mean the specifications, knowledge used in design, and the design solutions, respectively. If there are required specifications for design and knowledge to use, solutions can be derived from the specifications and the knowledge as the results of deduction. This idea can be found also in [27, 123].

Our experimental analysis also made clear that design had two issues which must be cared, i.e., parallelism and retractability of the design process. To deal with these, we introduce two non-standard logics, [59] *viz*., modal logic [56] and non-monotonic logic [93].

Modal logic can be seen as the logic of necessity and possibility and is defined as an extension of normal proposition logic or predicate logic. Modal logic is interpreted in multi-worlds, while the standard logic is interpreted in a single world. **L**p means that p is necessary and is valid in a certain world, if and only if predicate p is valid in every world which is accessible from that world. **M**p means that p is possible and is valid in a certain world, if and only if predicate p is valid in one or more worlds which is accessible from that world. We

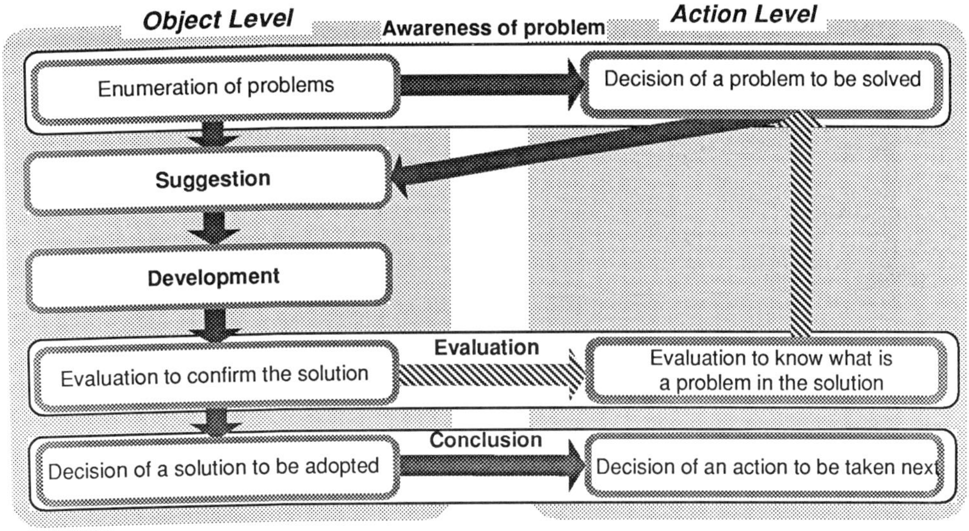

Fig. 7. The cognitive design process model.

use these properties to represent design processes, i.e., one world corresponds to one solution (or one proposal) and accessibility corresponds to the flow of design processes. In this interpretation **L**p represents what is always necessary through the entire design process, e.g., the required specifications. **M**p represents what holds during design process, e.g., a particular property of a particular solution.

Retractions in human thought processes cannot be expressed in standard logic. But, non-monotonic logic has a new symbol **A** which designates belief which is believed, if there is no contrary fact. For example,

$$p \rightarrow \mathbf{A}q$$

means that, "if p is true and there is no contrary to believe q, q is true." We use this type of non-monotonic expressions to express weak statements in design processes which may be retracted in later processes. For instance, we represent statements of suggestion as non-monotonic expressions.

We have translated the protocol data obtained in design experiments into this logical form using modal and non-monotonic logics (see Fig. 8). We can conclude from this attempt as follows:

(1) Most of design processes are represented as deductive processes.

(2) Modal expressions are useful to represent stepwise design processes and designers' standpoints.

(3) Backtracking and avoidance of inconsistence in design processes are similar to those in non-monotonic reasoning.

awareness-of-problem(mechanism-to-check-soldout(main-body, ?))
(world 1)**MA**mechanism-to-check-soldout(main-body, photo-sensor)
(world 1)**LA**high(cost(photo-sensor))
(world 2)**MA**mechanism-to-check-soldout(main-body, spring)
(world 2)mechanism-to-check-soldout(main-body, spring) → be-stressed(package)
(world 2)**M**be-stressed(package)
(world 2)**L**(weak(x) → ¬be-stressed(x))
(world 2)**L**weak(package)
(world 2)**L**¬be-stressed(x)
(world 2)**M**be-stressed(package) and **L**(¬be-stressed(x)) is contradiction
(world 2)**M**¬mechanism-to-check-soldout(main-body, spring)
(world 1)**L**¬high(cost(photo-sensor))
evaluation
conclusion(mechanism-to-check-soldout(main-body, ?), ?=photo-sensor)
Lmechanism-to-check-soldout(main-body, photo-sensor)

Fig. 8. Examples of logical formalization of the protocol data.

4.4.2. MTMS for Design Information Management. Assuming that design is a deductive reasoning process,

$$S \cup K \vdash Ds,$$

requests that for each world we have to manage both specifications S and knowledge K which represent a *snapshot* of the metamodel. Here by management of S and K, we mean that these two must be appropriately revised as the metamodel descriptions change. Such changes, or transitions, of the metamodel have three properties; i.e., sequentiality, branching, and retractivity. For this purpose, we have developed MTMS (Modal logic based Truth Maintenance System) to maintain relationships among worlds.

MTMS employs the concept of *possible worlds* in modal logic (we choose S4 system) to represent specifications and knowledge and *accessibilities between worlds* to represent transitions that are monotonic. A world contains two types of formulae, i.e., facts and rules. A fact is a positive or negative atomic formula like $p(a)$ and $\bar{}q(b)$. We use clause-like rules; a rule has a condition part consisting of conjunction of facts only and a conclusion part consisting of disjunction of facts only. Example rules are:

$$P \cap \neg Q \rightarrow R, \quad p(x) \rightarrow q(x), \quad \neg p(x) \rightarrow q(x) \cup r(x).$$

MTMS constructs a tree structure of possible worlds and generates a world corresponding to the currently valid set of specifications and knowledge (Fig. 9). MTMS automatically creates the accessibility graph corresponding to accessibilities among worlds. This graph is generated, such that a subsuming world is accessible from the subsumed world. Since we have decided transitions between worlds are monotonic, each world has only to preserve the differences from the subsumed world.

There are two types of operations of MTMS. One is local operations which can be used only within the current world and accessible worlds from it. They are used when the problem solver concerns only with the current state of the knowledge. The other is global operations which handles worlds globally. They are used when the problem solver needs to compare

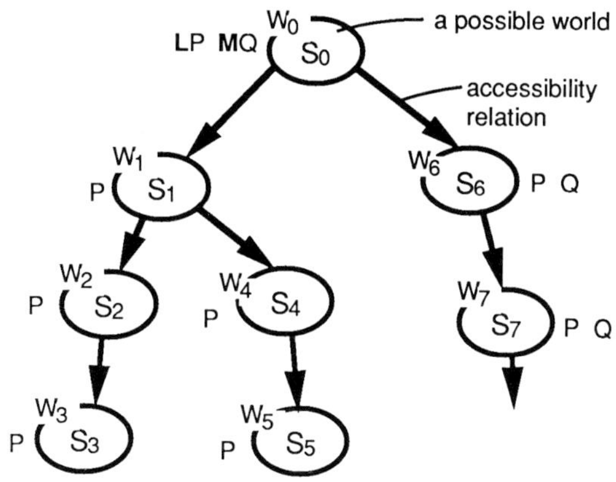

Fig. 9. Worlds in MTMS.

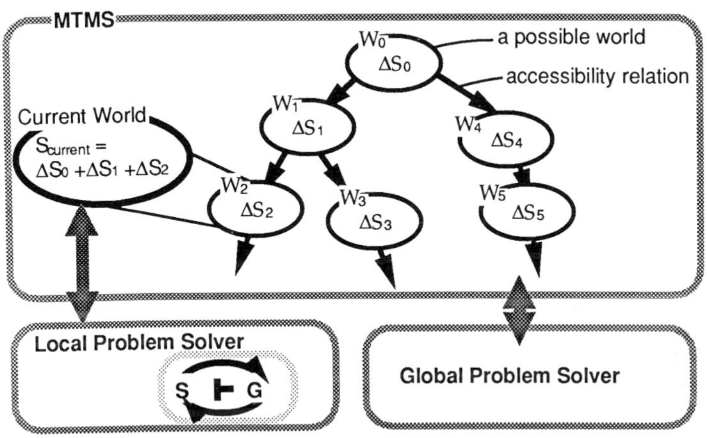

Fig. 10. The MTMS system.

several worlds, to look for a world which satisfies given requirements, to alter the initial or an intermediate state of the world, etc.

MTMS is basically a system that maintains relationships among worlds and can be applied to manage design information in the evolutionary design process where the metamodel descriptions can get detailed and be revised again and again. MTMS is similar to TMS (Truth Maintenance System) [31] in that all of the results when backtracking occurs are preserved, and ATMS (Assumption based TMS) [26] in that all labels are not computed. TMS maintains consistency among propositions derived from different justifications, when it is told a new proposition. When a contradiction is found, TMS tries to distinguish "what is believed'' from ''what is not believed'' using the dependency graph. ATMS aims at managing possibly contradicting worlds intelligently by maintaining *assumptions*. It is possible to directly switch from one world (or a set of beliefs) to another by changing assumptions, without tracing back the reasoning tree (i.e., backtracking), because ATMS maintains the differences among worlds as assumptions. Using ATMS for the maintenance of worlds is a good idea, because there is no backtracking. However, since in many cases worlds are used in a chronologically sequence for controlling inference, ATMS might not be cheap for such a task. MTMS is appropriate to represent incremental, chronological processes, like design processes.

Based on these ideas, a prototype MTMS system was implemented in Common Lisp on a Sun workstation. Figure 10 shows the structure of the MTMS system. The local problem solver tries to solve a design problem in the current world. A contradiction in a world corresponds to a situation in a real design session in which the designer finds that the candidate in that world has problems. If such a contradiction is found, the global problem solver (or the designer) tries to solve it by means such as retracting an assumption and abandoning the whole world, and changes the current world. MTMS allows for these changes at a cheaper cost than ATMS.

4.4.3. Design as a Non-Deductive Reasoning Process. In the previous discussions in this section, design was considered as a deductive reasoning process from specifications and design knowledge to design solutions. However, there are difficulties in trying to understand the whole of the design process in this way.

First, design is not always performed with complete information. This model requires complete descriptions for specifications, which is not the case in domains such as mechanical design where refinement of the specifications is a crucial part of the design process to obtain complete specifications from incomplete ones. For example, Maunier and Dixon modeled hierarchical mechanical system design as *iterative respecification* [76]. This implies that refinement of specifications and designing of objects are performed mutually in design; i.e., refinement of specifications recall next designing processes and results of designing objects request to refine specifications. Thus, not only deduction but also *abduction* [39] is needed for formalization of design processes to refine the specifications.

Secondly, knowledge in this model is concerned with how to design objects, i.e., what the designer should do for the given specifications. A typical example of this is, ''if there is a specification S_1, then use a design object D_1.'' Although it may be useful for routine design, it is not appropriate to more flexible and creative design in which e.g. knowledge on object properties and behaviors play an important role. We think knowledge on object properties and behaviors is more primary than knowledge about how to design, because a designer can design even when she/he faces a task to design a new product using such knowledge on object properties and behaviors.

The third problem, which is related to the second, is incompleteness and inconsistency of the knowledge. When the designed object does not satisfy the specifications, it should be regarded that the knowledge base was initially incomplete rather than inconsistent. Therefore, we need to deal with a method to make an incomplete knowledge base complete.

Here, we propose to regard design solutions and knowledge as the premise and the specification as the conclusion. A design process is formalized as a bidirectional process;

$$Ds \cup Ko \vdash P$$

where Ds is a set of logical formulae describing design solutions which the designer wants to obtain, Ko is knowledge on object properties and behavior, and P is properties which design solutions have. Required specifications are included in P. Given design knowledge Ko and the required properties P as the specifications, the designer tries to get a candidate which is expected to satisfy the specifications by abduction. While abduction merely proposes literally candidates, deduction is then performed to see if the candidate does not contradict with the given constraints including the specifications. This results in that the obtained candidate is detailed with complete descriptions. If the candidate does not satisfy the specifications, the designer either tries alternative candidates or modifies design knowledge and the specifications. This recalls further abductive or deductive processes, and finally complete descriptions of the solution and the specifications are obtained. If there is no more way to take, the design process terminates.

We can solve the first and second problems in this framework, but there still remains the third problem that we must deal with an incomplete knowledge base. We introduce *circumscription* [77] for solving this problem. We assume that every knowledge is valid, only when it is used in a certain situation. At the same time, it is not an easy task to explicitly describe applicable situations for every knowledge in advance. Therefore, we can only identify the applicability of knowledge when detecting a contradiction. For a given set of logical formulae, circumscription can be used to compute exceptions that caused the contradiction and to formulate them explicitly as a new situation. By doing so, the original knowledge is modified and becomes capable of handling incompleteness.

4.5. Computable Design Process Model

In this section, we show a computable model of design processes based on deduction, abduction, and circumscription, and we interpret the cognitive model described in Section 4.3 in terms of the computable model. A similar approach was discussed by Coyne *et al.* [22, 23] for building knowledge-based design systems and they put an emphasis on the rule-based approach.

The suggestion subprocess is a process the designer tries to find feasible solutions. This means that this subprocess is to obtain Ds from P and Ko and can be regarded as an *abduction* process. Peirce introduced abduction as an *ampliative reasoning*, i.e, it causes enlargement of what is known [39]. Peirce's abduction is considered to be a *weak* logical reasoning from a consequent to an antecedent, because it may commit an error of *the fallacy of affirming the consequent.*

On the other hand, the development and the evaluation processes are regarded as *deduction*. In these subprocesses, the designer applies her/his knowledge to the candidates and obtains what can be known at the moment. This is suitable for deduction, which was termed as *explicative reasoning* by Peirce. The development subprocess mainly uses knowledge to find out what properties the design object has, whereas the evaluation subprocess mainly uses knowledge to compare those properties obtained in the development subprocess with expectations. These two processes are to obtain P from Ds and Ko in our framework.

While the designer is developing or evaluating, she/he sometimes encounters a difficulty about the solution and defines a new problem yet to be solved. It is a jump from a development or evaluation subprocess to an awareness-of-problem subprocess. We interpret it as *circumscription*.

Difficulty on design appears as a contradiction in the theory[3]. For example, suppose the theory consists of

3. Here a *theory* denotes a set of logical formulae.

$$\{A \rightarrow B,\ A \rightarrow \neg C,\ \neg C \rightarrow \neg B,\ A\}.$$

If a contradiction is detected in the theory, we add literals of abnormal predicates to formulae in the theory and circumscribe these abnormal predicates with the theory.

$$\{A \cap \neg ab_1 \rightarrow B,\ A \cap \neg ab_2 \rightarrow \neg C,\ \neg C \cap \neg ab_3 \rightarrow \neg B,\ A\}$$

Then we obtain a set of modified formulae in which their abnormal predicates are substituted by non-empty formulae. For this example, we obtain a set of substitutions for the abnormal predicates, such as

$$ab_1 = \neg C,\ ab2 = false,\ ab3 = false.$$

Thus, the set is now modified to

$$\{A \cap C \rightarrow B,\ A \rightarrow \neg C,\ \neg C \rightarrow \neg B,\ A\}$$

Now we can avoid the contradiction, but we cannot conclude B, which represents the required specification, from the current design solutions. One possibility to conclude B is to manage to conclude C and this is a new problem to be solved. This is the process which makes a new problem from contradiction, and therefore it represents an awareness-of-process subprocess.

Although we discussed in Section 4.3 jumps from a development and an evaluation subprocess to an awareness-of-problem subprocess, we have not mentioned how to start a design cycle, i.e, an awareness-of-problem subprocess. These seem to be a problem of meta-level operations.

Metal-level architectures for reasoning are suggested in many ways. For example, Weyhrauch [131] proposed FOL which is a meta-level reasoning system on first-order logic. In our approach, operations on building theories and on how to do reasoning are introduced as meta-level operations to

- set up *Ds*,
- set up *P*,
- set up *Ko*,
- revise *Ds* by abduction from *P* and *Ko*,
- revise *P* by deduction from *Ds* and *Ko*, and
- modify *Ko* by circumscription on *Ds*, *P* and *Ko*.

Starting the design cycle is equivalent operations to set up *P* and *Ko*, for instance. Knowledge about how to design can be represented as a sequence of the operations in this level.

We do not interpret the conclusion subprocess in the logical framework. It is a decision making process to consider all information obtained by other types of reasoning and we believe this must be left with the designer, because we are aiming at CAD rather than DA. Figure 11 summaries the discussion and illustrates the correspondences between the subprocesses and different types of logical reasoning. This proposes, in fact, our computable design process model.

4.6. Design Simulation

We implemented a system that can *simulate* design processes based on the computable design process model described in the previous section. The system, called *Design Simulator* can demonstrate computer simulation of real design sessions by logically tracing back the protocol data obtained by design experiment.

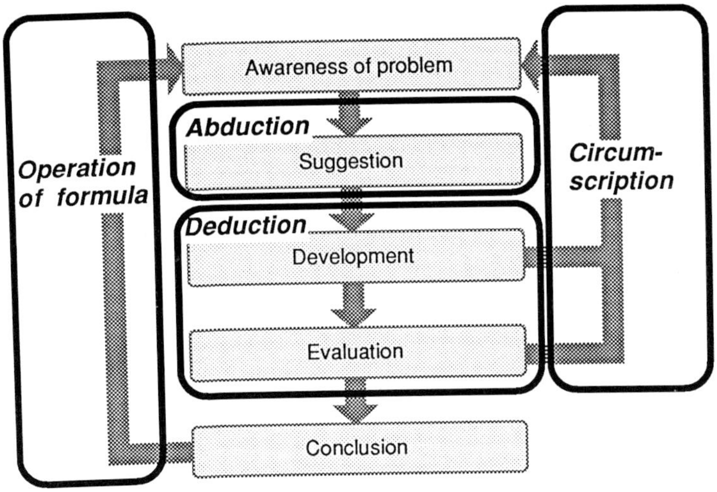

Fig. 11. The computable design process model.

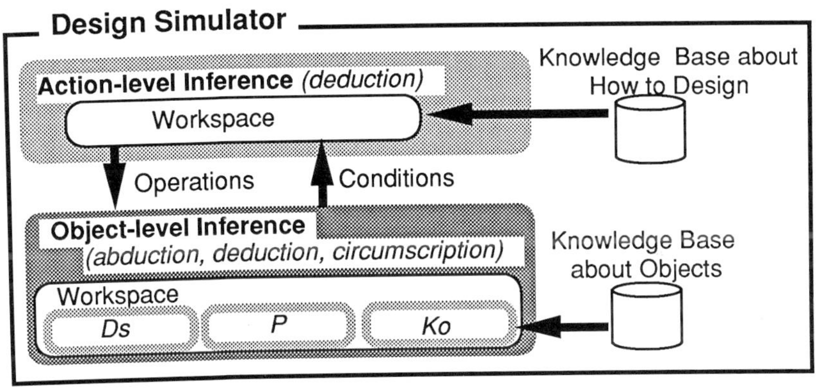

Fig. 12. Design Simulator.

It consists of meta-level inference, workspaces *Ds*, *P* and *Ko*, and three inference subsystems, which are deduction, abduction and circumscription subsystems (Fig. 12). The meta-level inference is done by a simple deduction system. Knowledge used on this level is concerned with how to design including knowledge about selecting knowledge bases and scheduling reasoning according to the condition of the object level. Results of this deduction is a sequence of operations on the object level. The object level inference is performed by abduction, deduction and circumscription that modify the current state of *Ds*, *P* and *Ko*. This may result in contradictions which are reported to the meta-level as the condition of the object level. *Ko* contains knowledge as Horn clauses, and *P* and *Ds* contain objects and their properties as atom formulae which have only a literal. The system asks the user when there are some alternatives, in particular when she/he has to make a decision in the conclusion subprocess.

The system is implemented in Allegro Common Lisp and X11 on a Sun-4 workstation. Figure 13 shows part of the protocol data used for design simulation. The task was to design a scale. Figure 14 shows a snapshot of the system display solving this example. It is obvious that this system does not really design as a human design does, because it has no ability e.g. to answer a question at the conclusion subprocess. This means that *semantical* or in our terminology, ontological information is an ingredient missing from the system. In the next chapter, we deal with this problem.

(1) What mechanism does a standard scale use?
(2) It measures the weight like this (Figure A).

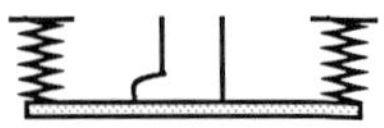

Figure A

...
(3) If we can use a rack and pinion (Figure B), we can measure the weight because the displacement is in proportion to the weight.
(4) Anyway, we think the indicator first.
(5) As it translates 5mm of the displacement to the 100kg weight, the displacement per 1kg is 0.05mm.

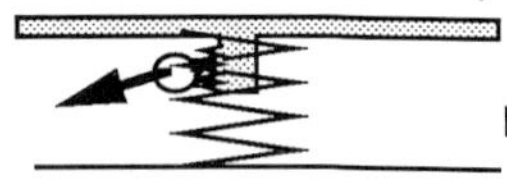

Figure B

(6) It is impossible to realize it like Figure B.
(7) If we don't mind the accuracy, it is possible by using many gears.
...
(8) But a standard scale must use a simpler mechanism.
...

Fig. 13. Design protocol data.

5. Theory of Design Objects

5.1. Theory of Design Objects and Ontological Knowledge

Although representation of design objects is perhaps the most developed area in CAD studies (e.g. geometric modeling [75]), yet there exist issues to be further studied [116]. First, typically a design process begins with ambiguous or rough descriptions of the design object and they will be gradually detailed. Design objects cannot be given fixed or rigid representation schemes.

Second, in engineering design we need to deal with the physical world anyway. Knowledge about the physical world must be incorporated into the system symbolically. For instance, consider developing an expert system which can perform a conceptual design of machines. The system must understand how basic functions are realized, e.g., by which kind of mechanism. This means the system requires deeper knowledge about mechanisms constructed through fundamental understanding of physical phenomena. *Qualitative physics* [12, 130, 132] is an approach to handling this type of knowledge and can be used for symbolically representing the structure and reasoning about dynamic behaviors of physical systems. The symbolic (or qualitative) nature of reasoning in qualitative physics is also useful to reason about behaviors of the design object from rough descriptions that will be gradually detailed.

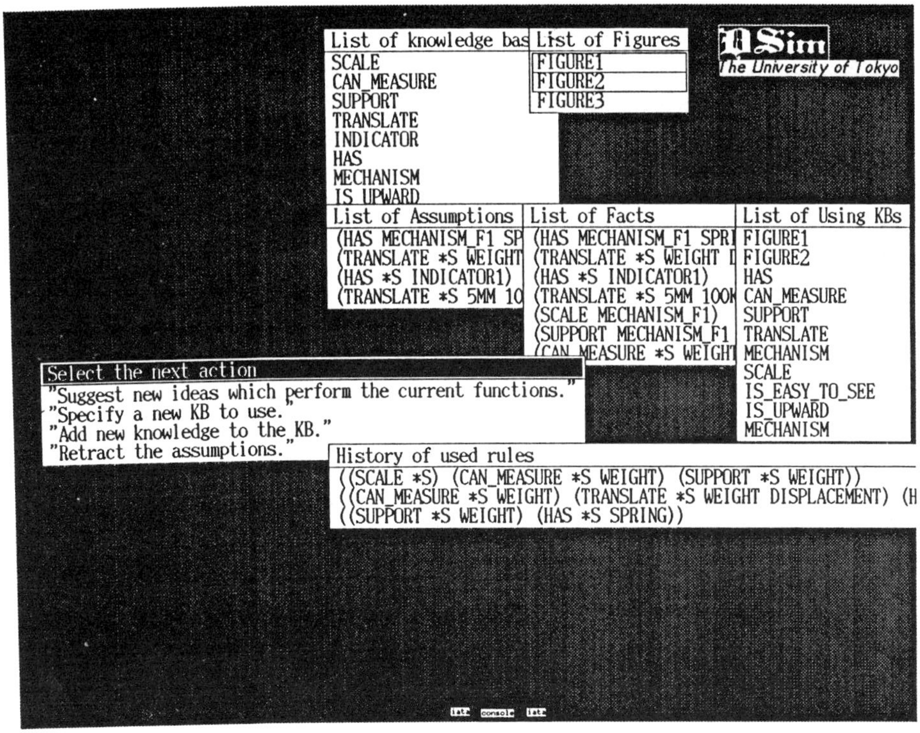

Fig. 14. Design simulation.

Third, we may realize that we simply do not know how to describe basic concepts, such as machine, function, attribute, etc.

Thus, we need a theory of design objects to deal with,

- knowledge about underlying principles of the task domain, i.e., *deeper* or *ontological* knowledge [51, 52] that is one of the major elements that are missing from conventional CAD, and
- how to describe basic concepts, such as machine structure, behavior, function, and attribute.

In Section 5.2, we propose to incorporate ontological knowledge that can be used in IIICAD, first of all, to envision physical phenomena and to generate models of the design object. Given a set of environment conditions, we can reason about what might happen and set up an appropriate object model as symbolic relationships between variables that denote physical parameters. This may solve the problem of representing structure, behavior, function, etc. Section 5.3 gives a brief survey about the concept of features, which is now considered to be a crucial issue in CAD research. In Section 5.4, we further discuss that ontological knowledge can be used as knowledge to manage multiple models in IIICAD, which is an integration issue.

5.2. Qualitative Physics

5.2.1. Basic Concepts. Qualitative physics has two roles, *viz*., to reason about dynamic behaviors of physical systems and to symbolically model their structure and framework [67]. Historically speaking, numerical and analytical methods have been dominating in engineering design. Physical systems are modeled in terms of differential equations that must be built prior to the analysis. Once these equations are described, we can predict behaviors of physical systems as chronological changes of variables representing physical quantities. Qualitative physics, on the other hand, deals with both building a symbolic model of a physical system and predicting the behavior qualitatively. In our view, the modeling aspect, i.e., building a symbolic model of a physical system, is of greater interest than predicting behaviors, because once such a model is constructed we will be able to use conventional numerical or analytical methods to find out behaviors.

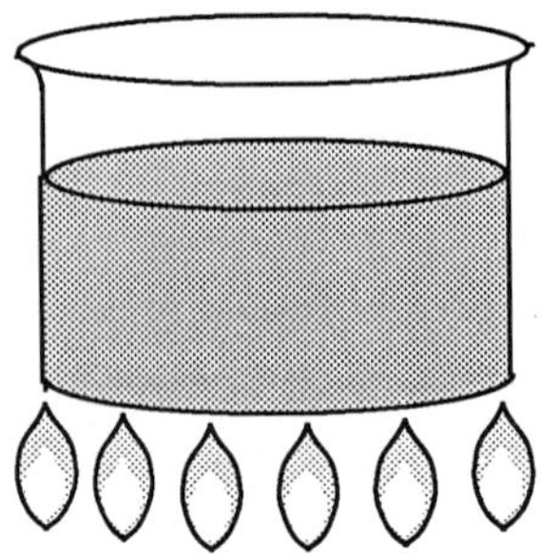

Fig. 15. Heating water.

We employ the basic ideas of Qualitative Process Theory [42] to represent physical phenomena for this purpose. The theory consists of three notions, i.e., individual view, process view, and history. An individual view is a category of existing entities, such as water, a container, and a heater (see Fig. 15). A process view is a category of physical occurrence that influences on entities. Heating is represented by a process view having influence on water to make its temperature rise. In mechanical systems, energy transformation, transmission, and vibration fall into this category. A history is represented by a sequence of individual views and activated process views. A history of heating, for example, begins with a process *heating* acting on water, which causes temperature to rise. If it reaches the boiling point, the process *boiling* becomes part of the history. Individual views and process views are supported by their own preconditions that justify their existence. In the example of heating water, the process *boiling* is supported by the process *heating*. When the process *heating* ceases, *boiling* cannot continue.

Since Qualitative Process Theory has the notion of processes that can represent physical phenomena, we call this type of qualitative physics *process oriented.* On the other hand, de Kleer proposed *device oriented* qualitative physics [25]. In this approach, an object is modeled by a device network. A *device* is an elementary object of which behavior is described as an input-output relationship. An arc in the network is called a *conduit* on which we define flow of energy, material, electric current, etc. Qualitative reasoning about such flow in the network takes place and *envisions* behaviors of the whole system from the behaviors of the parts. Because this device oriented approach assumes a rather fixed device network, the computational performance could be reasonably good for e.g. diagnostic tasks in which we can assume that the topology of the device network seldom change. However, it might be difficult to apply this method to tasks such as design in which we sometimes need to consider modifications even of the network.

Kuipers proposed the QSIM algorithm to solve differential equations about physical systems qualitatively [69]. For reasoning about behaviors in terms of increase and decrease of parameters, this is a fundamental technique. Faltings and Forbus [38] proposes Qualitative Kinematics to deal with behaviors of mechanical devices. Murthy proposes a method to envision behaviors of the target system even if its structural configuration changes [81]. Lenat is now conducting the Cyc project to construct a large scale knowledge base about physical systems [71]. The Cyc project aimes at collecting a big number of knowledge chunks about every aspect of physical, social, and psychological worlds. They believe that this is crucial to obtain so-called ontological knowledge.

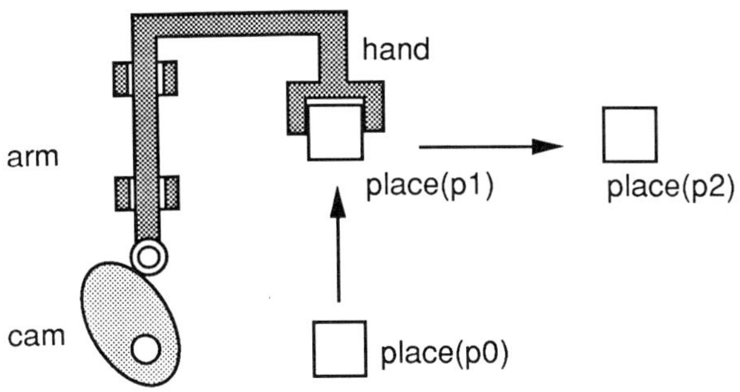

Fig. 16. Pick and place mechanism.

5.2.2. Examples. We have implemented a qualitative simulator to examine Qualitative Process Theory for qualitative representation of behaviors of machines from a view point of design. Figures 16 and 17 show an example of a simple mechanism for a "pick and place" job. A robot hand grips a work at the *place*(*w*0) and moves along the path *place*(*w*0), *place*(*w*1), and *place*(*w*2). The hand is connected to an arm, and as the arm is pushed up by the cam the hand follows. Figure 18 represents the phenomena happening from the time *t*0 when the work is at the *place*(*w*0) to the time *t*1 when the work is at the *place*(*w*1).

In this situation, three processes are taking place.

(1) The cam is pushing up the arm (process *move−by−cam−mechanism*).

(2) The arm is lifting the hand (process *move−by−connection*).

(3) The hand is lifting the work (process *move−by−grip*).

Process *move−by−cam−mechanism* is applicable to a pair of a cam and an arm is defined in the system as in Fig. 18. Figure 19 is the result of a simulation, showing which individual views and processes occurred in the situation. The simulation begins with the given initial situation, namely the set of existing individual views and the process views, and then instantiates possible individual views and process views. Processes either increase or decrease the value of variables as shown in the result. The qualitative simulator was implemented on Common Lisp running on a Sun workstation.

individual views

a−work, a−hand, an−arm, a−cam, a−gravity

processes

$(t0, t1)$ *force(upward, a−cam, an−arm)*
$(t0, t1)$ *force(upward, an−arm, a−hand)*
$(t0, t1)$ *force(upward, a−hand, a−work)*
$(t0, t1)$ *force(downward, a−spring, an−arm)*
$(t0, t1)$ *gravity(downward, a−cam)*
$(t0, t1)$ *gravity(downward, an−arm)*
$(t0, t1)$ *gravity(downward, a−hand)*
$(t0, t1)$ *gravity(downward, a−work)*
$(t0, t1)$ *move−by−cam−mechanism(upward, a−cam, an−arm)*
$(t0, t1)$ *move−by−connection(upward, an−arm, a−hand)*
$(t0, t1)$ *move−by−grip(upward, a−hand, work)*

transition

WORK: *place*$(w0) \rightarrow$ *place*$(w1)$
HAND :*place*$(h0) \rightarrow$ *place*$(h1)$
ARM :*place*$(a0) \rightarrow$ *place*$(a1)$
CAM :*place*$(c0) \rightarrow$ *place*$(c1)$

Fig. 17. Descriptions for the pick and place mechanism.

```
%define {
((type (process move-by-cam-mechanism))
 (localname local-cam local-object local-direction)
 (conditions                                            ; if
      (direction local-direction)
      (contact local-direction local-cam local-object)  ; a cam is contacting a follower in a direction,
      (rotating local-cam))                             ; the cam is rotating,
      (can-move local-direction local-object)           ; and the follower can move in the direction,
 (add-conditions                                        ; then
      (apply-force local-direction local-cam local-object) ; the cam applies force to the follower in the direction,
      (moving local-direction local-object))            ; and the follower moves,
 (relations
      (relation+
         (position local-direction local-object)        ; and position of the follower is
         (displacement local-direction local-cam))))}   ; proportional to displacement of the cam.
```

Fig. 18. Representation of phenomena

5.3. Features

5.3.1. The Concept of Features. The concept of features is now considered crucial in engineering design and CAD research. Early research on features was much motivated by the fact that the way to input geometry descriptions for CAD was cumbersome and most of the system terminology did not fit the designer's sense [83]. For instance, a *hole* should not be a negative geometric volume made when a cylinder is subtracted from a cube. The concept of

```
EPISODE 1
ACTIVE PROCESSES
 (CAM-ROTATE+
       (((PROCESS CAM-ROTATE)) (LOCAL (LC-CAM A-CAM))))
 (MOVE-BY-CAM-MECHANISM+
   (((PROCESS MOVE-BY-CAM-MECHANISM))
    (LOCAL (LC-CAM A-CAM) (LC-OBJECT AN-ARM) (LC-DIRECTION UPWARD))))
 (MOVE-BY-FIX+
   (((PROCESS MOVE-BY-FIX))
    (LOCAL (LC-OBJECT1 AN-ARM) (LC-OBJECT2 A-HAND)
        (LC-DIRECTION UPWARD))))
 (MOVE-BY-GRIP+
   (((PROCESS MOVE-BY-GRIP))
    (LOCAL (LC-HAND A-HAND) (LC-WORK A-WORK) (LC-DIRECTION UPWARD))))
 eight more processes are omitted

ACTIVE INDIVIDUALS
 (A-CAM (((IVIEW CAM)) (LOCAL)))
 (AN-ARM (((IVIEW ARM)) (LOCAL)))
 (A-HAND (((IVIEW HAND)) (LOCAL)))
 (A-WORK (((IVIEW WORK)) (LOCAL)))
 (A-SPRING (((IVIEW SPRING)) (LOCAL)))
 (UPWARD (((IVIEW DIRECTION)) (LOCAL)))
 (DOWNWARD (((IVIEW DIRECTION)) (LOCAL)))
 (THE-GRAVITY-FIELD (((IVIEW GRAVITY-FIELD)) (LOCAL)))

CHANGING VARIABLES
 (ANGLE A-CAM) INCREASING
 (DISPLACEMENT UPWARD A-CAM) INCREASING
 (POSITION UPWARD AN-ARM) INCREASING
 (POSITION UPWARD A-HAND) INCREASING
 (POSITION UPWARD A-WORK) INCREASING

POSSIBLE CHANGE OF ORDER
 FROM: (ANGLE A-CAM) < (MAX-ANGLE A-CAM)
 TO:  (ANGLE A-CAM) = (MAX-ANGLE A-CAM)
```

Fig. 19. Result of simulation.

geometric or form features, such as hole, rounding, wall, and rib, was formed and Fig. 20 shows examples of form features. Relevant features include pattern features such as a circular pattern that can be observed in the arrangement of bolt holes for a flange. It was also experimented to extract form features from geometric modelers [53, 98].

Dixon *et al.* proposed *designing with features* [30]. It is an important concept in that the designer models the design object with primary features that will be automatically converted to secondary features which are lower level expressions of geometry and topology. Feature-based modeling is an idea to construct a new type of geometric modeler that allows for more explicit representations of the designer's intentions [68, 100]. Primary features can thus be

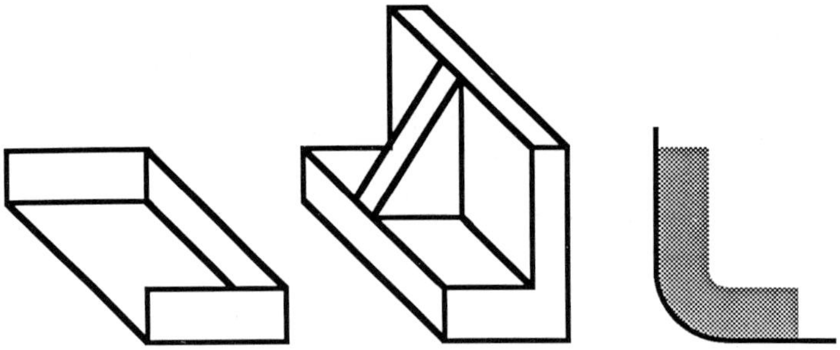

Fig. 20. Examples of form features.

formed only with respect to the concepts or intentions that the designer intends to express and manipulate.

The concept of features can be regarded as a method to symbolically manipulate geometrical information. Geometric reasoning techniques [6, 134] can be applied to symbolic reasoning about features [20, 120]. Rossignac *et al.* proposed parametric representations of features [95].

Features have problems, too. One of them is that exhaustiveness of, especially, secondary features: Are they mathematically complete to represent any possible geometric figures? Another important one is its ambiguity. For instance, two adjacent *slots* may form a *wall* if they are close enough (see Fig. 21). However, where will this *wall* become visible? The distance between the two slots has something to do with it, and thus not only shapes but also quantitative information is part of the feature *wall*. Moreover, a feature, e.g. a slot, is not a geometrical entity but a certain combination of surfaces. Conventional geometric modelers cannot have such a data structure explicitly and so-called non-manifold representations [128, 129] are considered useful for this purpose.

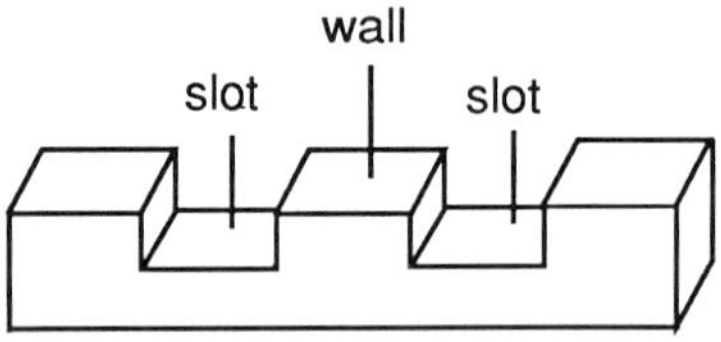

Fig. 21. Two slots and a wall.

Features may be formed according to applications. For instance, *manufacturing features* are features relevant to manufacturing methods, tool shapes, etc [24]. Thus, a feature is not necessarily a geometric entity and at this point, we can define a *feature* as an attribute or a set of attributes of an entity that has a *teleological* relationship with an abstract concept, such as topological relationships (pattern features), function (function features), manufacturing methods (manufacturing features), physical phenomena (physical features), etc.

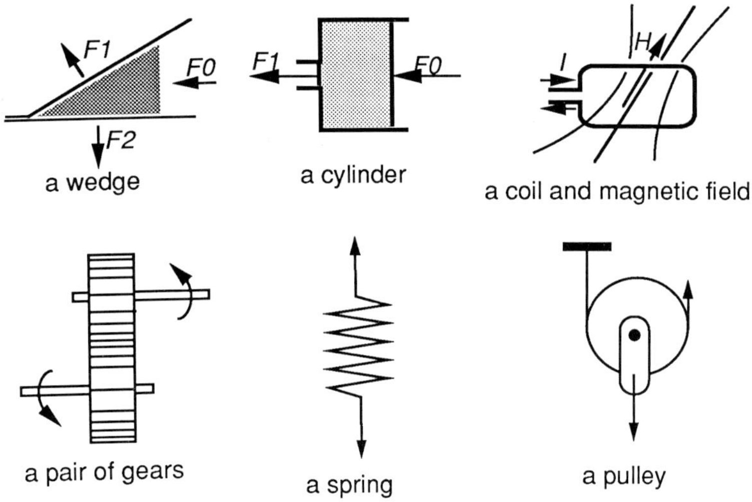

Fig. 22. Physical features.

5.3.2. Physical Features. A *physical feature* is an attribute or a set of attribute of an entity that is related with a physical phenomenon. Figure 22 illustrates examples of physical features. For instance, a wedge is a physical feature that causes diversion of force and prevents it from moving due to friction. Note, however, that geometrically speaking it is not a triangle object but anything that has two surfaces.

The metamodel concept in General Design Theory introduced in Section 4.2 requests that we describe behaviors of the design object in terms of physical phenomena. Physical features are expected to serve as a vocabulary for the metamodel. The exhaustiveness of the physical features (or compactness of the metamodel space) and must be guaranteed. Therefore, we need to build a large scale physical feature base. The Cyc project conducted by Lenat is its good example [71].

5.4. Integration of Design Object Models: Metamodel

5.4.1. Metamodel Mechanism. In design, particularly mechanical design, we use various kinds of models as a working place (consider drawings) to evaluate functionalities of the design object. They include a geometric model, a kinematic model, a dynamic model, a mathematical model, a strength model, etc. (We call such a model an *aspect* model as opposed to metamodel. See Fig. 23.) The problem here is that the level and focus of models are different from each other. For example, the information used in manufacturing is too detailed for structural analyses. Therefore, different attributes might be sometimes considered the same, although their actual values can be completely inconsistent with each other.

A *model* is a set of descriptions about the object world and it is constructed based on a *theory*. By observing the object world, we may select, extract, and abstract properties needed for building a model according to the theory. In this definition, *modeling* is a process where observed facts are filtered by a *theory* to formulate a world which is complete as far as the theory is concerned. For example, a geometric model is a model of this system with a focus

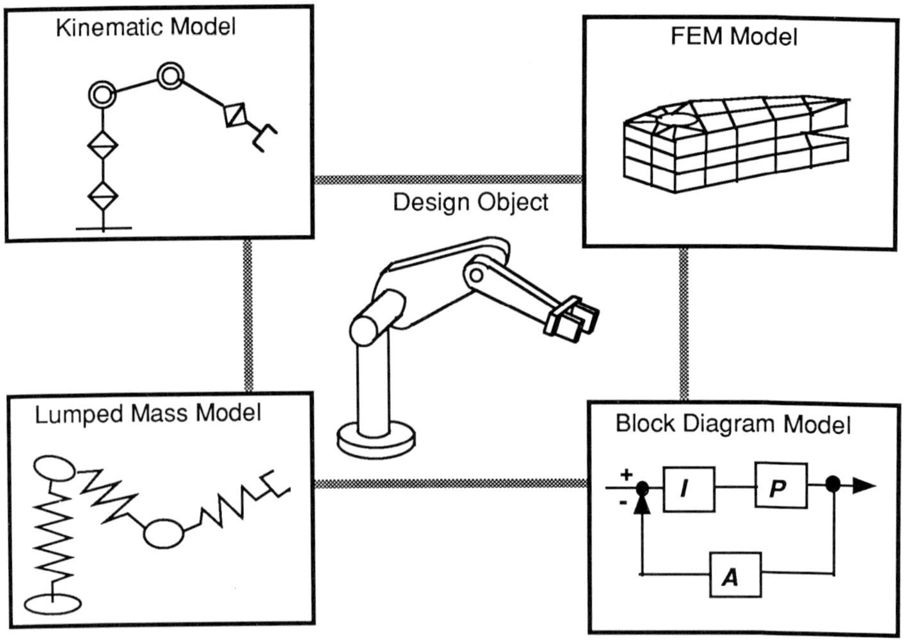

Fig. 23. A robot and its aspect models.

on its geometric properties such as surfaces, lines, curves, points, etc. The background theory behind the boundary representation geometric model is, perhaps, algebraic geometry, because those geometric entities are represented mathematically as algebraic equations. If there are two models, these models can be transformed to each other only when the background theories are compatible. It is impossible to transform an FEM model to a lumped mass model without additional knowledge about the background theories. Models and *representations* are different, too; a model can have many different representations. Figure 24 depicts this idea about how models are constructed from theories.

Suppose, for example, a kinematics model of a mechanism and its distorsion model. Changes in motion in the kinematic model may influence force modeled in the distorsion model. This can be inferred in such a way that, since acceleration of a solid object depends on force applied to it, changes in acceleration in the kinematic model should lead to changes in force in the distorsion model and as a result, e.g., bend must be recalculated. We proposed a new modeling framework, called (also) *metamodel*, to integrated various kinds of aspect models [66, 119, 126, 135]. The metamodel mechanism unifies various models which appear in design as a central model. By having a central model, we can avoid the combinatory explosion problem to implement data transfer programs between models and to keep consistency among them.

In order to find relationships among aspect models, knowledge on the level of the background theory is needed. It is knowledge about the modeling framework itself and should describe how a model is constructed using various fundamental concepts that are denoted in the background theories. Such knowledge is called ontological knowledge as discussed in Section 5.4 and to represent it we use Qualitative Process Theory [42].

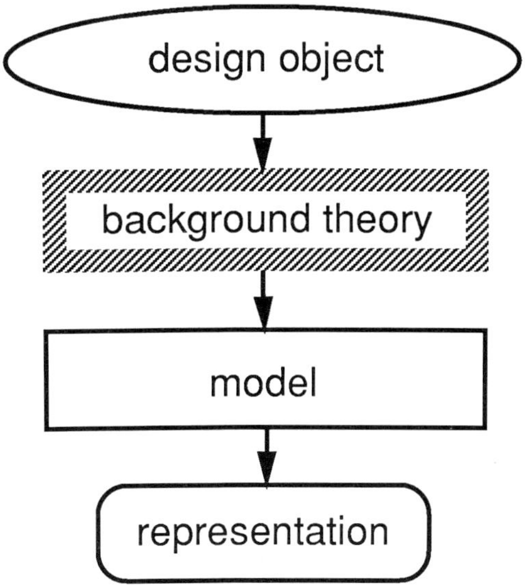

Fig. 24. Theories, models, and representations.

The metamodel mechanism has symbolic representations of concepts (i.e., physical parameters and phenomena) used to represent the design object. It also has a knowledge base (supposed to be fairly large for practical use, see [71]) about relationships among these physical concepts. The designer describes the design object as a combination of physical features that represent relationships between unit physical phenomena and entities (see Section 5.3). In this respect, a description of the design object described in terms of physical features serves as a mental model (see Section 3.2). A qualitative reasoner tries to figure out, first, if the combination of such physical features performs the desired behaviors given as the specifications and, second, helps the designer build necessary models for evaluation and further refinement of the design object. The metamodel mechanism maintains consistencies among such models. When one model is modified due to e.g. the results of an analysis, the change is propagated to other models accordingly through knowledge about relationships among concepts.

Figure 25 is a hardcopy of the display of the metamodel mechanism that integrates a geometric model and a kinematic model of a simple mechanism. The kinematic model has a concept *stroke* of which value (i.e. the slot length) should be calculated from the geometry that is available from the geometric model. However, since the calculation of the slot length depends on its shape, it is not desirable that we define direct relationships between the length and its geometry. The metamodel system, on the other hand, solves this problem by tracing through the network of these concepts. This metamodel system was implemented in Smalltalk-80 [50] on a Sun workstation.

5.4.2. Roles of the Metamodel. The metamodel concept has three roles. The first one is to serve as a central framework for integrating and unifying various models used in CAD systems. Integration of models might be achieved by constructing a common database that

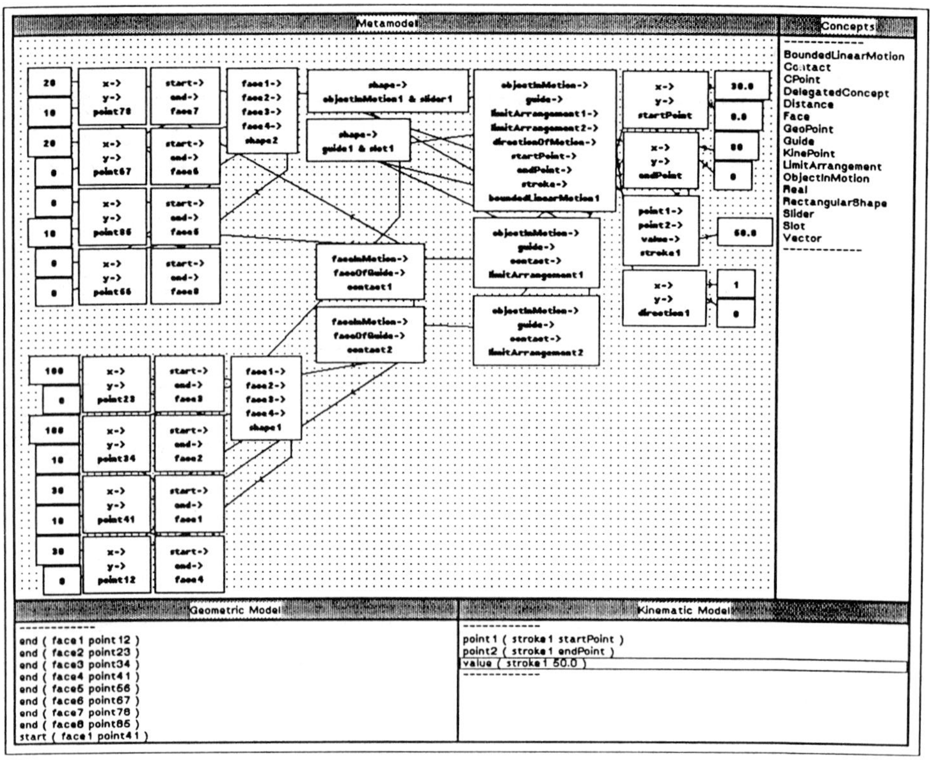

Fig. 25. Metamodel mechanism.

contains geometrical information, material properties, etc., and additional modules for generating models from the common database. This method of integration is an *ad hoc* approach and has drawbacks.

(1) If we want to incorporate another model, it is necessary to modify the entire modeling scheme.

(2) The level and focus of models can be different, thus direct coupling of models is not always possible.

The second role of the metamodel is as a mechanism to model physical phenomena and as a database of physical features. This view is supported by the definition of the metamodel in General Design Theory.

The third role is as a working database for the evolutionary design process model that was discussed in Section 4.2. In this sense, the metamodel is a mental model that reflects the evolving design object according to the progress of the design process. This view is justified by both the evolutionary design process model and the cognitive design process model. The concept of the metamodel is thus a key issue for building ICAD [119].

6. Theory for Representing Design Knowledge

6.1. Knowledge Representation for ICAD

A theory of knowledge is necessary, because IIICAD must be implemented as a tool for an intellectual process. Perhaps, we need epistemological theories to deal with the hierarchy of various levels of knowledge representation, such as metaphysics, philosophy, cognitive science, logic, and traditional knowledge representation theories [121]. Relevant issues include *conceptual modeling* in the database technology [15], and *knowledge base management* [99].

In codifying a piece of knowledge in a computer, we might need to proceed as follows.

(a) We must find the most appropriate knowledge representation schema to the application, such as Entity-Relationship model [18], the object oriented approach [13,21,63,88,89], and the semantic network representation.

(b) We then select a representation language.

(c) Finally, we start coding of knowledge.

A theory of knowledge is, thus, necessary as a guiding principle;

(1) to find the most appropriate representation schema,

(2) to organize the knowledge,

(3) to select the representation language, and

(4) to utilize the knowledge in a certain language.

The knowledge representation for IIICAD should be flexible and natural. By *flexible* we mean, for example, a multi-purpose data modeling scheme. By *natural* we mean using the terminology of the target domain. For instance, we implement programs for linear algebra in Fortran using *arrays* and *do-loops*; the language constructs of APL, on the other hand, include *matrix* and various matrix operations. A language for ICAD, in this way, should have language constructs that are naturally capable of describing design processes and objects.

6.2. Object Oriented Programming Paradigm for ICAD

In this chapter, as an example of knowledge representation schema, we examine the object oriented programming paradigm (OOPP) from a viewpoint of languages to implement ICAD [118]. Object oriented languages are becoming more and more popular and the ideas of the OOPP are considered indispensable for implementing applications like CAD, because the OOPP allows for usage of domain specific concepts in terms of *objects* that are in fact role players. An object can possess both behaviors and properties of the entity to be simulated. Simulations take place by sending and receiving messages. This is called *message passing* and by doing so, objects can capture the semantics of a real world written in the program as long as message passing is a good approximation of what is happening in the world: one does not need to cast his ideas into a mold made of programming language jargons, and he just concentrates to describe his ideas in his own terminology.

Message passing allows for *encapsulation* in terms of objects. An object understands a message and responds to it based on a *method*. A method must be defined in such a way that invoking the method should not require any additional knowledge on the implementation or internal structure of objects. This feature of *data abstraction* or *information hiding* results in another important concept of object oriented languages, *classes* and *instances*. The behavior of an object might be defined generally by a set of methods which as a whole defines a class. Objects in the same class respond to a particular message in exactly the same way. These objects would be called *instances* of this particular class.

Another key issue of the OOPS is *specialization* which, on the other hand, makes it possible for an object to behave *like something*. This is usually done through an *object hierarchy* (or class hierarchy) which can naturally realize the so-called *is-a hierarchy* [14] in AI. The object hierarchy allows for reuse of codes which contributes to the software engineering points of view of object oriented languages.

Most of object oriented languages have another important concept besides message passing and specialization. An object can have *internal structure*. For instance, Smalltalk-80 has concepts of *class variables* and *instance variables*. These are equivalent, to some extent, to *slots* in Misnky's frame theory [78] and inherited through the class hierarchy. CommonLoops [13], has a concept called *composite object*. These are ways to realize the *part-of structure* (or *hierarchy*) which is also an important issue in AI. Semantic networks, e.g., might also be used to represent the part-of structure.

Message passing represents the dynamic, procedural aspect of the OOPP; i.e., dynamic behaviors of objects are represented by sending and receiving messages. In Smalltalk-80, message passing is real communication between objects, whereas, in a language like ESP [19] which is based on the logic programming paradigm it is realized by assertions.

On the other hand, the static aspect of the OOPP is represented by these two types of hierarchies, the is-a and part-of hierarchies. Here, by static we mean static relationships among objects. The is-a hierarchy can be realized by an inheritance mechanism but this is not the only way. For example, Arbab [7] suggests that instead of inheritance the delegation concept [72] should be used especially in CAD applications due to inflexibility of the inheritance mechanisms. The delegation mechanism is a sort of selective, non-automatic inheritance mechanism. Unless clearly declared, an object does delegate only the class it belongs to. If it must be treated as another type of object, we must clearly declare.

Internal structures of objects should be avoided as well, because they give an object rigid characteristics that is particular to the class. One alternative is to have *plain objects* which have no internal structures and some additional mechanisms to represent the part-of and is-a hierarchies. For example, we can employ logical expressions only to represent static relationships among objects including the part-of and is-a hierarchies. If we have to use instance variables for one reason or another (e.g. to represent attributes of objects), instead we may use functions defined over objects.

7. A Prototype of IIICAD

7.1. Knowledge Representation Language for IIICAD

Efforts to establish a theory of CAD should result in a design knowledge representation language for ICAD. Such a design language must have language constructs representing concepts that appear in the design process. In IIICAD, it is called IDDL (Integrated Data Description Language) [9, 122, 127] which is capable of representing both design processes and design objects. Its design reflects major theoretical results obtained in the IIICAD project up to the present.

IDDL is the kernel language of the IIICAD system. System elements of IIICAD all speak IDDL and, in particular, the supervisor controls the system using scenarios. IDDL has the concepts of objects, attributes of objects and facts, and worlds to describe design objects. A world consists of objects and facts which describe relationships among these objects and it is in fact a partition of the database to preserve the results of design. An object of IDDL has attributes and we can define operations over these attributes as functions. IDDL has a class mechanism much the same as other object oriented languages, except that binding between objects is done through the delegation mechanism that allows much more useful specialization than the widely-used inheritance mechanism [118].

In order to describe the stepwise, refinement nature of design, IDDL has a scenario to represent the basic design cycle (see Section 4.3). A scenario consists of a set of objects and logical rules over these objects. A rule has the well-known if-then format and rules are *executed* in the same way as production rule systems. Calling subscenarios means executing design subprocesses. By entering a scenario in which a basic design cycle takes place, it fetches a set of relevant objects and creates a world where only relevant relationships among these objects can be seen. As a result of its execution, a scenario leaves objects a world in the database. A world is a partition in the database, such that worlds are independent from each other but can be linked, so that changes in one world can propagate to others. There must be always at least one world active in the database and this world is called active world and the execution of scenarios is done in this world. IDDL employs modality (namely the possibility and necessity operators) and default reasoning as the default operator. These operators are used to describe design processes more flexibly and to control executions of scenarios.

IDDL is, in principle, an object oriented language in that objects are sending and receiving messages to represent local, dynamic behaviors as function callings. The global, static behaviors of objects are described as relationships, i.e., as predicates. (In this sense IDDL is a combination between the object oriented and logic programming paradigms.) Sometimes, we not only want to determine relations among objects as building blocks, but also want to operate design objects directly. Functions are used for this purpose.

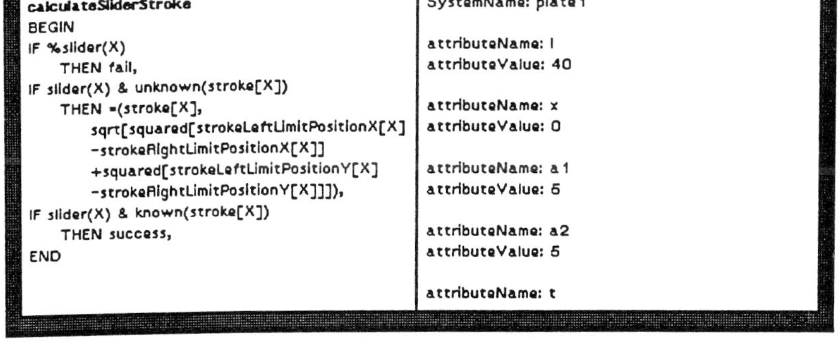

Fig. 26. IDDL browser.

Figure 26 shows a display hardcopy of an experimental version of IDDL that was implemented in Smalltalk-80 on a Sun workstation. The left side window of the IDDL browser is displaying a scenario, and the right side window is a browser for accessing the database. Figure 26 shows a scenario that is a part of the metamodel mechanism implemented in IDDL. We need to implement scenarios to perform the following tasks;

(1) to pick up or generate a candidate solution for the given specifications,

(2) to construct an aspect model from the metamodel,

(3) to evaluate the model, and

(4) to modify or detail the metamodel so that it meets the specifications.

A form feature extraction program was implemented in IDDL. This program combines IDDL with an application, i.e., a solid modeler written in C. The solid modeler executes numerical computation and the IDDL performs logical inference. Figure 27 is a display hardcopy of the system.

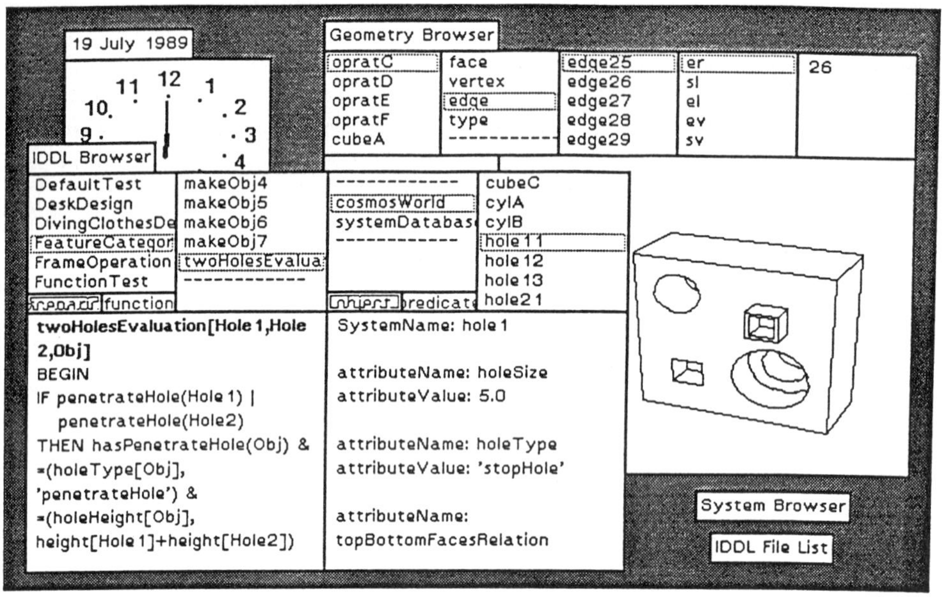

Fig. 27. Feature extraction in IDDL.

7.2. ICAD vs. CAD

We proposed the evolutionary design process model in Section 4.2, which is supported by the cognitive design process model derived from the results of design experiments. In Section 4.5 we demonstrated computer simulation of the evolutionary design process based on the computable model that was derived from the cognitive model. Chapter 5 discussed how to deal with ontological knowledge, or knowledge about physical systems in a symbolic way. The evolutionary model is based on the concept of metamodels that was formalized in General Design Theory as descriptions about ontological knowledge. In Section 5.4, we described the metamodel mechanism for integration of various aspect models. It also requires ontological descriptions about concepts in the physical world. In Section 7.1 it was demonstrated that a metamodel mechanism can be implemented in IDDL which is the kernel language for design knowledge representation of IIICAD.

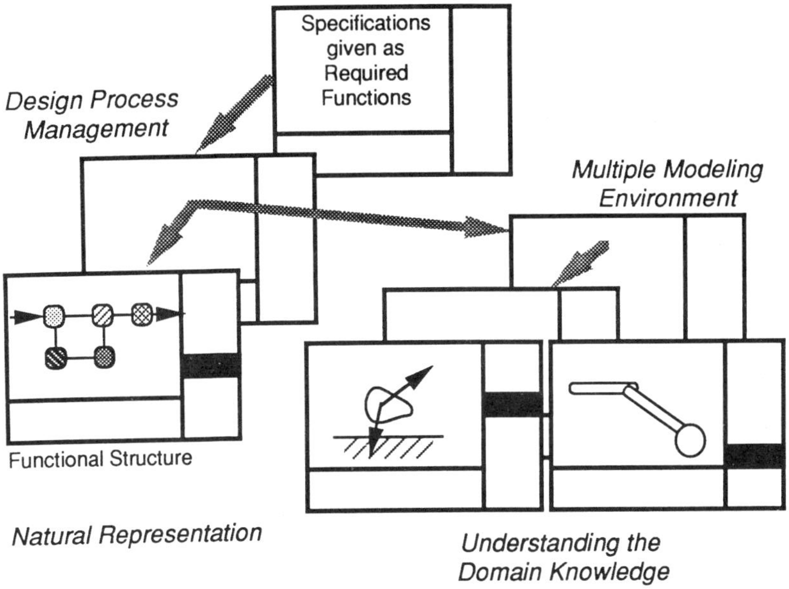

Fig. 28. Design with intelligent CAD.

Figure 28 summarizes the discussions above and depicts how design with ICAD (or IIICAD) will look like. In short, the system should have two types of design knowledge, *viz*., one about design processes and the other about design objects. The former is needed to *navigate design processes* and to *maintain design information*. The latter is necessary to *understand the domain knowledge* (or ontological knowledge) that is further useful to achieve user-friendly, natural representations for design knowledge and information. *Maintaining multiple models* is also an issue here: the concept of the metamodel is useful for this purpose.

As identified in Section 2.2.3, research trends are directed toward incorporating and utilizing wider range of design knowledge available in the system. IIICAD is supposed to serve as a general CAD framework to implement design knowledge that is composed of knowledge about design objects and design processes. Thus, the IIICAD architecture illustrated in Fig. 3 is now justified to incorporate such knowledge. Table 1 lists up goals of ICAD from viewpoints of representation of design knowledge and implementation.

Of course, there are missing elements of IIICAD yet to be developed. They include the followings.

- Improvement of the IDDL language specifications using the results of the computable design process model.
- Introduction of the metamodel mechanism.

- Development of other components of the system, such as *Intelligent User Interface, Supervisor,* and *Application Program Interface.* For example, it is expected that feature based user interfaces are promising [57].
- Collection of ontological knowledge.

Table 1. Goals of ICAD

Knowledge about design objects	Domain knowledge Knowledge integration framework Problem solving
Knowledge about design processes	How design proceeds Where design goes Designer's intention Meta knowledge
New implementation technology	Software engineering point of view Flexible, natural representation No system jargons

8. Conclusion

In this paper, we presented how future intelligent CAD systems should look like and be developed. ICAD should aim at not only intelligence but also integration and interactiveness to support designers better. To do so, it is crucial to codify design knowledge in a wide, deep, flexible, computable form. We proposed the concept and architecture of IIICAD. We find out that a theoretical approach is needed to deal with the complexity of design knowledge. Among other things, two elements are missing from the theoretical framework of conventional CAD systems, *viz*., notions of design processes and ontological knowledge. We have shown that it is possible to formalize design processes in a logical form, which further lends itself to establish a computable design process model. We have argued that qualitative physics can be useful to codify ontological knowledge. A prototype of ICAD was also demonstrated. Methods for design knowledge representation of both design processes and design objects are now obvious, including management of design processes and the metamodel mechanism.

We have also proposed the concept of the metamodel which has three roles, i.e., first as a central framework for integrating and unifying various models used in CAD systems, second as a mechanism to model physical phenomena and as a database of physical features, and third as a working database for the evolutionary design process model. It is now clear that such a concept is the key issue in developing ICAD. In order to arrive at the metamodel concept, the theoretical approach was useful. This justifies our approach towards ICAD and the directions towards ICAD are now clarified.

Acknowledgements

This tutorial paper was written based on the research results of both Yoshikawa and Tomiyama Laboratory at the University of Tokyo and Bart Veth IIICAD Group at the Centre for Mathematics and Computer Science in Amsterdam. I would like to thank Professor Hiroyuki Yoshikawa at the University of Tokyo for his encouraging advice and support. Contributions from the members of our laboratory were indispensable. Especially I am grateful to Yoshiki Ishida, Takashi Kiriyama, Hideaki Takeda, and Deyi Xue for their valuable ideas and excellent work. The IIICAD project was originally initiated by Bart Veth IIICAD Group, while the author was working at the Centre for Mathematics and Computer Science. I thank the members of the Group for their help: Paul J.W. ten Hagen gave continuing support to the project, and he also gave me this opportunity to present the results of the project as a tutorial for Eurographics '90. Many thanks go to Paul Veerkamp for his cooperation and to Professor Varol Akman at Bilkent University in Ankara for his moral support. Part of the research at the University of Tokyo is funded by research grant from Nippon Steel. The IIICAD project at the Centre for Mathematics and Computer Science is funded by NFI, a Dutch governmental organization.

References

1. Agogino, A. M. and Almgren, A. S., "Symbolic computation in computer aided optimal design," in *Expert Systems in Computer Aided Design*, Gero, J. (ed.), North-Holland, 1987, pp. 267-287.

2. Akman, V., Hagen, P. and Tomiyama, T.,"Design as a Formal, Knowledge Engineered Activity," CWI Report No. CS-R8744, Centre for Mathematics and Computer Science, Amsterdam, September 1987.

3. Akman, V. and ten Hagen, P. J. W., "The power of physical representations," in *Intelligent CAD Systems II: Implementational Issues*, Akman, V., ten Hagen, P. J. W. and Veerkamp, P. J. (eds.), Springer-Verlag, Heidelberg, Berlin, Heidelberg, New York, London, Paris, Tokyo, 1989, pp. 170-194.

4. Akman, V., ten Hagen, P. J. W. and Veerkamp, P. J. (eds.), *Intelligent CAD Systems II: Implementational Issues*, Springer-Verlag, Heidelberg, Berlin, Heidelberg, New York, London, Paris, Tokyo, 1989.

5. Akman, V., ten Hagen, P. J. W. and Tomiyama, T., "A fundamental and theoretical framework for an intelligent CAD system," *Computer-Aided Design*, 22(6), 1990, pp. 352-367.

6. Arbab, F. and Wing, J. M., "Geometric reasoning: A new paradigm for processing geometric information," in *Design Theory for CAD, Proceedings of the IFIP W.G. 5.2 Working Conference 1985 (Tokyo)*, Yoshikawa, H. and Warman, E. A. (eds.), North-Holland, Amsterdam, 1987, pp. 145-165.

7. Arbab, F., "A paradigm for intelligent CAD," in *Intelligent CAD Systems I: Theoretical and Methodological Aspects*, ten Hagen, P. J. W. and Tomiyama, T. (eds.), Springer-Verlag, Berlin, Heidelberg, New York, Tokyo., 1987, pp. 20-39.

8. Baker, K. D., Ball, L. J., Culverhouse, P. F., Dennis, I., Evans, J. S., Jagodzinski, A. P., Pearce, P. D., Scothern, D. G. C. and Venner, G. M., "A psychologically based intelligent design aid," in *Intelligent CAD Systems III: Practical Experience and Evaluation*, ten Hagen, P. J. W. and Veerkamp, P. J. (eds.), Springer-Verlag, Heidelberg, Berlin, Heidelberg, New York, London, Paris, Tokyo, to appear in 1991.

9. Bart Veth, "An Integrated Data Description Language for Coding Design Knowledge," in *Intelligent CAD Systems I: Theoretical and Methodological Aspects*, ten Hagen, P. J. W. and Tomiyama, T. (eds.), Springer-Verlag, Berlin, Heidelberg, New York, London, Paris, Tokyo, 1987, pp. 295-313.

10. Barthes, J. P. A. and El Dahshan, K. (eds.), *Intelligent CAD Systems IV: Added Value to Intelligent CAD Systems*, Springer-Verlag, Heidelberg, Berlin, Heidelberg, New York, London, Paris, Tokyo, to appear in 1991.

11. Bijl, A., "An approach to design theory," in *Design Theory for CAD, Proceedings of the IFIP W.G. 5.2 Working Conference 1985 (Tokyo)*, Yoshikawa, H. and Warman, E. A. (eds.), North-Holland, Amsterdam, 1987, pp. 3-31.

12. Bobrow, D. G. (ed.), *Qualitative Reasoning about Physical Systems*, North-Holland, Amsterdam, 1985.

13. Bobrow, D. G., Kahn, K., Kiczales, G., Masinter, L., Stefik, M. and Zdybel, F., "CommonLoops: Merging Lisp and object-oriented programming," *Proceedings of OOPSLA '86, special issue of SIGPLAN Notices*, **21**(11), 1986, pp. 17-29.

14. Brachman, R. J., "What IS-A is and isn't: An analysis of taxonomic links in semantic networks," *IEEE Computer*, **16**(10), October 1983, pp. 30-36.

15. Brodie, M. L., Mylopoulos, J. and Schmidt, J. W. (eds.), *On Conceptual Modelling: Perspectives from Artificial Intelligence, Databases, and Programming Languages*, Springer-Verlag, New York, Berlin, Heidelberg, Tokyo, 1984.

16. Brown, D. C. and Chandrasekaran, B., "Expert systems for a class of mechanical design activity," in *Knowledge Engineering in Computer-Aided Design, Proceedings of the IFIP W.G. 5.2 Working Conference 1984 (Budapest)*, Gero, J. S. (ed.), North-Holland, Amsterdam, 1985, pp. 259-290.

17. Chandrasekaran, B. and Mittal, S., "Deep versus compiled knowledge approaches to diagnostic problem-solving," in *Developments in Expert Systems*, Coombs, M. J. (ed.), Academic Press, 1984, pp. 23-34.

18. Chen, P. P., "The Entity-Relationship model — Toward a unified view of data," *ACM Transactions on Database Systems*, **1**(1), March 1976, pp. 9-36.

19. Chikayama, T.,"ESP Reference Manual," ICOT Technical Report No. Tech. Rep.-044, ICOT, Tokyo, Feb. 1984.

20. Chung, J. C. H., Cook, R. L., Patel, D. and Simmons, M. K., "Feature-based geometry construction for geometric reasoning," in *Proceedings of the 1988 ASME International Computers in Engineering Conference and Exhibition, Vol. 1*, Tipnis, V. J. and Patton, E. M. (eds.), ASME, New York, 1988, pp. 497-504.

21. Cox, B. J., *Object Oriented Programming: An Evolutionary Approach*, Addison-Wesley Publishing Company, Reading, MA, USA, 1986.

22. Coyne, R. D., Roseman, M. A., Radford, A. D. and Gero, J. S., "Innovation and creativity in knowledge-based CAD," in *Expert Systems in Computer-Aided Design, Proceedings of the IFIP W.G. 5.2 Working Conference 1987 (Sydney)*, Gero, J. S. (ed.), North-Holland, Amsterdam, 1987, pp. 435-471.

23. Coyne, R., *Logic Models of Design*, Pitman Publishing, London, 1988.

24. Cutkosky, M. R., Tenenbaum, J. M. and Muller, D., "Feature in process-based design," in *Proceedings of the 1988 ASME International Computers in Engineering Conference and Exhibition, Vol. 1*, Tipnis, V. J. and Patton, E. M. (eds.), ASME, New York, 1988, pp. 557-562.

25. de Kleer, J. and Brown, J. S., "A qualitative physics based on confluences," *Artificial Intelligence*, **24**(3), 1984, pp. 7-83.

26. de Kleer, J., "An assumption-based TMS," *Artificial Intelligence*, **28** , 1986, pp. 127-162.

27. Dietterich, T. A. and Ullman, D. G., "FORLOG: A logic-based architecture for design," in *Expert Systems in Computer-Aided Design, Proceedings of the IFIP W.G. 5.2 Working Conference 1987 (Sydney)*, Gero, J. S. (ed.), North-Holland, Amsterdam, 1987, pp. 1-24.

28. Dixon, J. R. and Simmons, M. K., "Computers that design: Expert systems for mechanical engineers," *Computers in Mechanical Engineering*, **2**(3), November 1983, pp. 10-17.

29. Dixon, J. R., "On research methodology towards a scientific theory of engineering design," *Artificial Intelligence for Engineering Design, Analysis and Manufacturing (AIEDAM)*, **1**(3), 1987, pp. 145-157.

30. Dixon, J. R. and Cunningham, J. J., "Research in designing with features," in *Intelligent CAD, I*, Yoshikawa, H. and Gossard, D. C. (eds.), North-Holland, Amsterdam, 1989, pp. 137-148.

31. Doyle, J., "A truth maintenance system," *Artificial Intelligence*, **12** , 1979, pp. 231-272.

32. Dyer, M. G., Flowers, M. and Hodges, J., "EDISON: An engineering design invention system operating naively," *Artificial Intelligence in Engineering*, **1**(1), 1986, pp. 36-44.

33. Eder, W. E. (ed.), *WDK 13, Proceedings of the 1987 International Conference on Engineering Design, (ICED 87)*, ASME, New York, 1987.

34. El Dahshan, K. and Barthes, J. P., "Implementing constraint propagation in mechanical CAD systems," in *Intelligent CAD Systems II: Implementational Issues*, Akman, V., ten Hagen, P. J. W. and Veerkamp, P. J. (eds.), Springer-Verlag, Heidelberg, Berlin, Heidelberg, New York, London, Paris, Tokyo, 1989, pp. 217-227.

35. Elmaraghy, W. H., Seering, W. P. and Ullman, D. G. (eds.), *Design Theory and Methodology — DTM '89*, ASME, New York, 1989.

36. Encarnacao, J. (ed.), *Computer Aided Design: Modelling, Systems Engineering, CAD-Systems*, Springer-Verlag, Berlin, 1980.

37. Ericsson, K. E. and Simon, H. A., "Verbal reports as data," *Psychological Review*, **87**(3), 1980, pp. 215-251.

38. Faltings, B., "Qualitative kinematics in mechanisms," *Proceedings of IJCAI '87*, 1987, pp. 436-442.

39. Fann, K. T., *Peirce's Theory of Abduction*, Martinus Nijhoff, The Hague, Holland, 1970.

40. Finger, S. and Dixon, J. R., "A review of research in mechanical engineering design. Part I: Descriptive, prescriptive, and computer-based models of design processes," *Research in Engineering Design*, **1**(1), 1989, pp. 51-67.

41. Proceedings of the First International Workshop on Formal Methods in Engineering Design, Manufacturing, and Assembly (January 15-17, 1990, Colorado Springs, Colorado, USA), 1990.

42. Forbus, K., "Qualitative process theory," *Artificial Intelligence*, **24**(3), 1984, pp. 85-168.

43. Forbus, K. D., "Intelligent computer-aided engineering," *AI Magazine*, **9**(3), Fall 1988, pp. 23-36.

44. Gero, J. S. (ed.), *Optimization in Computer-Aided Design, Proceedings of the IFIP W.G. 5.2 Working Conference 1983*, North-Holland, Amsterdam, 1985.

45. Gero, J. S. (ed.), *Knowledge Engineering in Computer-Aided Design, Proceedings of the IFIP W.G. 5.2 Working Conference 1984 (Budapest)*, North-Holland, Amsterdam, 1985.

46. Gero, J. S. (ed.), *Expert Systems in Computer-Aided Design, Proceedings of the IFIP W.G. 5.2 Working Conference 1987 (Sydney)*, North-Holland, Amsterdam, 1987.

47. Gero, J. S. (ed.), *Artificial Intelligence in Engineering Design*, Elsevier, Amsterdam, Oxford, New York, Tokyo, 1988.

48. Gero, J. S. (ed.), *Artificial Intelligence in Design*, Computational Mechanics Publications & Springer-Verlag, Southampton, Boston, 1989.

49. Goel, V. and Pirolli, P., "Motivating the Notion of Generic Design within Information-processing Theory: The Design Problem Space," *AI magazine*, **10**(1), 1989, pp. 18-47.

50. Goldberg, A. and Robson, D., *Smalltalk-80: The Language and its Implementation*, Addison-Wesley, Reading, MA, 1983.

51. Hayes, P. J., "The second naive physics manifesto," in *Formal Theories of the Commonsense World*, Hobbs, J. and Moore, R. (eds.), Ablex Publishing, Co., Norwood, New Jersey, 1985, pp. 1-36.

52. Hayes, P. J., "Naive physics manifesto I: Ontology for liquids," in *Formal Theories of the Commonsense World*, Hobbs, J. and Moore, R. (eds.), Ablex Publishing, Co., Norwood, New Jersey, 1985, pp. 71-107.

53. Henderson, M. R. and Anderson, D. C., "Computer recognition and extraction of form features: A CAD/CAM link," *Computers in Industry*, **6**(4), 1984, pp. 315-325.

54. Hubka, V. and the Programme Committee (eds.), *WDK 12, Proceedings of ICED 85 (Hamburg) — Theory and Practice of Engineering Design in International Comparison*, Heurista, Zurich, 1985.

55. Hubka, V. and Eder, W. E., *Theory of Technical Systems: A Total Concept Theory for Engineering Design*, Springer-Verlag, Berlin, Heidelberg, New York, London, Paris, Tokyo, 1988.

56. Hughes, G. E. and Cresswell, M. J., *An Introduction to Modal Logic*, Methuen and Company Ltd., London, 1968.

57. Ishida, Y., Xue, D., Tomiyama, T. and Yoshikawa, H., "A user-interface system for a design description language in intelligent CAD systems," in *Computer Applications in Production and Engineering, Proceedings of the Third International IFIP Conference on Computer Applications in Production and Engineering (CAPE '89, October 2-5, 1989, Tokyo)*, Kimura, F. and Rolstadas, A. (eds.), North-Holland, Amsterdam, New York, Oxford, Tokyo, 1989, pp. 617-624.

58. Ito, M., Kono, M. and Hayashi, K., "CONMOTO: A machine part description system based on designer's mental processes," in *Design Theory for CAD Proceedings of the IFIP W.G. 5.2 Working Conference 1985 (Tokyo)*, Yoshikawa, H. and Warman, E. A. (eds.), North-Holland, Amsterdam, 1987, pp. 167-198.

59. Jackson, P., Reichgelt, H. and van Harmelen, F. (eds.), *Logic-Based Knowledge Representation*, The MIT Press, Cambridge, London, 1989.

60. Johnson-Laird, P. N., *Mental Models*, Cambridge University Press, Cambridge, UK, 1983.

61. Joskowicz, L., "Shape and function in mechanical devices," *Proceedings of AAAI '87*, 1987, pp. 611-615.

62. Kalay, Y. E. (ed.), *Computability of Design*, John Wiley & Sons, New York, Chichester, Brisbane, Toronto, Singapore, 1987.

63. Kim, W. and Lochovsky, F. H. (eds.), *Object-Oriented Concepts, Databases, and Applications*, ACM Press, New York, and Addison-Wesley, Reading, MA, 1989.

64. Kimura, F., Sata, T. and Hosaka, M., "Integration of design and manufacturing activities based on object modelling," in *Advances in CAD/CAM, Proceedings of the 5th International IFIP/IFAC Conference on Programming Research and Operations Logistics in Advanced Manufacturing Technology (PROLAMAT 82, Leningrad, USSR)*, Ellis, T. M. R. and Semenkov, O. I. (eds.), North-Holland, Amsterdam, 1983, pp. 375-385.

65. Kimura, F., Suzuki, H. and Wingard, L., "A uniform approach to dimensioning and tolerancing in product modelling," in *Proceedings of CAPE '86, Second International Conference on Computer Applications in Production and Engineering*, Bo, K., Estensen, L. and Warman, E. A. (eds.), Copenhagen, 1986, pp. 165-171.

66. Kiriyama, T., Yamamoto, F., Tomiyama, T. and Yoshikawa, H., "Metamodel: An integrated modeling framework for intelligent CAD," in *Artificial Intelligence in Design*, Gero, J. S. (ed.), Computational Mechanics Publications, Southampton, Boston, 1989, pp. 429-449.

67. Kiriyama, T., Kurumatani, K., Tomiyama, T. and Yoshikawa, H., "Qualitative behavior representation and reasoning for intelligent CAD systems," in *Computer Applications in Production and Engineering, Proceedings of the Third International IFIP Conference on Computer Applications in Production and Engineering (CAPE '89, October 2-5, 1989, Tokyo)*, Kimura, F. and Rolstadas, A. (eds.), North-Holland, Amsterdam, New York, Oxford, Tokyo, 1989, pp. 29-36.

68. Krause, F. L., Vosgerau, F. H. and Yaramanoglu, N., "Implementation of technical rules in a feature based modeller," in *Intelligent CAD Systems II: Implementational Issues*, Akman, V., ten Hagen, P. J. W. and Veerkamp, P. J. (eds.), Springer-Verlag, Heidelberg, Berlin, Heidelberg, New York, London, Paris, Tokyo, 1989, pp. 195-208.

69. Kuipers, B., "Qualitative simulation," *Artificial Intelligence*, **29** , 1986, pp. 289-338.

70. Latombe, J., "Artificial intelligence in computer aided design: The TROPIC system," in *CAD Systems: Proceedings of the IFIP Working Conference 1976 (Austin, Texas, USA)*, Allan, III, J. J. (ed.), North-Holland, Amsterdam, 1977, pp. 61.

71. Lenat, D. B. and Guha, R. V., *Building Large Knowledge-Based Systems: Representation and Inference in the Cyc Project*, Addison-Wesley, Reading, MA, USA, 1989.

72. Lieberman, H., "Using prototypical objects to implement shared behavior in object-oriented systems," *Special Issue of ACM SIGPLAN Notices (Proceedings of Object-Oriented Programming Systems, Languages and Applications '86)*, **21**(11), November 1986, pp. 214-223.

73. MacCallum, K. J., "Knowledge-based systems for CAD," *Proceedings of CAPE '86, Second International Conference on Computer Applications in Production and Engineering*, Copenhagen, 1986, pp. 903.

74. Maher, M. L. and Fenves, S. J., "HI-RISE: An expert system for the preliminary structural design of high rise buildings," in *Knowledge Engineering in Computer-Aided Design, Proceedings of the IFIP W.G. 5.2 Working Conference 1984 (Budapest)*, Gero, J. S. (ed.), North-Holland, Amsterdam, 1985, pp. 125-146.

75. Mantyla, M., *An Introduction to Solid Modeling*, Computer Science Press, Rockville, Maryland, USA, 1989.

76. Maunier, K. L. and Dixon, J. R., "Iterative respecification: a computational model for hierarchical mechanical system design," in *Proceedings of the 1988 ASME International Computers in Engineering Conference and Exhibition*, Tipnis, V. A. and Patton, E. M. (eds.), 1988, pp. 25-32.

77. McCarthy, J., "Circumscription - A form of non-monotonic reasoning," *Artificial Intelligence*, **13** , 1980, pp. 27-39.

78. Minsky, M., "A framework for representing knowledge," in *The Psychology of Computer Vision*, Winston, P. H. (ed.), McGraw-Hill, New York, 1975, **pp. 211-277**.

79. Mistree, F., Karandikar, H. and Kamal, S., "Knowledge-based mathematical programming: A hybrid approach for decision making in design," in *Design Theory for CAD, Proceedings of the IFIP W.G. 5.2*

Working Conference 1985 (Tokyo), Yoshikawa, H. and Warman, E. A. (eds.), North-Holland, Amsterdam, 1987, pp. 201.

80. Mittal, S., Dym, C. L. and Morjaria, M., "PRIDE: An expert system for the design of paper handling systems," *IEEE Computer*, **19**(7), July 1986, pp. 102-114.

81. Murthy, S. S. and Addanki, S., "PROMPT: An innovative design tool," in *Expert Systems in Computer-Aided Design*, Gero, J. S. (ed.), North-Holland, Amsterdam, 1987, pp. 323-347.

82. Nagasawa, I., "Attributive modeling changes CAD," *Pixel*, **86** , November 1989, pp. 147-152. In Japanese.

83. Nakajima, N. and Gossard, D. C.,"Basic Study on Feature Descriptor," MIT CAD Laboratory Technical Report No. 1, Massachusetts Institute of Technology, Cambridge, MA, USA, 1982.

84. Newsome, S. L., Spillers, W. R. and Finger, S. (eds.), *Design Theory '88, Proceedings of the 1988 NSF Grantee Workshop on Design Theory and Methodologies*, Springer-Verlag, New York, Berlin, Heidelberg, London, Paris, Tokyo, 1989.

85. Ohsuga, S., "Conceptual design of CAD systems involving knowledge bases," in *Knowledge Engineering in Computer-Aided Design, Proceedings of the IFIP W.G. 5.2 Working Conference 1984 (Budapest)*, Gero, J. S. (ed.), North-Holland, Amsterdam, 1985, pp. 29-56.

86. Pahl, G. and Beitz, W., *Engineering Design: A Systematic Approach*, The Design Council, London, and Springer-Verlag, Berlin, Heidelberg, New York, London, Paris, Tokyo, 1988.

87. Pentland, A. and Williams, J., "Virtual manufacturing," in *Preprints of NFS Engineering Design Research Conference (June 11-14, 1989, Amherst, MA, USA)*, College of Engineering, University of Massachusetts, Amherst, MA, USA, 1989, pp. 301-316.

88. Peterson, G. E. (ed.), *Object-Oriented Computing 2: Implementations*, IEEE Computer Society Press, Los Angeles, CA, USA, 1987.

89. Peterson, G. E. (ed.), *Object-Oriented Computing 1: Concepts*, IEEE Computer Society Press, Los Angeles, CA, USA, 1987.

90. Pineda, L. A., Klein, E. and Lee, J., "GRAFLOG: Understanding drawings through natural language," *Computer Graphics Forum*, **7**(2), June 1988, pp. 97-103.

91. Pu, P. and Badler, N. I., "Design knowledge capture and causal simulation," in *Intelligent CAD, I*, Yoshikawa, H. and Gossard, D. C. (eds.), North-Holland, Amsterdam, 1989, pp. 201-212.

92. Rehak, D. R., Howard, H. C. and Sriram, D., "Architecture of an integrated knowledge based environment for structural engineering applications," in *Knowledge Engineering in Computer-Aided Design, Proceedings of the IFIP W.G. 5.2 Working Conference 1984 (Budapest)*, Gero, J. S. (ed.), North-Holland, Amsterdam, 1985, pp. 89-124.

93. Reiter, R., "A logic for default reasoning," *Artificial Intelligence*, **13**(1, 2), 1980, pp. 81-132.

94. Rodenacker, W., *Methodisches Konstruieren*, Springer, Berlin, Heidelberg, New York, 1971.

95. Rossignac, J. R., Borrel, P. and Nackman, L. R., "Interactive design with sequences of parameterized transformations," in *Intelligent CAD Systems II: Implementational Issues*, Akman, V., ten Hagen, P. J. W. and Veerkamp, P. J. (eds.), Springer-Verlag, Heidelberg, Berlin, Heidelberg, New York, London, Paris, Tokyo, 1989, pp. 93-125.

96. Ruttkay, Z., Allen, R. H. and Laczik, B., "A multiparadigm user interface for intelligent CAD systems," in *Intelligent CAD Systems I: Theoretical and Methodological Aspects*, ten Hagen, P. J. W. and Tomiyama, T. (eds.), Springer-Verlag, New York, Berlin, Heidelberg, Tokyo, 1987, pp. 242-255.

97. Rychener, M. D. (ed.), *Expert Systems for Engineering Design*, Academic Press, Boston, San Diego, New York, Berkeley, London, Sydney, Tokyo, Toronto, 1988.

98. Sakurai, H. and Gossard, D. C., "Shape feature recognition from 3d solid models," in *Proceedings of the 1988 ASME International Computers in Engineering Conference and Exhibition, Vol. 1*, Tipnis, V. J. and Patton, E. M. (eds.), ASME, New York, 1988, pp. 515-519.

99. Schmidt, J. W. and Thanos, C. (eds.), *Foundations of Knowledge Base Management*, Springer-Verlag, Berlin, Heidelberg, New York, London, Paris, Tokyo, Hong Kong, 1989.

100. Shah, J. J. and Rogers, M. T., "Expert form feature modelling shell," *Computer-Aided Design*, **20**(9), 1988, pp. 515-524.

101. Shortliffe, E. H., *Computer-based Medical Consultations; MYCIN*, American Elsevier, New York, 1976.

102. Smithers, T., Conkie, A., Doheny, J., Logan, B. and Millington, K., "Design as intelligent behavior: An AI in design research programme," in *Artificial Intelligence in Design*, Gero, J. S. (ed.), Computational Mechanics Publications, Southampton, Boston, and Springer-Verlag, Berlin, Heidelberg, New York, London, Paris, Tokyo, Hong Kong, 1989, pp. 294-334.

103. Smithers, T., "AI-based design versus geometry-based design or Why design cannot be supported by geometry alone," *Computer-Aided Design*, **21**(3), April 1989, pp. 141-150.

104. Sriram, D. and Adey, R. A. (eds.), *Applications of Artificial Intelligence in Engineering Problems*, Springer-Verlag, Berlin, Heidelberg, New York, Tokyo, 1986.

105. Sriram, D. and Leff, L., "Knowledge-based expert systems in engineering: An annotated bibliography," *ACM SIGART Newsletter*, July 1989, pp. 38-89.

106. Sriram, D., Logcher, R. and Fukuda, S. (eds.), *Proceedings of the MIT-JSME Workshop on Cooperative Product Development (November 20-21, 1989, Cambridge, MA, USA)*, Massachusetts Institute of Technology, Cambridge, MA, 1989.

107. Suh, N. P., *The Principles of Design*, Oxford University Press, New York, Oxford, 1990.

108. Sunde, G., "A CAD system with declarative specification," in *Intelligent CAD Systems I: Theoretical and Methodological Aspects*, ten Hagen, P. J. W. and Tomiyama, T. (eds.), Springer-Verlag, Berlin, Heidelberg, New York, London, Paris, Tokyo, 1987, pp. 90-104.

109. Sutherland, I. E.,"SKETCHPAD: A man-machine graphical communication system," MIT Lincoln Laboratory Report No. 296, Cambridge, MA, USA, May 1965.

110. Suzuki, H., Ando, H. and Kimura, F., "Synthesizing product shapes with geometric design constraints and reasoning," in *Intelligent CAD, II*, Yoshikawa, H. and Holden, T. (eds.), North-Holland, Amsterdam, 1990, pp. 309-324.

111. Szalapaj, P. J. and Bijl, A., "Knowing where to draw the line," in *Knowledge Engineering in Computer-Aided Design, Proceedings of the IFIP W.G. 5.2 Working Conference 1984 (Budapest)*, Gero, J. S. and Gero, J. S. (eds.), North-Holland, Amsterdam, 1984, pp. 149-169.

112. Takeda, H., Tomiyama, T. and Yoshikawa, H., "A logical formalization of design processes," in *Intelligent CAD, II*, Yoshikawa, H. and Holden, T. (eds.), North-Holland, Amsterdam, 1990, pp. 325-336.

113. ten Hagen, P. J. W. and Tomiyama, T. (eds.), *Intelligent CAD Systems I: Theoretical and Methodological Aspects*, Springer-Verlag, Berlin, Heidelberg, New York, London, Paris, Tokyo, 1987.

114. ten Hagen, P. J. W. and Veerkamp, P. J. (eds.), *Intelligent CAD Systems III: Practical Experience and Evaluation*, Springer-Verlag, Heidelberg, Berlin, Heidelberg, New York, London, Paris, Tokyo, to appear in 1991.

115. Tomiyama, T. and Yoshikawa, H., "An application of knowledge engineering to CAD," in *WDK 10, Proceedings of the International Conference on Engineering Design in Copenhagen 1983*, Hubka, V. and Andreasen, M. M. (eds.), Heurista, Zurich, 1983, pp. 607-614.

116. Tomiyama, T. and Yoshikawa, H., "Requirements and principles for intelligent CAD systems," in *Knowledge Engineering in Computer-Aided Design, Proceedings of the IFIP W.G. 5.2 Working Conference 1984 (Budapest)*, Gero, J. S. (ed.), North-Holland, Amsterdam, 1985, pp. 1-23.

117. Tomiyama, T. and Yoshikawa, H., "Extended general design theory," in *Design Theory for CAD, Proceedings of the IFIP W.G. 5.2 Working Conference 1985 (Tokyo)*, Yoshikawa, H. and Warman, E. A. (eds.), North-Holland, Amsterdam, 1987, pp. 95-130.

118. Tomiyama, T., "Object oriented programming paradigm for intelligent CAD systems," in *Intelligent CAD Systems II: Implementational Issues*, Akman, V., ten Hagen, P. J. W. and Veerkamp, P. J. (eds.), Springer-Verlag, Heidelberg, Berlin, Heidelberg, New York, London, Paris, Tokyo, 1989, pp. 3-16.

119. Tomiyama, T., Kiriyama, T., Takeda, H., Xue, D. and Yoshikawa, H., "Metamodel: A key to intelligent CAD systems," *Research in Engineering Design*, **1**(1), 1989, pp. 19-34.

120. Tomiyama, T. and Arbab, F. (eds.), "Special Issue on Features and Geometric Reasoning," *Computers & Graphics*, **14**(2), 1990.

121. Tomiyama, T. and ten Hagen, P. J. W., "Representing Knowledge in Two Distinct Descriptions: Extensional vs. Intensional," *Artificial Intelligence in Engineering*, **5**(1), 1990, pp. 23-32.

122. Tomiyama, T., Xue, D. and Ishida, Y., "An experience with developing a design knowledge representation language," in *Intelligent CAD Systems III: Practical Experience and Evaluation*, ten Hagen, P. J. W. and Veerkamp, P. J. (eds.), Springer-Verlag, Heidelberg, Berlin, Heidelberg, New York, London, Paris, Tokyo, to appear in 1991.

123. Treur, J., "A logical framework for design processes," in *Intelligent CAD Systems III: Practical Experience and Evaluation*, ten Hagen, P. J. W. and Veerkamp, P. J. (eds.), Springer-Verlag, Heidelberg, Berlin, Heidelberg, New York, London, Paris, Tokyo, to appear in 1991.

124. Ullman, D. G., Dietterich, T. G. and Stauffer, L. A., "A model of the mechanical design process based on empirical data: a summary," in *Artificial Intelligence in Engineering Design*, Gero, J. S. (ed.), Elsevier, Amsterdam, Oxford, New York, Tokyo, 1988, pp. 193-215.

125. van den Kroonenberg, H. H., "CAD applications in the creative phases of the methodological design process," in *Proceedings of CAPE '86, Second International Conference on Computer Applications in Production and Engineering*, Bo, K., Estensen, L. and Warman, E. A. (eds.), Copenhagen, 1986, pp. 339-348.

126. Veerkamp, P., Kiriyama, T., Xue, D. and Tomiyama, T., "Representation and implementation of design knowledge for intelligent CAD: Theoretical aspects," in *Preprints of the Fourth Eurographics Workshop on Intelligent CAD Systems (April 24-27, 1990, Mortefontaine, France)*, 1990, pp. 184-205.

127. Veerkamp, P., Pieters Kwiers, R. and Hagen, P. J. W., *Intelligent CAD Systems III: Practical Experience and Evaluation*, Springer-Verlag, Heidelberg, Berlin, Heidelberg, New York, London, Paris, Tokyo, to appear in 1991.

128. Weiler, K., "Boundary graph operators for non-manifold geometric modeling topology representations," in *Geometric Modeling for CAD Applications*, Wozny, M. J., McLaughlin, H. W. and Encarnacao, J. L. (eds.), North-Holland, Amsterdam, 1988, pp. 37-66.

129. Weiler, K., "The radial edge structure: A topological representation for non-manifold geometric broundary modeling," in *Geometric Modeling for CAD Applications*, Wozny, M. J., McLaughlin, H. W. and Encarnacao, J. L. (eds.), North-Holland, Amsterdam, 1988, pp. 3-36.

130. Weld, D. S. and de Kleer, J. (eds.), *Readings in Qualitative Reasoning about Physical Systems*, Morgan-Kaufmann Publishers, Inc., San Mateo, CA, 1990.

131. Weyhrauch, R. W., "Prolegomena to a theory of mechanized formal reasoning," *Artificial Intelligence*, **13** , 1980, pp. 133-170.

132. Widman, L. E., Loparo, K. A. and Nielsen, N. R. (eds.), *Artificial Intelligence, Simulation, and Modeling*, John Wiley & Sons, New York, Chichester, Brisbane, Toronto, Singapore, 1989.

133. Wilson, P. R. and Pratt, M. J., "A taxonomy of features for solid modeling," in *Geometric Modeling for CAD Applications*, Wozny, M. J., McLaughlin, H. W. and Encarnacao, J. L. (eds.), North-Holland, Amsterdam, 1988, pp. 125-136.

134. Woodbury, R. F. and Oppenheim, I. J., "An approach to geometric reasoning," in *Intelligent CAD, I*, Yoshikawa, H. and Gossard, D. C. (eds.), North-Holland, Amsterdam, 1989, pp. 149-168.

135. Xue, D., Kiriyama, T., Veerkamp, P. and Tomiyama, T., "Representation and implementation of design knowledge for intelligent CAD: Implementational aspects," in *Preprints of the Fourth Eurographics Workshop on Intelligent CAD Systems (April 24-27, 1990, Mortefontaine, France)*, 1990, pp. 206-226.

136. Yoshikawa, H., "General design theory and a CAD system," in *Man-Machine Communication in CAD/CAM, Proceedings of the IFIP Working Group 5.2 Working Conference 1980 (Tokyo)*, Sata, T. and Warman, E. A. (eds.), North-Holland, Amsterdam, 1981, pp. 35-58.

137. Yoshikawa, H., Arai, E. and Goto, T., "Theory of design experiment," *Journal of JSPE*, **47**(7), 1981, pp. 830-835. In Japanese.

138. Yoshikawa, H., "CAD framework guided by general design theory," in *CAD Systems Framework, Proceedings of IFIP Working Group 5.2*, Bo, K. and Lillehagen, E. M. (eds.), North-Holland, Amsterdam, 1983, pp. 241-253.

139. Yoshikawa, H., "Automation of thinking in design," in *Proceedings of CAPE '83, Second International Conference on Computer Applications in Production and Engineering, Amsterdam*, Warman, E. A. (ed.), North-Holland, Amsterdam, 1983, pp. 405-417.

140. Yoshikawa, H. and Warman, E. A. (eds.), *Design Theory for CAD, Proceedings of the IFIP W.G. 5.2 Working Conference 1985 (Tokyo)*, North-Holland, Amsterdam, 1987.

141. Yoshikawa, H. and Gossard, D. C. (eds.), *Intelligent CAD, I, Proceedings of the First IFIP Working Group 5.2 Workshop on Intelligent CAD, 6-8 October 1987, Cambridge, MA, USA*, North-Holland, Amsterdam, 1989.

142. Yoshikawa, H. and Holden, T. (eds.), *Intelligent CAD, II: Proceedings of the Second IFIP Working Group 5.2 Workshop on Intelligent CAD*, North-Holland, Amsterdam, 1990.

143. Yoshikawa, H. and Arbab, F. (eds.), *Intelligent CAD, III: Proceedings of the Third IFIP Working Group 5.2 Workshop on Intelligent CAD*, North-Holland, Amsterdam, in preparation, 1991.

Image Reconstruction for Medical Applications

David W. Townsend

1. Introduction

The goal of medical image reconstruction is to recover the spatial distribution of a parameter such as the X-ray attenuation coefficient, or radioisotope concentration, inside the body from external measurements, i.e. non-invasive. When the behaviour of the parameter is determined as a function of depth within the body, the resulting image is tomographic, and the procedure is termed tomographic image reconstruction. The essential feature of this procedure is that the image is reconstructed from *projections* of the underlying distribution. Image reconstruction from projections is a problem that has arisen repeatedly over the past thirty years in a wide variety of different disciplines as diverse as electron microscopy and radioastronomy.

One of the earliest developments of reconstruction techniques was due to Bracewell (1956) for use in radioastronomy. Cormack (1963,1964) published a reconstruction method with applications to radiology, and in the eight years from 1964, reconstruction algorithms appeared in the literature from a number of unconnected fields such as optics (Rowley, 1969; Berry and Gibbs, 1970), electron microscopy (DeRosier and Klug, 1968) and medicine (Muehllehner and Wetzel, 1971). The methods proposed independently included Fourier-based methods (Tretiak et al, 1969; Bates and Peters, 1971) similar to the method of Bracewell (1956), algebraic or iterative reconstruction (Gordon, Bender and Herman, 1970), and convolution-type algorithms (Ramachandran and Lakshminarayanan, 1971). It is interesting to note that a complete solution to the problem of the reconstruction of a function from an infinite number of projections was published by Radon (1917), at the time working on a problem in gravitation, although prior to 1972 his work was apparently unknown to almost all researchers in the field.

The introduction by Hounsfield (1973) of the computer-assisted brain scanner was a major breakthrough, for which he shared the 1979 Nobel Prize for physiology and medicine with Cormack. The appearence of the scanner had a profound effect not only in radiology, but also in other medical fields such as nuclear medicine, ultrasound and magnetic resonance, stimulating a period of intense mathematical development (see, for example, Herman 1980). Many of the algorithms which emerged were similar in nature, and much effort was expended in finding the most efficient numerical implementations. Subsequently, the methods have been applied in other fields such as, for example, radar, non-destructive testing and micro tomography.

In this tutorial, we shall review the common mathematical basis of these algorithms, and the particular problems associated with their digital implementation (see also Brooks and Di Chiro, 1976). While the principle mathematical results are summarised in these lecture notes, the tutorial will offer a more intuitive understanding of the techniques. They will be illustrated with examples taken mainly from the medical field, although reference will be made to other application areas where appropriate.

2. A Review of some Basic Concepts

In this section we present some of the basic formulae required for an understanding of image reconstruction. We assume implicitly that all functions we use are well-behaved and have properties that satisfy standard conditions of differentiability and integrability, etc. We shall explicitly state when this is not the case.

2.1 Notation

Following Rowland (1979), we define the functions:

$$\text{(1)} \qquad \begin{aligned} \mathrm{id}(x) &= x \\ \mathrm{abs}(x) &= |x| \\ \mathrm{rcp}(x) &= 1/x \\ \mathrm{sgn}(x) &= +1 \ \text{if} \ x > 0 \\ &= -1 \ \text{if} \ x < 0 \end{aligned}$$

The differential operator $\mathcal{D}$ is defined in the usual way by:

$$\text{(2)} \qquad [\mathcal{D}f](x) = \lim_{\Delta x \to 0} \frac{f(x+\Delta x) - f(x)}{\Delta x}$$

In some situations, a 1-D transform (e.g. differential, Fourier, etc.) will be applied to a function of two or more variables. In such cases, we will implicitly assume that the transformation is applied to the *first variable* of the function.

We define the 1-D Dirac δ-function, $\delta(x)$, by:

$$\text{(3)} \qquad \delta(x) = \int_{-\infty}^{+\infty} dy\, e^{-2\pi ixy}$$

We shall use this function principally for its sifting property:

$$\text{(4)} \qquad \int_{-\infty}^{+\infty} dx\, f(x)\, \delta(a-x) = f(a)$$

2.2 Fourier Transform

We define the 1-D Fourier transform of a function f(x) by:

$$(5) \qquad [\mathfrak{F}_1 f](X) = \int_{-\infty}^{+\infty} dx\, f(x)\, e^{-2\pi i\, xX} = F(X)$$

where $\mathfrak{F}_1$ denotes the Fourier transform operator with the dimensionality given by the subscript. F(X) is the Fourier transform of f(x) with frequency space coordinate X, so that f(x) and F(X) form a Fourier transform pair. This definition extends straightforwardly to two and three dimensions:

$$(6) \qquad [\mathfrak{F}_2 f](X,Y) = \int_{-\infty}^{+\infty} dy \int_{-\infty}^{+\infty} dx\, f(x,y)\, e^{-2\pi i\, (xX + yY)} = F(X,Y)$$

$$(7) \qquad [\mathfrak{F}_3 f](X,Y,Z) = \int_{-\infty}^{+\infty} dz \int_{-\infty}^{+\infty} dy \int_{-\infty}^{+\infty} dx\, f(x,y,z)\, e^{-2\pi i\, (xX + yY + zZ)} = F(X,Y,Z)$$

The Fourier transform of the derivative of a function may be written:

$$(8) \qquad [\mathfrak{F} \mathfrak{D} f] = 2\pi i\, id\, .\, [\mathfrak{F} f]$$

where $\mathfrak{D}$ and id have been defined in equations (1) and (2) above.

Analagously, the 1-D inverse Fourier transform $\mathfrak{F}_1^{-1}$ is defined by:

$$(9) \qquad [\mathfrak{F}_1^{-1} f](x) = \int_{-\infty}^{+\infty} dX\, F(X)\, e^{+2\pi i\, xX} = f(x)$$

with similar expressions in higher dimensions. We assume that, in any dimension, for all functions of interest f, we have $\mathfrak{F}^{-1}\mathfrak{F} f = \mathfrak{F}\mathfrak{F}^{-1} f = f$.

The space in which measurements are made and in which images are to be reconstructed is the *spatial domain*. Coordinates in the spatial domain are distances, expressed in cm, mm, etc. They will be denoted by symbols x, y, s, t, etc. Functions in the spatial domain are arguments of the Fourier transform, or result from inverse Fourier transform.

Functions resulting from a Fourier transform, or arguments to the inverse Fourier transform, are in the *frequency domain*. Coordinates in the frequency domain are spatial frequencies, expressed in cm^{-1}, mm^{-1}, etc. They will be denoted by the corresponding capital letters X, Y, S, T, etc, with obvious spatial domain equivalence. A function in the spatial domain with finite or compact support is *spatially limited*. A function in the spatial domain whose Fourier transform has compact support is *band limited*. A band limited function does not have compact support in the spatial domain.

We shall encounter some functions for which Fourier transformation is not so straightforward. For example, the function rcp defined above has a singularity at the origin, so that the Fourier integral is undefined. The Fourier integral may, however, be evaluated by resorting to *generalized function theory*, which is beyond the scope of this tutorial. When required, we will simply state the result without proof. Thus:

$$\mathfrak{F}_1 \mathrm{rcp} = -i\pi \, \mathrm{sgn} \tag{10}$$

2.3 Convolution

The convolution of two functions f(x) and h(x) is defined by:

$$[f * h](x) = \int_{-\infty}^{+\infty} dx' \, f(x') \, h(x - x') \tag{11}$$

where * denotes a 1-D convolution. Similar definitions exist in 2-D (**) and 3-D (***) for two and three dimensional functions. In 1-D, an element of the convolution, say at $x = x_1$, is obtained by superimposing the function h(x) on the function f(x), with h(x) centred on the point x_1. The value of the convolution at this point is then obtained by summing the product of h(x) with f(x) for all values of x.

By taking the Fourier transform of a convolution, it is easy to show that the following relation holds:

$$\mathfrak{F}[f * h] = \mathfrak{F}f \, . \, \mathfrak{F}h \tag{12}$$

where "." denotes point by point multiplication. This useful result is the Fourier convolution theorem, and analagous expressions exist in two and three dimensions. As will be seen, it is particularly useful to obtain a function, say f(x), when both the convolution (f * h) and the function h(x) are known.

The relationship *convolution* ↔ *product* holds equally from either domain. Thus, a product in the frequency domain becomes a convolution in the spatial domain.

It is important to note that, in equation (11), the function h depends only on the difference x-x' rather than on x and x' individually. This is the essential feature of the convolution integral. Thus, since the convolution at $x = x_1$ evaluates the sum of the products $f(x').h(x_1-x')$, it is necessary that the form of h does not depend on the coordinate x_1. Functions which exhibit this property are called *shift-invariant*, since their functional form is the same wherever they are positioned in x. As will be seen later, shift-invariant functions play a central role in image reconstruction from projections and the necessity to incorporate shift-variance increases the complexity of the reconstruction problem.

2.4 Hilbert Transform

The Hilbert transform $\mathcal{H}$ is just a special case of convolution with h = -1/π rcp. Thus,

$$(13) \qquad [\mathcal{H}f](x) = \int_{-\infty}^{+\infty} dx' \frac{1}{\pi} \frac{f(x')}{(x-x')} = -\frac{1}{\pi}[f * rcp](x)$$

At the point of discontinuity x = x', the Cauchy principal value is taken (assuming the limit exists). Applying the Fourier convolution theorem to the Hilbert transform, we find:

$$\begin{aligned} (14) \qquad [\mathcal{F}\mathcal{H}f] &= -1/\pi\,[\mathcal{F}\,rcp]\,.\,[\mathcal{F}f] \\ &= i\ sgn\,.\,[\mathcal{F}f] \end{aligned}$$

using equation (10). Combining equations (8) and (14), we obtain:

$$\begin{aligned} (15) \qquad [\mathcal{F}\mathcal{H}\mathcal{D}f] &= i\ sgn\,.\,[\mathcal{F}\mathcal{D}f] \\ &= -2\pi\ sgn\,.\,id\,.\,[\mathcal{F}f] \\ &= -2\pi\ abs\,.\,[\mathcal{F}f] \end{aligned}$$

and thus:

$$(16) \qquad [\mathcal{H}\mathcal{D}f] = [\mathcal{F}^{-1}(-2\pi\ abs\,.\,\mathcal{F}\mathcal{D}f)]$$

2.5 Discretization Effects

The operators and transforms defined above were applied to continuous functions. Radon's result, and others which will be described in the next section, are derived for reconstruction from an infinite number of projections, each projection being a continuous function in the projection variable. Obviously, in practice, these conditions cannot be met: only a finite number of projections are available, and each projection is sampled by the finite resolution of the detectors. The discrete nature of the data introduces a number of additional difficulties, necessitating a discrete form of the corresponding reconstruction algorithm (see later).

The reconstructed image will also be discretized as a 2-D matrix of elements called *pixels* (picture elements). There is a relationship between the reconstructed image resolution and the angular and radial data sampling which will be discussed later. When extended to three dimensions, the 3-D reconstructed image will be discretized as a 3-D matrix of *voxels* (volume elements).

2.5.1 Sampling Requirements

The sampling of a continuous function f(x) may be considered as multiplying the function by a set of unit impulses (Brigham, 1974). We denote the set, or train, of impulses (the shah function) by III(x), where:

$$(17) \qquad III(x) = \sum_{n} \delta(x - n\Delta)$$

Here the spatial domain sampling interval is Δ. The sampled version of f(x) is therefore f(x).III(x), which is equal to f(x) at the sample points $x = n\Delta$ and zero otherwise. If F(X) is the continuous Fourier transform of f(x), what is the Fourier transform of the sampled version of f(x)? Taking the Fourier transform of the sampled function in the spatial domain and applying the Fourier convolution theorem, we obtain:

$$(18) \qquad [\mathfrak{F} f.\mathrm{III}](X) = [\mathfrak{F} f](X) * [\mathfrak{F}\,\mathrm{III}](X) = F(X) * [\mathfrak{F}\,\mathrm{III}](X)$$

Thus, in the frequency domain, the sampling of f(x) in the spatial domain results in the *convolution* of F(X) with the Fourier transform of III(x). It can be shown that III(x) is its own Fourier transform:

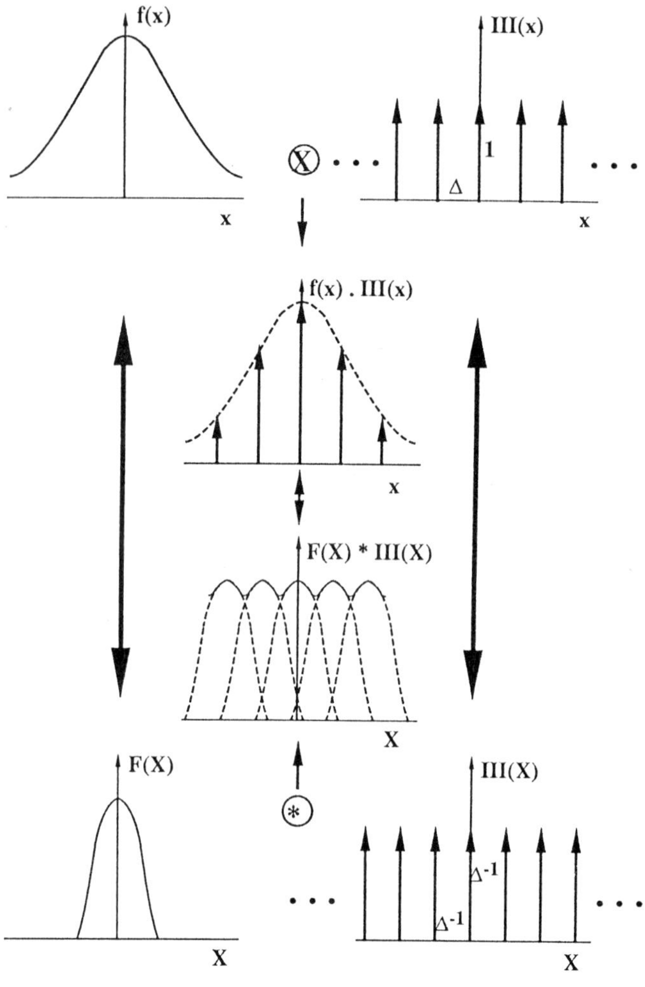

Fig.1 The Sampling Theorem and Aliasing

$$\text{(19)} \qquad III(X) = \frac{1}{\Delta} \sum_{n} \delta(X - n/\Delta)$$

which is a set of impulse functions with spacing $1/\Delta$. As shown in fig.1, the convolution in the frequency domain results in F(X) being repeated, with a spacing between the repetitions of $1/\Delta$. Therefore, if F(X) contains frequencies greater than $1/2\Delta$, the repetitions will *overlap* and the low frequencies of one period will be contaminated by high frequencies from the next period. This effect is called *aliasing*, (Bracewell, 1965) and it is the consequence of undersampling.

The condition to be satisfied for complete recovery of a function is known as the Sampling Theorem, which may be stated formally as follows: if a function f(x) is sampled in the spatial domain with interval Δ, then only frequencies up to $1/2\Delta$ can be recovered without aliasing. Alternatively, if a function contains frequencies up to $1/2\Delta$, then it must be sampled in the spatial domain at *twice* that rate in order to accurately represent it. Complete recovery of a function is theoretically possible, therefore, providing it is band-limited.

2.5.2 Discrete Convolution and FFT

Consider the discrete convolution of two functions each sampled at N points. From the definition of convolution as the overlap between the two functions, it is evident that the convolution will contain 2N-1 discrete values. In general, the convolution of an N-point function with an M-point function will contain N+M-1 values. In practice, if one or both of the functions are padded with zeros, the convolution may be small, or zero, outside the central N samples. As we shall see when we discuss the implementation of the algorithms, it is important to ensure that the functions are zero-padded to minimise edge effects.

The use of the Fast Fourier Transform (FFT) implementation of the Discrete Fourier Transform (DFT) requires that the number of samples be a power of 2. Since the measured samples do not always satisfy this requirement, we will again use zero-padding. It is important to ensure that the sampled functions decrease smoothly to zero (or small values) at the extremeties to avoid generating high frequencies (from sharp edges) in the frequency domain that will lead to aliasing artifacts.

3. Image Reconstruction in Two Dimensions

In this section, we describe a number of algorithms to reconstruct a two-dimensional image. First, however, let us clearly state the problem.

Consider a two-dimensional function f(x,y). The value of the function at each spatial position (x,y) represents the value of a certain parameter. In medical imaging, this parameter may be: the linear attenuation coefficient (electron density) in X-ray CT, the concentration of a radioactive tracer within an internal organ in single photon (SPECT) or positron emission tomography (PET), the acoustic refraction index in ultrasound tomography (US), or the proton density within tissue in magentic resonance imaging (MRI). Non-medical applications include the tracking of oil-flow in aero engines, reconstructing maps of the solar surface from microwave emissions, non-destructive testing using neutron radiographs of, for example, reactor cores, reconstructing complex biomolecules from electron micrographs, and mapping Fermi surfaces in metals from positron annihilation measurements.

3.1 The Radon Transform

The feature that all these methods have in common is that the desired function f(x,y) cannot be measured directly, but instead must be reconstructed from a set of measured *line integrals*. A line integral p(s, ϕ) of f(x,y) at angle ϕ is defined by:

$$(20) \qquad p(s,\phi) = \int dt\, f(s \cos\phi - t \sin\phi,\ s \sin\phi + t \cos\phi)$$

where, as shown in fig.2, integration is along the t-direction orthogonal to s. For the 2-D function f(x,y) the set of all 1-D line integrals is called the *Radon Transform* of the function and thus:

$$(21) \qquad [\mathcal{R}_2 f](s,\phi) = p(s,\phi)$$

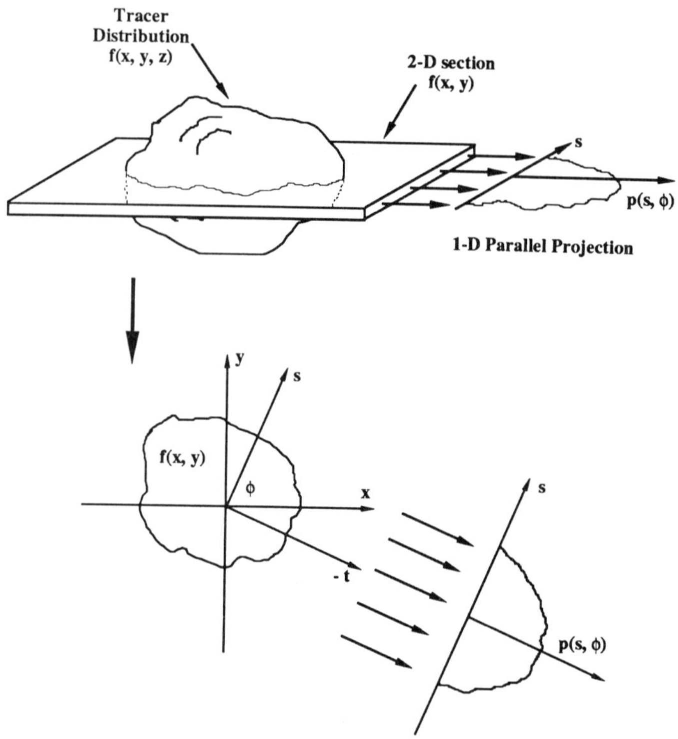

Fig.2 One dimensional Projection of a Two-dimensional Function

where the subscript indicates the Radon transform of a 2-D function. We will also discuss later the Radon transform in higher dimensions. In all the 2-D applications mentioned above, it is the Radon transform of the desired function which is measured by the detection system. For example, in X-ray CT the relationship between the incident beam intensity I_0 and the emerging beam intensity I is given by the usual exponential law:

$$(22) \qquad I = I_0 \, e^{-\int f(x,y)\, dt}$$

where f(x,y) is the linear attenuation coefficient for X-rays in tissue. Taking logarithms,

$$(23) \qquad -\log_e(I/I_0) = [\mathcal{R}_2 f]$$

Similarly, PET and SPECT scanners measure line integrals of tracer concentration through the body. Thus, the problem that interests us, and which is the topic of this tutorial, is the inverse problem: *Given the Radon Transform of a function, how do we recover the original function.* The inverse Radon Transform is the solution to this problem.

It is clear from fig.2 that a line integral is the projection of the function f(x,y) along the integration line. Imaging devices usually group sets of line integrals with a common property: for example, the set of all integrals with the same angle ϕ but different radial coordinates s is called a *parallel projection* of f(x,y), while the set of line integrals with different (s,ϕ) but all emerging from a single point is called a divergent or *fan-beam projection.* CT scanners generate fan-beam projections, data from PET and SPECT scanners are sorted into parallel beam projections. Inversion of the Radon transform is also called reconstruction from projections.

3.2 The Central Slice Theorem

Since it is not necessarily obvious that the inverse problem has a unique solution, it is useful to provide some insight into the relationship between the Radon transform and the original function. This insight is provided by the Central Slice, or Projection, theorem. Consider a parallel projection $p(s,\phi)$ for some ϕ, and let us take the 1-D Fourier transform with respect to the first variable, s.

$$(24) \qquad P(S,\phi) = \int ds \; p(s,\phi)\, e^{-2\pi i \, sS}$$

Now, we can substitute $p(s,\phi)$ from equation (20) to obtain:

$$(25) \qquad P(S,\phi) = \int ds \int dt \; f(s\cos\phi - t\sin\phi,\; s\sin\phi + t\cos\phi)\, e^{-2\pi i \, sS}$$

$$= \iint ds\, dt \; f(s\cos\phi - t\sin\phi,\; s\sin\phi + t\sin\phi)\, e^{-2\pi i \,(sS + tT)}$$

$$= [\mathcal{F}_2 f](X,Y) \;, \quad \text{with } S = \sqrt{(X^2 + Y^2)} \text{ and } \tan\phi = Y/X.$$

which is simply the 2-D Fourier transform of f(x,y) along the line T = 0, i.e. the line through the origin in the frequency domain making an angle ϕ with the Y-axis. Thus, the Fourier transform of any parallel projection of a function is *identical to* the Fourier transform of the original function along the line through the origin (hence, central slice) in the frequency domain at the same angle as the projection. This simple result immediately suggests one method to reconstruct f(x,y) from its projections: build up F(X,Y) in the frequency domain, radially line by line, and then take the inverse 2-D Fourier transform. While there are a number of practical problems with such an approach, and alternative algorithms, it demonstrates that measuring projections is equivalent to determining the function in the frequency domain, and hence inversion of the Radon transform should be possible.

3.3 Backprojection

Most of the algorithms which we will discuss involve a procedure called *backprojection*. As its name suggests, this procedure is formally the reverse of projection, or integration. Simple backprojection consists of taking a projection value p(s,ϕ) and redistributing it back along the original integration path. However, it is clearly not possible to redistribute the integral in the same way as it was originally distributed because this information has been lost in the integration process. Instead, the projection value is redistributed *uniformly* back along the integration path. Mathematically, this procedure, represented by the transformation $\mathfrak{B}$, is defined by:

$$(26) \qquad [\mathfrak{B}p](x,y) = \int_0^\pi d\phi \; p(x\cos\phi + y\sin\phi, \phi) = b(x,y)$$

At each point in the backprojection b(x,y) the function value is obtained by summing the values of *all* the integration lines passing through the point (x,y), i.e. lines with $s = x\cos\phi + y\sin\phi$. It is evident that b(x,y) is not the original function f(x,y), and we will see later how the two are related.

Equation (26) expresses the continuous version of backprojection. In practice, a discrete implementation is used where the integration is replaced by a summation over all projection angles.

3.4 The Inverse Radon Transform

We are now ready to derive formally the inverse Radon transform by combining the previous results. We will use 2-D polar coordinates (R,α) in the frequency domain, where:

$$X = R\cos\alpha \;, \quad Y = R\sin\alpha \;, \quad \text{and } R = \sqrt{(X^2 + Y^2)}$$

We begin with the identity:

$$f(x,y) = [\mathfrak{F}_2^{-1}\mathfrak{F}_2 f](x,y)$$

Expanding the inverse Fourier transform in polar coordinates gives:

$$f(x,y) = \int_0^{+\infty} R\, dR \int_0^{2\pi} d\alpha\, [\mathfrak{F}_2 f](R\cos\alpha, R\sin\alpha)\, e^{2\pi i R\,(x\cos\alpha + y\sin\alpha)}$$

$$f(x,y) = \int_{-\infty}^{+\infty} |R|\, dR \int_0^{\pi} d\alpha\, [\mathfrak{F}_2 f](R\cos\alpha, R\sin\alpha)\, e^{2\pi i R\,(x\cos\alpha + y\sin\alpha)}$$

Now, we know from equation (25) that the 2-D Fourier transform of f(x,y) is the 1-D Fourier transform of $p(s,\phi)$ at the same angle. Thus, substituting for $\mathfrak{F}_2 f$ and using equation (21) we get:

$$f(x,y) = \int_{-\infty}^{+\infty} |R|\, dR \int_0^{\pi} d\alpha\, [\mathfrak{F}_1 \mathfrak{R}_2 f](R,\alpha)\, e^{2\pi i R\,(x\cos\alpha + y\sin\alpha)}$$

$$= \int_0^{\pi} d\alpha \int_{-\infty}^{+\infty} dR\, [|R|\,.\,\mathfrak{F}_1 \mathfrak{R}_2 f](R,\alpha)\, e^{2\pi i R\,(x\cos\alpha + y\sin\alpha)}$$

Noting that the inner integral is an inverse Fourier transform, and re-writing this equation using the operator notation defined earlier, we find:

$$f(x,y) = \int_0^{\pi} d\alpha\, [\mathfrak{F}_1^{-1} [\text{abs}\,.\,\mathfrak{F}_1 \mathfrak{R}_2 f](x\cos\alpha + y\sin\alpha, \alpha)$$

Comparing this with equation (26) for backprojection:

$$(27) \qquad f(x,y) = \mathfrak{B}\mathfrak{F}_1^{-1}\, [\text{abs}\,.\,\mathfrak{F}_1 \mathfrak{R}_2 f](x,y)$$

Using equation (16), we obtain finally:

$$(28) \qquad f(x,y) = -1/2\pi\, [\mathfrak{B}\mathcal{H}\mathfrak{D}\mathfrak{R}_2 f](x,y)$$

This is the result, expressed in operator notation, that was first derived by Radon in 1917. To invert the Radon transform, we first differentiate the 1-D projection data with respect to the projection variable (s). We then take the Hilbert transform, or convolve the differentiated projection with rcp, and then finally backproject these modified projections to recover the original function. Note that the transformations prior to backprojection compensate for the uniform redistribution of the projection values during backprojection and result in the reconstruction of f(x,y) not of b(x,y). Replacing the operators by their integral transforms gives:

$$(29) \qquad f(x,y) = \frac{1}{2\pi^2} \int_0^{\pi} d\phi \int_{-\infty}^{\infty} ds' \frac{\partial\, p(s',\phi)/\partial s'}{s - s'}$$

Equation (29) is then the solution to the inverse problem of image reconstruction. While this is mathematically exact, it has been derived for continuous (noiseless) functions. Obviously, a major drawback is the appearance of the derivative: the inverse problem is ill-conditioned, and attempts to differentiate measured projection data containing noise will generally result in an increase in the noise. In practice it is necessary to find a better way to implement this inversion procedure, explicitly avoiding the differentiation step and re-expressing the singular integral of the Hilbert transform. The techniques used have been called *regularisation* techniques (see, for example, Herman, 1980).

3.5 The Convolution-Backprojection Algorithm for Parallel Projections

This is the form of the Radon inversion which has been implemented in the majority of commercial medical scanners. Returning to equation (27) and using the Fourier convolution theorem, we obtain:

$$(30) \qquad f(x,y) = \int_0^{\pi} d\phi \, \{[\mathfrak{F}_1^{-1} |S|] * p(s,\phi)\}$$

This expression shows that to reconstruct f(x,y) from p(s,ϕ), we simply convolve the projection data with the inverse Fourier transform of |S|, and then backproject. Alternatively, applying the Fourier convolution theorem to the integrand:

$$(31) \qquad f(x,y) = \int_0^{\pi} d\phi \, \{\mathfrak{F}_1^{-1} [|S|.\, P(S,\phi)]\}$$

which expresses the inner convolution as a product:- multiply the 1-D Fourier transform of the projection data by |S|, take the inverse transform and backproject. The alternative procedures of equations (30) and (31) are filtering operations. The filtering operation in the frequency domain involves multiplication by |S|, the absolute value of the frequency domain radial coordinate. It is called a *ramp* filter. In the spatial domain, this operation is replaced by the convolution with $\mathfrak{F}_1^{-1}|S|$. The function |S| is not integrable (the intregrand diverges), and hence does not possess a Fourier transform in the usual sense.

Two approaches are available. The first is to use the theory of generalised functions mentioned above (Lighthill, 1958), from which it can be shown that $\mathfrak{F}_1^{-1}|S| = -1/2\pi^2 s^2$. Such a function is non-local and has long tails. The second approach is to replace |S| with a windowed, or apodized, version (Rowland, 1979), denoted by |S| A(S), where A(S) is the apodizing function. The role of A(S) is two-fold: firstly, it limits the filter to some maximum frequency (i.e. A(S) is band-limited), and secondly it can be used to attenuate higher frequencies to avoid the excessive noise amplification which is intrinsic to inversion of the Radon transform. The simplest choice for A(S) is a rectangular function which has the value unity for $|S| \leq K$ and zero otherwise. We can define a function $h_K(s)$ by:

$$(32) \qquad h_K(s) = \int_{-K}^{K} dS \, |S| \, e^{-2\pi i S s}$$

An obvious choice of the maximum frequency K is that which satisfies the sampling theorem, i.e. $K = 1/2\Delta$, for projection data with a sampling interval of Δ. This integral may be evaluated by parts (Ramachandran and Lakshminarayanan, 1971) to give:

$$(33) \qquad h_K(s) = \frac{\sin(2\pi K s)}{\pi s} - \frac{\sin^2(\pi K s)}{\pi^2 s^2}$$

The first term in equation (33) behaves as sinx/x and thus the band-limited filter will have oscillatory behaviour. An alternative form was proposed by Shepp and Logan (1974) who chose a more smoothly varying behaviour for A(S). A common choice is to use a generalised Hamming window (Hamming, 1983):

$$(34) \qquad A(S) = \begin{cases} \alpha + (1-\alpha)\cos(\pi S/K) & \text{if } S \leq K \\ 0 & \text{if } S > K \end{cases}$$

The parameter α for a given K controls the way in which the higher frequencies are attenuated. A typical example, shown in fig.3, is for $\alpha = 0.5$, with a ramp filter ($\alpha = 1$) plotted for comparison.

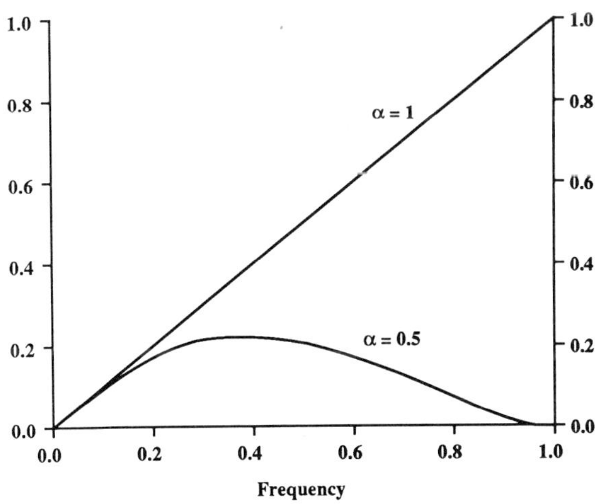

Fig.3 The ramp filter ($\alpha = 1$) and a generalised Hamming with $\alpha = 0.5$.

An apodized version of the spatial domain filter can be obtained from $-1/2\pi^2s^2 * a(s)$, where a(s) is the inverse Fourier transform of A(S).

3.6 Filtered Backprojection for Divergent Projections

A good discussion of this topic can be found in Herman (1980). The full treatment is beyond the scope of this tutorial, but a few points are worth noting. Interest in reconstruction from divergent projections arises because some imaging devices, the CT scanner in particular (Peters and Lewitt, 1977), acquire their data using a collimated source of photons and an arc of detectors centred at the source. The photons are emitted from the source in a fan, the fan angle corresponding to the detector arc. For the divergent geometry, the parallel projections $p(s,\phi)$ are replaced by $g(\sigma,\beta)$, where β is the angle of the source position and σ is the angle of a given projection line within the fan for the source at position β.

Obviously, each projection line (σ,β) also corresponds to a line (s,ϕ). It is essentially only the order in which the projection lines are acquired that is different. It is thus possible to *rebin* the divergent data into a set of parallel projections and then reconstruct the image using the algorithm presented in the previous section. Some interpolation may be required, first to form parallel projections with unequal sampling intervals, and then to sample each parallel projection uniformly.

The alternative approach is to reconstruct an image directly from the divergent projections. It has been found that a similar expression to equation (30) exists for the inverse Radon transform for divergent projections, and that by an appropriate change of variable, it can again be expressed in terms of convolution and backprojection. A reconstruction formula given by Herman (1980) for divergent projections $g(\sigma,\beta)$ is:

$$f(x,y) = \frac{D}{4\pi^2}\int_0^{2\pi} d\beta \frac{1}{W^2}\int_{-\delta}^{\delta} d\sigma \, [q_1(\sigma' - \sigma)\cos\sigma + q_2(\sigma' - \sigma)] \, g(\sigma,\beta)$$

where D is the radius of the circle of rotation of the source, W is a weighting factor and σ' an angular factor, both of which depend on β and the position of the reconstruction point (x,y). The divergent fan angle is 2δ. The functions q_1 and q_2 have the role of convolving or filter functions (analogous to $-1/2\pi^2s^2 * a(s)$ in the case of parallel projections), and thus the first term in the inner integral is the projection data weighted with a cosine function and convolved with q_1, while the second term is the projection data convolved with q_2. The resulting filtered projections are then backprojected with a weight $1/W^2$ which depends not only on the source position β but also on the position of the point (x,y). The main steps in the algorithm are thus similar to those for the parallel projection version.

It has been found that there is little difference between reconstructions made using the divergent projection algorithm and those made using rebinning and parallel projections. There may, however, be certain practical reasons to prefer the divergent algorithm over the rebinning procedure, particularly when there are large quantities of data to be rebinned.

3.7 The Rho-Filtered Layergram

An alternative, mathematically-equivalent formulation of the inverse Radon transform can be obtained by interchanging the backprojection and filtering operations. From the definition of backprojection, equation (26), with p(s,ϕ) replaced by the inverse Fourier transform of P(S,ϕ), we get:

$$\text{(35)} \qquad b(x,y) = \int_0^\pi d\phi \int_{-\infty}^{+\infty} dS\, P(S,\phi)\, e^{2\pi i\, Ss}$$

If we now rewrite this equation in polar coordinates, noting that in the spatial domain (r,α) the projection coordinate s = r cos(α-ϕ), and that in the frequency domain S is identical to the radial coordinate R:

$$\text{(36)} \qquad b(r,\alpha) = \int_0^\pi d\phi \int_{-\infty}^{+\infty} dR\, F(R,\phi)\, e^{2\pi i\, rR\cos(\alpha - \phi)}$$

where we have used the projection theorem to replace P(S,ϕ). This may be written:

$$\text{(37)} \qquad b(r,\alpha) = \int_0^\pi d\phi \int_{-\infty}^{+\infty} |R|\, dR\, \frac{F(R,\phi)}{|R|}\, e^{2\pi i rR\cos(\alpha - \phi)}$$

Examination of equation (37) shows that it represents the inverse Fourier transform of the function F(R,ϕ)/|R|, and hence:

$$\text{(38)} \qquad b(r,\alpha) = [\mathfrak{F}_2^{-1} F \,.\, \frac{1}{|R|}](r,\alpha)$$

$$= f(r,\alpha) ** [\mathfrak{F}_2^{-1} \frac{1}{|R|}](r,\alpha)$$

where we have used the Fourier convolution theorem. It can be shown, again using generalised function theory, that $\mathfrak{F}_2^{-1}(1/|R|) = 1/|r|$, and thus:

$$\text{(39)} \qquad b(r,\alpha) = f(r,\alpha) ** \frac{1}{|r|}$$

This equation shows that the backprojection b(x,y) is simply the original function f(x,y) convolved with the function 1/r. This function has long tails and introduces blurring and loss of contrast, which is why simple backprojection of unfiltered projections results in an unacceptable image. Taking the 2-D Fourier transform of both sides of equation (39) and rearranging:

$$\text{(40)} \qquad F(R,\phi) = B(R,\phi) \,.\, |R|$$

$$f(r,\alpha) = [\mathfrak{F}_2^{-1} B \,.\, |R|](r,\alpha)$$

This result was derived by Smith, Peters and Bates (Smith et al., 1973), and is called the rho-filtered layergram method because the authors used the symbol ρ for R. The steps of this version of the 2-D reconstruction algorithm are: backproject the unfiltered projection data to form b(x,y), take the 2-D Fourier transform of b(x,y) and multiply each point by the corresponding value of |R|, then take the inverse 2-D Fourier transform. The filtering function |R| is a 2-D ramp filter, and again, it is necessary to introduce an apodizing function to reduce the amplification of high frequency noise during filtering. This algorithm is mathematically equivalent to the filtered backprojection algorithm, but for a number of practical reasons the former is usually preferred.

3.8 The Point Response Function

Writing equation (39) explicitly as a 2-D convolution in cartesian coordinates:

$$(41) \qquad b(x,y) = \int_{-\infty}^{+\infty} dy' \int_{-\infty}^{+\infty} dx' f(x',y') \frac{1}{\sqrt{(x-x')^2 + (y-y')^2}}$$

Suppose the unknown function f(x,y) consists of a single impulse of unit amplitude positioned at the point (x_0,y_0). It may be represented by the 2-D δ-function $\delta(x-x_0, y-y_0)$. Inserting this function into equation (41) and using the sifting property (equation (4)) results in:

$$(42) \qquad b(x,y) = \frac{1}{\sqrt{(x-x_0)^2 + (y-y_0)^2}}$$

which shows that the simple backprojection of an impulse input at (x_0,y_0) behaves as 1/|r|, centred at the point (x_0,y_0). The function 1/|r| is the *system point response function.* The fact that it does not depend on (x_0,y_0), but only on distance, reflects the fact that we have a linear, shift-invariant system.

3.9 Discrete Implementation and Sampling

We shall discuss only the discrete implementation of the convolution backprojection algorithm. Similar considerations apply to the other algorithms. In practice, the projections are not measured as continuous functions, but are sampled at a number of points in discrete directions. Suppose that parallel projections are obtained at M equally-spaced angles $\phi_m = \pi m/M$ with m = 0,..,M-1, and suppose each parallel projection is sampled at N points $s_n = n\Delta s$, with n = -N/2+1,..,N/2. The convolution algorithm, equation (30), is discretized in two steps. First, convolve the projection with a filter function such as that in equation (32), to give a sampled, filtered projection:

$$(43) \qquad p_F(n\Delta s, \phi_m) = \Delta s \sum_{j=-N/2+1}^{N/2} p(j\Delta s, \phi_m)\, h_K(|n-j|\Delta s) \qquad n = -N/2,..,M/2$$

where we have used the trapezoidal quadrature rule to discretize the convolution integral. This summation approximates the filtering step in the range [(-N/2+1)Δs, N/2 Δs], and thus if the function $f(x,y) \neq 0$ outside a circle of radius N/2 Δs, reconstruction artifacts may result.

Backprojection, equation (26), of the filtered projections is discretized by:

$$(44) \qquad f(x,y) = \frac{\pi}{M} \sum_{m=0}^{M-1} p_F(x \cos\frac{\pi m}{M} + y \sin\frac{\pi m}{M}, \phi_m)$$

This sum is calculated at each point (x,y) in the image. However, for a given (x,y), the expression $x \cos(\pi m/M) + y \sin(\pi m/M)$ will not necessarily coincide with one of the measured sample points of $p_F(n\Delta s,\phi_j)$ and hence interpolation between adjacent measured samples will be required. Linear interpolation is often used as a good compromise between speed and accuracy.

Apart from the numerical problems which arise with discrete implementations, we would like to know to what extent the discrete reconstruction is a reliable estimate of the continuous solution. We would expect the discrete result to be a reasonable approximation to the continuous solution providing the data satisfies the conditions set down by the Sampling Theorem discussed in 2.5.1 above. We assume that the distribution f(x,y) we wish to reconstruct is zero outside a circular region of radius r. As noted earlier, in the frequency domain, such a function will have infinite extent, but assume it is essentially zero outside a circular region of radius ρ, i.e. the modulus of the maximum frequency we measure is ρ. Thus:

$$(45) \qquad F(X,Y) \approx 0 \ , \ \text{for} \ \sqrt{X^2 + Y^2} > \rho$$

For an accurate recovery of f(x,y), the sampling theorem requires that the data sampling satisfies:

$$(46) \qquad \Delta s \leq 1/2\rho \ \text{and} \ \Delta\phi < 1/2r\rho$$

Assuming that the sampling conditions are satisfied, and since Δs = 2r/N, we have the approximate relationship $M \approx N\pi/2$ between the number of angular and the number of radial samples for a good reconstruction.

We have implicitly assumed that the angular samples are distributed uniformly throughout the full angular range [0, π]. This is a necessary condition for a complete reconstruction. When there are significant gaps in the angular sampling, i.e. projections which are not measured for certain ranges of φ, we see from the projection theorem that this situation would correspond to regions in the frequency domain which are unsampled. Thus, when the inverse Fourier transform is taken, artifacts generated by these regions of zeros usually result. These reconstructions fall into the category of limited angle reconstruction (Davison, 1983). A number of techniques have been developed for such a situation, one approach being to complete the partially-measured transform by, for example, analytic continuation techniques. A full discussion of these techniques is beyond the scope of this tutorial, although we will briefly return to this point again in section 4 when we discuss 3-D reconstruction algorithms.

3.10 Iterative Techniques

The algorithms discussed above are classified as transform methods because they are based on direct inversion of the Radon transform. There is, however, an alternative approach that uses Series Expansion (Censor, 1983), or Iterative, techniques. For the direct inversion approach, we first derived a solution to the continuous problem, and then discretized the resulting formula in order to reconstruct real data. The series expansion approach, however, offers a solution directly to the discrete reconstruction problem. Iterative methods were known initially as algebraic reconstruction techniques (ART), or ART-type methods, and they were developed originally for electron microscopy applications (Gordon, Bender and Herman, 1970). As we shall see, iterative methods are usually computationally intensive, and for this and other reasons, direct transform methods have been preferred, even though in some cases iterative methods are able to produce better quality reconstructions. More recently, it has been found that, for emission imaging in particular, an iterative approach may offer a better treatment of the underlying statistical properties of the data, and hence there has been renewed interest and further developments.

To begin, let us take the continuous function f(x,y) we wish to reconstruct, discretize it into a matrix of elements (pixels), and write it as a 1-D vector $\lambda(b)$, b=1,..,B, where B is the total number of pixels in the matrix. For example, if the function is discretized into an LxL element matrix with L=64, then B=4096, and $\lambda(65)$ is the first element of the second row. Similarly, the projections $p(s,\phi)$ are discretized and written as a 1-D vector $n^*(d)$, d=1,..,D. For M projections, each sampled at N points, D=MxN, and, for example, $n^*(N+1)$ is the first sample point in the second projection, etc. It is evident if we discretize equation (20) that:

$$(47) \qquad n^*(d) = \sum_{b=1}^{B} m(b,d)\, \lambda(b)$$

where m(b,d) is a *projection matrix* with elements that specify which of the $\lambda(b)$ contribute to which projection values. For example, one row of the matrix for a given d selects all the image pixels which must be summed to obtain the projection value at that d. In matrix notation, equation (47) becomes (in the absence of noise):

$$(48) \qquad \mathbf{M}\lambda = \mathbf{n}^*$$

The projection matrix **M** is large (BxD), and sparse, since typically in one row of B elements, only $L = \sqrt{B}$ elements are non-zero. Special techniques are required to solve such a large system of equations, particularly since, in reality, the $\mathbf{n}^*$ contain measurement noise and it is necessary to add an error vector **e** to the left hand side of equation (48) to have an exact equality:

(49) $$\mathbf{M}\lambda + \mathbf{e} = \mathbf{n}^*$$

The discrete image reconstruction problem can then be stated as: *given* $\boldsymbol{n}^*$ *estimate the corresponding image vector* λ.

Although solving equation (49) by direct inversion of **M** has been tried (Kashyap and Mittel, 1973), there are obviously many difficulties, not least the large dimensions of **M** and the presence of noise. Alternatively, if the transpose of **M** is applied to both sides of equation (48), we obtain:

(50) $$\mathbf{M}^T \mathbf{M}\lambda = \mathbf{M}^T \mathbf{n}^*$$

$$\lambda = (\mathbf{M}^T\mathbf{M})^{-1} \mathbf{M}^T \mathbf{n}^*$$

The matrix $\mathbf{M}^T$ applied to $\mathbf{n}^*$ corresponds to the backprojection operation, equation (26) in matrix notation. As we have seen, this leads to an image of the function we require convolved with the point response function $1/|r|$. Multiplication by $(\mathbf{M}^T\mathbf{M})^{-1}$ is the matrix equivalent to deconvolving this $1/|r|$ factor. The matrix $(\mathbf{M}^T\mathbf{M})$ is a very large (BDxBD), square, dense matrix, and direct inversion presents a considerable problem. In fact, the solution for λ given by equation (50) is simply the minimum least squares solution, i.e. the λ which minimises:

(51) $$\|\mathbf{n}^* - \mathbf{M}\lambda\|^2 = \|\mathbf{e}\|^2$$

Instead of attempting to directly invert such large matrices, the approach has been to find a solution by a series of successive approximations (Herman, 1976; Eggermont et al, 1981). Thus, starting with an initial estimate, or 'guess', $\lambda_0(b)$, which may be, for example, a uniform image, the algorithm attempts to progressively improve upon this estimate, simultaneously ensuring that the estimate does not violate any known properties of the expected solution, e.g. pixel values should be positive. At each step, the current image estimate $\lambda_k(b)$ is used to generate a vector of projection data $n_k(d)$ which is compared with the measurements $n^*(d)$. The objective is to make the $n_k(d)$ consistent with $n^*(d)$ by modifying the image estimate $\lambda_k(b)$ to produce a new estimate $\lambda_{k+1}(b)$. Details of the modification procedure differ from one algorithm to another and a good review of the different possibilities may be found in Herman (1980). As an example, a simple procedure known as additive ART is to take:

(52) $$\lambda_{k+1}(b) = \lambda_k(b) + \frac{m(b,d)\,\Delta n_k(d)}{\sum_{b=1}^{B} m^2(b,d)}$$

where $\Delta n_k(d) = n^*(d) - n_k(d)$, and each $\lambda_k(b)$ receives a correction weighted by $m(b,d)$. The denominator in equation (52) is a normalisation factor.

The possibility to incorporate prior information, or constraints, into iterative methods is a significant advantage. Such prior information is particularly useful in guiding the algorithm towards an acceptable solution when the usual constraints imposed by the data are weak, for example in the case of low signal-to-noise or poor sampling. As mentioned above, one such constraint is positivity, which ensures that, since they are supposed to represent tracer concentration, successive $\lambda_k(b)$ are always positive. Note that the solution from the filtered backprojection algorithm is *not* guaranteed to be positive, negative values in the reconstructed image originating from negative values in the kernel $h_K(s)$.

As we have pointed out, iterative methods are computationally intensive, each iteration requiring approximately the same time as filtered backprojection, but with a complete reconstruction requiring many iterations. The number of iterations required depends, among other factors, upon the rate of convergence of the algorithm. The choice of the number of iterations is analagous to selecting the appropriate apodizing cut-off K in equation (34). Too few iterations, and the reconstruction is over-smoothed (K too small), while too many iterations and the reconstruction exhibits excessive noise amplification (K too large). The establishment of objective and efficient stopping rules has proved difficult.

In 1982, Shepp and Vardi proposed a method in which the statistical nature of the data could be incorporated into the reconstruction algorithm. They pointed out that m(b,d) is the probability that photons emitted from a pixel b are detected in the line integral, or projection element, d. They suggested that it should even be possible to incorporate some of the physics of the detection process into the m(b,d), and they considered PET in particular. In their model, they define $\lambda^*(d)$, which is the *expected* mean value of the measured $n^*(d)$ and is given by:

$$\lambda^*(d) = \sum_{b=1}^{B} \lambda(b)\, m(b,d) \qquad d=1,..D \tag{53}$$

The measurements $n^*(d)$ are therefore Poisson random numbers with means $\lambda^*(d)$. The aim of the reconstruction algorithm is then to maximise the likelihood that a set of Poisson processes with means $\lambda^*(d)$ gives rise to projection data $n^*(d)$. Since the m(b,d) are given, this procedure will find the image $\lambda(b)$ that is the most likely to have generated the projection data $n^*(d)$, where the likelihood is defined as:

$$L(\lambda) = \prod_{d=1}^{D} e^{-\lambda^*(d)} \frac{\lambda^*(d)^{n^*(d)}}{n^*(d)!} \tag{54}$$

In order to maximise this likelihood, Shepp and Vardi used the expectation - maximisation (EM) algorithm (Dempster et al, 1977). They showed that an image maximising the expression in equation (54) can be computed from the E-M iteration:

$$\lambda_{k+1}(b) = \lambda_k(b) \sum_{d=1}^{D} m(b,d) \frac{n^*(d)}{\sum_{b'} m(b',d)\, \lambda_k(b')} \tag{55}$$

with the m(b,d) normalised as

$$\sum_{d=1}^{D} m(b,d) = 1 \tag{56}$$

As the number of iterations increases we find that, as expected, initially the algorithm approaches a reasonable reconstruction, especially in low-count situations where the *true* mean value might vary considerably from the measurement. However, further investigation shows that if the iterations continue, the likelihood increases, whereas the image begins to degenerate, becoming increasingly noisy. It is, therefore, important to terminate the reconstruction before this degeneration begins, even though the likelihood function may not be a maximum. The origin of this effect lies in the fact that the measurements $n^*(d)$ are Poisson random variables with noise, and that insistence on an exact fit to the data will result in an image dominated by noise in a way similar to that resulting from the choice of a frequency cut-off K too large. The iteration procedure should then terminate when the fit to the data is as close as can be expected, within the noise level. However, as mentioned above, the choice of the stopping point is difficult, and research continues in order to define appropriate rules for use with real data (Llacer and Veklerov, 1989).

The E-M algorithm is an attractive approach since both the positivity of successive image estimates and correct normalisation are guaranteed, and it has been shown to yield images superior to those of filtered backprojection when the signal-to-noise ratio is small. This, and other similar algorithms, are therefore the subject of continuing research in an attempt to limit the effects of noise amplification and to accelerate convergence.

4. Image Reconstruction in Three Dimensions

In the preceeding section, we discussed algorithms to reconstruct a two-dimensional function f(x,y) from 1-D projections. In the remainder of this tutorial, we will consider the problem of reconstructing a three-dimensional function f(x,y,z), a problem which is of increasing interest. What is the reason for this interest ?

Medical imaging systems such as the CT scanner and PET and SPECT cameras make multiple transaxial section images of the internal organs of interest. The single section CT scanner achieves multiple section imaging by displacing the patient, while PET and SPECT cameras are capable of acquiring multiple sections simultaneously without patient movement. In some cases, patient movement may be necessary to scan the complete organ if the axial length of the scanner is less than that of the organ. The significant point is that all the sections are treated as separate and each is reconstructed independently using one of the algorithms described above. Then, by stacking the separate sections, a complete 3-D image of the particular organ is obtained, using only 2-D reconstruction techniques.

For the CT scanner, with a collimated X-ray beam and short scan times, the 2-D sectioning procedure is acceptable, although there may be problems, such as ensuring that the sections are parallel to one another. However, for emission imaging in PET and SPECT, the procedure is highly inefficient. Since photons are emitted from the patient in all directions, 2-D sectioning is only possible because lead or tungsten septa (collimators) are used to shield the detectors from photons which do not lie in one of the transaxial sections. Absorbing these photons (which nevertheless deliver a radioactive dose to the patient) with a collimator is a waste of potential information. Removal or redesign of the shielding to allow more of the photons to be detected has a number of important consequences: better use is made of the available photons, although there may also be an increase in the number of background events such as scatter; the radioactive dose administered to the patient can be reduced; the data must be reconstructed using a fully 3-D reconstruction algorithm.

The interest in 3-D reconstruction, therefore, lies in the need to improve the efficiency of these medical imaging devices. While there are evidently other problems associated with 3-D data collection, we shall restrict this tutorial to a discussion of 3-D reconstruction algorithms.

4.1 The 3-D Radon Transform

We will briefly mention the 3-D Radon transform, although owing to the way in which the data are collected by the scanners, the inversion of the 3-D Radon transform is not in practice appropriate for reconstruction, with the possible exception of MRI imaging (Shepp, 1980). Radon's work is applicable in any dimension where we wish to recover an m-dimensional function from a knowledge of its integrals over (m-1)-dimensional hyperplanes. Applications for $m > 3$ are, of course, rare; we have discussed the case of $m = 2$ in the previous section, and we now consider $m = 3$. In this case, a 3-D function is to be recovered from its integrals over 2-D planes, and it is because data from PET and SPECT scanners are not generally collected as integrals over planes that the inverse Radon transform is not applicable to these scanners.

We use a 3-D coordinate system in spherical polar coordinates (r, ϕ, θ) where, as shown in fig.4:

$$x = -r\cos\theta\sin\phi \qquad y = r\cos\theta\cos\phi \qquad z = r\sin\theta$$

To avoid cumbersome notation, we shall follow Barrett (1988) and represent the 3-D function by $f(\mathbf{r})$, where $\mathbf{r} = (r, \phi, \theta)$. Then:

$$(57) \qquad p(s,\mathbf{n}) = [\mathcal{R}_m f](s,\mathbf{n}) = \int_{-\infty}^{+\infty} d^3r\, f(\mathbf{r})\, \delta(s - \mathbf{r}.\mathbf{n})$$

where $\mathbf{n}$ is a unit vector in the projection direction. This equation applies for any m. For $m = 2$ it expresses equations (20) and (21) in a more general form. In 2-D, $\mathbf{n}$ is a vector within the 2-D section in the projection direction ϕ (i.e. $\mathbf{n}$ makes an angle ϕ with the y-axis). The δ-function is one dimensional and in the 2-D case restricts one integration to points on the line $s = \mathbf{r}.\mathbf{n}$, i.e. the projection coordinate s. In 3-D, the δ-function restricts one integration to points lying on the *plane* $s = \mathbf{r}.\mathbf{n}$, i.e. again, the coordinate s is orthogonal to the integration directions. If we now write the inverse, 3-D Fourier transform (see equation (7)) in polar coordinates, we obtain:

$$(58) \qquad f(\mathbf{r}) = [\mathcal{F}_3^{-1} F](\mathbf{r}) = \iint_{2\pi} d\Omega \int_{-\infty}^{+\infty} R^2\, dR\, F(\mathbf{R})\, e^{2\pi i \mathbf{r}.\mathbf{R}}$$

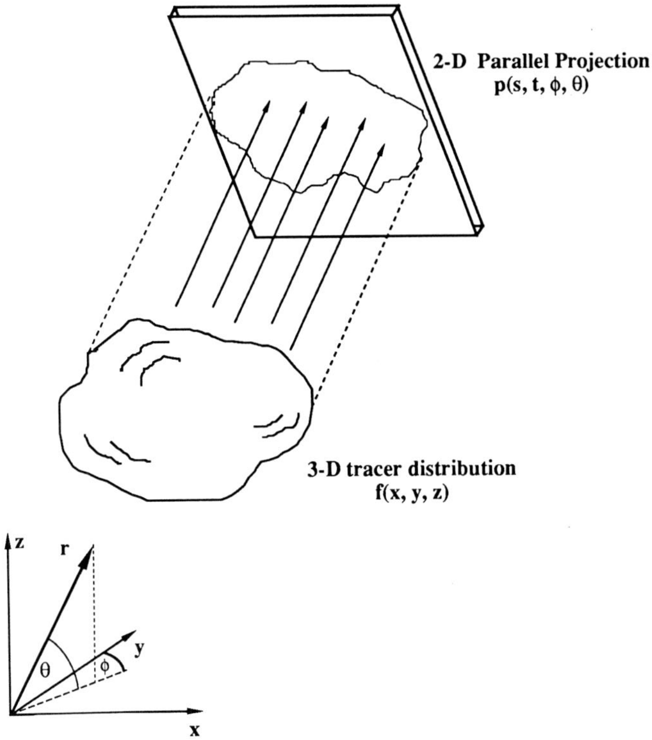

Fig.4 Two dimensional projections and the three-dimensional coordinate system

where $d\Omega = \cos\Theta \; d\Theta \; d\Phi$ is an element of solid angle in the frequency domain. We can again use the Central Slice theorem: in this case we have a 1-D function p(s,**n**) along the line in the direction **n**, with function values which are obtained by integrating f(**r**) over planes orthogonal to **n**. The Fourier transform of this function is P(S,**n**), and from the Central Slice theorem, we know that this is just F(**R**) with **R** = S**n**. Thus,

$$(59) \qquad f(\mathbf{r}) = [\mathcal{R}_3^{-1} p](\mathbf{r}) = \int_{-\infty}^{+\infty} S^2 \, dS \iint_{2\pi} d\Omega_n \, P(S,\mathbf{n}) \, e^{2\pi i S \mathbf{r}.\mathbf{n}}$$

where Ω_n is the solid angle containing all the projection directions **n**. This equation may be rewritten as:

$$(60) \qquad f(\mathbf{r}) = \iint_{2\pi} d\Omega_n \left\{ \int_{-\infty}^{+\infty} dS \, S^2 \, P(S,\mathbf{n}) \, e^{2\pi i s S} \right\}_{s = \mathbf{r}.\mathbf{n}}$$

where s = **r.n** restricts the 3-D backprojection operation to a smearing over the original plane of integration. Thus, inversion of the Radon transform in 3-D, as given by equation (60), requires a 1-D Fourier transform of each projection, multiplication by S^2, inverse 1-D Fourier transform, backprojection of each filtered projection over the original plane, and then integration over all projection directions (the outer integral). In practice, as in 2-D, to limit noise amplification, it may be necessary to use an apodized version, $S^2A(S)$.

This result may be re-expressed using the Fourier derivative theorem (equation (8)), to give:

$$(61) \qquad f(\mathbf{r}) = -\frac{1}{4\pi^2} \iint_{2\pi} d\Omega_n \, [p''(s,\mathbf{n})]_{s=\mathbf{r}.\mathbf{n}}$$

where p"(s,**n**) is the second derivative of p(s,**n**). Thus, an alternative algorithm is to take the second derivative of the projection with respect to the projection coordinate, backproject it, and then integrate over all projection directions. This result shows that inversion of the Radon transform in 3-D is better-behaved than the 2-D case. Instead of convolution with the function $1/s^2$ with long tails, we have a simple second derivative, which is a local operation. The difference arises because |S| has a slope discontinuity at the origin, while S^2 and all its derivatives are continuous.

As for the case of the rho-filtered layergram, we can commute the operations in equation (61) to give:

$$(62) \qquad f(\mathbf{r}) = -\frac{1}{4\pi^2} \nabla^2 \iint_{2\pi} d\Omega_n \, \{ p(s,\mathbf{n}) \}_{s=\mathbf{r}.\mathbf{n}}$$

where ∇^2 is the Laplacian operator. This form of the inversion requires backprojection, integration over all projection directions, and then the Laplacian of the resulting 3-D function. Note that the Laplacian operation replaces the deconvolution of the 1/|r| function required in the case of the rho-filtered layergram.

It is also interesting to note that, in analogy with equation (35), the result of backprojecting the unfiltered projection data, i.e. the backprojection b(**r**), where

$$(63) \qquad b(\mathbf{r}) = \iint_{2\pi} d\Omega_n \, p(s,\mathbf{n})$$

can be shown to be:

$$(64) \qquad b(\mathbf{r}) = f(\mathbf{r}) *** \frac{\pi}{r} \qquad \text{with } r = |\mathbf{r}|$$

which is the 3-D analogue of equation (39). Thus, even though the backprojection requires smearing over a plane rather than a line, we have exactly the same relationship between b(**r**) and f(**r**) as in the 2-D case, i.e. they are both based on the same point response function.

4.2 The X-ray Transform

While the results of the preceeding subsection follow from a generalisation to 3-D of the results of section 3, it has been pointed out that, with the possible exception of MRI (Shepp, 1980), data for emission tomography are not collected in the form of integrals over planes. Instead, data are again acquired as line integrals, but with the lines having any direction in space, rather than being constrained to a 2-D plane as before. As shown in fig.4, the projection data in this case are not the 1-D sets of 2-D *plane* integrals of the preceeding subsection, but are instead 2-D sets of 1-D *line* integrals grouped into parallel projections. The projections are therefore denoted by p(**s**,**n**), where now **s** = (s,t) are the coordinates of a point within the plane of the projection, and **n** is the unit normal to the projection plane, with direction cosines (- $\sin\phi \cos\theta$, $\cos\phi \cos\theta$, $\sin\theta$), as shown in fig.5.

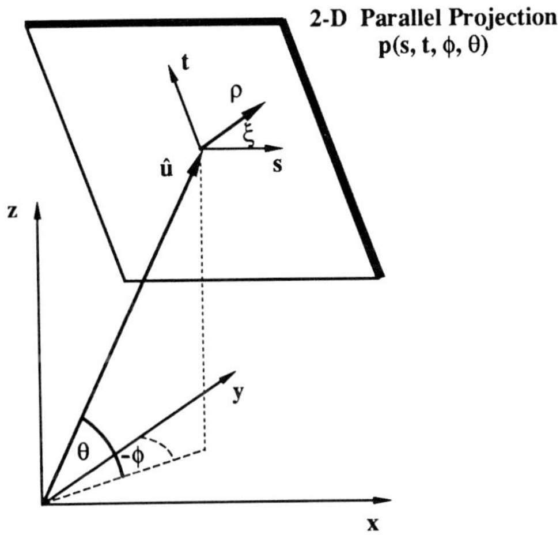

Fig.5 The 2-D projection plane

The transformation between the function f(x,y,z) and p(**s**,**n**) is not therefore the Radon transform. It has been called instead the X-Ray Transform (Solmon, 1976), and it may be written as (Defrise et al, 1989):

$$(65) \qquad p(\mathbf{s},\mathbf{n}) = \int_{-\infty}^{+\infty} d\ell \; f(\mathbf{s} + \ell \mathbf{n})$$

where ℓ is the coordinate along the integration line (corresponding to t in the 2-D case), and we have $\mathbf{s}.\mathbf{n} = 0$. In 2-D, the X-Ray transform is identical to the Radon transform.

The unit normals **n** belong to a set of directions in space, denoted by Ω_n, as in the previous case of the 3-D Radon transform above. By integrating over 2π in equations (58) to (63) we assumed implicitly that the Radon transform was available in all possible directions. In practice, of course, this is rarely the situation since, for emission tomography in particular, a spherical detector geometry would be required. Ω_n is therefore a subset of all possible directions, and we may ask what are the conditions Ω_n must fulfil in order to ensure that we can find a unique solution for f(x,y,z).

To answer this question, let us apply the Central Slice theorem in 3-D. The Radon transform of f(x,y,z) were measurements of F(**X**), with $\mathbf{X} = (X,Y,Z)$, along one *line* (through the origin) in the frequency domain, and by measuring $[\mathcal{R}_3 f]$ in all directions F(**X**) was completely determined. The X-ray transform, on the other hand, are measurements of F(**X**) over central *planes* in the frequency domain. In general, some of these planes will intersect, and thus F(**X**) will be sampled by more than one projection. To ensure that we can recover f(x,y,z), F(**X**) must be sampled at least once at each frequency, so for a unique solution, for each frequency **X**, there must be at least one projection which satisfies $\mathbf{X}.\mathbf{n} = 0$. This necessary and sufficient condition was first published by Orlov (1976), who expressed it geometrically by requiring that the set of projection directions Ω_n must intersect all great circles on the unit sphere. We note that this condition is satisfied for 2-D reconstruction when $0 \le \phi \le \pi$, as we assumed throughout section 3.

It is important to note that we *do not* require $\Omega_n = 2\pi$ for a unique 3-D reconstruction. From the Central Slice theorem, the set of all 2-D projections with $\theta = 0$ and $0 \le \phi \le \pi$, fully samples F(**X**). Projections with $|\theta| > 0$ provide further measurements of F(**X**) at the same frequency samples, and therefore serve to *improve* our estimate of F(**X**). Each additional 2-D projection improves the statistical quality of the reconstruction, but we do not *require* all projections with $|\theta| > 0$ for the reconstruction to be unique; the basic set with $\theta = 0$ and $0 \le \phi \le \pi$ ensures that Orlov's condition is satisfied. What is required, however, is that if a 2-D projection is measured, then it is *completely* measured. The difficulty with 3-D imaging devices is not that they have $\Omega_n < 2\pi$, but that some of the projections within Ω_n are only partially measured. As we shall see, this problem relates to the fact that the 3-D point response function is not shift-invariant. Inversion of the X-ray transform is then not quite so straightforward.

4.3 The Inverse X-Ray Transform

We will assume initially that all projections within Ω_n have been completely measured. The X-ray transform, equation (65) can be inverted by a generalisation to 2-D projections of the filtered backprojection algorithm, equations (30) to (32) (Schorr et al., 1983). Thus, a 2-D apodized filter function $h_K(s,\mathbf{n})$ is convolved with the projections $p(s,\mathbf{n})$ to form filtered projections $p_F(s,\mathbf{n})$ given by:

$$(66) \qquad p_F(s,\mathbf{n}) = \int_{-\infty}^{+\infty} ds'\; p(s',\mathbf{n})\; h_K(s - s', \mathbf{n})$$

As in 2-D, this convolution operation is more efficiently carried out as a frequency domain multiplication by the 2-D Fourier transform of $h_K(s,\mathbf{n})$, i.e. $H_K(S,\mathbf{n})$, with $\mathbf{S}.\mathbf{n} = 0$. In 2-D, the tomographic filter is unique, except for different apodizing procedures, and, as we saw in equation (31), behaves as $|S|$ in the frequency domain. In 3-D, the filter $H_K(\mathbf{S},\mathbf{n})$ is not unique, and a number of alternatives have been published (Colsher, 1980; Ra et al., 1982; Schorr et al., 1983). It has been shown (Defrise et al., 1989) that all valid filters must satisfy:

$$(67) \qquad \iint_{\Omega_n} d\Omega_n\, H(\mathbf{X}, \mathbf{n})\, \delta(\mathbf{X}.\mathbf{n}) = 1$$

where the δ-function selects the planes for which $\mathbf{X}.\mathbf{n} = 0$, and the integration is over all projection directions. Equation (67) is interpreted as follows: select a frequency component $\mathbf{X}$ and then integrate the filter values for all planes $\mathbf{n}$ which contain $\mathbf{X}$, where $\mathbf{X}.\mathbf{n} = 0$. The result of this integration is unity for a valid filter. The filter essentially compensates for the different number of measurements of $F(\mathbf{X})$.

Defrise et al (1989) have shown that, for 3-D reconstruction, the filter due to Colsher (1980) has optimal noise properties. This filter is symmetric in ϕ, but has a θ-dependence due to the fact that, in practice, cylindrical imaging systems measure 2-D projections at θ angles out to some maximum Ψ. Colsher's filter, to be applied to each 2-D projection, is conveniently expressed in frequency domain polar coordinates (ρ,ξ):

$$(68) \qquad H(\rho\cos\xi\,, \rho\sin\xi\,, \theta\,) = \frac{\pi\rho}{\arcsin\dfrac{\sin\Psi}{\sin\Theta}} \qquad \text{if } \sin^2\Theta > \sin^2\Psi$$

$$= \qquad 2\rho \qquad \text{if } \sin^2\Theta \le \sin^2\Psi$$

where $\sin^2\Theta = (\cos^2\xi + \sin^2\xi\, \sin^2\theta)$ and $|\theta| \le \Psi$. Note that the filter again depends upon the modulus of the 2-D frequency, $|\rho|$. Similar noise amplification considerations apply as in 2-D, and in practice $H(\mathbf{s},\mathbf{n})$ must include an apodizing function, $A(\mathbf{S})$.

After the inverse 2-D Fourier transform, the filtered projections $p_F(s,\mathbf{n})$ (equation (66)) are backprojected in the same way as in 2-D (equation (31)) to give:

$$(69) \qquad f(\mathbf{x}) = \iint_{\Omega_n} d\Omega\; p_F(s,\mathbf{n})$$

At each point $\mathbf{x}$, $f(\mathbf{x})$ is reconstructed by integrating the contibutions from all backprojection lines $\mathbf{n}$ which pass through $\mathbf{x}$. This procedure therefore inverts the X-Ray Transform in 3-D.

4.4 The Response Function in 3-D

As in 2-D, the order of filtering and backprojection can be commuted to give the 3-D analogue of the rho-filtered layergram approach described in 3.7. Although this approach has been used for 3-D reconstruction (Chu and Tam, 1977; Schorr et al., 1983), the filtered backprojection formulation is usually preferred. Nevertheless, it is interesting to note that the backprojection of the *unfiltered* 2-D projections, may be written:

$$b(\mathbf{r}) = \iint_{\Omega_n} d\Omega \; p(\mathbf{s},\mathbf{n}) \tag{70}$$

Substituting for p(**s**,**n**) from equation (65), it can be shown that (for $\Omega_n = 2\pi$):

$$b(\mathbf{r}) = f(\mathbf{r}) *** \frac{1}{r^2} \tag{71}$$

in analogy to equations (39) and (64). The function $1/r^2$ is the 3-D system point response function, corresponding to 1/r in the 2-D case. Since this response function falls off more rapidly than 1/r, the 3-D backprojection is intrinsically less blurred than the equivalent 2-D function. Thus, in 3-D, the backprojection of the X-Ray Transform gives the true function f(**r**) convolved with $1/r^2$, while the backprojection of the Radon transform gives the true function convolved with 1/|r|. Note, however, that for $\Omega_n = 2\pi$ the inverse three-dimensional Fourier transform of $(1/r^2)$ is 1/R (Lighthill, 1958), and thus the 3-D version of the rho-filtered layergram filters the 3-D backprojection with a ramp function in the frequency domain (Pelc and Chesler, 1979). When $\Omega_n < 2\pi$, the appropriate filter includes a θ-dependent factor (Schorr et al, 1983).

4.5 Shift-Invariance in 3-D

In practice, emission imaging devices have $\Omega_n < 2\pi$, because they are usually a truncated cylindrical or spherical design. Thus, as a point source of radioactivity is moved around inside the scanner, its geometrical appearance varies (Rogers et al, 1987), i.e. although the system point response function still behaves as $1/r^2$, the geometrical envelope (or support) of the function is no longer spherically symmetric but changes with position. This variation is equivalent to the fact that not all the 2-D projections are completely measured. As θ approaches the maximum acceptance angle of the scanner (Ψ), the 2-D projections are increasing truncated by the edge of the detector. In such a situation, the filtered backprojection algorithm cannot be applied without some procedure to compensate for the shift-variance.

However, as explained before, it is important to preserve the simplicity of the filtered backprojection approach and maintain the convolution relationship expressed by equation (71). A number of algorithms have been published which address this problem (Defrise et al., 1987; Clack et al., 1989; Kinahan et al., 1989). The approach we discuss (Kinahan et al, 1989) introduces an additional step into the algorithm of filtered backprojection in order to complete the partially-measured projections. The problem of how to complete partially-measured projections is resolved by using the one set of complete 2-D projections that are measured, i.e. those for $\theta = 0$, to reconstruct an initial image with the 2-D reconstruction algorithm described in section 3. From this initial estimate, it is then possible to simulate the projection process mathematically and *create* the unmeasured parts of a projection by 'forward projecting' (Joseph, 1982) along projection lines that do not exist in the actual scanner. The procedure is equivalent to simulating a scanner with a greater effective axial extent.

To summarise, then, the steps in the algorithm that invert the X-Ray transform of a projection set with a shift-variant response function are as follows:

1. Reconstruct a first estimate of $f(\mathbf{x})$ using only the 2-D parallel projections with $\theta = 0$ and a 2-D reconstruction technique such as equation (31) above.
2. Based on this estimate, reproject the unmeasured projection lines in order to complete the partially-measured projections for $|\theta| > 0$. If desired, $|\theta|$ can extend out to Ψ, the maximum acceptance angle of the tomograph. However, at these angles the number of measured projection lines may be small compared with the number that have been obtained by reprojection.
3. With a set of complete projections for all $|\theta|$, reconstruct a final image incorporating all projections, using equations (66), (68) and (69) above.

In the ideal situation of continuously-sampled and noise-free data, the final reconstruction from step 3 will be identical to the initial estimate from step 1. It is only in the presence of statistical noise that the incorporation of the additional projections with $|\theta| > 0$ serves to improve the signal-to-noise ratio in the final 3-D reconstruction.

The discretization of this algorithm follows a similar procedure to that used in 3.9 for the 2-D case. However, it may be necessary to re-express the backprojection equation (69) in terms of the variables actually measured by a particular scanner.

Acknowledgement

I am indebted to my colleague Dr Michel Defrise of the Vrije Universiteit Brussels, Belgium, for the derivation and discussion of many of the results presented in section 4.

References

Barrett H.H. (1988) The Fundamentals of the Radon Transform. In Proceedings of the NATO ASI on Mathematics and Computer Science in Medical Imaging, Il Ciocco, Italy. Series F, 39. pp. 105-125.

Bates R.H.T. and Peters T.M. (1971) Towards improvements in tomography. N.Z.J. Sci. 14, pp. 883-896.

Berry M.V. and Gibbs D.F. (1970) The interpretation of optical projections. Proc. R. Soc. A, 314, pp. 143-152.

Bracewell R.N. (1956) Strip integration in radio astronomy. Aust. J. Phys. 9, pp. 198-217.

Bracewell R.N. (1965) The Fourier Transform and its Applications. New York, McGraw-Hill.

Brigham E.O. (1974) The Fast Fourier Transform. Prentice-Hall, Englewood Cliffs, N.J.

Brooks R.A. and Di Chiro (1976) Principles of Computerized tomography (CAT) in radiographic and radioisotopic imaging. Phys. Med. Biol. 21, p. 689.

Censor, Y. (1983) Finite series-expansion reconstruction methods, Proc. IEEE, 71 p. 409.

Chu G. and Tam K.C. (1977) 3D imaging in the positron camera using Fourier techniques, Phys. Med. Biol. 22, p. 245.

Clack R., Townsend D.W. and Defrise M. (1989) An algorithm for three-dimensional reconstruction incorporating cross-plane rays, IEEE Trans. Med. Imag. MI-8, p. 32.

Colsher J.G. (1980) Fully three-dimensional Positron Emission Tomography, Phys. Med. Biol., 25, p. 103.

Cormack A.M. (1963) Representation of a function by its line integrals, with some radiological applications. J.Appl. Phys. 34, pp. 2722-2727.

Cormack A.M. (1964) Representation of a function by its line integrals, with some radiological applications. II. J.Appl. Phys. 35, pp. 2908-2913.

Davison M.E. (1983) The ill-conditioned nature of the limited angle tomography problem, SIAM J. Appl. Math. 43, 428.

Defrise M., Kuijk S. and Deconinck F. (1987) A new three-dimensional reconstruction method for positron cameras using plane detectors, Phys. Med. Biol. 33 , p. 43.

Defrise M, Townsend D.W., Clack R. (1989) Three-dimensional image reconstruction from complete projections. Phys. Med. Biol. 34, pp. 573-587.

Dempster A.P., Laird N.M. and Rubin D.B. (1977) Maximum Likelihood from incomplete data via the Expectation Maximization algorithm, J. Royal Stat. Soc., B39, p. 1.

DeRosier D.J. and Klug A. (1968) reconstruction of three-dimensional structures from electron micrographs. Nature 217, pp. 130-134.

Eggermont, P.P.B., Herman G.T. and Lent, A. (1981) Iterative algorithms for large partitioned linear systems, with applications to image reconstruction, Linear Algebra and its Applications, 40, p. 37.

Gordon R., Bender R., and Herman G.T. (1970) Algebraic reconstruction techniques (ART) for three-dimensional electron microscopy and X-ray photography, J. Theor. Biol. 29 p. 471.

Hamming R.W. (1983) Digital Filters Prentice Hall, Englewood Cliffs, NJ.

Herman G.T., Lakshminarayanan A.V. and Naparstek A. (1971) Convolution reconstruction techniques for divergent beams, Comp. Biol. Med. 6, p. 259.

Herman G.T. and Lent A. (1976) Iterative Reconstruction Algorithms. Comput. Biol. Med. 6, pp. 273-294.

Herman, G.T. (1980) Image Reconstruction from Projections: the Fundamentals of Computerized Tomography. Academic Press, New York.

Hounsfield G.N. (1973) Computerized transverse axial scanning tomography: Part I, description of the system. Br. J. Radiol. 46, pp. 1016-1022.

Joseph. T.M. (1982) An improved algorithm for reprojecting rays through pixel images, IEEE Trans. Med. Imag. MI-1, p. 192.

Kashyap R.L. and Mittel M.C. (1973) in the First Int. Joint Conf. Pattern Recognition, Washington DC, PP. 286-292.

Kinahan P.E. and Rogers J.G. (1989) Analytic 3D image reconstruction using all detected events, IEEE Trans. Nucl. Sc. NS-36, p. 964.

Lighthill M.J. (1958) Introduction to Fourier analysis and generalized functions. Cambridge University Press.

Llacer J. and Veklerov E. (1989) Feasible images and practical stopping rules for iterative algorithms in emission tomography, IEEE Trans. Med. Imag. MI-8, p. 186.

Muehllehner G and Wetzel R.A. (1971) Section imaging by computer calculation. J. Nucl. Med. 12, pp. 76-84.

Orlov S.S. (1976) Theory of three-dimensional reconstruction. 1. Conditions of a complete set of projections, Sov. Phys. Crystallography 20 p.312.

Pelc N.J. and Chesler D.A. (1979) Utilization of cross-plane rays for three-dimensional reconstruction by filtered back-projection, J. Comput. Assist. Tomogr. 3, p. 385.

Peters T.M. and Lewitt R.M. (1977) Computed tomography with fan-beam geometry, J. Comput. Assist. Tomogr. 1, p. 429.

Ra J.B., Lim C.B., Cho Z.H., Hilal S.K., Correll J. (1982) A true three-dimensional reconstruction algorithm for the spherical positron emission tomograph, Phys. Med. Biol. 27, p. 37.

Radon, J. (1917) Uber die Bestimmung von Funktionen durch ihre Integralwerte langs gewisser Manningsfaltigkeiten, Ber. Verh. Saechs. Akad. Leipzig, *Math. Phys. Kl.* , 69, 262, 1917. Translation by Parks P.C. (1986) in IEEE Trans. Med. Imag. MI-5 p.170.

Ramachandian G.N. and Lakshminarayanan A.V. (1971) Three-dimensional reconstruction from radiographs and electron micrographs: application of convolution instead of Fourier transform, Proc. Nat. Acad. Sc. USA 68 p. 2236.

Rogers J.G., Harrop R., Kinahan P.E. (1987) The theory of three-dimensional image reconstruction, *IEEE Trans. Med. Imaging*, MI-6, p. 239.

Rowland S.W. (1979) Computer implementation of image reconstruction formulas. In Image Reconstruction from Projection : Implementation and Applications. Ed. Herman G.T., Springer-Verlag, Berlin p. 9.

Rowley P.D. (1969) J. Opt. Soc. Am. 59, pp.1496-1498.

Schorr B., Townsend D. and Clack R. (1983) A general method of 3D filter computation, Phys. Med. Biol. 28, p. 1009.

Shepp L.A. and Logan B.F. (1974) The Fourier reconstruction of a head section. IEEE Trans. Nucl. Sci. NS-21, pp.21-43.

Shepp L.A. (1980) Computerized tomography and nuclear magnetic resonance. J. Comput. Assist. Tomogr. 4, pp. 94-107.

Shepp L.A. and Vardi V. (1982) Maximum Likelihood reconstruction for Emission Computed Tomography, IEEE Trans. Med. Imag., MI-1, p. 113.

Smith P.R., Peters T.M. and Bates R.H.T. (1973) Image reconstruction from a finite number of projections. J. Phys. A6, pp. 361-382.

Solmon D.C. (1976) The X-ray transform J. Math. Anal. Appl. 56 p. 61.

Tretiak O.J., Eden M, Simon W. (1969) Internal structure from X-ray images. Proc. 8th Int. Conf. on Med. Biol. Eng., Chicago, Session 12-1.

Direct Manipulation Techniques for the Human-Computer Interface

Jürgen E. Ziegler

1 Introduction

Over the past few years, a new concept of human-computer interaction has gained considerable relevance for most areas of software applications and products and is now rapidly developing into a de facto standard for some classes of systems. In many respects, this concept marks a transition to a new generation of software technology for the design of the user interface as the development of 4th generation languages has done for the design of database systems. Direct manipulation or object-oriented user interfaces, as the concept is often called, is replacing low-level general-purpose user interface styles like command languages with techniques which are more concrete, meaningful, transparent and effective with respect to the human user's intentions, knowledge and skills.

The origins of this new technique for human-computer interaction lie in studies done at the Xerox Palo Alto Research Center which led to the development of the Star, an office system which was designed with the focus of providing a new type of user interface (Smith et al. 1983). The novelty of this user interface consisted in presenting on the screen symbols of familiar office objects which could be selected and manipulated by means of a mouse. The desktop metaphor is an image of a real office environment which also simulates as much as possible the behaviour and constraints of the physical objects. The same techniques were used for the document editing facilities of the system using principles like WYSIWIG (What you see is what you get.)

The approach of using object manipulation as the major paradigm for the user interface bears many similarities to object-oriented programming languages like Smalltalk (cf. Goldberg and Robson 1983) which was developed in the same research environment. Some salient similarities are the extensive use of object attributes for representing the functionality or generic commands which may apply to a wide range of object classes while retaining the same meaning for the user. Despite these similarities, there are also differences. The abstract concept of message passing, for instance, does not become visible at the user interface which conveys the impression of concrete, direct manipulation of objects.

In this paper, the major characteristics and design issues of direct manipulation user interfaces will be discussed. We will first review relevant definitions and descriptions of the term direct manipulation and discuss its psychological implications. In a second part, the main components of direct manipulation interfaces along with guidance for their design are presented. Relevant style guides and tool kits are introduced. In the third part, we focus on design guidelines and empirical studies of direct manipulation.

2 Characteristics of Direct Manipulation

2.1 Definitions

Direct manipulation (abbreviated DM in the rest of this paper) was introduced by Shneiderman (1982, 1983) as a collective term for user interfaces exhibiting the following characteristics:

- Continuous representation of the object of interest
- Physical actions or labelled button presses instead of complex syntax and command names
- Rapid incremental reversible operations whose impact on the object of interest is immediately visible.

Shneiderman describes a number of examples which show typical characteristics of DM: A screen editor as opposed to line-oriented editors displays the document in its actual form. Some editors present the text exactly as it will look on the print-out, with immediate feedback on modifications (WYSIWYG principle). Spreadsheets employ the metaphor of an accountant´s worksheet to convey an easily comprehensible visual representation of the data with their complex arithmetic and logical relationships. The presentation is always kept up-to-date with respect to the actual state of the calculations. Spatial management systems and graphical browsers may use DM principles for orientation and navigation in large complex data structures. Video games, CAD/CAM systems or query-by-example database retrieval (Zloof 1977) are other examples of applications where DM can be found.

Shneiderman claims that a number of favourable usability characteristics can be achieved by DM interaction techniques:

- Novices can learn basic functionality quickly (usually through a demonstration).
- Experts can work extremely rapidly to carry out a wide range of tasks, even defining new functions and features.
- Knowledgeable intermittent users can retain operational concepts
- Error messages are rarely needed
- Reduced anxiety of the user because of the easy reversibility of actions.

We will discuss the validity of these claims later on the basis of a number of empirical studies. In general, we can say that more research is needed to prove that the principles of DM are superior to other interaction techniques.

Hutchins, Hollan and Norman (1986) describe DM as a complex concept which cannot be captured by a list of surface features and which is difficult to define: "... DM is not a unitary concept nor even something that can be quantified in itself. It is an orienting notion."

They cite a number of examples which show characteristics of DM, like Sutherland´s Sketchpad of 1963, a graphical design program, the constraint-based system Thinglab (Borning 1979) and Steamer (Hollan, Hutchins and Weitzman 1984), a knowledge-based system which also provides tools for constructing interactive graphical user interfaces.

Hutchins et al. base the discussion of DM on a scheme of human-computer interaction. This scheme is based on the notion of two "gulfs" which separate the user´s goals and intentions from the concepts and operations represented in this system (Fig. 1). The "gulf of execution" refers to the required transformation of the user´s goals into input actions. The "gulf of evaluation" signifies the problem of bringing the system reactions into a representational form which can be perceived, interpreted and evaluated by the user with respect to his or her task goals. The user interface should provide means to bridge these two gulfs by an appropriate input and output language.

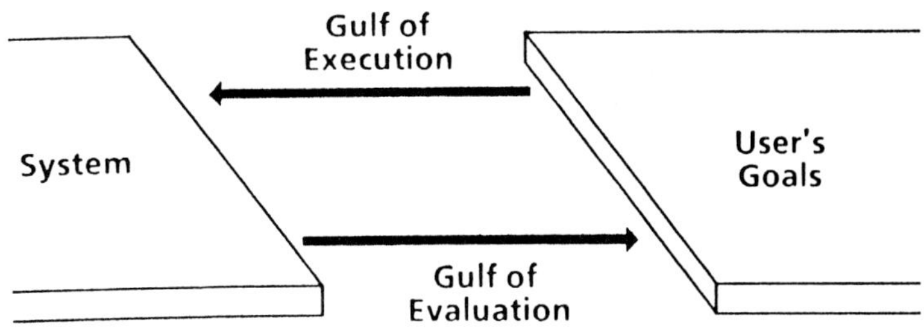

Fig. 1: The gulfs of execution and evaluation (from Hutchins et al. 1986)

DM facilitates the bridging of these gulfs by providing the facility to use elements of the system´s output directly as components of the user´s input language. A user can then select an output and manipulate it directly. This capability is called "interreferential I/O" by Hutchins et al. This term means that both the user as well as the system can refer to objects on the screen.

Altmann (1987) describes the concept of DM in a more abstract manner as the design of user interfaces as a model action world. The real world as mapped to the system by means of metaphors and corresponding graphical representations. The user can change the state of this model through manipulative actions and perceive immediately the effect of these operations. Hutchins (1989) makes the distinction between user interfaces as "conversation" as it can be found in conventional command languages and user interfaces as "model-worlds".

In the conversational paradigm, the user and the system communicate through subsequent messages which cannot be changed once they have been sent. In DM interfaces, in contrast, the user and the system exchange information via a shared (visual) representation, the model world. Every manipulation of this model (by the user and the system) leads to a changed state which can serve as a basis for further incremental modifications.

2.2 Classification of Manipulative Techniques

The properties of DM systems can be more precisely elaborated within the framework of a general model of interactive systems (Ziegler 1987). This model employs three different levels with associated components which serve for defining different interaction techniques. Layered models for describing human-computer interaction have been proposed by several authors (cf. Foley 1981, Moran 1981, Nielsen 1986).

- The conceptual level describes the tasks which can be carried out with the system as well as the semantic objects and operations used for accomplishing these tasks. A component of the interactive system is defined at this level which is called the internal conceptual model.

- The dialogue level describes the structure of user's navigation between the objects of the conceptual level and the syntactical composition of inputs and outputs (dialogue component).
- The input/output level describes the structure (e.g. two-dimensional arrangement) and form of the elements of the input /output (external, observable model).

An interaction with the system requires transformations of information between the conceptual level (internal model) and the input/output level (external model). The different mappings which are involved in this process constitute relevant dimensions along which human-computer interaction techniques can be characterised.The following terms shall be used for these different mappings: the mapping of the internal system state (conceptual level) to the output shall be called *representation*. The term *reference* describes how the user can refer to conceptual objects by means of input/output elements. The temporal structuring and sequencing of the interaction process is called *interactivity* (Fig. 2).

Within this framework, the following distinctions can be established for defining manipulative interaction techniques:

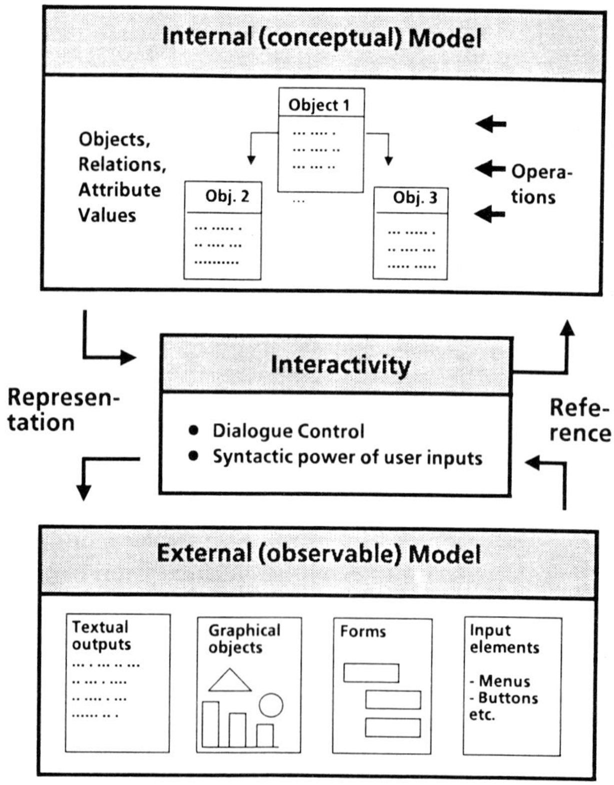

Fig. 2: Representation, reference and interactivity as basic dimensions of interaction techniques

Representation: For DM interfaces, the objects that are presented on the screen have an internal representation, i.e. there are data structures in the system memory which correspond to the actual contents of the screen (display objects are kept "alive"). This is different from, for instance, command language interaction where the contents of the screen is solely dependent on the (accidental) sequence of inputs and outputs. For command language interfaces, the output is basically managed by means of display operations without preserving the data structure corresponding to the object displayed (cf. Mallgren 1983).

In DM systems, the user can modify the internal model by manipulating the visible external model. According to the range of modifications possible, we can distinguish several stages which are shown in Fig. 3:

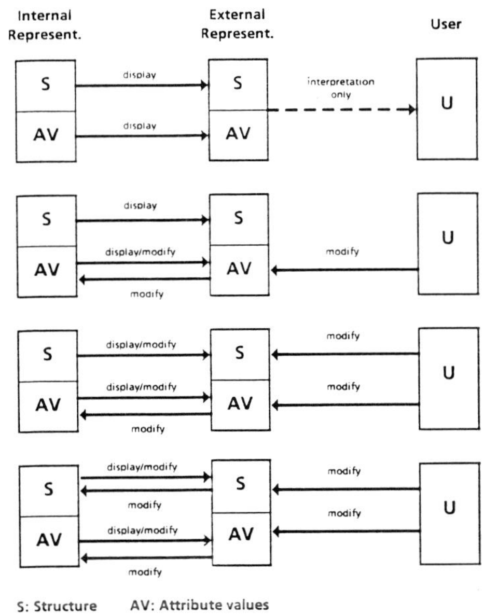

Fig. 3: Four types of representation (explanations in the text)

1) The topmost part of Fig. 3 shows the case which is typical for conventional command language interfaces. The objects displayed on the screen cannot be used for input, they can only be read and interpreted by the user. Of course, the user can cause new objects to be displayed e.g. by typing in a command.

2) In the second case, the system displays a fixed structural layout of objects which is determined by some internal state. The values of some object attributes are accessible and modifiable both by the user and the system. If the user changes an externally visible attribute (e.g. a field value) the internal attribute value is also changed. A typical example of this type are screen forms.

3) In the third case, attribute modifications are possible as in the previous case. In addition, the user can change the (external) layout of objects which does, however, not change the internal structure of the objects displayed. An example of this type of manipulations are

window system operations by which the user can influence the layout of the screen objects without changing their internal state.

4) In the bottom part of Fig. 3, both structure and attribute values of the internal objects can be modified by manipulating their external equivalents. In this case, the surface representation has to be an operational model of the internal data. Only on this level, we can have user operations like <move-object> which are associated with some function on the structure of the internal representation. While writing this document, for example, I can change the structure of the paper by directly moving nodes in the outline structure with the mouse (Fig. 4).

All types of representation from 2) to 4) typically occur in DM interfaces but the scope and power of manipulation by the user is different. Type 4) provides the highest manipulative power whereas type 2) is found in many conventional systems

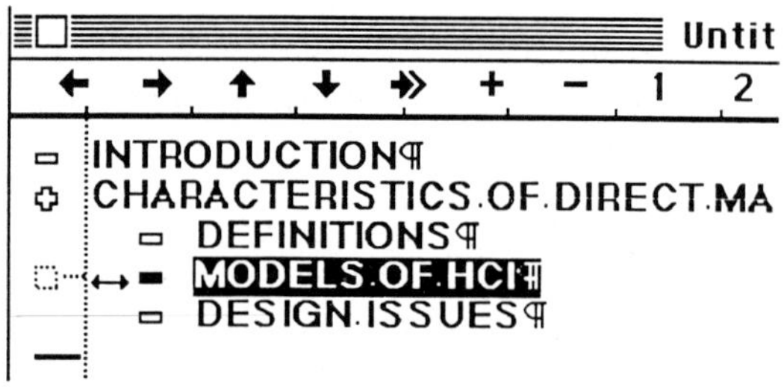

Fig. 4: Direct manipulation of a document outline structure (Microsoft Word™) Nodes can be moved horizontally (to higher or lower levels) or vertically (before or after other nodes) by simply pulling them around with the mouse.

Reference: Users can refer to objects or functions (1) by pointing at them or by more general forms of gesture (like lassoing a group of objects), (2) by using a name or (3) by using a description of some sort. In user interfaces, these types can occur in nested forms. Manipulative interactions must allow referencing by means of pointing operations (deictic reference). In a broader sense, hard or soft buttons or function keys which are often found in DM systems can also be subsumed in this category.

Interactivity: Manipulative systems are characterized by a high degree of interactivity. This means that each input action is immediately interpreted, an appropriate change of the internal system state is effected, and feedback on this change is provided to the user. In contrast, other types of interactivity (which are not characteristic for manipulative systems) allow the specification of functions with several parameters which are interpreted only after the full entry is completed. In most DM systems, however, we can also find components with low interactivity like, for instance, (modal) dialogue boxes which allow to change a number of parameter settings which become only effective after some termination.

The dimensions described above determine a space of interaction techniques. Although typical features of DM can be identified, most real systems exhibit a mixture of different techniques. The above analysis constitutes a basis for defining manipulative interactions. The concept of directness describes the psychological implications of the interaction technique and is elaborated in the following section.

2.3 Directness

When does manipulation turn into *direct* manipulation? In the previous section, we have illustrated that manipulative techniques can be regarded as properties of the interactive system itself. Directness, however, can only be assessed by taking into account the user, his or her mental concepts, intentions, and plans and thereby is a psychologically mediated usability characteristic. In the framework of the model presented before, directness can be understood as a measure of the degree to which the implemented user interface fits the mental concepts and expectations of the user. Directness can therefore be examined at each level of this model. Therefore we may define several different types of directness. The concepts of semantic and articulatory directness were suggested by Hutchins et al. (1986). Additionally, we may consider aspects of directness at the dialogue level, referred to as operational directness. The term formal directness (used by Hutchins et al., in a draft of their paper) is used to refer to the surface form of the input and output tokens (the different levels together with examples of directness are also shown in Table 1).

Semantic Directness. Semantic directness is determined by the distance between the user´s intentions and the semantic objects and operations provided by the system. For the user, it is essential that (1) he or she can, at all times, communicate his or her intentions to the system and (2) that this can be expressed in a simple and concise manner. To achieve these goals, it is necessary that the system provide the appropriate functionality as well as conceptual objects and operations at a level of abstraction that is appropriate to the user. This problem is well-known from the domain of higher-level programming languages which adapt the language constructs directly to the problem domain.

Semantic directness is low if in order to work with one conceptually coherent object of a task domain several different objects have to be manipulated or composed. Semantic directness is also low if a certain intended operation can be achieved only by invoking several system functions in a sequence. When directness is low, the mental effort for planning the task is greater. For example, if the task is to create a rectangle and only lines are known to the system as objects, it takes a greater amount of planning and interaction effort than if the rectangle is available as an object. Low semantic directness can therefore lead to low interaction efficiency. DM systems for document processing, for instance, should for this reason provide basic objects at an appropriate level of abstraction (e.g. business graphics objects, tables etc.). If these basic objects are not sufficient for the specific task, the user should be able to define additional objects which can be reused if the task occurs again. User-defined object classes are a promising means to keep the semantic distance small.

Operational Directness. At the dialogue level, the temporal aspects of directness must be considered. A dialogue sequence is indirect if the user intends to follow a path of action which is different from the one provided by the system. Selecting an icon with the mouse, for instance, and immediately being able to move it on the screen is direct in an operational sense because the action is not subdivided by additional command input (like pressing a <move> button). It would be an example of low operational directness if the user has to open several nested windows in order to specify one command.

It is usually difficult to make valid assumptions about the user´s intended action sequences. Most DM systems therefore try to make all visible objects accessible in an user-initiated manner and to support the evaluation of a sequence of actions by immediate feedback after each step.

Formal Directness. This aspect of directness refers to the immediate comprehensibility of the system´s output and an easy and efficient handling of the input elements and devices (commands, buttons, mouse handling, etc.) The use of obvious iconic representations, object and function selections instead of symbolic command names, a well-structured layout of the screen, and comprehensible naming of function keys are all important aspects that can increase formal directness. The WYSIWYG principle, which allows documents to be perceived on the screen in exactly the same form as they will look on the print-out, is an important factor of formal directness.

The degree of directness depends on the user's experience and knowledge and will therefore change with continuous progress in learning. What appears direct to the novice may not be appropriate for the more complex action plans of the expert. Therefore, a certain degree of flexibility and extendability of the system may be necessary in order to maintain the user´s impression of directness.

Table 1: Examples of direct and indirect user interface design

Level	Direct	Indirect
Semantic directness	- use business graphics object - use sort function for sorting a list	- compose business graphic from lines, rectangles etc. - sort by repetitive use of move function
Operational directness	- move an icon by selecting and keeping button pressed while moving - effect of property changes immediately visible	- select, invoke move function and point to target position - effect only visible after trigger operation
Formal directness	- Font size etc. directly displayed - Function keys associated with virtual keys on the screen	- Font, size etc. indicated through a code - Combinations of special keys

3 Design of Direct Manipulation Interfaces

In this chapter, the different interaction elements and components of DM user interfaces will be described and guidance provided for the development of interfaces which are designed for optimal usability. The appearance and behaviour of the single elementary interaction objects are currently in the process of being standardised through the emerging industrial de facto standards. We will therefore first discuss the role of these standards in the design of user interfaces.

3.1 Style Guides and Toolkits

One of the most pervasive problems in the design of human-computer interfaces has always been the issue of lacking consistency. Users who have to switch between different systems, tools or application programmes are regularly experiencing a whole range of incompatibilities: keyboards with different key layouts, different meaning of mouse or function keys, menus or buttons which are activated differently, functions with similar names but different effects and many others. As long as users were mainly working with a couple of screens of some specialised application and had basically no access to other software, this problem was not considered acute. For people, however, who use PCs or workstations for a whole range of tasks with heterogeneous software products, this issue is of paramount importance. Inconsistent design requires more learning and is particularly adverse to highly skilled actions because users have to make these automated mechanisms conscious again when they switch to a new system. For these reasons, inconsistency causes errors and can considerably decrease user performance.

Over the past few years, a number of so-called look-and-feel standards or style guides have been developed which try to overcome the consistency problem for a particular system or hardware/software environment. These style guides are being promoted by either individual companies or industrial groups and are rapidly gaining importance for the design and implementation of graphical direct manipulation interfaces. What makes these style guides particularly attractive, is the fact that they are in most cases supported by corresponding software toolkits which make the implementation of user interfaces following the standard considerably more productive. At present, the following style guides can be considered as being the most relevant ones:

- OSF/Motif™ (Open Software Foundation)
- Open Look™ (AT&T, UNIX International)
- Human Interface Guidelines (Apple Computer Inc.)
- Common User Access (IBM)

All these style guides describe the visual appearance and the behaviour of user interface elements like windows, menus or buttons and provide as well more general guidelines. Consistency is a central concern of the style guides: " Above all else, an application must be consistent. It must be consistent within itself; but to be truly successful in the marketplace, it must be consistent with other applications that share the same environment" (OSF 1989).

While there is not sufficient space here to describe the relevant look-and-feel standards in detail, we will frequently refer to the design options offered by them in the rest of the paper.

3.2 Components of Direct Manipulation Interfaces

In the following, we will discuss the different components of DM interfaces. At the top level of a DM system or application we usually find a graphically represented *metaphor* like a desktop which serves for managing documents, applications and auxiliary tools. Through this top level structure, the user can access applications which are displayed in windows. Various means for generating or selecting objects, invoking and controlling functions are available in windows, subwindows or as components of the global desktop view (e.g. menu bar). The following components are typically used for manipulating objects and controlling functions:

- *Handles*: These are controls which are directly attached to an application specific object like a circle in a drawing programme. They are usually made visible after selection of the object and can be grabbed with the mouse for performing a wide range of manipulations like moving, resizing, stretching, rotating and the like. Handles as application specific components are typically not addressed by the style guides mentioned above apart from handles attached to standard objects like windows.
- *Controls* comprise elementary means for invoking functions or for input of parameters. The Motif style guide lists the following controls:
  - Buttons (push buttons, radio buttons, check buttons)
  - Boxes (list boxes, entry boxes, pre-formatting entry boxes)
  - Valuators (scales, scroll bars, application specific valuators)
- *Menus* may be considered as aggregations of elementary controls which are composed in a typical arrangement. In Open Look, menus are actually just collections of buttons which may be activated by pressing a button stack. Frequently used forms of menus are pull-down, pop-up and cascading menus.
- *Dialog boxes* are used for just displaying some message, for soliciting the user for some decision (e.g. "Save changes before quitting?") or for any input of parameters or data. The typical characteristic of dialog boxes is that they are modal, i.e. the user explicitly has to terminate interaction with the dialog box before being able to move the input focus to some other part of the application. The effect of the input usually only becomes visible after an <apply> or <OK> function has been activated. In this respect, dialog boxes are less direct manipulative than the other features addressed in this section because of their lower degree of interactivity.

Other components of DM interfaces are related to the presentation of information, like *icons* which may or may not be associated with a certain behaviour. Most often, they either behave like buttons or exhibit the specific behaviour of desktop objects, i.e. they can be dragged around, opened etc.

3.3 Metaphors and Conceptual Models

Metaphors are one of the most powerful means to make the usage of computer systems more natural, transparent and intuitive. They can direct the user's understanding and behaviour by establishing some analogy between domains and concepts in the real world and the objects and operations of the computer system. According to the type of domain the metaphor is drawn from, Hutchins (1989) distinguishes the following classes of metaphors:

- Activity metaphors refer to the user's highest level goals and structure expectations and intentions with respect to the outcome of the interaction. Typical activity domains may be "controlling a process", "writing documents" or "playing games".

- Mode of interaction metaphors organise understandings about the nature of interaction with the computer without regard for the particular task the user wishes to accomplish. The computer may be viewed as a conversational partner, an environment for action or a tool box and materials.
- Task domain metaphors provide the user with a structure for understanding the nature of particular tasks as presented by the computer. An example is the file system metaphor where the user can behave as if information is stored in files that have properties like those of paper files stored in file cabinets.

There are two relations which have to be maintained if metaphors are to be used successfully for the design of user interfaces. The system designer is developing a conceptual model which is a mapping from some state of affairs in the real world to the data model and functionality of the system. The metaphor represented in the user interface is a visible, graphical image of this conceptual model. The user interface metaphor therefore has to match both the conceptual model built into the system as well as the domain of the real world it represents.This can sometimes only partly be achieved. A spreadsheet, for instance, although simulating the visual appearance of an accountant's sheet of paper has a totally different behaviour which would be difficult to achieve with non-computer objects of the real world.

Most metaphors are drawn from certain task domains. The best known metaphor is certainly the one which represents the computer screen as a desktop (Fig. 5). It has by now become a standard component of many systems for the top level file management activities. The desktop metaphor, too, is only partially corresponding to real world offices. There are many breakdowns in the analogy: Folders (at least German ones) cannot arbitrarily be nested into each other, waste paper baskets do not empty themselves, things you send by mail are gone unless you copy them. Despite these differences, the desktop provides a graphical environment for action which most users find quite natural.

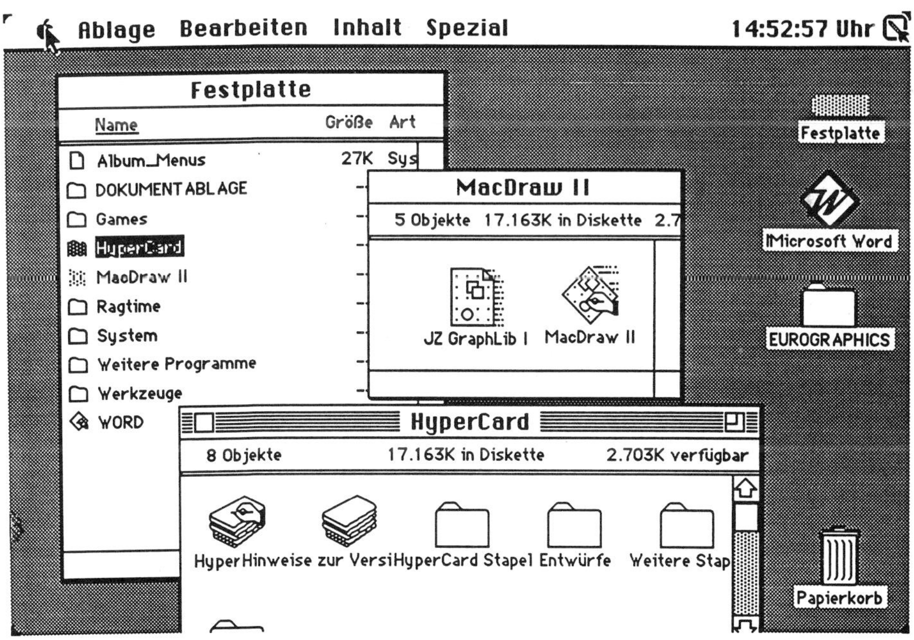

Fig. 5: Desktop metaphor (Apple Macintosh)

The desktop is also an example of the restrictions for the design of the system which are implied by the use of metaphors. In software systems, references to a certain object can easily be kept at different places providing access to this object from different contexts. This cannot be done with physical documents which have to be copied if they are to be stored at different locations. The user, however, could often work much more efficiently if multiple references to the same object can be filed at different places (Apple, for instance, is introducing this capability in the Macintosh Finder Version 7.0). Crossing the boundaries of a metaphor as it is derived from the known world of physical objects can therefore result in much more power for the user. In the design of metaphors for the user interface, one clearly has to make a trade-off between the learnability and transparency of the metaphor and the power it offers to the user for achieving his or her goals.

User interface metaphors vary considerably concerning their scope and complexity. Whereas a desktop may be a component global to the entire system supporting a complex structure and a multitude of different operations, other metaphors may be specific to a particular application or a part of it. Even a low level control element as, for example, a slider constitutes a metaphor, taken from the domain of hifi equipment or other electronic devices.

Specific task domains are sources for many possible user interface metaphors. For manufacturing systems, for instance, the model of a shop floor with people, machines, materials and tools can be used to provide access to the relevant data of the manufacturing process (Fig. 6). Another example is an electronic scheduling board which supports the planning and scheduling of work orders for a certain shop floor (Fig. 7). Physical equivalents of such scheduling boards can nowadays be found in many factories and many people are familiar with them. This concept is being taken up in decentralised software systems for shop floor planning and control. The first generation of systems in this domain has focussed on simulating the manual operation of a physical scheduling board, whereas more recent developments are transgressing the boundaries of this simple metaphor.

Other metaphors may represent a chemist's laboratory desk, a film cutter's materials and tools, models from molecular biology, an electronics laboratory, process control environments etc. Many models used in CAD also have characteristics of metaphors like wire frame models and others.

Even if metaphors are only partly corresponding to the domain they are taken from, their use can offer a number of advantages for the user:

- They offer a visual environment for concrete actions which reduces memory load and helps to develop a feeling of directness.
- They allow to maintain certain constraints automatically and in a transparent way by the system, thus relieving the user from tedious activities which are not in the focus of his or her task. An example is the automatic calculation of values in spreadsheet programs. In this case, the constraints can even be defined by the user. Metaphors should be implemented in such a way that the effect of some user operation on other dependent parts of the structure can be immediately evaluated and visualised (if a numerical entry field and a bar chart are coupled then changing the numerical value should immediately show its effect on the graphical representation and vice versa).
- By maintaining operational constraints (enabling and disabling operations according to the current context) syntactic errors can be made almost impossible. Of course, the user can still perform an action which is not matching his or her intentions (semantic errors).

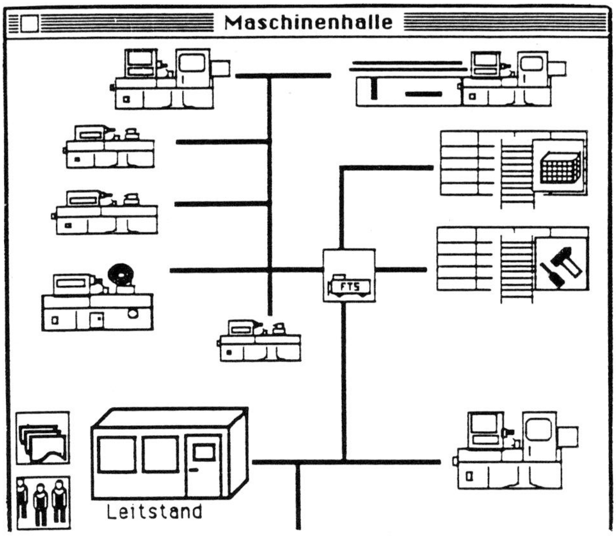

Fig. 6: Representation of a shop floor (Development: Fraunhofer Institute IAO Stuttgart)

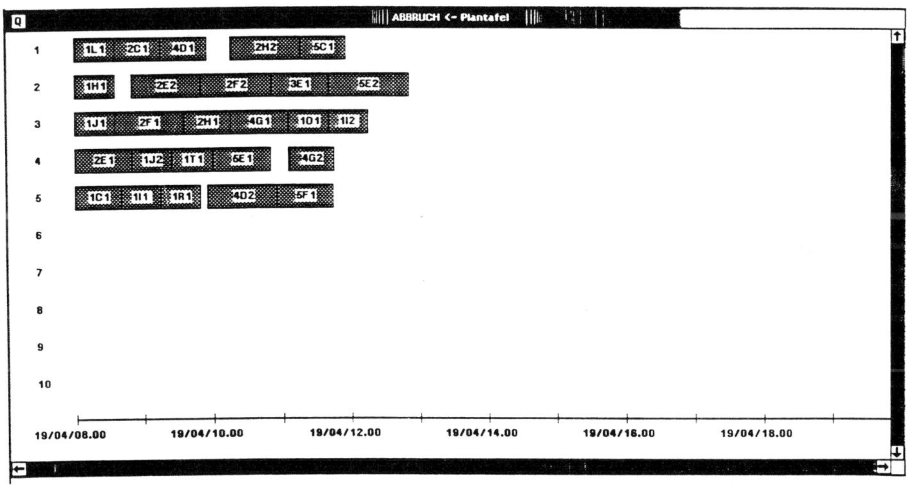

Fig. 7: Electronic scheduling board (Development: Fraunhofer Institute IAO Stuttgart)

3.4 Design of Objects and Functions

DM interfaces should be designed with the goal of a clear separation of data objects and functions which manipulate them. There is a complementary relationship between the complexity of the objects and the number and complexity of different functional concepts in a system. In the UNIX system, for instance, it requires the application of a specific function to display a list of files in a particular layout, say in a three column format. In a typical DM system like the Macintosh, the display of files as icons or as a list of textual entries can be controlled through an attribute of the respective window. The setting of the attribute is kept in memory and maintains its effect until it is changed again. Another example is the difference between a text formatter like Troff and a WYSIWIG editor. In the first case, the layout of the document is determined by textual commands which are interspersed with the actual contents of the document. In a WYSIWIG editor, the user can change the attributes of each single textual object and immediately see the effect of this change.

As a result of the increased amount of information which is stored with an object , we need less different functions in order to perform the same tasks. In such a system, the user can also more easily handle defaults by setting standard attribute values. In many cases, inheritance-like mechanisms can be used in order to increase user performance, like defining complex style templates for text objects. The facilities for defining styles or templates by the user considerably enhance the flexibility and tailorability of the system.

Generic Functions

In conventional systems, we find typically numerous different functions which perform some semantically similar operation for different types of objects. Deleting a file requires a command which is different from the one needed for deleting a word from a text , and the latter may again be different from the one which deletes a character. This variety of commands is very confusing particularly for the non-expert user and puts a high strain on the user's memory. Their complexity is mainly due to the fact that they identify at the same time an object and an operation.

Object-oriented interfaces, in contrast, make extensive use of so-called generic functions, i.e. functions which are applicable over a wide range of object types or classes. This is made feasible by the fact that a typical manipulative interaction is divided in two distinct steps:

1.) Selecting the object of interest with the pointing device

2.) Invoking the function which manipulates the selected object

As the identification of the object is now no longer part of the identification of the operation, much less different operations are needed at the user interface to achieve the same results. In addition, both steps are supported by visual representations on the screen or by labelled hard keys. Typical generic functions found in DM are:

- moving objects to a different location
- deletion of objects
- copying
- cutting and pasting
- opening and closing files

An important mechanism for providing more generic functionality is to replace unary operations by binary ones: The function <print object> e.g. can be replaced by <move object to

printer icon>. Although the concept of printing is still present through the printer icon, the user can now apply the very basic move operation.

The use of generic functions is one of the most powerful mechanisms for increasing the consistency of user interfaces. Users can, for instance, manipulate a text string in basically the same way regardless whether it occurs in a text document, in a field of a data input form or as part of a technical drawing. Generic functions are hence one of the major factors for enabling a positive transfer of user knowledge between different applications or systems.

Generic functions alone are usually not sufficient for realising an applicaton, because of specific application requirements as well as for reasons of user performance. They can, however, form the basis for developing a set of operational skills which the user should be able to apply reliably across different applications and systems.

3.5 Activation of Functions

Although the visual appearance as well as the detailed behaviour of controls or menus which are used to activate functions of the computer system, varies considerably with the different style guides introduced earlier, they can be classified with respect to their logical properties. The basic types can be found in all relevant style guides. In the following sections we will present the most frequently used interaction objects and discuss their behaviour and appearance.

3.5.1 Buttons

Buttons are sensitive areas on the screen which the user can hit with the mouse pointer. The button is activated by pressing a mouse button (usually the left button in the case of mice with two or three buttons). Buttons have typically two visual components: a graphical image that represents the button and a label or icon describing the action invoked by the button. The label may be positioned inside or outside the button image.

Push buttons represent the most simple type of button. Push buttons activate some arbitrary function when pressed. They have no internal logical state; however, they may have several different visual representations which are used in their interaction behaviour: one is used for the the inactive state, a second one may indicate that the selection mouse button is currently pressed on this button. This leads to a small, but critical design issue. Should the push button function be activated on pressing or releasing the mouse button? Releasing the mouse button for starting the action appears to be the better solution because users can still move the cursor away from a button they have pushed unintentionally without the function being triggered. This is particularly helpful if many sensitive areas are visible on the screen which the user may just be trying to identify by moving the cursor around. This does, of course, not hold for buttons used for functions which are depending on the duration of pressing the button (like incrementing the value of a numerical field).

In some instances, buttons are activated differently according to the context. In Open Look, the standard activation mechanism works by moving the pointer into the button area. In modal dialog boxes, however, the pointer is trapped in a region below the buttons to be selected. The mouse button must be pressed while the pointer is outside the button area. Such behavioural differences cause difficulties for intermittent or transfer users because in the standard paradigm of DM the user is always in control of the pointer.

Radio buttons are actually groups of two or more buttons which represent mutually exclusive choices. Only one button can be activated at a time, pressing a button other than the currently selected one resets the previous selection. Radio buttons represent typically parameter settings or options.

Check buttons represent choices which are not mutually exclusive. Most style guides make visual distinctions between radio buttons and check boxes. Motif uses different button shapes, whereas OpenLook distinguishes between touching (exclusive choice) and separated (non-exclusive choice) rectangles. The golden rule is here: same behaviour = same image.

Fig. 8 shows the different types of buttons for the Motif, Open Look and Apple Macintosh styles.

Button defaults. Representing predefined default settings requires no additional visual elements in the case of radio or check buttons; they are simply shown with the default button(s) selected. In the case of push buttons, the default should be marked by a specific visual cue like an additional border line, because these defaults should be distinguishable and can usually also be activated by an accelerator (e.g. return key).

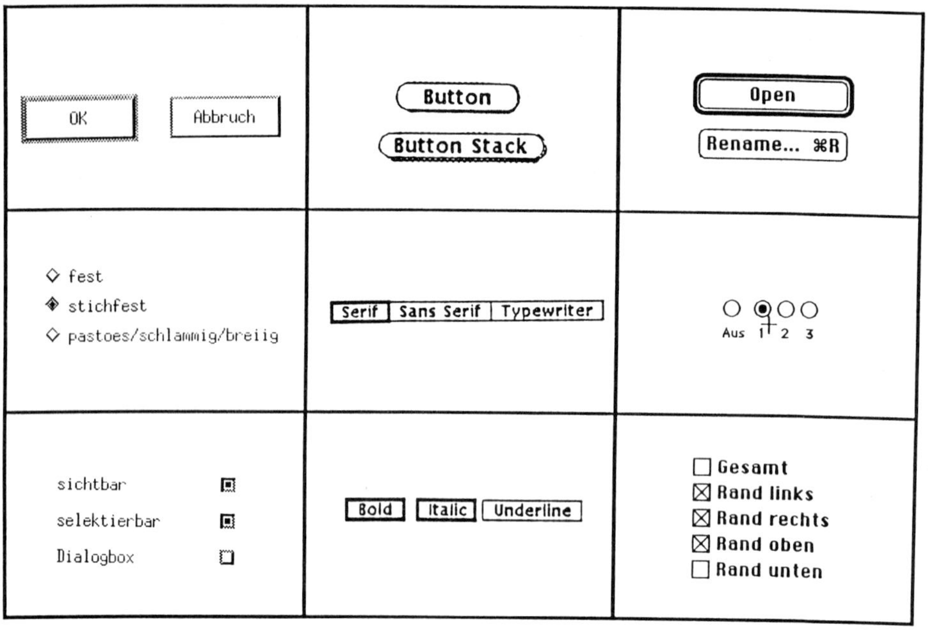

Fig. 8: Different types of buttons in different look-and-feel standards.Top row: push buttons, middle row: radio buttons, bottom row: check buttons.Styles (from left to right): OSF/Motif, Open Look, Apple.

3.5.2 Menus

Menus are generally advantageous for novices as well as discretionary users, who do not possess a thorough understanding of the application program, as well as for all applications with a complex & elaborate function/attribute structure which would be difficult to access by keyboard (Shneiderman 1986). In many application programs, however, some or all commands accessible via a menu may also be invoked by keyboard entry. This enables the same program to be used by non-experts and experts. In this case, the menu may be considered an abbreviated help facility, showing the available function names along with their key commands.

An arrangement of menu items in a window or a window subarea shall be called a menu panel. Menu panels can be members of a menu structure, a hierarchy or network as the case may be. There are generally three conditions under which a hierarchy or network should not be used, i.e. where a flat menu will be appropriate: all options have to be accessible in only one step; the number of options is not large; the options do not fall into logical or conventional groups.

Items in a menu may be labels for a submenu as indicated above or names for the application´s objects, functions or attributes. Thus components of a menu panel may be items demanding further user inputs, e.g. via dialogue boxes, executable items or checkable (two-state) items. Some items have keyboard equivalents, also called accelerators, others don´t.

There are a number of different menu panel features, which have to be considered here. Menu designs may be distinguished on four orthogonal dimensions: menu access, menu layout, item access, and item layout, which will be explained now.

Panel Access

Permanent menus: Permanently accessible menus are appropriate, if the user should have quick and frequent access to the menu options. Because the permanent menu might cover the working area, i.e. the object to be edited, the menu needs to be movable or to occupy a reserved region on the screen. For the same reasons, the menu should not automatically disappear, after the user has made a selection. Menus which may only be cancelled by the user, should leave a permanently visible icon or other representative on the screen.

Occasional menus: If the user needs occasionally reference to some menu, that menu may best be implemented as a non-permanent one. This implies, that it will disappear immediately after the selection of an item.

Panel Layout

Although any menu may be thought of as a single list of options from which the user may select one or more, the physical appearance of menus and their associated items on the screen may be quite different. We have found it helpful to distinguish the following four layout variants.

Window-like menus: These are menus, whose items are arranged in two-dimensional screen space without any inherent constraints on their position. However, the items will always appear in the same position, when using the menu. This type of menu is useful, when e.g. the items are positioned on a background picture intended to enhance the interpretation of the items.

Row-like menus: Menus whose items are horizontally arranged are appropriate for small menus or if the screen space reserved for the menu should be minimized. It may be very screen-efficient, if icons or other graphical symbols are used for the menu items.

Column-like menus: Menus whose items are vertically arranged are appropriate if their items are alphabetically sorted or for menus with relatively many verbal items.

Array-like menus: These are menus, whose items are arranged in rows as well as in columns on the screen. This type is applicable if the number of items in the menu is large, such that it is not feasible to present them in either a row-like or a column-like menu, and if the items themselves are arranged according to two features which correspond to the rows and columns of a two-dimensional array.

Item Presentation

Although most menus have their items represented as text, a growing number of applications incorporate menus with iconic options, partly or completely. The reason is straightforward: often it is difficult, sometimes even impossible to assign a name to or describe the option referred to (see also the discussion of icons as special symbols). Of course, a combination of text and icon for one or more items is possible, in particular if the designer wants to be sure that all users will understand the option in the same way or if the icon is used for a class of objects, each instance of it bearing a different name.

Text items: The option is named or described in the users´s natural or professional language.

Icon items: The option is represented by a well-chosen graphical symbol, i.e. an icon, which uniquely identifies the option by visual similarity or by convention.

Pull-Down and Cascaded Menus

The term pull-down menu refers to a particular arrangement where a permanently visible menu bar is hit with the mouse and submenus open either immediately or on pressing the mouse button. It is usually preferable to use an explicit activation of the pulldown menu. Pull-down menu selection is a very efficient process if it is not separated by unnecessary button presses. The action sequence of moving the pointer to the menu bar, pressing the button, moving to the menu item and releasing the button appears to be the best solution in terms of user performance. It has been shown that pull-down menu selection is faster and safer than pop-up menus with one submenu (which is logically equivalent) even if the menu bar is relatively far away from the current working position. This is probably due to the fact that the first-level choices are already visible at the beginning of the action.

Cascaded menus use a second-level panel which is usually attached to the left or right of the item which is its parent (Fig. 9). Two mechanisms can be found: (1) the submenu pops up as soon as the main entry is touched, (2) the pointer hits the main entry and is then moved to the right (pull-right menu). Most users find the first version more usable and less error-prone.

Cascaded menus are especially appropriate if the second-level menu items belong to one common category (e.g. fonts) or represent an ordered set of options (e.g. font sizes).

Pop-Up Menus

Pop-up menus are in most aspects similar to pull-down menus apart from the fact that they can appear at arbitrary locations on the screen, depending on the current position of the pointer. Their contents, however, is in most cases depending on the respective screen area the pointer is currently located at. Their main advantage is that the user is not forced to leave the current focus of work with the mouse. Items should be selectable with one button press- release cycle.

Often, we find pop-up menus which are fixed to certain objects on the screen like, for instance, a data entry field with a limited set of possible entry options. They behave much like pull-down menus but are not attached to some standard menu bar. The current setting of the entry field and the default value should be indicated by positioning the pop-up menu in such a way that the field is in alignment with the respective menu entry. An additional visual cue should be used for the default setting (Fig. 10).

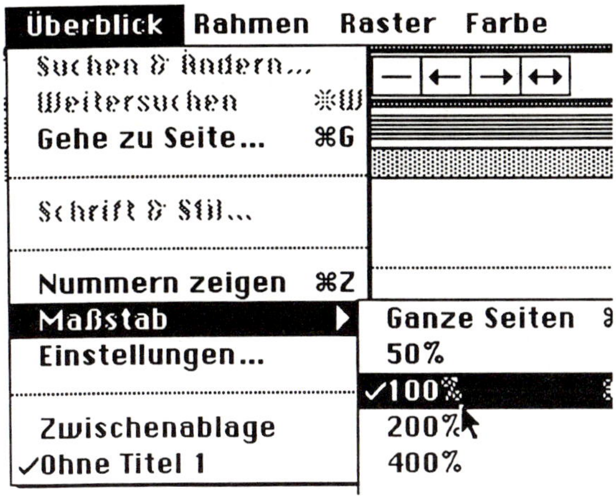

Fig. 9: Pull-down menu with cascaded menu (Apple Macintosh)

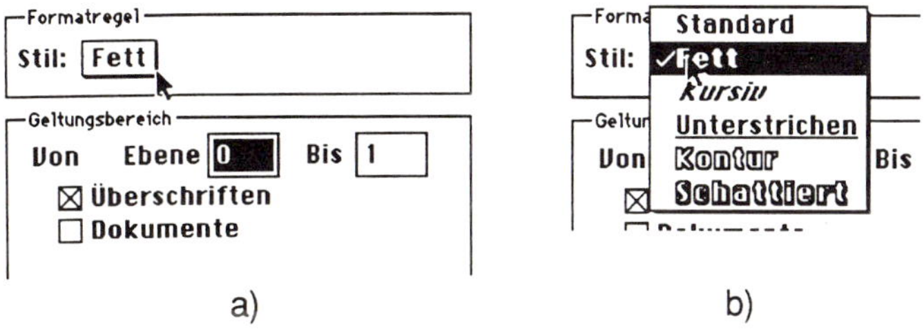

Fig. 10: Pop-up menu attached to data field. a) Parameter field is selected,b) Menu pops up with the current setting marked and aligned with the button position (MORE™ on Macintosh).

Tear-off and Push-pin Menus

Pop-up and pull-down menus are modal, i.e. they disappear after an item has been selected. Quite often, however, users find it useful to have a menu permanently available, e.g. when performing repetitively the same operations. Tear-off and push-pin menus can be forced by the user to stay on the screen. This is done by "tearing off" a menu panel from a pull-down menu and placing it at some other position on the screen (Macintosh style) or by explicitly pressing a push-pin button at the top of the menu panel (Open Look Style, see Fig. 11).

Fig. 11: Menu panel with a push pin button (Open Look). When the push pin button is pressed the menu stays on the screen until the button is pressed again.

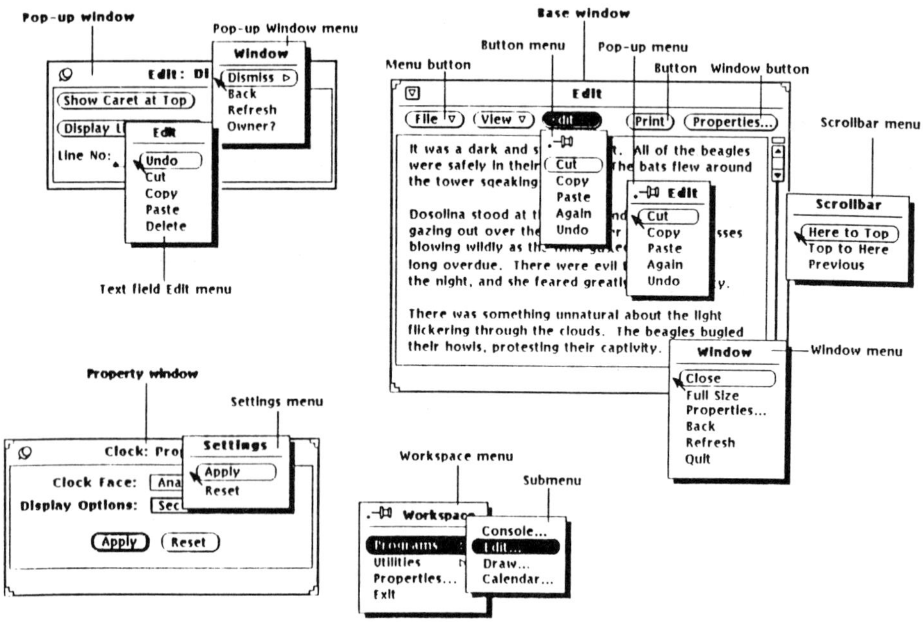

Fig. 12: Overview of Open Look menus.

3.6 Syntactic Modes and Feedback

DM has often been called a modeless interaction technique. This is, of course, not true; otherwise the user would not be able to achieve anything. What is true, however, is that the user can access much more functionality from the normal working context. Persistent syntactic modes - as e.g. command and entry modes of command-oriented editors - are basically avoided. Intransparent or nested modes are a major source of errors and short term memory load.

DM is an interaction technique which can exhibit a large number of syntactic "micro-modes". The usual syntactic composition of a DM interaction is <select object> followed by <activate function>. After the object selection, a mode <object selected> is entered which should be visualised by an appropriate highlighting of the object. After activation of the function, a new mode may be active, e.g. when waiting for a further parameter, like the target position of a move operation. In this case, the shape of the cursor is a useful means for informing the user about the current mode (Fig. 13).

Persistent modes may also be useful, for instance, when creating a series of objects. Some graphics editors provide menu bars with functions for creating geometric objects which can be activated either as transitory modes (single mouse click) or persistent modes (double mouse click). If persistent modes are used, it should be obvious to the user how to finish it. Some readers may have seen users fighting with the end of a polygon they have just created, and not being able to get rid of this mode.

Meaning	Cursor	Meaning	Cursor
- Standard form Text and graphics	↖	- Copy Properties	
- Move		- Enter Object in File	→
- Copy		- Wait	⌛
- Target undefiend	?	- Extended Selection	
- Copy, Move Folder		- Menu Selection	←
- Copy, Move Document		- Drawing	+
- Pagination, Paging in Document	1	- Copy Table Columns	↓

Fig. 13: Mode feedback through different cursor shapes (Siemens 5800, after: Lauter 1987)

3.7 Presentation of Information

Bitmap displays are usually used for DM systems although some DM characteristics can be achieved with alphanumeric displays. This makes it possible to present text with different font sizes as well as object-oriented graphics. A high-quality typography facilitates the uptake of information by the user considerably. Positive displays are preferable for bitmap screens because of their close resemblance to the printed output.

Icons

The use of icons constitutes an important aspect of DM, because the graphical representation allows abstract entities and technical artifacts to be displayed as "real" objects which can be manipulated by the user. Whereas objects which are visual by their very nature, like text or graphic objects, are relatively easy to display, abstract objects, like files or functions like "delete", are more difficult to portray because there is no familiar symbol that corresponds to the meaning of the concept. This leads to the use of metaphors which map the objects of the application or problem domain on a visual world which is familiar to the user.

According to Gittins (1986), icons can be classified by their form, type and colour. The form of an icon can either portray certain characteristic(s) of the object or it can suggest some of the cognitive characteristics of the task. Concerning the type, static and dynamic objects can be distinguished. As in the design of pictograms, icons should be constructed with as few graphical components as possible (usually not more than two or three components). Too much detail hinders perception rather than facilitating it.

Icons usually represent classes of objects rather than individual objects. To distinguish different icons of the same class, additional names are usually needed. If there are, for instance, two types of objects - documents and folders - the icon shape helps to distinguish between the two types whereas names are needed to identify a specific document or folder. If many icons of the same type are displayed in a window, alphabetic or sequential lists may be used to direct the user to a specific icon. It should therefore be possible to switch between iconic and textual representation .

Icons not only facilitate the identification of an object and its meaning, they can also support the user in inferring attributes of objects, relations among objects, and potential operations. This fact may also imply danger of misinterpreting the visual representation if the metaphor is not consistent with or too far removed from the actual problem domain.

Window Arrangement and Layout

With the DM style of interaction, only those objects which are visible on screen can be manipulated. For this reason, the user should be able to arrange the contents of the screen according to his needs. The parallel display of different contexts is essential. For this, window systems are needed which allow a flexible arrangement of different information and interaction contexts. Switching between windows should be easy and quick, e.g., by clicking with a mouse in the next window of interest. The use of window systems, however, has a tendency to clutter the screen with overlapping windows which may make access to a specific window difficult .

Bly and Rosenberg (1986) compared tiled (non-overlapping) and overlapping windows. Their results indicated that non-overlapping windows might be preferable if the contents of the windows basically conform to a predefined arrangement of window size and placement and if the user does not wish to be distracted by managing the windows. However, there are yet no sound guidelines to determine the appropriateness of overlapping and non-overlapping windows.

For the layout of windows, consistent design rules should be applied. The most important factors are (a) the division of the window in consistently used areas like work area, dialog area etc., (b) spatial grouping of semantically related information and (c) the use of horizontal and vertical alignments. Fig. 14 shows the layout of a form in Motif style.

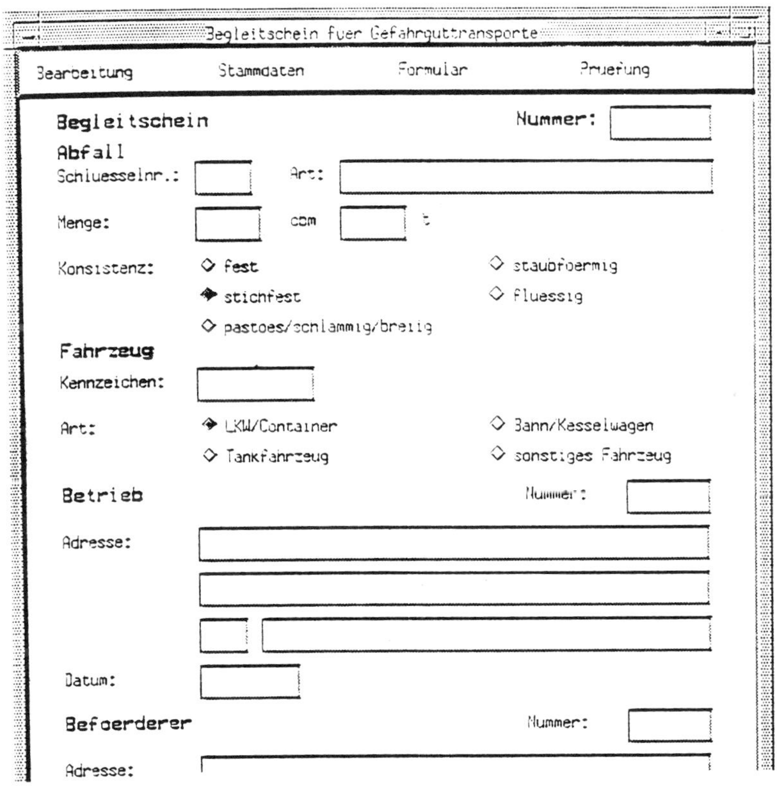

Fig. 14: Window layout in a Motif application

4 Evaluations and Guidelines

4.1 Empirical Studies

There have been only a few empirical studies on the suitability and application of DM in particular task areas. One of the first studies was undertaken by Whiteside et al. (1985) and involved an empirical comparison of the usability characteristics of seven systems, two of which had a DM iconic interface. The others were menu systems and command language with and without help facilities. The objective was to compare user performance and preference for several standardized filing tasks. Seventy-six subjects participated. They were classified either novice-, transfer-, or system users and received only a short introduction. The following results were obtained:

- There are large difference in learnability and usability between the systems, even for the two "iconic systems".
- Subject performance or preference did not depend on the type of system.

In addition, the experiment revealed a number of specific design problems:

- Feedback was often incomprehensible or was not understood/recognized.
- There were inconsistencies in the input syntax. In particular, the syntax of the mouse manipulation, including number of button activations, was surprisingly difficult to learn and led to errors.
- Help messages were often unhelpful, misleading, or confusing.
- In the DM systems, subjects often used incorrect positioning strategies.

This study found no general advantage of DM, which contradicts the high subjective ratings attributed to this form of interaction by many specialists. However, the question remains open whether the scope of tasks and the time span used in the experiment could give a complete assessment of the technique.

Frese et al.(1987) compared learning and performance with word processors using different interaction techniques. The systems investigated were a DM style application (Macintosh: MacWrite) and a command-driven system (Wordstar). Novices performed text editing tasks in a series of experimental sessions. User performance with DM system was found to be consistently better, except for the first experimental session which was comparable in terms of performance with the Whiteside et al. experiment. No differences were found for this first session which is consistent with Whiteside´s findings. However, the superiority of the DM system increased with the duration of the experiment and with the degree of complexity of the tasks which was higher for later sessions. These findings indicate that the initial learning requirements for the novice are about equal for simple tasks, but that further learning is facilitated by the DM interface, maybe because of a higher consistency of the interface and a better retention of the operations required.

In this study, further factors were found which improve learning: training methods which allow the user´s mental model to develop in a self-paced and integrated way as well as plan-orientation and problem-solving competence of the user.

A study comparing different text-editors was described by Card et al. (1983). Differences in user performance were investigated with five different editors for four different tasks (creating text, editing text, editing standard text, creating tables). Two of the editors were "display-oriented", mouse-controlled editors. The subjects were all experts and had over a year´s experience with their respective editors. Time differences between the "fastest" and "slowest" editors lay, depending on the task, between factors of 1.4 and 2.3, the display-oriented editors being superior for text editing tasks.

Ziegler, Vossen and Hoppe (1986) carried out an experiment on learning and transfer with a DM system. The "cognitive complexity theory" (Kieras and Polson 1985) was taken as a basis from which learning times and also transfer could be predicted using a production system model of each task (a model of the user´s procedural behaviour).

Eighty-eight subjects performed four different types of tasks. The tasks consisted of text editing and generation of graphics. The assumption was made that common rules and methods can be transferred completely across different tasks. Thus common rules resulting from the generic functions leads to high transfer of skill.

The results of the investigation confirmed the predictions of the cognitive complexity models and thus underline the importance of the consistency of an interface in order to enable transfer of skill. Detailed modelling also showed syntactic differences between methods which, superficially, seem quite similar (e.g., selecting text and graphics objects with the mouse).

In a recent study, Shneiderman and Margono (1987) compared simple file manipulation tasks using command language and DM systems. Thirty inexperienced subjects learned to perform the tasks with either DOS or Macintosh systems. The tasks consisted of "open document", "copy document", "change document name" and "delete document". Performance time and errors were recorded after an introductory and training period, and questionnaires were used to obtain subjective ratings. The results showed that DM was superior with respect to learnability, time to complete tasks, and subjective rating. According to the authors, this was due to the lower memory load and the easy and efficient handling of the mouse and the pull-down menus in the DM interface.

4.2 General Guidelines

As a summary, a list of general user interface design guidelines is presented in the following section which has been compiled from the literature. The guidelines have been selected with respect to their applicability for DM user interfaces. The guidelines were taken from the following sources: Apple (1986), Smith and Mosier (1983), Ilg and Ziegler (1988), Gardiner and Christie (1987), Shneiderman (1982), Jacob (1989). Further guidelines may be found in DIN 66234, part 8 (DIN) and VDI 5005 (VDI). A set of user interface design guidelines is also currently under discussion in ISO TC159 SC4 WG5 "Software Ergonomics and Man-Machine Dialogue".

Actions should be initiated by the user; the system waits for useful user input .

User input is made by "recognizing and pointing" instead of "remembering and typing" .

The interface must be simple; it should not be overloaded by too many or complex elements .

DM systems are usually operated in one main mode. If the system is in a specific mode, the current mode must always be identifiable by sufficient visual cues. One possible solution is to modify the shape of the cursor.

For the design of documents which can be printed, the WYSIWYG-principle (What You See Is What You Get) is recommended.

Care for reversibility: Reversibility may be defined in terms of its violation (Monk 1990): A hard to reverse effect is given if consequences of one user action requires many actions to reverse or cannot be reversed at all. If such effects can not be avoided, at least a warning should be displayed by the system.

Care for predictability: a dialogue is ambiguous if a user action can have different effects which can not be predicted by the user from the current state of the display alone. Often, ambiguous displays imply a hidden mode.

Objects

User interfaces should be organised into single manipulative objects and single, generic actions.

Objects which are manipulated must be visually represented on the screen and must be directly accessible .

Selection of an object may be implicitly combined with the execution of an action.

Information output on the screen is itself displayed as an object which immediately can be manipulated by the user (Hancock 1989).

Icons representing objects should "behave and react" similar to reality.

Example: The icon of a message should disappear after sending the message via an electronic letter box, but after copying it, the message should remain visible.

Supplementing icons with textual descriptions (names) may improve comprehensiveness.

If the use of a metaphor or icon is meaningful only for a specific part of the user interface, every situation in which it cannot be used must be indicated (e.g. by visual cues).

Actions

User input must be done consistently with the same interaction syntax, either object selection before action selection or consistently the other way round.

For DM systems, the object-action syntax is more natural to the user. For creating objects, the function must first be specified.

Generic actions should be provided for semantically similar functions.

Example: A uniform delete command should be available for different classes of objects.

Accelerator mechanisms (e.g. keyboard commands) should be available for expert users in order to allow for increased performance.

Use simple, concrete actions (in analogy to real physical modifications of objects) instead of complex commands.

After every user action, immediate visual feedback should be presented on the screen .

Every single user action should be reversible .

It must be always clear, which actions are currently available.

For specific tasks a typical sequence of actions may be necessary. Interrupting or cancelling the sequence must be possible at any stage.

Attributes

Defaults or current values should be displayed by appropriate visual means.

Often needed specifications of properties may also be implemented as single actions to enhance efficiency .

Example: the formatting of text may be inefficient, if each single attribute must be specified in a property sheet. It is more effective to offer a command which sets all attributes to the required values in one action.

Property sheets may be more efficient than menus if many attributes have to be changed at a time.

5 References

Altmann, A.(1987): *Direkte Manipulation: Empirische Befunde zum Einfluß der Benutzeroberfläche auf die Erlernbarkeit im Textsystem.* Zeitschrift für Arbeits- und Organisationspsychologie H. 3, 108-114 .

Apple Computer Inc.(1986): *Human Interface Guidelines: The Apple Desktop Interface.* Cupertino.

Borning, A., (1979). Thinglab: A constraint-oriented simulation laboratory, *Technical Report SSL-79-3*, Palo Alto: Xerox PARC.

Bly, S. and Rosenberg, J.(1986). A comparison of tiled and overlapping windows. *Proceeding of CHI'86*, 101-106, New York, NY: ACM.

Card, S.K., English, W.K., Burr, B. (1978). Evaluation of mouse. Rate-Controlled Isometric Joystick, Step Keys and Text Keys for Text Selection on a CRT. *Ergonomics, 21*, 601-613.

Card, S.K. (1983). The Psychology of Human Computer Interaction. New Jersey: Lawrence Erlbaum Associates.

DIN (1988): Bildschirmarbeitsplätze - Grundsätze ergonomischer Dialoggestaltung. DIN 66234, Part 8, Berlin: Beuth-Verlag.

Foley, J, Wallace, V. and Chan, P. (1981): The human factors of graphic interaction tasks and techniques. Tech. Rep. GWU-11st-81-3. Washington: The George Washington University.

Frese, M., Schulte-Göcking, H., Altmann, A. (1987): Lernprozesse in Abhängigkeit von der Trainingsmethode, von Personenmerkmalen und von der Benutzeroberfläche. In Schönpflug & Wittstock (Eds.): Software-Ergonomie 87, Stuttgart: Teubner.

Gardiner, M. M., Christie, B. (1987): *Applying cognitive psychology to user-interface design.* Chichester: John Wiley & Sons.

Gittins, D. (1986). Icon-based human-computer interaction. *International Journal of Man Machine Studies, 24*, 519-543.

Goldberg, A. and Robson, D. (1983). Smalltalk 80: The language and its implementation, Reading, MA: Addison-Wesley.

Hancock, Chignell (1989): *Intelligent Interfaces.* Amsterdam: North-Holland.

Hollan, J.D., Hutchins, E., and Weitzman, L. (1984). STEAMER: An interactive inspectable simulation-based training system. *AI Magazine, 5*, 15-27.

Hutchins, E. (1989): Metaphors for Interface Design. In Taylor, Néel and Bouwhuis: The Structure of Multimodal Dialogue, Amsterdam: North-Holland.

Hutchins, E.L., Hollan, J.D. and Norman, D.A. (1986): Direct Manipulation Interfaces. In: D.A. Norman, W.S. Draper (Eds.): User Centered System Design: New perspectives in Human-Machine Interaction, Hillsdale London: Lawrence Erlbaum.

Ilg, R., Ziegler, J.(1988): *Direkte Manipulation.* In: Balzert, H. u.a.(Eds.): Einführung in die Software-Ergonomie. Berlin, New York: Walter de Gruyter.

Jacob, R.(1989): *Direct manipulation in the intelligent interface.* In: Hancock & Chignell: Intelligent Interfaces. Amsterdam, NewYork, Oxford: North-Holland.

Kieras, D. and Polson, P. (1985): An approach to the formal analysis of user complexity. *International Journal of Man-Machine Studies, 22*, 365-394.

Lauter, B. (1987): Software-Ergonomie in der Praxis. München: Oldenbourg.

Mallgren, W.R. (1983). Formal specification of interactive graphical programming languages. Cambridge, MA: MIT Press.

Moran, T.P. (1981). The command language grammar - a representation for the user interface of intercative computer systems. *International Journal of Man-Machine Studies, 15*, 3-50.

Monk, A.(1990): Action-effect rules: a technique for evaluating an informal specification against principles. Behaviour & Information Technology, Vol. 9, No. 2, 147-155.

Nielsen, J. (1986). A virtual protocol model for computer-human interaction. *International Journal of Man Machine Studies, 24*, 3.

OSF (1989): OSF/Motif Style Guide, Revision 1.0. Cambridge (Mass.): Open Software Foundation.

Rosenberg, J.K. and Moran, T.P. (1984). Generic commands. In: Shakel, B. (Ed.) *Proceedings of Interact'84*, Amsterdam: North-Holland.

Shneiderman, B. (1982). The Future of Interactive Systems and the Emergence of Direct Manipulation. *Behaviour and Information Technology, 1*, 237-256.

Shneiderman, B. (1983). Direct Manipulation: A Step beyond Programming Languages. *IEEE Computer, 16*, 57-69.

Shneiderman, B.(1986): Designing the User Interface: Strategies for Effective Human-Computer Interaction. Reading (Mass.): Addison-Wesley.

Shneiderman, B. and Margono, S. (1987). A Study of File Manipulation by Novices Using Commands vs. Direct Manipulation. *Proceedings of 26th Annual Technical Symposium of the Washington, D.C. Chapter of the ACM, Gathersburg*, MD: National Bureau of Standards.

Smith, D.C., Irby, D., Kimball, R. Verplank, B. and Harslem, E. (1983). Designing the STAR User Interface. In: Degano, P. and Sandewall, S. (Eds.): Integrated Interactive Computing Systems, Amsterdam: North-Holland.

Smith, S.L. and Mosier, J.N. (1986): Guidelines for Designing User Interface Software. Report 7 MTR-10090, Esd-Tr-86-278, Bedford (Mass.): Mitre Corporation.

Sun Microsystems, Inc. (1989): Open Look Graphical User Interface - Functional Specification. Reading (Mass.): Addison-Wesley.

VDI (1988): Software-Ergonomie in der Bürokommunikation. VDI Guideline No. 5005 (Draft). Düsseldorf: Verein Deutscher Ingenieure.

Whiteside, J, Joes, S., Levy, P., Wixon, D. (1985). User Performance with Command, Menu and Iconic Interfaces. *Proceedings of CHI'85*. New York: ACM.

Ziegler, J.E., Vossen, P. and Hoppe, H.U. (1986). On using production systems for cognitive task analysis and prediction of transfer of cognitive skill. *Third European Conference on Cognitive Ergonomics*, Paris.

Ziegler, J. (1987). Grunddimensionen von Interaktionsforman . In: Schönplug und Wittstock (Eds.): *Software-Ergonomie'87*, Stuttgart: Teubner.

Zloof, M. (1977). Query by Example: A database language. *IBM Systems Journal, 16*, 321-343.

List of Contributors

W.F. Bronsvoort, F.W. Jansen, F.H. Post
Faculteit der Technische Wiskunde en Informatica, Technische Universiteit Delft
Julianalaan132, 1628 BL Delft, The Netherlands

M.F. Cohen, J.S. Painter
Department of Computer Science, University of Utah, 3190 Merrill Engineering Building
Salt Lake City,Utah 84112, USA

F. Crow
Palo Alto Research Center, Xerox Corporation, 3333 Coyote Hill Road, Palo Alto
California 94304, USA

Th. Huang
Coordinates Sciences Laboratory, University of Illinois, 1101 West Springfield Avenue
Urbana, Illinois 6181, USA

A.E. Kaufman
Department of Computer Science, State University of New York at Stony Brook
Stony Brook, New York 11794-4400, USA

M. Kunt
Laboratoire de Traitement des Signaux, Ecole Polytechnique Fédérale de Lausanne
EPFL-Ecublens, CH-1015 Lausanne, Switzerland

S.W. Thomas
Artificial Intelligence Laboratory, Department of Electrical Engineering and Computer Science
University of Michigan, 1101 Beal Avenue, Michigan 48109-2110, Ann Arbor, USA

S.J. Thorpe
Département des Neurosciences de la Vision, Université P. et M. Curie
9 quai Saint Bernard, F-75005 Paris, France

T. Tomiyama
Department of Precision Machinery, Faculty of Engineering, University of Tokyo
Hongo 7-3-1 Bunkyo-ku, Tokyo 113, Japan

D.W. Townsend
Division de Médecine Nucléaire, Hôpital Cantonal Universitaire de Genève
24 rue Michel du Crest, CH-1211 Genève, Switzerland

J.E. Ziegler
Fraunhofer-Institut für Arbeitswirtschaft und Organisation IAO, Senefelderstrasse 26
W-7000 Stuttgart 1, Federal Republic of Germany

EurographicSeminars

Tutorials and Perspectives in Computer Graphics

Eurographics Tutorials '83. Edited by P. J. W. ten Hagen.
XI, 425 pages, 164 figs., 1984

User Interface Management Systems. Edited by G. E. Pfaff.
XII, 224 pages, 65 figs., 1985

Methodology of Window Management. Edited by F. R. A. Hopgood, D. A. Duce, E. V. C. Fielding, K. Robinson, A. S. Williams.
XV, 250 pages, 41 figs., 1985

Data Structures for Raster Graphics. Edited by L. R. A. Kessener, F. J. Peters, M. L. P. van Lierop. VII, 201 pages, 80 figs., 1986

Advances in Computer Graphics I. Edited by G. Enderle, M. Grave, F. Lillehagen.
XII, 512 pages, 168 figs., 1986

Advances in Computer Graphics II. Edited by F. R. A. Hopgood, R. J. Hubbold, D. A. Duce. X, 186 pages, 96 figs., 1986

Advances in Computer Graphics Hardware I. Edited by W. Straßer.
X, 147 pages, 76 figs., 1987

GKS Theory and Practice. Edited by P. R. Bono, I. Herman.
X, 316 pages, 92 figs., 1987

Intelligent CAD Systems I. Theoretical and Methodological Aspects.
Edited by P. J. W. ten Hagen, T. Tomiyama. XIV, 360 pages, 119 figs., 1987

Advances in Computer Graphics III. Edited by M. M. de Ruiter.
IX, 323 pages, 247 figs., 1988

Advances in Computer Graphics Hardware II. Edited by A. A. M. Kuijk, W. Straßer.
VIII, 258 pages, 99 figs., 1988

CGM in the Real World. Edited by A. M. Mumford, M. W. Skall.
VIII, 288 pages, 23 figs., 1988

Intelligent CAD Systems II. Implementational Issues. Edited by V. Akman, P. J. W. ten Hagen, P. J. Veerkamp. X, 324 pages, 114 figs., 1989

Advances in Computer Graphics IV. Edited by W. T. Hewitt, M. Grave, M. Roch.
XVI, 248 pages, 138 figs., 1991

Advances in Computer Graphics V. Edited by W. Purgathofer, J. Schönhut.
VIII, 223 pages, 101 figs., 1989

User Interface Management and Design. Edited by D. A. Duce, M. R. Gomes, F. R. A. Hopgood, J. R. Lee. VIII, 324 pages, 117 figs., 1991

Advances in Computer Graphics Hardware III. Edited by A. A. M. Kuijk. VIII, 214 pages, 88 figs., 1991

Advances in Object-Oriented Graphics I. Edited by E. H. Blake, P. Wisskirchen. X, 218 pages, 74 figs., 1991

Advances in Computer Graphics Hardware IV. Edited by R. L. Grimsdale, W. Straßer. VIII, 276 pages, 124 figs., 1991

Advances in Computer Graphics VI. Edited by G. Garcia, I. Herman. IX, 449 pages, 186 figs., 1991

In preparation:

Intelligent CAD Systems III. Practical Experience and Evaluation. Edited by P. J. W. ten Hagen, P. J. Veerkamp. Approx. 280 pages, 1991